Fiji

Dean Starnes
Nana Luckham

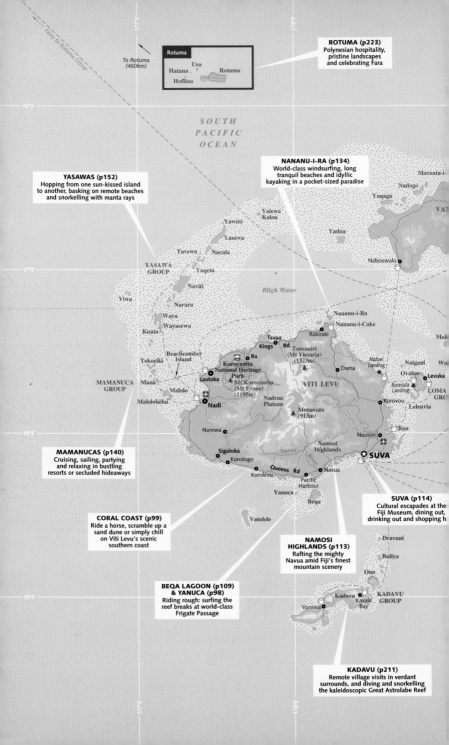

Rotuma

Uea
Hatana
Rotuma
Hofliua

ROTUMA (p223)
Polynesian hospitality,
pristine landscapes
and celebrating Fara

To Rotuma
(460km)

Ferry to Rotuma Group

16°S

172°E

174°E

SOUTH
PACIFIC
OCEAN

NANANU-I-RA (p134)
World-class windsurfing, long
tranquil beaches and idyllic
kayaking in a pocket-sized paradise

YASAWAS (p152)
Hopping from one sun-kissed island
to another, basking on remote beaches
and snorkelling with manta rays

Macuata-i-
Nadogo
Yaqaga
VA

Yalewa
Kalou

Yawini
Yasawa

Yadua

Nabouwalu

Tavewa   Nacula
YASAWA
GROUP   Yaqeta

17°S

Bligh Water

Naviti

Viwa

Narara
Waya
Wayasewa

Nananu-i-Ra
Nananu-i-Cake

Rakiraki

Tavua
Kings   Rd

Mak

Kuata

Tokoriki

Beachcomber
Island

Tomanivi
(Mt Victoria)
(1323m)

Dama

Natovi
Landing

Naigani
Ovalau   Wa
Levuka
Burelala
Landing   LOMA
GRC

Wa

MAMANUCA
GROUP

Mana

Ba
Koroyanitu
National Heritage
Park
McKoroyamitu
(Mt Evans)
(1195m)

Lautoka

VITI LEVU

Korovou

Malolo

Nadrau
Plateau

Leleuvia

Malololailai

Nadi

Monavatu
(913m)

Korovou

Nausori

Bau

Narewa

Namosi
Highlands

Navua

SUVA

18°S

MAMANUCAS (p140)
Cruising, sailing, partying
and relaxing in bustling
resorts or secluded hideaways

Sigatoka
Korotogo
Korolevu

Queens   Rd

Navua
Pacific
Harbour

SUVA (p114)
Cultural escapades at the
Fiji Museum, dining out,
drinking out and shopping h

Yanuca

Beqa

CORAL COAST (p99)
Ride a horse, scramble up a
sand dune or simply chill
on Viti Levu's scenic
southern coast

Vatulele

**NAMOSI
HIGHLANDS (p113)**
Rafting the mighty
Navua amid Fiji's finest
mountain scenery

Dravuni

Buliya

Ono

**BEQA LAGOON (p109)
& YANUCA (p98)**
Riding rough: surfing the
reef breaks at world-class
Frigate Passage

Kadavu   Kavala
Bay

KADAVU
GROUP

19°S

Vunisea

KADAVU (p211)
Remote village visits in verdant
surrounds, and diving and snorkelling
the kaleidoscopic Great Astrolabe Reef

172°E

178°E

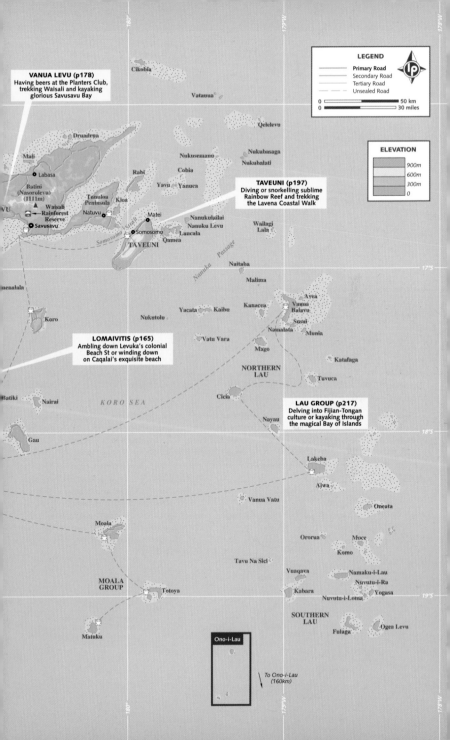

VANUA LEVU (p178)
Having beers at the Planters Club,
trekking Waisali and kayaking
glorious Savusavu Bay

TAVEUNI (p197)
Diving or snorkelling sublime
Rainbow Reef and trekking
the Lavena Coastal Walk

LOMAIVITIS (p165)
Ambling down Levuka's colonial
Beach St or winding down
on Caqalai's exquisite beach

LAU GROUP (p217)
Delving into Fijian-Tongan
culture or kayaking through
the magical Bay of Islands

LEGEND

	Primary Road
	Secondary Road
	Tertiary Road
	Unsealed Road

0   50 km
0   30 miles

ELEVATION

	900m
	600m
	300m
	0

Cikobia

Vatauua

Qelelevu

Druadrua

Nukusemanu
Cobia
Nukubasaga
Nukubalati

Mali

Labasa

Rabi

Batini
(Nasorolevu)
(1111m)

Yavu
Yanuca

VU

Waisali
Rainforest
Reserve

Tunuloa
Peninsula

Kioa

Natuvu

Matei

Nanukulailai
Nanuku Levu
Laucala

Wailagi
Lala

Savusavu

Somosomo

TAVEUNI

Qamea

Naitaba

Malima

nenalala

Koro

Yacata

Kaibu

Kanacea

Ayea

Vanua
Balavu

Nukutolu

Vatu Vara

Susui

Namalata

Munia

Mago

Katafaga

**NORTHERN
LAU**

Tuvuca

Batiki

Nairai

KORO SEA

Cicia

Nayau

Gau

Lakeba

Aiwa

Vanua Vatu

Oneata

Moala

Ororua

Muce

Komo

Tavu Na Sici

Vuaqava

Namaku-i-Lau

Nuvutu-i-Ra

**MOALA
GROUP**

Totoya

Kabara

Nuvutu-i-Loma

Yogasa

**SOUTHERN
LAU**

Matuku

Ogea Levu

Fulaga

Ono-i-Lau

↘ To Ono-i-Lau
(160km)

On the Road

DEAN STARNES Coordinating Author

Clocks run slow in Fiji, and slower still in the Yasawas. Every day felt like a lazy Sunday, and on some days my biggest dilemma was deciding under which palm I should spread my towel. Not that the crew of the *Yasawa Flyer* (p155) would agree – they maintain that I was on and off the boat so often that they should buy me a uniform. I'm pictured here on the boat's top deck, enjoying the view between island stops.

NANA LUCKHAM It was a gloomy day in Savusavu, so we donned wetsuits and headed underneath the water. When we reached Split Rock (p183) – a beautiful coral column with a distinctive split on one side – the sun came out, illuminating a ton of colourful clown fish and, deep in the shadows, a sinister-looking moray eel.

For full author biographies see p266.

FIJI FAVOURITES

While Fiji may be a mere speck on most world maps, it manages to pack a lot into its tiny frame. Its white-sand beaches, coral reefs, clear waters and world-class surf make this one of the Pacific's most alluring playgrounds. Inland the fun continues; there are rainforests to explore, villages to visit, canyons to raft and hot springs to soak in, and with two vibrant and famously friendly cultures, these sunny isles are so warm they sizzle.

Island Escapes

With more than 300 islands scattered across 1 million sq km, Fiji is more water than land. While the mainland is an island, it is the smaller outer islands that have the best beaches. The Yasawa and Mamanuca Groups are Fiji's favourite sons. If you are after a week of sun, tepid water and cold refreshments, they are an excellent choice.

2

① Beachcomber Island

Beachcomber Island (p144) has earned its stripes as Fiji's premier party destination. Head here to strut your stuff on the sand-covered dance floor, and snooze all day on a coconut palm–studded beach.

② Yasawas

Lacing their way up the west coast of Fiji, the Yasawas (p152) comprise 20 volcanic islands famous for crystal-blue lagoons, ruggedly handsome landscapes and heavenly beaches. Top picks include the sand bridge between Waya and Wayasewa (p156), and Nacula's sheltered Long Beach (p163).

③ Navini, Likuliku Lagoon, Vomo & Tokoriki

Beachside dinners, private plunge pools and candle-lit massages – these intimate, adult-only resorts in the Mamanuca Group (p140) leave no pillow unfluffed when it comes to providing honeymooners with some serious island-style pampering.

④ Monuriki

Ever since Tom Hanks' *Cast Away* was filmed here, tiny Monuriki (p147) has become Fiji's biggest star. Its broad lagoon and gorgeous beach have most day trippers wondering why Tom ever left.

⑤ Caqalai

Just south of Ovalau, Caqalai (p175) is the Lomaiviti Group's answer to your prayers. Owned by the Methodist Church, this tiny island is ideal for those looking to escape the hype of the Yasawas and Mamanucas for a slice of solitude and a stretch of secluded sand.

⑥ Ono Island (Kadavu)

Enclosed by the Great Astrolabe Reef, Ono island (p215) off the northern tip of Kadavu is a well-kept secret. Deserted, gold-sand beaches backed by dense tropical forest make this another fine alternative to the busier western groups.

Hiking

Fiji's rugged interior is best appreciated by those prepared to hike a few hills. It's culturally inappropriate to simply hike anywhere, but there are some well-marked trails in Fiji's national parks and reserves that take in some expansive views over surrounding hills and offshore islands. Taveuni offers the widest scope for trekkers, with challenging ascents and coastal ambles.

1 Colo-i-Suva Forest Park

The Colo-i-Suva Forest Park (p121) offers a network of trails between forest-fringed swimming holes, and gorgeous views. Only 11km from downtown Suva, Colo-i-Suva is not only the most accessible park in Fiji, it is also one of the most scenic.

2 Lovoni

Follow a local guide up and over Ovalau's rugged spine to Lovoni (p174), a village built in a broad, flat-bottomed volcanic crater and surrounded by a lush and verdant forest.

3 Sigatoka Sand Dunes

A millennium in the making, the massive Sigatoka Sand Dunes (p101) are one of Fiji's natural highlights. Keep an eye out for pottery shards and archaeological treasures, which the shifting sands occasionally uncover.

4 Koroyanitu National Heritage Park

Options at Koroyanitu National Heritage Park (p96) include treks through Dakua forests in search of waterfalls, and sweaty scrambles up mountain peaks for breathtaking views. Community-based projects mean it's possible to incorporate villagestays and a night in Fiji's highest *bure* in most excursions.

5 Lavena Coastal Walk

Skirting the forest's edge, the 5km Lavena Coastal Walk (p209) links beautiful white- and black-sand beaches to isolated villages. Saving the best for last, trekkers can cool off with a brave leap into a pool carved from basalt by twin waterfalls.

6 Taveuni's Interior

Nature lovers are rewarded for the challenging slog to the top of Des Voeux Peak (p202) with incredible birdwatching opportunities; and for battling through the knee-deep mud at Lake Tagimaucia (p202) with a glimpse of Fiji's national and exceedingly rare *tagimaucia* flower.

Water Sports

Whether it's diving under, floating on or sailing over – the waters that surround Fiji are a mecca for water-sport aficionados. Even seasoned snorkellers are impressed by the water clarity, which can extend to 40m. Top facilities for yachties, surfers and divers ensure that Fiji remains one of the South Pacific's top water-sport destinations.

❶ Kayaking

For a unique turtle's-eye view of the coast, consider one of the multiday kayak excursions through the Yasawa (p154), Kadavu (p213) and Lau (p218) Groups. Paddlers get to savour secluded bays and beaches seldom visited by others.

❷ Diving

Coral-encrusted canyons, schools of oceanic pelagics, shark-feeding encounters, gentle drift dives and walls of feathery soft corals, such as those seen at the numerous dive sites in the Somosomo Strait off Taveuni (see p71), have justifiably earned Fiji considerable praise among diving enthusiasts all over the world.

❸ Yachting

A permanent fixture on the Coconut Milk Run, Fiji has long drawn yachtspeople from all over the globe. For many, picturesque Savusavu Bay (p179) is the first port of call before fanning out through Fiji's extensive archipelago.

❹ Snorkelling

Virtually all of Fiji's offshore islands boast beautiful multihued reefs teeming with colourful marine life. It seems miserly to suggest one spot above the rest, although watching the manta rays near Naviti island (p158) is a thrilling start.

❺ Surfing

While the colossal left-handers of Cloudbreak and Namotu Left (see p141) are enough to make most mortals shiver in their wetsuit, there are many other breaks. The underrated surf at Frigate Passage (p113) is also capable of producing some adrenalin-laced rides.

❻ Windsurfing

From May to July, reliable trade winds, warm water and a good selection of budget accommodation make the small island of Nananu-i-Ra (p134) our recommendation for Fiji's top windsurfing spot.

❼ River Trips

Geology looms large in the humid Namosi Highlands (p113). Sheer canyon walls crowd the Wainikoroiluva River, forming dramatic curtains of rock and the backdrop for Fiji's most scenic river-rafting trip.

Unexpected Treasures

From horse riding to mud slinging, there's more to Fiji than can ever be seen from a beach towel, and since most resorts post listings of daily activities on their blackboards, there is little excuse for not sampling some of Fiji's 'other' delights.

① Horse Riding along Natadola Beach

Sit tall in your saddle and take in a slice of Viti Levu's finest stretch of sand – Natadola Beach (p98). If trotting along the foreshore doesn't suit, riding the cane train along the Coral Coast Scenic Railway (p98) may be just the ticket.

② Sabeto Foothills

Tucked in a valley overlooked by the Sabeto Mountains, the Garden of the Sleeping Giant and the Sabeto Hot Springs (p90) make for an interesting day trip from Nadi. The garden is flushed with orchids, and the springs are dirty (but wholesome) fun for kids large and small.

③ Cruising to the Blue Lagoon

Whether you arrive on your own yacht, aboard the *Yasawa Flyer* or on a luxury cruise, the turquoise waters and crystalline beaches of the aptly named Blue Lagoon (p161) are a powerful fix for any beach addict.

④ Sawa-i-Lau

Hollow Sawa-i-Lau (p164) hides a secret. Beneath its mantle of limestone lies eerie caverns and underwater grottoes inscribed with etchings of forgotten meaning. The only way to see them all is with a nervous dive between caves via an underwater passage.

⑤ Waitavala Water Slide

Only for the brave and bruise-resistant, the Waitavala Water Slide (p202) is a natural chute through water-worn rocks, which dumps swimmers unceremoniously into a pool below.

Culture & History

Few escape without downing at least one shell of *kava*, but those who delve deeper will also discover a fascinating history and a rich tapestry of cultural threads including intriguing traditional etiquette, the kaleidoscopic culture of the Indo-Fijian community, diverse influences of neighbouring South Pacific nations and a Western missionary–inspired Christian inheritance.

1 Sri Siva Subramaniya Swami Temple

Nadi's Sri Siva Subramaniya Swami Temple (p80), the Indo-Fijian community's finest, is painted every hue under the South Sea sun. It is one of the few places outside of the subcontinent showcasing traditional Dravidian architecture.

2 Levuka's Colonial Streets

In Levuka (p169), which was once a refuge for deserters, drunks, freebooters and whalers, you can still catch a whiff of the town's wild and immoral colonial days. It also served as the nation's capital when Fiji was ceded to the British Crown (see p34).

3 Navala village

Nestled in the Nausori Highlands, Navala village (p137) is Fiji's last bastion of traditional architecture, and one of country's most striking villages. From the chief's house to the outhouses, all are built using traditional techniques utilising woven-bamboo walls and thatched roofs.

4 Fiji Museum

The Fiji Museum (p119) traces the country's cultural evolution, from its first Austronesian settlers to the more-recent Indian indentured labourers, with a treasure trove of war clubs, cannibal utensils, chiefly ornaments, ocean-going canoes and intricate *masi* (tapa) cloth creations.

5 Village Homestay

A homestay at a village such as those within the Koroyanitu National Heritage Park (p96), can be an unexpected highlight and a unique insight into everyday life. Bring a *sevusevu* of *yaqona* (*kava*) root and a loud barracking voice for the village rugby-field sidelines.

6 Sunday Church

Throughout Fiji, Sunday church services are filled with beautiful songs and skilfully harmonised vocals. Our favourite? The hymns sung by the congregation at Taveuni's Wairiki Catholic Mission (p201), which will have confirmed atheists believing they've died and gone to heaven.

7 Suva Nightlife

Surprisingly, most Fijians are urban rather than rural dwellers and spending a night on the dance floors of Suva (p128) is not only fun but it may force you to reevaluate preconceived ideas of Fijian youth and Fiji's cultural landscape.

Festivals

Fijians love to sing and many resorts have weekly *meke* nights, including *lovo*-cooked meals and traditional song and dance performances. While most ethnic Fijians reserve their melodious best for church, the isolated islands of Rotuma and Lau have retained some unique, interesting celebrations. On the mainland, the Indo-Fijian Hindi festivals are feted with the most flair.

① Indo-Fijian Fire-walking

To be awestruck by the commitment exhibited by Hindi devotees, witness them pierce their bodies with metal skewers and walk over a bed of hot embers during a fire-walking festival (p124).

② Hibiscus Festival

Fijis largest festival, this nine-day event (p124) draws large crowds that converge on Suva's Albert Park to partake of the stalls, carnival rides and free entertainment.

③ Fara

Few travellers ever make it as far as remote Rotuma, but those who do would be wise to ensure their trip coincides with Fara (p224), the highlight of the Rotuman year. Part Christmas party, part street party – revellers sing their way from house to house.

Contents

On the Road 4

Fiji Favourites 5

Destination Fiji 19

Getting Started 21

Itineraries 26

History 31

The Culture 40

Indo-Fijian History & Culture 49

Food & Drink 56

Environment 61

Diving 67

Viti Levu 75

NADI & THE WEST 78
Nadi 78
Around Nadi 88
Lautoka 92
Koroyanitu National Heritage Park 96
Momi Bay 96
Robinson Crusoe Island 97
Natadola Beach 98
Yanuca & Around 98
CORAL COAST 99
Sigatoka 99
Around Sigatoka 101
Korotogo & Around 104
Korolevu & Around 105
Pacific Harbour 108
Around Pacific Harbour 112
Offshore Islands 113
SUVA 114
History 115
Orientation 116
Information 117
Dangers & Annoyances 119

Sights 119
Activities 122
Walking Tour 123
Tours 124
Festivals & Events 124
Sleeping 125
Eating 126
Drinking 128
Entertainment 129
Shopping 129
Getting There & Away 130
Getting Around 130
KINGS ROAD 130
Nausori & the Rewa Delta 131
Korovou to Dama 132
Naiserelagi Catholic Mission 133
Rakiraki & Around 133
Nananu-i-Ra 134
Tavua 136
Ba 137
Nausori Highlands 137

Mamanuca Group 140
South Sea Island 143
Bounty Island 143
Beachcomber Island 144
Treasure Island 144
Vomo 144
Navini 145
Mana 145
Matamanoa 146
Monuriki 147
Tokoriki 147
Castaway Island 147
Wadigi 148
Malolo 148
Malololailai 149
Namotu 150
Tavarua 151

Yasawa Group 152
Kuata 155
Wayasewa 156
Waya 157
Naviti & Around 158
Tavewa 160
Nanuya Lailai 161
Matacawalevu & Yaqeta 162
Nacula 163
Nanuya Levu (Turtle Island) 164
Sawa-i-Lau 164
Yasawa 164

Lomaiviti Group 165

OVALAU	168
Levuka	169
Lovoni	174
Rukuruku	174
Arovudi (Silana)	174
OTHER LOMAIVITI ISLANDS	175
Yanuca Lailai	175
Moturiki	175
Caqalai	175
Leleuvia	176
Wakaya	176
Koro	176
Naigani	177

Vanua Levu 178

Savusavu & Around	179
North of Savusavu	188
Tunuloa Peninsula	189
Offshore Islands	189
Labasa	190
Around Labasa	194
Nabouwalu & Around	195
Namenalala	195
Wainunu Bay	195

Taveuni 197

Waiyevo, Somosomo & Around	201
Southern Taveuni	203

Matei	205
Eastern Taveuni	208
OFFSHORE ISLANDS	209
Matagi	209
Qamea	210
Laucala	210

Kadavu Group 211

Orientation	212
Information	212
Dangers & Annoyances	212
Activities	213
Sleeping	214
Eating	216
Getting There & Away	216
Getting Around	216

Lau & Moala Groups 217

LAU GROUP	219
Vanua Balavu	219
Other Northern Lau Islands	220
Lakeba	221
Other Southern Lau Islands	221
MOALA GROUP	222
Moala	222

Rotuma 223

History	224
Information	224

Sights & Activities	224
Sleeping & Eating	224
Getting There & Away	225

Directory 226

Transport 241

Health 252

Language 258

Glossary 264

The Authors 266

Behind the Scenes 268

Index 272

GreenDex 279

Map Legend 280

Regional Map Contents

ROTUMA p224

VANUA LEVU pp180–1

YASAWA GROUP p154

TAVEUNI p198

MAMANUCA GROUP p142

VITI LEVU pp76–7

LOMAIVITI GROUP p167

LAU & MOALA GROUPS p219

KADAVU GROUP p212

Destination Fiji

Most who visit Fiji want little more than a white-sand beach, a cloudless sky and the opportunity to fall into a sun-induced coma under a palm tree. On this score, Fiji doesn't disappoint. The Mamanuca and Yasawa islands arc north like a stingray's tail from the body of Viti Levu and are Fiji's movie stars, dangled in front of the world as idyllic South Sea Edens – their reefs and cobalt blue waters providing cinematic eye candy for films such as Tom Hanks' *Cast Away* and Brooke Shields' vehicle to stardom, *The Blue Lagoon*.

Fiji has been in the tourism business for decades and the Nadi and Denarau island-hopping-escape itinerary has proven to be a winning formula. Those who arrive with notions of sipping cocktails on alabaster beaches are seldom disappointed. The underwater scenery is spectacular and some of the finest, and most accessible, dives in the Pacific can be found here. Its reputation as the 'soft coral capital of the world' is well justified and, with the opening of the country's first overwater bungalow resort on Malolo, Fiji remains flushed with sunburnt tourists despite the 2006 coup.

Northwest of Fiji's largest island, Viti Levu, is the Yasawa Group, a chain of volcanic islands set to rival the better-known Mamanucas in the popularity stakes. A daily catamaran threads its way from one bay to the next, dropping off and picking up travellers as it goes. The Yasawas are sparsely populated and the rainless dry spells that once made life so difficult for villagers is proving to be their greatest asset now. Local communities, inspired by the successes achieved further down the line, have opened budget 'resorts' and tout their coral gardens and laid-back charm as 'the real Fiji'.

But the Yasawas and Mamanucas – as lovely as they are – are only part of the equation and there's more to Fiji than can ever be seen from a beach towel.

To get to grips with the national psyche you have to spend some time on either of the two main islands, Viti Levu and Vanua Levu. Two-thirds of the population live in urban centres and it is on Viti Levu that you'll find the country's two cities: Suva, the capital, and Lautoka, a port town reliant on the sugar-cane farms that surround it.

Fijians are politically savvy and their politics fascinates them. Newspaper editorials are choked with letters elaborating on the subtle ramifications of the latest government proposal or pouring scorn on surreptitious political manoeuvrings. And they have much to comment on: since 1987, Fiji has had four coups. The last was in 2006 when Commodore Frank Bainimarama staged a military takeover from the prime minister he himself had appointed after the 2000 coup. He alleged that corruption and systemic racism was his prime motivator and disbanded the Great Council of Chiefs, that (until then) had wielded considerable political clout.

The coups, and the underlying unrest they represent, barely make it across the radar of most travellers. They don't, as the locals are quick to point out, threaten tourist safety. The locals are just as likely to blame irresponsible scaremongering by overseas interests (particularly the New Zealand and Australian governments) as the primary reason for the downturn in their economy as they are their own country's political instability.

The 2006 coup and the proposed People's Charter underpin one of Fiji's most contentious issues – who qualifies to be a 'Fijian' and enjoy the rights that go with it? In the late 1870s, Britain brought indentured Indian labourers to work the sugar-cane fields. More than 130 years on, Indo-Fijians are yet to enjoy the civil liberties enjoyed by indigenous Fijians.

FIJI IN A COCONUT SHELL

Population: 861,000

GDP: $4.6 billion

GDP growth: -6.6%

Number of international airports: 2

Largest export: sugar (18%)

Length of coastline: 1129km

Chiefs in the Great Council of Chiefs: 55

Number of coups since independence: 4 and counting

Percentage of Indo-Fijians in the population: 37% and falling

Number of people eaten by Ratu (Chief) Udreudre: 872

Today the tension between the ethnic Fijian landowners and the entrepreneurial Indo-Fijians is one of the key problems facing Fiji. The fallout from this couldn't have come at a worse time. Fearful of an Indian-led government, many Fijian landowners have refused to renew Indo-Fijian sugar-cane farmers' land leases. Farmers and their families have suddenly found themselves homeless, and have drifted into a cycle of poverty in squatters' camps around the main centres. Meanwhile, a declining sugar yield and the EU's decision to cut sugar subsidies is dealing a double blow of woe to Fiji's beleaguered main industry.

'Within minutes of landing at Nadi's airport the word *bula* (cheers! hello! welcome!) will be burnt into your vocabulary'

While this may sound all doom and gloom, Fijians themselves have a deep well of optimism, and it is their unfailing friendliness and unrestrained warmth that has so endeared them to travellers the world over. Within minutes of landing at Nadi's airport the word *bula* (cheers! hello! welcome!) will be burnt into your vocabulary. Fijians are also noteworthy for their elastic sense of time; for some travellers the transition between the fast-food, quick-fix West and the chilled-out, take-it-as-it-comes islands can be frustrating. This languid pace is called 'Fiji time' and it refers as much to a philosophy of *kerekere* (a concept that time and property is communal) as to anything that can be read off a clock.

'Fiji time' creeps even slower north of Viti Levu. The country's second largest island, Vanua Levu, is surprisingly undeveloped and its deeply indented coastline and rugged interior continue to challenge road builders and civil engineers. Daily flights from Nadi and Suva, however, have made this island fortress quite accessible. Few travellers make it beyond a handful of resorts; Savusavu, often the first port of call for visiting yachts, is the island's most visited area. Indeed, Fiji is a great maritime nation and has long been defined by the ocean it drifts in. When Captain Cook's crew first met the Fijians in Tonga they described them as 'formidable warriors and ferocious cannibals, builders of the finest vessels in the Pacific'. It was this vast stretch of water, which both protected and isolated the locals, that fostered the culture Cook's men described. Perhaps then, it is only fitting that Fiji today has become a permanent fixture for yachties on the 'Coconut Milk Run' between the US and New Zealand.

In Fiji's vast territorial waters, spinning on the periphery around the hub of Viti Levu, are 321 other islands. Taveuni, the Garden Island (so called because of its abundant tropical growth and beautifully weathered mountains), and further south, Kadavu, with its kaleidoscopic Great Astrolabe Reef, are but two. Life on these islands revolves around church, village etiquette and gardening. For the moment, locals here are happy to sit back and observe, with wry commentary, the political goings-on in Suva.

Getting Started

Fiji has it all – beautiful beaches, pristine reefs, welcoming faces, abundant sunshine, a rich culture and a genuine zest for tourism. Travelling around the mainland and to the Yasawa and Mamanuca islands couldn't be easier. The mainland is ringed by a road and well serviced by buses, and the Yasawa and Mamanuca Groups are serviced by a fleet of modern catamarans. Virtually everyone speaks English. There are dive centres, honeymoon retreats, backpacker camps, fishing charters and kayaking tours on offer all over the place. For those wishing to indulge in some serious R&R, five-star resorts can arrange everything from a helicopter shuttle to a champagne lunch on a deserted atoll. With only minimal planning, independent travellers to these areas can make use of a good transport network and numerous accommodation options.

Peak-season travel requires more thought, as will reaching the more remote areas such as Vanua Levu, Taveuni and Kadavu. Here roads deteriorate and infrastructure becomes less reliable. Factor in the cost of an internal flight and be prepared for small boats to transport you along the coast. These islands, however, are the place to head to if you want to get off the tourist trail and explore the archipelago independently.

Whatever your preferred approach to travel, bear in mind that Fiji is not a 'budget' destination per se and caters better to midrange wallets. That said, plenty of backpackers head here and travel comfortably enough without spending a ransom.

WHEN TO GO

The best time to visit is during the so-called 'Fijian winter' or 'dry season', from May to October. This time of year is more pleasant, with lower rainfall and humidity, milder temperatures and less risk of meteorological hazards such as cyclones. Consequently these six months make up the high season, when airfare and accommodation costs are at their highest. Expect costs to peak in June and July.

See Climate Charts (p233) for more information.

Fiji's 'wet season' is from November to April, with the heaviest rains falling from December to mid-April. This is when tropical cyclones, or hurricanes, are most likely to occur. Strong, destructive cyclones are, however, a fairly

---

DON'T LEAVE HOME WITHOUT...

- Insect repellent, which is sold only in city pharmacies but needed most elsewhere
- Plenty to read – bookshops are only found in the cities
- Reef shoes to protect yourself and the reefs that surround most of Fiji's islands
- A Zenlike patience to cope with 'Fiji time', which is more official here than GMT
- Wedding rings if you're here to get hitched (see p229)
- Your own snorkel and mask, because they'll probably get a daily workout
- Checking the current visa situation (p239)
- Keeping abreast of the current political climate – Fiji has experienced several coups
- A waterproof camera to capture your marine encounters and make your friends jealous
- Sunscreen and a raincoat to combat tropical climate conditions
- Seasickness tablets if you don't have sea legs – with over 300 islands, there are a lotta boats in Fiji!

rare phenomenon in Fiji. The country has been hit by an average of 10 to 12 cyclones per decade, with only two or three of these being very severe.

A once-in-a-generation spate of tropical storms wreaked havoc across western Viti Levu in January 2009, causing a declaration of a state of emergency there. At least 11 people died during the week of torrential rains and the resulting floods forced thousands of villagers from their homes and into shelters. Hundreds of tourists were left stranded and many roads and bridges were destroyed by floodwaters and mud.

If you're travelling during the wet season it's best to head to drier regions such as the Mamanuca and Yasawa island groups. That said, December and January are also busy months as they coincide with school holidays in both Australia and New Zealand, and with Fijians visiting relatives. In February, March and November, however, Fiji sees fewer tourists and you're more likely to get bargains on your accommodation. The temperature during these months is also fairly appealing, so you get the best of both worlds.

Fijian school holidays can have an impact on accommodation availability. They generally last for two weeks from late April to early to mid-May and mid-August to early September. Summer holidays run from early December to late January.

COSTS & MONEY

Although cheaper than many Pacific countries, Fiji doesn't provide travellers with the same value as, say, Southeast Asia. Many backpackers are surprised to discover that Fiji is not a US$20-a-day destination.

Regardless of your budget, accommodation and food will easily be your greatest expense. Local transport and markets are extremely good value, particularly in more remote areas; however, anything geared for tourists is far more expensive. On average, budget travellers can expect to pay about $100 to $150 per day for food, transport and accommodation. If you stay in dorms and dine on corned beef, you can do it for a little less. Island-hopping is generally fairly pricey: if you're planning to move around a lot, it's a good idea to stay within one island chain.

Solo midrange travellers can expect to pay around $190 per day, and couples can expect to pay around $150 per person per day. These costs are based on transport, comfortable hotel (but not resort) accommodation and eating out three times a day. Abundant self-catering options enable travellers in this price bracket to reduce their overall costs significantly. Families benefit the most from self-contained units, because children are often charged either heavily discounted rates or nothing at all.

Resorts usually include all meals and plenty of activities in their tariffs, and hover around $300 to $600 per night for a room suitable for a couple or a family of four. Children often stay for free and sleep on divan-type beds that are left as couches when the room occupancy is only for two. Kids clubs are often free and some of the activities kids most enjoy, such as swimming and snorkelling, are also free.

Top-end options can cost anywhere up to $3000 a night for accommodation, food, alcohol and activities.

Most budget and midrange accommodation includes Fiji's 12.5% VAT (value-added tax) and the new 5% hotel turnover tax in the advertised rates, but this is not always the case, so check before you book. Many will also charge an additional 3% if you settle by credit card. Again, you should check this before you book. All rates quoted in this book are peak season rates, which tend to be 10% to 20% higher than low season rates. See p226 for more information on accommodation and p58 for more information on eating costs.

HOW MUCH?

Taxi in Nadi or Suva $5-12

Snorkel hire $5-10

Local bus ride $0.75

Coffee $3

Cocktail $8-15

TRAVELLING RESPONSIBLY

Because of its relative isolation in the middle of the earth's largest ocean, travelling to Fiji clocks up a lot of carbon emissions. Some airlines support charities aimed specifically at offsetting carbon credits and you can enquire about these when you book your flight. There is also a lot that can be done whilst in Fiji, such as travelling on public transport or hiring bicycles. Divers and snorkellers do a lot of damage standing on fragile corals, destroying decades of growth in a single misplaced step. See the boxed texts, p71 and p66, for advice on how to minimise your impact on the ecology.

A peculiarity to Fiji is that most land is owned by traditional *mataqali* (landowning groups) and they earn substantial rents from the land they lease to international resorts. You can rest easy knowing that no matter where you stay, chances are that at least some of the money you spend is going to nearby communities. However, by choosing to spend your money with locally owned operators, even more Fijians will directly benefit from your stay. Beyond this, the GreenDex (p279) lists environmentally sound hotels and socially responsible businesses.

Fiji is an archipelago of 322 islands and a further 500 smaller islets covering a total area of more than 1.3 million sq km, with a land area of 18,300 sq km.

TRAVEL LITERATURE

If there is one country that lends itself to whiling away the hours with a good book, it is Fiji. Consider packing something that offers a little local insight as well as the latest bestseller. Many of the books listed here can be ordered online through the **USP Book Centre** (Map p116; ☎ 323 2500; www .uspbookcentre.com; University of the South Pacific, Suva) or bought on the campus. Other books can be purchased at the Fiji Museum (p119) in Suva.

On Fiji Islands, by Ronald Wright, is an oldie but a goody. It's a great read to get your head around the history, culture and flavour of the country, complemented by personal anecdotes of the author's travels.

Getting Stoned with Savages, by J Maarten Troost, is a humorous personal account of the author's tireless devotion to *kava* (mildly narcotic, muddy and odd-tasting drink made from the aromatic roots of the Polynesian pepper shrub) and the Fijians and Vanuatans he drank it with.

Geoff Raymond's *Footprints in Fiji* is also good for a beautifully humanistic impression of the country. It is an endearing and humorous memoir of an Australian family that moved to Fiji in the mid-'80s to run a resort abandoned by its previous owners.

Yesterday's Child: Once Upon an Island in the Fijis, by Wesley Hall, is a light-hearted romance, set at the end of WWII, and follows the fortunes of a man's quest for fame, love and favour from a lesser god.

Kava in the Blood, by Peter Thomson, is a strong, evocative autobiography of a white Fijian who became a senior civil servant and was imprisoned by Lieutenant Colonel Sitiveni Rabuka during the 1987 coup.

There are two excellent photographic books: *Children of the Sun,* by Glen Craig, which gets under the skin of the country by capturing its diverse population; and *Fiji: The Uncharted Sea,* by Federico Busonero, which is a visual celebration of the archipelago's exquisite marine life and beaches.

INTERNET RESOURCES

The web is an absolute goldmine for travellers. Before leaving home you can research your trip, hunt down bargain airfares, book hotels, check on weather conditions or chat with locals and other travellers about where to go and where to steer clear of.

TOP 10   FIJI

FESTIVALS & EVENTS

Fijians love to celebrate, and barely need a reason to do so. The country's festivals calendar is enhanced by two distinct cultures and the following are 10 reasons to get stuck into it. See p234 for more details.

1 Hindu Holi (Festival of Colours; nationwide), February or March

2 Ram Naumi (Birth of Lord Rama; Suva), March or April

3 Bula Festival (Nadi), July

4 Hibiscus Festival (Suva), August

5 Hindu Ritual Fire Walking (nationwide), August

6 Fiji Regatta Week (Musket Cove), September

7 Lautoka's Sugar Festival (Lautoka), September

8 Ram Leela (Play of Rama; Labasa), October

9 Diwali (Festival of Lights; nationwide), late October or early to mid-November

10 South Pacific World Music Festival (Savusavu), November

MUST-SEE FLICKS

Stoke your enthusiasm for a trip by getting an eyeful of the scenery and a mindset of the culture. Although Fiji hasn't exactly been the subject of many films, the following were filmed, if not also set, here. They range from the outstanding, award-winning *The Land Has Eyes* to the swashbuckling, tacky, iconic and plain ridiculous. See p45 for reviews of some of them.

1 *The Land Has Eyes* (2004) directed by Vilsoni Hereniko

2 *Coral Reef Adventure* (2002) distributed by Macgillivray Freeman

3 *No 2* (2006) directed by Toa Fraser

4 *Flynn* (1993) directed by Frank Howson

5 *Cast Away* (2000) directed by Robert Zemeckis

6 *Mr Robinson Crusoe* (1932) directed by Edward Sutherland

7 *The Blue Lagoon* (1979) directed by Randal Kleiser

8 *The Dove* (1974) directed by Charles Jarrott

9 *His Majesty's O'Keefe* (1953) directed by Byron Haskin

10 *Anacondas: The Hunt for the Blood Orchid* (2004) directed by Dwight Little

DIY CULTURAL EXPERIENCES

Plenty of travellers come to Fiji on package holidays to avoid having to think too hard about how to enjoy what the country has to offer. But delving into the real Fiji on your own is so easy it requires minimal effort and brain cells. The following are some of the best cultural experiences to be had in this archipelago; all are unmissable.

1 Visiting a village (p231)

2 Watching a *meke* (dance performance that enacts stories and legends; p46)

3 Drinking *kava* (p57)

4 Witnessing fire-walking (p109)

5 Eating at a *lovo* (feast cooked in a pit oven; p57)

6 Rafting on a *bilibili* (bamboo raft; p231)

7 Offering *sevusevu* (presentation of a gift; p40)

8 Appreciating a Hindu temple (p80)

9 Catching a rugby match (p41)

10 Shopping for souvenirs and saris (p238)

Try the following websites for useful information on Fiji.

Fiji Times (www.fijitimes.com.fj) Fiji's daily newspaper online.

Fiji Village (www.fijivillage.com) Excellent site updated with daily news and links to local events, including music, movies and sport.

Fiji Visitors Bureau (www.bulafiji.com) Fiji's official tourist site, offering information on accommodation, activities and getting around, with links and an email directory.

Lonely Planet (www.lonelyplanet.com) Get started on your Fiji planning with snapshots of the country, travel links, postcards from other travellers, and the Thorn Tree travel forum.

South Pacific Tourism Organisation (www.spto.org) Useful travel directory with info on South Pacific countries.

Itineraries
CLASSIC ROUTES

ISLAND FLING
10-14 Days / Mamanucas & Yasawas

Begin your fling in **Nadi** (p78), taking a day to acclimatise in the hot springs near the **Sabeto Mountains** (p90). Suitably relaxed, board the *Yasawa Flyer* to begin your island-hopping excursion through the **Yasawas** (p152). Spend the next few days on the sliver of sand that connects **Wayasewa** (p156) to **Waya** (p157) before drifting north to **Naviti** (p158) to snorkel with manta rays. Reboard the *Flyer* for a dash up to **Nacula** (p163), or **Nanuya Lailai** (p161), where you can paddle in the **Blue Lagoon** (p161). From here, leapfrog your way back down the chain stopping at **Matacawalevu** (p162), and Naviti once more. Spend a night or two partying at **Beachcomber Island** (p144), and then change boats and loop through the rest of the **Mamanucas** (p140). Here the resorts go upmarket and it's a difficult choice between the romantic **Tokoriki** (p147), versatile **Matamanoa** (p146) and the picture-perfect **Castaway Island** (p147). Before returning to Nadi, be sure to take a day trip to **Monuriki** (p147).

This 190km route is the ultimate beach fling – nothing but sun, sea and snorkelling – winding its way through the Yasawas' secluded beaches before visiting the Mamanucas' holiday hot spots. To make the most of Fiji, combine it with the Once Around the Block itinerary.

ONCE AROUND THE BLOCK
Two-Three Weeks / Viti Levu & A Yasawa Or Mamanuca Island

Assuming you start in **Nadi** (p78) – although you could begin anywhere – follow the Coral Coast Hwy to the **Momi Guns** (p97), and **Natadola Beach** (p98) for some horse riding. Chug into the verdant interior on the **Coral Coast Scenic Railway** (p98) or don your sneakers and trek to the top of the **Sigatoka Sand Dunes** (p101). Kids will love feeding the wildlife at the **Kula Eco Park** (p104), while mum and dad might enjoy a few days poolside at a resort in **Korolevu** (p105). Amble into **Pacific Harbour** (p108) to go diving with sharks in **Beqa Lagoon** (p109) or take a boat trip out to surf the underrated **Frigate Passage** (p113). Don't miss the opportunity to raft the canyons of the **Navua River** (p112) before heading to **Suva** (p114). Check out the Fiji Museum and then spend a day swinging, Tarzan-style, into the refreshing pools at **Colo-i-Suva Forest Park** (p121). Complete the circuit via the northern Kings Road, windsurfing at **Nananu-i-Ra** (p134) or scuba diving at **Rakiraki** (p133). From here, head back to sugar country and visit **Lautoka** (p92), the second largest city. This is a great base to explore the **Nausori Highlands** (p131), and to trek in the **Koroyanitu National Heritage Park** (p96). Wind the whole thing up with a well-deserved rest on one of the **Yasawa** (p152) or **Mamanuca** (p140) islands.

For those who can't sit still, this tour is easily combined with the other itineraries and could be run in either direction. It takes a bus 12 hours to run the circuit, but allow 14 to 21 days to see it all. All up, you'll cover 450km.

ROADS LESS TRAVELLED

THE NORTHERN LOOP   10 Days / Suva to Vanua Levu

This route takes in Fiji's other 'mainland' – Vanua Levu. Trek, shop, eat and drink here before hopping over to neighbouring Taveuni, which has spectacular snorkelling, diving, mountains and water slides. In total this trip covers about 480km.

Beginning in **Suva** (p114), spend a morning at the excellent Fiji Museum and then an afternoon stocking up on souvenirs at the craft market. After exhausting Suva's nightlife, hop on a flight to **Vanua Levu** (p178) and land yourself in **Labasa** (p190), a sugar town where you can smell the molasses in the air. Visit the Wasavula Ceremonial Site and take a side-trip to the mystifying **Cobra Rock** (p194) inside the Naag Mandir Temple.

Continue your Vanua Levu adventure by jumping on a bus and heading south to **Savusavu** (p179). Spend a day or two taking in the sights, and the evenings talking with visiting skippers over a beer at the Savusavu Yacht Club. Take a day trip to the rich and colourful **Waisali Rainforest Reserve** (p188), or rent a 4WD and brave the roads to the lesser-travelled **Tunuloa Peninsula** (p189).

Then it's time to head to gorgeous **Taveuni** (p197). If you've got sea legs, catch a ferry, if not, the flight provides some spectacular views. **Somosomo** (p201) is a good base from which to explore the surrounding area. First might be a day snorkelling or diving at the magnificent **Rainbow Reef** (p199). Satisfied with the quality of the undersea ecology, trek the **Lavena Coastal Walk** (p209) to see what's topside. Or, for a view of both, climb to the top of the world…well, to the top of **Des Voeux Peak** (p202), which is just as good. Before heading back to Suva scare yourself silly on the **Waitavala Water Slide** (p202).

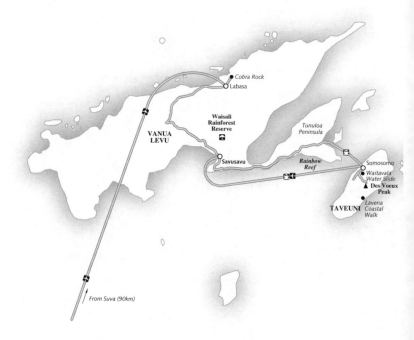

MIDDLE OF NOWHERE   Two Weeks / Lomaiviti & Lau Groups

If you really want to get off the beaten track, head to the **Lomaiviti Group** (p165). The easiest way is to fly (via the Bureta Airstrip), but the adventurous can take the ferry from Natovi Landing (via Buresala Landing) to **Levuka** (p169), which was the original capital and is one of Fiji's most picturesque towns. Spend a few days making the most of the sights in this town littered with colonial buildings, and boasting a harmonious multicultural population. Since you have come so far, it would be criminal not to dive **Levuka Passage** (p166), or climb Gun Rock to take in the view. Spend one day in the village of **Lovoni** (p174), which is nestled in a crater in the centre of Ovalau, and another in **Arovudi** (Silana; p174), which has a remarkable church.

Once you've had your urban fix, book a passage to the coral island of **Caqalai** (p175) and leave consumer crutches – but not your mask and snorkel – behind. Take a day or two to explore this tiny island (it only takes 15 minutes to circumnavigate it), making the most of its dazzling beaches and beautiful offshore reefs. It's more of the same on **Leleuvia** (p176), the next island down. But don't linger too long; there's a plane to catch in Suva and you'll need to catch a boat from either Caqalai or Leleuvia to make it in time.

Before catching the once-weekly flight to the Lau Group – yes, you'll be there for a week – stock up on provisions to share with your soon-to-be new-found friends on **Vanua Balavu** (p219), where you might swim in the spectacular Bay of Islands or hike to the Meeting House of the Gods.

> Reset your watch to 'Fijian time': take your time exploring the Lomaiviti islands and Levuka's colonial heritage; return to Suva by leapfrogging between two coral islands; and, if you are game, fly to the remote Lau group. Excluding the plane trip you travel 200km.

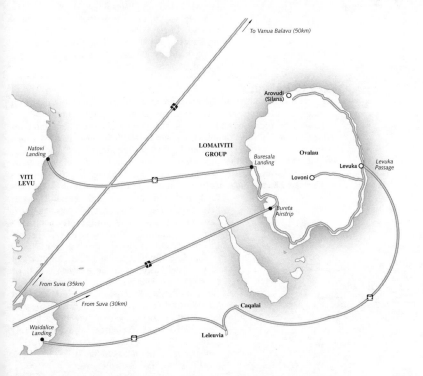

TAILORED TRIPS

IN PURSUIT OF THE PERFECT BEACH

It's no accident that Fiji is synonymous with sun, sand and sea. Boasting over 300 islands, the archipelago offers copious versions of the perfect beach. The Mamanucas are a good place to start, with wide sandy beaches, populated by partygoing backpackers on **Beachcomber Island** (p144), or families indulging in innumerable water sports on **Treasure Island** (p144). If you're looking for something more exclusive, the intimate beaches at **Matamanoa** (p146) and **Tokoriki** (p147) should be just the ticket.

The Yasawa islands are home to two of Fiji's finest: Oarsman's Bay's sublime beach on **Nacula** (p163) and the exquisite beach of the Blue Lagoon on **Nanuya Lailai** (p161). On **Waya** (p157), the Sunset Beach Resort sits on a beautifully thick curve of beach; while Botaira Beach Resort on **Naviti** (p158) is planted on a long stretch of soft, white sand.

Glorious **Natadola Beach** (p98) is Viti Levu's best stretch of shoreline and the **Tunuloa Peninsula** (p189) on Vanua Levu boasts dramatic views and 5.5km of superb coast.

Minuscule **Caqalai** (p175) in the Lomaivitis is a coral island renowned for its perimeter of lovely beach. Prime beaches can also be found on nearby **Leleuvia** (p176) and **Naigani** (p177).

Matagi (p209) and **Qamea** (p210), on Taveuni, have world-class diving and divine beaches, and on **Kadavu** (p211) you'll find gorgeous swimming beaches at Dive Kadavu and Nagigia Island Resorts.

BACK TO NATURE

Here's a quick rundown on where to swim in, walk through, surf on, raft down or hike up some of the country's most spectacular natural attractions.

To work the pins you need look no further than Viti Levu's mountainous interior. Close to Nadi and Lautoka, **Koroyanitu National Heritage Park** (p96) is a must for hikers, who can take either a four-hour trail to the summit of Castle Rock or a full-day trek through the park; afterwards, soothe weary joints in the nearby Sabeto Hot Springs. Also on Viti Levu, you can raft through beautiful canyons in the steamy **Namosi Highlands** (p113) rainforest or ride a horse along **Natadola**

Beach (p98). On Vanua Levu, the **Waisali Rainforest Reserve** (p188) features a short but stunning trek descending to a waterfall, while on **Taveuni** (p197) there's the stunning Lavena Coastal Walk – a 5km trail through forests, beaches and villages.

For those who believe that it's better wetter, suit up for a shark dive in the **Beqa Lagoon** (p109), or snorkel with the manta rays in the **Yasawas** (p158). Taveuni's **Rainbow Reef** (p199) and Kadavu's **Great Astrolabe Reef** (p213) have enough dive spots to keep most divers happy for several holidays.

The Mamanucas' **Cloudbreak** and **Namotu Left** (p141) are surf breaks that attract the world's top surfers, while **Nananu-i-Ra** (p136) has Fiji's most reliable wind for windsurfing.

History

VITIAN ARRIVALS

The original inhabitants of Fiji called their home Viti. Based on pottery remains found in the area, archaeologists believe these people were Austronesians, who arrived about 1220 BC and stayed for only a short while before mysteriously disappearing from the archaeological record. Their descendants, who became assimilated with new arrivals from Melanesia, were coastal dwellers.

Around 500 BC a shift from a coastal, fishing lifestyle towards agriculture occurred, along with an expansion of population – probably due to further immigration from other parts of Melanesia – that led to an increase in intertribal feuding. Cannibalism became a ritual for humiliating defeated foes. New architecture developed around this martial culture, with villages moving to ring moat-fortified sites during times of war. Around AD 1000 Tongan incursions began, continuing until the arrival of Europeans.

Eventually the islands became known to Europeans as Fiji. The story goes that Captain James Cook asked the Tongans what the name of the islands to their west was. He heard 'Feegee', the Tongan pronunciation of Viti: so 'Fiji' came from an Englishman's mishearing of a Tongan's mispronunciation.

While there were extended periods of peace, Fiji was undergoing intense social upheaval at the time of the first European settlement in the early 19th century, and these regular tribal skirmishes led Europeans to believe that it was in a constant state of war.

There's a widespread legend that the first Fijians arrived from Tanganyika, East Africa, in the ancestral canoe *Kaunitoni*.

EUROPEAN ENCOUNTERS

Europeans sailed the Pacific during the 17th and 18th centuries, ostensibly to find *terra australis incognita*, the great 'unknown southern land' later called Australia. Some of them bumped into Fiji on the way. The lure of exotic trade goods also brought many fortune hunters.

The first European to sail the area was a Dutchman, Abel Tasman, who sailed past in 1643 on his way back from Van Diemen's Land. His descriptions of treacherous reefs kept mariners away for the next 130 years. English navigator James Cook stopped over on Vatoa in the southern Lau Group in 1774 and his countryman, Captain Bligh, passed between Vanua Levu and Viti Levu after he was thrown off the *Bounty* in 1789. The channel is known as Bligh Water in memory of the mutinied captain.

Tongans had long traded colourful *kula* (a type of parrot) feathers, *masi* (printed bark cloth) and weapons with the eastern Fiji islands, but from the early 19th century new trading partners appeared. European whalers and

According to indigenous Fijians' oral history, the first arrivals in the area came with a great chief known as Lutunasobasoba, who landed at Vuda.

TIMELINE

1220 BC	500 BC	AD 1000
The Austronesian people arrive, choosing to settle only along the coast and to live off fishing, just as they did in Tonga before gradually moving to Samoa.	Melanesians from elsewhere in the Pacific arrive and begin permanent settlement, which includes moving inland and establishing farms and other more-sustainable ways of life.	Tongan and Samoan warriors begin a series of incursions into Vitian territory, forcing Fijians to create fortified sites and adopt a warlike lifestyle.

traders of sandalwood and bêche-de-mer began to visit as better maps of the surrounding reefs were available.

Fragrant sandalwood was highly valued in Europe and Southeast Asia. Tongans initially controlled trade, obtaining sandalwood from the chiefs on Vanua Levu and then selling it to the Europeans. But when a ship-wrecked survivor of the *Argo*, Oliver Slater, discovered the location of the supply, news quickly spread of its whereabouts. In 1805 Europeans began to trade directly with Fijians, bartering metal tools, tobacco, cloth, muskets and gunpowder. By 1813 the sandalwood supply was exhausted, but firearms and the resulting increase in violent tribal warfare were lasting consequences.

The other commodity that brought trade to the area, bêche-de-mer, was an Asian delicacy. The intensive harvesting and drying required to process the seafood required hundreds of workers at each bêche-de-mer station. Chiefs who sent their villagers to work boosted their own wealth and power, with an estimated 5000 muskets traded during this period. Bêche-de-mer was also a short-lived trade, lasting only from 1830 to 1850.

> Samples of Lapita pottery found at the Sigatoka Sand Dunes, which is now open to the public, suggests this was one of the earliest settlements in Viti.

King of Fiji

By 1829 the chiefdom of Bau, in eastern Viti Levu where European trade was most intense, had accumulated great power. Bauan chief Cakobau, known to foreigners as Tui Viti (King of Fiji), was at the height of his influence in the 1850s when he first offered to sell the islands to Britain, despite having no real claim over most of Fiji.

In 1848 a Tongan armada of war canoes captured Vanua Balavu in northern Lau, and by 1860 Tongans controlled several of the eastern islands, posing a serious threat to Cakobau's power.

> For a clear, concise and readable overview of Fijian and regional history, dip into *Worlds Apart: A History of the Pacific Islands* by IC Campbell.

Cakobau needed some serious allies both militarily and financially. In 1862 he again proposed to Britain's consul that he would cede the islands to Queen Victoria, in return for the payment of his debts. The consul declined, doubting Cakobau's claims on the kingdom, but the rumours caused a large influx of settlers to Levuka, who bickered among themselves. Disputes also erupted with Fijians over land ownership and the town became a lawless and greedy outpost, on the verge of anarchy and racial war. Cakobau's huge debt was not cleared until 1868 when the Australian Polynesia Company agreed to pay it in exchange for land (see p115).

GOD OR GREED

In the 1830s London Missionary Society (LMS) pastors and Wesleyan Methodist missionaries arrived in southern Lau to find converts and preach against cannibalism.

Conversion of chiefs became the most successful strategy, with the powerful Cakobau adopting Christianity in 1854. This was a triumph for the

1643	**1774**	**1789**
Dutchman Abel Tasman's ship is almost wrecked off the northern islands; he manages to chart the eastern portion of Vanua Levu so that others can avoid it.	After landing at Australia, Captain Cook visits – although he limits his contact, due to the islands' reputation as the Cannibal Isles; he hears 'Viti' pronounced as 'Fiji', and gives the country another name.	Captain William Bligh and 18 others make rough navigation charts while drifting between the Vitian islands after being cast adrift near Tonga following the *Bounty* mutiny.

TABUA

Tabua (carefully polished and shaped whales' teeth) were believed to be shrines for the ancestor spirits. They were, and still are, highly valued items and essential to diplomacy. The acceptance of a *tabua*, which is a powerful *sevusevu* (a gift presented as a token of esteem or atonement), binds a chief to the gift-giver. Traditionally, a chief's body was accompanied to the grave by a *tabua*.

Originally *tabua* were rare, obtained only from washed-up sperm whales or through trade with Tonga. However, European traders introduced thousands of whale teeth and replicas made of whalebone, elephant tusk and walrus tusk. These negotiation tools became concentrated in the hands of a few dominant chiefdoms, increasing their power.

Methodist Church, who later sent Reverend Thomas Baker out to spread the gospel in the western highlands of Viti Levu. However, in 1867 he was eaten by locals who resented his manner and the imposition of ideas associated with Bau (see p138).

Acceptance of Christianity was made easier because of its similarity to the existing beliefs of *tabu* (sacred prohibitions) and *mana* (spiritual power), with most Fijians adopting it in parallel with traditional spirituality. Villagers continued to worship ancestral gods through such practices as the *kava* ceremony, *tabu* areas and codes of conduct, and the symbolic *tabua* (see the boxed text, above).

Commercial Settlers

A whaling settlement was established at Levuka, on Ovalau, in the 1830s, and became a major port in the South Pacific for traders and warships. In 1840 Charles Wilkes led a US expedition that produced the first reasonably complete chart of the Fijian islands. He also negotiated a port-regulation treaty under which Cakobau and his subchiefs were paid for the protection of foreign ships and the supply of provisions.

However, this seemingly mutually beneficial relationship was fraught with tension. Relations began to deteriorate in 1841 when Levuka was razed by fires, which the settlers suspected Cakobau of instigating. Later, during the 1849 US Independence Day celebrations, the Nukulau island home of US consul John Brown Williams was also destroyed by fire, and locals helped themselves to his possessions. Williams held Cakobau (as nominal King of Fiji) responsible for the actions of his people and sent him a substantial damages bill, which was a significant source of Cakobau's debts.

Blackbirding

When the American Civil War created a worldwide cotton shortage, Fiji enjoyed a cotton boom that indirectly stimulated blackbirding, a trade in labourers. Europeans brought other Pacific Islanders, particularly from the

Missionaries developed written Fijian language – called Bauan – from the dialect spoken in the powerful chiefdom of Bau during the 1830s.

1804	**1830**	**1840**
After trading with Tongans, Europeans discover sandalwood on Vanua Levu and begin a direct trade, which utterly depletes the supply by 1813; some chiefs become briefly wealthy.	The first London Missionary Society pastors arrive from Tahiti and begin to devise a written language, which they will teach in schools and use to record early-contact culture.	The first US navy visit, commanded by Captain Charles Wilkes, arrives; an incident at Malolo island results in the deaths of two sailors and over 70 Fijians.

Solomon Islands and New Hebrides (now Vanuatu), to labour on the Fijian cotton (and copra and sugar) plantations.

Initially, people were coaxed into agreeing to work for three years in return for minimal wages, food, clothing and return passage. Later, however, chiefs were bribed and men and women traded for ammunition. By the 1860s and '70s the practice had developed into an organised system of kidnapping. Stories of the atrocities and abuses inflicted by recruiters resulted in pressure on Britain to stop the trade, and in 1872 the Imperial Kidnapping Act was passed; but it was little more than a gesture, as Britain had no power to enforce it.

THE COLONIAL PERIOD

The end of the American Civil War in 1865 brought a slump in the world cotton market, which severely affected the Fijian economy. In the following years, new arrivals brought diseases to Fiji, such as measles, which had dramatic effects on the Fijian population. Both were factors of rising social unrest in Fiji. Nevertheless, the Australian Polynesia Company continued to invest in the islands, acquiring land around Suva.

By 1873 Britain was interested in annexing Fiji, citing the need to abolish blackbirding as justification. In reality, they were also interested in protecting Commonwealth commercial interests and bailing out an economy that was drastically overspent. Taking advantage of this interest, Cakobau again approached the British consul (see p32) and negotiated to cede the islands to Queen Victoria. Fiji was pronounced a British crown colony on 10 October 1874, at Levuka.

To ensure the cooperation of the chiefs, the colonial government protected Fijian land rights by forbidding sales to foreigners. This successfully retained land rights for the indigenous owners, and 83% of the land is still owned by indigenous Fijian communities today. Give or take a dissenting chief or two, it also helped to maintain peace.

Fiji's first coup took place 108 years to the day after the arrival of the Leonidas carrying the first group of Indian indentured labourers.

From Girmitiyas to Indo-Fijians

To maintain good relations with its subjects, the colonial government combated exploitation of indigenous Fijians by prohibiting their employment as plantation labourers. However, plantation crops such as cotton, copra and sugar cane, while extremely profitable, demanded large pools of cheap labour. If the colony were to avoid blackbirding then a new labour source had to be found.

In 1878 negotiations were entered into with the Indian colonial government for indentured labourers to come to Fiji on five-year contracts. After this term the labourers (known as *girmitiyas*) would be free to return to India, though free passage for the return trip was only available under certain conditions. Indian indentured labourers began arriving in Fiji at a rate of about 2000 per year.

1867	1874	1875
After several conversions in coastal areas, Methodist minister Reverend William Baker heads into the Western Highlands, but villagers disagree with him about his god and the pastor is killed and eaten.	After much debate and negotiation, Cakobau and 12 other chiefs cede Fiji to Queen Victoria and Britain on 10 October in a ceremony at Levuka.	Without the benefit of the immunity that Europeans had built up to the disease, a third of the population is killed by a savage measles outbreak, creating further tensions in the colony.

The *girmitiyas* were a diverse group from all over India, with 80% Hindu, 14% Muslim and the remainder mostly Sikhs and Christians. Overcrowded accommodation gave little privacy, different castes and religions were forced to mix, and social and religious structures crumbled. Despite the hardship, most *girmitiyas* decided to stay in Fiji once they had served their contract and many brought their families across from India to join them. For more information on Indo-Fijian history and culture, see p49.

By the early 1900s India's colonial government was being pressured by antislavery groups in Britain to abolish the indenture system. In 1916 recruitment stopped and indenture ended officially in January 1919. By this time, 60,537 indentured labourers were in Fiji.

Fiji's colonial government discouraged interaction between Indians and indigenous Fijians. Indo-Fijians, as they came to be called, were restricted from buying Fijian land and moved instead into small business, or took out long-term leases as independent farmers.

The 1920s saw the first major struggle for better conditions for Indo-Fijians and increasing labour unrest. By siding with the indigenous Fijians, Europeans diverted attention from their own monopoly on freehold land, along with their power and influence in the civil service. Playing the 'race card' of blaming all problems on the Indian community and exacerbating fears that the size of the Indian population would surpass that of indigenous Fijians served European interests well.

> Contact with the firearms and diseases of Europeans had a marked impact on Fiji's ethnic population, which has only recently returned to its 18th-century level.

Fiji in Arms

Fiji had only a minor involvement in WWI, as colonial authorities prevented many from enlisting. Nevertheless, about 700 of Fiji's European residents and about 100 Fijians served in Europe.

The conflict in the Pacific during WWII was much closer to home. Fiji itself was used as an Allied training base from an airstrip at Nadi that today has become the international airport. Around 8000 Fijians were recruited into the Fiji Military Force (FMF) and from 1942 to 1943 fought against the Japanese in the Solomon Islands. At the same time, the people of Fiji were also fighting domestically, with Indo-Fijians striking over better pay conditions in the sugar industry, which created greater divisions between European and indigenous Fijians.

INDEPENDENCE & ETHNIC TENSION

The 1960s saw a movement towards Fijian self-government and, after 96 years of colonial administration, Fiji became independent on 10 October 1970. In the rush towards independence important problems such as land ownership and leases and how to protect the interests of a racially divided country were not resolved. Fiji's first election was won by the indigenous Fijian Alliance Party (FAP). Despite an economic boom in the immediate

1879	1882	1951
Following the outlawing of blackbirding, Britain introduces the first group of *girmitiyas* (Indian indentured labourers) to work in the labour-intensive sugar-cane fields of the main island.	As Levuka's difficult geography impeded further expansion, the government is forced to relocate; Suva officially becomes the capital, although the town has barely a dozen buildings.	Fiji Airways, called Air Pacific since 1971, is founded by Australian aviator Harold Gatty, offering one of the first services to another new capital, Canberra, Australia.

FIJI'S FAVOURITE SON

Born in 1888 to a chiefly family on Bau, Ratu Sir Lala Sukuna was well educated, attending an Indo-Fijian school before going on to college in New Zealand. Through his family connections he began to study at an English university, but when WWI erupted Ratu Sukuna was keen to be involved. The British, however, would not allow Fijians to join the armed forces. Ratu Sukuna joined the French Foreign Legion, fighting until he was wounded in 1915. Even this didn't stop him and he returned to service in the newly formed Native Transport Detachment. He was awarded the Croix de Guerre, France's highest military honour.

After the war he studied law, and became the first Fijian to receive a degree. Following the death of his father, in 1920, he returned to Fiji to take up his place as clan chief. He served as chief assistant on the Native Lands Commission, and was later appointed to the Legislative Council. The greatest honour came in 1938 when he was anointed as Tui Lau, a senior chiefly title which had been unfilled for several years – effectively, it made him the most powerful of the chiefs. In 1942 he was also granted an Order of the British Empire (CBE). In the same year he recruited Fijians to fight in WWII, which was permitted by a pronounced change from the WWI policy of not accepting Fijian enlistees.

His greatest achievement was the formation of the Native Land Trust Board, which consolidated individual leases between clan landowners and Indo-Fijian farmers into a consistent agreement, and meant longer leases and a greater sense of security. In the postwar period, Ratu Sukuna cautiously advocated for independence, citing the need to create a form of democracy that all Fijians could live with. He supported the formation of Fiji's first political party, the Fijian Association. He died while sailing back to Britain just 12 years before independence.

---

postindependence years, by the early 1980s the price of sugar had fallen and the country's dependence on it resulted in massive foreign debt.

Economic woes exacerbated ethnic tensions. In Fiji most shops and transport services were (and still are) run by Indo-Fijian families. Stereotypes developed portraying Indo-Fijians as money obsessed, despite the fact that most belonged to poorer working classes and – unlike indigenous Fijians – could never secure land tenure on their farming leases.

The FAP was associated with economic failure, and greater unity among workers led to the formation of the Fiji Labour Party (FLP). In April 1987 an FLP government was elected in coalition with the National Federation Party (NFP). Despite having an indigenous Fijian prime minister, Timoci Bavadra, and a cabinet comprising an indigenous Fijian majority, the new government was labelled 'Indian dominated' because the majority of its MPs were Indo-Fijian.

The Early Coups

With the FLP labelled 'Indian dominated', racial tensions got out of hand. The extremist Taukei movement played on Fijian fears of losing their land rights and of Indo-Fijian political and economic domination. On 14 May

1963	1970	1977
Indigenous Fijian men and women are given the vote, and the 38-member Legislative Council is divided almost equally into indigenous Fijian, Indo-Fijian and European groups.	After 96 years of colonial rule Fiji becomes independent (on 10 October), adopting a British model of parliament with two houses, including a 'House of Lords' made up of Fijian chiefs.	The National Federation Party wins an election but fails to put together a government, so election results are overturned by the governor-general. The following election is a landslide for the Alliance Party.

1987, one month after the elections, Lieutenant Colonel Sitiveni Rabuka took over from the elected government in a bloodless coup, and formed a civil interim government supported by the Great Council of Chiefs.

In September 1987 Rabuka again intervened with military force. The 1970 constitution was invalidated, Fiji was declared a republic and Rabuka proclaimed himself head of state. The following month, Fiji was dismissed from the Commonwealth of Nations.

The coups returned power to an elite minority, with Indo-Fijians effectively removed from the political process. Conflicts resurfaced: between chiefs from eastern and western Fiji, between high chiefs and village chiefs, between urban and rural dwellers, and within the church and trade-union movement. Economically the coups were disastrous, with the two main industries, tourism and sugar, severely affected. Development aid was suspended, and from 1987 to 1992 about 50,000 people, mostly Indo-Fijians, emigrated.

Tipping the Scales

On 25 July 1990 a new constitution was proclaimed. It asserted the political power of the Great Council of Chiefs and the military, while diminishing the position of Indo-Fijians in government. Indo-Fijian political leaders immediately opposed the constitution, claiming it was racist and undemocratic. As the 1992 elections approached, the Great Council of Chiefs disbanded the multicultural FAP and in its place formed the Soqosoqo-ni-Vakavulewa-ni Taukei (SVT; Party of Policy Makers for Indigenous Fijians).

Rabuka returned to the scene as interim prime minister and party leader of the SVT. Changing his hardline approach, he was twice elected: in 1992 and 1994.

WHERE ARE THE CHIEFS?

One of Fiji's most powerful institutions (when active) is the Great Council of Chiefs, which was founded by British colonisers in 1876. The Council consists of 55 members, who are mostly hereditary chiefs, charged with safeguarding the political system. It gained even greater power after the military coups of the 1980s and introduction of the 1990 constitution. The Council appointed presidents, who in turn appointed judges, in consultation with the Judicial & Legal Services Commission. It also has authority over any legislation related to land ownership and common rights.

The Council supported the 2000 coup, as well as the controversial 2005 Promotion of Reconciliation, Tolerance and Unity Bill. When Commodore Frank Bainimarama seized power the Council refused to recognise his power, insisting that Lasenia Qarase be present at meetings. Bainimarama suspended the Council in 2007 and installed his own president. Recently there has been talk of reviving the Council, which would ensure a place for chiefs in contemporary Fijian politics.

1979	**1987**	**1990**
A remake of *The Blue Lagoon,* in the Yasawas, catapults Brooke Shields to teenage stardom and puts Fiji on the top of the romantic-holidaymakers' list.	Two military coups take place in quick succession under the leadership of Lieutenant Colonel Sitiveni Rabuka; Fiji is expelled from the Commonwealth and becomes a republic.	A new constitution is created, which asserts ethnic Fijians' role in the political system, marginalises Indo-Fijians and reserves two seats for the army in the cabinet.

Rewriting the Constitution

In 1995 a Constitutional Review Commission (CRC) presented its findings. It called for a return to a multiethnic democracy and, while concluding that the position of president should be reserved for an indigenous Fijian, proposed no restriction on ethnicity for the prime minister. The government acted on most of the CRC's recommendations and a new constitution was declared in 1997.

In the same year, Rabuka apologised to Queen Elizabeth for the 1987 military coups and presented her with a *tabua* as a gesture of atonement; in the following month Fiji was readmitted to the Commonwealth.

New Coup

In the May 1999 elections voters rejected Rabuka's SVT. The FLP won the majority of seats and its leader, Mahendra Chaudhry, fleetingly became Fiji's first Indo-Fijian prime minister.

Many indigenous Fijians feared for their traditional land rights and began protesting. Many refused to renew expiring 99-year land leases to Indo-Fijian farmers. On 19 May 2000, armed men entered the parliamentary compound in Suva and took 30 hostages, including Prime Minister Chaudhry. Failed businessman George Speight quickly became the face of the coup, demanding the resignation of Chaudhry and President Ratu Sir Kamisese Mara. He also wanted the 1997 multiethnic constitution rescinded.

Support for Speight was widespread and Indo-Fijians suffered such harassment that many fled the country. Chaudhry refused to resign, so President Ratu Mara unwillingly announced that he was removing Chaudhry from power. Speight's group demanded Mara's resignation as well and, with lawlessness increasing, Ratu Mara relinquished power. The head of Fiji's military, Commodore Josaia Voreqe 'Frank' Bainimarama, instituted martial law. After long negotiations between Speight's rebels and Bainimarama's military, the 1997 constitution was revoked.

In March 2001 the appeal court decided to uphold the 1997 constitution and ordered that Fiji be taken to the polls to restore democracy. Lasenia Qarase, heading the Fijian People's Party (SLD), won 32 of the 71 parliamentary seats in the August 2001 elections. Claiming that a multiparty cabinet would be unworkable in the current circumstances, Qarase defied the constitution by including no FLP members in his 18-strong cabinet. In the meantime, Speight pleaded guilty to treason. He was given a death sentence that was quickly commuted to life imprisonment, likely out of fear of further unrest.

THE 2006 COUP

While Speight's coup was quick, there was much that was unresolved. The Qarase government's draft Promotion of Reconciliation, Tolerance and Unity (PRTU) Bill divided the country during 2004 and 2005. Though the aim was to heal the wounds of the past, opponents saw the amnesty provisions for those in-

---

For daily news, views and sports check out *Fiji Village* (www.fijivillage.com), a Fijian-based media source that remains surprisingly honest.

If you can't tell your coup from a cuckoo, then *Islands of Turmoil: Elections and Politics in Fiji*, by Brij V Lal, is one of the best history books to read.

1997

Under increasing public pressure, Rabuka unveils a new constitution, which calls for a return to multiethnic democracy; it will lead to more democratic elections and includes a Bill of Rights that outlaws racial discrimination.

1998

Mahendra Chaudhry becomes the first Indo-Fijian prime minister, promising change, which unnerves many indigenous Fijians and leads to protests in the capital and around the country.

2000

Failed-businessman George Speight heads a 19 May coup; 30 hostages are held in parliament for eight weeks as Speight demands the resignation of Mahendra Chaudhry and the president. Speight is later jailed.

PEOPLE'S CHARTER

When Commodore Frank Bainimarama ousted Lasenia Qarase he pushed aside the constitution and sought to create the People's Charter, which he aimed to release prior to democratic elections to sit beside a new constitution. Released on 6 August 2008, the document seeks to remove the racism and corruption that Bainimarama perceived in the Qarase regime, with ideas such as teaching Fijian and Hindi in schools and referring to both Indo-Fijians and indigenous Fijians just as 'Fijians'.

Critics of the document point to key features that formalise the military's role in governing the country and charge courts with the authority to dissolve political parties that 'engage in activities that breach important values of the constitution'. While the Fiji Labour Party, including leader Mahendra Chaudhry, officially supported the charter, many Fijians don't.

The Methodist Church called it 'an illegal, dangerous document' and point to the fact that it comes from a government that seized power during a coup and not from the people. At the time of research, the Fijian Teachers Association was opposing the teaching of the charter in schools.

---

volved in the coup as untenable. One of the opponents of the bill, Commodore Frank Bainimarama, presented a list of demands including dropping the PRTU and other controversial bills. He gave a deadline of 4 December 2006 to Qarase, and began military exercises around Suva to support his intention.

Qarase met several of the demands, agreeing to put three contentious bills on ice, but it wasn't enough. On 5 December, President Ratu Josefa Iloilo dissolved parliament on Bainimarama's order and Qarase was put under house arrest. Several key groups did not approve of Bainimarama's coup, including the Methodist Church and the Great Council of Chiefs. When Bainimarama called on the council they refused to meet without Qarase and continued to recognise President Iloilo, who Bainimarama had ousted by declaring a state of emergency. Bainimarama dissolved the council and has acted as interim prime minister since.

Needless to say, international reaction was scornful. New Zealand Prime Minister Helen Clark compared Bainimarama to Zimbabwean dictator Robert Mugabe, refused to allow him to attend Pacific Islands Forum events in New Zealand, and imposed travel restrictions on Fijians. Bainimarama responded by not attending the forum, which led to widespread international condemnation. The expulsion of the New Zealand High Commissioner and Australian journalists led those countries to advise their nationals against travel to Fiji. The tourism and textile industries have both suffered, creating greater pressure on the Fijian economy.

In January 2007 Iloilo was sworn back in as president, though many speculate that he is now purely a figurehead with little influence. A High Court case in October 2008 ruled that the coup was legal under the country's constitution, but Bainimarama has told the UN that the promised elections of 2009 may be pushed back to 2010. Democracy in Fiji has been postponed yet again.

In 2006, the discovery of an ancient Fijian village possibly dating back as far as the 13th century brought excitement to the village of Kuku in Nausori. Locals have been rebuilding the site in the hopes of creating a tourist attraction.

2001

In a tough general-election campaign, interim Prime Minister Lasenia Qarase emerges victorious, defeating Mahendra Chaudhry; George Speight (using the name Ilikimi Naitini) is also briefly elected before being prevented from taking his seat.

2006

After making several demands about upcoming bills, Commodore Frank Bainimarama begins military manoeuvres in Suva that eventually depose the government of Lasenia Qarase, and declares himself acting president of Fiji.

2007

Bainimarama restores Ratu Josefa Iloilo to the presidency, who in turn appoints Bainimarama prime minister – a role he continues to occupy until the next election.

The Culture

THE NATIONAL PSYCHE

Most places you go in Fiji you'll be met with a cheery '*bula*' (cheers! hello! welcome!; literally 'life') and a smile. Fijians welcome *kaivalagi* (foreigners; literally 'people from far away') by going out of their way to help and chatting in shops and cafes, which makes for comfortable travelling. Not wishing to disappoint, a Fijian 'yes' might mean 'maybe' or 'no'; this can be disconcerting for visitors, so be sensitive to reluctance and be generous.

Despite its recent history of internal conflict, face-to-face confrontation is rare in Fiji and is frowned upon. Impersonal forms of dissent and argument are common, though, as a look at the letters page of any Fijian newspaper shows. The presence of Indo-Fijians (descendants of indentured workers) remains both one of the great strengths of, and challenges to, the sense of national identity in the country (see p49 for more on this).

For a look at the indigenous Fijian diaspora, search out *No 2* (2006), a New Zealand film about a Fijian family living in Auckland and the resulting breakdown of their traditional family structure.

LIFESTYLE

Food has always been relatively easy to grow in Fiji's tropical climate, which has in many ways made for a relatively stable society. Generally, the carefree island life means people live well and long, with an average life expectancy of 70.

However, the downsides of modern life are creeping up on the island paradise. A quarter of all households live below the poverty line and urban crowding is a very real problem, particularly on Viti Levu. But extended family networks, whose village members often support the town-dwellers with food, remain strong. Town-dwellers in turn support villagers when they come to town for schooling, medical treatment or work. Beyond Fiji, family members often send back part of their pay from the armed forces to support the larger family unit.

In rural areas, many aspects of an interdependent way of life also remain strong. Indigenous Fijian villagers live in land-owning *mataqali* (extended family groups) under a hereditary chief, who allocates land to each family for farming, and clans gather for births, deaths, marriages, *meke* (traditional dances) and *lovo* (feasts cooked in a pit-oven). *Yaqona* (also know as *kava*) drinking is still an important social ceremony (see the boxed text, p57) and communal obligations have to be met. Such obligations include farming for the chief, preparing for special ceremonies and feasts, and village maintenance.

Village life is conservative: independent thinking is not encouraged and being too different or too ambitious is seen as a threat. Concepts such as *kerekere* and *sevusevu* are still strong, especially in remote areas. *Kerekere* is unconditional giving based on the concept that time and property is communal; this can prove difficult, for example, for anyone attempting to start up a village shop. *Sevusevu* is the presentation of a gift such as *kava* for, say, permission to visit a village, or, more powerfully, a *tabua* (whale's tooth; see p33) as a token of reconciliation or as a wedding gift.

English is the official language of Fiji, literacy stands at 97% and Fiji is still regarded as an educational centre of the Pacific.

Urbanisation is one of Fiji's biggest challenges, with traditional values and the wisdom of elders often being less respected in towns and cities. Many young people travel to the cities for education, employment or to escape the restrictions of village life, but the increased freedom comes with challenges such as competition for jobs, a less-supportive social structure, and TV programs and the internet that present different values and contradictory messages to those associated with village life.

The population drift to urban centres is a disturbing reality in Fiji, with squatter-settlements on the edges of many towns (see p115). As with anywhere else, high levels of deprivation have led to an obvious presence of beggars and street kids, the increased use of alcohol and drugs, and accompanying crime. Problems such as people smuggling and child-sex tourism are also becoming major issues in Fiji's biggest towns.

Even for those in work, disposable income is almost nonexistent. As wages for government workers are around $150 a week – and just $50 for unskilled workers – paying the rent is often hard enough. There are exceptions of course, and the salaries of some executives are on par with the Western world. Spacious houses with big gardens reflect this occasional affluence, but most homes are modest and often crowded.

About 30% of the population is of school age. Education is heavily subsidised by the government, so almost all children attend primary school and most complete lower-secondary education. While not officially segregated, many schools are run by the major religions: Indo-Fijian children tend to go to Hindu or Muslim schools; indigenous Fijians tend to go to Christian schools and there's also a Chinese-Fijian school in Suva.

Suva is very much an educational hub, not just for Fiji but also for the Pacific. The University of the South Pacific (USP) was established in 1968 as a Pacific regional university, with its main campus in Suva. The Fiji School of Medicine (FSM) and the Fiji Institute of Technology (FIT) are also in the capital.

Visit FRIEND (Foundation for Regional Integrated Enterprises 'N' Development; www.fijifriend .com) – an NGO focused on helping rural women sell locally produced jams, handicrafts and clothing – to partake in some ethical tourist spending.

ECONOMY

Fiji's sugar plantations have historically been the greatest money-spinners, with special concessions to European markets. However, the EU's decision to cut sugar subsidies will have an impact on Fijian trade, and the crop that represents a third of the nation's industry is in for difficult times.

Tourism was to be the modern cash-cow – as well as the resort-based tourism, there's also a large cruise-ship market that briefly visits the islands. However, although some international players have been able to weather the boom-bust economy brought about by the coups, locals have suffered from dwindling visitor numbers. Further, international textile manufacturers, Rip Curl and Billabong, were forced to shut down their large factories on Viti Levu because of the coups. Similarly, international aid, which makes up an important part of the economy, has been suspended due to bellicose politics.

POPULATION

Population growth has almost halved in the last 30 years or so, with Fijians opting to have smaller families, and about 30% of Fijians are now aged under 15. Emigration of Indo-Fijians has also had a substantial impact.

Despite the island stereotypes, two-thirds of Fijians are now urban dwellers, which is a high proportion given that urban centres are few. For example, several thousand people from the island of Rotuma have moved to 'mainland' Fiji to pursue a level of education and work that their remote northern island couldn't offer. I-Kiribati from Banaba island and Tuvaluans from Vaitupu island have resettled on Rabi and Kioa islands off Vanua Levu.

To break into the cult of Fijian rugby union, ruck into Planet Rugby (www .planet-rugby.com), a huge site that has a dedicated Fiji page with the latest news.

SPORT

Almost a religion amongst indigenous Fijians, rugby union is the one sport that has continually put Fiji on the world stage since the first match between Fijian and British soldiers in 1884. Fijians are prized internationally as players, often having contracts in Europe, NZ or Australia that prevent them from playing for Fiji. Still, Fiji has won the most Pacific Tri-Nations titles and is a tough draw for any international side. The rugby season is from April to September and every village in Viti Levu seems to have its own rugby field.

Women's rugby is also gaining acceptance but has nowhere near the resources of the men's game. However, netball has the same popularity among

HOME & HOSTED: VILLAGE ETIQUETTE

If you visit a village uninvited, ask to see the headman at once; it's not proper to just turn up and look around. Never wander around unaccompanied: beaches, reefs and gardens are all someone's private realm. Complex codes of behaviour are in operation; do as you're asked, and discreetly find out why later.

- Dress modestly; sleeves and *sulu* (skirt or wrapped cloth, worn to below the knees) or sarongs are fine for both men and women. You will rarely see adult Fijians swimming and when they do they cover up with a T-shirt and *sulu*. Wear slip-on shoes: they're easier to take off when entering houses or temples.

- Take off your hat and sunglasses, and carry bags in your hands, not over your shoulder; it's considered rude to do otherwise.

- It is rare to see public displays of affection between men and women so curtail your passions in public to avoid embarrassing or offending locals.

- Bring *yaqona (kava)* with you. This is for your *sevusevu,* requesting permission to visit the village from the *turaga-ni-koro* (hereditary chief) and, in effect, the ancestral gods. He will welcome you in a small ceremony likely to develop into a *talanoa* (gossip session) around the *tanoa* (*yaqona* bowl) so be prepared to recount your life story. The custom throughout Fiji is to finish drinking *yaqona* before dining. Be warned – this can result in some very late meals.

- Check with your host if you can take photos and wait until after the *sevusevu* to start snapping.

- Stoop when entering a *bure* (thatched dwelling) and quietly sit cross-legged on the pandanus mat. It is polite to keep your head at a lower level than your host's. Fijians regard the head as sacred – never ever touch a person's head.

- If you're staying overnight, and had planned to camp but are offered a bed, accept it; it may embarrass your hosts if they think their *bure* is not good enough. If you'll be bathing in the river or at a shared tap, wear a *sulu* while you wash.

- The custom of *kerekere* means that people may ask you for things. If you don't want to give an item away, just say that you can't do without it; but be sensitive to people's lack of material goods, and take minimum gear on village visits.

- Travel with thank-you gifts of tea, tinned meat or sugar, or contribute some cash to cover costs.

- Sunday is for church and family so avoid visiting then.

Fiji's women as rugby does with men, and the country was due to host the 2007 World Netball Championship – until the coup interrupted. The Fijian team is consistently in the top 10 in the world and you'll see local games on weekends throughout the islands.

Basketball is popular with both genders, and soccer is also popular with Indo-Fijians. Even if you're not a footy fan, it's worth going to a rugby or soccer match just to watch the excited crowd.

The British also brought golf to Fiji; one of the world's current top golfers, Vijay Singh, is Indo-Fijian. There are golf courses on Denarau island, at hotels along Viti Levu's Coral Coast and in Suva.

Islanders from Banaba (Ocean Island), Kiribati, were resettled on Rabi, Vanua Levu, after their homeland was stripped bare by phosphate mining.

MULTICULTURALISM

Always a vexed issue in Fiji, the not-quite-equal numbers of Fijians (57%) and Indo-Fijians (37%) has long had an impact on Fiji's culture and politics. Since colonial days the notion of racial integration and sense of one national identity has been discouraged (see p34), and the legacy has been maintained by successive Fiji administrations.

The government categorises people by their racial origins, as you'll notice on the immigration arrival card. 'Fijian' means indigenous Fijian, and while many Indo-Fijians have lived in Fiji for several generations, they are referred to as 'Indian', just as Chinese-Fijians are 'Chinese'. Fijians of other Pacific Island descent are referred to by the nationality of their ancestors. Australians, Americans, New Zealanders and Europeans are 'Europeans'. Mixed Western and Fijian heritage makes a person officially 'part-European'.

There is ongoing tension between land-owning ethnic Fijians and entre-preneurial Indo-Fijians; or more simply, there is tension between those with power but little capital and those with capital but little power. There's little intermarriage between the groups and some areas have distinct ethnic looks, particularly in Suva. However, a recent proposal in the People's Charter (p39) wants to call all of the population simply Fijians.

Visitors, though, rarely notice this tension, and the upside of Fiji's cultural heritage is a heady mix of laid-back Melanesian lifestyle and Indian commercial street scenes. See p49 for more information on Indo-Fijian culture.

MEDIA

Fiji's media climate is stormy, and the government keeps a close eye on journalists. In 2008 two Australian publishers, from popular English-language papers the *Fiji Sun* and *Fiji Times*, were deported. Other journalists have been detained or questioned. Newspapers, printed in English, Fijian, Hindi and Chinese, are lively forums for issues that people rarely discuss face-to-face, such as race. To avoid controversy, great attention is paid to local and human-interest stories, and political journalism treads warily around government sensitivities.

There are several Fiji radio stations, mostly of the music and chat variety, with Radio Australia also offering several news and other programs specifically for the Pacific on the FM band. The BBC World Service is also broadcast on FM. FemTALK's 'radio-in-a-suitcase' broadcasts community radio geared towards women's issues.

Fiji once had a single government-run local free-to-air TV station, called, sensibly, Fiji One. In 2008, however, a new station, Mai TV, began broadcasting with a mix of international (including Al Jazeera news) and local programming including current affairs. Several pay-TV channels are received via satellite in most hotels and bars including Australia Network and Sky Fiji.

RELIGION

Since the 1830s Christianity has been developing in Fiji and remains an important part of cultural and political life. Indigenous Fijians maintain their traditional culture but extreme practices such as cannibalism and ancestor worship were erased by Christian values.

Today 53% of Fijians are Christian, the majority of whom (about 34%) are Methodist, and the church remains a powerful force in internal affairs. There's a Catholic minority of around 7%, and evangelical Christian churches are becoming increasingly popular. The arrival of Indian indentured labour brought other religions to Fiji: Hinduism is practised by 34% of the population, and Islam by about 7%.

Religious officials have traditionally been sought as a way of legitimising power structures, particularly after coups. However, there are now calls for a greater separation between church and state; the current differences between Commodore Frank Bainimarama and the powerful Methodist church may assist implementation of this pronounced change (see p39 for more on the Methodist church's position on Bainimarama's actions).

WOMEN IN FIJI

With the focus on ethnic tensions in modern Fiji, gender equality has been left behind. While women received the right to stand for parliament in 1963,

With the media under fire, new media blogs have boomed (and been busted by the government in a few cases). Try Intelligentsiya (http://intelligentsiya.blogspot.com), Digital Fiji (http://dfiji.blogspot.com) and Stuck in Fiji MUD (http://stuckinfijimud.blogspot.com) for some differing opinions.

Look out for images and statues of Degei, a traditional Fijian snake god who judges dead souls by either sending them to paradise or throwing them into a lake.

INTO THE FIRE *Dean Starnes*

Hindu fire-walking is part of a religious festival and the culmination of a 10-day period of absti-
nence, meditation and worship. During this time it is believed that the participants are cleansed
of all physical and spiritual impurities. On the final day, devotees bathe in the ocean and have
their tongues, cheeks and bodies pierced with three-pronged skewers. In an almost-trancelike
state they then dance to the temple, where, in front of a statue of the goddess Maha Devi, they
walk across a pit of charred wood raked over glowing coals.

The day after the festival, and seemingly none the worse for their ordeal, I spoke to one of
these extraordinary men.

Is this the first time that you have participated in the festival? This is my fourth time. I didn't
walk over the ash on my first year – it came slowly to me. I walked at first because my mother
and uncle wanted me to but now the rewards outweigh the sacrifices.

What is the most difficult aspect of fire-walking? The preparation is the most difficult. You
must give up many things – meat, cigarettes, *kava* (mildly narcotic, muddy and odd-tasting
drink made from the aromatic roots of the Polynesian pepper shrub), alcohol, sex and all impure
thoughts. As for the pain – if you have the blessing of the Goddess, the piercing of the skewers
feels only like the bites of small ants.

Why do you walk? I walk to show my devotion, and I take vows for my wishes to be granted.
I hope for business success; others pray for their illness to be cured, success in exams or for a
child.

What is the secret to fire-walking? Why is it that you don't get burnt? There is no secret.
Anyone with a true heart and who has meditated with their teacher and abstained from meat
and sex will not be hurt. If it happens that your mind is upset or if you think of your girlfriend or
wife instead of remaining focused on the goddess, then you might be burnt.

they still hold only 7% of seats; even though more women have stood for
office since the coups of 2000, numbers have actually fallen below their pre-
2000 representation. While more than half of senior officials and managers
are women, they earn only a third of their male counterparts' salary. Given
the traditionally patrilineal nature of inheritance (though women can inherit
personal wealth and land), the Great Council of Chiefs very much remains
an old boys' club.

Despite the slow nature of change, there's an active **Fiji Women's Rights
Movement** (www.fwrm.org.fj), which helped push the Family Law Bill through
parliament in 2004. Women now have the right to pursue child custody,
access and maintenance. Paid maternity leave, while rarely matching a full-
time wage, makes it easier for working women to spend more time with
their babies.

In much of Fiji, domestic violence disguised as a cultural norm prevails.
According to the **Fiji Women's Crisis Centre** (www.fijiwomen.com), two-thirds of men
in Fiji consider it acceptable to hit the women in their family, and incidents
of random violence against women are common.

ARTS

Traditional arts and crafts such as woodcarving and weaving, along with
dancing and music, remain an integral part of life in many villages and a
major tourist attraction. These traditions have inspired much of the small but
thriving Fijian contemporary arts scene, of which Suva is the epicentre.

The USP's Oceania Centre for Arts & Culture (Map p116) provides working space for artists, musicians and dancers. The Fiji Arts Club has an annual
exhibition, usually in August or September, in Suva. Suva is also the literary
hub for Fiji, hosting occasional readings by members of the Pacific Writing
Forum, and performances of work by Fijian playwrights and poets.

Literature

The strong oral-storytelling tradition in Fiji, especially in rural areas, means that you're more likely to hear good stories than read them. When stories are transcribed it's usually in English, and *Myths and Legends of Fiji & Rotuma,* by AW Reed and Inez Hames, gives a good selection. For another perspective, *Bittersweet: An Indo-Fijian Experience* features writings by Ahmed Ali, Mohit Prasad and Brij V Lalabout about the *girmitiya* (Indian indentured labourers) experience.

Fiji's small but strong community of poets and writers creates work that's gritty and realist. Joseph C Veramu's 1994 novel *Moving Through the Streets* is an eye-opener about Suva's disaffected youth, while Daryl Tarte's *Stalker on the Beach* pits global capitalism against Fijian nationalism in a book that makes uncomfortable resort reading.

Beyond Ceremony: An Anthology of Fiji Drama showcases Fiji's playwrights including Vilsoni Hereniko, Sudesh Mishra, Jo Nacola, Raymond Pillai and Larry Thomas; look out for occasional performances of their work in Suva.

Since the 1960s Indo-Fijian writers have increasingly worked in English, including Subramani, Satendra Nandan and Rohitash Chandra, and poet Mohit Prasad, who wrote *Eating Mangoes* (2001). Of course, the injustice of indenture and coups rates highly in Indo-Fijian literature.

Collections of women writers' poetry include *Of Schizophrenic Voices,* by Frances Koya, and *Nei Nim Manoa,* by Teresia Teaiwa. Writers from Fiji and the nearby region are well represented in poetry and prose in two anthologies, *Nuanua: Pacific Writing in English since 1980* and *Niu Waves: Contemporary Writing from Oceania.*

Check out the latest literary offerings from and about Fiji and the Pacific online at the University of the South Pacific's bookshop (www .uspbookcentre.com).

Cinema

White-sand beaches and clear blue waters would seem to make Fiji a perfect movie location, but Hollywood has been wary since the 2006 coup. The original paradise picture, *Blue Lagoon,* was filmed in the Yasawas in 1948 and remade there in 1979. The less-successful *Return to the Blue Lagoon,* with Milla Jovovich, was shot on Taveuni in 1991. In 2001 Tom Hanks chatted with a volleyball called Wilson in *Cast Away,* filmed on Monuriki in the Mamanuca islands, where Jodie Foster's 'heaven' sequence in the sci-fi movie *Contact* was also filmed. The filming in Fiji of two schlockers, *Anacondas: The Hunt for the Blood Orchid* (2004) and *Welcome to the Jungle* (2007), and the TV series *Survivor: Fiji* (2007) raised hopes of attracting more big-budget films, but political instability has led to the suspension of productions.

Fiji's first home-grown feature film, *The Land Has Eyes,* is set during the last gasp of colonialism in 1960s Rotuma. Made in Rotuman language with English subtitles, and a mostly local cast, it's a wonderfully genuine insight into a changing community.

Formed in 2002, the **Fiji Audio Visual Commission** (www.fijiaudiovisual.com) aims to attract more film-makers with significant tax incentives. Yaqara Studio City, a huge and hi-tech audiovisual complex, was planned for western Viti Levu, though the coup has delayed this project.

For the latest in Fijian and Pacific literature, grab a copy of *Dreadlocks,* the USP's journal of creative and critical writing, which is edited in Suva.

Music

Fiji has an active music scene influenced by reggae, hip hop (see the boxed text, p46) and rock. Popular older acts include Seru Serevi, Lia Osborne and Daniel Rae Costello, and bands such as Delai Sea and Voqa ni Delai Dokidoki. Black Rose is one of Fiji's most successful rock bands. For most Fijian musicians, such as rappers D Kamali who moved to Auckland or Hawaiian-based performer Fiji, success means moving overseas.

Sunday church services usually feature fantastic choir singing. The Oceania Centre produces CDs of Pacific music with a contemporary twist; listen to, for example, Sailasa Tora's album *Wasawasa*.

Indo-Fijian singer Aiysha is a big hit in India, and local Indo-Fijian band The Bad Boys play at venues around Fiji. Music from Bollywood films, and Indian dance and pop music is popular, as are classical *qawali* and Hindu devotional *bhajans*. Vocal, *tabla* (percussion) and sitar lessons are given at Indian cultural centres.

Film-maker Steve James' 'family vacation' meant moving his clan to remote Taveuni and opening a cinema to show free movies. The amazing documentary *Reel Paradise* (2006; www.reelparadise.com) tells the story.

Dance

Most visitors first encounter Fijian dance when they're welcomed at resorts and hotels with *meke*, a performance that enacts ancient lore. Traditionally, *meke* were accompanied by a chanting chorus or by 'spiritually possessed seers'. Rhythm was supplied by clapping, the thumping and stamping of bamboo clacking sticks and the beating of slit drums. The whole community participated in *meke*. In times of war, men performed the *cibi* (death dance), and women the *dele* or *wate,* a dance in which they sexually humiliated enemy corpses and captives. Dancing often took place by moonlight or torchlight, with the performers in costume and with bodies oiled, faces painted and combs and flowers decorating their hair.

Traditional Chinese dancing is also still practised in Fiji, and Indian classical dance, including Bharat Natyam and *kathak,* is taught at Indian cultural centres.

Modern dance takes on international forms including hip hop and ballet. For a more contemporary dance experience, look out for performances by the Oceania Dance Theatre (p121) in Suva.

Architecture

TRADITIONAL

The village of Navala (p137), nestled in the Viti Levu highlands, is an exemplar of traditional Fijian architecture. It's the only village remaining where every home is a *bure*. *Bure*-building is a skilled trade passed from father to son, although the whole community helps during construction and many people know how to maintain its woven walls and thatched roof. Today, however, most villagers live in simple, rectangular, pitched-roof houses made from industrialised materials requiring less maintenance. For more information on *bure,* see the boxed text, p48.

COLONIAL

Historic Levuka (p169) was once the capital of Fiji and has been nominated for World Heritage listing. A number of its buildings date from its heyday of the late 19th century, particularly the main street, which is surprisingly intact.

FIJIAN HIP HOP WORLDWIDE

Young Fijians have embraced hip hop and several new artists have emerged recently. The Suva scene is particularly strong, thanks mostly to Underdawg Productions, which was set up by rapper Sammy G and often features other MCs including Mr Grin, up-and-coming Redchild and Tukaine. Influenced by gangsta and reggae, lyrics are a frank exploration of Fiji's current social issues with references to coups, drug use and Fijians serving overseas in the army.

An essential track is Sammy G and Mr Grin's *Suva City,* in which Sammy G likens his relationship with his home town to a divorce, all the while waving a baseball bat. Another stand-out is Knox's *Jah Love, Jah Crucify,* a reggae-tinged paean to the difficulties of urban life. To check out the latest hip hop head for Underdawg's YouTube channel (www.youtube.com/user/udawgfiji).

MELODIOUS MEASURES

Replaced by guitars and keyboards, traditional indigenous instruments are a rare find in Fiji these days. Yet once upon a time, nose flutes were all the rage. Made from a single piece of bamboo, some 70cm long, the flute would be intricately carved and played by your typical laid-back Fijian, reclined on a pandanus mat and resting his or her head on a bamboo pillow. Whether it was the music or the pose, flutes were believed to have the power to attract the opposite sex and were a favourite for serenading.

Other traditional instruments had more practical purposes, such as shell trumpets and whistles, which were used for communication. Portable war drums were used as warnings and for communicating tactics on the battlefield. One instrument you are still likely to see (and hear) is the *lali*, a large slit drum made of resonant timbers. Audible over large distances, its deep call continues to beckon people to the chief's *bure* or to church.

The British influence on Suva is reflected in its many grand colonial buildings, including Government House, Suva City Library and the Grand Pacific Hotel (see the boxed text, p122).

MODERN

Fiji's modern architecture combines modern technology with traditional Fijian aesthetics. Notable buildings include the parliament complex (p120), USP campus (p120) and Great Council of Chiefs complex in Suva, and the *bure bose* (meeting house) at Somosomo (p201) on Taveuni.

Most resorts have faux-traditional *bure* huts, while others use it as a point of departure for grander structures. Resorts with distinctive architecture include the upmarket Vatulele Island Resort (p114), Koro Sun Resort (p186) near Savusavu and Raintree Lodge (p125) outside Suva.

Pottery

Pottery has a 3000-year history in Fiji, thought to have first been brought by the Lapita people, and some modern potters still use traditional techniques. The pots are beaten into shape with wooden paddles of various shapes and sizes, while the form is held from within using a pebble anvil. Coil and slab-building techniques are also used. Once dried, pots are fired outdoors in an open blaze on coconut husks, and are often sealed with resin varnish taken from the *dakua* tree.

Two of Fiji's best-known pottery villages, Nakabuta (p102) and Nasilai (p131), receive visitors. Pottery demonstrations take place every Tuesday and Thursday on the verandah of the Fiji Museum (p119) in Suva.

Fiji's Treasured Culture (www.museum.vic .gov.au/fiji) is an online exhibition of fabulous artefacts held in Museum Victoria (in Melbourne, Australia) and Suva's Fiji Museum.

Woodcarving

Traditional woodcarving skills are largely kept alive by the tourist trade, providing a ready market for war clubs, spears and cannibal forks. *Tanoa* (drinking bowls) and *bilo* (*kava* cups of coconut shell) remain part of everyday life. *Tanoa* shaped like turtles are thought to have derived from turtle-shaped *ibuburau*, vessels used in indigenous Vitian *yaqona* rites.

The Fiji Museum (p119) is the best place to see authentic traditional woodcarvings, and there are usually carvings in progress at USP's Oceania Centre for Arts & Culture (Map p116) in Suva. Many 'handmade' artefacts for sale at handicraft centres may have actually been mass-produced by a machine.

Bark Cloth

Masi (also known as *malo* or *tapa*) is bark cloth with rust-coloured and black printed designs. In Vitian culture, *masi* was invested with status and associated with celebrations and rituals. It was worn as a loincloth by men

TRADITIONAL BURE

Fijian villagers once resided in traditional thatched dwellings known as *bure*. Travellers to Fiji will become familiar with the term almost immediately as it is now a synonym for accommodation at every price range.

In the past, these homes were dark and smoky inside, with no windows, usually only one low door and hearth pits for cooking. The packed-earth floor was covered with grass or fern leaves and then finely woven pandanus-leaf or coarse coconut-leaf mats. Sleeping compartments were at one end, behind a bark-cloth curtain, with wooden headrests.

Traditional *bure* are usually rectangular in plan, with timber poles and a hipped or gabled roof structure lashed together with coconut-fibre string. Thatch, woven coconut leaves or split bamboo is used as wall cladding, and roofs are thatched with grass or coconut leaves. *Bure* are cheap, relatively quick to build and withstand the elements well. Communities band together to finish a *bure* in a few weeks and rethatch every couple of years. Most villages still have some traditional-style *bure* but, as village life breaks down and natural materials become scarcer, most Fijians find it easier and cheaper to use concrete block, corrugated iron and even flattened oil drums.

The *bure* advertised on your resort brochure is likely to be a long stretch from its forebear. Although budget resorts offer rustic dwellings, most resort *bure* are mock structures to provide travellers with a dose of indigenous Fijian culture without losing the creature comforts.

Bure Kalou

In the days of the old religion, every village had a *bure kalou* (ancient temple), which was also used as a meeting house. These buildings had a high-pitched roof and usually stood on terraced foundations. The *bete* (priest), who was an intermediary between the villagers and spirits, lived in the temple and performed various rituals, including feasting on slain enemies and burying important people. A strip of white *masi* (bark cloth) was usually hung from the ceiling, to serve as a connection to the spirits. The construction of such a temple reputedly required that a strong man be buried alive in each of the corner-post holes.

during initiation rituals and renaming ceremonies and as an adornment in dance, festivity and war. *Masi* was also an important exchange item, used in bonding ceremonies between related tribes. Chiefs were swathed in a huge puffball of *masi*, later given to members of the other tribe.

While men wore the *masi*, production has traditionally been a woman's role. Made from the inner white bark of the paper mulberry bush that has been soaked in water and scraped clean, it's then beaten and felted for hours into sheets of a fine, even texture. Intricate designs are done by hand or stencil and often carry symbolic meaning. Rust-coloured paints are traditionally made from an infusion of candlenut and mangrove bark; pinker browns are made from red clays; and black from the soot of burnt *dakua* resin and charred candlenuts.

It is difficult to see *masi* being made, though you'll see the end product used for postcards, wall hangings and other decorative items. Textile designers have also begun incorporating traditional *masi* motifs in their fabrics.

Mat & Basket Weaving

Most indigenous Fijian homes use woven *voivoi* (pandanus leaf) to make baskets, floor coverings and fine sleeping mats. Traditionally, girls living in villages learned to weave, and many still do. Pandanus leaves are cut and laid outdoors to cure, stripped of the spiny edges, and boiled and dried. The traditional method of blackening leaves for contrasting patterns is to bury them in mud for days before reboiling. The dried leaves are made flexible by scraping with shells and then split into strips of about 1cm to 2cm and woven. Mat borders are now often decorated with brightly coloured wools instead of the more traditional parrot feathers.

Indo-Fijian History & Culture Clement Paligaru

It would be hard to imagine Fiji without Indo-Fijians. With enterprise and resilience, they have forged a presence that permeates throughout the country. Despite mostly being the descendants of indentured labourers who arrived in the country up to 130 years ago, Indo-Fijians are still considered *vulagi* (visitors) by many indigenous Fijians. But this has never stopped them making the most of life on the islands, adding their own touch to the rich mosaic of Fiji's cultural traditions.

For a visitor, this Indo-Fijian presence is vividly evident. Fiji may well be best known for indigenous ceremonies, *lovo* (earth ovens), leis and crafts; however, Indo-Fijian culture provides another dimension – food, shopping, temples and festivals, as colourful as you would find in Rajasthan but with an undeniably Fijian character.

In recent decades, an intriguing portrait of the Indo-Fijian has emerged – one shrouded in the dark shadows of numerous coups. Yet, at the same time, the Indian presence in Fiji has been so colourful and flavoursome, even indigenous Fijian life will never be the same again.

Clement Paligaru is an Indo-Fijian journalist. He has reported on Asia Pacific affairs for the Australian Broadcasting Corporation for over 15 years. Clement is a presenter on ABC Radio Australia's *In the Loop* program and the Australia Network's TV program *Pacific Pulse*, which profile the peoples and cultures of Oceania.

COMINGS & GOINGS: A HISTORY

The earliest Indian arrivals in Fiji were indentured labourers brought by the British to work in the sugar industry in the 1870s. As the newcomers adapted to life as labourers, they also forged the foundations of a unique Indo-Fijian cultural identity, later bequeathed to the generations that followed.

It did not take the workers long to realise plantation life was too tough and restrictive to accommodate the strict social and religious codes of India. Labourers began socialising, eating and marrying across caste and religious lines. They still maintained religious and cultural practices, but got rid of many social hang-ups. The 'subversive' practice of choosing only the Indian customs that suited life on the islands had begun.

After their labour contracts expired, many Indians remained in Fiji. For many, it was because they were not eligible for, or couldn't afford, the costly passage to India. Some also feared being kicked out of their communities at home for breaking Indian mores, making the idea of starting anew in Fiji a much more attractive option. Little did they realise that the bountiful future they envisaged would also be fraught with ethnic tension.

By the time indentured labour was abolished in 1919, independent sugarcane, cotton, tobacco and rice farms had been set up by Indo-Fijians, mostly on land leased from indigenous Fijians. Other migrants ran small stores or became public servants or maids. The big move into commerce began in the 1930s, following the arrival of a second wave of business migrants from India. There was no doubt Indo-Fijians were hard-working and becoming prosperous. Some indigenous Fijians found they didn't make bad friends either. But their success did not impress everyone.

As the new migrants set about laying the foundations for their future, many indigenous Fijians began to feel increasingly uneasy. The customs and ambitions of Indo-Fijians were deemed offensive by some. And some Fijians regarded the migrants as usurpers of their land, despite laws introduced in the late 1800s forbidding the sale of native land, and forever guaranteeing indigenous Fijians ownership of more than 80% of land in Fiji. This, however, did not stop the

To visualise the lives of Fiji's early Indo-Fijian settlers, visit the Fiji Museum's Indo-Fijian gallery in Suva. It reconstructs the history of Indo-Fijian indentured labourers, and their customs and traditions, with the help of family heirlooms, artefacts and personal belongings.

Indo-Fijians from demanding rich, arable land for lease. As the Indo-Fijian farmers and business people became prosperous, many indigenous groups became wary of being eclipsed economically. The seeds were sown for decades of dispute between the two ethnic groups, primarily over land leases.

By the mid-20th century, the Indo-Fijians had become indispensable to the economy, dominating agriculture, business and the public service. They also outnumbered indigenous Fijians. But the lack of political power and land-ownership rights remained a source of insecurity for the Indo-Fijians. A previously fledgling campaign for political equality began gaining momentum, despite facing stiff resistance from Europeans and Fijians.

By the time independence from Britain was attained in 1970, the campaign for equality had laid the foundations for race-based politics in the country. After much debate, the new constitution set out an electoral system arranged along racial lines – allocating some elective seats to particular ethnic groups, to be elected by voters enrolled as members of that ethnic group. The politics of ethnicity was now institutionalised. To win easy votes, political parties could now play the race card.

The word *girmit* is used to describe the indenture system. It entered the Indo-Fijian lexicon when the *girmitiyas* (early labourers) mispronounced the word agreement.

After independence, Indo-Fijians felt fairly secure under the rule of Prime Minister Ratu Sir Kamisese Mara, whose Alliance Party promoted multi-racialism. National celebrations included vibrant Indo-Fijian presentations. But some Fijians were troubled by this increased acceptance of Indo-Fijian culture. In the mid-1970s the Alliance Party's concessions to Indo-Fijians on issues such as land leases, combined with the lack of prosperity among indigenous Fijians, led to a backlash by nationalists. Warning of an Indo-Fijian takeover, they demanded that 'visitors' leave.

As the Alliance Party scrambled to introduce pro-indigenous policies in the mid-1980s, Indo-Fijian voters turned to the new Fiji Labour Party (FLP) and its platform of social reform. The FLP, in coalition with an Indo-Fijian–dominated party, won the elections in 1987. But, soon afterwards, it was overthrown by Lieutenant Colonel Sitiveni Rabuka's military coup. The reason? Although the government was led by an indigenous Fijian, Dr Timoci Bavadra, the idea of an Indo-Fijian–dominated coalition was too much for the nationalists. To ensure the pendulum didn't ever swing back to favour Indo-Fijians, Rabuka introduced a racially biased constitution in 1990. Thousands of skilled and professional Indo-Fijians fled the country.

At the end of the decade, Rabuka, now prime minister, gave in to internal and international pressure for a review of the 1990 constitution and its indigenous bias. A new constitution, declared in 1997, incorporated a complex system of governance that promoted power-sharing between political parties, across racial lines. It was marginally fairer to Indo-Fijians, but many seats remained race based.

Under this new constitution Fiji's first Indo-Fijian prime minister, FLP leader Mahendra Chaudhry, was elected. Within a year, however, the Chaudhry government was overthrown following a coup led by nationalists who despised his social reform agenda and personal style. The nationalists also opposed Chaudhry's campaigns for the rights of Indo-Fijian farmers whose land leases were expiring.

New Zealand's governor-general, Anand Satyanand, describes his ancestry as Indian and Pacific. His Indo-Fijian parents were both born in Fiji, while he was born in New Zealand.

After a lengthy series of court battles relating to the coup, Fiji returned to the polls in 2001. The election of a nationalist prime minister, Lasenia Qarase, led to a renewed exodus of Indo-Fijians. But many more chose to remain in the country they call home.

In 2006 Indo-Fijians found themselves divided over the country's fourth coup, despite the perception that this time Indo-Fijians would have most to gain. Military chief Commander Voreqe Bainimarama ousted Qarase's government, promising a future free of discrimination against Indo-Fijians.

A number of high-profile Indo-Fijians threw their support behind Bainimarama. Many became key advisors and members of his interim cabinet, including the former Indo-Fijian prime minister, Mahendra Chaudhry, and the high-profile attorney-general, Aiyaz Sayed-Khaium. But others, including Indo-Fijian religious organisations, the Indo-Fijian–dominated National Federation Party, some trade unions and Indo-Fijian civil society leaders, denounced the military action.

Despite the dissenting voices, there is a strong perception in the country that what happened in 2006 was an 'Indo-Fijian coup' and that most Indo-Fijians support the Bainimarama-led interim government. This is unlikely to change as the military commander and interim prime minister pushes ahead with his agenda for social reform.

The most potent proposal is for the creation of a manifesto known as the People's Charter, aimed at ending decades of discrimination against Indo-Fijians. Debate still rages about the appropriateness of such a blueprint, but Bainimarama and his interim government are refusing to allow for general elections until and unless the People's Charter is signed, sealed and delivered. Whether or not such a document will change the course of history for Indo-Fijians remains to be seen.

> The Indo-Fijian social and cultural experience is very similar to the experience of descendants of Indian indentured labourers in the West Indies, Surinam and Mauritius. Shared traditions include food, spoken dialects and religious rituals.

THE FIJIAN IN INDO-FIJIAN

Compared with the Indians of the subcontinent, Indo-Fijians are recognised as very relaxed and friendly. And it's not surprising, as they have now lived alongside the infectiously laid-back Fijians for more than a century. The distance from India and its strict mores has also allowed Indo-Fijians to discard the rigidities of India's caste and social structure. So Indo-Fijians socialise and engage freely across socioeconomic groups, without many of the restrictions that are observed by society in India. For example, in Fiji, city and townsfolk enjoy attending wedding celebrations in rural areas where relatives are often economically disadvantaged. These are opportunities to renew ties and introduce younger family members to folk traditions. Such disregard for social codes would be frowned upon in India.

As in India, marriages in Fiji are sometimes still arranged, but Hindu wedding practices have changed somewhat. While still distinctly Indian, they have largely been standardised and are an amalgam of various traditions. The Fiji Hindu nuptials are attended by family and friends, and last at least an hour. In contrast, wedding rituals in some parts of India last just a few minutes, and in other parts they are sometimes witnessed only by a handful of family members.

One of the more significant departures from Indian cultural has been the emergence of a unique Hindi dialect. Known as 'Fiji-Hindi', it is an amalgam of regional dialects once spoken by the indentured labourers from India. For some useful words and phrases in Fiji-Hindi, see inside front cover and p264.

THE INDIAN IN INDO-FIJIAN

With some five generations of history in Fiji, the Indo-Fijian community has forged a strong identity in its adopted homeland. This identity is a unique blend of Fijian and Indian cultures. For an Indo-Fijian, being ethnic Indian as opposed to being indigenous Fijian is about a certain type of upbringing and way of life. The outlook and aspirations of Indo-Fijians emphasise the importance of education and hard work to ensure a secure future. Add thriftiness for good measure and you have the core of the Indo-Fijian package.

India remains an important cultural beacon for Indo-Fijians, influencing rituals, culinary traditions, dress and entertainment. Today these influences

> Even though they are far away from the India, the heartland of vedic astrology, many Indo-Fijians regularly consult with pundits (priests) for readings and predictions about the future.

provide some of the more obvious signs of cultural distinction between Indo-Fijians and indigenous Fijians.

Indo-Fijians love homemade rotis (traditional breads). Steaming curries are served with roti and rice, with condiments completing the meal. Indo-Fijians generally have a weakness for *mithai* (traditional sweets). Out of the home, the curry combo also finds its way to schools, the workplace and the outdoors.

Tradition, pride and identity have also ensured that saris, the colourful Indian dress worn by women, remain popular in Fiji. More recently, there has been a revival of medieval fashions such as *lehenga choli* (skirt, blouse and veil) and the *salwaar kameez* (pants and dress) thanks to Bollywood influences. Most Indo-Fijians are practising Hindus, Muslims or Sikhs, and across the country, temples and mosques lend a particularly Indian feel to the landscape. The domes, minarets and red flags atop bamboo poles in backyards also serve as a reminder of the strength of Indo-Fijian adherence to the faiths of India.

Entertainment and recreation continue to have a decidedly subcontinental flavour for many Indo-Fijians, with the local cinemas providing a regular dose of Hindi-language Bollywood film and music. In Indo-Fijian homes, entertainment systems are often tuned to provide Bollywood on tap. Apart from the pure escapism value, Bollywood films also provide many with the only connection they have with India and subcontinental Hindi.

Most Indo-Fijians will never visit India. Few now dream of going there. Some of those who do visit are motivated by a desire to explore their cultural heritage, religion and ancestry, while others simply visit out of curiosity. However, few are compelled to take the journey as an affirmation of their identity; it is Fiji they turn to for that.

ETHNIC TENSIONS

Most aspects of Indo-Fijian lifestyle and culture have comfortably coexisted with the indigenous Fijian way of life for more than a century. A quick look around reveals that large numbers of Indo-Fijians and indigenous Fijians live side by side, work together and go to the same schools. But apart from attending some sports, entertainment and special occasions together, the two groups still tend not to engage socially. Their economic, educational, cultural and social priorities, including *tabu* (that which is forbidden or sacred), differ. These differences have proven rich fodder for political agitators seeking to exploit the insecurities of indigenous Fijians.

For decades nationalists have pointed to Indo-Fijian economic success to fan the coals of resentment. Yet many Indo-Fijians remain economically disadvantaged. The threat of 'eventual Indian domination' has been a recurring theme in Fiji politics.

Quite often, Indo-Fijian success and material wealth serve as convenient reminders of what makes Indo-Fijians different, as well as threatening. The perceived lack of Indo-Fijian respect for Fijian customs also serves to annoy many indigenous Fijians. For example, when people are sitting down at a

---

Arranged marriages remain a serious option for many young Indo-Fijians seeking a life partner. A high proportion of Indo-Fijians who have migrated overseas still consider returning home to find a bride or bridegroom.

At least 15 distinct Indo-Fijian religious and cultural associations exist around Fiji, through which communities can maintain cultural, regional and religious affiliations with India. One of the Hindu organisations established the new University of Fiji near Lautoka in 2005.

MILAAP – DISCOVER YOUR ROOTS PROJECT

A small but growing number of Indo-Fijians are now retracing their ancestral roots in India. Sydney-based documentary maker Satish Rai has made documentaries about his and others' experiences, including *Milaap: Discover Your Indian Roots* (2001), *Milaap: The Land of South Indian Girmitiyas* (2006) and *In Exile at Home: A Fiji Indian Story* (2008). See www.girmitunited.org for more information, and some of his work.

meeting on the ground or floor, Fijian custom requires that you pass them in a crouching motion. The tendency for Indians to walk upright in such situations is seen as arrogant and disrespectful. One coup leader even referred to the way Indians 'look different and smell different' when justifying his actions to the international media.

The Indo-Fijian 'threat' has in fact often served as a perfect smokescreen for other agendas. After the 2000 coup there was much debate about who benefited – the disenfranchised or, as speculation would have it, an elite group of indigenous and nonindigenous opportunists. But the subsequent Qarase and Bainimarama regimes have left Indo-Fijians in no doubt that they remain central to the dilemma facing the country. And there is little guarantee that the roller-coaster ride that began after the 1987 coup will stop.

Under the nationalist Qarase government, Indo-Fijians witnessed the tide slowly turning against them, so many continued leaving the country. Qarase's efforts to transfer marine fishing rights to indigenous Fijians and release perpetrators of the 2000 coup only reinforced the sense of disempowerment among Indo-Fijians. On the other hand, while the policies of the Bainimarama regime aim to extinguish the legacies of race-based politics, these efforts have not stemmed the flow of emigration. Many Indo-Fijians prefer not to discuss the merits of the supposedly pro-Indian regime. This reticence suggests they are still cautious about the fault lines that have run through their island society for over a century.

> Today's Indo-Fijians are among some 10 million descendants of indentured Indian labourers who live outside India.

COMING TOGETHER

Despite the differences between Indo-Fijians and indigenous Fijians, the way the two groups coexist and influence each other is testament to over a century of shared experiences. In many ways Fiji is already witnessing the synergy that has resulted from cooperation between these two communities. Many Indo-Fijians may be leaving the country in search of stability, yet this has not stalled the momentum of a mutual cultural exploration by Indo-Fijians and indigenous Fijians.

Increasing numbers from both communities speak each other's language. In Fiji's sugar-cane belts on the western side of Viti Levu and around Labasa on Vanua Levu, many indigenous cane farmers who work alongside Indo-Fijians speak Fiji-Hindi fluently, while their families immerse themselves in Bollywood films. Indo-Fijian music and songs have even been recorded and released commercially by indigenous Fijian artists. Elsewhere, Indo-Fijians in rural communities, including former Christian mission settlements, also speak Fijian. A few hundred indigenous Fijians, including a prominent nationalist politician, Apisai Tora, have also converted to Islam.

> There are hundreds of small Hindu clubs called *mandalis* around Fiji. Once a week they hold musical recitals of Indian epics, such as Ramayana, as part of devotional rituals.

In larger urban centres, popular culture and fashion are also breaking down barriers. Visit Fiji during the Hindu Diwali festival (held in October or November) and you will see many indigenous Fijian women wearing Indian outfits. The country's fashion designers are using sari cloth and Indian motifs in their designs. Nightclubs are playing Bollywood DJ-mixes and bars are serving bowls of curry with drinks the way Indo-Fijians do in their homes. Across the country, sport, especially soccer, brings both communities together. When victorious national rugby sides return from overseas, Indian dancers greet them alongside the thousands of Fijian spectators.

> Today, Fiji-style Indian roti curry combinations are an essential part of indigenous Fijian celebrations. At community events overseas they are even replacing the *lovo* (earth-oven baked meals) as the food of choice to celebrate Fiji identity.

Perhaps the most amazing transformation that has taken place is the elevation of Indian food in indigenous Fijian life. In many homes, almost every second meal is a curry. So be prepared: if you accept an invitation to an indigenous Fijian home, you may not be served islander food.

Intermarriage, however, remains one area few are willing to explore. For many the cultural, religious and social differences remain insurmountable.

***THE BOLLYWOOD BEAUTY* BY SHALINI AKHIL, PENGUIN AUSTRALIA (2005)**

Kesh is feminist, loves pubs, swears a lot and was born and raised in Australia. Her Indo-Fijian cousin Rupa is the exact opposite. She diligently cooks curries, wears saris and is heading for an arranged marriage. When Rupa comes to live with Kesh in Melbourne, their worlds collide. Wicked humour and disarming honesty spice up this tale of culture clash, identity struggle and the Indo-Fijian way.

Read Shalini Akhil's blog at www.iwriter.blogspot.com.

Among Indo-Fijians, notions of cultural differences and religious purity have placed intermarriage firmly in the too-hard basket. Early colonial policy prohibiting racial intermingling has also been blamed for limiting interaction and understanding between the communities. There is a minuscule, but growing, number of intermarriages taking place; this is testament to the resolve of the few who are risking ostracism and breaking *tabu*.

The early indentured-labourer experience and postcoup reflections have inspired countless pages of Indo-Fijian poetry and fiction by authors such as Satendra Nandan, Raymond Pillai, Subramani, Sudesh Mishra, Mohit Prasad and Kavita Nandan.

Elsewhere, film-makers, NGOs and artists often push the boundaries of cross-cultural experimentation to promote national unity and understanding. Cultural groups such as the Shobna Chanel Dance Group and the Oceania Centre for Arts and Culture fuse rhythms and traditions of Indo-Fijian and indigenous Fijian cultures at national and international events. Femlinkpacific, a community-based organisation, promotes cross-cultural themes in its media activities. Indo-Fijian filmmaker James Bhagwan has been recognised internationally for documentaries promoting cultural tolerance. Similarly visual and multimedia artists, including Sangeeta Singh and Frances Koya, explore gender, identity and sexuality, referencing their Indo-Fijian and cross-cultural experiences.

CULTURAL IMMERSION

The best way to experience Indo-Fijian culture is to share a meal at the home of an Indo-Fijian. To increase the chances of being invited, you can always meet sociable Indo-Fijians at some of their favourite celebrations, haunts, shops and cultural venues around urban centres. If you are lucky enough, you may meet someone who could take you to an Indo-Fijian settlement to enjoy rural hospitality. That could mean anything from a refreshing glass of *sharbaat* (country-style lemon juice) to a village-style curry feast. Just remember to take some sweets or biscuits with you as a gift for your hosts.

In the absence of strong ancestral ties with India, a growing number of Indo-Fijian Hindus and Muslims are making annual pilgrimages to sacred sites overseas, including Mecca and temples in India, to consolidate their religious and cultural identities.

There are many fantastic eateries serving home-style meals in cities and towns. But try to also explore some of the places that cater for Indo-Fijians in smaller towns. They often serve seasonal vegetables such as *duruka* (Fijian asparagus), *katahar* (jackfruit) and *kerela* (bitter melon). Do not forget to ask for pickles and chutneys made from local fruits such as mangoes, *kumrakh* (star-apple) and tamarind. Remember, even some of the locals do not know these places exist. So put some effort into asking around and you're likely to experience a culinary adventure you will never forget. NGOs such as **FRIEND** (www.fijifriend.com) help disadvantaged and rural women produce and market their Indian condiments for tourists and locals.

Annual festivals and events also offer the visitor a chance to experience Indo-Fijian culture. Diwali (Festival of Lights) takes place across the nation in October or November. You can join in the fun by wearing some traditional gear (or a *bindi* on the forehead) and sharing *mithai* and candles. Popular events include temple fairs where thousands of Indo-Fijians gather to watch rituals and enjoy folksy meals. In Suva, the South Indian fire-walking festival (see p124) takes place at the Mariamma Temple during July or August. In Vanua Levu, the Ram Leela festival is held at the Mariamman Temple in

Vunivau (east of Labasa) around October. If you want to explore Hindu mysticism, try the Naag Pathaar Mandir temple north of Labasa, where a shrine is built around a large rock that devotees believe is growing in the shape of a cobra (see p194). Another interesting event is the annual **South Indian Sangam convention** (www.sangamfiji.com.fj), which takes place around Easter. During the rest of the year, visitors are welcome at Hindu and Sikh temples.

Fairground activities accompany Fiji's soccer season, which runs from February to October. Major tournaments include the **Interdistrict** (www.fijifootball.com) as well as the **Fiji Muslim League Soccer Championship** (☎ 990 8566). On the sidelines at these events there is fierce culinary competition under tin sheds, where *pulau* (aromatic fried rice), curry and roti are sold. Be prepared to eat with your fingers and put up with distorted Bollywood and folk music blaring around you.

If you want to hear and watch authentic Bollywood, there are cinemas in all major towns and cities with regular sessions of Hindi films (without subtitles); newspapers carry screening details. Bollywood music tapes and CDs are usually available in duty-free shops, as well as at music stores. In major Indo-Fijian shopping areas, such as Toorak and Cumming Sts in Suva, there is a wide variety of stores selling Indian spices, saris and knick-knacks. And if you want to leave the country with the Indian stamp of approval, treat yourself to traditional henna body art by popular mehndi artists including Usha Chauhan at **Jack's Little India** (www.jacksfiji.com) in Suva.

Although his appearances in Fiji are rare, professional golfer Vijay Singh (two-time winner of the PGA Championship, known on the circuit as 'The Big Fijian') is Fiji's most famous Indo-Fijian, and his achievements are regularly mentioned on websites about the global Indian diaspora.

Food & Drink

Fiji's food reflects the country's position as the multicultural hub of the Pacific, with its blend of indigenous Fijian, Polynesian, Indian, Chinese and Western tastes. Starchy carbohydrates play a big part in Pacific diets, but a spending spree at a fabulous local fruit and veggie market will increase your intake of the other food groups.

STAPLES & SPECIALITIES

Traditional Fijian foods include *tavioka* (cassava) and *dalo* (taro) roots, boiled or baked fish, and seafood in *lolo* (coconut cream). Meat is usually fried and accompanied with *dalo* and *rourou* (boiled *dalo* leaves in *lolo*), though you'll often find the colossally popular corned beef substituting for the real thing. *Kokoda* is a popular dish made of raw fish marinated in *lolo* and lime juice, with a spicy kick. See also p58 for details on popular local snacks.

Indo-Fijian dishes are usually spicy, and a typical meal comprises meat (but never beef or pork), fish or veggie curry with rice, *dahl* (lentil soup) and roti (a type of Indian flat bread). Chinese food is generally a Western-style takeaway affair with stir-fries, fried rice, chop suey, chow mein and noodle soups.

The ubiquitous corned beef became easier to preserve (and serve) after the 1875 invention, in Chicago, of the tapered corned-beef can.

DRINKS
Nonalcoholic Drinks

Ask locally if the tap water's OK to drink – in some places it is, in others it's not and will need to be boiled – but local and imported mineral water and soft drinks are available. Most milk is long life or powdered. Fresh local fruit juices and smoothies are great, but 'juice' on a menu often means sickly sweet cordial. The chilled water from green coconuts is refreshing.

Alcoholic Drinks

A variety of local and imported spirits and beer is available in bottle shops, most restaurants, and some supermarkets. Fiji Bitter and Fiji Gold are locally brewed beers, and the Malt House Brewery in Suva brews its own. Most wine is from Australia or New Zealand, and the price for a decent-enough bottle starts around $22. You can expect to pay about $6 for a beer in a bar, more at upmarket resorts. A 750mL bottle of Fiji Rum costs about $32.

TRAVEL YOUR TASTEBUDS

A wander through a busy Saturday market is a must – you'll have some fun encounters asking stallholders what they're selling, and how to cook it.

Follow your nose to the seafood. That bright-green mini bubble-wrap is actually *nama*, a seaweed that is made into a cold salad to accompany fish; the yellow bird-nesty mass is *lumi*, another seaweed, which gets cooked into a sort of jelly. Plates of scary-looking raw peeled shellfish are sold with a squeeze of lime and fresh chilli, and the less said about the rubbery bêche-de-mer the better. Don't know if you'll recognise bêches-de-mer? They're also known as sea cucumber, and that's just what they look like.

If you prefer something sweet, look for stalls with piles of things wrapped in banana-leaf. Try teeth-jarringly sweet *vakalolo*, made of cassava. It may look as though it's been passed through the digestive system of a large animal, but it's actually delicious.

KAVA

Kava, also called *yaqona* or grog, is as much a part of Fiji as beaches and *bure* (traditional thatched dwellings). It is mildly narcotic, looks like muddy water and makes your tongue go furry. You won't escape trying it!

Yaqona is an infusion prepared from *Piper methysticum,* a type of pepper plant. It holds a place of prominence in Fijian culture – in the time of the 'old religion' it was used ceremonially by chiefs and priests only, but today, *kava* is a part of daily life across the country and across the races. 'Having a grog' is used for welcoming and bonding with visitors, for storytelling sessions or merely for passing time. When visiting a village you will usually be welcomed with a short *sevusevu* ceremony (whereupon you'll present a gift to the village chief), during which you will be initiated into *kava* culture (see p42).

There are certain protocols to be followed at a *kava* ceremony. Sit cross-legged, facing the chief and the *tanoa* (large wooden bowl). Women usually sit behind the men. Never walk across the circle of participants, turn your back to or point your feet at the *tanoa,* or step over the cord – if there is one – that leads from the *tanoa* to a white cowrie shell, which represents a link with the spirits.

The dried and powdered root, wrapped in a piece of cloth, is mixed with water in the *tanoa* and squeezed out; you will be offered a drink of the resulting concoction from a *bilo* (half a coconut shell). Clap once, accept the *bilo,* say *'bula'* (meaning 'cheers' or, literally, 'life') and drink it down in one go. Clap three times in gratification. The drink will be shared until the *tanoa* is empty. You are not obliged to drink every *bilo* offered to you, but it is polite to drink at least the first. Despite rumours, it doesn't taste that awful (kind of like a murky medicine) and the most you're likely to feel from one *bilo* is a furry tongue. After a few drinks you may feel a slight numbness of the lips. Long sessions with stronger mixes can make you very drowsy, and some heavy drinkers develop *kanikani* (scaly skin).

Kava is a mild narcotic and has been used as a diuretic and stress reliever for pharmaceutical purposes. It has properties that combat depression, reduce anxiety and lower blood pressure – news that spread like wildfire through health-obsessed Western countries in the 1990s. When trade in *kava* peaked in 1998, Fiji and neighbouring Vanuatu were exporting US$25 million worth of *kava* each year. But the good times didn't last. A German study done in 2001 indicated that *kava* potentially caused liver damage, and in late 2002 most of Europe as well as Canada and the USA had either banned or put warnings and restrictions on *kava.*

After further research and lobbying, in 2005 the World Health Organization gave its support for reviving *kava* sales, and in mid-2007 the bans were lifted in Germany and eased elsewhere.

CELEBRATIONS

Fijians love food. The communal selection, preparation, cooking and eating of enormous multiple servings all play a central role in ceremonies and celebrations.

Lovo are traditional indigenous Fijian banquets in which food is prepared in an underground oven. A hole is dug in the ground and stones are put inside and heated by an open fire. The food – whole chickens, legs of pork, fragrant stuffed *palusami* (meat or corned beef, onions and *lolo*) or *dalo* – is wrapped in banana leaves and slowly half baked and half steamed on top of the hot stones. Delicious! Traditionally, *lovo* is served for family get-togethers as well as for more formal occasions such as church festivals and funerals.

If you're fortunate enough to be around Indo-Fijian Hindus during Diwali (Festival of Lights; p235), you'll be served fabulous vegetarian food during the three-day celebratory period, plus an astonishing array of sweets such as *gulab jamun* (deep-fried dough served in a sugar syrup) and *barfi* (Indian confectionery made from milk and sugar) on the day itself.

Lunar New Year is celebrated by Fiji's Chinese community with multi-course banquets accompanied by lion dancers and drummers.

WHERE TO EAT & DRINK

Nadi and Suva have a good variety of eateries ranging from cheap cafes in town to fine dining on the waterfront. Most places serve a combination of adapted Chinese, Fijian, Indian and Western dishes, and Japanese and Korean speciality restaurants are increasingly popular. Cheap restaurants and food halls charge between $4 and $8 for main meals; in decent city restaurants and resorts expect to pay upwards of $20 for a dish. Locals don't often linger over the dinner table and restaurants close early; you won't find many places open after 9pm.

Quick Eats

Fijians, like many peoples of the world, are forgoing traditional foods for readily available fast foods, but interesting (and often nutritionally better) local snack foods can also be found at street stalls and in the markets.

You haven't truly eaten locally until you've had a roti parcel. Easy food for travelling and breakfast, it's Indian flat bread wrapped around a serve of some sort of curried meat or spicy vegetable; most food stalls sell it.

You'll find some neat Fiji food and folklore stories by following the 'restaurant' link at www .fijilive.com/fijimagic.

In the markets you'll see all manner of anonymous cooked foods wrapped in banana-leaf packages. These will almost certainly be something starchy, probably *tavioka*, which has been grated and mixed with coconut, slightly sweetened, then baked or steamed. They're filling, with the ultimate biodegradable packing.

Around town you'll see Indian *mithai la gaadi* – sweet stalls that also sell cheap snacks such as roasted salted peas or cassava chips. They're often stationed around school entrances.

Be sensible about what you try. It's not a good idea to scoff down cooked meat that's been sitting around for a while, but if it comes from an icebox and is cooked in front of you – like the street barbecues that spring up at night – it's probably fine.

Self-Catering

Test your culinary skills and enjoy fabulous food photos from a Fijian kitchen at www.fijibure .com/namatakula/food .htm.

Every large town in Fiji has a fresh fruit-and-vegetable market and at least one supermarket where you can buy basic groceries. Most villages have a small shop but, as villagers grow their own fresh produce, stock is often limited to tinned fish, corned beef and packets of instant noodles. If your accommodation has cooking facilities, it will generally sell (very) basic supplies; but you'll be better off stocking up in town.

VEGETARIANS & VEGANS

Being vegetarian in Fiji is pretty easy, especially if you're partial to Indian food. Many Indo-Fijians are strict vegetarians, so most Indo-Fijian restau-

---

FIJI'S TOP FIVE RESTAURANTS

- Bad Dog Cafe (p126) is one of the hippest spots in the South Pacific, with mouth-watering pizza and a wine list to match.
- Seaview Restaurant (p95) is a long-time favourite Lautoka institution, with hearty meals and reasonable prices.
- Mantarae Restaurant (p112) is the place to splurge in Pacific Harbour. Ocean-side jazz, sunny day beds and contemporary Fiji fusion cuisine.
- Surf and Turf (p187) serves sublime steaks and lobster with alfresco dining and incredible Savusavu views.
- Whale's Tale (p173) in Levuka has great-value set meals and some of the best fish and chips in Fiji and is a perfect people-watching spot.

DOS & DON'TS

▪ Don't start serving yourself or eating until asked to do so by your host – there may be prayers to be said beforehand.

▪ Do have a snack before joining a *kava* session; you won't eat until it's finished – and this may take some time.

▪ Tipping is not expected but is, of course, welcome; 10% of the bill is sufficient if you feel so inclined.

---

rants have lots of veggie options, and there are Govinda's or Hare Krishna vegetarian restaurants in most sizeable towns. Most resorts and tourist restaurants have at least one token veggie meal on the menu.

The only time a person's vegetarianism can prove tricky is on visits to indigenous Fijian villages. If you are planning to go on a tour, be sure to tell the tour operator of your eating requirements when you book, because your hosts may find it strange – and perhaps offensive – that you'd refuse meat that they may not easily be able to afford. Communicating that your religious beliefs or your health won't allow you to eat meat are probably the most acceptable explanations.

EATING WITH KIDS

You'll have no problem feeding children in resorts, where kids' menus are on offer. Food halls in Suva are good value with a variety of food styles, and most will hold back on the chilli or cook up a special request out the back.

For fussy eaters, there's always the standby of a bunch of fresh bananas and fresh bread from Fiji's many hot bakeries. There's Western-style fast food in Suva and Nadi. Baby food is available in supermarkets, and it's probably wise to use boiled or bottled water for infants. See also p232.

HABITS & CUSTOMS

People rise at first light in Fiji, so breakfast – of fresh bread, or roti – is taken early. Fijians snack regularly in the gaps between eating a big lunch and a big, early dinner. Many people prefer to eat with their hands, and most restaurants have hand-washing basins available. In villages or in homes people often eat seated on a mat on the floor; men generally eat first, along with any visitors. As a guest, you'll be served the best food available; if it's not to your taste, accept and eat it graciously.

Muslim Fijians observe the fasting month of Ramadan by not eating during daylight hours. It doesn't make much difference to eating options for visitors, but your taxi driver or tour guide might be less energetic than normal during this period.

Public eating places are often theoretically nonsmoking, though this is rarely enforced. In the larger towns, bars and nightclubs are open until the early hours of the morning, and the party animals only get going after 10pm.

EAT YOUR WORDS

If you thought *kokoda* was a WWII walking trail in Papua New Guinea, think again. For a better taste of the language, see the pronunciation guidelines, p258.

Useful Phrases

breakfast	*katalau*
lunch	*vakasigalevu*
dinner	*vakayakavi*

Can't tell a mango from a mangosteen? You will once you've savoured *A Taste of the Pacific*, a regional food guide and recipe book by Susan Parkinson, Peggy Stacy and Adrian Mattinson.

Fiji's flag illustrates three of the country's main food crops – sugar, bananas and coconuts.

Food Glossary
(FH = Fijian-Hindi)

achar	Indian pickles
baigan	eggplant
barfi	Indian confectionery made from milk and sugar
bêche-de-mer	sea cucumber
bele	green leafy vegetable, served boiled
bhaji	spinach, or any leafy green vegetable
bhindi	okra
bu	green coconut
bulumakau	beef
čā (FH)	tea
dalo	taro, a starchy root served boiled or baked
dhaniya	coriander
duruka (FH)	Fijian asparagus
gulab jamun	deep-fried dough served in a sugar syrup; an Indian dessert
ika	fish
jalebi	Indian sweet
jira	cumin
katahar (FH)	jackfruit
kava/yaqona	mildly narcotic, muddy and odd-tasting drink made from the aromatic roots of a *Piper methysticum* (Polynesian pepper) shrub
kerela (FH)	bitter melon
kokoda	raw fish marinated in lime juice and *lolo*, served with chilli and onion…yum
kumrakh (FH)	star-apple
lauki	a type of gourd
lolo	coconut cream
lovo	food cooked on hot stones in an underground oven
lumi	a seaweed that is commonly cooked into a jelly
masala	curry powder
mithai	Indian sweets
nama	a seaweed commonly served as an accompaniment to fish…not so yum
palusami	corned beef (or meat), onions and *lolo* wrapped in *dalo* leaves and baked in *lolo*
pulau (FH)	aromatic fried rice
puri	deep-fried, Indian flat bread
roti	Indian flat bread
rourou	boiled *dalo* leaves in *lolo*
seo	Indian savoury snack
sharbaat (FH)	country-style lemon juice
tavioka	cassava
thali	Indian dish with several vegetarian dishes
toa	chicken
ura	freshwater prawns
uto	breadfruit, usually boiled or baked in a *lovo*
vakalolo	a sweet made from cassava
walu	butter fish

One of Fiji's efforts to combat obesity was an import ban in 2000 of high-fat 'lamb flaps' (don't ask) from New Zealand.

Legend has it that the plant that *kava* is made from sprung from the grave of a Tongan princess who died of a broken heart.

Environment

THE LAND

Fiji is south of the equator and north of the tropic of Capricorn. The country's territorial limits cover an enormous 1.3 million sq km, but only about 18,300 sq km of this – less than 1.5% – is dry land. The 180-degree meridian cuts across the island group at Taveuni, but the International Date Line has been doglegged eastward so that all of the islands fall within the same time zone – 12 hours ahead of GMT.

The more than 300 islands vary in size from tiny patches of land a few metres in diameter, to four larger islands (Viti Levu, Vanua Levu, Taveuni and Kadavu). Viti Levu, the main island, is 10,390 sq km and includes Fiji's highest point, Tomanivi (1323m; also called Mt Victoria), near the northern end of a range of mountains that separates the island's east and west. This mountain range also acts as a weather barrier; Suva, the country's capital, is located on the island's wetter side, while both Nadi, home of the country's main international airport, and Lautoka, the second-most important port after Suva, are on the drier, western side of the island.

Vanua Levu, the second-largest island (60km northeast of Viti Levu), is also mountainous and has many bays of various shapes and sizes. Taveuni, the third-largest, is rugged and, with rich volcanic soil, is known as the Garden Island. Kadavu, south of Viti Levu, is formed by three irregularly shaped land masses linked by isthmuses, and boasts beautiful reef lagoons, mountains, waterfalls and dense vegetation.

Fiji's first piece of national environmental protection legislation, the Environment Management Act, came into force in 2005.

WILDLIFE

Like many isolated oceanic islands, Fiji's native wildlife includes a few gems but is otherwise relatively sparse. Many of the plants and animals are related to those of Indonesia and Malaysia, and are thought to have drifted in on the winds and tides.

Animals

Fiji's main wildlife attraction is its bird life, but birdwatching in the wet season (roughly November to April) is hard work.

More than 3500 years ago the first settlers introduced poultry, Polynesian rats, dogs and pigs to Fiji. This was good for the people but not so good for native animals; two big-footed, mound-building birds and a giant flightless pigeon immediately became extinct.

In his wonderfully strange novel *The Island of the Day Before*, Umberto Eco reveals his captivation with the time-shifting possibilities of the 180-degree meridian that bisects Taveuni, and with the island's fabulous orange dove.

NATIVE MAMMALS

The only native terrestrial mammals in Fiji are six species of bat, of which you'll almost certainly see *beka* (large fruit bats or flying foxes), flying out around sunset to feed, or roosting during the day in colonies in tall trees. Two species of insectivorous bats are cave dwellers and are seldom seen.

Dolphins and whales are found living in Fijian waters, with several additional species passing by on their annual migration. *Tabua* (the teeth of sperm whales) have special ceremonial value for indigenous Fijians (see p33).

INTRODUCED MAMMALS

All other land-dwelling mammals have been introduced to their Fijian habitat from elsewhere. The common Indian mongoose was introduced in 1883 to control rats in sugar-cane plantations. Unfortunately, the mongoose mostly chose to eat Fiji's native snakes, frogs, birds and birds' eggs instead, and the rats are still there. Domestic animals that have turned feral include pigs introduced by the Polynesian settlers and goats brought by missionaries.

In the 19th century Europeans inadvertently but inevitably brought with them the brown-and-black rat and the house mouse.

BIRDS

Of the 57 bird species that breed in Fiji, 26 are endemic; but despite the fairly short distances between islands some birds, such as the orange dove of Taveuni and the cardinal honeyeater of Rotuma, are found on one or two islands only.

In urban areas you're likely to see the chunky collared lory (a common parrot) and the brilliant emerald, red-headed parrot finch. Aggressive introduced species, such as Indian mynahs, have forced many native birds into the forest, where you'll hear barking pigeons and giant forest honeyeaters. Some 23 tropical sea birds are also seen in Fiji. Fiji's rarest bird, the *kacau* (petrel), as seen on the back of the $50 note, is only found on Gau in the Lomaiviti Group.

Taveuni and Kadavu islands, and Colo-i-Suva Forest Park outside Suva, are good birdwatching spots.

REPTILES & AMPHIBIANS

Fiji's 27 species of reptiles are mostly lizards. The endemic crested iguana, only identified in 1979, is found on the Yasawas and, mostly, on Yadua Taba off the west coast of Vanua Levu. Its ancestors are thought to have floated to Fiji on vegetation from, unusually, South America. The banded iguana is also found in Fiji.

There are also two native terrestrial snakes (a small, nonpoisonous Pacific boa and the Fiji burrowing snake) and four sea snakes found in Fiji. Most are rarely seen, except for the *dadakulaci* (banded sea krait), which occasionally enters freshwater inlets to mate and lay its eggs on land. Although the *dadakulaci* are placid and can't open their jaws wide enough to bite humans, their venom is highly poisonous so it is worth being careful around them.

Five turtle species are found in Fijian waters: the hawksbill, loggerhead, green (named after the colour of its fat), Pacific Ridley and leatherback. As in many other parts of the world, turtle meat and eggs are considered a delicacy in Fiji. However, the taking of eggs and the capture of adults with shells under 46cm is banned. Although, because most turtles only reach breeding age at a size much larger than this, the ban isn't particularly effective in ensuring that the species procreates.

The cane toad was introduced in 1936 to control insects in the cane plantations. It's now become a pest itself, preying upon native ground frogs in coastal and lowland regions, as well as competing with them for food. The native tree frog and ground frog have retreated deep into the forests and are rarely seen.

MARINE LIFE

Fiji's richest animal life is underwater. There are hundreds of species of hard and soft coral, sea fans and sponges, often intensely colourful and fantastically shaped.

As coral needs sunlight and oxygen to survive, it's restricted to depths of less than 50m; wave breaks on shallow reefs are a good source of oxygen. Corals on a reef-break are generally of the densely packed varieties, such as brain coral (which looks like human brains), which are able to resist the force of the surf. Fragile corals such as staghorn grow in lagoons where the water is quieter.

Birders visiting Fiji should try to obtain copies of two essential illustrated pocket guides: *Birds of the Fiji Bush*, by Fergus Clunie, and Dick Watling's *Birds of Fiji – Sea & Shore Birds*.

Check out the (mostly) encouraging results of Birdlife International's 'Important Bird Areas in Fiji' project online at www.birdlife.org/world wide/national/fiji/index .html.

Can't tell a batfish from a butterflyfish? *Tropical Reef Life – a Getting to Know You & Identification Guide*, by Michael Aw, gives an informally detailed overview of underwater life, plus photographic tips.

CORAL WARNING: GLOBAL WARMING

One of the most obvious effects of global warming is the melting of polar caps and consequential rises in sea levels – estimated at 0.5m to 1m in the next 100 years. Rising sea levels will eventually cause devastating flooding and coastal erosion in many low-lying Pacific countries; the island of Gau, in Fiji's Lomaiviti group, has already lost 200m of coast. As well as the loss of land, the rising seawater table will poison crops and reduce the available fresh groundwater.

To date, Fiji's greatest warning of global warming has been coral bleaching. When physiologically stressed by raised water temperatures, coral loses the symbiotic algae that provide its colour and nutrition. If water temperatures return to normal, coral can recover; however, with repetitive bleaching entire reefs can be degraded and die. In 2001 and 2002 Fiji's reefs experienced huge amounts of bleaching, affecting 65% of reefs and killing 15%. As one of the most productive ecosystems on earth, reefs provide habitat and food for 25% of marine species; they also protect Fiji's smaller islands, provide food for local people and are a major source of income through tourism. As the bleaching occurs in shallow waters it has so far had no effect on Fiji's dive-tourism industry, but continued degradation could quickly spell disaster. Fiji signed the Kyoto Protocol on Climate Change in 1998.

Fiji's tropical fish are exquisite. Among the many you're likely to see are yellow-and-black butterflyfish; coral-chomping, blue-green parrotfish; wraithlike needlefish; and tiny, territorial, black-and-white clownfish guarding their anemone home. Fat-fingered blue starfish and delicate feathered starfish are common. Some marine creatures, such as fire corals, scorpionfish and lionfish, are highly venomous; if in doubt, don't touch! And watch where you put your bare feet.

Small black- and white-tipped reef sharks cruise along channels and the edges of reefs. The open sea and deeper waters are the haunt of larger fish, including tuna, swordfish and rays.

Plants

Most of Fiji is lush with fragrant flowers and giant, leafy plants and trees. There are 1596 identified plant species here, and about 60% of these are endemic. Many are used for food, medicine, implements and building materials.

RAINFOREST PLANTS

Forest giants include valuable timbers such as *dakua* (Fijian kauri), a hard, durable timber with a beautiful grain, used for furniture making. Of the many different fern species in Fiji, a number are edible and known as *ota*. The *balabala* (tree ferns) of Fiji are similar to those in Australia and New Zealand; once used on the gable ends of *bure* (traditional thatched dwellings), the trunks are now commonly seen carved into garden warriors – the Fijian counterpart of the Western gnome. The Pacific Islands are famous for their palm trees and Fiji has 31 species that reside in the rainforest and on the coasts.

You'll see *noni* (evergreen) products – cordials and soaps – for sale throughout Fiji. Noni produce a warty, foul-smelling, bitter-tasting fruit, which, despite its unattractive properties, is gaining credibility worldwide for its ability to help relieve complaints including arthritis, chronic fatigue, high blood pressure, rheumatism and digestive disorders.

The *tagimaucia,* with its white petals and bright red branches, is Fiji's national flower (see the boxed text, p202). It only grows at high altitudes on the island of Taveuni and on one mountain on Vanua Levu.

Orchids are abundant. Vanilla is a common orchid and there's a renewed commercial interest in its cultivation for use as a natural food flavouring.

FIJI'S ISLANDS & REEFS

The majority of the Fijian islands are volcanic in origin, but you'll also encounter coral and limestone islands. Fiji's reefs take three different forms: fringing, barrier and atoll.

Volcanic Islands

Volcanic islands generally have a series of conical hills rising to a central summit. Pinnacles indicate the sites of old volcanoes, with crystallised lava flows reaching the coast as ridges, forming cliffs or bluffs. Between these ridges are green valleys, with the only flat land to be found along the river basins of larger islands. The coasts are lined with beaches and mangroves, and the wetter sides of the islands – facing the prevailing winds – support thriving forests. The leeward hills are home to grasslands with only a sparse covering of trees.

There are no active volcanoes in Fiji but there is plenty of geothermal activity on Vanua Levu. In Savusavu some locals use the hot springs to do their cooking! Viti Levu and Kadavu are also volcanic islands.

Limestone Islands

Limestone islands are characteristically rocky land masses that have risen from the sea. Volcanic materials thrust up through the limestone, and the islands are often made up of cliffs, undercut by the sea and topped with shrubs and trees, and a central depression, forming a basin, surrounded by fertile, undulating hills. Vanua Balavu in the Lau Group is a limestone island.

Coral Islands

If you're looking for somewhere to swim or snorkel, head to one of Fiji's coral islands. Small and low, they are generally found in areas protected by barrier reefs, with surface levels at the height at which waves and winds can deposit sand and coral fragments. Their coasts have

COASTAL & RIVER PLANTS

Mangroves are the most distinctive plant communities along the coasts of Fiji. They provide important protection for seashores, against erosion, and are breeding grounds for prawns and crabs. Mangrove hardwood's value as firewood and for building houses has led to the destruction of many mangrove areas.

Casuarina, also known as ironwood or *nokonoko*, grows on sandy beaches and atolls. As its name suggests, the timber is heavy and strong and was used to make war clubs and parts of canoes.

An icon of the tropics, the coconut palm continues to support human settlement. Coconuts provide food and drink, shells are used for making cups and charcoal, leaves are used for baskets and mats, and oil is used for cooking, lighting, and as body and hair lotion.

Several species of pandanus are cultivated around villages. The leaves provide raw material for roof thatching, and for weaving baskets and mats.

Other common coastal plants include the beach morning glory, with its dawn-blooming purple flowers, and beach hibiscus, with its large, yellow flowers and light wood once used for canoe building. The *vutu* tree flowers only at night; its highly scented blooms are white and pink with a distinctive fringe, and were traditionally used as fish poison.

Find out what climate change means for the Pacific at the World Wildlife Fund's website, www.wwfpacific.org.fj, or see how Greenpeace's Pacific fisheries campaign is going at www.green peace.org.au/oceans.

GARDEN PLANTS

Botanist John Bates Thurston brought many plants to Fiji in the 19th century. Introduced African hibiscus is Fiji's most common garden plant, and is used for decoration, food and dye, and a medicine for treating stomach pains can be distilled from the leaves and fruit. Bougainvillea and yellow allemanda are also common, both introduced from Brazil. The flowers of the bright, white-sand beaches, and mangroves are found in the lagoon shallows. Examples of coral islands are Beachcomber and Treasure Islands in the Mamanucas, and Leleuvia and Caqalai in the Lomaivitis.

Fringing Reefs
Narrow fringing reefs link to the shore of an island, stretching seaward, and are exposed during low tide. Often the bigger fringing reefs have higher sections at the open-sea edge and drainage channels on the inside, which remain water filled and navigable by small boats. Where rivers and streams break the reefs, fresh water prevents coral growth. The Coral Coast on southern Viti Levu is an extensive fringing reef.

Barrier Reefs
Barrier reefs are large strips of continuous reef, broken only by occasional channels some distance from the coastline. Fiji's Great Sea Reef extends about 500km from the coast of southwestern Viti Levu to the northernmost point of Vanua Levu. A section of this lying between 15km and 30km off the coast of Vanua Levu is unbroken for more than 150km. The Great Astrolabe Reef circling Kadavu is a barrier reef, as are the smaller reefs encircling Beqa.

Atolls
Atolls are small rings of coral reef with land and vegetation on top, just above sea level and enclosing a lagoon. Despite their idyllic representation in tales of the South Pacific, most have inhospitable environments. The porous soil derived from dead coral, sand and driftwood retains little water and is often subject to drought. The vegetation is made up of hardy pandanus, coconut palms, shrubs and coarse grasses. Of Fiji's few atolls the best-known is Wailagi Lala in the Lau Group.

bua (frangipani) are strongly scented and are therefore often used in soaps and perfumes, or tucked into people's hair.

NATIONAL PARKS & RESERVES
Fiji has several protected conservation areas, though lack of resources means that conservation is hard to ensure. The Bouma National Heritage Park and Ravilevu Nature Reserve now protect over 40% of Taveuni's land area and contain several well-maintained walking tracks. Koroyanitu National Heritage Park, near Lautoka in the highlands of Viti Levu, is also well established.

Other significant sites include the Sigatoka Sand Dunes (p101) on Viti Levu's Coral Coast, Colo-i-Suva Park (p121) and Garrick Reserve near Suva, and Tunuloa Silktail Reserve near Navua on Vanua Levu. For permits to go to Yadua Taba (home to the crested iguana), Garrick Reserve and several other sites of ecological and historical importance you will need to contact the **National Trust for Fiji** (Map p118; ☎ 330 1807; nationaltrust@is.com.fj; 3 Maafu St) in Suva.

Suva's beautiful (but underresourced) public gardens, opened in 1913, are named after botanist John Bates Thurston, who introduced many ornamental plants to Fiji.

ENVIRONMENTAL ISSUES
Ecotourism is a buzzword in Fiji, as elsewhere. In areas of intense tourism it has become trendy for resorts and tours to tack an 'eco' onto their name; some are more environmentally aware than others (see the GreenDex, p279, for a list of the more environmentally savvy operators). However, while remote villages can benefit from the income brought by low-impact tourism, it also brings additional pollution and rapid cultural change.

Greenpeace and the World Wildlife Fund both have offices in Suva, and campaign regionally on issues such as ocean fisheries and climate change.

RESPECT & PROTECT

Many of Fiji's endangered animals and plants are protected by the Convention on International Trade in Endangered Species (CITES). Others are protected by national legislation. If you buy a souvenir made from a protected or endangered species and don't get a permit, you're breaking the law and chances are that customs will confiscate it at your overseas destination. In particular, remember the following:

- *Tabua* are *tabu* (sacred) – whale's teeth are protected.
- Turtle shell looks best on live turtles.
- Leave seashells on the seashore; protected species include giant clams, helmet shells, trochus and tritons.
- Tread lightly. Stepping on live coral is like stepping on a live budgie: you'll kill it.
- Many plants, including most orchids, are protected.

Trash & Carry

Your litter will become someone else's problem, especially on small islands; where possible, recycle or remove your own.

Don't Rush to Flush

Fresh water is precious everywhere, especially on small islands; take short showers and drink boiled or rainwater rather than buy another plastic bottle.

Air Pollution

Out of town, air quality is generally good, though there's often a smoke haze from burning domestic rubbish. In towns, lack of maintenance means that many vehicles emit thick exhaust; local authority spot-checks and fines are an attempt to address this. In 2005 a deep toxic fire burned for days in the Suva municipal rubbish tip, provoking debate on the problem of solid-waste management for island states.

For encouraging and creative examples of how communities can manage their own resources, check out the Communities and Coasts web page of the Foundation of the Peoples of the South Pacific International, www.fspi.org.fj.

Erosion & Deforestation

Burning of forests and land-clearing for agriculture has resulted in the erosion of fertile topsoil. Sugar-cane and other steep-slope farming have increased erosion even further. Pine plantations (though they have drawbacks in other ways) and the reintroduction of sustainable agricultural practices are ongoing attempts to restore soil quality and quantity and jobs.

Water Pollution

About 59% of the population has access to a sustainable water source. In urban centres water quality is generally good but not everywhere; Lautoka residents, for example, boil their water before drinking.

The sea around the busy ports of Suva and Lautoka is polluted with sewage seepage, oil spills and litter dumping. Destructive fishing techniques, such as the use of explosives, are still used without much control, and coral harvesting for the aquarium industry can be a problem. The use of drift nets for fishing is illegal. These and other issues are being addressed by local and international NGOs, which work with local people on community-based coastal management projects aiming to improve community livelihoods and protect biodiversity.

Diving Jean-Bernard Carillet

Diving in Fiji is truly amazing, offering innumerable underwater sights that will make even the most world-weary diver dewy-eyed. The water is warm, clear and teeming with life. You'll see a myriad of multihued fish, canyonlike terrain and vertigo-inducing walls festooned with exquisite soft and hard corals resembling a lush flower garden in full bloom. You can also have heart-pounding experiences such as drifting with the current in Somosomo Strait or going nose-to-nose with massive bull sharks in Beqa Lagoon. Whatever your level of expertise and your inclinations, you'll find your slice of underwater heaven.

DIVING CONDITIONS

Although Fiji is diveable year-round, the best season is from April to October. November to March tends to see the most rainfall, which can obscure visibility off the main islands with river run-off.

Keep in mind that many dives are subject to currents, which vary from barely perceptible to powerful. Visibility varies a lot, from a low of 10m at certain sites up to 40m at others.

Water temperatures range from 23°C in August to 29°C in January. You won't need anything more than a thin neoprene or a 3mm wetsuit to remain comfortable whilst diving.

A dive instructor and incorrigible traveller, Jean-Bernard Carillet has written widely for various French publications and has also coordinated and coauthored Lonely Planet diving guides.

DIVE SITES

For well-informed divers, Fiji equals soft corals. Dive Somosomo Strait off Taveuni and you'll know what we mean. But soft corals and drift dives are not the only raison d'être of diving in Fiji. You will also find majestic reefs ablaze with technicoloured critters and a spectacular underwater topography. The only weak point is the dearth of impressive wrecks. But the dive repertoire is endless, with diving on offer on all islands. In fact, it's hard for divers to decide where to go: there are so many fabulous dive sites. Just as the individual islands have their distinct flavours, so too do the dive sites have their own hallmark. Just take your pick!

The following are some of Fiji's top dive sites.

For Beginners

Breath Taker (Nananua-i-Ra, Viti Levu) Great pelagic action on an incoming tide including Spanish mackerel and reef sharks.

Gotham City (Mamanuca Group) Reef species aplenty and excellent coral.

Dreadlocks (Vanua Levu) An aquariumlike setting, with a host of kaleidoscopic tropicals.

Yellow Wall (Kadavu) An atmospheric site resembling a fairy-tale castle.

Lekima's Ledge (Yasawa Group) An underwater cliff and a feast for the eyes.

Fiji is dubbed 'the soft coral capital of the world', and rightly so.

For Experienced Divers

Great White Wall (Taveuni) Possibly the best soft-coral dive in Fiji.

Shark Reef (Beqa Lagoon, Viti Levu) Bull sharks galore – a once-in-a-lifetime experience.

Nigali Passage (Shark Alley, Lomaiviti Group) An exhilarating drift dive spiced up with regular sightings of grey sharks.

Nasonisoni Passage (Vanua Levu) Another rip-roaring drift dive in a narrow passage.

Split Rock (Kadavu) A maze of faults, canyons and tunnels.

E6 (Bligh Water, Lomaiviti Group) A phenomenal seamount that brushes the surface; a magnet for pelagics.

Viti Levu

Viti Levu is normally the visiting diver's first glimpse of Fiji. Although less charismatic than Taveuni or Kadavu, it boasts a fair share of underwater wonders and deserves attention for its variety of sites. The best diving is found off Nananu-i-Ra island to the north and in Beqa Lagoon to the south, but there are also some interesting options off Toberua island to the east and in Navula Passage to the west. Most dive sites are suitable for all skill levels.

But what sets it apart is the diving at Shark Reef in Beqa Lagoon, where you can witness a phenomenal shark-feeding session (see the boxed text, opposite). Here you're almost certain to go nose-to-nose with massive predators.

Of course there are much-less-intimidating sites around Viti Levu. In Beqa Lagoon the quality of the corals is not the strong point but you'll like the underwater scenery at Caesar's Rock, which has a multitude of pinnacles riddled with tunnels and caves. A long-standing favourite, Side Streets features a collection of small coral pillars scattered in a reef passage. ET features a vast tunnel more than 30m long and 5m in diameter. The sides of the tunnel are densely blanketed with sea fans and soft corals. Carpet Cove (also known as Seven Sisters) is a good spot, with the wreck of a Japanese trawler that was scuttled in 1994, at about 25m.

In 2000, high water temperatures resulted in severe coral bleaching throughout Fiji but a recent report put out by the Coral Reef Initiative for the South Pacific indicates that the reefs are recovering surprisingly quickly.

Diving along the northern shore of Viti Levu is focused on the offshore islands and reefs near Rakiraki, including Nananu-i-Ra. This area is a real treat for divers, with a good balance of scenic seascapes, elaborate reef structures and dense marine life. Dream Maker ranks among the best sites in the area. You'll enjoy weaving your way among large coral heads lavishly blanketed in a bright mosaic of sea fans and gorgonians – a typical Fiji dive. Breath Taker is famous for its dense concentration of colourful tropicals and the quality of its corals. To the northwest, off Charybdis Reef, Spud Dome is renowned for its dramatic scenery while Heartbreak Ridge offers a chance of spotting pelagics.

Mamanuca Group

Due to their proximity to Nadi and Lautoka on Viti Levu, the Mamanuca islands are very popular among divers and can easily be reached from these two towns by boat. You could also base yourself at any of the island resorts because diving infrastructure is readily available throughout the Mamanuca Group. Most dive sites are scattered along the Malolo Barrier Reef or off the nearby islets. Diving is probably less spectacular than in other areas of Fiji but it's still rewarding, with diverse marine life, good visibility and a varied topography, as well as a glut of easy sites that will appeal to novice divers.

Two well-regarded sites are the Plantation Pinnacles, notable for its three deep-water rock towers, and Sherwood Forest, which has beautiful gorgonian sea fans. Inside the barrier-reef lagoon, Gotham City comprises several coral heads surrounded by a smorgasbord of reef fish in less than 20m. Other sites to look for include Namotu Reef, the Big Ws (where you'll see some big fish) and Bird Rock. Wreck buffs will explore the *Salamanda,* a 36m vessel that was sunk as an artificial reef. She rests upright on a rubble sea-floor in the 20m range and is partly encrusted with a variety of glowing soft corals and anemones. There's usually abundant fish life hanging around.

Yasawa Group

Less crowded and fewer dive boats: this is diving in the Yasawas. This chain of ancient volcanic islands offers excellent corals, pristine reefs and good visibility – not to mention superb topside backdrops. Check out Lekima's Ledge, a stunning underwater cliff off Vawa island, suitable for novice divers, and Paradise Wall, another recommended wall dive off the western side of

UP CLOSE & PERSONAL WITH THE OCEAN'S MOST FEARED CREATURES

We've done it, and we won't forget it. Believe us: you'll experience the adrenaline thrill of a lifetime. A few kilometres off the Viti Levu coast near Pacific Harbour lies Shark Reef. You won't come here to marvel at soft or hard corals. Instead, this spot is home to phenomenal shark-feeding sessions. For a list of operators who run this dive see p109.

In other parts of the world, shark feeding usually involves grey reef sharks and, if you're lucky, lemon sharks and nurse sharks. Here, up to eight different types of sharks turn up: tawny nurse sharks, white-tip, black-tip and grey reef sharks, sicklefin lemon sharks, silvertips, massive bull sharks (the star performers, with up to 25 individuals at a time) and even the heavyweight of them all – tiger sharks! Handfeeding these monsters seems suicidal. However, the two feeders from Beqa island have become experts in 'taming' the predators. They claim they are protected by traditional magic. Apparently, this protection is effective as no incident has ever been recorded in their more than six years of diving.

There are two distinct dives. The first one is at 30m. On a coral rubble patch, the divers form a line, behind a purpose-built small coral wall, a few metres away from the feeders. The feeder dips into a huge bin and pulls out hunks of dead fish. He is soon in the middle of a maelstrom. For several minutes at a time it may be hard to work out what is happening in the swirl of tails and fins as one shark after another materialises, ripping and tearing at the bait. It's definitely (in)tense, but there's no frenzy to speak of. The sharks approach in surprisingly orderly fashion, even the ponderous-looking bull sharks. Being within touching distance of these predators is absolutely awesome, but you'll also be enthralled by the other fish species that are invited to this free meal, including schools of giant trevally, snapper, grouper and surgeonfish.

The second dive takes you down to 17m. Again, you sit on a clear arena behind a small wall. Now the hefty bull sharks and the lemon sharks are more inquisitive and come even closer to the feeder. But wait! The adrenaline level has not reached its maximum. If the arena suddenly clears, then you know that a 4m tiger shark is going to make its appearance. When it takes the bait from the feeder, you can see its cavernous maw…

Let's put it frankly. This is more a show than a dive. Fish feeding is a controversial subject among diving operators all over the world. On the one hand, these artificial encounters undeniably disrupt natural behaviour patterns. Sharks that grow dependent on 'free lunches' may unlearn vital survival skills. Some have developed dangerous Pavlovian responses to the sound of revving boat motors. On the other hand, some experts think that these shows have educational virtue and raise awareness among divers; a diver who has viewed these often-misunderstood creatures up close becomes an instant shark lover with a positive image of these feared denizens of the deep.

Whatever your stance on the issue, these dives are conducted in a very professional way. There's a comprehensive briefing prior to the dive and divers are watched over by dive masters with large poles. At no time do you feel a sense of threat.

Take note that bull sharks leave the spot from October to January to mate.

Yasawa island. There are also some interesting caves to explore off Sawa-i-Lau island. The passage between Nanuya Balavu and Drawaqa is frequented by giant manta rays, and although the use of scuba equipment is prohibited, this is an amazing snorkelling experience. The resorts around Nacula, Tavewa and Nanuya Lailai islands offer diving in the Blue Lagoon; although the fish numbers are high here, the coral has been damaged. Bonsai, the Maze and the Zoo are all recommended alternatives, as is the Saturday shark-encounter dive.

Lomaiviti Group & Bligh Water

Central Fiji roughly covers the area between the country's two main landmasses – it extends from Bligh Water in the west to Namenalala and the Lomaiviti Group in the east. Most sites in this 'golden triangle' can only be accessed by live-aboards (see p72) and remain largely untouched. One of the most spectacular dive regions in Fiji, it boasts a unique configuration

CORAL'S TRUE COLOUR *Justine Vaisutis*

The Yasawa islands are home to some of the most-vivid coral in the world and excellent visibility provides snorkellers and divers with plenty of opportunity to appreciate it. Although its flowery exterior appears plantlike, coral is actually an animal, and a hungry, carnivorous one at that.

Corals belong to the same class of animals as sea anemones and jellyfish. The true reef-building corals or Scleractinia are distinguished by their lime skeletons. This skeleton forms the reef and as new coral continually builds on old, dead coral the reef gradually builds up.

All coral formations are made up of polyps, the tiny, tubelike, fleshy cylinders that look very like their close relation, the anemone. The top of the cylinder is open and ringed by waving tentacles, which sting any passing prey and draw them into the polyp's stomach. This is why coral cuts can be quite painful – when you graze your skin on coral you're actually receiving a sting. Although this is reason enough to avoid touching coral, it's more important to remember that coral is quite fragile, so if you break it you're essentially killing decades of growth and life.

Each polyp is an individual creature, but each can reproduce by splitting to form a coral colony of separate but closely related polyps. Although each polyp catches and digests its own food, the nutrition passes between the polyps to the whole colony. Most coral polyps only feed at night; during the daytime they withdraw into their hard limestone skeleton, so it is only at night that a coral reef can be seen in its full colourful glory.

Hard corals take many forms. One of the most common and easiest to recognise is the staghorn coral, which grows by budding off new branches from the tips. Brain corals are huge and round with a surface looking very much like a human brain. They grow by adding new base levels of skeletal matter and expanding outwards. Flat or sheet corals, such as plate coral, expand at their outer edges.

Like their reef-building relatives, soft coral is made up of individual polyps, but does not form a hard limestone skeleton. Without the skeleton that protects hard coral, it would seem likely that soft coral would fall prey to fish, but it seems to remain relatively immune either due to toxic substances in its tissues or to the presence of sharp limestone needles, which protect the polyps. Soft corals can move around and will sometimes engulf and kill hard coral.

When diving or snorkelling be careful to respect the underwater environment; admire but don't touch. If your expedition takes you to the ocean floor, look what's beneath you before touching the bottom. Corals may appear resilient and hardy but they are extremely vulnerable and preserving them ensures a healthy ecological balance for all marine life in the area.

consisting of an intricate maze of vast barrier reefs surrounding large lagoons and islands, all exposed to both nutrient-rich run-off and clean ocean water. This constant interplay of ecosystems ensures prolific marine life and reefs abloom with corals.

The Great Fiji Butterfly-Fish Count takes place every November. Volunteers – especially divers and snorkellers – are required. Go to www .fijibutterflyfishcount .com for details.

E6 is consistently rated as one of the best sites in Fiji. This seamount in Vatu-i-Ra Channel rises from 1000m to the surface and acts as a magnet for pelagics in search of easy pickings. You might come across schooling barracuda, hammerheads and eagle rays. On the leeside you'll marvel at soft corals and fans in full blossom. A huge swim-through in the seamount, called the Cathedral, creates a magical atmosphere, especially when beams of sunlight filter through the cracks in the ceiling.

Another spectacular seamount reaching from 1000m to just below the surface, Mt Mutiny is sheer delight, with a colourful collection of throbbing coral communities adorning the wall. Keep an eye out for cruising pelagics.

In the mood for an adrenaline rush? Off Gau island, Nigali Passage (also known as Shark Alley) is the right place. A drift dive by essence, this narrow channel is one of the most active in this region. The site's biggest claim to fame is the almost ever-present squadron of grey sharks (up to 20 individuals) that haunt the passage, as well as schooling trevally, barracuda, snapper and the occasional ray. A less-challenging site on the northwest side of Gau's barrier reef, Jim's Alley features a collection of coral boulders that bottom out at 24m.

Off the southeastern coast of Vanua Levu, the reef surrounding Namenalala is another hot spot, with several breathtaking sites, including Chimneys, in less than 25m. As the name suggests, you'll see several towering coral pillars, all coated with soft corals, sea fans and crinoids. Numerous reef species hide in the undercuts. Finish your dive in the shallows atop the pinnacles, where constellations of basslets and blennies flit about the coral structures. Some instructors also swear by North-Save-a-Tack, located in a current-swept passage renowned for its copious fish life and healthy corals.

Off Wakaya island, make a beeline for Blue Ridge. This site derives its name from the abundance of bright-blue ribbon eels. Although they lead the show, many other species will vie for your attention, including dartfish, gobies and leaf fish and, if you're lucky, hammerheads and manta rays.

Vanua Levu

Fiji's second-largest island, Vanua Levu, is a true gem, with numerous untouched sites for those willing to venture away from the tourist areas. Most dive sites are in or around Savusavu Bay. The underwater scenery is striking, the walls are precipitous and the fish population (which includes pelagics) is diverse.

Experienced divers shouldn't miss Nasonisoni Passage, a rip-roaring drift dive in a narrow, current-swept channel. During tidal exchange, divers are sucked into the passage and propelled through the funnel by the forceful current.

Do you like tiny critters? Dreadlocks, right in the middle of Savusavu Bay, is an enchanting site that will appeal to all levels. A jumble of coral pinnacles in less than 20m harbours numerous kaleidoscopic tropicals, including harlequin filefish, lionfish, butterflyfish, gobies, nudibranchs, sweetlips…

As the name suggests, Barracuda Point is famed for schooling barracuda that can be spotted at about 25m. Batfish are also regularly seen here. Healthy staghorn corals and gorgonians complete the picture.

Dreamhouse refers to a small seamount that seems to attract a wealth of pelagics, including grey reef sharks, jacks and tuna. If the current is not running, all you do is spiral up around the coral mound and marvel at the luxuriant setting.

Taveuni

Blessed with lush rainforests, cascading waterfalls and a profusion of tropical plants and flowers, Taveuni is called the Garden Island. It's more or less the same story below the waterline. The Somosomo Strait, a narrow stretch of ocean that is funnelled between Taveuni and Vanua Levu, has achieved

---

RESPONSIBLE DIVING

The Fiji islands are ecologically vulnerable. By following these guidelines while diving, you can help preserve the ecology and beauty of the reefs:

- Encourage dive operators to establish permanent moorings at appropriate dive sites.
- Practise and maintain proper buoyancy control.
- Avoid touching living marine organisms with your body and equipment.
- Take great care in underwater caves, as your air bubbles can damage fragile organisms.
- Minimise your disturbance of marine animals.
- Take home all your trash and any other litter you may find.
- Never stand on corals, even if they look solid and robust.

LIVE-ABOARDS

A couple of live-aboards ply the Fiji waters, usually with week-long itineraries. A live-aboard dive trip is recommended for those looking to experience unchartered and uncrowded dive sites beyond the reach of land-based dive operations, especially the sites in Bligh Water and off the Lomaiviti Group. Take a look at the following operators:

Fiji Aggressor (www.aggressor.com)
Nai'a (☎ 345 0382; www.naia.com.fj)
Republic of Diving (☎ 628 2736; www.republicofdiving.com)
Sere-ni-Wai (☎ 336 1171; www.sere.com.fj)

Shangri-la status in the diving community, and for good reason. Strong tidal currents push the deep water back and forth through the passage, providing nutrients for the soft corals and sea fans that form a vivid and sensual tapestry on the reefs. This area is often called Rainbow Reef. As if that weren't enough, vertical walls add a touch of drama.

Start with the aptly named Purple Wall. And what a wall: it is suffused with a dense layer of purple soft-coral trees, whip corals and sea fans wafting in the current. Numerous overhangs and arches harbour soldierfish and squirrelfish. At the entrance of Somosomo Strait, Great White Wall is one of Fiji's signature dives. It's an awesome wall and drift dive, with a phenomenal concentration of white soft coral (it's actually pale lavender), resembling a snow-covered ski slope. When the current is running, soft-coral trees unfurl from the wall to feed and feature an almost heavenly glow – a truly ethereal sight. In the same area, don't miss Rainbow Passage. Once again a photogenic spot, it features a large, submerged reef offering a wealth of marine life and spectacular bouquets of soft corals. A number of pinnacles protruding from the reef are wreathed with luxuriant soft-coral trees in every colour of the rainbow. Look closely for the rich resident fish-and-invertebrate population, including nudibranchs, Christmas-tree worms, crinoids and clown fish.

In the middle of Somosomo Strait, Annie's Bommies is an explosion of colour, with several big boulders liberally draped with soft corals and surrounded by swirling basslets. Unlike other sites, it's not a wall dive, so you can leisurely weave your way among the boulders and stare at coral exuberance. Other sites include Cabbage Patch, Blue Ribbon Eel Reef, the Ledge, the Pinnacle, Yellow Grotto and the Zoo.

But there's more to Somosomo Strait than coral splendour and vertigo-inducing walls. The nutrient-rich water also produces pelagic sightings. It's not uncommon to encounter manta rays, white-tip reef sharks, kingfish, barracuda and, with a bit of luck, even leopard sharks.

There are also superb dive sites around neighbouring Matagi, Qamea and Laucala islands and at Motualevu Atoll, some 30km east of Taveuni. Check out the Edge, off Motualevu Atoll. This breathtaking drop-off is adorned with a wide variety of soft and hard corals and carved by numerous overhangs and windows at various depths. Another renowned site, Noel's Wall is a feast for the eyes. The wall is showered in soft-coral bushes covering the whole colour spectrum. Due to the isolation of the site, you've got a reasonable chance to spot bronze whalers, tuna, barracuda, jacks and manta rays.

Currents bring life to the reef. They constantly channel nutrients in and out with the tides, attracting all forms of sealife along the food chain. When the current flows, the corals bloom with flowerlike beauty. When it's absent, the corals withdraw into their spicules.

Kadavu

Kadavu's main claim to fame is the Great Astrolabe Reef, a barrier reef that hugs the south and east coasts of the island for about 100km. For divers, this is a gem of a reef, with a vibrant assemblage of exquisite hard and soft-coral formations and breathtaking walls beginning as shallow as 10m. The dramatic seascape is another highlight, with a network of passages, swim-throughs and crevices sheltering a stunning variety of reef species. You can't get bored here. Unlike Taveuni, currents are probably easier to handle in this area, but be prepared for rough seas and reduced visibility when it's raining or when the winds blow, especially from November to April.

On the western side of the Great Astrolabe, recommended dive sites include Broken Stone, Split Rock and Vouwa. They more or less share the same characteristics, with a mind-boggling combination of twisting canyons, tunnels, caverns and arches. If you like scenic underwater seascapes, you'll be in seventh heaven here.

In the mood for an adrenaline-pumping ride? Try Naiqoro Passage, just off the east coast of Kadavu. This narrow channel is frequently swept by strong tidal currents and offers rewarding drift dives along steep walls.

The northwestern side of Kadavu is a bit overshadowed by the Great Astrolabe Reef but it also features dives that are superb in their own right. Novice divers will feel comfortable here – the dive conditions are less challenging than anywhere else in Kadavu but still offer excellent fish action. If you want a relaxed dive, Mellow Reef does the trick. It consists of several boulders in less than 20m. It's an ideal site to refresh your skills before taking on deeper dives. Another easy dive, Yellow Wall is a very atmospheric site in the 20m range, featuring several pinnacles graced with yellow soft corals. Wend your way around these rocks and marvel at the colourful fauna fluttering about. Once you've had your fill of soft corals and drift dives, you might want to explore the *Pacific Voyager*, a 63m-long tanker that was in 1994 intentionally sunk in 30m of water as an artificial reef. It's nothing spectacular but it makes for an interesting change.

> The only downside in Somosomo Strait is the average visibility. It does not exceed 15m to 20m when the currents flow.

DIVE CENTRES

Dive centres are open year-round, most of them every day. Many are attached to a resort and typically offer two-tank dive trips. Try to book at least a day in advance. Operators offer a whole range of services, such as introductory dives, night dives, exploratory dives and certification programs.

Diving in Fiji is rather good value, especially if you compare it with other South Pacific destinations. If you plan to do many dives on one island, consider buying a multidive package, which comes out much cheaper. Generally, prices don't include equipment rental, so it's not a bad idea to bring all your gear. Most dive shops offer free pick-ups from your accommodation and accept credit cards.

There's one recompression chamber in Suva (see p117).

FREE THRILLING RIDES

Drift diving is an integral part of Fiji diving. As the tide rises and falls, enormous volumes of water flow in and out of the channels, across the reefs and along the walls, forming bottlenecks and creating strong currents. The current becomes a great buddy, helping propel you through the water with amazing ease. All you do is immerse yourself in the ocean and let yourself be sucked through the channel, until the effects of the current weaken. Because the distances covered during drift dives are huge, a boat follows divers' progression by tracking their bubbles. At the end of the dive, the instructor inflates a brightly coloured marker buoy to signal the exact position of the group, and the boat picks up the divers.

Drift diving is very exciting because you feel as though you're flying or gliding through the channels. But it's an advanced activity that requires specific skills, including a perfect control of buoyancy. Such dives are more suitable for intermediate or advanced divers. Local dive centres usually check divers out before taking them to these sites.

DIVING & FLYING

Most divers get to Fiji by plane. While it's fine to dive soon *after* flying, it's important to remember that your last dive should be completed at least 12 hours (some experts advise 24 hours) *before* your flight, to minimise the risk of residual nitrogen in the blood causing decompression. Careful attention to flight times as compared with diving times is necessary in Fiji because so much of the interisland transport is by air.

Beginner Divers

Fiji is a perfect starting point for new divers, as the warm water in the shallow lagoons is a forgiving training environment.

Just about anyone in reasonably good health can sign up for an introductory dive, including children aged eight years and over. There are various programs on offer, including Discover Scuba, which takes place in a pool, and Discover Scuba Diving, which is a guided dive in open water.

If you choose to enrol in an Open Water Course while in Fiji, count on it taking about three days, including classroom lectures and training. Another option is to complete the classroom and pool sessions in your home country, and perform the required open-water dives in a dive centre in Fiji that is affiliated with the Professional Association of Diving Instructors (PADI) or Scuba Schools International (SSI). Once you're certified, your C-card is valid permanently and recognised all over the world.

HOW MUCH?

Introductory dive: about $130

Two-tank dive: about $210, including equipment rental

Open Water certification course: about $625

Choosing a Dive Centre

There are at least 30 professional dive centres in Fiji. All of them are affiliated with one or more internationally recognised certifying agencies, usually PADI or National Association of Underwater Instructors (NAUI). In general, you can expect well-maintained equipment, good facilities and knowledgable staff, but standards may vary from one centre to another. On islands with several operators, do your research and opt for the one that best suits your expectations. Dive centres are detailed in the destination chapters.

Documents

If you're a certified diver, bring your C-card; it's a good idea to have your dive logbook with you as well. Centres welcome certification from any training agency (Confédération Mondiale des Activités Subaquatiques, PADI, NAUI etc), but may ask you to do a test dive to assess your skills.

Viti Levu

Like a grand chief presiding over a tribal council, Viti Levu, the largest of the Fijian islands, squats roundly and self-assuredly in the centre of those it governs. And, like all great chiefs, Viti Levu wields considerable power; it is the pivotal point about which politics, commerce and industry revolve and where around three-quarters of the population resides.

Sultry Suva is the largest city in the South Pacific and the confluence of island cultures and Indo-Fijian traditions has given the capital a vibrant nightlife, a rich heritage and the country's best restaurants.

The Queens and Kings Roads run the perimeter of the island, occasionally skirting into the lush interior. From Nadi, Fiji's sunny gateway, the Queens Road hugs the Coral Coast. Disappointingly, the coast doesn't quite live up to its name; the beaches of Viti Levu (with the exception of Natadola), run a poor second to those on the outer islands. Scratch deeper though and travellers will discover a Fiji beyond the gimmicky hype. Opportunities to foray into the interior's dramatic highlands or marvel at the views from elevated Tongan forts abound. For the adventurous, it is possible to explore giant sand dunes and dive with truly massive tiger sharks.

The Kings Road completes Viti Levu's northern loop. Surprisingly few tourists visit here but those in the know – usually savvy windsurfers and divers – head for Nananu-i-Ra island, home to consistent winds and the beautiful 'breath-taker' reef.

HIGHLIGHTS

- Slip and slide over the **Sigatoka Sand Dunes** (p101) on the lookout for ancient burial relics
- Catch a local bus into the Nausori Highlands to **Navala** (p137), Fiji's sole remaining traditional *bure* village
- Get to grips with the traditional culture on display at Suva's **Fiji Museum** (p119) and compare it with today's vibrant urban culture at **Suva's bars** (p128)
- Kayak or raft the mighty **Navua River** (p112) in the rugged Namosi Highlands
- Stifle knocking knees and dive with the resident tiger sharks in **Beqa Lagoon** (p109)
- Gallop along the beautiful **Natadola Beach** (p98) on a local's horse
- Feed baby turtles and stroke an iguana at the **Kula Eco Park** (p104)
- Head to **Nananu-i-Ra** (p135) to windsurf and snorkel on the island's best reefs

- POPULATION: 585,000
- AREA: 10,400 SQ KM

VITI LEVU

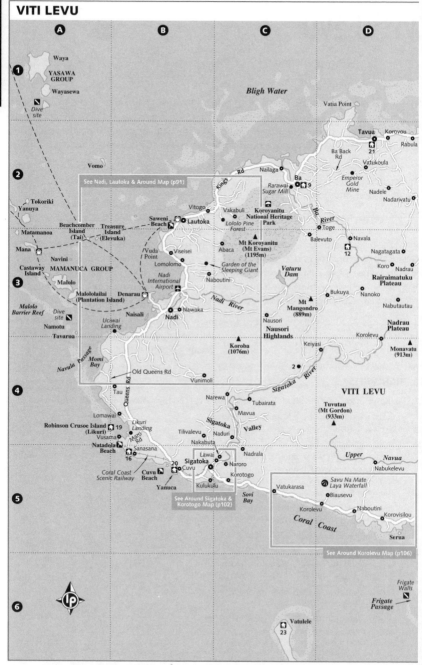

See Nadi, Lautoka & Around Map (p91)

See Around Sigatoka & Korotogo Map (p102)

See Around Korolevu Map (p106)

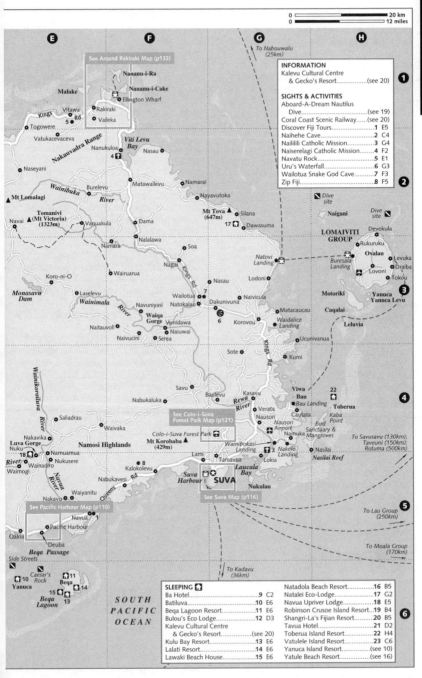

See Around Rakiraki Map (p133)

To Nabouwalu
(25km)

INFORMATION
Kalevu Cultural Centre
& Gecko's Resort..............(see 20)

SIGHTS & ACTIVITIES
Aboard-A-Dream Nautilus
Dive............................(see 19)
Coral Coast Scenic Railway......(see 20)
Discover Fiji Tours.....................1 E5
Naihehe Cave.............................2 C4
Naililili Catholic Mission..............3 G4
Naiserelagi Catholic Mission.......4 F2
Navatu Rock.............................5 E1
Uru's Waterfall.............................6 G3
Wailotua Snake God Cave.........7 F3
Zip Fiji.....................................8 F5

Nananu-i-Ra
Malake
Nananu-i-Cake
Ellington Wharf
Kings   Vitawa   Rakiraki
5 Rd   Vaileka
Togowere
Vatukacevaceva
Viti Levu
Bay
Nanukuloa   Nasau
4
Naseyani

Dive
site
Naigani
Dive
site
LOMAIVITI
GROUP
Devokula

Wainibuka   Burelevu
River   Matawailevu   Namarai
Nayavutoka

Mt Tova
(647m)   Silana
17   Dawasuma

Rukuruku
Ovalau   Levuka
Buresala   Draiba
Landing   Lovoni   Tokou

Mt Lomalagi
Tomanivi
(Mt Victoria)
(1323m)
Navai   Vanuakula
Dama
Nalalawa   Soa

Natovi
Landing
Lodoni

Motoriki
Yanuca
Yanuca Levu

Koro-ni-O
Monasavu
Dam   Laselevu
Wainimala
River   Navuniyasi
Naitauvoli   Naiuwai
Naivucini   Serea

Nagai
Nasau
Wailotua   7
Natokalau   Dakunivuna   Naivicula
6   Matacaucau
Korovou   Waidalice
Landing
Kings   Rd

Caqalai
Leluvia
Ucunivanua

Waiqa
Gorge
Vuhidawa

Sote
Kumi

Wainikoroiluva
Saliadrau
Waivaka
Nakavika
Luva Gorge
Nuku   Namuamua
River   Nukusere
Waimogi   Waimadiro

Savu
Nabukaluka
Baulevu
Rewa
River
Verata
Nausori   Nakelo
Namuka   Landing
Nausori
Airport
Wainibokasi
Landing   3
Lami   Tanavua
Lokia
Nailasi

Viwa
Bau   22
Bau Landing   Toberua
Cautata
Kaba
Point
Bird
Sanctuary &
Mangroves
To Savusavu (130km);
Taveuni (150km);
Rotuma (500km)

Nasilai Reef

See Colo-i-Suva
Forest Park Map (p121)
Colo-i-Suva Forest Park
Mt Korobaba
(429m)

Namosi Highlands
Kalokolevu   8
Nabukavesi
Queens   Rd
Waiyanitu
Nakavu

Laucala
Bay
SUVA
Suva
Harbour
Nukulau

See Suva Map (p116)

To Lau Group
(250km)

See Pacific Harbour Map (p110)
Navua   1
Pacific Harbour
Qaloa
Deuba
Beqa
Passage
Side Streets
Caesar's
Rock
Yanuca   10   11   Beqa
15   14
Beqa   13
Lagoon

To Moala Group
(170km)

To Kadavu
(36km)

SOUTH
PACIFIC
OCEAN

SLEEPING
Ba Hotel.....................................9 C2
Batiluva...................................10 E6
Beqa Lagoon Resort.................11 E6
Bulou's Eco Lodge....................12 D3
Kalevu Cultural Centre
& Gecko's Resort..............(see 20)
Kulu Bay Resort.......................13 E6
Lalati Resort............................14 E6
Lawaki Beach House.................15 E6
Natadola Beach Resort............16 B5
Natalei Eco-Lodge....................17 G2
Navua Upriver Lodge...............18 E5
Robinson Crusoe Island Resort..19 B4
Shangri-La's Fijian Resort........20 B5
Tavua Hotel.............................21 D2
Toberua Island Resort..............22 H4
Vatulele Island Resort..............23 C6
Yanuca Island Resort.............(see 10)
Yatule Beach Resort..............(see 16)

0 ___ 20 km
0 ___ 12 miles

E   F   G   H
1
2
3
4
5
6

VITI LEVU

Geography & Geology

At 10,400 sq km, Viti Levu (Great Fiji) is Fiji's largest island. The roughly oval-shaped island (146km from east to west and 106km from north to south) has a mountainous interior scattered with remote villages. The highest Fijian peak, Tomanivi (Mt Victoria; 1323m), is at the northern end of a high backbone running north to south. Rugged ranges and hills slope steeply down to the low-lying coast. Viti Levu has four large rivers: the Rewa and the Navua Rivers form fertile delta regions near Suva; the Sigatoka River flows south to the Coral Coast; and the Ba River flows north.

Orientation

Suva, the country's capital, largest city and main port, is in the southeast. Most travellers, however, arrive in the west at Nadi International Airport, which is 9km north of central Nadi and 24km south of Lautoka.

Nadi and Suva are linked by the sealed Queens Road along the 221km southern perimeter of Viti Levu, which contains a scattering of villages and resorts and is known as the Coral Coast. Many minor roads lead off this road to isolated coastal areas and into the highlands. Most of these minor roads are unsealed and often too rough for non-4WD vehicles. Between the wetter months of November and April, some roads can become impassable. The fertile Sigatoka Valley, formed by Fiji's second-largest river, extends far into the highlands.

Heading north from Suva, the Kings Road is mostly sealed and travels for 265km through Nausori (where Suva's airport is located), the eastern highlands, Rakiraki and Ba on the north coast, and on to Lautoka.

There are three roads leading up from the coast to the Nausori Highland villages of Navala and Bukuya (beginning at Ba, Nadi and Sigatoka).

Getting There & Away

Most travellers arrive in Fiji at Nadi International Airport. See p241 for contact details of airline offices. Nadi is also a main domestic transport hub. From here there are flights to many of the other larger islands and reliable boat services and cruises to offshore islands. See p245 and individual island chapters for information on interisland flights and boat services.

Getting Around

For those in a hurry or after a scenic flight, there are cheap, regular light-plane flights between Nadi and Suva for around $160.

Viti Levu has a regular and cheap bus network. Express buses operated by Pacific Transport and Sunbeam Transport link the main centres of Lautoka, Nadi and Suva, along both the Queens and Kings Roads. Most will pick up or drop off at hotels and resorts along these highways. Look for timetables at their offices in Lautoka. Slower, local buses also operate throughout the island and even remote inland villages have regular (though less frequent) services. These trips might take a while as they stop often along the way. Before heading to an isolated area, check that there is a return bus so you don't get stranded without any accommodation – sometimes the last bus of the day stays at the final village.

Companies and services available:

Coral Sun Fiji (☎ 672 3105; www.coralsunfiji.com) Runs comfortable, air-conditioned coaches between Nadi and Suva ($20, four hours, twice daily), stopping only at resorts on the Coral Coast.

Feejee Experience Offers hop-on-hop-off coach packages from $396. See p251.

Pacific Transport Limited Lautoka (☎ 666 0499; Yasawa St); Nadi (☎ 670 0044); Sigatoka (☎ 650 0088); Suva (☎ 330 4366) About six express buses run daily between Lautoka and Suva ($14.20, five hours express or six hours regular) via the Coral Coast. Generally it's OK to turn up at the bus station, but you can book in advance.

Sunbeam Transport Limited Lautoka (☎ 666 2822; Yasawa St); Suva (☎ 338 2122/2704) Around four Lautoka–Suva express services go daily via the Queens Road ($14.75, five hours). Also, around six services daily travel via the Kings Road.

Minibuses and carriers (small trucks) also shuttle locals along the Queens Road. Taxis are plentiful, but drivers don't always use meters, so confirm the price in advance. Viti Levu is also easy to explore by car or motorcycle, although for the unsealed highland roads you'll generally need a 4WD. See p249 for rental details.

NADI & THE WEST

NADI
pop 31,400

Everyone usually goes to Nadi (*nan*-di) twice, whether they like it or not. Its indecently warm air slaps you in the face when you first step from the plane and its airport is the last place to buy sunburn remedies when you leave. For some that's twice too often and many travellers aim to minimise their Nadi exposure to the briefest time possible. Others pause long enough to make the most of the infrastructure before heading out to more picturesque locales. Not that this bothers Nadi. The shops, restaurants, cafes and tour operators strung along Main St are happy making a living from the plane loads of arriving and departing tourists.

There are no must-sees in Nadi itself – it's something of a perennial adolescent in constant pursuit of an identity, not quite sure whether it's a city, tourist junction or business hub – but there are a few interesting possibilities in the surrounding areas. Lautoka, the Sabeto Mountains, Natadola Beach, the Mamanuca islands and Sigatoka are all within striking distance and the tourist companies in those areas have representatives here.

Orientation

From Nadi airport the Queens Road heads north to Lautoka and 9km south to downtown Nadi. Nadi's Main St extends southward from the Nadi River for about 800m to the T-junction at the large Swami temple. From here the Queens Road continues right to Suva, while Nadi Back Rd bypasses the busy centre and rejoins the Queens Road back near the airport. The road to the Nausori Highlands leads off into the mountains from Nadi Back Rd.

Just north of downtown, between the mosque and the Nadi River, Narewa Rd leads west for 6km to Denarau island, where you'll find Nadi's most upmarket resorts, and Denarau Marina, where boats depart for the Mamanucas and Yasawas.

Near Martintar village, Wailoaloa Rd also turns west off the Queens Road towards Wailoaloa and New Town Beaches.

Information

EMERGENCY
Ambulance (☎ 911, 670 1128)
Fire (☎ 911, 670 0475)
Police (Map p83; ☎ 917, 670 0222; Koroivolu Ave)

INTERNET ACCESS
Internet access is easy to find in downtown Nadi and costs around $3 per hour. Most backpacker lodges offer internet connections.

MEDICAL SERVICES
DSM Centre (Map p83; ☎ 670 0240; www.dsmcen trefiji.com.fj; 2 Lodhia St; ☻ 8.30am-4.30pm Mon-Fri, till 12.30pm Sat) Specialises in travel medicine and has radiology and physiotherapy departments. Consultations $50 to $65.

MONEY
At the airport arrivals concourse there is an ANZ bank (open for all international flights). Main St has several currency exchange stores and all the main banks – ANZ, Westpac and Colonial National Bank have ATMs.

POST
Post office Airport (Map p81; ☎ 672 2045; Nadi International Airport); Downtown (Map p83; ☎ 670 0001; Sahu Kahn Rd)

TOURIST INFORMATION
Fiji Visitors Bureau (FVB; Map p81; ☎ 672 2433; www.fijime.com; Suite 107, Colonial Plaza, Namaka; ☻ 8am-4.30pm Mon-Thu, to 4pm Fri) Fiji's official tourism bureau is excellent. Friendly and helpful staff provide accurate information.

TRAVEL AGENCIES
The travel agents at the airport will find you before you've had time to hail a taxi. The major and more reputable companies have offices and representatives on the ground floor to meet arriving clients, while the 13 agencies upstairs are smaller, local operators who take turns pouncing on anyone with a backpack. Many of these specialise in budget accommodation and offer good deals, particularly for the islands, but be mindful that you're not receiving independent advice. The commission they earn, not the colour of the coral, governs their advice. Popular hotels and backpackers all have tour desks where you can book trips, although again, their advice isn't always impartial.

Domestic plane tickets can be bought directly from the Air Fiji and Pacific Sun offices in the arrivals concourse.

Recommended agencies:
ATS Pacific (Map p81; ☎ 672 4667; www.atspacific .com; Nadi airport concourse) Principally an international operator working with overseas agents but maintains travel desks at many of the Denarau resorts.
Coral Sun Fiji (Map p81; ☎ 672 2268; www.atspacific .com; Nadi airport concourse) Operates the daily Suva– Nadi/Nadi–Suva scheduled bus services and transfers to Coral Coast hotels as well as arranging private tours.

VITI LEVU FOR KIDS

Fiji's main island has plenty to offer families with young tackers in tow. If you're staying in the Nadi area try a day cruise to one of the **Mamanuca** (p141) or **Yasawa islands** (see the boxed text, p155) or the ever-popular **Robinson Crusoe Island** (p97).

The Coral Coast is home to a number of attractions that will appeal to kids. A day on the **Coral Coast Scenic Railway** (p98) is a fun way to gain an appreciation of Fiji's landscape, and the barbecue lunch is a family-oriented affair. Nearby, the **Kalevu Cultural Centre** (p99) showcases Fijian singing, dancing and ceremonies that will entertain children. A little more kitsch and flashy are the demonstrations, boat tours and mock battles at the **Arts Village** (p109) in Pacific Harbour. You could also take them horse riding at **Natadola Beach** (p98) or show them Fiji's less-domesticated wildlife at the excellent **Kula Eco Park** (p104).

The **Fiji Museum** (p119) is chock-full of exhibits (including cannibal utensils – eeeewwwww) that will capture inquisitive young minds. Off the northern coast, **Nananu-i-Ra** (p134) is only a short hop from the mainland and offers calm seas for child-friendly swimming and snorkelling, and self-catering accommodation. Kids can also partake in kayaking and windsurfing here.

Many of the resorts have abundant activities to occupy children. Some kid-friendly resorts:

- Shangri-La's Fijian Resort (p99)
- Hideaway Resort (p108)
- Sonaisali Island Resort (p92)
- Radisson Resort Fiji (p89)
- Naviti Resort (p107)

Great Sights Fiji (Map p81; ☎ 672 3311; enquiries@greatsightsfiji.com; Nadi airport concourse) Specialising in 4WD day tours to Navala ($179 per person), Nausori Highlands ($99), Koroyanitu National Heritage Park ($119) and Abaca ($109). Children aged five to 12 half price.

Rosie Holidays (Map p81; ☎ 672 2755; www.rosiefiji.com; Nadi airport concourse) The largest and best resourced agency in Fiji. Rosie's organises multiday treks into the central highlands (six days $1147 per person) and the Sigatoka valley (four days $828) and day treks to the Nausori Highlands ($115) as well as bus loads of road tours to Sigatoka Valley/Kula Eco Park, Viseisei village/Garden of the Sleeping Giant and Pacific Harbour. It is also the agent for Thrifty Car Rental.

Travel Fiji Holiday (Map p83; ☎ 670 3276; cnr Main St & Andrews Rd)

Dangers & Annoyances

According to some shopkeepers, you're still on the plane if you haven't tried *kava* (a mildly narcotic, muddy and odd-tasting drink made from the aromatic roots of the Polynesian pepper shrub), but their disingenuous offer to mix some then-and-there is little more than a preamble to a sales pitch. There's nothing wrong with the *kava*, just know that you'll feel obliged to buy something afterwards. Oh, and the free trinket at the end – you'll be expected to give a trinket of your own in return – preferably something wallet-sized and made of paper. The southern end of Main St is considerably rougher than the northern end and we don't recommend the nightclubs there. Otherwise common sense applies; avoid wandering around at night or alone along deserted stretches of Wailoaloa and New Town Beaches.

Sights & Activities

SRI SIVA SUBRAMANIYA SWAMI TEMPLE

At the base of Main St, away from Nadi's boisterous main drag, this peaceful Hindu **temple** (Map p83; ☎ 670 0016; admission $3.50; 5.30am-7pm) is one of the few places outside of India where you can see traditional Dravidian architecture. The whole place is painted in colours bright enough to make your eyes ache and looks fantastic against cloudless, blue skies. The wooden carvings of Hindu deities travelled all the way from India, as did the artists who dressed the temple in its colourful coat and impressive ceiling frescos. New murals are still being commissioned and it's quite possible that you'll see resident artist, MA Sreekandan Pusnpa, lying, Michelangelo-style, on scaffolding as he paints the temple's ceilings.

If you are having trouble sorting out Lord Shiva's reincarnations and manifestations ask

Mr Prakash Reddy, a temple custodian employed to answer questions and make sense of the Hindi deities.

Nadi's festivals, such as Karthingai Puja (held monthly), Panguni Uthiram Thiru-naal (in April) and Thai Pusam (January), attract worshippers from around the world. Devotees circle the temple where they offer banana,

smash a coconut, burn some camphor and receive blessing from the priest. Some of these festivals last several days and it's worth attending if they coincide with your plans.

Visitors are welcome as long as they wear neat and modest dress and remove their shoes at the temple entrance. It is fine to take photos in the grounds but not inside the temple,

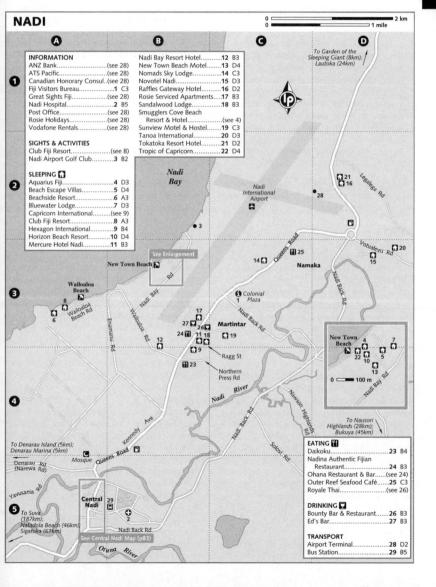

NADI

INFORMATION	
ANZ Bank.............................(see 28)	
ATS Pacific...........................(see 28)	
Canadian Honorary Consul..(see 28)	
Fiji Visitors Bureau...................**1** C3	
Great Sights Fiji....................(see 28)	
Nadi Hospital.........................**2** B5	
Post Office...........................(see 28)	
Rosie Holidays.....................(see 28)	
Vodafone Rentals.................(see 28)	
SIGHTS & ACTIVITIES	
Club Fiji Resort.......................(see 8)	
Nadi Airport Golf Club............**3** B2	
SLEEPING	
Aquarius Fiji............................**4** D3	
Beach Escape Villas...............**5** D4	
Beachside Resort....................**6** A3	
Bluewater Lodge.....................**7** D3	
Capricorn International...........(see 9)	
Club Fiji Resort.......................**8** A3	
Hexagon International..............**9** B4	
Horizon Beach Resort............**10** D4	
Mercure Hotel Nadi...............**11** B3	

Nadi Bay Resort Hotel...........**12** B3	
New Town Beach Motel..........**13** D4	
Nomads Sky Lodge................**14** C3	
Novotel Nadi.........................**15** D3	
Raffles Gateway Hotel............**16** D2	
Rosie Serviced Apartments....**17** B3	
Sandalwood Lodge.................**18** B3	
Smugglers Cove Beach	
Resort & Hotel.................(see 4)	
Sunview Motel & Hostel.........**19** C3	
Tanoa International................**20** D3	
Tokatoka Resort Hotel............**21** D2	
Tropic of Capricorn................**22** D4	

To Garden of the
Sleeping Giant (8km);
Lautoka (24km)

Nadi
Bay

Nadi
International
Airport

New Town Beach

Wailoaloa
Beach

New Town
Beach

0 ——— 100 m

Namaka

Colonial
Plaza

Martintar

Ragg St

Northern
Press Rd

Nadi River

To Nausori
Highlands (28km);
Bukuya (45km)

To Denarau Island (5km);
Denarau Marina (5km)

Denarau
Rd
(Narewa Rd)

Mosque

Queens Road

Kennedy Ave

Yavusania Rd

To Suva
(187km);
Natadola Beach (46km);
Sigatoka (61km)

Central
Nadi

Nadi Back Rd

See Central Nadi Map (p83)

Oriuna River

EATING	
Daikoku..............................**23** B4	
Nadina Authentic Fijian	
Restaurant.......................**24** B3	
Ohana Restaurant & Bar......(see 24)	
Outer Reef Seafood Café.....**25** C3	
Royale Thai.........................(see 26)	
DRINKING	
Bounty Bar & Restaurant.......**26** B3	
Ed's Bar..............................**27** B3	
TRANSPORT	
Airport Terminal..................**28** D2	
Bus Station..........................**29** B5	

0 ————————— 2 km
0 ————————— 1 mile

VITI LEVU

HINDU SYMBOLIC RITES

Around 35% of Fijians practise Hinduism, and the distinctive and sometimes flamboyant temples and shrines in which they worship are dotted liberally around Viti Levu. Sculptured deities and colourful frescos pose photogenically against a tropical or mountain background; taking a reverent five minutes to pay your respects can be a cathartic experience regardless of your religious persuasion. The most celebrated of Fiji's Hindu temples is the Sri Siva Subramaniya Swami Temple in Nadi, which was constructed and decorated in part by craftsmen flown in from India.

A Hindu temple symbolises the body, the residence of the soul. Union with God can be achieved through prayer and by ridding the body of impurities (meat cannot be eaten on the day of entering the temple).

Water and fire are used for blessings. Water carried in a pot with flowers is symbolic of the Great Mother (the personification of nature), while burning camphor symbolises the light of knowledge and understanding. A trident is used to represent fire, the protector and the three flames of purity, light and knowledge.

Hindus also believe that the body should be enslaved to the spirit and denied all comforts. Consequently fire-walking is practised in order to become one with the Great Mother. Hindus believe life is like walking on fire and that a disciplined approach, like the one required in the ceremony, helps them to achieve balance, self-acceptance and to see good in everything.

Before entering a Hindu temple always ask permission and remove your shoes. Photography outside the temple is generally OK but considered offensive inside.

---

and non-Hindus are asked not to enter the inner sanctum, which is reserved for devotees bringing offerings.

FISHING
Club Fiji Resort (Map p81; ☎ 672 0150; www.clubfiji -resort.com; Wailoaloa Beach Rd) Has fantastic-value fishing trips. Game fishing costs $40 for a day and line fishing costs $30.

Crystal Blue Adventures (Map p83; ☎ 670 3276; www.crystalbluefiji.com; cnr Main St & Andrews Rd) Full- and half-day ($1200 and $750) deep-sea fishing charters. Prices include all equipment and the boat takes a maximum of eight.

SURFING
Fiji Surf Company (Map p83; ☎ 670 5960; www.fijisurfco .com; 2nd fl, cnr Main St & Hospital Rd) Local surf legend Ian Muller is the man to talk to about all things surfing. He passionately promotes surfing within Fiji and can draw on a wealth of local knowledge. The shop sells, repairs, makes and rents ($30 to $40 per board per day) short and long boards. Ian also runs surf school day trips to Natadola and Sigatoka beaches (one, two or three people costs $200, $150 or $100 per person) and a 'road/boat shuttle operation' to the monster Mamanuca reef breaks (see p141).

Tours
Nadi is a good base to explore the west side of Viti Levu. From here it is possible to visit the Koroyanitu National Heritage Park (p96), Nausori Highlands (p137), and Namosi Highlands (p113) near Pacific Harbour. Many out-of-town tour companies will pick up and drop off from Nadi, so be sure to consult other destination chapters for inspiration.

The Mamanuca and Yasawa island groups, with their necklaces of coral gardens, are the most popular of all the day trips out of the Nadi area. Boats depart from Port Denarau (p88) several times daily and offer free hotel pick-ups and drop-offs. See p141 to read about your Mamanuca options and p153 to read about boats leaving for the Yasawas. Organised trips to Robinson Crusoe Island (p97) just south of Nadi are also an easy and fun day excursion.

Sleeping
Regardless of what the websites or brochures promise there are no appealing beaches in the Nadi area. That said, the resorts located at the grey-sand New Town and Wailoaloa Beaches are fairly isolated and peaceful, while those in Martintar and along the Queens Road are conveniently placed on the main bus route.

On arrival at Nadi International Airport you will be bombarded with a huge range of accommodation options. Most hotels have free transfer vehicles awaiting international flights, so it's best to already have some idea of where to go for the first night.

BUDGET
Along the Queens Road

Nomads Sky Lodge (Map p81; ☎ 672 2200; www.nomadsskylodge.com.fj; Queens Rd, Namaka; 8-/6-/4-bed dm $25/28/31, tw & d $78-128; ✗ ✗ 🖳 🖵) This is a great choice as there's oodles of space and the rooms are spotlessly clean, if somewhat Spartan. The more expensive 'superior' rooms are much larger than the 'standard' doubles, but both have air-con, private bathrooms, phone, TV, fridge and towels. There's a large pool with plenty of sun loungers, a decent restaurant (mains $10 to $18), pool tables, nightly activities, a travel desk, volleyball courts and a games room – it's a little like a school camp for grown-ups.

Capricorn International (Map p81; ☎ 672 0088; www.capricornfiji.com; Queens Rd, Martintar; dm $25, r incl breakfast $105-125, f incl breakfast $175; ✗ ✗ 🖳 🖵) Everything about the Capricorn is middle-of-the-road. The rooms are dated and faded but essentially still comfortable, and while the pool is small, it's clean and inviting. The pricier deluxe rooms come with a balcony, and if you stay in the 17-bed, all-white dorm, you may well have the place to yourself. Children under 12 stay free, otherwise it's only $20 for an extra guest.

Sunview Motel & Hostel (Map p81; ☎ 672 4933; hsunviewmotel@connect.com.fj; 14 Gray St, Martintar; dm incl breakfast $25, d with/without air-con $60/50, tr $80-100; ✗ ✗ 🖳) Leave party plans at the gate; this is a modest and quiet option for those wanting to escape the backpacker circuit. The upstairs bathrooms are shared by those in the double rooms and have the only hot-water showers. Once those staying downstairs cotton on, everyone wants in.

Nadi Bay Resort Hotel (Map p81; ☎ 672 3599; www.fijinadibayhotel.com; Wailoaloa Rd, Martintar; dm $27-30, s/d without bathroom from $71/84; s with bathroom $82-100, d with bathroom $96-118, ✗ ✗ 🖳 🖵) This is one of Nadi's best-equipped budget resorts and the two pools have a high-tide line of British backpackers. It's well suited to social animals and the overhead planes leaving the airport are the only interruption to lively banter. The restaurant's outstanding (mains $11 to $24), the rooms are comfortable and clean, and there's even a free

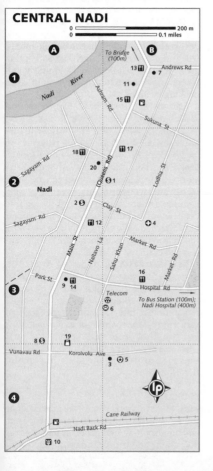

CENTRAL NADI

0 _____ 200 m
0 _____ 0.1 miles

INFORMATION	
ANZ Bank	**1** B2
Colonial National Bank	**2** A2
Divisional Registrar	**3** B4
DSM Centre	**4** B2
Police	**5** B4
Post Office	**6** B3
Travel Fiji Holiday	**7** B1
Westpac Bank	**8** A3

SIGHTS & ACTIVITIES	
Crystal Blue Adventures	(see 7)
Fiji Surf Company	**9** A3
Sri Siva Subramaniya Swami Temple	**10** A4
Sunsail Fiji	**11** B1

EATING 🍴	
Bo Hai Seafood Restaurant	**12** A2
Bulaccino	**13** B1
Curry House	**14** A3
Mama's Pizza	**15** B1
Market	**16** B3
RB Patel Supermarket	**17** B2
Saffron & Corner Café	**18** A2

SHOPPING 🛍	
Handicraft Market	**19** A3

TRANSPORT	
Jack's Handicrafts	**20** A2

VITI LEVU

mini movie-theatre. Indeed, the only fly in the *kava* is that the tour desk charges a 5% 'hotel turnover tax' (which should only be applied to hotel services) on all tours they book.

Hexagon International (Map p81; ☎ 672 0044; www .hexagonfiji.com; Queens Rd, Martintar; r $66-97, apt $159; ❌ 🖥 🚌) This two-storey complex surrounds a central, tiled pool and while the rooms are sparsely furnished they offer excellent value for the budget traveller. There's a poolside bar and restaurant (dinner $21 to $27), wi-fi hot spots and massage facilities available at the beauty spa next door.

Rosie Serviced Apartments (Map p81; ☎ 672 2755; reservations@rosie.com.fj; Queens Rd, Martintar; apt $79-135; ❌ 🔅) This block of apartments has all the appeal of a car park, but while it may be a bit of an ugly duckling from the outside, these studio, one- and two-bedroom apartments are great value for self-caterers. There's enough room (even in the studios) to swing several cats and each apartment comes with a fully equipped kitchen and use of the laundry and pool in the Mercure Hotel Nadi.

Sandalwood Lodge (Map p81; ☎ 672 2044; san dalwood@connect.com.fj; Ragg St, Martintar; s $84-103, d & tw $94-113; 🔅 🖥 🚌) This hotel offers perky, self-contained rooms (there's no restaurant here) with blindingly colourful decor, small kitchenettes and TVs. They're neat and great value for self-caterers and families, plus the location off the main road promises a good night's sleep. Garden Wing rooms on the ground floor have patio doors leading to the picturesque, free-form pool, while the Orchid Wing rooms upstairs have balconies and more modern and spacious interiors.

New Town Beach

A haul from downtown and the main road, New Town Beach offers budget travellers a cluster of backpacker resorts amid a smattering of wealthy residential properties. It's a peaceful area with great views of the Sabeto Mountain Range across the water.

Tropic of Capricorn (Map p81; ☎ 672 3089; chop kins@bigpond.net.au; 11 Wasawasa Rd; dm $15-27, d $80-95; ❌ 🚌) Mama's big smiles and warm welcome means that this place gets rave reviews from those seeking a home-away-from-home. The older, fan-cooled rooms are still here but the new two-storey block occupies the prime beachfront location and the pool is oddly sandwiched between the two. The meals (mains $10 to $18) are good value and Mama

cooks up a mean mash – reason enough for many to stay.

Horizon Beach Resort (Map p81; ☎ 672 2832; www .horizonbeachfiji.com; 10 Wasawasa Rd; dm with/without air-con $22/15, d with air-con $65-80, d without air-con $50, f with air-con $115-155; ❌ 🔅 🖥 🚌) Popular with the backpacker crowd who stay in the cheaper rooms and use the upmarket facilities of Smugglers Cove next door. Cunning.

Bluewater Lodge (Map p81; ☎ 672 8858; bluewaterfiji@ connect.com.fj; New Town Beach; dm/d incl breakfast $23/90; ❌ 🔅 🚌) Small and unassuming, this place is the pick of the bunch for travellers beating a retreat from the hollering crowds. The rooms are spotlessly clean, light and airy, with only three beds in a dorm. The wee restaurant and bar (mains $16 to $25) opens for dinner only.

Beach Escape Villas (Map p81; ☎ 672 4442; www .beachescapefiji.com; off Wasawasa Rd; dm with/without air-con $23/19, d & tw $42-68; ❌ 🔅 🖥 🚌) This place is a village of villas – some contain six-bed dorms and others contain two double rooms, which share a small lounge. The $68 option gives you the whole villa to yourself and for an additional $20 they'll throw in some cooking facilities.

Aquarius Fiji (Map p81; ☎ 672 6000; www.aquarius .com.fj; 17 Wasawasa Rd; dm incl breakfast $26-30, d incl break-fast $90-115; ❌ 🔅 🖥 🚌) This former luxury home was converted into a professionally run backpackers in 2003 and has never looked back. The whole place swims with warm party vibes. There's a lively restaurant and, for those who overdo it on the nightly cocktail specials, it's only a short stagger around the pool to the hangover-soothing hammocks. All rooms have attached bathrooms, although the larger (and cheaper) 12-bed dorms are slightly airless and cramped when full.

New Town Beach Motel (Map p81; ☎ 672 3339; newtownbeach@connect.com.fj; s/d/tr/f $40/50/60/80; ❌ 🚌) One of the originals, this place has now been overshadowed by the larger and flashier newcomers. It still offers excellent value, even if the rooms look as if somebody's grandmother decorated them in the early '70s. The restaurant opens for breakfast and lunch ($2 to $5) but you'll have to pop next door for dinner.

MIDRANGE

Most of the midrange hotels are located along the Queens Road between downtown Nadi and the airport. Rooms generally have air-con, TV, phone and fridge, and most hotels have tour desks, luggage storage, courtesy airport transfers and restaurants open for breakfast, lunch and dinner.

Along the Queens Road

Raffles Gateway Hotel (Map p81; ☎ 672 2444; www .rafflesgateway.com; Queens Rd, Namaka; d & tw $98-155, tr/f $172/196; ✗ ✗ ☐ ☎) Directly opposite the airport, and behind the mock-colonial entrance, Raffles is a sound choice. The small water slide gets the kids squealing and those under 16 stay free. The cheaper standard rooms are pinchy but cool and crisp, while the superior rooms are a leap in value with their lounge furniture, TVs and private patios. There's a poolside restaurant (mains $13 to $28) and a grassed central courtyard flanked by massive bougainvilleas that give an accurate idea of the age of this long-time favourite.

Mercure Hotel Nadi (Map p81; ☎ 672 2255; reserva tions@mercurenadi.com.fj; Queens Rd, Martintar; s $149-169, d & tw $179-209; ✗ ✗ ☎) This hotel (formerly the Dominion International) was renovated in 2004 and given a tasteful, if slightly predictable, colour scheme. The 85 rooms aren't huge, but they're big on creature comforts, including a glossy bathroom, Sky TV and a well-stocked fridge. Most rooms face the pretty pool area, and the extensive grounds encompass a sprawling alfresco restaurant (mains $20 to $30, Saturday Mongolian barbecue $35 per person) and tennis court out back.

New Town Beach & Wailoaloa Beach

Smugglers Cove Beach Resort & Hotel (Map p81; ☎ 672 6578; www.smugglersbeachfiji.com; Wasawasa Rd; dm incl breakfast $28, r incl breakfast $98-185, f incl breakfast $198; ✗ ☐ ☎) Young and brash, Smugglers Cove opened in 2006 and immediately upstaged some of the older establishments along the beach. There's a bunch of amenities including a tour desk, restaurant, minimart, coin-operated laundry and disabled access. Kayaks and use of the Nadi Airport golf course are free for guests and all the rooms are modern and comfortable. The dark and cavernous dormitory has 34 bunk beds divided into cubicles of four and isn't as appealing as the other facilities here.

Beachside Resort (Map p81; ☎ 670 3488; www .beachsideresortfiji.com; Wailoaloa Beach Rd; s incl breakfast $68-145, d incl breakfast $76-153, tr incl breakfast $138-149; ✗ ✗ ☐ ☎) The moniker's a tad misleading, but this compact and private resort (away from the beach) provides more comfort than a backpackers and is easier on the wallet than

a resort. The rooms are stylish and immaculate and dressed with cheery Fijian prints. Cheaper rooms are tucked behind the main complex, while the pricier ocean-view suites have balconies overlooking the central pool. The Coriander Cafe (mains $18 to $22) has a blackboard menu of tasty treats.

Club Fiji Resort (Map p81; ☎ 672 0150; www .clubfiji-resort.com; Wailoaloa Beach Rd; d $94-188, f $288; ✗ ✗ ☎) If you want to stay in Nadi but you're looking for beachside atmosphere, this is a good option. The duplex *bure* are comfortable and clean, and there's a great selection of daily activities, including free windsurfing and kayaking. The fishing trips are particularly well priced here ($30 to $40). The restaurant (mains $18 to $30) boasts Australian steaks, Asian noodles and English roasts.

TOP END

See p89 for details on Denarau island's mega-resorts.

Novotel Nadi (Map p81; ☎ 672 2000; reservations@ novotelnadi.com.fj; Votualevu Rd, Namaka; r $158-198; ✗ ✗ ☐ ☎) Formerly the Mocambo, when the name changed the whole place got a facelift. All the rooms now have internet connections, flat-screen TVs and a very chic brown-on-beige colour scheme. The rooms aren't huge but they are very comfortable and walk-in guests (or those who telephone ahead) can usually swing sizeable discounts off the rack rates quoted here. There's a boutique, business centre, ninehole golf course, day spa and pool. Children under 16 stay for free.

Tokatoka Resort Hotel (Map p81; ☎ 672 0222; res ervations@tokatokaresort.com.fj; Queens Rd, Namaka; s & d $189, villas $211-349; ✗ ✗ ☐ ☎) This sprawling, low-rise resort is a 'village' of villas connected by a series of covered, mazelike walkways. We got embarrassingly lost – twice. Some of the villas sleep up to seven and are self-contained (although the kitchens are dated), so are ideal for groups. Although most rooms are too worn to justify their high-end prices, the designer pool with its sunshade sail and water slide are top notch. Other facilities include a restaurant (mains $24 to $42) and wheelchairaccessible rooms.

Tanoa International (Map p81; ☎ 672 0277; tonoahotels@connect.com.fj; Votualevu Rd; d $220-280; ✗ ✗ ☐ ☎) Another flashy, self-contained resort loaded with facilities and distractions (including flood-lit tennis courts, a beauty spa and a gym), making it very popular

VITI LEVU

with package pool addicts and families. The whole place oozes Fijian tropicana, from the lush gardens to the Bula Bar and Mint Café. The restaurant here (mains $22 to $32) has a Saturday curry and Sunday roast buffet (each for $28). Again, substantial discounts are given to those who phone ahead and ask for local rates. Kids 12 and below stay free.

Eating

Nadi is a tourist town catering well for a variety of tastes and budgets. Most places serve a mixture of traditional Fijian, Indian, Chinese and Western dishes, and there are lots of cheap lunchtime eateries downtown. Some of the resorts have special *lovo* nights, where food is cooked in a pit oven.

RESTAURANTS
Central Nadi

Bo Hai Seafood Restaurant (Map p83; ☎ 670 0178; above the Bank of Baroda, Main St; mains $6-25; ☒ lunch & dinner) Giving the curry houses a run for their money, Bo Hai has an extensive menu with a heavy emphasis on seafood. Adventurous souls should try the bêche-de-mer combination hotpot. Tasty meals and low prices (many mains go for around $8) mean it's often recommended by locals.

Mama's Pizza (Map p83; ☎ 670 0221; Main St; mains $8-22; ☒ lunch & dinner; ☒) The smell from the wood-fired oven is a great introduction to Mama's downtown, cool, dark interior. Traditionalists may want to stick to the proven crowd pleasers, but the more adventurous should check out the flip-side of the menu for gourmet treats like garlic-glazed chicken, smoked *walu* (butter fish) and eggplant and sun-dried tomato combos. Other stores have opened at Port Denarau and Colonial Plaza – all are good, although cheese quantities vary.

Curry House (Map p83; ☎ 670 0798; Hospital Rd, Nadi; mains $15-25; ☒ breakfast, lunch & dinner) This is one of three curry joints on this busy intersection and indecisive diners will often be given a discount to entice them inside. One-meal-a-day portion sizes make it great value and even a basic vegetable curry comes with roti, rice, dhal, soup, a pappadum, a small salad and a dollop of chutney.

Saffron & Corner Café (Map p83; ☎ 670 1233; Jacks Mall, Sagayam Rd; mains $15-25; ☒ lunch & dinner Mon-Sat, dinner Sun; ☒) Two restaurants, one kitchen – a hard choice. The cafe serves light lunches, burgers and noodles while the adjoining, and

more upmarket, Saffron serves up healthy curries, birianis and kormas behind swanky, plate-glass windows. It's worth scanning the menu for some interesting Fijian twists on Indian favourites.

Other Locations

The restaurants at most hotels in Nadi and at Denarau welcome nonguests.

Royale Thai (Map p81; ☎ 672 8940; 79 Queens Rd, Martintar; mains $12-18; ☒ dinner; ☒) In the style of Thai restaurants around the world there are plenty of tacky pictures on show and kitschy, billowing blue cloth hung from the ceiling. Thankfully, old favourites like chicken and cashew, and prawn *tom yum* soup, are faithfully represented here. Best of all, the dishes are MSG free, even if they are swimming in oil.

our pick Nadina Authentic Fijian Restaurant (Map p81; ☎ 672 7313; Queens Rd, Martintar; mains $20-30; ☒ lunch & dinner) Putting the *bula* into *bulumakau* (beef), this is one of the few restaurants in town specialising in Fijian cuisine beyond *lovo* buffets. Both the grated cassava in caramel sauce and the pan-fried *walu* in coconut milk make a great introduction to island fare; and as it's BYO, you'll get to polish off that duty-free you brought along. Meals are served on the terrace or in your own small, open-sided garden *bure* (traditional thatched dwelling).

Ohana Restaurant & Bar (Map p81; ☎ 672 2900; Queens Rd, Martintar; mains $22-30; ☒ lunch & dinner) The 'skytop' Ohana is a great place to shoot the breeze, with an open-air, rooftop terrace. The music is mellow, contemporary and heavy on the bass. Bar nibbles and light meals are available, although for something a little more refined (and pricier) you'll have to head downstairs to the 'fine dining' Ohana and order something from the 'pasta corner' or one of 'Ron's catches'.

Daikoku (Map p81; ☎ 670 3622; cnr Queens Rd & Northern Press Rd; mains $26-52; ☒ lunch & dinner Mon-Sat) You'll need to brush up on your chopstick skills if you are to match those of the table-side chefs who slice, dice, flip and serve delicious Japanese teppan-yaki at this purpose-built restaurant. If teppan-yaki seems too theatrical, head downstairs for more intimate dining.

CAFES

Bulaccino (Map p83; ☎ 672 8638; Main St; light meals & snacks $4-16; ☒ breakfast & lunch; ☒ ▣) Bulaccino is arguably the best cafe on Main St although, to be fair, it doesn't have a lot of competition. Lunching alongside the Nadi River on the fan-cooled verandah is bliss, but after a hard day's haggling you might want to bypass the Bircher muesli, gourmet sandwiches and scrummy salads in favour of shots of caffeine and one of the scrummy cakes.

ourpick **Outer Reef Seafood Café** (Map p81; ☎ 672 7201; Lot 2, Queens Rd, Namaka; sandwiches $6-10, mains $29-48; ⏱ breakfast, lunch & dinner; ☒) Up front, this former seafood market turned trendy cafe serves deli sandwiches and coffee, while out back the courtyard has been transformed into a secret oasis specialising in fine seafood dining. From Friday to Sunday a guitar, keyboard and vocalist trio perform classics, take requests and encourage diners to push aside their tables and dance.

QUICK EATS
The bottom end of Main St in downtown Nadi has a number of cheap curry houses, all of which expend far more energy on the cheap nosh than on the dim surrounds. You can lunch for around $4.

SELF-CATERING
Nadi has a large produce **market** (Map p83; Hospital Rd), which sells lots of fresh fruit and vegetables. Good-quality meat, however, is not so easy to come by. There are several large supermarkets and bakeries downtown including **RB Patel Supermarket** (Map p83; ☎ 670 1577; Main St).

Drinking
Ed's Bar (Map p81; ☎ 672 4650; Lot 51, Queens Rd, Martintar) From the roadside there's little to recommend Ed's Bar, but this is one of Nadi's best watering holes and a step up from the grog shops in town. Cheap beer, friendly staff, pool tables and the occasional live band draw locals and visiting social animals alike. There's a small dining section inside, but the bar is the main event. Tables outside catch the breeze but they generally fill by late afternoon, so you'll have to strap on your beer boots early to nab one.

Bounty Bar & Restaurant (Map p81; ☎ 672 0840; 79 Queens Rd, Martintar) This convivial restaurant-cum-bar is named in honour of the local rum, and the old barrels, large seafaring mural and glass floats provide enough maritime atmosphere to keep most drunken sailors happy. There's a large TV screening important sporting events and a band plays here Friday, Saturday and Sunday, during which times

things get loud, beery and fun. Although we wouldn't jump ship for it, the restaurant here serves passable surf and turf–type meals.

The bars at the Aquarius Fiji (p84) and Nadi Bay Resort Hotel (p83) are also atmospheric options for a beer. Each of the flashy Denarau resorts (p89) have a six-pack of bars, all tastefully decorated and with attentive staff.

Shopping
Nadi's Main St is largely devoted to souvenir and duty-free shops, although sadly most items are mass-produced and you're unlikely to find anything truly unique. Worse still, much of it isn't even particularly Fijian, just vaguely tribal. We saw Papua New Guinean masks, Balinese statues, Chinese Buddhas and African soapstone carvings (the hippos were a giveaway) for sale in stores promoting Fijian handicrafts. The four biggest stores in town (you'll spot them) are all cut from this same (*tapa*) cloth and stock more or less identical merchandise aimed unashamedly at the tourist wallet. Your best bet for locally produced souvenirs include printed designs on *masi* (bark cloth), *tanoa* (*kava* drinking bowls), cannibal forks, war clubs and wood-turned bowls. See p238 for general information.

You may pick up something more authentic at the **handicraft market** (Map p83; Koroivolu Ave), but check out the prices in the shops beforehand to ensure you really are getting a bargain.

Getting There & Around
Nadi International Airport is 9km north of downtown Nadi and there are frequent local buses just outside the airport that travel along the Queens Road to town ($0.65); otherwise a taxi is $10. Most of the hotels have free transfer vehicles awaiting international flights. From Nadi bus station (in downtown Nadi) there are buses to Lautoka and Suva and nonexpress buses can be caught at regular bus stops along the Queens Road.

Buses depart from New Town Beach for downtown Nadi ($0.73, 15 minutes, six daily, Monday to Saturday). A taxi costs $6, $10 or $15 to the Queens Road junction, downtown or the airport.

For details of domestic flights from Nadi, see p245.

Most boat companies, including Awesome Adventures Fiji and South Sea Cruises, provide free transfers between Nadi hotels and Port

Denarau for clients using their island-bound boats. You can get to Denarau island independently: **West Bus Transport** (☎ 675 0777) has six buses Monday to Saturday (fewer on Sunday) from Nadi bus station and outside Jack's Handicrafts to Denarau island. The first is at 8.30am and the last at 5pm ($0.70, 30 minutes).

Taxi drivers are always on the look out for business. They don't use meters, so confirm prices in advance. Remember, if they are returning to base, you pay less. See p249 for a list of car-rental companies.

AROUND NADI
Denarau

Proving that money loves company, this upmarket island (2.55 sq km) is laden with fancy resorts manicured to perfection with heavenly pools and designer suites. Although it's only 6km west of Nadi town, the disparity couldn't be starker and staying here offers little insight into everyday Fijian life. But if you're looking to splash some cash, enjoy a dose of pampering and avoid Nadi altogether, then Denarau is the place to go. Be warned though – what the brochures and websites don't advertise is that Denarau is built on reclaimed mangrove mudflats and the beach has dark-grey sand and murky water unsuitable for snorkelling.

ACTIVITIES
Adrenalin Watersports (☎ 675 1288; www.adrenal infiji.com; per 30min adult/child $85/40) Has the licence to run the water-sports shops at all of the Denarau resorts and at Port Denarau Retail Centre. It specialises in jet-ski tours

to Beachcomber, Castaway or Malololo Islands (solo riders $386, $216 per person for tandem riders). Adrenalin also offers parasailing ($110), wakeboarding ($83) and diving (PADI Open Water Course/two-tank dive $695/220).
Adrenalin Jet (☎ 675 0400; www.jetfiji.com; per 30min adult/child $79/38) Roars around the Nadi River mangroves in a jet boat at hair-raising speeds.
Denarau Golf & Racquet Club (☎ 675 9711; info@ denaraugolf.com.fj) This club caters mainly to guests of the Sheraton hotels. It has an immaculately groomed 18-hole golf course with bunkers in the shape of sea creatures. Green fees are $125 for 18 holes and $85 for nine holes.
Dive Tropex (☎ 675 0944; www.divetropex.com; WorldMark by Wyndham resort) Hidden in the WorldMark by Wyndham timeshare resort, Dive Tropex offers a two-tank dive for $220, or PADI Open Water Course for $695. Snorkelling trips to the outer reefs cost $70 per person.
Yacht Help (☎ 675 0911; VHF Marine channel 16; www .yachthelp.com; Shop 5, Port Denarau) This extremely efficient aid to skippers can arrange Lau cruising permits, assemble provision orders and contact tradesmen, and it publishes *The Fiji Marine Guide.* Berth facilities at the marina include rubbish disposal, dock-side water and fuel, and showers, but no immigration or customs clearance.

Offshore Islands
Denarau Marina is the port used by catamarans departing to and from the offshore

SIGHTS & ACTIVITIES	
Adrenalin Jet...(see 7)	
Adrenalin Watersports.................................(see 7)	
Denarau Golf & Racquet Club....................**1** A2	
Dive Tropex...**2** A2	
Fiji's Finest Tours...(see 7)	
Island Hoppers...(see 7)	
Yacht Help..(see 7)	

SLEEPING 🏠	
Fiji Beach Resort & Spa Managed by the Hilton......**3** B1	
Radisson Resort Fiji....................................**4** A2	
Sofitel Fiji Resort & Spa.............................**5** A1	
Westin Denarau Island................................**6** A1	

EATING 🍴	
Amalfi Ristorante Italiano..........................(see 7)	
Hard Rock Cafe Fiji......................................(see 7)	
Indigo...(see 7)	

SHOPPING 🛍	
Port Denarau Retail Centre........................**7** B2	

TRANSPORT	
Awesome Adventures...................................(see 7)	
Bus to Nadi..**8** B2	
Captain Cook Cruises..................................(see 7)	
Denarau Marina...(see 7)	
Malolo Cat I & II..(see 7)	
Port Denarau...(see 7)	
Sea Fiji..(see 7)	
South Sea Cruises.......................................(see 7)	

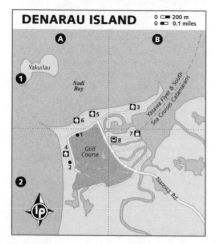

DENARAU ISLAND

0 ⸺ 200 m
0 ⸺ 0.1 miles

islands. It can be a hive of activity as suitcases are loaded, tired children are soothed and buses drop off guests from their hotel pick-ups. See p141 to read about your Mamanuca options and p153 to read about boats leaving for the Yasawas.

TOURS

Like those in Nadi, many tour companies based as far away the Nausori Highlands and Namosi Highlands will organise pick-up/drop-off from Denarau. **Fiji's Finest Tours** (Port Denarau) is a collection of tour companies operating under an umbrella moniker. Inside the shop are representatives from Robinson Crusoe Island (p97), Sea Fiji water taxis (p143), Feejee Experience (p251), Exclusive Tours and Beachcomber Island (p144).

In addition to island transfers, **Island Hoppers** (☎ 675 0670; www.helicopters.com.fj; Port Denarau) offers scenic helicopter flights over the islands and reefs of the Mamanuca Group and the water-falls and gorges of the Koroyanitu (Mt Evans) Ranges. Ten-, 20- and 35-minute flights cost $99, $220 and $330 per person respectively. A romantic lunch on a secluded island beach costs $1800 per couple.

SLEEPING

The rates at all of these resorts vary drastically with season and occupancy. You can be sure that rooms in the following resorts are taste-fully decorated and of a high standard, but none offers complimentary snorkelling trips or a beach that compares with those found on the islands.

Sofitel Fiji Resort & Spa (☎ 675 1111; www.sofitel .com; r $240-400; ✖ ✖ ▫ ▣) The large pavilion-style lobby is flanked by columns of polished, vine-entangled tree trunks on one side and an impressive mezzanine bar overlooking the free-form pool on the other. The Sofitel gets top marks for its Salt restaurant with alfresco dining and water's-edge location (mains $15 to $35) but didn't score as highly with its 296 rooms in uniform blocks flanking either side of the main building.

Radisson Resort Fiji (☎ 675 6677; www.radisson .com/fiji; r $333-575; ✖ ✖ ▫ ▣) The Radisson, Denarau's newest resort, wins the prize for Fiji's best pool; even from reception the pool's giant waterfall dominates. It has a series of lagoons, sandy beaches with child-friendly inclines, a white-water tunnel, adult areas and an island containing a day spa. The kids club

here is $20 per day and there are free kayaks, windsurfers and catamarans. There are 270 rooms and all suites are self-contained.

Fiji Beach Resort & Spa Managed by the Hilton (☎ 675 6800; www.fijibeachresortbyhilton.com; r $389-889; ✖ ✖ ▫ ▣) A series of seven rectangular, interlocking pools surrounded by artistically simple day beds is a nice architectural change from the other resorts. The long beachfront (the best Denarau has to offer) can be seen from all rooms (most with kitchens), and Nuku, argu-ably Denarau's top restaurant (mains $35 to $56), is on site. While it tops the dining list, it has the worst lobby and fails to impress when first arriving. The kids club here is free.

Westin Denarau Island (☎ 675 0000; www.westin .com/denarauresort; r $435-865; ✖ ✖ ▫ ▣) The beautifully designed lobby is a synthesis of dark timber and pale sandstone. A series of alternating high and low ceilings lead past the resort's many facilities to a designer pool and beachside restaurants. The Westin is more adult oriented, although children are welcome (a kids club is available for a one-time $55 fee) and there's a small artificial beach, held in place by a bank of stones. Fire-walkers perform here on Wednesdays and Saturdays ($85 including buffet meal). The Westin gets the award for Denarau's (if not Fiji's) most beautiful day spa. There are no free water sports here.

EATING & DRINKING

Each of the Denarau resorts has a handful of restaurants and it's easy to sample any of them by jumping on the free interresort '*bula* bus'. Indeed, for many, this is one of the attrac-tions of staying here. At Port Denarau, **Indigo** (☎ 675 0026; mains $18-35; ☺ lunch & dinner) serves Indian and Asian dishes and is a good choice for vegetarians, the steak at **Amalfi Ristorante Italiano** (☎ 675 0020; mains $27-38; ☺ lunch & dinner) is popular and there is also the **Hard Rock Cafe Fiji** (☎ 675 0032; mains $13-35; ☺ lunch & dinner). The clubhouse at the golf course also makes a nice change from the resorts.

SHOPPING

Port Denarau Retail Centre (www.portdenarau.com.fj) is trying hard to supplant Nadi's Main St as the place to shop, and the ever-expanding list of tenants currently includes beachwear, souve-nir and video shops. Most find it more pleas-urable to shop here than contend with the hassles in town. The only thing is, it does tend to feel strangely…what's the word? White?

The noticeboard at the back of the complex posts a list of free daily activities provided for children.

To see fit young men twirl knives and perform South Pacific dances to prerecorded music, attend one of the free cultural dance performances held in front of the fountain. Again, times are posted on the noticeboard.

GETTING THERE & AWAY

The local 'West Bus' operates between Nadi (catch it at the main station or outside Jack's Handicrafts) and Denarau Island ($0.70). You'll recognise the free interresort '*bula* bus' as it has a thatched roof on it – who said money can't buy taste? A taxi from Nadi town costs $12 and from the airport $24.

Foothills of the Sabeto Mountains

The undulating countryside between Nadi and Lautoka is a lovely area to explore. All of the following sights could be visited in a day and are easily accessible from Nadi.

The **Garden of the Sleeping Giant** (Map p91; ☎ 672 2701; Wailoko Rd; adult/child/family $12/6/30; ⏰ 9am-5pm Mon-Sat, to noon Sun) was established in 1977 by the actor and orchid-enthusiast, Raymond Burr (of *Perry Mason* and *Ironside* fame). There are now over 1500 varieties of orchid, representing 160 species; and although they won't all be flowering simultaneously (peak flowering season is June to July and November to December), expect a brilliant display year-round. A 50m-long shade cloth–covered walkway leads to a jungle boardwalk that showcases indigenous flora and other tropical beauties. The whole place takes about 45 minutes to walk around, unless you bring a picnic and stay longer.

A few kilometres further inland, the **Sabeto Hot Springs** (Map p91; admission $10; ⏰ 9am-5pm Mon-Sat) is the place to come clean while getting dirty. There is a series of geothermal hot pools and a mud pool. The soft and silty, knee-deep mud is covered by a top layer of leaves and the contrasting texture is a little freaky when you first sink into the ooze. The temptation to scoop up a handful of mud to smear over your friends may prove overwhelming. Solo women should decline any offers of massages from men they do not know.

A taxi from Nadi will cost around $15 to either the orchid garden or the hot springs. The Wailoko bus ($1.50) leaves Nadi at 9am, 1pm and 4pm and returns at 11am, 2pm and 5pm.

There is an abandoned battery of guns, known as **Lomolomo Guns** (Map p91), on a low rise at the foot of the Sabeto Mountains. The graffiti-covered guns were built in WWII to protect Nadi Bay and while they are hardly a 'must see', the walk up the hill offers some fine views across sugar-cane fields to the Yasawas. To get there, take the second turn-off on the right, 400m after the Lomolomo police station. Follow the dirt road (taking the left when it forks) for as far as you are able, before continuing on foot.

SLEEPING & EATING

Stoney Creek Resort (Map p91; ☎ 672 2206; www .stoneycreekfiji.net; Sabeto Rd; dm $28, s/d without bathroom $50/64, r with bathroom $80-110; 💻 🐾) When you tire of lying on your beach towel, head here to replace the aqua-blue seascape of the outer islands with the velvet-green landscape of Sabeto Valley. There's a load of activities on site and nearby, including mountain biking ($22 for half-day or $35 for full-day hire), village visits, guided waterfall treks (October to April, $80) and swimming in the river. Be warned though, the whole place is very relaxing and many guests spend their time just chilling by the pool, playing board games. The 'Love Shack' dorms are reminiscent of train carriages with shuttered windows and the *bure* are cosy and private; both have sweeping mountain views. Rates include breakfast and free internet. There is a sunken bar, and a restaurant (mains $10 to $30) that caters well to both meat-eaters and vegetarians, on site.

The resort provides a free airport shuttle for guests staying a minimum of two nights and there are regular 'Sabeto' buses from Nadi bus station, every 1½ hours between 8am and 5.30pm, for $1.70. Otherwise catch a Lautoka–Nadi bus to the Sabeto and Queens Roads' junction and a carrier from there. A taxi from the airport costs $13, and from downtown $18.

Viseisei & Vuda Point

About 12km north of Nadi is **Viseisei** village, which, according to local lore, is the oldest settlement in Fiji. The story goes that the *mataqali* (extended family) here are descendants of the first ocean-going Melanesians who landed 1km north of here c 1500. As if to follow tradition, Fiji's first Methodist missionaries also chose to land here, in 1835, and the Centennial Memorial in front of the

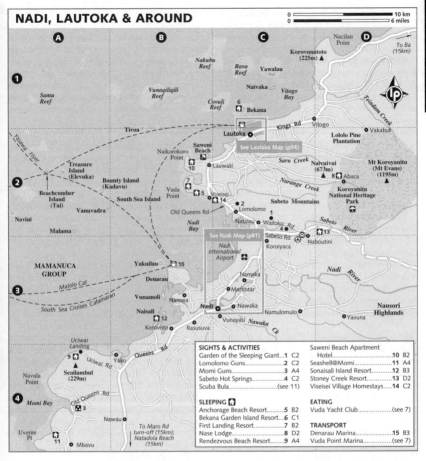

NADI, LAUTOKA & AROUND

SIGHTS & ACTIVITIES		
Garden of the Sleeping Giant...**1**	C2	
Lomolomu Guns...**2**	C2	
Momi Guns...**3**	A4	
Sabeto Hot Springs...**4**	C2	
Scuba Bula...(see 11)		

SLEEPING		
Anchorage Beach Resort...**5**	B2	
Bekana Garden Island Resort...**6**	C1	
First Landing Resort...**7**	B2	
Nase Lodge...**8**	D2	
Rendezvous Beach Resort...**9**	A4	

Saweni Beach Apartment Hotel...**10**	B2	
Seashell@Momi...**11**	A4	
Sonaisali Island Resort...**12**	B3	
Stoney Creek Resort...**13**	D2	
Viseisei Village Homestays...**14**	C2	

EATING		
Vuda Yacht Club...(see 7)		

TRANSPORT		
Denarau Marina...**15**	B3	
Vuda Point Marina...(see 7)		

church is the focal point for 10 October (Fiji Day) celebrations. Fiji's current president, Ratu Josefa Iloilo, who holds the chiefly title of Tui Vuda, still uses the ceremonial *bure* opposite the memorial on important occasions and both Queen Elizabeth and Prince Charles have been received here. To look around you'll need to pay $3 to the ladies who run the tiny **craft market** (8am-6pm Mon-Sat), remove your hat and wear something that covers your shoulders and knees. A bypass on Queens Road skips Viseisei so be sure to check with the driver that the Nadi to Lautoka bus you catch actually calls by the village.

The **Vuda Point Marina** (Map p91; 666 8214; www .vudamarina.com.fj) is a well-organised and thriving boaties lure. Facilities include free showers, an excellent noticeboard, a coin-operated laundry, sail makers, a general store, yacht-repair specialists and a chandlery. Berths per foot, per day, cost $0.50 and electricity costs $3.50 per day.

SLEEPING & EATING
The beaches around Vuda Point are better than those found near Nadi, but are far from Fiji's best and offer little for the avid snorkeller. Some find staying here a little isolated for anything more than a few days.

Viseisei Village Homestays (Map p91; www.fijibure .com/holidaysinfiji.htm, www.fijianfamilies.com, www.couch surfing.com; per person $50-60) A number of families offer homestays in Viseisei, although they may be hard to contact. If trawling through the websites listed here doesn't help, contact Finau Bavadra (☎ 925 5370; dawfintravel@consultant.com), who often welcomes couch surfers.

Anchorage Beach Resort (Map p91; ☎ 666 2099; www.anchoragefiji.com; r incl breakfast $150-350; ✗ ❄ ⚲) The hilltop wedding *bure* has panoramic views of Nadi Bay and the Mamanucas and the grassy lawn can accommodate large numbers. The resort was renovated in 2004 and the newer villas have spa baths built into their private decks. Most of the rooms here are large and a sliding internal window means you can enjoy the views from the bath. A ho-hum beach, the main restaurant (mains $25 to $30) and a sparkling pool are a five-minute walk down the hill.

First Landing Resort (Map p91; ☎ 666 6171; www.firstlandingfiji.com; r incl breakfast $820-920, 2-bed villa incl breakfast $820-920; ✗ ❄ ⚲) Perched on the water's edge and dripping in palms and colourful foliage, this resort is made-to-order for those who enjoy package holidays. The *bure* and villas are like cheerful hotel rooms with bright, tiled bathrooms and mosquito-screened verandahs. The more expensive villas have private plunge pools and, although the beach isn't great, there's an artificial island in the shape of a footprint and a lagoon-style pool to accommodate sunbathers. The restaurant serves excellent seafood (mains $25 to $38), fairly bland pasta, and wood-fired pizza.

Vuda Yacht Club (Map p91; ☎ 666 8214; Vuda Point Marina; mains $13-18; ☿ lunch & dinner) It screams 'members only' from a sign out front, but that's all bravado and travellers are more than welcome. Dinner mains consist of Cajun steak, curries and stir-fries.

Naisali

Like Denarau, Naisali (42 hectares) is on the edge of mangroves, the beaches aren't ideal for swimming and the dark sand disappoints some. This long, flat island is just 300m off the mainland and about 12km southwest of Nadi.

There's plenty of white sand at **Sonaisali Island Resort** (Map p91; ☎ 670 6011; www.sonaisali.com; r incl breakfast $495-682, ste incl breakfast from $891; ✗ ❄ ⏲ ⚲), but unfortunately none of it's on the beach – being mainly used in landscaping the grounds. While the glossy brochure and slick website tend to oversell the resort, there is a large pool with a swim-up bar and

an endless array of activities to keep everyone happy (including a free kids club). The meal plan ($70 for adults and $35 for children) is the way to go for big eaters, although you may want to sample the food first before upgrading. Bring plenty of duty-free – the drinks are pricey (cocktails $22). The hotel rooms in the double-storey building are getting tired, whereas the semidetached *bure* are far nicer, with spa baths built into the verandahs.

Naisali is a 25-minute drive followed by a three-minute boat shuttle (free for guests) from Nadi airport. A taxi from the airport costs $32, the resort shuttle $55.

Uciwai Landing

Uciwai Landing, used by surfers to access the Mamanuca breaks and island resorts on Namotu and Tavarua, is 18km southwest of Nadi. Surfing is really the only reason to head here.

The lingo and 'tude hang thickly in the air at **Rendezvous Beach Resort** (Map p91; ☎ 628 4427; www.surfdivefiji.com; camping per person $20, dm $30, s with/without bathroom incl breakfast $80/60, d with/without bathroom incl breakfast $125/70; ❄ ⏲ ⚲), which caters predominantly to surfers on a budget and Japanese studying English. It's an interesting combination. Quick access to the Mamanuca surf breaks and dive sites are the attraction and the idea is to spend as much time away from the resort as possible. Accommodation is rudimentary, although the better beach huts have air-con. There are no facilities for self-caterers, but meal plans are available for $35. Internet access is included in the room rates. The staff here are as languid as the seasoned surfers who visit.

The daily surf boat goes to Cloudbreak (Saturdays only), Wilkes, Desperations, Mini Cloud or the Swimming Pools (see p141) and costs $65 for three to four hours surfing. A two-tank dive costs $200 and PADI Open Water Course $580, with the on-site instructor.

Resort transfers are available from Nadi ($40) and the airport ($60), or there are local buses to Uciwai from Nadi bus station ($1.50) departing at 8am, 1.30pm and 5.30pm weekdays, and 7am, 1pm and 5pm Saturday.

LAUTOKA
pop 52,900

According to legend, Fiji's second-largest city derives its name from a battle cry that means 'spear-hit'. The story goes that when an argument erupted between two local chiefs, one cried out the words *lau toka* as he killed the other by spearing him through the chest, simultaneously stating the obvious and naming the location. Lautoka's recent history is entwined with the fortunes of sugar and it is the cane on which Lautoka depends that gives rise to its other name, Sugar City.

Lautoka doesn't have much to detain the traveller although it is a pleasant enough spot with wide streets steeped in foliage, a picturesque esplanade, a relaxed ambience and the backdrop of the Koroyanitu (Mt Evans) Range to remind everyone that the urban reaches are well and truly finite.

Information

EMERGENCY

Ambulance (☎ 911)

Police (Map p94; ☎ 911, 666 0222; Drasa Ave) There is also a police post on Tui St.

INTERNET ACCESS

Internet access seems to be incredibly cheap and plentiful in Lautoka. It is not uncommon to pay only $1 per hour, including at the **JC Internet Cafe** (Map p94; Namoli Ave; ☺ 8am-10pm) in the Village 4 Cinema Complex.

MEDICAL SERVICES

Avenue Clinic (Map p94; ☎ 665 2955; 47 Drasa Ave) Consultation $30.

Lautoka Hospital (off Map p94; ☎ 666 0399; Thomson Cres) South of the Botanical Gardens.

MONEY

There are several banks downtown that will change money and travellers cheques. There are ANZ bank ATMs on Vitogo Pde, Yasawa St and near the cinema on Namoli Ave.

POST

Post office (Map p94; cnr Vitogo Pde & Tavewa Ave) Has public phones.

Sights & Activities

Fiji has the highest percentage of Hare Krishnas per capita in the world, and the **Sri Krishna Kaliya Temple** (Map p94; ☎ 666 4112; 5 Tavewa Ave; ☺ 8am-6pm) is the foremost International Society for Krishna Consciousness (ISKCON) temple in the South Pacific. Visitors are welcome anytime, but an interesting time to

visit is during the noon *Puja* (prayer) on Sunday. Sit according to your gender and expect a whole lot of drum beating, bell ringing, conch blowing and chanting, which is the way Krishnas approach God and achieve transcendental bliss. Keep a donation handy for the tray that a child circulates at the end of the service. Everyone, whether you give money or not, is invited to the 1pm vegetarian 'feast' that follows.

Lautoka has broad streets and Marine Dr makes a nice promenade along the waterfront. From here it is possible to walk to the **Lautoka Sugar Mill** (off Map p94; Nadovu Rd), the backbone of the local economy. The mill opened in 1903 and is now reputably the largest sugar mill in the southern hemisphere. There are no tours, but you should be able to the see the conveyors and pipeline for loading sugar, woodchips and molasses into the waiting cargo boats.

There is no beach at Lautoka and locals frequent the unappealing but popular **Saweni Beach** (Map p91) 8km out of town.

Blue Lagoon Cruises (Map p94; 183 Vitogo Pde) operates its Yasawa cruises from Lautoka Port. See p153 for details.

Sleeping

TOWN

Cathay Hotel (Map p94; ☎ 666 0566; www.fiji4less.com; Tavewa Ave; dm $22-24, s & d $55, tr $74; ✕ 🖳) The dorms here are good value with only four to a room and each with its own bathroom. Otherwise, choose between spacious rooms with air-con and simpler but still roomy, fan-cooled rooms with shared bathrooms. There's an upstairs bar overlooking a small pool and the central location means it's handy to the downtown restaurants (which are preferable to the one here).

Lautoka Hotel (Map p94; ☎ 666 0388; ltkhotel@connect.com.fj; 2-12 Naviti St; r without bathroom $35-45, r with bathroom $60-80; ✕ 🖳) On the bright side, Lautoka Hotel is very reasonably priced. On the down side, the hotel prescribes to the pay-for-what-you-get school of thought. The cheapest rooms have shared facilities while the air-con rooms are comfortably worn. The hotel sprawls above, and is sandwiched between, two nightclubs. The music will make you feel like dancing!

Sea Breeze Hotel (Map p94; ☎ 666 0717; fax 666 6080; Bekana Lane; s $52-68, d $58-74; ✕ 🖳 🔊) From the outside the Sea Breeze resembles a jaunty blue-and-white apartment building. Inside,

VITI LEVU

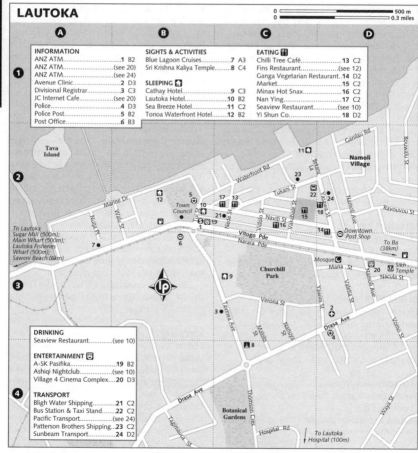

LAUTOKA

INFORMATION
ANZ ATM.................................**1** B2
ANZ ATM............................(see 20)
ANZ ATM............................(see 24)
Avenue Clinic.........................**2** D3
Divisional Registrar................**3** C3
JC Internet Cafe...................(see 20)
Police.....................................**4** D3
Police Post.............................**5** B2
Post Office.............................**6** B3

SIGHTS & ACTIVITIES
Blue Lagoon Cruises................**7** A3
Sri Krishna Kaliya Temple........**8** C4

SLEEPING 🛏
Cathay Hotel..........................**9** C3
Lautoka Hotel.......................**10** B2
Sea Breeze Hotel..................**11** C2
Tonoa Waterfront Hotel........**12** B2

EATING 🍴
Chilli Tree Café.....................**13** C2
Fins Restaurant...................(see 12)
Ganga Vegetarian Restaurant..**14** D2
Market.................................**15** C2
Minax Hot Snax....................**16** C2
Nan Ying..............................**17** C2
Seaview Restaurant.............(see 10)
Yi Shun Co............................**18** D2

DRINKING
Seaview Restaurant............(see 10)

ENTERTAINMENT 🎭
A-SK Pasifika.........................**19** B2
Ashiqi Nightclub..................(see 10)
Village 4 Cinema Complex....**20** D3

TRANSPORT
Bligh Water Shipping............**21** C2
Bus Station & Taxi Stand......**22** C2
Pacific Transport................(see 24)
Patterson Brothers Shipping..**23** C2
Sunbeam Transport..............**24** D2

the piously austere rooms are a clean and tranquil sanctuary to noise-weary travellers. Cheapest are the fan-cooled digs, but the more expensive sea-view rooms with air-con are the nicest. There's also a TV lounge where breakfast is available ($4 to $10).

Tonoa Waterfront Hotel (Map p94; ☎ 666 4777; www .tonoahotels.com; Marine Dr; r $128-188; ✗ ✗ 🖥 🛒) Lautoka's top hotel has a top waterfront location. The cheapest rooms are spotlessly clean and have the ambience and trimmings of a midrange US hotel chain. The more expensive rooms have contemporary interiors, flat-screen TVs and small balconies overlooking two pools. There is a gym, a coin-operated laundry, a small children's playground, a bar and Fins Restaurant (see opposite) on site.

OUT OF TOWN

Saweni Beach Apartment Hotel (Map p91; ☎ 666 1777; www.fiji4less.com; dm $23, apt $95-120; ✗ ✗ 🛒) Situated 8km southwest of town, this hotel offers a series of one-bedroom, self-contained apartments in two long complexes. In addition there are two dorms that have a total of eight beds and share a communal kitchen and lounge area. All up, it's an inexpensive option for self-caterers and those looking for a base to explore the nearby highlands, but you'll want your own wheels and imagination – there's little to do at the hotel but paddle in the pool.

Bekana Garden Island Resort (Map p91; ☎ 664 0180; www.bekanaislandfiji.com.fj; d $150-350; ✗ ✗ 🖥 🛒) This downward-spiralling resort occupies a small island close to Lautoka and has not been well maintained in recent years. There are three types of *bure*, the largest of which is split-level, right on the water and can accommodate a family of four. On site are a restaurant and bar, and the resort offers a plethora of activities including windsurfing, snorkelling and kayaking, although these all cost extra. The resort runs a regular shuttle service from Lautoka Fisheries Wharf (off Map p94) although departure times can be whimsical.

Eating

Lautoka has fewer restaurants than Nadi or Suva; however, there are lots of inexpensive lunchtime eateries frequented by locals.

Minax Hot Snax (Map p94; ☎ 666 1306; 56 Naviti St; meals $5; ☻ breakfast & lunch) This unassuming, family-run restaurant is the best place in town to sample authentic South Indian food. Meals are prepared using fresh ingredients including jackfruit, okra, *lauki* (a kind of gourd) and local spinach.

ourpick Seaview Restaurant (Map p94; ☎ 666 4592; cnr Naviti & Tui Sts; mains $5-12; ☻ breakfast, lunch & dinner) This has been a long-time favourite with locals and travellers alike for good reason. The relaxed family atmosphere, pleasant bar, reasonable prices and delicious food served in huge portions leave little room for the competition to get a look in. You can order anything from roast chicken to masala dosa, and the family-sized pizza can feed a whole tribe.

Chilli Tree Café (Map p94; ☎ 665 1824; 3 Tukani St; meals $6-12; ☻ breakfast & lunch Mon-Sat; ✗) This corner cafe is the best place to grab a paper and coffee, build a sandwich and settle into a chair for some serious people watching behind the plate-glass windows.

Nan Ying (Map p94; ☎ 665 2668; Nede St; mains $13-30; ☻ lunch & dinner Mon-Sat, dinner Sun; ✗) Twinkly lights, backlit pictures and fake flowers give this place an air of Chinatown authenticity that would do San Francisco proud. Fragrant poultry and noodle dishes, sizzling seafood hotplates and fried-rice specials demonstrate that these cooks know their way around their chopsticks.

Also recommended:

Ganga Vegetarian Restaurant (Map p94; cnr Naviti & Yasawa Sts; meals $2-5; ☻ breakfast & lunch) Popular Hare Krishna restaurant serving good vegetarian meals.

Fins Restaurant (Map p94; ☎ 666 4777; Marine Dr; mains $19-32; ☻ breakfast, lunch & dinner) The $15

barbecue dinner on Saturdays is good value, but the tiled floors ricochet noise terribly.

Self-caterers can stock up at **Yi Shun Co** (Map p94; ☎ 666 4615; Sugar City Mall, Yasawa St) for Chinese groceries, or at the produce market, which is part of the larger, town **market** (Map p94; ☻ 7am-5pm Mon-Fri, to 3pm Sat).

Drinking & Entertainment

Lautoka lacks the sophistication of Suva and the small number of pubs and clubs are generally on the seedy side. Fighting and drinking are a popular pastime for some and, if you haven't noticed, Fijian men aren't exactly petite; we don't recommend nightclubbing for solo travellers. But, for those with friends, a fun night out dancing can be had at **Ashiqi Nightclub** (Map p94; Lautoka Hotel, Tui St; ☻ 8pm-1am Fri & Sat), which plays Bollywood hits at alarming decibels.

A-SK Pasifika (Map p94; ☎ 666 8989; 151 Vitogo Pde; ☻ 5pm-1am Mon-Sat) Popular with Fijians who flock here on 'sponsored nights' when the beer is cheaper. A $5 cover charge applies on Friday and Saturday when a band or DJ plays.

Seaview Restaurant (Map p94; cnr Naviti & Tui Sts) The small bar at this restaurant is frequented by expats and it's a nice spot to grab a table and enjoy a few beers before dinner.

Village 4 Cinema Complex (Map p94; Namoli Ave) Besides the Suva cinema, this is the only other mainstream cinema in Fiji. Tickets are $4 for children and $5 for adults, except on Tuesday when both are $1 cheaper.

Getting There & Around

Lautoka's bus station is a busy little place. Local buses depart for Nadi (33km, $2.10, one hour) via the airport every 15 minutes. Sunbeam Transport and Pacific Transport have offices in Yasawa St opposite the market and both have frequent services to and from Suva ($14.20, six hours) via Queens Road. Sunbeam also has seven daily departures to Suva via Kings Road ($17, seven hours).

Local buses connect Lautoka with Saweni Beach ($1, 45 minutes, six daily). Alternatively any local bus to Nadi will drop you at the turn-off, from where it is an easy walk along 2km of unsealed road. A taxi from Saweni will cost approximately $10 to Lautoka, or $35 to Nadi airport.

On-again, off-again ferries run to Savusavu from Lautoka. Turn to p247 for details.

Arriving yachts wishing to clear customs and immigration at **Lautoka Port** (☎ 666 0722; VHF Marine channel 16; ⏰ 8am-1pm, 2-4.30pm Mon-Fri) will need to announce their arrival to port authorities who will issue instructions on where to moor.

KOROYANITU NATIONAL HERITAGE PARK

An hour's drive from Lautoka, the **Koroyanitu National Heritage Park** (Map p91; admission $8) is deep within Viti Levu's interior and a world away from the Mamanucas and Yasawas, which are visible from the summit of Castle Rock. There are six small and largely self-sufficient villages within the park that cooperate as part of an ecotourism project intended to protect Fiji's only un-logged tropical montane forest. The villagers maintain the landscape and tracks, and sub-sequently earn tourist dollars through villagestays and manning the visitor centre.

It's best to contact the **Abaca visitor centre** (☎ 666 6644, after the beep dial 1234) before setting out, as recent landowner issues have seen the centre keep erratic hours. If you can't get through, check with the Fiji Visitors Bureau in Nadi (p239) for any recent developments. Abaca (am-*bar*-tha) village is at the base of **Mt Koroyanitu** (Mt Evans) and has beautiful walks through native *dakua* forests and grasslands, birdwatching, archaeological sites and waterfalls.

Trekking

From Nase Lodge a marked track leads its way up to **Castle Rock**, which has some impressive views; it takes about three hours (one way) up some steep inclines, so wear something grippy.

There is also a two-hour hike that takes in a waterfall, the terraced gardens at Tunutunu and the Navuratu village site. A full-day hike to Mt Koroyanitu also visits the remains of a fortified village. Guides can be arranged at the visitor centre for around $20.

It's also possible to make a day trek to and from Fiji's sleeping giant, Mt Batilamu, although this is a more strenuous hike and guides are recommended. However, in 2008 a landslide destroyed the path and it was closed until the landslide can be cleared. As there were no definite plans to reopen them at the time of research, contact the visitor centre or one of the tour agencies listed here for

an up-to-date status report on the path and tour options.

Mount Batilamu Trek (☎ 664 5747; fax 664 5547) organises tours up the Sabeto Valley. The three-day option starts with a 4WD up to the village of Navilawa for a *sevusevu* ceremony (presentation of a gift to the village chief). After a night in the village community hall you will be taken on a five- to eight-hour walk up Mt Batilamu, where you'll spend the night in Fiji's highest *bure* (about 1150m). The following day, you head down to Abaca where you're transported back to Nadi or Lautoka. The all-inclusive tour costs $430 per person, including transport to and from Nadi and Lautoka hotels. Scaled-down versions include an overnight trek ($250 person) and a day trek ($150) to the summit.

Great Sights Fiji (p80) and Rosie Holidays (p80) also sometimes run overnight excursions to Mt Batilamu.

Sleeping

Nase Lodge (dm $35), which is maintained by the villagers of Abaca, is an old colonial lodge about 400m uphill from the village. It has 12 bunk beds, no electricity or showers (try the swimming hole in the nearby river), but there is a flush toilet, mosquito netting around the beds, and a main lounge to unwind in. You can order meals from the ladies at the village, but you should also take some groceries as there is only a small village shop. Make bookings at the Abaca visitor centre, which can also arrange homestays for $45 per person including meals.

Getting There & Away

There are no buses to Abaca, but if you contact the Abaca visitor centre, it can advise if the local carrier has resumed running. Alternatively, it can arrange a car to collect you from Nadi ($100 each way). A cheaper option would be to rent a car and drive yourself.

If driving from Nadi, turn right off the Queens Road at Tavakubu Rd, past the first roundabout after entering Lautoka. Continue for about 6.5km, past the police post and the cemetery, then turn right at Abaca Rd. It is a further 10km of gravel road up to the village, suitable for 4WDs only.

MOMI BAY

The first interesting detour off Queens Road is 18km south of Nadi, along a sealed road that threads its way between barren hills, pine plantations and sugar-cane fields to Momi Bay and the more impressive **Momi Guns** (Map p91; adult/child/family $3/1/6; ☉ 9am-5pm). The two 6in guns were installed here by the New Zealand 30th Battalion in 1941 to defend Fiji against the Japanese. Fiji was, like most other islands, poorly equipped to take on the might of the Imperial Army; an army that had already swept through Papua New Guinea, the Solomon Islands and parts of what is now Vanuatu. A quick scan of the horizon will reveal why this spot was chosen for the battery. The guns (and now tourists) have unobstructed views to Malolo Barrier Reef, the Mamanuca islands and Navula Passage, the only entry into western Fiji for large ships. The war raged on but the guns were only fired once in anger – at a New Zealand Navy ship that failed to signal correctly.

Recently Momi has seen a new battle rage – a legal one. Construction was well underway on the JW Marriott Fiji Resort and Spa, Fiji's second overwater *bure* resort, until work came to a grinding halt in 2006. Local speculation runs rife as to why the project has stalled. All anyone really knows though is that Momi Bay is now home to a first-class golf course on which no one has ever played.

Scuba Bula (Map p91; ☎ 628 0190; www.scubabula .com) is an excellent, independently owned company based at the Seashell@Momi resort. It has exclusive rights to a large stretch of coast and dive master 'Scuba Sam' has 20 years' experience on local reefs. A two-tank dive including equipment costs $165 and PADI Open Water Course $575, and staff will collect four or more divers from Nadi for free (one to three divers pay $80 for the car). Snorkellers are welcome and are charged $40 for a two-session outing.

Seashell@Momi (Map p91; ☎ 670 6100; www.sea shellresort.com; dm incl meals $86, s/d with shared facilities incl breakfast $47/70, r incl breakfast $158-190, apt incl breakfast $231-315; ☒ ☒ ☐ ☒) has an undiscovered air about it and while it's far from upmarket, it offers excellent value if you don't mind the dated decor. Accommodation comes in all shapes and sizes, from self-contained *bure* and apartments to roomy suites, inexpensive lodges and roomy dorms. On-site facilities include a tennis court, a children's playground, two pools, a restaurant (mains $10 to $20) and enough palm trees for a whole island. People don't come here for the beach (although if

you walk around the rocky point there's a larger bay with better sand), but for access to some of Fiji's hottest dive spots and premier surf breaks. A 7am surf trip departs daily for a three- to four-hour session ($60 per person, minimum of two people, board rental $30 per day) at Wilkes Passage, Mini Clouds or Desperations (p141).

Getting There & Away

Airport transfers by resort minibus are $25 per person each way (minimum charge $50) and taxis cost $55. **Dominion Transport** (☎ 670 1505) buses leave Nadi Bus Station for Momi Bay at 8am, 12.30pm, 2.30pm and 4pm and cost $2. The 11.15am bus from Sigatoka costs $3.80. Both buses pass the Momi Guns and the resort, but do not operate on Sundays.

ROBINSON CRUSOE ISLAND

Like bees to Bacardi, budget travellers in the 18- to 30-year-old bracket swarm to Likuri, which is now known as **Robinson Crusoe Island Resort** (Map pp76-7; ☎ 628 1999; www.robinsoncrusoeislandfiji .com; dm/s/d incl meals from $86/103/206; ☒), a small, coral island fringed by gorgeous white sand. The entertainment program is intense and some will undoubtedly find it a little tacky – your boat is 'attacked by cannibals' on your arrival. On the days when day trippers visit (Tuesday, Thursday and Sunday, $89 for adults and $45 for children including Nadi and Coral Coast transfers, which can generally be arranged through your accommodation's tour desk), the entertainment ramps up to overdrive and before long you'll find yourself buying into activities you'd be ashamed to be associated with back home. The crab racing is oddly addictive and clearly crab 42 was a ring-in.

The accommodation is basic: some of the thatched private *bure* are barely bigger than the bed, and the shared facilities are no more than bucket showers. There are 24 bunk beds in a dorm that looks like a wooden army barracks decorated for a South Sea musical but, with the right attitude, it can be a blast and kids, old and young, love it. Buffet meals are served in a large horseshoe-shaped shelter surrounding a sandy central area used for performances.

The run-off from the mainland has killed much of the coral and consequently the snorkelling isn't particularly good. If you are keen to see more spectacular marine life, suit up with long-time operators, **Aboard-A-Dream Nautilus Dive** (Map pp76-7; ☎ 628 2736; www .aboardadream.com), which operates a concession here. Nautilus also picks up clients staying at Natadola Beach, from the Robinson Crusoe Island Jetty, upon request. A two-tank dive including equipment costs $180 and a PADI Open Water Course $599.

The only way to get stranded on Crusoe is with a bus/boat return-transfer from Nadi operated by the resort ($79).

NATADOLA BEACH

Gorgeous Natadola Beach is Viti Levu's best. Its vast bank of white sand slides into a cobalt sea providing good swimming regardless of the tide. Natadola's strong currents often defy the brochures: instead of glassy, still conditions, you may find sufficient chop for good body surfing – just watch the undertows.

Local villagers tie up their horses under the trees near the car park and pounce on tourists as soon as they arrive. They are fairly persistent and you'll shock them if you don't want a **horse ride**. A ride along the beach to a nearby cave costs anything-they-can-get, but according to a local hotel operator you should only pay $10. Good luck with that. Graduating from the same school of high-pressure sales tactics are the coconut and seashell sellers. They're great if you want coconuts or shells but tiring if you don't.

Natadola's peace and tranquillity, however, face more serious threats than a few locals eking out a living from day-tripping tourists. When we passed, gangs of construction workers were busier than bees with bum-fuls of honey. The mammoth **InterContinental Resort Fiji** (www.natadolafiji.com) is set to open here in 2009, and further up the road the 18-hole Vijay Singh Golf Course was also under construction.

Sleeping & Eating

Yatule Beach Resort (Map pp76-7; ☎ 672 8004; reser-vation@yatuleresort.com.fj; villas $200-$320, f villa $530; ✕ ✕ ✕) The thatched roofs of the self-contained *bure* make this resort look like a Fijian village. Originally built to house the bigwigs involved in the building of the InterContinental, it now offers some excellent beachside accommodation. All the villas have minikitchens, bedrooms and separate lounges. The family villa has four separate bedrooms and is ideal for teenage kids who

need privacy. The restaurant (mains $18 to $26) has a fantastic beachside location and is a great place for a beer.

Natadola Beach Resort (Map pp76-7; ☎ 672 1001; www.natadola.com; r $225, villas $275; ✕) This small, intimate resort has only 11 suites in two blocks and, since there are no children under 16 allowed, it's ideal for couples. The resort was built in the faux–Spanish colonial style popular a few years back, and has a certain 'Casa del Fiji' charm about it. Each room has a spacious bathroom, small private courtyard and tiled interior. The pool meanders through tropical gardens and there's plenty of poolside shade for those wishing to snooze. When all that R&R gets too much, grab a boogie board and cross the road to the beach. The restaurant-bar (mains $27 to $32) is open to nonguests and is a popular lunch stop with day trippers.

Getting There & Away

Natadola Beach is fairly isolated and most people visit as part of a day tour from Nadi or the Coral Coast. The Coral Coast Scenic Railway (below) is a particularly nice way to arrive. For those with a rental car, turn off Queens Road onto Maro Rd 36km from Nadi. The road is sealed and the beach is signposted. For those with energy, you can walk here in 3½ hours, by following the track from Yanuca, and catch the train or bus back.

Paradise Transport buses head to Natadola from Sigatoka ($3, one hour, four daily on weekdays), otherwise catch any bus and ask to be let off at the Maro Rd junction and catch a taxi from there ($7). A taxi costs $72 each way from Nadi.

YANUCA & AROUND

Past the turn-off to Natadola, the Queens Road continues southeast, winding through hills and down to the coast at Cuvu Bay and Yanuca, about 50km from Nadi. Yanuca itself is a blink of a village, but it's home to a couple of good attractions.

The station for the **Coral Coast Scenic Railway** (Map pp76-7; ☎ 652 0434; Queens Rd) is at the cause-way entrance to Shangri-La's Fijian Resort. It offers scenic rides along the coast in an old diesel sugar train, past villages, forests and sugar plantations, to beautiful Natadola Beach. The railway was once used for transporting cane and passengers to the Lautoka Mill. The 14km trip takes about 1¼ hours, leaving at 10am on Tuesdays, Thursdays, Saturdays and Sundays and returning at 4pm ($91 including barbecue lunch). On Mondays, Wednesdays and Fridays a Sigatoka shopping trip runs east and costs $38. Children under 12 pay half price.

Directly opposite the Scenic Railway station, the **Kalevu Cultural Centre & Gecko's Resort** (Map pp76-7; ☎ 652 0200; www.fijiculturalcentre.com; 1hr/half-day guided tour $20/55, tw without bathroom incl breakfast $58, d with bathroom incl breakfast $120, self-contained f incl breakfast $150-175; ☾ tours 9am-4pm; ✕ ☷ ⌨ ⌘) has experienced a rocky road in recent years. In 2000, a fire burnt down four *bure* and destroyed irreplaceable artefacts and now many of the items displayed are replicas. The purpose-built centre is under new management, keen to extend it beyond the current cultural shows and mediocre static displays. The half-day tour includes a *lovo* lunch and South Pacific dancing, but requires a minimum group of eight. The accommodation here has recently expanded to include 28 new, simple-but-nice hotel rooms and the shared twins are particularly good value as accommodation includes admission to the cultural village. The restaurant (mains $12 to $49) is recommended, particularly the steaks, and if you can round up a group of 15 they'll throw in a complimentary South Pacific dance show for everyone.

Anchored offshore on its own private island, the **Shangri-La's Fijian Resort** (The Fijian; Map pp76-7; ☎ 652 0155; www.shangri-la.com; r incl breakfast from $490; ✕ ☷ ⌨ ⌘) is one of the Coral Coast's premier hotels. Linked to the mainland by a causeway, the resort's recently upgraded 442 rooms come in a variety of configurations and packages. Depending on how you book (online or through a travel agent), your room rate may include incredible waist-expanding breakfasts ($33) and free meal packages for the kids. While mum and dad nip off for a round of golf ($33) or toddle down to one of Fiji's swanky day spas, they can shunt junior (lovingly) into the child-care centre. All of this five-star luxury (well 4½ actually) doesn't come cheap, and since you charge everything back to your room, the bill can be a shock. If you like big resorts, and armies of squealing kids don't daunt you, you'll enjoy the three swimming pools, excellent restaurants, tennis courts and possibly even the wedding chapel.

Getting There & Away

The Fijian is about a 45-minute drive from Nadi and 11km west of Sigatoka. There are regular express buses, minibuses and carriers travelling along the Queens Road. A taxi to Nadi airport is about $75, or the **Coral Sun Fiji** (☎ 672 3105; www.coralsunfiji.com) coach costs $12 if you book it yourself.

CORAL COAST

A wide bank of coral offshore gives this stretch of coast between Korotogo and Pacific Harbour its name. Flanked by waves of richly vegetated hills and a fringing reef that drops off dramatically into the deep blue of the South Pacific Ocean, it's the most scenic slice of the Queens Road and resorts of all standards exploit the views. That said, the Coral Coast's beaches are poor cousins to those on Fiji's smaller islands and most swimming is done in hotel pools. Travellers are better off focusing on highlights such as the Sigatoka Sand Dunes, Tavuni Hill Fort, Sigatoka Valley and, near Pacific Harbour, river trips in the Namosi Highlands and diving in the Beqa Lagoon. Lounging in a resort is also a prime pursuit in these parts.

Much of the coast experiences tidal fluctuations that leave a lot of the reef exposed for long lengths of time and (except for some lagoons) it is only possible to swim and snorkel at high tide. Sovi Bay, 2.5km east of Korotogo, is one of the better swimming beaches, but be wary of strong channel currents. The photos, so often seen, of white, sandy Fijian beaches are unlikely to have been taken along the Coral Coast.

SIGATOKA
pop 9500

Sigatoka (sing-a-*to*-ka) is the largest town on the Coral Coast and serves as the commercial hub for the farming communities that grow sugar cane and vegetables upriver in the fertile swathe of the Sigatoka Valley.

Because of its pretty riverside location and accessibility, Sigatoka is a popular day trip from Nadi and the nearby Coral Coast resorts. There is a bustling produce market in the heart of town, a few souvenir shops, a large mosque and a fantasy-style, privately owned mansion overlooking the lot. The Sigatoka River, the second largest in Fiji, flows along

VITI LEVU

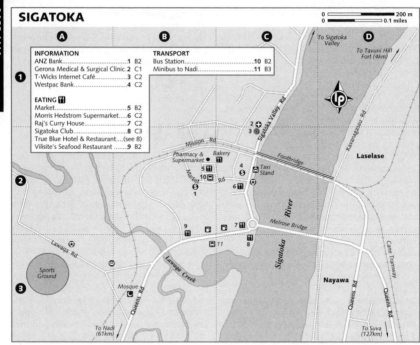

SIGATOKA

0 — 200 m
0 — 0.1 miles

INFORMATION
ANZ Bank...............................1 B2
Gerona Medical & Surgical Clinic.2 C1
T-Wicks Internet Café..............3 C2
Westpac Bank........................4 C2

EATING 🍴
Market..................................5 B2
Morris Hedstrom Supermarket....6 C2
Raj's Curry House...................7 C2
Sigatoka Club........................8 C3
True Blue Hotel & Restaurant....(see 8)
Vilisite's Seafood Restaurant 9 B2

TRANSPORT
Bus Station..........................10 B2
Minibus to Nadi.....................11 B3

To Sigatoka Valley

To Tavuni Hill Fort (4km)

Laselase

Nayawa

Sports Ground

Mosque

To Nadi (61km)

To Suva (127km)

the eastern edge of town – if you find your enthusiasm for souvenirs exhausted, stroll across the smaller of the two bridges (the one damaged in a 1994 hurricane) to see if you can spot the shark god, Dakuwaqa, swimming in the murky waters beneath.

Sigatoka's major draws – the sand dunes (opposite), surfing (opposite) and the Tavuni Hill Fort (p103) are all a few kilometres out of town, but easily reached by a short taxi ride.

Information

Westpac and ANZ have banks in town.
Gerona Medical & Surgical Clinic (☎ 652 0128; Sigatoka Valley Rd; ☽ 8.30am-1pm, 2-4pm, 7-8pm Mon-Fri, 8.30am-1pm Sat)
T-Wicks Internet Café (☎ 652 0505; 50 Sigatoka Valley Rd; per hr $12) There's cheaper ($3.50 per hour) dial-up connections on the machines out back; CDs and DVDs can be burnt here for $7.50 and $10 respectively.

Tours

Adventures in Paradise (☎ 652 0833; www.adventuresinparadisefiji.com; tours per person incl Coral Coast/Nadi hotel transfers $99/119, child 5-12yr half-price) Offers day trips to the Naihehe Cave (p103) on Tuesdays, Thursdays

and Saturdays. Lunch and a *bilibili* (bamboo raft) ride downstream are included – children love it. The Savu Na Mate Laya Waterfall tour leaves Mondays, Wednesdays and Fridays and involves nonstrenuous walking to a waterfall-fed swimming hole.
Sigatoka River Safari (☎ 650 1721; www.sigatokariver.com; jet-boat tours per person incl Coral Coast/Nadi hotel transfers $195/215, child 4-15yr $89) The half-day jet-boating trips include a 45km whirl up the Sigatoka River, a village visit and lunch.

Sleeping & Eating

Sigatoka doesn't offer any outstanding accommodation or dining options. You're better off heading to nearby Korotogo (p104).

True Blue Hotel & Restaurant (☎ 650 1530; Sigatoka Club Bldg, Queens Rd; dm $20, s/d $35/45, mains $8-24; ☽ lunch & dinner; ⊠ 🐾) The draw here is the elevated position and lovely views from the cavernous, dancehall-like restaurant up the mangrove-lined Sigatoka River. The food, however, is hit and miss – some of it's only a small step up in quality from that served in local fast-food joints. Be sure to ask for the menu as it's often considerably cheaper than the blackboard 'specials' shown to tourists. Unfortunately the rooms aren't much and many patrons choose only to stay for an hour.

Vilisite's Seafood Restaurant (☎ 653 0054; Queens Rd; mains $8-17; ☺ breakfast, lunch & dinner; ☒) Picture a tropicana restaurant from the late '70s with faded polyester *lei* and dusty bamboo ceilings and you'll have an idea of what to expect from this local favourite. There are Chinese and curry options on the menu but everyone recommends seafood followed by a rolled ice cream ($2) from the shack outside.

Raj's Curry House (☎ 650 1470; Queens Rd; mains $8-19; ☺ lunch & dinner) Under the glare of fluoro tubes in a windowless room, locals test their mettle here on a regular basis with curries that make your tastebuds dance. Vegetarians are well catered for and you can order takeouts from the lighter and brighter entrance next door.

Sigatoka Club (☎ 650 0026; mains $8-24; ☺ lunch & dinner) Downstairs from the True Blue Restaurant, this club is the best drinking-hole in town. Grab a seat in one of the waterfront booths or help prop up the horseshoe-shaped bar with the locals. The place is very informal. 'We don't get many visitors from the resorts,' we were told jokingly. 'But when we do, we expect 'em to wear shoes.'

Self-caterers can stock up at the market and the Morris Hedstrom supermarket.

Getting There & Around

In addition to a multitude of slower, local buses, Pacific Transport and Sunbeam Transport run several express buses a day between Nadi and Sigatoka ($4.50, 1¼ hours) and between Sigatoka and Suva ($8.50, three hours) via Pacific Harbour ($5.40, two hours).

Carriers, minibuses and taxis ply the same Queens Road route. Minibuses will take you to Nadi for $6, Suva for $11 or Pacific Harbour for $8; taxis cost $70 to Nadi, $120 to Suva or $90 to Pacific Harbour.

AROUND SIGATOKA
Sigatoka Sand Dunes

One of Fiji's natural highlights, these impressive **dunes** (adult/child/family $8/3/20, child under 6yr free; ☺ 8am-4.30pm) are a ripple of peppery monoliths skirting the shoreline near the mouth of the Sigatoka River. Wind blown and rugged, they stand 5km long, up to 1km wide and on average about 20m high, but rising to about 60m at the western end. Do not expect golden

Sahara-like dunes, as the fine sand is a greybrown colour and largely covered with vines and shrubs. The dunes have been forming over millions of years as sediments brought down by the Sigatoka River are washed ashore by the surf and blown into dunes by the prevailing winds. A mahogany forest was planted in the 1960s to halt the dunes' expedition onto the Queens Road and the state-owned part of the area was declared Fiji's first national park in 1989.

Since the coastal margin of the dunes is largely unstable, human bones and early pottery are sometimes exposed and in many cases destroyed by slipping slope faces and eroding winds. Archaeological excavations here have uncovered pottery more than 2600 years old and one of the largest burial sites in the Pacific. The **Sigatoka Sand Dunes visitor centre** (☎ 652 0243; ☺ 8am-4.30pm) houses a few pottery shards and ceramic pots from some of these excavations.

To access the national park, enter through the visitor centre at the western end of the dunes, 4.5km southwest of Sigatoka on the Queens Road. Take care to stick to the designated trails and allow one hour for the round-trip walking tour. Take plenty of water and sunscreen and if by chance you do come across a thighbone jutting from the sand, know that you'll be cursed forever if you attempt to remove it.

Most buses (excluding express) travelling between Nadi and Sigatoka can drop you right outside the visitors centre on the main highway. A taxi from Sigatoka town costs $3.

Kulukulu

Viti Levu's premier **surfing** spot and the country's only beach break can be found in the Kulukulu area between the Sigatoka Sand Dunes National Park and Maunivanua Point at the mouth of the Sigatoka River. Most other areas have fringing reefs but here the fresh water has prevented their formation and the waves break over a large, submerged rock platform covered in sand.

However, surfers should be aware that after heavy rains the murky water flowing from the river mouth can run at about 10 to 15 knots, creating strong currents and undertows as well as being laden with floating logs, coconuts and debris. On top of all that, the place is sharky and in 2006 a local surfer had his hand badly bitten while surfing here.

VITI LEVU

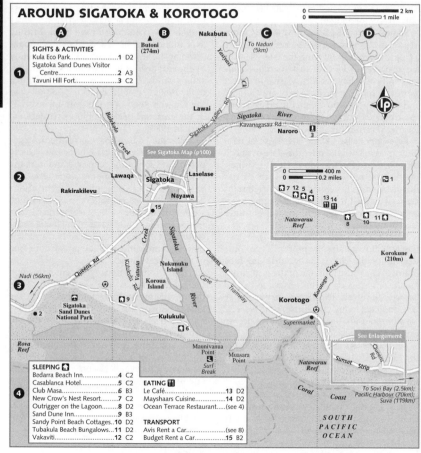

AROUND SIGATOKA & KOROTOGO

0 — 2 km
0 — 1 mile

SIGHTS & ACTIVITIES
Kula Eco Park.............................1 D2
Sigatoka Sand Dunes Visitor
  Centre...................................2 A3
Tavuni Hill Fort........................3 C2

Butoni
(274m)

Nakabuta

To Naduri
(5km)

Lawai

Sigatoka River
Kavanagasau Rd

Naroro

See Sigatoka Map (p100)

Lawaqa

Laselase

Sigatoka

Rakirakilevu

Nayawa

0 — 400 m
0 — 0.2 miles

Natawarau
Reef

Korokune
(210m)

Nadi (56km)

Queens Rd

Nukunuku
Island

Koroua
Island

Korotogo

Supermarket

Sigatoka
Sand Dunes
National Park

Kulukulu

Natawarau
Reef

Sunset Strip

Rova
Reef

Maunivanua
Point
Surf
Break

Muasara
Point

Coral
Coast

To Sovi Bay (2.5km);
Pacific Harbour (70km);
Suva (119km)

See Enlargement

SOUTH
PACIFIC
OCEAN

SLEEPING
Bedarra Beach Inn...................4 C2
Casablanca Hotel.....................5 C2
Club Masa.................................6 B3
New Crow's Nest Resort.........7 C2
Outrigger on the Lagoon........8 D2
Sand Dune Inn.........................9 B3
Sandy Point Beach Cottages..10 D2
Tubakula Beach Bungalows...11 D2
Vakaviti...................................12 C2

EATING
Le Café....................................13 D2
Mayshaars Cuisine.................14 D2
Ocean Terrace Restaurant.....(see 4)

TRANSPORT
Avis Rent a Car.......................(see 8)
Budget Rent a Car.................15 B2

There are two places to stay near the beach **Sand Dune Inn** (☎ 650 0550; dm $25, tent sites $10, meals $6) is closer to the road and **Club Masa** (dm $28) is a 1km walk further down the dirt road beyond the locked gate. Club Masa is under new management and slowly being improved after long years of neglect. Both places open and close erratically, are extremely basic and get mixed reviews. If you stay at either you'll probably have the place to yourself.

Sunbeam buses run between Sigatoka and Kulukulu (Monday to Saturday, eight daily, $0.75) and a taxi costs $6 to the locked gate.

Lower Sigatoka Valley

The Sigatoka River's tributaries originate as far away as Tomanivi (Mt Victoria) and the Monasavu Dam. The river has long provided a line of communication between mountain peoples and coast dwellers. Almost 200 archaeological, cultural or historically significant sites have been found in and around the valley, but many are being taken over by farms or housing.

This fertile river valley is known as Fiji's 'salad bowl'. Cereals, vegetables, fruits, peanuts and sugar cane are grown here, mostly on small-scale farms. Much of the produce ends up at the municipal markets, and vegetables such as eggplant, chilli, okra and root crops such as *dalo* (taro), *tavioka* (cassava) and yams are exported to Canada, Australia, New Zealand and the USA.

Two valley villages are known for their **pottery**: Lawai and Nakabuta. Both welcome visitors, who are charged $5 to look around. None of the pots is made using machines or even a potter's wheel. Instead, local sand and clay is mixed together using the heel of the foot and the somewhat uneven pots are then formed by hand. These are sun dried and fired in open fires, along with other small and saleable items like pottery pigs and *bure*.

Paradise Valley 'green valley' buses travel up the Sigatoka Valley on the western side of the river to Naduri, and pass Lawai and Nakabuta ($0.70, one every one to two hours). Lawai is about 2.5km north of Sigatoka. Nakabuta is twice as far ($5 by taxi or a 10-minute drive). On weekends services are less frequent.

It is possible to catch a morning bus to Keiyasi village (55km upriver) and back for around $5.50 (four hours return). Be aware that the afternoon buses overnight in Keiyasi, so check with the driver before departing.

Upper Sigatoka Valley

The **Naihehe cave** (Map pp76–7), about an hour's drive upriver from Sigatoka, was once used as an underground fortress by hill tribes and has the remains of a ritual platform and cannibal oven. The large cathedral-like chamber is quite impressive with its stalactites, flowstones and underground springs. Adventures in Paradise (p100) offers guided tours of the area.

Tavuni Hill Fort

Built in the 18th century by Tongan chief Maile Latumai, this **fort** (Map p102; adult/child $12/6; 🕑 8am-5pm Mon-Fri, 8.30am-1.30pm Sat) was a defensive site used in times of war and is one of Fiji's most interesting historical sights. It provides an excellent insight into the strong precolonial links between Tonga and Fiji and although there are many like it scattered all over Fiji, this is the most accessible for visitors. The information centre here was set up in a combined effort between the Ministry of Tourism and the people of Naroro, and received funding from the EU. Unfortunately the local villagers, whose ancestors once lived in the fort, have grown increasingly divided on how the money is best spent.

CANNIBALISM

Archaeological evidence from food-waste middens shows that cannibalism was practised in Viti Levu from 2500 years ago until the mid- to late 19th century, during which time it had become an ordinary, ritualised part of life. In a society founded on ancestor worship and belief in the afterlife, cannibalising an enemy was considered the ultimate revenge. A disrespectful death was a lasting insult to the enemy's family.

Bodies were either consumed on the battlefield or brought back to the village spirit house and offered to the local war god, then butchered, baked and eaten on the god's behalf. The triumph was celebrated with music and dance. Men performed the *cibi* (death dance) and women the *dele* or *wate* (an obscene dance in which they sexually humiliated corpses and captives). Torture included being thrown alive into ovens, being bled or dismembered, being forced to watch their own body parts being consumed or eat some themselves!

Mementoes of the kill were kept to prolong the victor's sense of vengeance. Necklaces, hairpins or ear-lobe ornaments were made from human bones, and the skull of a hated enemy was sometimes made into a *tanoa* (*kava* drinking bowl). Meat was smoked and preserved for snacks, and war clubs were inlaid with teeth or marked with tally notches. To record a triumph in war, the highlanders of Viti Levu placed the bones of victims in branches of trees outside their spirit houses and men's houses, as trophies. The coastal dwellers had a practical use for the bones: leg bones were used to make sail needles and thatching knives. Sexual organs and foetuses were suspended in trees. Rows of stones were also used to tally the number of bodies eaten by the chief.

The growing influence of Christianity had a great impact on cannibalism and the practice began to wane in the mid-1800s. By all accounts, it had ended by the turn of the century. Western fascination with the gruesome practice has remained alive and well, however, and souvenir cannibal forks are sold in abundant quantities. Traditionally, chiefs used these because it was forbidden for human flesh to touch their lips. Considered sacred relics, these forks were kept in the spirit house and were not to be touched by women or children. Today, it would appear, they make interesting wall features.

The eldest son of a king, Maile Latumai fled Tonga to escape a dispute during an era of political and social upheaval. He and his entourage of servants sailed all the way in a double-hulled canoe and arrived in the Sigatoka area in about 1788. They originally set up in Korotogo (originally Koro-Tonga or 'village/gathering of Tonga') but were kept on the move by constant tribal warfare. Eventually the local tribes accepted the newcomers, and the chief was given some land and a local wife.

The steep limestone ridge, about 90m high, at the edge of a bend in the Sigatoka River was an obvious strategic location for a fortification. From this position the surrounding area could easily be surveyed, both upstream and downstream, and the views are spectacular. Substantial earthworks were carried out to form *yavu* (bases for houses) and terraces for barricade fencing. There are also a number of grave sites, a *rara* (ceremonial ground) and a *vatu ni bokola* (head-chopping stone), as well as some beautiful curtain figs and an *ivi* (Polynesian chestnut tree), on the site.

The fort is about 4km northeast of Sigatoka on the eastern side of the river, above Naroro village. The local buses that pass Tavuni Hill ($0.75) leave Sigatoka bus station and travel along Kavanagasau Rd heading for Mavua seven times a day on weekdays. Besides the bus station, a good place to catch these buses is at the eastern end of the main bridge in Sigatoka. It is possible to walk to the fort by following either the cane railway or road for about an hour. A taxi is $8 one way but the drivers ask tourists for more.

KOROTOGO & AROUND

The start of the Coral Coast begins in earnest at this condensed group of hotels flanking the water. Korotogo itself is a small village, but travellers will find themselves outside of its confines. Korotogo is the best area to lodge when exploring the sights around Sigatoka.

Sights & Activities
KULA ECO PARK

This **wildlife sanctuary** (Map p102; ☎ 650 0505; www.fijiwild.com; adult/child $20/10; ☒ 10am-4.30pm) is a must for fans of the furred, feathered and scaled. Supported by the National Trust for Fiji and several international parks and conservation bodies, the park showcases some magnificent wildlife, including hawksbill sea turtles (hand-fed at 11am, 1pm and 3.30pm daily); Fiji's only native land mammal, the Fijian flying fox; and an aviary full of quarrelsome kula parrots, Fiji's national bird and the park's namesake (look out for the sole dark mutation!).

The park has come a long way since 1997, when most of the birds here were either dead or dying and today it runs invaluable breeding programs, with success stories for the Pacific black duck (Fiji's only remaining duck species) and the crested and banded iguana. Guided ($25) and behind-the-scenes ($35) tours are also available, the latter including a visit to the park's incubation centre and the room housing the biological filtration system, which allows the aquarium to support living coral.

Ambling down the wooden walkway, poking in and out of the aviaries and reading the labels on the indigenous flora is a lot of fun and since the park is 80% funded by gate receipts, it's great to know that your money is well spent. The park also has great wheelchair access.

Sleeping
BUDGET

Vakaviti (Map p102; ☎ 650 0526; www.vakaviti.com; Sunset Strip; dm $20, r $100-150; ☒) Tumbling down a steep and densely vegetated embankment, Vakaviti is a bit of a mixed bag. The small, clean dormitory is quite dark and the bathroom has only cold water, whereas the split-level motel rooms are far nicer and overlook the pool. Down on the flat there are some comfortable *bure*, ideal for families as children under 12 stay free. All rooms have kitchenettes.

Tubakula Beach Bungalows (Map p102; ☎ 650 0097; www.fiji4less.com/tuba.html; dm $26, s/tw $58/63, ste $115-164; ☒ ☒) If it weren't for the palm trees, swimming pool and waterfront setting, this low-key resort would be right at home in the mountains. Simple dorms, singles and twins have shared facilities, and the excellent A-frame chalets have strapping timber frames, modern kitchens, and verandahs with slouchy wooden seats. It's perfect for self-driving, self-catering, self-sufficient types wishing to escape the crowds. It's right on the beach, there are nightly movies and free snorkel equipment, and the restaurant is excellent value (mains $8 to $15, open for breakfast and dinner).

Casablanca Hotel (Map p102; ☎ 652 0600; Casablanca@connect.com.fj; Sunset Strip; s/d $50/65; ☒) This mock-Moroccan mansion offers eight self-contained rooms that are cheap and cheerful but look like they were decorated with furniture picked up at a garage sale. The four rooms on the 2nd floor have fantastic views.

Sandy Point Beach Cottages (Map p102; ☎ 650 0125; cbcom@connect.com.fj; s/d/tr/f $90/110/110/160; 🖳) Five beachside cottages built in the style of roomy Kiwi *baches* (holiday homes) from the '70s.

MIDRANGE

New Crow's Nest Resort (Map p102; ☎ 650 0230; www .crowsnestfiji.com; Sunset Strip; r $135-145; 🗶 🗶 🖳 🖳) Perched on the hillside like a...er...crow, these split-level timber bungalows have lovely balconies and ocean views and, having undergone a recent facelift, are good value. The slightly more expensive rooms are self-contained, but all can accommodate a family of four (kids stay free). The restaurant (mains $15 to $25) faces the hillside pool and has a cosmopolitan menu.

Bedarra Beach Inn (Map p102; ☎ 650 0476; www .bedarrafiji.com; Sunset Strip; r incl breakfast $167-180; 🗶 🖳) This place is a gem. It offers spacious, spotlessly clean rooms with tiled floors and plenty of natural light, genuinely friendly staff and just the right mix between resort-style comfort and do-it-yourself practicality. Everyone who stays here seems to rave about it and most of the clientele are returning Australians. The new bar is uniquely designed so that social types can face each other as they sip cocktails.

TOP END

Outrigger on the Lagoon (Map p102; ☎ 650 0044; www .outrigger.com/fiji; r from $567; 🗶 🗶 🖳 🖳) The 7m outrigger canoe suspended from the ceiling in the main lobby and the stunning balcony views create a powerful impression of this much-touted resort. From the main building, an artificial stream meanders through lush gardens to a huge, lagoon-style pool, but as this is the only pool, it can get noisy with excited kids, and the pool loungers are in hot demand. The *bure* (from $990), with their high, hand-painted *masi* ceilings are fabulous, as is the day spa with its superb hilltop location. There's an okay kids club and children eat for free – depending on which package you have. All in all, the Outrigger is stylish, although we don't know if it truly deserves its five-star rating – the gym is dated and, even by resort standards, the food pricey ($49 for steak). Not to be missed, however, is the Fijian fire-walking show (per person $18) every Tuesday night (nonguests welcome). Dive Away Fiji (p106) runs the dive shop here.

Eating

Mayshaars Cuisine (Johnny's, Beachside Restaurant, Ice Bar; ☎ 652 0584; Sunset Strip; mains $8-15; 🕑 breakfast, lunch & dinner) This place may have changed its name more times than its cooking oil, but the food here is still pretty good. Diners take their seats on picnic tables in front of a small supermarket and, while the setting is utterly unsophisticated, most people are pleasantly surprised by the tasty meals. As for the menu, you name it, they've got it – Chinese, Fijian, Italian and Western.

Le Café (☎ 652 0877; Sunset Strip; mains $10-20; 🕑 breakfast, lunch & dinner) Just west of the shops, Le Café has a Swiss chef who cooks European-style food – tasty pizzas are the speciality. There's also a daily happy hour from 5pm to 7pm.

Ocean Terrace Restaurant (☎ 650 0476; Bedarra Beach Inn; mains $20-30; 🕑 lunch & dinner) Slightly pricier than its neighbours, but serving the best food in the area, this hotel restaurant often lures guests from the Outrigger. As the name suggests, you get a pleasant view from the terrace, out over the pool to the reef. It's a great place to try some creative Fijian fusion dishes like *ika vakalolo* (fish poached in coconut milk) served with cassava, but for the less adventurous there's steak, pizza and curries. A children's menu is also available.

Getting There & Around

Pacific Transport and Sunbeam Transport run regular buses along the Queens Road, stopping at resorts along the way (about $5 from Nadi, 1½ hours). Coral Sun Fiji has air-conditioned coaches that also stop outside resorts ($12 from Nadi, 1½ hours). The cheapest way from Korotogo to Sigatoka is to walk to the roundabout and catch a local bus for $1. A taxi to Sigatoka is $6, and around $70 to Nadi.

KOROLEVU & AROUND

Further east, the section of the Queens Road between Korotogo and Korolevu is the most beautiful. The road winds along the shore, with scenic bays, beaches, coral reefs and mountains; photo opportunities beg around every bend. It's an especially spectacular trip at sunrise or sunset. A good range of

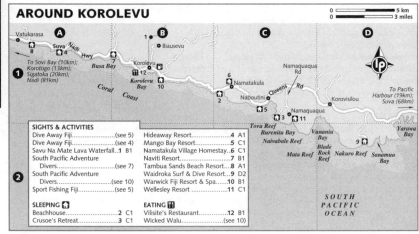

AROUND KOROLEVU

0 ————— 5 km
0 ————— 3 miles

SIGHTS & ACTIVITIES
Dive Away Fiji.........................(see 5)
Dive Away Fiji.........................(see 4)
Savu Na Mate Lava Waterfall..**1** B1
South Pacific Adventure
  Divers.................................(see 7)
South Pacific Adventure
  Divers................................(see 10)
Sport Fishing Fiji....................(see 5)

Hideaway Resort.....................**4** A1
Mango Bay Resort....................**5** C1
Namatakula Village Homestay..**6** C1
Naviti Resort...........................**7** B1
Tambua Sands Beach Resort...**8** A1
Waidroka Surf & Dive Resort...**9** D2
Warwick Fiji Resort & Spa.......**10** B1
Wellesley Resort **11** C1

SLEEPING
Beachhouse...........................**2** C1
Crusoe's Retreat.....................**3** C1

EATING
Vilisite's Restaurant...............**12** B1
Wicked Walu.........................(see 10)

SOUTH
PACIFIC
OCEAN

accommodation peppers the coast, each pocketed within its own private cove.

East of Korolevu, the Queens Road turns away from the shore and climbs over the southern end of Viti Levu's dividing mountain range. To the east of this range the road improves and the scenery changes to lush rainforest as the road winds its way past wider bays.

Activities

Besides slumming it at the beach, the most popular activity is **snorkelling** and resorts ferry guests to and from the outer reefs daily for close encounters of the marine kind.

This area is well served by the tour companies at Sigatoka (p100) and Pacific Harbour (p110), which all pick up from the hotels. There is a small waterfall, the Savu Na Mate Lava, 2.5km inland from the turn-off to **Biausevu** village, which is a 15-minute drive east of Hideaway Resort. The waterfall is an easy 15- to 30-minute walk from the village, but be sure to read about village etiquette (p42) before arriving.

Based at Mango Bay Resort, **Sport Fishing Fiji** (Tropical Fishing; ☎ 653 0069; www.sportfishing fiji.com) runs three-quarter–day ($900) and full-day ($1200) game-fishing charters on an 8.5m boat. The boat can accommodate five anglers at a time and drinks, lunch and all equipment are provided. Danny and his crew won the Fiji 2004 International Game Fishing Championship and know these waters well.

DIVING

The Korolevu stretch of coast offers some spectacular diving within close distance to the shore. Some notable sites include Wonderwall, with its 'snowdrift' of white soft corals, and, for the experienced, the Gunbarrel, which is an adrenalin-laced dive riding a strong current through a narrow gorge amid schools of snapper and surgeon fish.

Dive Away Fiji (☎ 650 1124; www.diveaway-fiji.com) Runs the dive shops at the Beachhouse and the Outrigger, Hideaway and Mango Bay Resorts. Most guests are ferried to Hideaway or Mango Bay from where the dive boats depart. A two-tank dive costs $180 and PADI Open Water Course $725 at the upmarket resorts, but guests at Mango Bay, Hideaway and the Beachhouse get the same thing cheaper.

South Pacific Adventure Divers (☎ 653 0555 ext 609; www.spadfiji.com) Dive operators for the Warwick and Naviti resorts but, like Dive Away, they'll collect from other nearby hotels. A two-tank dive costs $190 and PADI Open Water Course $680. To travel as far afield as Beqa Lagoon costs an extra $35.

Sleeping
BUDGET & MIDRANGE

Beachhouse (☎ 653 0500; www.fijibeachouse.com; sites per person/dm/d incl breakfast $23/30/93;) Aimed squarely at backpackers, this long-time favourite combines simple digs with heady social activities in a winning formula. The dorms (including a women-only dorm) are in two-storey houses and the doubles are in colourful duplex bungalows. All facilities are shared. A big advantage here is that buses will stop right outside, and there's a pretty pool, a cheap cafe and on-site cooking facilities. Activities include horse riding ($20 per hour) and a recommended 'jungle trek' to a waterfall ($8), for which sandals are a must.

our pick Mango Bay Resort (☎ 653 0069; www .mangobayresortfiji.com; dm incl breakfast $36-45, d incl breakfast $90-270, 4-person luxury tents incl breakfast $189; ✕ ▣ ☙) The dorm, safari tents, lodges and *bure* are scattered through parklike grounds, which seem to attract a disproportionally large number of frogs (watch for them at night – you'll feel bad when you squish one underfoot, like we did). Facilities are far better than those found in your average backpackers and the restaurant is excellent. The dorms are modern and new, the *bure* have atrium showers and the beach is one of the best on the Coral Coast. Mango targets the 18- to 35-year-old set with plenty of activities of the full moon–party and sunset-bonfire variety. Snorkelling and diving are with Dive Away Fiji, and game fishing can be arranged through Sport Fishing Fiji (opposite). Many of the Feejee Experience crowd brought here opt to stay an additional night or two. Wise people.

Namatakula Village Homestay (www.fijibure.com/ namatakula/index.htm; per adult/child incl meals $70/35) This village homestay is popular with Intrepid Travel groups and with good reason – it's the real deal, so expect basic accommodation, large meals and an excellent opportunity to see a traditional Fijian village first hand.

our pick Tambua Sands Beach Resort (☎ 650 0399; www.tambuasandsfiji.com; d $130-170; ☙) Smeared across a pretty slice of coast, this friendly resort will suit intrepid travellers looking to indulge. The *bure* have large, shuttered windows, and are consequently light and bright. If occupancy levels are high enough, there are nightly cultural activities and a live band. Village tours, reef-walking excursions and the tour desk keep guests busy and the manicured lawns are littered with enough sun loungers to keep a herd of sloths happy. For the best snorkelling, ask to be taken to the channel, but be mindful of the powerful currents that run there. The restaurant (mains $15 to $34) has great palm-framed views and a good à la carte menu. Children stay free.

Waidroka Surf & Dive Resort (☎ 330 4605; www .waidroka.com; dm incl meal package $195, d incl breakfast $240-295, ste incl breakfast $250; ▣ ☙) Over a hilly dirt road, Waidroka caters to serious surfers and divers looking for an upmarket alterna-

tive to the Yanuca island surf camps. There's a small flotilla of boats on hand to take guests to local breaks ($45, nonguests $55) and Frigate Passage (p113; $85, nonguests $95). Boris is exceptionally skilled at finding the best waves and runs the only dive operation to Frigate Walls (p109; a two-tank dive costs $170 to $195 and PADI Open Water Course $750). Surf and dive 'widows' are also well catered for with free snorkelling and kayaking, game fishing ($250 to $1250), shopping trips, beachside massages and an excellent restaurant (meal packages $65). Guests stay in either bright orange *bure* or the adjoining terrace rooms. Both are very smart. Taxis from Nadi cost $140 but it is cheaper if you take a bus to Korovisilou village and ask to be collected from there ($18 per car).

TOP END

Wellesley Resort (☎ in Fiji 603 0664, New Zealand booking office 04 474 1308; www.wellesleyresort.com.fj; Man Friday Rd; d incl breakfast & Nadi transfers $189-399; ✕ ⛱ ▣ ☙) Oozing comfort, style and tranquillity, this boutique resort is ideal for couples seeking a romantic retreat or as a venue for an intimate wedding. The 15 suites saddle a small valley that leads to a pretty cove and even the most ardent adrenalin junkie will soon rediscover their inner sloth. If they don't, they may find this place a little too isolated (even though tours are available) as it's 4.5km down a dirt road.

Crusoe's Retreat (☎ 650 0185; www.crusoesretreat .com; r incl breakfast $240-370; ▣ ☙) Crusoe's may lack the polish of the larger resorts, but its sublime location – hidden by lush hills and boasting a white coral beach – makes up for that. Its isolation is enhanced by the fact that there are no TVs, radios or newspapers available. Many of the 28 spacious and fan-cooled *bure* are located on a hillside and the stairs are not ideal for older guests. The pool is small but the restaurant (mains $15 to $25) serves classy fare. Dive Crusoes (www.divecrusoes. com) charges $246 for a two-tank dive and $784 for a PADI Open Water Course. Hotel transfers from Nadi airport are $130 per person return. A taxi is around $150 or $15 if you take a bus to the Warwick first.

Naviti Resort (☎ 653 0444; www.navitiresort.com .fj; r incl breakfast/all-inclusive $299/508, ste incl breakfast/ all-inclusive $522/615; ✕ ⛱ ▣ ☙) Heavy on the greenery and light on the concrete, the colossal Naviti has all the goodies – four restaurants, five bars, a nine-hole golf course, a swim-up bar, a health spa and a kids club. Unlike other resorts, the all-inclusive package includes beer, wine, Sigatoka shopping excursions, a sunset cruise and a choice between à la carte or buffet dining (although the food is only average at both). The two tiny islands offshore are used for weddings and, coral be damned, they are dredging themselves an all-tide-swimming lagoon to compensate for the poor beach.

Hideaway Resort (☎ 650 0177; www.hideawayfiji.com; d & tr $345-463, f $550; ☒ ☒ ☐ ☒) Since many of the neighbouring resorts have undergone recent renovations, the Hideaway looks a little tired by comparison and unless a package deal can offer substantial discounts on the rack rate listed here, you may be better off elsewhere. Nonetheless, the water slide, kids club and cruise-ship-like entertainment prove popular with families. The manicured grounds include artificial sand alcoves and plenty of grassy sun-baking plots. Guests wear coloured wristbands that denote their package entitlements and the tiled restaurant is very noisy at meal times. Dive Away Fiji (p106) is based here.

Warwick Fiji Resort & Spa (☎ 653 0555; www.warwickfiji.com; s & d incl breakfast $350-550, ste incl breakfast $740; ☒ ☒ ☐ ☒) Owned by the same crowd that own Naviti (there's a free shuttle between the two and guests can use each other's facilities), the Warwick is another feature-laden, activity-rich resort. The trendy rooms feature wooden floors, cane furniture and soft brown furnishings. There are five restaurants, seven bars (one of which has Middle Eastern water-pipes) and lagoons with all-tide swimming areas. As you would expect, most of the nonmotorised water sports are free, but the Warwick does charge to use its gym ($10) and kids club ($5 per day). South Pacific Adventure Divers is based here and at Naviti resort.

Eating

Vilisite's Restaurant (☎ 650 1030; Queens Rd; mains $12-38; ☯ breakfast, lunch & dinner) If you have a Hawaiian shirt you'll feel right at home, as this place drips tropical garb. With its sweeping ocean views, it's the nicest restaurant in the area outside of the flashy resorts. There's Chinese, seafood curries and lobster on offer, although everyone seems to order the fish and chips.

The three major resorts here – the Warwick, Naviti and the Hideaway – all have multiple restaurants and bars catering to different budgets and are welcoming to nonguests. The pricey Wicked Walu at the Warwick (try saying that after a few beers) has particularly good steak and seafood (mains $30 to $50) and a prominent setting on its own island. However, it's only open for dinner and reservations are required.

Entertainment

The Warwick has fire-walking on Mondays and Fridays ($15) and Polynesian dancing on Tuesdays ($45 with beach barbecue). The same fire-walkers also perform at Naviti on Wednesdays ($15) and at the Hideaway on Thursdays (also $15). The **nightclub** (nonguests $10; ☯ Wed-Sat until 1am) at the Warwick has a DJ who plays mostly soul and house rhythm.

Getting There & Around

There are plenty of buses shuttling along the Queens Road (getting to Suva or Nadi costs about $7) and drivers will pick up and drop off at resort gates. The Warwick and the Naviti have a free shuttle bus for guests to Nadi International Airport. A taxi to Sigatoka takes two minutes and costs around $10.

PACIFIC HARBOUR

Leaving the glorious vegetation and hilly passes of Korolevu in its wake, Queens Road sweeps across a small bridge into Pacific Harbour, the self-labelled 'Adventure Capital of Fiji'. A range of unique activities, guaranteed to have hearts racing and knees knocking, backs up the claim.

Pacific Harbour began in the 1970s as a canal development and once the surrounding swamps were drained roads were laid, waterways formed and holiday homes built. The resulting maze of culs-de-sac, manicured lawns and orderly river settings are more 'soccer mum and bridge parties' than anything Fijian, and although the large grassy blocks are brochure-perfect, many are still waiting to be filled by the anticipated boom. It is so at odds with the rest of Fiji that you may feel you've crossed some unseen line and dipped your toes into the Twilight Zone.

Information

Attached to the Arts Village is the Arts Village Marketplace, an open-air shopping mall of mock-colonial eateries, an ANZ Bank (with ATM), a supermarket and several souvenir shops selling Fiji-style resort wear and some good but pricey handicrafts. **Rosie's Tours** (☎ 345 0655) has a tour desk and can book all of the activities within the area. Internet can be found at the Water's Edge restaurant for $5 an hour.

Sights & Activities

ARTS VILLAGE

This faux **village** (☎ 345 0065; www.artsvillage.com; tours per adult/child from $55/28; 🕑 9am-4pm Mon-Sat) is unashamedly 'Fiji in a theme park' and within its Disneylike confines are a temple, chiefly *bure*, cooking area with utensils and weaving hut. Fijian actors dressed in traditional costumes carry out mock battles, preach pagan religion and demonstrate traditional arts. Tours include an Island Boat Tour (for the kids), Island Temple Tour and Arts Village Show. The fire-walking and *meke* (a dance performance that enacts stories and legends) show every Tuesday, Thursday and Saturday at 10.45am ($75 per adult and $37 per child) is the best and includes a *lovo* feast. It's good fun for families, but a far cry from authentic village life.

DIVING

There are more than 20 dive sites near Pacific Harbour, mostly within **Beqa Lagoon**, but the main attraction here are the sharks – and we're not talking wimpy white-tips. Beqa Lagoon is one of the few places where it's possible to dive with massive, barrel-chested bull and tiger sharks without being caged (or sedated).

Other impressive dives include **Side Streets** (soft corals, coral heads and gorgonian fans) **Frigate Walls** (a 48m wall in Frigate Pass, with large pelagic fish) and **Caesar's Rocks** (coral heads and swim-throughs). See p68 and the boxed text, p69, for further details about these dives.

The companies listed here run the shark dives; for an extra $50 you can relive the frenzy with a DVD of 'the feeding'. The prices quoted include equipment and the marine park entrance fees.

Aqua-Trek Beqa (☎ 345 0324; www.aquatrek.com; Pearl South Pacific) A two-tank dive costs $170, two-tank shark-feeding dive $200 and PADI Open Water Course $700. The shark-feeding dives are available Mondays, Wednesdays, Fridays and Saturdays.

ourpick **Beqa Adventure Divers** (☎ 345 0911; www .fiji-sharks.com; Lagoon Resort) Has shark-feeding dives on Mondays, Tuesdays, Thursdays and Saturdays. The dive masters here are very professional and knowledgable about the sharks in these waters. A two-tank dive costs $190, two-tank shark-feeding dive $230 and PADI Open Water Course $650.

SURFING & SWIMMING

There is world-class surfing at Frigate Passage (p113) but it's easiest accessed from the surf camps on Yanuca island (p114) or through Waidroka Surf & Dive Resort (p107).

Pacific Harbour's main beach, **Deuba Beach**, is reasonable for swimming, although no match for the islands. The snorkelling 500m out from Uprising Beach Resort is surprisingly good.

SOME LIKE IT HOT

Of all Fiji's cultural rituals, the extraordinary art of fire-walking is perhaps the most impressive. Watching men display the poise of a lead ballerina while they traverse a pit of blazing embers without combusting is truly baffling. Even more mystifying is the fact that, originally, this ritual was practised in Fiji only on the tiny island of Beqa. Indigenous Fijian fire-walking is known as *vilavilairevo* (literally 'jumping into the oven'). The ability to walk barefoot on white-hot stones without being burned was, according to local legend, granted to a local chief by the leader of the *veli*, a group of little gods. Now the direct descendants of the chief *(tui qalita)* serve as the *bete* (priests) who instruct in the ritual of fire-walking.

Preparations for fire-walking used to occupy a whole village for nearly a month. Firewood and appropriate stones had to be selected, costumes made and various ceremonies performed. Fire-walkers had to abstain from sex and refrain from eating any coconut for up to a month before the ritual. None of the fire-walkers' wives could be pregnant, or it was believed the whole group would receive burns.

Traditionally, *vilavilairevo* was only performed on special occasions in the village of Navakaisese. Today, though, it's performed only for commercial purposes and has little religious meaning. There are regular performances at the Pacific Harbour Arts Village (above), at the larger resort hotels and at Suva's annual Hibiscus Festival.

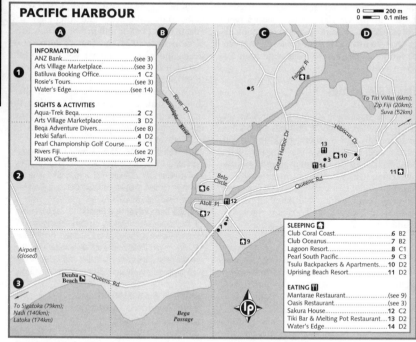

PACIFIC HARBOUR

VITI LEVU

INFORMATION	
ANZ Bank	(see 3)
Arts Village Marketplace	(see 3)
Batiluva Booking Office	1 C2
Rosie's Tours	(see 3)
Water's Edge	(see 14)

SIGHTS & ACTIVITIES	
Aqua-Trek Beqa	2 C2
Arts Village Marketplace	3 D2
Beqa Adventure Divers	(see 8)
Jetski Safari	4 D2
Pearl Championship Golf Course	5 C1
Rivers Fiji	(see 2)
Xtasea Charters	(see 7)

SLEEPING	
Club Coral Coast	6 B2
Club Oceanus	7 B2
Lagoon Resort	8 C1
Pearl South Pacific	9 C3
Tsulu Backpackers & Apartments	10 D2
Uprising Beach Resort	11 D2

EATING	
Mantarae Restaurant	(see 9)
Oasis Restaurant	(see 3)
Sakura House	12 C2
Tiki Bar & Melting Pot Restaurant	13 D2
Water's Edge	14 D2

FISHING

Pacific Harbour reefs, shoals, bait schools, current lines and drop-offs are ideal for both trolling and popping. Wahu, mahi mahi, marlin and yellow fin tuna are all regularly caught.

Xtasea Charters (☎ 345 0280; www.xtaseacharters .com; 1 Atoll Pl) caters to serious fishos on the 12m game boat, MV *Wai Tadra*. A half-day's reef fishing costs $1500 and full-day game fishing $2500. These rates are for the vessel, which accommodates up to eight anglers, and includes all fishing gear and tackle but not lunch ($50).

Sport Fishing Fiji (p106) and Waidroka Surf & Dive Resort (p107) also fish these waters.

GOLF

Even though the **Pearl Championship Golf Course** (☎ 345 0905; 18 holes with/without club hire $71/47, 9 holes with/without club hire $42/24) has more sand bunkers than some beaches, the main reason it's challenging is that in 2004, during a change of ownership, it was left unmaintained for four months. It's still recovering; but don't fret – for those who get hot (and bothered) there's a swimming pool and clubhouse

(mains $12 to $25, open for lunch only) to soothe frayed nerves.

ZIPLINE

Zip Fiji (Map pp76-7; ☎ 930 0545; www.zip-fiji .com; ☽ 8am-8pm) lets squealing thrill-seekers whoosh from one platform to another in a series of eight aerial ziplines. The rainforest canopy tour costs $120 per adult and $60 per child but, as it's in a jungle setting 20km from Pacific Harbour, you'll need to factor in another $20 per person for return transfers.

Tours

Rivers Fiji (☎ 345 0147; www.riversfiji.com; Pearl South Pacific) offers excellent kayaking and whitewater rafting trips into the Namosi Highlands (p113) north of Pacific Harbour. The day trip ($205 per person, including lunch) to Wainikoroiluva (Luva Gorge) is highly recommended and the scenery alone is worth the two-hour bumpy carrier trip up to Nakavika village. After the obligatory *kava* session with the chief, you paddle downstream (four hours) by inflatable kayak over stretches of gentle rapids and past waterfalls to Namuamua village. Here, where the 'Luva River joins the Upper Navua, the tour is completed with a motorised longboat ride.

For spectacular gorges and grade-two rapids, try the day trip to the Upper Navua River ($275 per person). It is more physically demanding and involves seven hours on the water. The one-hour road trip to Nabukelevu village is very scenic.

Jetski Safari (☎ 345 0933; www.jetski-safari.com; 158 Kaka Pl) takes travellers on a four-hour, full-throttle, 60km jet-ski tour (solo rider $400, twin share $215 per person) around Beqa Lagoon. Lunch, snorkelling gear, wetsuits and life jackets are included. Book at least a day in advance.

Based just out of town in Navua, but also working the Pacific Harbour hotels, is Discover Fiji Tours (p112), which offers tours into the Navua River area.

Sleeping

BUDGET & MIDRANGE

Club Oceanus (☎ 345 0498; info@cluboceanus.com; 1 Atoll Pl; dm/d/f $25/85/120; ✗ ☷ ⚉) This riverside resort has 10 recently painted, self-contained flats in a long, compact block. It's good value, located in a convenient spot on the canal and plans are well underway to open a cafe.

Tsulu Backpackers & Apartments (☎ 345 0065; www.tsulu.com; dm $30-34, d $150, 1-/2-/3-bed apt $160/210/485; ☷ ▦ ⚉) This place is the kind of psychedelic trip that would give Austin Powers a hard-on. Attached to the Arts Village, the Tsulu has picked up the artistic gauntlet and really, and we mean really, run with it. The walls (and in some cases the ceilings) of the dorms, double rooms and self-contained apartments are painted in vibrant murals. One room is bright blue with life-size fish, coral gardens and a snorkeller painted on the ceiling above. Does it make you horny baby? Who knows.

OUR PICK **Uprising Beach Resort** (☎ 345 2200; www.uprisingbeachresort.com; dm incl breakfast $35, d incl breakfast $160-180; ▦ ⚉) The Uprising is the new kid in town and already it's got quite the reputation. The 12 spacious *bure* have nifty outdoor showers (although the novelty of these wears thin if it rains) and bifolding doors to catch the ocean breeze. The 'treehouse' dorm is spotlessly clean and although it isn't in a tree, it does afford beautiful views from the verandah. The restaurant (mains $14 to $24) serves mainly Tex-Mex cuisine and even if the bar

is not quite the hot spot it claims to be, there are enough barflies buzzing around to give it a cheery vibe. Horse riding (4km, $20), wakeboarding ($60, 15 minutes) and snorkelling trips to Beqa Lagoon ($55) can all be booked at reception, which also has free internet.

Club Coral Coast (☎ 345 0421; clubcoralcoast@connect .com.fj; Lot 12 Belo Circle; d with bathroom $90-120, d without bathroom $40; ⚉) Occupying its own bend in the river, Club Coral Coast has seven rooms with kitchenettes and baths, in two blocks as well as an on-site pool and tennis court.

TOP END

Lagoon Resort (☎ 345 0100; www.lagoonresort.com; Fairway Pl; r $170-295, ste $325; ✗ ☷ ⚉) This grandiose colonial hotel was built in the '80s as a bordello for wealthy Arabs and then painted pink by Korean owners in 1995, before being sold to the present owners in 1999 (it's now, thankfully, a pristine white). Since then it has hosted South Pacific leaders and the cast of *Anaconda 2*. As you might imagine, there's plenty to talk about and the staff and management are extremely friendly. On Wednesdays, the tables are pushed together so that the men can swap seats with every course served (the three-course meal is $30), although they are encouraged to go home with the person they came with.

OUR PICK **Pearl South Pacific** (☎ 345 0022; www .thepearlsouthpacific.com; Queens Rd; r $248-314, ste $582-666; ✗ ☷ ▦ ⚉) Revamped and reworked with industrial-strength Botox, this is now one of Fiji's finest hotels. No expense is spared in the Fijian-Asian fusion rooms that come themed in six flavours including French Provincial and Moody Blues. Style gurus will overdose on the marble bathrooms, low-slung beds and private decked alcoves with cushioned sun loungers. There's no kids club here (a nanny service is available) but there are plenty of activities to keep adults happy: a day spa, Sunday afternoon jazz, discounted fees at the affiliated golf course and two boats available for fishing ($80 per hour) and surfing (four hours at Frigate Passage for $250) charters.

Tiri Villas (☎ 345 0552; www.tirivillas.com; d $289-389, f $240; ☷ ▦ ⚉) At first glance you may wonder where the villas are, but this ecoretreat has gone to considerable pains to blend the thatched villas and *bure* into the environment. There are no concrete walkways here, the driftwood is left undisturbed on the beach and while the thickets of mangroves are not everyone's cup of tea, birders will go cuckoo over the river-mouth location (23 species spotted so far). Tiri is 6km and a $7 taxi fare away from the Arts Village.

Eating

Tiki Bar & Melting Pot Restaurant (☎ 345 0065; Arts Village Marketplace; mains $8-30; ⏱ lunch & dinner) In keeping with the faux-Fijian theme of the Arts Village, this open-air eatery is on the sand banks of a swimming pool. Overlooked by an 18m tall, Azteclike tiki head, this place is great for kids, who can swim in the pool or pickle themselves in the cannibals' 'hot pot' spa. Oh…and the food's not bad either.

Water's Edge (☎ 345 0145; Arts Village Marketplace; mains $8-28; ⏱ Mon-Thu breakfast & lunch, Fri-Sun breakfast, lunch & dinner) The deckside dining at Water's Edge is surrounded by the water-lily pond and is a great place for lunch. The menu is strong on pizza (available to take away), pasta and vino. Meals come with 30 minutes of complimentary internet.

Oasis Restaurant (☎ 345 0617; Arts Village Marketplace; mains $16-36; ⏱ breakfast, lunch & dinner; ✗ 🖳) Burgers, sandwiches, tortillas, curries and a whole lotta seafood is served at this local favourite. The secondhand books for sale are mostly the kind of romance novels you might be embarrassed to be seen with on a sun lounger.

Sakura House (☎ 345 0256; River Dr; mains $20-35; ⏱ dinner) Although it features other Asian dishes, the Japanese tempura, sashimi, shabu-shabu (thinly sliced meat and vegetables cooked tableside in a pot of boiling water) and teriyaki are Sakura's speciality.

ourpick **Mantarae Restaurant** (☎ 345 0022; Pearl South Pacific; mains $34-38; ⏱ dinner Tue-Sat) This place is worth the splurge; the mouth-watering, contemporary, fusion-style cuisine has diners dribbling their way from the main course to dessert. Sprawled out on a day bed, or sequestered behind the bar that has a mirror-backed water feature, it's fine dining all the way – with a wine list to match.

Getting There & Around

There are frequent Pacific Transport and Sunbeam Transport buses travelling the Queens Road between Lautoka and Suva, as well as vans and carriers, and they all call in at Pacific Harbour.

The first bus from Pacific Harbour to Nadi ($15, 3½ hours) leaves at about 7.50am and

the last at around 7pm. The first bus to Suva ($4.15, one hour) leaves at 10.15am and the last is at 9.40pm. Coral Sun buses stop opposite Rosie's Tours at 8.20am and 4.45pm for Nadi ($17) and at 10.50am and 4pm for Suva ($9).

A taxi to Suva costs $40; call **Ratan's Taxi** (☎ 346 0329). Ratan provides excellent commentary and manages to make friends out of every fare. Taxis to Nadi cost about $145.

AROUND PACIFIC HARBOUR
Navua

There would be little to bring a traveller to Navua if it were not the base for several interesting trips up the Navua River to the Namosi Highlands. If you are staying on the bus, the town's most notable feature is the blindingly purple house that showcases the local proclivity for bright homes.

Early in the 20th century, sugar cane was planted in Navua and a sugar mill built, but this activity ceased as the drier western region proved more productive. Farmers of the delta region then turned to dairy farming, rice and other crops.

The regular express buses along the Queens Road stop at Navua and there are market boats and local buses to and from Namuamua and Nukusere villages, about 20km up the Navua River. The trip can take up to two hours ($10 each way), depending on the river's water level and general conditions. The boats leave any time between 10am and noon, but do not always return before the next morning (sometime between 6am and 7am). Before visiting a village, see the boxed text, p42.

Discover Fiji Tours (Jewel of Fiji Tours, Great Adventures; Map pp76-7; ☎ 345 0180; www.discoverfijitours.com) has several tours to the Navua River area. Tours include waterfall visits, 4WD trips, trekking, kayaking and white-water rafting, and cost from $115 to $122, including transfers from Pacific Harbour or Suva. All tours last 10 to 12 hours and include lunch. Some also include *bilibili* rafting, but avoid the Sunday village tours as they don't include the *kava* ceremony. Phoning first and making your own way to Navua normally pays off with a substantial discount.

There are also one- to three-day guided treks across the Namosi Highlands, camping overnight in villages.

Navua Upriver Lodge (Map pp76-7; ☎ 336 2589; navrest05@yahoo.com; Nuku Village; dm/d incl meals $65/90)

Situated about 25km north of Navua town, this Fijian-run lodge offers travellers a genuine river-village experience. Accommodation and food is simple and the surrounding environment is simply stunning. Call the lodge from Navua and they'll arrange a *bilibili* transfer. The 1½-hour ride up the Navua passes some 20 waterfalls.

Namosi Highlands

The steamy Namosi Highlands north of Pacific Harbour have Fiji's most spectacular mountain scenery (including dense lush rainforests, steep ranges, deep river canyons and tall waterfalls). If you have your own wheels (preferably 4WD), take a detour as far inland as you can from Nabukavesi, east of Navua. If you intend to visit a village, take along some *kava*. Sunday is observed as a day of rest.

Tour companies Rivers Fiji (p110), Wilderness Ethnic Adventure Fiji (p124) and Discover Fiji Tours (opposite) offer trips to this beautiful area that travellers otherwise rarely see.

OFFSHORE ISLANDS

World-class diving and surfing are to be had in the waters that surround the islands off southern Viti Levu and are the principal reason for visiting. The easiest way to dive or snorkel on the surrounding coral reefs is with one of the dive shop operators (p106) based in Pacific Harbour.

For surfers, the left-hand waves at **Frigate Passage**, also known as Kavu Kavu Reef, break on the western edge of Beqa Barrier Reef, 11km from the nearest land and southwest of Yanuca island. With long rides and reliable barrels, the surf here can reach 6m when the swell is coming from the southeast to southwest. At other times it is far smaller and suitable for intermediate surfers. The break has three sections, which join up under the right conditions: a large take-off zone; a long, walled speed section with the possibility of stand-up tubes; and an inside section breaking over the shallow reef and finishing in deep water. Access is by boat (it's in the middle of nowhere) with Waidroka Surf & Dive Resort (p107) or one of the Yanuca island hotels (p114) specialising in surfing.

Beqa

The high island of Beqa (area 36 sq km), about 7.5km south of Pacific Harbour, is visible from Queens Road and even from Suva. The island is about 7km in diameter, with a deeply indented coastline and rugged interior sloping steeply down to the coast. The villagers of Rukua, Naceva and Dakuibeqa are known for their tradition of fire-walking (see the boxed text, p109), but the best place to see it isn't on Beqa; it's now performed chiefly for tourists at the Coral Coast resorts.

Beqa Lagoon Resort (Map pp76-7; ☎ 330 4042; www.beqalagoonresort.com; r $200; 🍽 🖳 🈂) The 25 *bure* here come with opulent bathrooms and traditional interiors. Families are booked into the newer two-bedroom *bure*. The surrounding landscape and sea lends itself to excellent snorkelling, kayaking, hiking to waterfalls and village visits. There's a large restaurant-lounge *bure* serving fabulous food (meal package $75) and a pool on a coconut tree–fringed beach. Diving and surfing trips can be arranged and boat transfers from Pacific Harbour are $75 per person one way.

Lawaki Beach House (Map pp76-7; ☎ 992 1621, 368 4088; www.lawakibeachhouse.com; sites incl meals $68, dm/s/tw incl meals $78/96/192; 🖳) Aptly named, this small resort sits in front of an isolated beach on the southwestern side of Beqa island. Comprising two double *bure* with en-suites and verandahs, and a six-bed dorm, the unobtrusive and cosy set-up blends well with the surrounding environment. Guests mingle together in the communal TV lounge, soaking up the relaxed mood. There is good snorkelling off the secluded, pristine white-sand beach, as well as visits to the nearby village, diving and surfing ($225 for the boat, plus $15 per hour). The resort offers transfers from Pacific Harbour on a covered aluminium boat ($70 per person one way). Alternatively, you can catch the small public ferry from the Navua Jetty. The ferry usually leaves between noon and 2.30pm from Monday to Saturday, and costs $30 per person one way. It returns to Navua at 7am every day but Sunday.

Two more five-star options:

Lalati Resort (Map pp76-7; ☎ 347 2033; www.lalati-fiji.com; s/d/tr incl meals from $600/880/1170; 🍽 🈂) Intimate and lavish with only seven *bure*.

Kulu Bay Resort (Map pp76-7; www.kulubay.com; per person $1740; 🍽) A five-star romantic hideaway. Rates include all meals and most activities.

Yanuca

Tiny Yanuca island is a hilly speck inside Beqa Lagoon, about 9km west of Beqa. It has comely beaches, good snorkelling and is close to the humbling breaks of Frigate Passage (p113). Unsurprisingly, it lures avid surfers; many of whom come for a week, slip into the lifestyle and stay for a month. If living in your swimmers 24/7 is your idea of bliss, then you've found utopia.

The long-standing camp **Batiluva** (Map pp76-7; ☎ 345 1019, 992 0019; www.batliuva.com; dm/d incl meals $175/350) is the stuff of surfers' dreams. The sturdy accommodation houses three spotless and airy dorms, as well as two double rooms. The per-person price is the same for each, but couples get first dibs on the doubles. 'Gourmet jungle meals' are included in the tariff, but more importantly, so too is the daily boat out to Frigates for the surf-till-you-drop clientele. The beach here is quite pretty, but for good snorkelling you need to go on a short boat trip (free of charge). Transfers from Pacific Harbour are $50 return, per person (see the booking office at Pacific Harbour, Map p110).

Yanuca Island Resort (Map pp76-7; ☎ 336 1281, 997 8958; www.frigatesreef.com; per person incl meals $150) is a simple camp, etched into a protected, grassy groove of the island. There is one dorm with solid timber bunks and mosquito nets, plus two cabins with private bathrooms attached. Meals are served in an open-air dining area. Snorkelling straight off the tiny beach is good, but most guests head out to the reef each day. Daily boat transfers to Frigate Passage are included, but the return transfers from Pacific Harbour are $50 per person.

Vatulele
pop 950
The beautiful island of Vatulele (31 sq km) is 32km south of Korolevu, off Viti Levu's southern coast, and west of Beqa Lagoon. It is 13km long and mostly flat; the highest point is just 33m above sea level, and there is scrub and palm vegetation. The western coast is a long escarpment broken by vertical cliffs, formed by fracturing and uplifts. A barrier reef up to 3km offshore forms a lagoon on the eastern and northern ends, with two navigable passages at the northern end.

Vatulele has four villages and one exclusive resort. The villagers live mostly off subsistence farming and fishing and are one of Fiji's two main producers of *masi*. Vatulele has **archaeological sites**, including ancient rock paintings

of faces and stencilled hands, and unusual **geological formations**, including limestone caves and pools inhabited by red prawns that are considered sacred.

Vatulele Island Resort (Map pp76-7; ☎ 672 0300; www.vatulele.com; d $1630-3000), an exclusive and intimate place, is definitely one of Fiji's best top-end resorts, with a price to match. The location is idyllic and the architecture stunning: a mix of thick, Santa Fe–style rendered walls with the lofty thatched roofs of traditional Fijian *bure*. The 19 open-plan, split-level villas are well spaced for privacy, each with an outdoor terrace and its own stretch of white-sand beach and turquoise lagoon. Gourmet meals, alcohol and most activities are included in the rate. Those who stay here usually arrive by plane ($775 per person return, 25 minutes from Nadi).

SUVA
pop 194,300
Suva (*soo*-va), the heart of Fiji, is home to half of the country's urban population and, as the largest city in the South Pacific, it has become an important regional centre. Swimming in the urban milieu is the influence of every island and background, a vibrant Indo-Fijian community, university students from around the Pacific, Asian sailors on shore leave, and a growing expat community of Australians and New Zealanders.

Downtown is as diverse architecturally as the populace is culturally. A jigsaw of colonial buildings, modern shopping plazas, abundant eateries and a breezy esplanade all form the compact central business district. Small passages transport you to a city somewhere in India with curry houses, sari shops and bric-a-brac traders. Bollywood and Hollywood square off at the local cinema and within the same hour you're likely to see politicians in traditional *sulu* (skirt or wrapped cloth worn to below the knees) sharing a few shells of *kava* and denim-clad youth heading off to the hottest clubs in the country.

Beyond downtown Suva there is a string of pretty suburbs dribbled along the hills that crowd the capital's busy port. If Suva is indeed Fiji's heart, there are signs that it may be sick; the ballooning settlement camps of tin sheds on the city outskirts are proof that when 'coup-coup land' misses a beat, the whole country shudders.

On a less serious but equally grey note, clouds tend to hover over Suva and frequently dump rain on the city (around 300mm each year), which accounts for the lush tropical plants and comparative lack of tourists.

HISTORY

Suva's contemporary history has its roots in the fickle mismanagement of Chief Cakobau of Bau, who, with the help of King George of Tonga, proclaimed himself Tui Viti, or King of Fiji, in the 1850s. Cakobau promptly took it upon himself to give away bits and pieces of Fiji to foreign settlers, while concurrently accumulating giant debts with American immigrants. By 1862 his inability to repay the debts became apparent when he attempted to cede Fiji to Britain in exchange for debt clearance.

Up until this time, the only Europeans in the Suva area had come from Melbourne, Australia, seeking new sources of fortune after the decline of the gold rushes and subsequent downturn in the Australian economy. In 1868 the opportunistic Aussies formed the Australian Polynesia Company and agreed to clear Cakobau's debts with the Americans in return for the right to trade in Fiji and a large chunk of land, 90 sq km of which covered the Suva Peninsula.

While it was not his land to trade, the powerful Chief Cakobau had the Suva villagers relocated and welcomed new Australian settlers to the area in 1870. The settlers cleared dense reed from what is now downtown Suva and attempted, unsuccessfully, to grow cotton and sugar cane. In an effort to increase land values, two Melbourne merchants, Thomson and Renwick, encouraged the government to relocate the capital from Levuka to Suva with incentives in the form of land grants. As Levuka had little room for expansion, the government officially moved to Suva in 1882. In the 1880s Suva was a township of about a dozen buildings, but by the 1920s it was a flourishing colonial centre.

Suva's recent history is inevitably linked to the coups. In May 2000, Suva's parliament buildings became the site of a hostage drama when George Speight and his militia held 36 government officials captive for almost two months (see p38). More recently, in 2006,

---

HOME AWAY FROM HOME

On the outskirts of Suva, away from the flashy shops and colonial homes, tens of thousands of people are living in settlements of tiny, corrugated-iron huts. These dilapidated settlements have little sanitation and often no water or electricity. In 2008, an estimated 35% of Fijians were living below the poverty line and as long as the country's unresolved land issues remain, more and more of the poor are expected to drift towards the urban centres.

Indigenous Fijians have traditional ownership rights to over 80% of the country's land mass, large tracts of which they've leased to Indo-Fijian farmers for the past century. However, with these leases coming to an end and ethnic friction heightened by recent political events, many indigenous landowners are turfing Indo-Fijian farmers off property where their families have lived for generations. Ironically, in many cases the farms that had once been profitably worked by the Indo-Fijian tenants are now lying idle and overgrown. Consequently, the sugar-cane harvest has plummeted from up to 4.3 million tonnes a year at the time of George Speight's coup in 2000 to about 3.2 million tonnes in 2006, only fuelling further economic woes.

Meanwhile, the now-landless Indo-Fijians are fleeing to the cities for safety. Unfortunately, with their livelihood gone, many families are ending up in suburban squatter settlements. However, these impromptu, crowded towns are not strictly Indo-Fijian. The substantial pay cuts and rise in unemployment that have followed the country's coups have left many urban indigenous Fijians unable to pay the rent. Their only means of survival is also to head for the squatter settlements.

The government does acknowledge the severe impact this issue has on Fiji's social and economic fabric and millions have been spent on squatter resettlement, mostly in the form of estates (primarily around Lautoka) and new housing developments, but for many this has been too little, too late. With farming leases continuing to expire, it looks certain that the rural-to-urban migration trend will continue and for families who have lost their land, the immediate future continues to look dim.

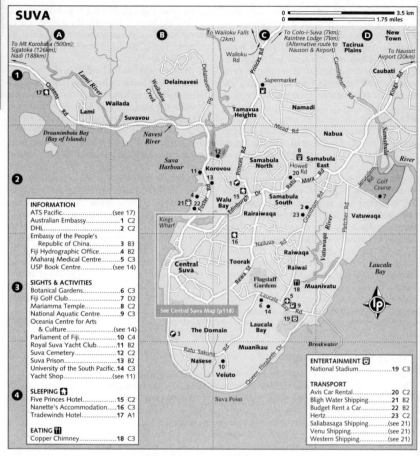

SUVA

VITI LEVU

INFORMATION
ATS Pacific..........................(see 17)
Australian Embassy....................1 C2
DHL.....................................2 C2
Embassy of the People's
  Republic of China...................3 B3
Fiji Hydrographic Office...............4 B2
Maharaj Medical Centre................5 C3
USP Book Centre..................(see 14)

SIGHTS & ACTIVITIES
Botanical Gardens......................6 C3
Fiji Golf Club.........................7 D2
Mariamma Temple........................8 C2
National Aquatic Centre................9 C3
Oceania Centre for Arts
  & Culture........................(see 14)
Parliament of Fiji....................10 C4
Royal Suva Yacht Club.................11 B2
Suva Cemetery.........................12 C2
Suva Prison...........................13 B2
University of the South Pacific.......14 C3
Yacht Shop.......................(see 11)

SLEEPING
Five Princes Hotel....................15 C2
Nanette's Accommodation...............16 C3
Tradewinds Hotel......................17 A1

EATING
Copper Chimney........................18 C3

ENTERTAINMENT
National Stadium......................19 C3

TRANSPORT
Avis Car Rental.......................20 C2
Bligh Water Shipping..................21 B2
Budget Rent a Car.....................22 B2
Hertz.................................23 C2
Saliabasaga Shipping.............(see 21)
Venu Shipping....................(see 21)
Western Shipping.................(see 21)

Suvanites, and indeed the whole country, were once again plunged into political turmoil when Frank Bainimarama seized power (see p38).

ORIENTATION

Suva is on a peninsula about 3km wide by 5km long, with Laucala Bay to the east and Suva Harbour to the west. Most of the peninsula is hilly, apart from the narrow strip of land on the western edge of the city where you'll find Suva's main drag, Victoria Pde, as well as the market and wharf.

The suburb of Toorak tumbles up onto the hill east of Suva Municipal Market. Originally Suva's posh neighbourhood (named after one of Melbourne, Australia's exclusive suburbs),

it has fallen from grandeur. In this area, Waimanu Rd passes the hospital in the northeast and then rolls down into town, becoming Renwick Rd at Nubukalou Creek and then Victoria Pde.

Victoria Pde holds many of the city's restaurants, shops and clubs. Heading south, it continues past the Government Buildings, Albert Park and Thurston Gardens (and the museum). Beyond Albert Park, the road is renamed Queen Elizabeth Dr and heads out past Suva Point and around to the University of the South Pacific (USP) and National Stadium on the eastern side of the peninsula.

Drivers may find central Suva's one-way streets, angled intersections and contorted loops a bit challenging at first. There are three major roads in and out of the city: Queens Road from Nadi; Princes Rd to the north (the scenic route to Nausori); and Kings Road from Nausori and the international airport. Kings Road meets Princes Rd closer to Suva, where it turns into Edinburgh Dr. Edinburgh Dr and Queens Road converge at Walu Bay roundabout; if you're heading downtown, head south from here onto Rodwell Rd, which you can follow past the bus station and market, across Nubukalou Creek and into central Suva.

Maps

Beyond the maps found at the front of each telephone book, the **Map Shop** (Map p118; ☎ 321 1395; Room 10, Department of Lands & Surveys; ☯ 8am-3.30pm Mon-Thu, till 3pm Fri) in the Government Buildings stocks a good map of Suva and the surrounding areas, as well as large survey maps of the rest of Fiji.

Yachties after navigational charts of the Yasawas, Kadavu, eastern Vanua Levu and the Lau Group can buy them for $32 each at the **Fiji Hydrographic Office** (Map p116; ☎ 331 5457; cnr Freeston Rd & Amra St, Walu Bay). The rest of Fiji is covered by the British Admiralty Charts available for $97 each at **Carpenters Shipping** (Map p118; ☎ 331 2244; 22 Edinburgh Dr).

INFORMATION
Bookshops

Bookleaders (Map p118; ☎ 330 4304; 173 Victoria Pde) Good range of guidebooks, paperbacks and more.

Fiji Museum (Map p118; ☎ 331 5944; www.fijimuseum.org.fj; Thurston Gardens; ☯ 9.30am-4.30pm Mon-Sat) The gift shop stocks a good selection of Fijian books on history, cooking and birds.

Suva Flea Market (Map p118; Rodwell Rd) Great secondhand bookshop out the back.

USP Book Centre (Map p116; ☎ 323 2500; www.uspbookcentre.com; University of the South Pacific) Excellent selection of local and international novels, Lonely Planet guides and Pacific nonfiction. Pricey, but you can order online and they deliver.

Emergency

Ambulance (☎ 911, 330 2584)
Fire (☎ 911, 331 2877)
Police (Map p118; ☎ 911, 331 1222; Pratt St) There is also a police post on Cumming St.

Internet Access

Internet access is cheap and abundant in Suva.

Connect Internet Café (Map p118; ☎ 330 0777; Post Office Bldg, 10 Thomson St; per hr $3; ☯ 8.30am-8pm Mon-Fri, 9am-8pm Sat) Broadband access in 15-minute intervals.

Fintel (Map p118; ☎ 331 2933; 158 Victoria Pde; per hr $5; ☯ 8am-8pm Mon-Sat) This office has Fiji's only VOIP (voice-over-internet protocol) telephones, with international calls costing only $0.20 per minute.

Skynet Café (Map p118; ☎ 331 6967; Upstairs, cnr Victoria Pde & Gordon St; per hr $3.50; ☯ 24hr) Midnight specials and popular with gamers, plus DVD-burning for $6 a disk.

Medical Services

Visits to general practitioners are usually $15 to $25.

Colonial War Memorial Hospital (Map p118; ☎ 331 3444; Waimanu Rd)

Fiji Recompression Chamber Facility (off Map p118; ☎ 999 3506, 851 0434; recompression@connect.com.fj; cnr Amy & Brewster Sts) Call ahead as it only opens in emergencies.

Maharaj Medical Centre (Map p116; ☎ 327 0164; Sports City Centre, Laucala Bay Rd, Laucala Bay; ☯ 9am-1pm, 2-6pm Mon-Fri, 9am-1pm Sat & Sun) Private medical centre.

Pharmacy Plus (Map p118; ☎ 330 5300; 190 Renwick Rd) Large and well-stocked pharmacy.

Money

There are plenty of ATMs and Western Union–affiliated currency exchange shops scattered along Victoria Pde. Both the banks listed here have foreign-exchange counters and cash travellers cheques.

ANZ bank (Map p118; ☎ 132 411; 25 Victoria Pde)
Westpac bank (Map p118; ☎ 132 032; 1 Thomson St)

Post

Post Fiji (Map p118; ☎ 321 8450; Thomson St)

Tourist Information

Fiji Visitors Bureau (FVB; Map p118; ☎ 330 2433; www.fijime.com; cnr Thomson & Scott Sts; ☯ 8am-4.30pm Mon-Fri, to noon Sat) Friendly, knowledgable and unbiased staff can advise on local tours and accommodation options throughout Fiji. Ask for a copy of *Kulcha Vulcha*, a fortnightly newsletter with what's-on listings.

Travel Agencies

See p247 for contact details of interisland ferry agencies and p130 for airline offices.

ATS Pacific Holiday Inn (Map p118; ☎ 330 1600; Victoria Pde); Tradewinds Hotel (Map p116; ☎ 336 4086; Queens Rd, Lami) Books local tours and activities, including those at nearby Pacific Harbour.

VITI LEVU

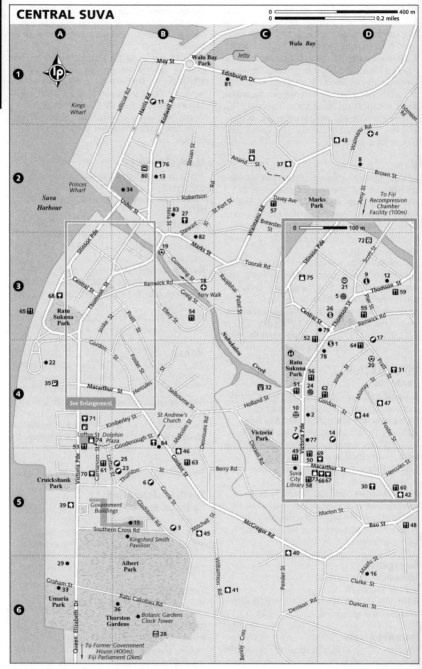

CENTRAL SUVA

INFORMATION
ANZ Bank.................................**1** D4
ATS Pacific...........................(see 39)
Bookleaders...........................**2** C4
British Consulate.....................**3** B5
Carpenters Shipping...............(see 81)
Colonial War Memorial Hospital..**4** D2
Connect Internet Café...............**5** D3
Embassy of Nauru...................(see 73)
Embassy of Tuvalu....................**6** B5
European Union Representative...**7** C4
Fiji Disabled People's Association..**8** D2
Fiji Museum..........................(see 28)
Fiji Visitors Bureau...................**9** D3
Fintel..................................**10** C4
French Embassy......................(see 12)
German Embassy.....................**11** B1
Hunts Travel..........................**12** D3
Japanese Embassy...................(see 12)
Korean Embassy......................(see 56)
Lau Provincial Council..............**13** B2
Malaysian Embassy..................**14** D4
Map Shop.............................**15** B5
Ministry of Fijian Affairs...........(see 15)
National Trust for Fiji...............**16** D6
Netherlands Embassy...............(see 78)
New Zealand Embassy..............**17** D3
Pharmacy Plus.......................**18** B3
Police..................................**19** B3
Police..................................**20** D4
Post Fiji...............................**21** D3
Registrar General's office..........**22** A4
Representative of the Federated
    States of Micronesia.............**23** B5
Skynet Café...........................**24** C4
South Pacific Tourism
    Organisation......................(see 74)
Suva Flea Market....................(see 76)
US Embassy...........................**25** B5
Westpac Bank........................**26** D3

SIGHTS & ACTIVITIES
Centenary Methodist Church....**27** B2
Fiji Museum............................**28** B6

Grand Pacific Hotel..................**29** A6
Holy Trinity Cathedral..............**30** D5
Roman Catholic Cathedral........**31** D4
Shree Laxmi Narayan Temple....**32** C4
Suva Bowls Club......................**33** A6
Suva Municipal Market.............**34** B2
Suva Olympic Swimming Pool....**35** A4
Thurston Gardens....................**36** B6

SLEEPING
Annandale Apartments............**37** C2
Colonial Lodge........................**38** C2
Holiday Inn............................**39** A5
Peninsula International Hotel....**40** C5
South Seas Private Hotel...........**41** C6
Southern Cross Hotel...............**42** D5
Studio 6 Apartments................**43** D2
Sunset Apartment Motel...........**44** D4
Suva Motor Inn.......................**45** B5
Tanoa Plaza Hotel....................**46** B5
Town House Apartment Hotel.. **47** D4

EATING
Aberdeen Grill........................**48** D5
Ashiyana...............................**49** C5
Bad Dog Cafe.........................**50** C5
Barbecue Stands......................**51** C4
Boulevard Medical Centre........(see 54)
Capital Palace.........................**52** C3
Daikoku Restaurant..................**53** A4
Dolphin Plaza.........................(see 74)
Downtown Boulevard
    Shopping Centre.................**54** B3
Esquires Coffee House..............**55** D3
Esquires Coffee House..............(see 74)
Focaccia Café.........................**56** C4
Korea House...........................**57** C2
Maya Dhaba..........................**58** C5
MHCC Department Store..........**59** D3
Mona Lisa.............................**60** D5
Old Mill Cottage.....................**61** A5
Roma's Hook and Chook..........**62** D4
Shabu-Shabu..........................**63** B5
Shanghai Seafood House..........**64** D4

Superfresh.............................(see 59)
Suva Municipal Market............(see 34)
Tiko's Floating Restaurant.........**65** A3
Victoria Wines & Spirits...........(see 69)

DRINKING
Bad Dog................................(see 50)
Bar 66..................................(see 74)
Birdland R&B Club...................**66** D5
Bourbon Bluez........................**67** D5
JJ's on the Park.......................**68** A3
O'Reilly's...............................**69** D5
Ranch..................................**70** A5
Traps Bar..............................**71** A4

ENTERTAINMENT
Village 6 Cinema Complex.......**72** D3

SHOPPING
Government Crafts Centre........**73** C5
ROC Market...........................**74** A4
Suva Curio & Handicraft
    Market..............................**75** C3
Suva Flea Market....................**76** B2

TRANSPORT
Air Fiji.................................**77** C4
Air New Zealand.....................**78** D4
Air Pacific.............................**79** D3
Bus Station............................**80** B2
Carpenters Shipping................**81** C1
Consort Shipping....................(see 12)
Consort Shipping....................(see 81)
Pacific Blue............................**82** B3
Pacific Sun.............................(see 79)
Patterson Brothers
    Shipping............................**83** B2
Qantas.................................(see 79)
Taxi Stand............................(see 80)
Thrifty Car Rental....................**84** B4

Hunts Travel (Map p118; ☎ 331 5288; huntstravel@
connect.com.fj; 1st fl, Dominion House Arcade, Thomson
St) Avoid the queues at Air Pacific and book your domestic
and international flights here.

DANGERS & ANNOYANCES

Suva suffers many of the same dangers as
most urbanised centres. Pickpockets roam,
so keep your valuables out of sight, particularly
in crowded areas such as the market or on
dance floors. Walking around during daylight
hours is perfectly safe, but as night descends
it's preferable to catch a taxi; they are metered,
cheap and safe.

The infamous Suva sword sellers, who
flogged tacky swords by carving into them
the names of tourists, are largely a thing of the
past. Tourists have wised up and local handicraft sellers have returned to more traditional
bartering tactics.

SIGHTS
Fiji Museum & Thurston Gardens

This excellent **museum** (Map p118; ☎ 331 5944; www
.fijimuseum.org.fj; Ratu Cakobau Rd; adult/child $7/5; ☉ 9am-
4.30pm Mon-Sat) captivates visitors with a journey
into Fiji's archaeological, political, cultural
and linguistic evolution. To enjoy the exhibits
in chronological order, start with the displays
behind the ticket counter and work your way
clockwise around the room. Original examples of musical instruments, cooking appara-
tus, jewellery – including chiefs' whale-tooth
necklaces – and a daunting array of Fijian war
clubs and cannibal utensils give a vivid insight
into traditional life. Taking centre stage is the
massive Ratu Finau (1913), Fiji's last *waqa
tabus* (double-hulled canoe), which measures
13.43m long and includes an enclosed deck
for inclement weather.

The growing influence of other South Pacific and European cultures is documented in a hall on the other side of the museum shop. It is here that you'll find the well-chewed, but ultimately inedible, shoe of Thomas Baker (see the boxed text, p138), a Christian missionary eaten for his indiscretions in 1867. Upstairs, a small Indo-Fijian hall chronicles some of the contributions made by the Indian workers and their descendants who were brought to Fiji in the 1870s as indentured labourers. Also on the same floor is a gallery of beautiful *masi* by some of Fiji's finest contemporary artists.

The museum continually undertakes archaeological research and collects and preserves oral traditions. Many of these are published in *Domodomo*, a quarterly journal on history, language, culture, art and natural history that is available in the museum's gift shop. It also organises craft demonstrations; contact the museum for times.

After visiting the museum, ponder on your new-found knowledge with a wander through the compact but beautiful **Thurston Gardens** (Map p118). The dense conglomeration of native flora and surrounding lawns are less manicured and growing more haphazard with every coup, but it was here that the original village of Suva once stood. It's a lovely spot for a picnic – particularly if you camp yourself under one of the grand and stately fig trees.

Parliament of Fiji

Opened on June 1992, the **parliament complex** (Map p116; ☎ 330 5811; www.parliament.gov.fj; Battery Rd; admission free) must be one of the world's most striking political hubs. It was designed in the post-1987 atmosphere (see p36 for information on the 1987 coup) and the aim of maintaining indigenous Fijian values is apparent through the open-air corridors, traditional arts and struc-

tures and *masi* cloths throughout. The main building, *vale ne bose lawa* (parliament house), takes its form from the traditional *vale* (family house) and has a ceremonial access from Ratu Sukuna Rd. The complex is 5km south of the city centre. It's easiest to reach by taxi; however, you can hop on a bus along Queen Elizabeth Dr and walk along Ratu Sukuna Rd for 1km.

It's advisable to call ahead if you want to tour the grounds, but you can also obtain a visitor's pass from the guard at the main entrance. It's also possible to sit in on a parliamentary session by phoning in advance.

Suva Municipal Market

The beating heart of Suva is the **Suva Municipal Market** (Map p118; Usher St; ☺ 6am-6pm Mon-Fri, to 4.30pm Sat) and it's a great place to spend an hour or so poking around with a camera. The boys with barrows own the lanes and they aren't afraid to mow down a few tourists to deliver their cassava on time. Besides the recognisable tomatoes, cabbages and chillies, look out for bitter gourds, *rourou* (boiled *dalo* leaves in *lolo*), *kava*, jackfruit, *dalo* and sweet potatoes.

Head upstairs to buy your *sevusevu*. *Yaqona (kava)* root costs anything from $24 to $40 a kilo and a gift of these guarantees 100-watt smiles. Only cheapskates opt for the powdered, less potent stems.

University of the South Pacific

While hardly a must-see from a tourist's perspective, the **University of the South Pacific** (USP; Map p116; ☎ 331 3900; www.usp.ac.fj; Laucala Bay Rd) is the foremost provider of tertiary education to the island nations of the Pacific region. The governments of 12 Pacific countries jointly own the university and mingling among the Fijian students you're likely to see young academics from the Cook Islands, Kiribati,

---

WINGING IT

Charles Kingsford Smith was the first aviator to cross the Pacific, flying in his little Fokker trimotor, *The Southern Cross*, from California to Australia. The longest leg of the flight was the 34-hour trip from Hawaii to Fiji. Suva's Albert Park, with its hill at one end and the Grand Pacific Hotel at the other, was made into a makeshift landing strip for his arrival. Trees were still being cleared after Smith had already left Hawaii. Kingsford Smith and his crew arrived on 6 June 1928, and were welcomed by a crowd of thousands, including colonial dignitaries who had gathered at the Grand Pacific Hotel to witness and celebrate this major event. Because the park was too short to take off with a heavy load of fuel, Smith had to unload, fly to Nasilai Beach and reload for take off to Brisbane and Sydney. Kingsford Smith and his crew were presented with a ceremonial *tabua* (whale's tooth) as a token of great respect.

Tonga, Vanuatu and Western Samoa. As this is a fee-paying institution, many of the 11,000 or so students rely on scholarships, and the competition for them is fierce. The USP's main campus (built on the site of a New Zealand seaplane base) offers some fascinating people-watching and picturesque strolling through a small **botanical garden**. But even this much-lauded example of regional cooperation has its share of ethnic tension and the graffiti in the toilet stalls is an eye-opening vitriol of anti-Indian sentiment.

On most weekday mornings, the Oceania Dance Theatre and other performance groups can be found rehearsing in the **Oceania Centre for Arts & Culture** (Map p116), where you can also see temporary exhibits of paintings and carvings.

Colo-i-Suva Forest Park

This lush rainforest **park** (Map p121; ☎ 332 0211; adult/child $5/1; ☽ 8am-4pm), pronounced tholo-ee-*soo*-va, is a 2.5-sq-km oasis teeming with vivid and melodic bird life and tropical flora. The 6.5km of walking trails navigate clear natural pools and gorgeous vistas. Sitting at an altitude of 120m to 180m, it's a cool and peaceful respite from Suva's urban hubbub.

Slipping and sliding through the forest over water-worn rocks is the Waisila Creek, making its way down to Waimanu River and forming the water catchment for the Nausori and Nasinu areas. The creek gives rise to natural swimming holes, and the Lower Pools have a rope swing guaranteed to bring out the Tarzan in anyone.

The mahogany and pines were planted after a period of aggressive logging in the 1940s and '50s, to stabilise the topsoil without impinging on the indigenous vegetation. Among the wildlife are 14 different bird species, including scarlet robins, spotted fantails, Fiji goshawks, sulphur-breasted musk parrots, Fiji warblers, golden doves and barking pigeons.

The visitor information centre is on the left of the road as you approach from Suva; buy your ticket here and then head to the entrance booth on the other side of the road. The recommended route is to follow Kalabu Rd as it skirts the park, turning up Pool Rd to the car park. From here you take the Nature Trail to the Lower Pools for swimming, and the aforementioned rope swinging and, if you remembered to bring it, lunch. It's a sweaty, uphill walk back to the main road via the Falls Trail. Nonstop this loop takes about 1½ hours to complete.

Before entering the park, ask the guards about the security situation, as there have been some distressing attacks over the years. If concerned, solo travellers can pay an additional fee (on asking) to have a guard accompany them and it is obviously wise to leave valuables back in your hotel room. The park receives an annual rainfall of 420cm and the trails can be extremely slippery, so sturdy footwear is essential.

The Sawani bus leaves Suva bus station every half hour ($1.80, 30 minutes). If driving, take Princes Rd out of Suva, past Tamavua and Tacirua villages.

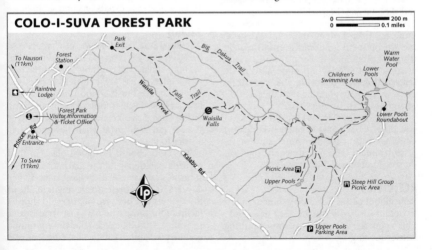

COLO-I-SUVA FOREST PARK

GRAND DESIGNS

A short stroll along Suva's foreshore towards Albert Park brings you to one of Fiji's most dignified, and yet most neglected, buildings – the Grand Pacific Hotel (Map p118). In his book, *The World is My Home*, James A Michener describes it as having '…a huge central dining area filled with small tables, each meticulously fitted with fine silver and china…and the barefoot Indians who served the meals [here] had a grace that few hotels in the world could offer and none surpass'.

Built in 1914 by the Union Steamship Company, the splendid white facade still hints at the hotel's former glory, but it has remained abandoned and in a continuing state of decay since its closure in 1992. Today the floorboards upstairs have rotted, shutters hang from glassless windows and the wallpaper peels from decaying walls. A string of redevelopment plans and backers had failed to give new life to this grand old dame, until 2006 when new plans were unveiled to restore the Grand Pacific to its former grandeur. Two years on and little has changed; the army has now moved in and if you're lucky enough to poke around inside, you'll see their tents pitched in the disused rooms.

Churches & Temples

Despite their cosmopolitan lifestyle, the majority of Suva's Indo-Fijians and indigenous Fijians are still very religious and dash off to temple or church on a regular basis. While few of these buildings are interesting in themselves, a couple are worth a gander if you're in the neighbourhood.

Just east of downtown, the bright orange and blue **Shree Laxmi Narayan Temple** (Map p118; Holland St) generally has a caretaker around to let you in for a look.

Holy Trinity Cathedral (Map p118; cnr Macarthur & Gordon Sts), with its unique boat-shaped interior, interesting Fijian tapestries and wood-beamed ceiling, is a peaceful retreat. The gigantic tree in front of the church is a showcase of Pacific plants, with cacti and ferns making themselves at home in its branches. The 1902 **Roman Catholic Cathedral** (Map p118), at the corner of Murray and Pratt Sts, is built of sandstone imported from Sydney and is one of Suva's most prominent landmarks; unfortunately, it's most often locked. For a rousing chorus of song on a Sunday morning, head to the **Centenary Methodist Church** (Map p118; Stewart St); the pitch is more invigorating than dulcet and it often fills the surrounding streets.

If you entered town via the Queens Road, you likely passed **Suva cemetery** (Map p116). Graves are dug by the inmates from the prison, built in 1913, just down the road and then decorated with bright cloth.

ACTIVITIES

Suva all but closes down on a Sunday, so try to organise activities in advance or attend a Fijian church service to hear some uplifting, boisterous singing.

Trekking

Colo-i-Suva Forest Park (p121) is an easy place for bushwalking close to Suva. You can also hike to **Mt Korobaba** (off Map p116), about a one- to two-hour walk from the cement factory near Lami. **Joske's Thumb** is an enticing spectacle for serious climbers; check with FVB about getting permission to climb it. A climb to this peak was featured in the film *Journey to the Dawning of the Day*. Unfortunately, **Wailoku Falls** (off Map p116), between Suva and Colo-i-Suva, is not a good place for a dip as muggings are a *very* common occurrence.

Keen trekkers should contact the Rucksack Club for weekly walking adventures either inland or to other islands. Ask the FVB for the latest contact number because the membership changes regularly, as most of the 80 to 100 members are expats on contract in Fiji.

Sailing

The **Royal Suva Yacht Club** (Map p116; ☎ 331 2921; rsyc@kidanet.net.fj; ☯ office 8am-5pm Mon-Fri, 9am-1pm Sat) is a popular watering hole for yachties and locals alike. It has great sunset views of the Bay of Islands but the food is only hit-and-miss at best. Even without a yacht, overseas visitors are welcome and the atmosphere at the bar can be lively and salty; everyone has a story to tell.

The noticeboard is a good place to find crewing positions and the marina has dockside fuel and water. Anchorage fees are $8 per day or $30 if you prefer to overnight in one of the six berths. There are laundry and shower facilities for those who have just arrived, and the office should be able to advise on immigration procedures. Contact the **Yacht Shop** (Map p116; ☎ 331 3832; ysrsyc@tradewinds.com.fj) if you need to order parts or arrange repairs.

Sports

As Suva is without a beach, the two best places for a swim are at the **National Aquatic Centre** (Map p116; ☎ 331 8185; Laucala Bay Rd, Laucala Bay; admission $3; 🕑 6am-8pm Mon-Sat year-round, 9am-6pm Sun Oct-Jun, 10am-6pm Sun Jul-Sep), which was built for the 2003 South Pacific Games, and the fantastically cheap **Suva Olympic Swimming Pool** (Map p118; 224 Victoria Pde; adult/child $1.65/0.80; 🕑 10am-6pm Mon-Fri & 8am-6pm Sat Apr-Sep, 9am-7pm Mon-Fri & 7am-7pm Sat Oct-Mar).

Nonmembers are welcome at the **Fiji Golf Club** (Map p116; ☎ 338 1184; 15 Rifle Range Rd; 🕑 7am-last tee-off at 3pm) except on Saturdays and from noon to 3pm on Tuesdays when the greens are reserved for local competitions. The green fees on this par-72 course are $15 for nine holes, and $20 for 18.

Lawn bowlers may roll up at the **Suva Bowls Club** (Map p118; ☎ 331 0596; cnr Graham St & Victoria Pde; green fees $5; 🕑 9am-5pm Mon-Sat), but don't underestimate the breadth of talent in this club. There are only 50 playing members here, but Fiji won silver in the 2008 world championship and the top male player here is ranked 6th in the world, the top female player 8th.

WALKING TOUR

Downtown Suva has a scattering of colonial buildings and places of interest in between the shops and office blocks, making it a pleasant place to wander around. Give yourself several hours for this tour, taking lunch and other pit stops into consideration.

Start your pedestrian journey on Stinson Pde at the **Suva Curio & Handicraft Market** (1; p129). Have a good look around but don't make any purchases yet – there are a few more shops on the itinerary. Cross to the opposite side of the street and follow the esplanade south, taking in the gorgeous views of Suva Harbour and Joske's Thumb. Once you reach **Tiko's Floating Restaurant** (2; p126), one of Suva's finest eateries, cross the road and amble through the tree-lined **Ratu Sukuna Park** (3) to Thomson St. Continue south down Victoria Pde, past the pale, colonial 1926 **Fintel building** (4) and the 1904 **old town hall** (5). Now home to several restaurants, the old town hall building was once used for dances, bazaars and performances. The **Suva Olympic Swimming Pool** (6) is set back between this building and the 1909 **Suva City Library** (7).

Continue down Victoria Pde. On your left-hand side are the stately **Government Buildings** (8), built between 1939 and 1967. Presiding over the manicured green lawns are statues of Ratu Cakobau and Ratu Sukuna. In the block south of the Government Buildings is **Albert Park** (9), a large sporting field where you can often catch rugby union teams in action or training. The park is named after Queen Victoria's husband and was given to the Fijian Government by the Australian Polynesia Company as an incentive for moving the capital to Suva (see p115 for more on this). Towards the back of the park are a cricket ground and tennis courts. The **Kingsford Smith Pavilion** (10), named after the famous aviator who landed here, is on Southern Cross Rd. On the seaside opposite the park is the glorious

WALK FACTS

Start Stinson Pde
Finish Stinson Pde
Distance 3.5km
Duration Two to four hours

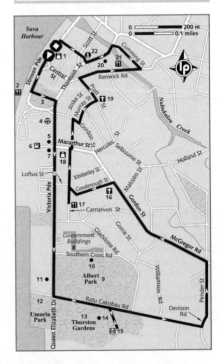

old **Grand Pacific Hotel** (11; see the boxed text, p122), a haunting reminder of a bygone age. Just past Ratu Cakobau Rd you'll stumble across **Umaria Park (12)**, where you can take a breather. If you've got kids in tow, they'll enjoy scrambling over the colourful monkey bars and playground. A scattering of concrete picnic tables and benches make this a popular spot for picnicking families on the weekend.

Cross the road at the corner of Ratu Cakobau Rd and Queen Elizabeth Dr and enter **Thurston Gardens** (13; p119). Meander through this colourful and balmy park, which was built in 1913 and named after Sir John Bates Thurston, an amateur botanist who introduced many ornamental plant species to Fiji. Within the grounds is the **Botanic Gardens Clock Tower (14)** and the **Fiji Museum (15;** p119).

Keep walking east along Ratu Cakobau Rd and climb into the escalating inner suburbs. Turn left at Pender St and left again at McGregor Rd. Amid the tranquil residential streets you'll find sweeping views of the city below. Continue along McGregor Rd, which turns into Gordon St and leads back to the city centre. Turn left at Goodenough St, with **St Andrew's Church (16)** on the corner. Follow Goodenough St and dog-leg onto Carnarvon St. If you need a pick-me-up, drop into the **Old Mill Cottage** (17; p126) for a traditional Fijian feast.

Stroll north past the bars and clubs of this little back road and duck into the **Government Crafts Centre (18)** on Macarthur St. This small outlet sells some of the finest crafts in Fiji. Continue walking north along Carnarvon St, crossing Gordon St to Murray St. At the corner of Murray and Pratt Sts is the sandstone **Roman Catholic Cathedral (19;** p122), one of Suva's most prominent landmarks.

Turn left onto Pratt St and then right onto Renwick Rd. Window-shop your way to Cumming St. Turn left to immerse yourself in Suva's little India, with curry houses, sari sellers, souvenir shops and the scent of incense thick in the air. In the 1920s this street was known for its *kava* saloons and 'dens of iniquity'.

Turn left onto Thomson St and make your way past the stately old **Garrick Hotel (20)**. Built in 1914, it's now home to shops and the **Shanghai Seafood House (21;** p127). Make a right at the 1912 **FVB building (22)** and head towards the water and your starting point at the Curio & Handicraft Market. If you've got any energy left, spend it on a bout of souvenir shopping.

TOURS

Many of the tour companies based in Pacific Harbour (see p110) and Navua (see p112) also pick up from Suva hotels.

Wilderness Ethnic Adventure Fiji (☎ 331 5730; www.wildernessfiji.com.fj) runs village tours to the Namosi Highlands (p113) and on-demand tours requiring a minimum of four to Nasilai village on the Rewa Delta (p131). Trips cost $99 per person including transport from Suva. Rafting trips from Navua cost $109 per person but can be combined with a village trip for heavily discounted prices.

FESTIVALS & EVENTS

Since its inception in 1956, the **Hibiscus Festival** (www.hibiscusfiji.com) has grown into a nine-day event, drawing large crowds from around Vitu Levu. It is held every August to coincide with the second-term school break. The annual beauty pageant and the crowning of the 'Hibiscus Queen' are the chief draws, but families also flock to Albert Park to ride creaky rides in the amusement park, browse stalls and listen to the free entertainment. Some might find it a little archaic, but if you are in the market for cheap sunglasses and loud shirts, you've struck gold.

The extraordinary **South Indian fire-walking festival** is held at the **Mariamma Temple** (Map p116; ☎ 337 2773, 338 2357; Howell Rd, Samabula) annually in either July or August. On the day of the ritual, yellow-clad devotees gather at Suva Point, near the National Stadium, to bathe in the sea and make their final preparations for the fire-walking ahead. Temple pundits (Hindu priests) pierce the tongues, cheeks and bodies of the devotees with three-pronged skewers and smear their faces with yellow turmeric, a symbol of prosperity and a powerful totem over disease. At around 2pm the participants dance the 3km back to the temple, arriving at Mariamma Temple around 4pm where a large crowd waits. Fire-walking over a bed of hot ash and coals is seen as a sign of devotion and self sacrifice, the culmination of a 10-day ascetic period during which devotees rely solely on the offerings from the local Hindu community, abstain from sex and eating meat, and meditate to worship the goddess Maha Devi. It is believed that if the fire-walkers are cleansed of physical and spiritual impurities and thus focused on the divine Mother, they will feel no pain.

SLEEPING

Accommodation options in the capital aren't as modish as those found in the more tourist-oriented towns elsewhere on the island. Suva's three top hotels are nowhere near the standard set by the resorts in Denarau and cater more to businessmen than vacationers. Similarly, without the steady stream of backpackers that Nadi enjoys, quality budget accommodation is also rather thin on the ground. The only price point well represented in Suva is the mid-range bracket. Besides the midrange hotels listed here, there are many more to be found along Robertson Rd, particularly the loop it forms between Anand St and Waimanu Rd. A quiet word of warning – some of these are the haunts of prostitutes and their clients; if you notice no other travellers and a lot of traffic, you may want to move on.

Budget

South Seas Private Hotel (Map p118; ☎ 331 2296; www
.fiji4less.com; 6 Williamson Rd; dm/s/d/f without bathroom $19/35/46/54, s & d with bathroom $58; ⊠) The art deco sign out front sets the scene for this grand old dame of the Pacific. The sweeping interior verandah, classic white exterior, high ceilings and wide halls speak of the romance of a bygone era. This large colonial house and former girls-only hostel welcomes backpackers with the best dorms in walking distance of central Suva. The rooms are fan cooled, simple and clean.

ourpick Raintree Lodge (Map p121; ☎ 332 0113; www
.raintreelodge.com; Princes Rd, Colo-i-Suva; dm/d/tw $25/65/65, bure $165; ⊠ 🖳 🏊) It is hard to believe that the tranquil, rainforest-fringed lake that provides such a lush backdrop here was once a rock quarry. There are rumoured to be two trucks and a bulldozer lying abandoned beneath the lake's glassy surface from when the quarry closed in the 1970s. On Tuesdays, Thursdays and Sundays, Feejee Experience stays here and guests make the most of the three dormitories, communal kitchen and double and twin rooms with shared bathrooms. There are also five *bure* set amongst the trees and these offer excellent value with plump beds, private decks, TV and DVD players (movies available). The lakeside bar and restaurant (mains $15 to $28) serve excellent food. The only drawback is the 11km taxi ride ($9) back to town. Alternatively, the Tacirua Transport bus to Sawani passes the Raintree Lodge ($1.80, 30 minutes), half-hourly from Monday to Saturday.

Colonial Lodge (Map p118; ☎ 330 0655; www.colonial
lodge.com.fj; 19 Anand St; dm/s/d/tr with shared bathroom & incl breakfast $30/38/80/100; 🖳) Run by a friendly and boisterous family, this budget homestay is a rabbit warren of interconnected rooms with shared bathrooms and ad hoc additions. If you end up in one of the airless rooms with low ceilings, you'll appreciate the homely lounge. Evening meals here cost $12.

Peninsula International Hotel (Map p118; ☎ 331 3711; www.peninsula.com.fj; cnr McGregor Rd & Pender St; d/tr $85/105; ⊠ 🔁 🏊) Pleasantly situated in a leafy residential area, the Peninsula is a little confused and tired but does its best to provide reasonable value. From the outside it looks like an apartment block and is recognisable by the overhanging window canopies (which get in the way of what would have been excellent views). There is a pool, restaurant and bar on site. If you plan to stay here, aim high – the rooms get better the higher you go.

Studio 6 Apartments (Map p118; ☎ 330 7477; stu
dio6@unwired.com.fj; 1-3 Walu St; s/d $60/110; 🔁 🏊) The 105 motel rooms are starting to look shabby but are essentially clean and comfortable. There are six different room types (including many self-contained options) and it's seldom full, so ask to see a few before settling on one. This hillside location affords some terrific harbour views.

Nanette's Accommodation (Map p116; ☎ 331 6316; www.nanettes.com.fj; 56 Extension St; r incl breakfast $89-125, apt incl breakfast $150-175; ⊠ 🔁 🖳) Resort-weary travellers can find solace here in unassuming comfort and Jo's warm hospitality. This former residence is only a 10-minute walk to downtown Suva, but set a world away in tranquil gardens. The four upstairs rooms of varying size share a communal TV lounge and kitchen and all have bathrooms, some with enticingly large tubs. Downstairs are three comfortable apartments with their own spacious kitchens and bedrooms.

Two further, but less appealing, cheapies:

Sunset Apartment Motel (Map p118; ☎ 330 1799; townhouse@connect.com.fj; cnr Gordon & Murray Sts; dm/d from $17/74; 🔁) The cheap rooms are often full with long-term residents; we recommend bringing a sleeping sheet if you're going to sleep here, because there were reports of bed bugs at the time of research.

Town House Apartment Hotel (Map p118; ☎ 330 0055; townhouse@connect.com.fj; 3 Foster St; s/d $69/79; 🔁) The rooms have seen more action than the government has coups and are consequently tired.

VITI LEVU

Midrange & Top End

Suva Motor Inn (Map p118; ☎ 331 3973; www.hexagonfiji.com; cnr Mitchell & Gorrie Sts; d $117-183; ⊠ ⊡) Fab for families, the Suva Motor Inn is a little humble with its title. The four-storey hotel (no lift) is shaped like a 'U' around a small pool into which snakes a water slide. All rooms have balconies (the best with views to Albert Park) and the larger two-bedroom apartments sleep four and have kitchens. The rooms are large, but the TVs tiny – it's a solid midrange choice.

Five Princes Hotel (Map p116; ☎ 338 1575; www.fiveprinceshotel.com; 5 Princes Rd; d $155, d with kitchenette $185, villas $300; ⊠ ⊡ ⊡) The aged 1920s exterior belies the transformation that this one-time colonial villa has undergone on the inside. Solid teak furniture, polished timber floors, power showers, satellite TV and broadband internet connections are all to be had in timelessly appointed rooms. The stand-alone villas are similarly decorated but also include kitchenettes and private verandahs.

Tanoa Plaza Hotel (Map p118; ☎ 331 2300; www.tanoahotels.com; cnr Gordon & Malcolm Sts; r $159-178, ste $323; ⊠ ⊠ ⊡ ⊡) The rooms here are comfortable, functional and forgettable. It's sleek and sophisticated in that mini bar, pamper products in the bathroom, kind of way. The views, though, are impressive and it's one of Suva's best.

Tradewinds Hotel (Map p116; ☎ 336 2450; www.tradewindssuva.com.fj; Queens Rd, Lami; d with garden/ocean view $210/236; ⊠ ⊠ ⊡) Now part of the Accor group, this one-time starlet was getting a long overdue renovation at time of research. Walk-in rates were 60% of the rack rates quoted here, but the un-refurbished rooms were fairly plain and devoid of personality. The great waterfront location and the views across Draunimbota Bay requires no improvement.

Holiday Inn (Map p118; ☎ 330 1600; reservations@holidayinnsuva.com.fj; Victoria Pde; r $290-590; ⊠ ⊠ ⊡ ⊡) This inn occupies a great location on the harbour shore, across from the Government Buildings and near the museum. Rooms are generically spacious, cool and comfortable and will please picky travellers. The inn patently appeals to business travellers and those on coach tours and it has the facilities to match.

There are many more midrange options to be found around Suva including the following:

Annandale Apartments (Map p118; ☎ 331 1054; 265 Waimanu Rd; r $55-80, f $120-150; ⊠ ⊡) The cheap prices accurately reflect the quality here at this friendly joint.

Southern Cross Hotel (Map p118; ☎ 331 4233; southerncross1@connect.com.fj; 63 Gordon St; r $95-115; ⊠ ⊡) Good-value, modest rooms around a courtyard pool. French restaurant on site.

EATING

For a compact city, Suva offers a relatively diverse and multicultural array of eateries. It's the best place in Fiji to try authentic Fijian and Indo-Fijian food, but there are plenty of Western-style options on offer if your tummy and palate are timid.

Restaurants

WESTERN & FIJIAN

Old Mill Cottage (Map p118; ☎ 331 2134; 49 Carnarvon St; dishes $5-12; ☺ breakfast & lunch Mon-Sat) Officials and government aides from the nearby embassies cram the front verandah of this Suva institution to dabble in authentic Fijian fare. Exotic dishes including *palusami* (meat, onion and *lolo* – coconut cream – wrapped in *dalo* leaves and baked in a *lovo*) are displayed under the front counter alongside Indian curries and vegetarian dishes. The restaurant occupies two adjoining and somewhat dilapidated cottages. One serves breakfast, the other lunch.

our pick Bad Dog Cafe (Map p118; ☎ 330 4662; cnr Macarthur St & Victoria Pde; mains $15-25; ☺ breakfast, lunch & dinner Mon-Sat, lunch & dinner Sun; ⊠) This trendy drinking hole serves tasty bar snacks and crowd-pleasing mains. The cheery clink of wine glasses and the constant stream of food from the kitchen attest to its popularity. The Cajun chicken, Thai curries, squid rings and potato wedges were all good, but it was the smoothies that made our toes curl.

Mona Lisa (Map p118; ☎ 310 0233; 59 Gordon St; mains $17-30; ☺ lunch & dinner Tue-Sat, dinner Mon; ⊠ ⊠) With elegant settings and opera playing softly in the background, Mona Lisa goes beyond mere gnocchi and ravioli; the Italian owners pride themselves on their authentic antipasti, sinful *dolci* (desserts) and a constantly evolving menu. One guess who the portrait on the wall is of.

Aberdeen Grill (Map p118; ☎ 330 0384; 16 Bau St, Flagstaff; mains $20-35; ☺ lunch & dinner) This stately restaurant has the interior of an old boys' club: with plenty of dark wood, brass, mock-antique seating and wide bay windows. The food is similarly conservative, but is done well. European-influenced chicken, seafood and steak are the predominant stars of the carnivores' menu.

Tiko's Floating Restaurant (Map p118; ☎ 331 3626; off Stinson Pde; mains $25-40; ☺ lunch & dinner Mon-Fri, dinner Sat) The only way you could be any more harbourside would be if you were standing in the water. This permanently moored, former Blue Lagoon cruise ship is best enjoyed when there's little motion in the ocean. The excellent surf-and-turf fare includes New Zealand steak, fresh local fish (*walu* and *pakapaka*) and an extensive wine list.

INDO-FIJIAN

In addition to the three options listed here, there are plenty of hole-in-the-wall, easy-on-the-wallet, curry houses in Suva to set heads spinning and mouths watering, .

Ashiyana (Map p118; ☎ 331 3000; Old Town Hall Bldg, Victoria Pde; mains $8-16; ☽ lunch & dinner Tue-Sat, dinner Sun) This pint-sized restaurant is a long-standing Indian favourite with some of the best butter chicken in town and curries so spicy even the taxi drivers consider them hot.

Maya Dhaba (Map p118; ☎ 331 0045; 281 Victoria Pde; mains $8-17; ☽ lunch & dinner; ✗ ☎) Refined Maya Dhaba screens hip-gyrating Bollywood musicals on flat-screen TVs in Suva's most urbane restaurant. The meals are excellent and you can wrap your naan around any number of Indian classics.

Copper Chimney (Map p116; ☎ 327 0260; 37 & 38 Sports City, Laucola Bay Rd; mains $12-20; ☽ lunch & dinner Mon-Sat, dinner Sun; ✗ ☎) Vegetarians will like the *nauraataan korma*, which features nine different fruit and vegetables cooked in an almond sauce. Others may lean towards the interesting Indo-Chinese fusion dishes.

CHINESE

Capital Palace (Map p118; ☎ 331 6088; 64 Victoria Pde; mains $10; ☽ lunch & dinner; ✗) Unimposing from the outside but surprisingly big on the inside, Capital Palace is a Sunday yum cha institution. The rather curt service here does little to dampen the appetite of the happy diners. The menu offers plenty of Chinese classics and a few dishes straight out of *Fear Factor*. Try the stretched sea cucumber soup or the fish bones rice noodles soup – whatever they are.

Shanghai Seafood House (Map p118; ☎ 331 4865; 6 Thomson St; mains $13-20; ☽ lunch & dinner) In the heart of the shopping district, this 1st-floor restaurant is plush in a kitschy, fake-flower kind of way. The encyclopaedic menu and alfresco seating on the balcony induce long and lazy lunches.

KOREAN & JAPANESE

Korea House (Map p118; ☎ 331 1711; 178 Waimanu Rd; mains $12-25; ☽ lunch & dinner) The interior of this restaurant may lose its oomph once you pass the grand entrance (flanked by a Korean mural), but the food does not. Greenpeace supporters may want to skip the shark-fin soup and stick to the pungent kimchi (pickled vegetables) and sticky Korean barbecue.

Shabu-Shabu (Map p118; ☎ 331 8350; Ramarama Bldg, 91 Gordon St; mains $15-50; ☽ lunch & dinner Mon-Sat, dinner Sun) Some things in life seem just wrong – Fijians wearing kimonos would be one. If you can get past this oddity, you'll be able to enjoy the delicately presented sushi, tempura, udon (wheat noodles), soba (buckwheat noodles) and signature shabu-shabu.

Daikoku Restaurant (Map p118; ☎ 330 8968; Victoria Pde; mains $19-30; ☽ lunch & dinner Mon-Sat) Upstairs past the closet-sized bar, the acrobatic culinary skills of Daikoku's teppanyaki chefs are reason enough to spend an evening here. The seafood, chicken and beef seared on the sizzling teppanyaki plates would hold up in any Tokyo restaurant. Sushi and sashimi is also on the menu and a happy chatter fills the room.

Cafes & Quick Eats

Focaccia Café (Map p118; ☎ 330 9117; Vanua Arcade, Victoria Pde; meals $7; ☽ breakfast & lunch Mon-Sat) This bustling city eatery serves fresh burgers, wraps, rolls, kebabs and focaccias at counter seating or tables in the arcade lobby (it sounds incongruous but it works).

Roma's Hook and Chook (Map p118; ☎ 368 1071; Gordon St; meals $5-15; ☽ lunch & dinner) Traditional fish 'n' chips and rotisserie chicken go up-market in this takeaway-cafe hybrid. The fish (from swordfish to parrot fish) comes with either regular or spicy batter or, for the health nut – grilled, diced and threaded on skewers with veggies.

Esquires Coffee House (☽ breakfast, lunch & dinner; ✗ ☎ ; Dolphin Plaza Map p118; ☎ 330 0333; Dolphin Plaza, Victoria Pde; Downtown Map p118; ☎ 330 0828; Renwick Rd) Both outlets serve good coffee ($3.50 to $5.50) but only average cakes and sandwiches ($3 to $9). Based on the same fair trade and organic bean model as the New Zealand parent company, these cafes also offer free wi-fi access in air-conditioned comfort.

The teams of cooks at the **barbecue stands** (Map p118; Ratu Sukuna Park Intersection; meal boxes $5; ☽ 5pm-4am Tue-Sat) serve Suva's best-value meals into the wee hours of the night. Styrofoam boxes are crammed with enough carbs and cholesterol (taro, sausage, chops, cassava, lamb steak and fried eggs) to arrest the heart of a marathon runner. There are no knives, forks or napkins to be had and eating the runny eggs is a messy proposition.

Suva's food courts, especially the ones at **Downtown Boulevard Shopping Centre** (Map p118; Ellery St), **Dolphin Plaza** (Map p118; cnr Loftus St & Victoria Pde) and **MHCC Department Store** (Map p118; Thomson St; ⊙ 9am-9pm), have large selections of cheap eats.

Self-Catering

Suva Municipal Market (Map p118; Usher St) is the best place for fish, fruit and vegetables. For something to wash it all down with, try **Victoria Wines & Spirits** (Map p118; ☎ 331 2884; Victoria Pde; ⊙ 11am-9pm Mon-Fri, till 2pm Sat). The best supermarket in town is **Superfresh** (Map p118; Thomson St) in the MHCC Department Store. You can also pick up fresh bread and muffins from the bakery on the ground floor.

DRINKING

Suva has a good mix of drinking and dancing dens. The place to be on Friday and Saturday nights is at the bars around Victoria Pde and Macarthur St. Generally, dress standards are very relaxed and although some of the bars may seem rough, the ones listed here are all fairly safe. If a band is playing, or the hour late, expect to pay a small cover charge (usually no more than $5). On the other hand, if you arrive early, entry is free and drinks are discounted between the happy hours of 6pm and 8pm.

Be cautious of the other nightclubs in this area. Many of these tend to become dodgier as the night progresses and most locals attend them only with a group of friends; you should do the same. Watch out for pickpockets on the dance floor and always take a taxi after dark, even if you're in a group. The *Fiji Times'* entertainment section lists upcoming events and what's on at the clubs.

ourpick **O'Reilly's** (Map p118; ☎ 331 2322; cnr Macarthur St & Victoria Pde) O'Reilly's kicks the evening off in relatively subdued fashion: relaxed punters playing pool or watching sport on the numerous TVs. But it brews quite a party as the hours tick by and come 11pm-ish the place is generally throbbing with a diverse crowd shaking their bits to Europop, soft metal, techno, peppy rock-pop…basically anything that keeps the crowd moving. It is one of the few pubs where a reasonably

smart dress code prevails, so dig out your best threads. Aside from the name on the door and the token Guinness on tap, there is nothing particularly Irish about O'Reilly's, other than it'll have you seeing wee leprechauns by midnight.

Bad Dog (Map p118; ☎ 331 2322; cnr Macarthur St & Victoria Pde) Connected by a back door to O'Reilly's, this restaurant turns into a swanky drinking spot at night. It's one of the few bars to open on Sunday so you can grab a jug of sangria, glass of wine or an imported beer and booze it up under the trippy lights at the bar or in the more intimate booths, seven days a week.

Traps Bar (Map p118; ☎ 331 2922; Victoria Pde) Something of a subterranean saloon bar with a series of cavelike, dimly lit rooms. Take a seat in the pool room with wide-screen TV (yes, with sports) or join the happy din at the main bar. The crowd is generally young, trendy and dancing by 11pm. Live music is frequent (usually on Thursdays), as are Bob Marley singalongs.

Bar 66 (Map p118; ☎ 330 8435; Loftus St) This place, above Dolphin Plaza, is popular with jean-clad uni students and one of the few places where both Fijians and Indo-Fijians socialise. The crowd is younger, the vibe cooler and everyone dances to the hip hop, funk and rap skilfully mixed by the resident DJ.

Bourbon Bluez (Map p118; ☎ 330 0945; cnr Macarthur St & Victoria Pde) Two rooms, two bars and two sets of speakers playing different music at the same time. You'll never quite know what to expect here and if you stand anywhere near the middle of the bar, you'll hear it all. When we arrived, one room was playing ABBA and the other Guns N' Roses. When we left (which wasn't long after), the band was trying to make itself heard over an enthusiastic karaoke singer.

JJ's on the Park (Map p118; ☎ 330 5005; Stinson Pde) This classy eatery also has a long bar, which is a nice place to sip a cocktail or glass of red. The atmosphere is refined and relaxed and caters to an older crowd. There are views to the ship-studded harbour, service is attentive and a pianist often (Monday to Thursday) taps the ivories in the background.

Slightly dodgy alternatives:

Birdland R&B Club (Map p118; ☎ 330 3833; 6 Carnarvon St) This underground bar plays Fijian hip hop/jazz and rhythm to an older crowd. The smoky air certainly adds the appropriate bouquet to the blues-den feel.

MOVING TO THE BEAT OF A DIFFERENT DRUM

Dancers pay homage to the steady beat of the drums, seemingly oblivious to the spectators. The poorly lit room is crowded with both tourists and locals yelling 'bula' to one another over the din. As a big, indigenous Fijian man – who better meets the image you may have of a traditional Fijian chief – approaches with a flower behind his ear and a pitcher of beer on his tray, you don't need any reminding that this is no *meke* (dance performance that enacts stories and legends). This is Saturday night in Suva, when the country's urban youth let down their hair and pole dance to pop music.

Fiji's urban youth face many of the same difficulties as young people around the globe: teenage parenting, crime, drugs and skyrocketing unemployment (only one in eight school leavers finds a job). However, these youths also find themselves straddling two opposing worlds: the traditional, conservative society of the villages many have left behind, where life was filled with cultural protocols; and the liberal, individualistic lifestyle of the modern and increasingly Westernised city. With 90% of its airtime devoted to Western sitcoms, young people watch TV filled with an irrelevant and often unattainable world. On the positive side, the rising club and cafe culture is bringing together youths from indigenous and Indo-Fijian backgrounds, in the midst of a city filled with ethnic tension. On the negative side, many have difficulty finding a job; and returning 'home' to a village sporting dreadlocks and skin-tight jeans isn't much easier. Youth have little room to voice their own opinions and it's not entirely surprising that many look for routes out of the country.

This is not the Fiji of postcards, of grass skirts and beachside *lovo* (feast cooked in a pit oven); however, it's well worth grabbing a cappuccino or putting on your dancing shoes to check out Fiji's rising urban youth culture. It's an unexpected eye-opener.

Ranch (Map p118; ☎ 992 7901; Carnarvon St) Hokey cowboy songs get a Fijian makeover and the band makes every 'somebody done me some wrong' song quite cheery.

ENTERTAINMENT
Cinemas
Village 6 Cinema Complex (Map p118; ☎ 330 6006; Scott St; adult/child $5.50/4.50) Recently released Hollywood and Bollywood films battle it out at Suva's flashy cinema complex.

Check out the *Fiji Times'* entertainment section for cinema listings.

Sport
Fijians are fanatical about their rugby and, even if you aren't that keen on the game, it's worth going to a match. The season lasts from April to September and teams tough it out at the **National Stadium** (Map p116; Laucala Bay Rd, Laucala). The atmosphere is huge. Ask at the FVB if there will be a match during your stay.

You can also catch players training hard at Albert Park during the week.

SHOPPING
Your best chance of finding something truly unique is to skip the mass-produced stuff found in the chain tourist stores (which are carbon copies of their Nadi parents; see p87) and head straight to the markets.

Suva Curio & Handicraft Market (Map p118; Stinson Pde) Strap on your barter boots; this market has endless craft stalls and, if you know your stuff, can offer some fantastic deals. Just be aware that not many of the artefacts are as genuine as the vendor would like you to believe. Only pay what the object is worth to you. A 2.1m by 1.2m *ibe* (mat) goes for between $45 and $75 (depending on how fine the weaving is) and a completely plain white *tapa* cloth costs around $45 for a 3.6m-by-0.6m length.

Suva Flea Market (Map p118; Rodwell Rd) Less touristy than the handicraft market previously mentioned, this is another great place to buy *masi* and traditional crafts, although you might have to sort through the Hawaiian shirts to find them.

ROC Market (Map p118; Dolphin Plaza, Victoria Pde) The Dolphin Plaza holds a small but eclectic market on the third Sunday of every month. Stalls feature homemade food, and arts and crafts at reasonable prices.

Government Crafts Centre (Map p118; ☎ 331 5869; Macarthur St) Money spent here assists rural artisans and you can be guaranteed that the generally high-quality items for sale aren't imported from Indonesia. Prices are fixed.

GETTING THERE & AWAY

Suva is well connected to the rest of the country by air and interisland ferries, and to western Viti Levu by buses and carriers. Most international flights, however, arrive at Nadi International Airport.

Air

Nausori International Airport is around 23km northeast of central Suva. **Nausori Taxi & Bus Service** (☎ 331 2185) has regular shuttle buses between the airport and the Holiday Inn hotel in Suva ($10). Otherwise, a taxi from the airport to or from Suva costs a standard $27 (taxi drivers generally won't budge on this).

See p245 for domestic flight routes.

Airline offices in Suva:

Air Fiji (Map p118; ☎ 331 5055; www.airfiji.com.fj; 185 Victoria Pde)

Air New Zealand (Map p118; ☎ 331 3100; www .pacificislands.airnewzealand.com; Queensland Insurance Bldg, Victoria Pde)

Air Pacific & Pacific Sun (Map p118; ☎ 330 4388; www.airpacific.com, www.pacificsun.com.fj; Colonial Bldg, Victoria Pde)

Pacific Blue (Map p118; ☎ 331 5311, www.virginblue .com.au; 81/85 Marks St)

Qantas (Map p118; ☎ 331 1833; fax 330 4795; Colonial Bldg, Victoria Pde)

Boat

From Suva there are regular ferry services to Ovalau, Vanua Levu, Taveuni and Kadavu, plus less regular, and far less comfortable, boats to the Lau and Moala islands. Not many travellers use these boats, and conditions are a far cry from anything the words 'a cruise on the South Pacific' might imply. For details about these interisland boats see p247.

Bus & Carrier

There are frequent buses operating along the Queens Road and Kings Road from Suva's main **bus station** (Map p118; Rodwell Rd). If you can cope with busy bus stations and sometimes crowded buses, these buses are more fun and better value than tourist buses and will stop at resorts along the way upon request. **Sunbeam Transport** (☎ 382 122) runs several express buses daily to Lautoka via both the southern (Queens Road), and northern (Kings Road), routes. **Pacific Transport** (☎ 330 4366) also runs several daily express buses to Lautoka ($14.20) via

Queens Road, with stops at Pacific Harbour ($3.60), Korolevu ($6.70), Sigatoka ($8.50) and Nadi ($9.35).

Minibuses travelling west along Queens Road depart from behind the cinema. They are slightly faster than normal buses and depart when full. It costs $5 to Pacific Harbour, $10 to Sigatoka, $15 to Nadi and $17 to Lautoka (per person).

The Coral Sun bus leaves the Holiday Inn at 7.30am and 3.50pm, calling at the major Coral Coast resorts as it travels to Nadi International Airport. One-way fares cost $9 to Pacific Harbour, $15 to the Outrigger Hotel and $20 to Nadi airport, per person. Tickets can be booked at the ATS Pacific tour desk in the Holiday Inn.

GETTING AROUND

Local buses are cheap and plentiful and depart from the main bus station. There are relatively few buses in the evening and barely any on Sundays.

Taxis are cheap for short trips ($3 to $5), and in Suva they actually use the meter! The city's one-way looping streets may make you think the taxi driver is taking you for a ride; drivers along Victoria Pde may get caught on a long run around the market and wharf area. To order one call **Jason's Taxis** (☎ 337 2220), **Carnarvon Taxi** (☎ 331 5315), **Sanyo Cabs** (☎ 330 4541) or **Piccadilly Taxis** (☎ 330 4302; ☾ 24hr).

See p249 for more information, and a list of car-rental companies in Suva.

KINGS ROAD

Carving a scenic route between Suva and Lautoka, the Kings Road is every bit as spectacular as the faster and more popular Queens Road route. Much fuss is made of the pothole-ridden roads, the ageing buses and the general lack of infrastructure in northern Viti Levu, but for those who don't mind a few bumps – and that's all they'll be – a lush interior and gorgeous views over the Wainibuka River awaits.

The road coils and extends for around 256km, linking the country's two largest cities via the mainland's least developed coast. Promises to upgrade the road have been in the pipeline for many years, but work appears to be carried out at an excruciatingly cautious rate. At the time of research, the road between Korovou and Dama remained unsealed, but had recently been remetalled. Whether this was a precursor to more ambitious plans or a quick fix until the next rainy season, who can tell? A Sunbeam express bus can take up to seven hours to trundle between Suva and Lautoka, although most travellers layover at Rakiraki or Nananu-i-Ra.

NAUSORI & THE REWA DELTA
Nausori
pop 25,000

The township of Nausori is on the eastern bank of the Rewa River, about 19km northeast of downtown Suva. It has the country's second-largest airport. Nausori is a bustling service centre and transport hub for the largely agricultural- and manufacturing-industry workers.

The town developed around the CSR sugar mill that operated here for eight decades until 1959, when everyone realised that the canes actually grew better on the drier western side. D'oh! Now Nausori is a major rice-producing region and the old sugar mill has been put to good use as a rice mill.

There are many eroded ring-ditch fortifications in the Rewa Delta. About 10m wide with steep, battered sides and a strong fence on the inner bank, they were necessary for the survival of a village in times of war, protecting it against a surprise attack.

GETTING THERE & AROUND
The Kings Road from Suva to Nausori is the country's busiest and most congested stretch of highway; regular buses ($1.85, 30 minutes) travel this route. The Nausori bus station is in the main street. Sunbeam Transport has regular buses to Lautoka via the Kings Road ($15.80, 5½ hours).

Regular buses run from Nausori to nearby boat landings: Bau Landing, Wainibokasi Landing (for Nasilai village) and Nakelo Landing (for Toberua). From Nakelo Landing there are local village boats, which you may be able to join or hire to explore the area.

Nausori International Airport
The airport is about 3km southeast of Nausori, 22km from Suva. This is primarily a domestic airport used principally by Air Fiji and Pacific Sun (although Pacific Sun flies to Tonga and Tuvalu from here).

See p245 for details of flying domestically within Fiji.

Nasilai Village & Naililili Catholic Mission
Nasilai village is home to the well-known potter, Taraivini Wati. Pottery is a major source of income for the village and when large orders are placed everyone participates in the process – helping to collect and prepare the clay and make the pots. When a baby girl is born in the village, a lump of clay is placed on her forehead. It's believed she will then automatically know how to carry on the pottery-making tradition.

Catholic missionaries from France built the **Naililili Catholic Mission** (Map pp76–7) at the turn of the century. The stained-glass windows were imported from Europe and incorporate Fijian writing and imagery.

Wilderness Ethnic Adventure Fiji (p124), based in Suva, occasionally offers full- and half-day tours to this seldom-visited area.

There are regular buses to Wainibokasi Landing from Nausori bus station. If driving from Nausori, head southeast for 6km on the road that runs parallel to the Rewa River. Pass the airport entrance and turn right at the T-junction. The landing is a further 1km, before the bridge across the Wainibokasi River. There you can catch a boat to the Naililili Catholic Mission, which is almost opposite the landing, or take a short trip downriver to Nasilai village. Ask a local for permission to visit the village and take along some *kava* for a *sevusevu*.

Bau
It is bizarre to think that in the 19th century such a tiny speck of land was the power base of Cakobau and his father, Tanoa (see p32). In the 1780s, there were 30 *bure kalou* (ancient temples) on the small chiefly island, including the famous Na Vata ni Tawake, which stood on a huge *yavu* faced with large panels of flat rock. Also of interest are its **chiefly cemetery**, **old church** and a **sacrificial killing stone** on which enemies were slaughtered prior to being cooked and consumed.

Bau is not an official tourist attraction and to visit (and possibly stay the night) you must first be invited by someone who lives there. If you dress conservatively, show polite and genuine interest, take a large *waka* (bunch of *kava* roots) for presentation to the *turaga-ni-koro* (chief) and ask around at Bau Landing, you'll probably be invited to visit. Failing that, ask for permission from the **Ministry of Fijian Affairs** (Map p118; ☎ ask for Peni Leweniqila 330 4200; Government Bldgs, Suva).

There are regular buses from Nausori bus station to Bau Landing, which is northeast of Nausori airport. If you are driving from Nausori, turn left before the airport and after about 4km turn left at the intersection and follow the road to its end. Boats cross to nearby Bau. Boats also leave Bau Landing for the island of **Viwa**, where missionaries lived during Cakobau's time.

Toberua

This small island (2 hectares) is just off Kaba Point, the easternmost point of Viti Levu, about 30km from Suva.

Toberua Island Resort (Map pp76-7; ☎ 347 2777; www.toberua.com; s/d/tr from $439/495/619, s/d/tr incl meals from $636/776/899, children under 16yr stay free; 🏊) is the perfect island hideaway for those seeking some South Pacific solitude. Originally built in 1968 as an American millionaire's hideaway, it's since reinvented itself to cater to unfussy couples and families. The 15 waterfront *bure* scattered along the beach have gloriously high roofs, minibars, sun decks and stylish bathrooms. Toberua only receives about one-third of Suva's annual rainfall so the climate is balmy for most of the year. At low tide the beach is used for golf and there is snorkelling, paddle boating, and tours to the nearby bird sanctuary and mangroves. A two-tank dive costs $210 and PADI Open Water Course $680. Transfers involve a taxi from Nausori airport ($20) or Suva ($40) to Nakelo Landing, followed by a boat trip ($80 per adult and $40 per child return, 40 minutes).

KOROVOU TO DAMA

While the Kings Road is mostly sealed, the 56km section between Korovou and Dama is not. Although locals tackle the route in 2WDs, it's best traversed with a 4WD and a prayer to the god of suspension. After a downpour you can throw the complication of mud into the equation. The reward is an untouched landscape, devoid of a coastline and commercial infrastructure. It's one of the most scenic road trips in the country; travelling by bus will afford the views without the hassle.

Korovou is not much more than a transport intersection, about 50km north of Suva. From here the Kings Road continues to the northwest and over the hills. Another unsealed road follows the coast to Natovi Landing (below), a 20-minute drive from where there are bus-ferry services to Labasa (Vanua Levu) and Levuka (Ovalau). See p248 for details. Arranged boat pick-ups to resorts on Leluvia and Caqalai islands are from Waidalice Landing, southeast of Korovou.

About 14km from Korovou on the Kings Road you'll pass the beautiful **Uru's Waterfall** (Map pp76–7), which descends over a rocky slope on the northern side of the road and ends its journey in a serene pool surrounded by colourful foliage. It's possible to swim here – just ask one of the villagers for permission.

Wailotua Snake God Cave (Map pp76–7), 23km west of Korovou, is reputedly one of the largest caves in the world. The name derives from six glittering stalactites in the shape of snakes' heads. During times of war, the village would pack up en masse and seek shelter in the cave's pitch-black labyrinth, which culminates in a huge chamber inhabited by bats. To get here, hop on one of the Suva–Lautoka buses and ask the driver to let you off at Wailotua village. Ask the first person you approach if you can visit the cave; they'll organise a couple of lads to guide you through it by lantern. This is the village's main source of income and a $15 donation is well worth the tour and commentary. Wailotua village also entertains Feejee Experience groups, which call in for *bilibili* rafting and visits to local schools on their way to Rakiraki.

Between Korovou and Rakiraki, the Kings Road crosses dairy-farming country (land given to returned soldiers after WWII), winds through hills and along the Wainibuka River, and passes many villages.

Natovi Landing

There is a general store at Natovi Landing, but little else. Patterson Brothers offers a bus-ferry-bus service from Suva to Labasa via Natovi Landing for $55. It also has a Suva–Natovi–Ovalau bus-ferry service ($25, daily except Sunday) to Levuka.

It is possible to travel north by road and meet the Kings Road again further on, but the road deteriorates significantly as you approach Mt Tova.

Natalei Eco-Lodge (Map pp76-7; ☎ 949 7460; vic torkoyanaivole@connect.com.fj; dm/r incl meals $80/180) is a village-based tourism project in Nataleira and a great opportunity to swerve right off the beaten track and into a cultural adventure. The double and dorm *bure* are frugal, but exploring the surrounding landscape is the real appeal here. Close to Mt Tova, the area offers some excellent hiking and Bligh Water is renowned for snorkelling and diving. There are buses from Suva ($12, three hours) departing at 10am, 1pm and 2pm daily and returning at 7am and 4pm.

NAISERELAGI CATHOLIC MISSION

About 25km southeast of Rakiraki is this 1917 mission (Map pp76–7) overlooking Viti Levu Bay. The church is famous for its mural depicting a black Christ, painted in 1962 by Jean Charlot. The three panels of biblical scenes depict Christ on the cross in a *masi sulu* (skirt or wrapped cloth worn to below the knees) with a *tanoa* at his feet. Indigenous Fijians are shown offering mats and *tabua* (whale's tooth), and Indo-Fijians presenting flowers and oxen. Visitors are welcome and a small donation is appreciated.

From Vaileka, or the Kings Road intersection, take the Flying Prince local bus ($2, 30 minutes, five to eight daily), ideally before 9am when buses are more regular. Otherwise it will cost $36 return by taxi. Naiserelagi is just south of Nanukuloa village, on the right past the school. The mission is on the hill, about 500m up a winding track.

RAKIRAKI & AROUND

The scenery is stunning along the Kings Road, winding down the mountains from Dama past Viti Levu Bay and to the beautiful region of Rakiraki, Viti Levu's northernmost tip. The climate on the northern side of the **Nakauvadra Range** is similar to that of western Viti Levu, drier and suited for growing sugar cane, although far windier. According to local legend, the imposing mountains are the home of the great snake-god Degei, creator of all the islands. The opening and closing of his eyes prompt night and day, and thunder is said to be Degei turning in his sleep.

The turn-off to **Ellington Wharf** is about 5km east of Rakiraki junction and it is here that resorts collect their guests for the short boat ride across to Nananu-i-Ra.

West of Rakiraki junction, there is a turn-off that leads past the sugar mill to the small service town of **Vaileka**. This is where those arriving by bus will be deposited, and it's a good

place to stock up on provisions before heading offshore. Besides the bus station itself, town amenities include a New World supermarket, a taxi rank, a produce market, Westpac and ANZ banks (both with ATM machines), several greasy fast-food restaurants and upstairs in a small shop – identified simply by its sign saying 'Internet' – near Sunbeam Buses, reliably fast internet for $2 an hour.

Sights & Activities

If you have commandeered your own taxi, it's worth asking the driver to show you **Udreudre's Tomb**, the resting place of Fiji's most notorious cannibal (see the boxed text, p134). The tomb isn't very impressive, just a rectangular block of concrete often overgrown with weeds but, as it's just by the roadside (on the left about 100m west of the Vaileka turn-off), drivers don't mind stopping for a few minutes.

About 10km west of Rakiraki, near Vitawa, is a large outcrop known as **Navatu Rock** (Map pp76–7). There was once a fortified village on top of the rock and it was believed that from here spirits would depart for the afterlife.

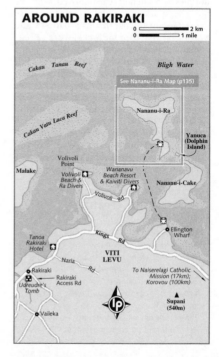

AROUND RAKIRAKI

0 —————— 2 km
0 —————— 1 mile

Cakau Tanau Reef

Bligh Water

See Nananu-i-Ra Map (p135)

Nananu-i-Ra

Cakau Vatu Laca Reef

Yanuca (Dolphin Island)

Volivoli Point

Malake

Volivoli Beach & Ra Divers

Wananavu Beach Resort & Kaiviti Divers

Nananu-i-Cake

Volivoli Rd

Ellington Wharf

Tanoa Rakiraki Hotel

Kings Rd

VITI LEVU

Naria

Rd

Rakiraki

Rakiraki Access Rd

Udreudre's Tomb

To Naiserelagi Catholic Mission (17km); Korovou (100km)

Vaileka

Supani (540m)

VITI LEVU

One of the principal reasons to visit the Rakiraki area is the excellent **scuba diving** to be had on the nearby Cakau Vatu Lacca and Cakau Tanau Reefs. Volivoli Beach (below) and Wananavu Beach Resort (right) have on-site dive operators, and there is also an operator on Nananu-i-Ra (see opposite). All three share spots and all three will happily collect divers from anywhere in the area (usually for around $40, depending on how far they had to come). See the diving section, p68, for a general overview of what lies beneath.

Sleeping & Eating

Located on the northernmost point of Viti Levu, **Volivoli Beach** (☎ 669 4511; www.volivoli.com; Volivoli Rd; dm/d/villa $26/105/336; 🏊) has a unique location and offers some of the best budget accommodation in Fiji. The eight-person dorms are in a modern and spotlessly clean hillside lodge. Each dormitory shares a huge deck and comes with two bathrooms (allowing the girls to annex one and the boys the other). Further up the hill is another lodge divided into four doubles that share a communal lounge, bathroom and wide hall that doubles as a kitchen. Far removed from the noisy backpackers and on the opposite side of the restaurant and bar (mains $10 to $18, and $2 for a bowl of fruit for brekkie) are 13 self-contained, two-bedroom villas with sweeping ocean views and modern, crisp interiors. If you are disappointed by the mangrove-lined beach, you'll be pleasantly surprised by the picturesque sand spit only a minute's walk around the corner. It is here you will find **Ra Divers** (☎ 669 4511; www.radivers.com), which charges $165 for a two-tank dive or $550 for a PADI Open Water Course. Volivoli also offers some great value dorm-and-dive packages (four nights and the Open Water

Course for $559). Ra also rents snorkel gear for $10 and shuttles snorkellers to the outer reef for $25.

Part of the Tanoa chain, **Tanoa Rakiraki Hotel** (☎ 669 4101; www.tanoahotels.com; Kings Rd; dm $33, r $75-130; 🅿 🏊) is an ageing midrange hotel, which also offers dorms and cheap singles ($60) in a lodge out back. Located 1.8km east of the Vaileka turn-off and currently running a poor second to neighbouring options, there is little, beyond a bowling green, to tempt travellers.

Wananavu Beach Resort (☎ 669 4433; www.wananavu.com; garden/ocean bure incl breakfast $200/270, beachfront bure incl breakfast $350-380, f incl breakfast $450; 🅿 🏊) has a restaurant (mains $32 to $39) with gorgeous views over the beautiful pool area and out to Nananu-i-Ra island. All the *bure* have timber floors, panelled walls, air-con and their own small decks and are surrounded by pretty palm- and bougainvillea-filled gardens. While the *bure* are all very similar, the price climbs dramatically as you head down the hill towards the water. The beach here is entirely artificially created and although the landscapers have done an excellent job, with strategically placed palm trees perfect for slinging a hammock between, most guests end up swimming in the pool. Diving and snorkelling are provided by **Kaiviti Divers** (☎ 669 4522; www.kaivitidivers.com), which are based at the resort's small marina. A two-tank dive costs $232 and PADI Open Water Course $550 including equipment.

Getting There & Around

The best way to reach the resorts of Rakiraki and Nananu-i-Ra island is to catch a Sunbeam express bus along Kings Road from either Suva ($10.60, 4½ hours) or Nadi ($9.50, 2¼ hours) and get off at Vaileka, Rakiraki's main town. Keep hold of your bus ticket because the conductors on this route are tirelessly dedicated to checking them. A taxi costs $15 (the price is fixed) to either Volivoli, Wananavu Beach Resort or Ellington Wharf (to catch your prearranged boat to Nananu-i-Ra).

Your other option is to time it for the 7am or 8.30am Flying Prince local bus that runs directly to Ellington Wharf from Vaileka, or catch any Kings Road local bus and walk the 1.3km from the junction.

NANANU-I-RA

This pocket-sized paradise is a must on any northern Viti Levu itinerary. The 3.5-sq-km island is beautifully hilly, and is surrounded

---

AN UNEARTHLY APPETITE

In 1849, some time after the death of Ratu Udreudre (p133), the Reverend Richard Lyth asked Udreudre's son, Ratavu, about the significance of a long line of stones. Each stone, he was told, represented one of the chief's victims, and amounted to a personal tally of at least 872 corpses. Ratavu went on to explain that his father consumed every piece of his victims of war, sharing none. He ate little else, and had an enormous appetite.

by scalloped bays, white-sand beaches and mangroves. There are, however, neither roads nor villages, and accommodation standards are very basic. Cattle grazing has cleared much of the dense vegetation and today rolling hills of grass inhabit the interior. It's only 3km north of Ellington Wharf, but the atypical landscape and small enclave of wealthy holiday homes exaggerates the distance. Nananu-i-Ra's original inhabitants were wiped out by disease and tribal war, and their land was sold by their surviving heirs, mostly to Fijians of European descent.

Nananu-i-Ra is renowned for windsurfing and it can get very windy on the east side of the island from May through to July and again from late October to December during the cyclone season. The narrow strip of land that separates the west (Front Beach) from the east (Back Beach) is only 200m wide and no matter which way the wind blows, it's only a short walk to the calmer side.

At one stage there was talk of developing the island, including resurrecting the now-defunct Nananu Lodge as a five-star hotel. So far it's just talk.

Dangers & Annoyances

It would seem that a place as small as Nananu-i-Ra wouldn't be particularly dangerous – and as a rule, it's not – but client poaching can be a problem. If anyone, particularly another hotel operator, tells you that the place where you intend to stay is closed, wait until you arrive on the island and see for yourself before committing to anywhere else.

Activities

TREKKING

The island is great for trekking and has wonderful views to the mainland. A common sight from the southern side of the island are billowing white clouds swallowing the volcanic Nakauvadra mountain range. The grassy hilltops also provide bird's-eye views of the surrounding turquoise reefs and the aptly named **Sunset Point** where Ed Morris, a past president of the International Brotherhood of Magicians, has constructed his **labyrinth**. It may sound like something out of *Harry Potter*, but it's nothing more than some rope pegged to the ground. If you are lucky, Ed will be around to explain what it all means.

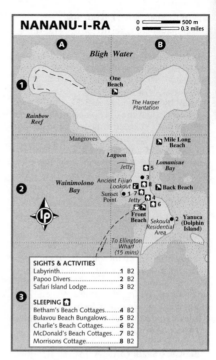

SIGHTS & ACTIVITIES
Labyrinth	1 B2
Papoo Divers	2 B2
Safari Island Lodge	3 B2

SLEEPING
Betham's Beach Cottages	4 B2
Bulavou Beach Bungalows	5 B2
Charlie's Beach Cottages	6 B2
McDonald's Beach Cottages	7 B2
Morrisons Cottage	8 B2

If you time it right with the tides, you can walk around the island in about four to five hours (passing the mangroves at low tide). Part of the island is rocky so shoes are recommended.

DIVING & SNORKELLING

Snorkelling offshore you can expect to see some coral, abundant fish and, on the north side of the island, many sea snakes. The surrounding reefs and especially Bligh Water to the north have some amazing dive sites (see p68).

You can snorkel off the jetty (lots of colourful fish) or do day trips to the reefs at Bligh Water ($25 per person, minimum four people).

Papoo Divers (☎ 944 4726; papoodivers@mobilee mail.vodafone.com.fj) is the only dive shop based at Nananu-i-Ra and the dive instructor has 19 years' experience in these waters. It charges $150 for a two-tank dive including equipment and $500 for an open-water course. The dive boat has plenty of shade and Ginger, the cat, usually accompanies every outing.

WINDSURFING & KITEBOARDING

The climate here is relatively dry and the island's exposure to the southeast trade winds make it especially suited for windsurfing. Many windsurfers come here from May to July when winds are generally 10 knots or more most days.

Safari Island Lodge (☎ 669 3333, 669 3700; www .safarilodge.com.fj) is the only place on the island that has both kiteboarding and windsurfing gear for hire (beginner equipment is $350 per week, and advanced $500) and an experienced instructor. Because of the reef, and the possibility of torn sails, a first-time, one-off lesson ($85) is advisable to access your coral-avoiding skills.

Sleeping & Eating

Take cash and plenty of change, as not all places accept credit cards. Many of the budget places are well set up for self-caterers and both Betham's and McDonald's Beach Cottages have an outdoor cafe with limited menus and small stores selling the basics. Vegetarians might want to bring their own fruit and vegetables from the mainland to ensure supply.

Expect cold-water showers and the generator to be switched off around 10pm.

Betham's Beach Cottages (☎ 669 4132; www .bethams.com.fj; dm/tw/cottages $20/110/130) Betham's has some sound, old-fashioned beach-house accommodation options. The duplex beachfront cottages have large kitchens, tiled floors and can sleep up to five people. The double rooms are good value and there is a large communal kitchen that is shared by those in the spacious eight-bed dorm. The open-air restaurant (mains $17 to $23) here serves hearty meals, if you place your order by 1pm.

Charlie's Beach Cottages (☎ 628 3268; charlie's@ connect.com.fj; dm/d $25/100, extra person $10) Charlie's has a large beach cottage made of concrete blocks and is of a fairly basic standard. There's a double bed in the bedroom and the lounge can take a further four single beds if required. There is also a seven-bed dorm in a similar but smaller cottage. Set evening meals cost $16.

McDonald's Beach Cottages (☎ 628 3118; www .macsnananu.com; dm & tw $27, cottages tw/f $89/131) McDonald's offers a scattering of supertidy cabins on a nicely landscaped property right in front of the jetty. The cute blue and yellow cottages are self-contained and it's popular

with do-it-yourself types. The outdoor restaurant serves great pizza ($17), which is probably the best food on the island (although it is a very small island). There is no snorkelling gear available but kayaks are free and, weather permitting, kayaking around the island takes four to five hours.

ourpick Bulavou Beach Bungalows (☎ 669 3755; www.bulavoubeachbungalowsfiji.com; dm/d/tr/q $30/150/150/150) This is by far the nicest accommodation on the island and, as it is no dearer than elsewhere, it's the logical place to stay. There are three newly constructed, double-storey chalets with a unit on each floor. Each unit has two rooms furnished with a queen-sized bed, a set of bunks and two single beds, as well as modern bathrooms, hot water and spacious lounges. The units are let on a per-bed ($30) or per-room ($150) rate. Meal packages are available ($55 for breakfast and dinner) and if you catch a fish on one of their fishing trips ($200 for six hours), they'll cook it for you.

Morrisons Cottage (☎ 628 1075, 988 9451; tip ple@connect.com.fj; dm/cottages $30/140) The self-contained cottage here can sleep four and there is also a simple dorm. This place was in the process of changing hands when we called and its future unclear. Phone first to check that it is still operating. There is no restaurant here.

Getting There & Around

Nananu-i-Ra is just a 15-minute boat ride from Ellington Wharf. All the resorts on Nananu-i-Ra have their own boat transfers. Arrange your pick-up in advance (there is also a phone at Ellington Wharf). Boat transfers for the budget resorts are around $30 to $40 per person return. Coming back you should spot the taxi that usually waits at the wharf for returning travellers. If there are none, phone **Susnil Sharma** (☎ 830 6786) to come and collect you. A taxi costs $15 to Vaileka, to Lautoka $100 and to Nadi $130.

TAVUA

pop 2400

Tavua is a small, quiet agricultural town with lots of temples, churches and mosques. The Emperor Gold Mining Company mined here from the 1930s until 2006 when DRD Gold of South Africa announced it was no longer viable and the mine was closed. Until then, most of the mine's 1800 workers lived in

Vatukoula, a purpose-built town 9km south of Tavua. The Emperor Gold Mining Company had been Fiji's largest private employer and its subsequent closing has placed considerable hardship on local communities.

The only place to stay is at the **Tavua Hotel** (Map pp76-7; ☎ 668 0522; Vatia St; dm/s/d $27/68/100; ☒).

Nadarivatu, Navai & Koro-Ni-O

In the dry season head up to the forestry settlement of Nadarivatu (30km southeast of Tavua), from where you can hike to Fiji's highest peak, **Tomanivi** (1323m, also known as Mt Victoria), or to **Mt Lomalagi** (meaning 'sky' or 'heaven' in Fijian). The Mt Lomalagi hike has great views (three hours return). The **Forestry Office** (☎ 668 9001) can arrange camping or a homestay with a local family (bring provisions and give money or groceries to your hosts to cover costs).

You can walk from Navai, which is 8km southeast of Nadarivatu, to Tomanivi's peak. Allow at least five hours (return) to hike from the village. Guides can be hired for $15. The last half of the climb is practically rock climbing and can be very slippery.

The Wainibuka and Wainimala Rivers (eventually merging to form the Rewa) originate around here, as does the Sigatoka River. Past Navai the road deteriorates and is recommended for 4WD vehicles only. Koro-ni-O (meaning 'village of the clouds') and the **Monasavu Dam** are about 25km to the southeast. The Wailoa/Monasavu Hydroelectric Scheme here provides about 93% of Viti Levu's power needs.

GETTING THERE & AWAY

The turn-off to the hills, crossing Fiji's highest mountain range and eventually ending up in Suva, is about 3km east of Tavua. The windy, rough gravel road climbs sharply, affording spectacular vistas of the coast and takes about 1½ hours by 4WD. Local bus services from Tavua ceased operating due to poor road conditions. The road from Navai to Suva is barely passable; avoid it unless you have a 4WD or are getting a lift in a carrier.

BA

pop 15,800

Although few find reason to visit Ba, it is Fiji's fifth largest town and characterised by its sizeable Indo-Fijian and Muslim population –

most of whom are soccer mad. Ba boasts Fiji's best racecourse and the town's **horse-racing** and **bougainvillea festivals** are in September.

Most who make it to Ba are there to change buses and catch onward transport into the Nausori Highlands. If you want to break your journey, overnight at the bright pink and purple **Ba Hotel** (Map pp76-7; ☎ 667 4000; bahotel@connect.com.fj; 110 Bank St; s & d $69; ☒ ☒) near the Westpac Bank. The rooms are comfortably worn and have hot-water showers and tea- and coffee-making facilities. The restaurant next to the public bar is open from breakfast to dinner.

Sunbeam buses travelling between Lautoka ($2, 55 minutes) and Suva ($15, five to six hours) call in at the bus station throughout the day.

NAUSORI HIGHLANDS

In stark contrast to the dense rainforests of the eastern highlands, the Nausori Highlands ascend into the interior in a panorama of grassy moguls. Massive folds of pale green tussle and tumble into the background as the coastline diminishes along the horizon. There are patchy areas of forest and small villages scattered in the hills; the more remote, the more traditional the villagers are in their ways. Sunday is a day of rest and worship, so visits to villages on this day may be disruptive and unappreciated. The villagers in Navala are Catholic, while in Bukuya they are Methodist.

If you have your own transport, the loop from Nadi to Ba, going part of the way to Bukuya and then either back down to Nadi, or down via the Sigatoka Valley, is a fun and usually easy day trip. You'll need a 4WD, and you should check road conditions and fill your tank before heading for the hills.

TOURS

Nadi tour operators, Great Sights Fiji and Rosie Holidays, arrange tours in the Nausori Highlands, including day trips to Navala. See p79 for details.

Navala

pop 800

Nestled in rugged, grassy mountains, Navala is by far Fiji's most picturesque village. Navala's chief enforces strict town-planning rules: the dozens of traditional thatched *bure* are laid out neatly in avenues, with a central promenade

---

THE REVEREND BAKER'S LAST SUPPER

Thomas Baker, a Wesleyan Methodist missionary, was killed on 21 July 1867 by the Vatusila people of Nubutautau village (also known as Navatusila), deep in the isolated Nausori Highlands. A few years earlier, Baker had been given the task of converting the people of the interior to Christianity. Baker's predecessors had been able to convert many groups peacefully and he was advised to keep to these areas. But out of impatience, martyrdom, foolhardiness or the urge for success, he ignored the advice and with it crucial cultural know-how.

The highlanders associated conversion to Christianity with subservience to the chiefdom of Bau. As they were opposed to any kind of extended authority, knocking off the reverend may well have been a political manoeuvre. However, a second and more widely believed theory maintains that it was Baker's own behaviour that brought about his nasty end. Apparently, the local chief had borrowed Baker's comb to festoon his voluptuous hairdo. Insensitive or forgetful of the fact that the chief's head was considered sacred, Baker grabbed the comb from the chief's hair. Villagers were furious at the missionary for committing this sacrilege and killed him and ate him in disgust.

In 2003, believing they had suffered a curse of bad luck as a result of their ancestors' culinary habits, the people of Nabutautau held a tribal ceremony to apologise to the descendants of the missionary. Around 600 people attended, including Thomas Baker's great-great-grandson and Prime Minister Lasenia Qarase.

---

sloping down the banks of the Ba River. All of the houses here are built with local materials; the only concrete block and corrugated iron in sight is for the school, Catholic church and radio shed (housing the village's emergency radio telephone). The rectangular-plan houses have a timber-pole structure, sloping stone plinths, woven split-bamboo walls and thatched roofs. Kitchens are in separate *bure*, and toilets in *bure lailai* (little houses).

Navala is a photographer's delight, but you need to get permission and pay the $15 entrance fee before wandering around. If arriving independently, ask the first person you meet to take you to the *turaga-ni-koro* (the chief-appointed headman who collects the entrance fee). As the village charges a fee to enter, a traditional *sevusevu* is not required although all other village etiquette rules outlined on p42 apply. Recently some enterprising locals have been charging visitors $25 and pocketing the extra $10 for themselves, or insisting that guides are mandatory. If you visit the *turaga-ni-koro* first, or arrive with Tui from Bulou's Eco Lodge, you should be able to circumvent these hassles.

SLEEPING & EATING

Bulou's Eco Lodge (Map pp76-7; ☎ 628 1224, 666 6644, after the beeps dial 2116; dm/bure per person incl meals $65/75) To experience Fijian hospitality at its finest, a night (or two) spent with the retired couple Seresio and Bulou N Talili, and their

son Tui is highly recommended. Their home and ecolodge is 1km past Navala village, so phone ahead so they can send their tiny truck to meet you at the bus stop. Guests are totally spoilt; expect to be encouraged to 'eat more' of the traditional food that is prepared in staggering quantities. Tui is an excellent guide and he accompanies all their guests around the village introducing them to his relatives and friends. He will also guide nonguests around for $10 (per group up to four).

There are two traditional *bure* in the garden and a 10-bed dorm attached to the house; there are cold-water showers and flush toilets but no electricity. It is polite to bring a small *sevusevu* (a $5 pack of ground *kava* is enough) to present the hosts during the *kava* ceremony (although they will neither ask for nor expect it). Bulou sells her handicrafts (pandanus mats and printed *masi* cloth) for reasonable prices and when you tire of swimming in the backyard river Tui can arrange horse riding ($25) and trekking ($20) in the surrounding hills.

GETTING THERE & AWAY

The local buses from Ba to Navala ($2.60) leave Ba bus station at 12.30pm and 5.15pm Monday to Friday and at noon, 4.30pm and 5.15pm on Saturday. Buses return to Ba at 6am, 7.30am and 1.45pm Monday to Saturday. Locals pay $45 one way to charter a carrier but it is unlikely you will be able to get it for this price. The rough, gravel road has a few patches of bitumen on the really steep bits. While only 26km away, Navala is about a 1¼-hour drive from Ba, past the Rarawai Sugar Mill, through beautiful rugged scenery.

If driving from Ba, there are a couple of turns to watch out for – at the police post take the left turn passing a shop on your right, and at the next fork in the road, keep left. The road is rough and rocky, but usually passable as long as the car has high clearance. The Ba River floods occasionally and the concrete bridge just before the village becomes impassable.

Bukuya
pop 700

The village of Bukuya is at the intersection of the gravel roads from Sigatoka, Nadi and Ba. The drive from Sigatoka up the Sigatoka Valley is a stunning 1½ hours, as is the journey from Ba via Navala. From Nadi along the Nausori Highlands Rd it takes about 1½ to two hours.

Bukuya is a little more commercial than Navala, but still a worthy cultural experience. The easiest way to visit this area is by renting your own car or on an organised tour. See p79 for details.

GETTING THERE & AWAY

All roads to Bukuya are rough and unsealed, and are best suited to a 4WD or, if the weather is fine, at least a vehicle with high clearance. It's a bone-crunching ride in the back of a carrier, which will cost around $60 to or from Ba or $18 to or from Navala.

Mamanuca Group

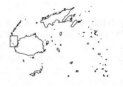

Grab your favourite boardies or bikini – this is it. Fiji's crown jewels. The much-trumpeted, widely promoted, photographed and romanticised Mamanuca isles. A series of picture-perfect coral atolls and small volcanic islands, the Mamanucas are valued more for their natural beauty than any contribution they make to the national culture.

Like a string of pearls, the 20 or so islands arc west through the large lagoon formed by the Malolo Barrier Reef and Viti Levu. Pacific currents sweep nutrients through the passages around tiny Namotu and with them come turtles, reef sharks and vast schools of multicoloured tropical fish. With more dive operators, world-class surf, five-star retreats and family-oriented resorts than any other group, the Mamanucas are anything but a well-kept secret.

Each morning a small army of day trippers, fortified with beach towels and factor 15, fan out from the mainland to conquer the white-sand beaches. They meet with no resistance. Most of the habitable islands (and many others that rely on desalination plants or freshwater deliveries) support resorts; this small string of islands forms the backbone of the Fijian tourist industry.

Perhaps because they box so far above their weight when it comes to hauling in the cash, life here bears little resemblance to the harsh realities experienced by most Fijians. Only two resort islands, Mana and Malolo, support Fijian villages but even here tourists outnumber locals. Not that they mind – almost all resorts lease their land from local communities and so, while heavy rain clouds hang over the mainland (both physically and metaphorically), the sun always shines on the magical Mamanucas.

HIGHLIGHTS

- Wax up your board – the mighty surf breaks of **Cloudbreak** and **Restaurants** (opposite) await
- Dive among big fish and harmless sharks at amazing sites such as **Gotham City** and **The Supermarket** (p68)
- Reenact your favourite scene from Tom Hanks' *Cast Away* on **Monuriki** (p147), the island where the film was shot
- Kick up your heels, and the sand on the dance floor, at **Beachcomber Island** (p144)
- Enjoy an intimate break with your partner at stunning **Likuliku Lagoon** (p149), peaceful **Navini** (p145), romantic **Tokoriki** (p147) or beautiful **Vomo** (p144)
- Treat the kids to a holiday they'll never forget at **Malolo Island Resort** (p148) or **Castaway Island** (p147)

Activities

The Mamanucas are all about water sports and extreme relaxation. Whether you are staying for a week or visiting for a day, nonmotorised water sports (like snorkelling, windsurfing, kayaking and sailing in catamarans) are nearly always provided free of charge. However, the moment an engine is fired you can expect to be billed. Waterskiing, parasailing and wakeboarding cost about $80 for 15 minutes. Village trips or snorkelling on the outer reef cost between $20 and $40 per person, and reef-fishing trips average around $150 per hour for four people. Island-hopping tours cost anywhere between $78 and $165 per person, depending on how many islands are visited and whether lunch is included. But, whatever you do, don't forget your book – hammocks just aren't the same without one.

DIVING

Mamanuca dive sites teem with fantastically gaudy fish circling psychedelic corals. The visibility here astounds first-time divers and you can see for 30m to 40m through the water much of the year. Turn to p67 for general information on diving and p68 for a brief description of some of the local spots. The companies in the following list are the big fish in the diving pond, with multiple dive shops on multiple islands.

Aqua-Trek (Vitu Water Sports; ☎ 670 2413; www .vitiwatersports.com) Based at Mana and Matamanoa Island Resorts. A two-tank dive costs $215 and a PADI Open Water Course $780.

Reef Safari (☎ 675 0566; www.reefsafari.com.fj) Has dive shops at South Sea, Bounty and Amunuca Island Resorts. A two-tank dive costs $200 and a PADI Open Water Course $575.

Subsurface Fiji (☎ 666 6738; www.subsurfacefiji.com) Runs the dive shops at Malolo and Beachcomber, Musket Cove and Treasure Islands. It also offers diving with free pick-ups for guests at Namotu, Navini and Tavarua Island Resorts, Wadigi Island Lodge, Resort Walu Beach, Funky Fish Beach Resort and Likuliku Lagoon. A two-tank dive costs $230 (except for those staying at Beachcomber Island Resort, who pay $195), and a PADI Open Water Course is $740.

SURFING

The reefs off the southern Mamanuca islands have some of the world's most formidable breaks, but you'll need big bucks (and a lion's share of courage) to gain access. Locals hold that the Fisheries Act (which provides for the maintenance of traditional fishing grounds) extends to the surf breaks and they are not above using threats and violence to protect their exclusivity. Currently, two American-owned resorts – Namotu (p150) and Tavarua Island Resorts (p151) – lease these rights and it is with them that you must stay in order to test your mettle against legendary **Cloudbreak** and **Restaurants** (Tavarua) or **Namotu Left** and **Swimming Pools** (Namotu). Failing this, your only opportunity is to surf the Saturday timeslot during the resort changeover period. Put your name down well in advance and pray on your little surf booties that you will be allocated one of the 17 Saturday spots.

The public-access breaks of **Wilkes Passage**, **Mini Clouds** and **Desperations** should not be underestimated. They are easily reached by boat from Funky Fish Beach Resort (p148) and any resort on Malololailai (p150) for around $40 per person (Cloudbreak $70 per lucky person with a Saturday spot). In brief, the breaks are as follows:

Cloudbreak World famous and for experienced riders only. Hollow left breaking on a reef. Best with southwest offshore winds when tubes of up to 250m form.

Restaurants A powerful, superfast, left-hander over shallow coral. Up to 200m long for advanced surfers.

Namotu Left A hollow, carving left-hander up to 150m long.

Swimming Pools A fun, easy right. Good for longboarders.

Wilkes Passage Short, fast, down the line, right. Swell magnet and can get as mean as Cloudbreak on some days. Crowded.

Mini Clouds High-tide break. Best on a south to south-west swell.

Desperations Ideal in small swell conditions. Right and left.

Tours & Cruises

Many, but not all, of the island resorts accept day trippers and every morning a whole armada of launches and yachts leave Port Denarau with boat-loads of people keen to spread their beach towels on some of that glorious white sand.

Captain Cook Cruises (Map p88; ☎ 670 1823; www .captaincook.com.au) Offers a day cruise from Denarau island to Tivua, a tiny coral island, on board the sailing ship *Ra Marama* (a 33m former governor's brigantine) for $139 for adults and $69.50 for children. The sunset romance dinner cruise ($99 per adult and $49.50 per child for three hours) includes a three-course meal. Captain Cook Cruises also has popular three-day, two-night cruise/camping trips to the Mamanucas and southern Yasawas.

MAMANUCA GROUP

MAMANUCA GROUP

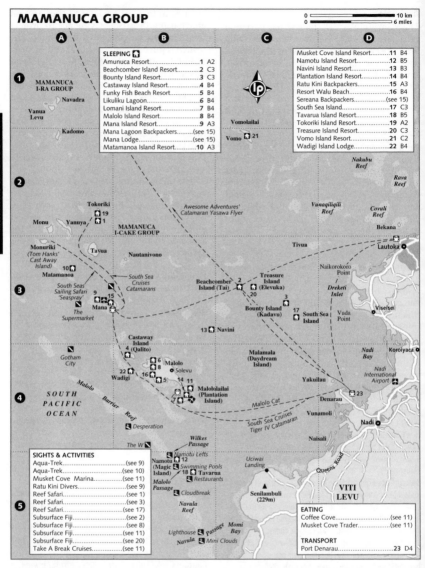

MAMANUCA GROUP

0 — 10 km
0 — 6 miles

SLEEPING
Amunuca Resort	1 A2
Beachcomber Island Resort	2 C3
Bounty Island Resort	3 C3
Castaway Island Resort	4 B4
Funky Fish Beach Resort	5 B4
Likuliku Lagoon	6 B4
Lomani Island Resort	7 B4
Malolo Island Resort	8 B4
Mana Island Resort	9 A3
Mana Lagoon Backpackers	(see 15)
Mana Lodge	(see 15)
Matamanoa Island Resort	10 A3

Musket Cove Island Resort	11 B4
Namotu Island Resort	12 B5
Navini Island Resort	13 B3
Plantation Island Resort	14 B4
Ratu Kini Backpackers	15 A3
Resort Walu Beach	16 B4
Sereana Backpackers	(see 15)
South Sea Island	17 C3
Tavarua Island Resort	18 B5
Tokoriki Island Resort	19 A2
Treasure Island Resort	20 C3
Vomo Island Resort	21 C2
Wadigi Island Lodge	22 B4

SIGHTS & ACTIVITIES
Aqua-Trek	(see 9)
Aqua-Trek	(see 10)
Musket Cove Marina	(see 11)
Ratu Kini Divers	(see 9)
Reef Safari	(see 1)
Reef Safari	(see 3)
Reef Safari	(see 17)
Subsurface Fiji	(see 2)
Subsurface Fiji	(see 8)
Subsurface Fiji	(see 11)
Subsurface Fiji	(see 20)
Take A Break Cruises	(see 11)

EATING
Coffee Cove	(see 11)
Musket Cove Trader	(see 11)

TRANSPORT
Port Denarau	23 D4

MV Sundancer (☎ 672 0786; www.sundancerfiji.net; per day $4000) If you've got the cash and you're looking for something more intimate, charter this 13m yacht for day trips including fishing and snorkelling gear and lunch. It can accommodate up to six people, all of whom will be thoroughly pampered.

Sailing Adventures Fiji (☎ 623 2001; www.sailingadventuresfiji.com) Targets backpackers with a three-day sailing cruise to the Yasawas returning via Monuriki, Mana and Malolo for $415 per person. Accommodation on the 15m yacht, *Pelorus Jack*, is in dormitory-style bunk beds.

Seaspray (☎ 675 0500; www.ssc.com.fj; cruise per adult/child $165/89) This full-day combination catamaran and sailing cruise aboard the famous *Seaspray*, a two-masted schooner that featured in the *Adventures of the Seaspray* TV series, is run by South Sea Cruises. You cruise by three uninhabited islands (including Monuriki of the movie *Cast Away* fame), stop for snorkelling, a barbecue lunch and a village visit. Travel is by catamaran to Mana island where *Seaspray* is docked. Don't expect much sailing; even with favourable winds the sails are seldom unfurled.

South Sea Cruises (Map p88; ☎ 675 0500; www.ssc .com.fj) Apart from the catamaran transfers, these boats are used to ferry day trippers from Port Denarau to various islands and between the islands themselves. The two modern catamarans call in to nearly all of the Mamanuca islands on their routes throughout the day, including South Sea Island (adult/child \$59/110), Beachcomber (\$50/99), Mana Island resort (\$70/130), Castaway Island (\$99/140), Treasure Island (\$70/130), Bounty (\$70/125), Malolo Island Resort (\$70/135) and Amunuca (\$95/135). Cruises include lunch, the use of the resort facilities and pick-up and drop-off from Nadi. Half-day options are also available.

Sunsail Fiji (Map p83; ☎ 670 5192; www.malamalais land.com; Main St, Nadi) Offers three cruises daily (half day for \$89 or full day for \$99 for adults, children four to 14 are half price) to Malamala, a small, uninhabited island, for a day of beach lounging and snorkelling. Lunch included.

Getting There & Around

Thanks to their proximity to both Port Denarau and Nadi airport, the Mamanuca islands are easily reached by catamaran, speedboat, plane or helicopter. Most people arrive on one of the four high-speed catamarans departing from Port Denarau. All the following boat companies (except Sea Fiji) provide free pick-up and drop-off from Nadi hotels.

Awesome Adventures Fiji (Map p88; ☎ 675 0499; www.awesomefiji.com) runs the *Yasawa Flyer* (also known as the 'Yellow Boat'), which connects with South Sea Island (\$68 one way), Bounty Island (\$60 one way), Beachcomber Island (\$68 one way) and Vomo (\$135 one way in the captain's lounge) on its way north to the Yasawas. See the boxed text, p155, for more information on this boat.

Malolo Cat I & II (Map p88; ☎ 672 2444, 672 2488, 675 0205) are owned and operated by Plantation Island and Musket Cove Resorts, which use them to bring clients directly to Malololailai. A boat leaves Port Denarau at 10.30am, 2pm and 5pm, and returns at 9am, 12.30pm and 3.30pm. The trip takes 50 minutes.

South Sea Cruises (Map p88; ☎ 675 0500; www .ssc.com.fj) operates two fast catamarans that run five or six loops from Denarau to most of the Mamanuca islands, including South Sea Island (\$50), Bounty Island (\$60), Beachcomber Island (\$68), Treasure Island (\$68), Mana (\$83), Matamanoa (\$105), Castaway Island

(\$78), Tokoriki (\$105) and Malolo (\$78). All fares are one way; children aged five to 15 pay half price, and those aged under five travel free.

To avoid spending a night on the mainland, you might consider a water taxi. A trip to Mana island with **Sea Fiji** (Map p88; ☎ 672 5961; www.seafiji.net) costs \$585 for up to four people and \$665 for five to eight people.

Alternatively, the price of a light-plane ticket is comparable with catamaran prices, and the flight over tropical islands with whitesand beaches is more scenic and much quicker (no more than 15 minutes). **Pacific Sun** (☎ 330 4388; www.pacificsun.com.fj) has daily flights from Nadi to Mana (adult/child \$88/58 one way) and Malololailai (adult/child \$71/40 one way). **Turtle Airways** (☎ 672 1888; www.turtleairways.com) and **Pacific Island Seaplanes** (☎ 672 5644; www.fi jiseaplanes.com) offer more expensive seaplane charters to the Mamanuca resorts, as does helicopter outfit **Island Hoppers** (☎ 675 0670; www.helicopters.com.fj).

SOUTH SEA ISLAND

South Sea Island is the smallest of the island resorts and little more than a bump of sand with some trees growing on top. You can walk around the whole island in three minutes; if you hurry, you could make it in two. Being so small it can sometimes feel a little overrun with the day trippers brought here by South Sea Cruises (see left).

Many backpackers spend a night at **South Sea Island** (☎ 675 0500; www.ssc.com.fj/South_Sea_Island .aspx; dm \$89; 🖭) on their way to, or from, the Yasawas. Prices include three meals of varying quality and the use of all nonmotorised water-sport equipment including snorkelling gear, kayaks and a sailing catamaran. The only accommodation is in the 32-bed dorm above the communal lounge; and we recommend bringing a sleeping sheet to help avoid being bitten by bed bugs, which were evident at the time of research. The beach is good for swimming and OK for snorkelling, and there is a small freshwater swimming pool. Reef Safari (p141) runs the dive shop here. Transfers are by South Sea Cruises (left) or the *Yasawa Flyer* (see the boxed text, p155).

BOUNTY ISLAND

Bounty Island, also known as Kadavu, is a 20-hectare coral island just 15km offshore from the mainland. It's bigger than its immediate neighbours but it still only takes 20 minutes to walk around or, if you don't stop to tease the clown fish, 1½ hours to snorkel. Halfway around the island are the decaying remains of the TV set used in the British reality series, *Celebrity Love Island*. Enough said. The white-sand beach attracts both endangered hawksbill turtles and the all-too-common day tripper (see South Sea Cruises on p143 for prices).

Bounty Island Resort (☎ 628 3387; www.fiji-bounty .com; dm incl meals $85-90, bure d incl meals $276; ❌ ☒) is a notch above South Sea Island in terms of quality and a few decibels quieter than Beachcomber Island. Many people come here for a few days R&R between the mainland and the Yasawas. The 12 *bure* with tiled floors, air-con and attached bathrooms are fairly basic by Mamanuca standards but those returning from the Yasawas will appreciate the hot showers, fridges and round-the-clock electricity. There's a small pool, but we weren't keen to brave the suntan-oil slick on top. The dorms are in a large, partitioned building out the back. Some have air-con and six beds to the room and others are fan cooled with enough bunks for 20. The prices listed here include the compulsory meal plan. Nonmotorised sports are free and diving can be arranged with Subsurface Fiji (p141). Transfers are with South Sea Cruises (p143) or the *Yasawa Flyer* (see the boxed text, p155).

BEACHCOMBER ISLAND

Tiny Beachcomber Island (Tai) is 20km offshore from the mainland. It is circled by a beautiful, coconut palm–studded beach.

Beachcomber Island Resort (☎ 666 1500; www .beachcomberfiji.com; dm incl meals $101, s/d incl meals $231/309, bure d incl meals $400-446; ❌ ☐ ☒) has the reputation of being *the* party island and tales of drunken debauchery are told far and wide. The truth: over recent years some of the shine has rubbed off Beachcomber's disco ball and, depending on the crowd on the night, the only interesting thing you see might be some weird choreography on the dance floor. Nonetheless, with a huge bar, live music and nightly activities involving the inappropriate use of alcohol, it remains a fun place to spend a night or two. Accommodation options include rooms in the lodge and some clean but basic *bure*, although most people opt for a bed in a double-storey *bure* that sleeps 120. This may sound like dormitory hell but it is

actually quite nice. The food at Beachcomber is excellent, particularly the buffet breakfasts, which are far better than you'll find at comparable backpackers elsewhere. Snorkelling equipment is free but, unlike other Mamanuca resorts, you'll have to pay for everything else. Diving is with Subsurface Fiji (see p141).

Both Awesome Adventures Fiji's and South Sea Cruises' catamarans call in here (see p143).

TREASURE ISLAND

Treasure Island (Elevuka) is another tiny island that takes mere minutes to walk around and is no more than a flyspeck on most maps. The beaches are similar to those found at Bounty, South Sea and Beachcomber Islands.

Treasure Island Resort (☎ 666 6999; www.fiji -treasure.com; bure/duplex $450/890; ❌ ☐ ☒) caters well for families. The new pool has plenty of sloping 'beaches' for toddlers and the turtle feeding and miniputt course are ideal for older kids. It has 66 comfortable, but tired, air-conditioned units housed in 34 duplex *bure* with roofs that resemble witches' hats. Standards at Treasure have been slipping and the quality of food, friendliness of staff and overall cleanliness has fallen below that of other island resorts. Optional meal packages cost $77/94 for two/three meals daily (half price for kids under 12), and diving trips are organised with Subsurface Fiji p141).

The island is serviced by South Sea Cruises catamarans (p143).

VOMO

This wedge-shaped, 90-hectare island rises to a magnificent high ridge, has two lovely beaches (one or the other will be sheltered if it is windy) and some of the best snorkelling in the Mamanuca islands. It's large enough to be interesting – it takes an hour to walk around – but small enough to be intimate. All in all, Vomo is the very definition of postcard-perfect Fiji.

ourpick **Vomo Island Resort** (☎ 666 7955; www .vomofiji.com; villas incl meals from $1300; ❌ ☐ ☒) could make even the most laconic guests wax lyrical. The *bure* are stunningly appointed in dark brown Pacificana with indigenous wooden floors and separate living areas. The beachside *bure* are so close to the beach you could walk to the water with your flippers on and the hillside *bure* have fantastic views (particularly from Nos 28, 29 and 30). If money is no object, the new 'private residence' has four bedrooms (all with private living areas) in three separate pavilions that frame a private pool. It comes with a dedicated butler and more mod-cons than Inspector Gadget. Vomo is the only five-star resort to accept children, but because the grounds are so spacious they have little impact on the tranquillity. The 'honeymoon island', Vomolailai, is just offshore and newly-weds can be dropped here with bubbly, lunch and a two-way radio. Rates include divine meals (all of which are three courses), daily snorkelling trips, access to the nine-hole, pitch 'n' putt golf course and nonmotorised water sports.

Most guests arrive by helicopter or seaplane (p143) or by Awesome Adventures Fiji's catamaran (p143).

NAVINI

From a distance, Navini looks like a round wafer biscuit topped with thick pesto. Up close, this small island is just as delicious. It is surrounded by a white-sand beach and offshore reef. It's owned by the people of Solevu on Malolo, who once held chiefly meetings and fished here. That was until fishing was banned many years ago and a marine sanctuary established. Beware of friendly fish!

our pick Navini Island Resort (☎ 666 2188; www.navinifiji.com.fj; bure $545-695; 🖳) is a boutique, ecofriendly resort, which has only 10 *bure*, each spacious and tastefully decorated. The standard *bure* have two rooms and the larger 'premier' *bure* (sleeping three) have verandahs at either end. The honeymoon *bure* has a courtyard tiled with pebbles and a private spa. Since all the *bure* are beachfront, every couple gets their own slice of sand, plus a few hammocks and sun loungers to go with it. Guests usually eat at the same long table and meals are a social occasion. More intimate beachside dining can also be arranged, and the hibiscus and bougainvilleas that surround each *bure* mean privacy is assured. The compulsory meal package ($98/88 three/two meals daily for adults; child rates available) still allows guests to choose from a daily menu and, as there are more staff than guests, the service can't be faulted.

Return transfers by resort speedboat ($198/99/594 per adult/child/family) allow you to maximise your time on the island no matter what time your plane arrives or leaves.

MANA

The beautiful but divided island of Mana is about 30km northwest of Denarau and home to the upmarket Mana Island Resort and several budget backpackers next to the village on the southeastern end. Incredibly, a high fence, and occasionally even a guard, separates the *bure*-bunnies from the dorm-dwellers and signs throughout Mana Island Resort warn 'nonguests' that they are not welcome in their restaurants or shops. For their part, the budget resorts welcome everyone but seem unable to cooperate amongst themselves and, although the situation has much improved, there is a history of bad blood between the families who established these budget digs.

Fence or no fence, the beaches are open to all and it takes three hours to walk around the island. Bring shoes to negotiate the rocky parts and don't be alarmed if you find sea snakes basking in the warm shallows. On the northern coast, keep an eye out for the rectangular building with polystyrene statues out front. This is the set used for 'tribal councils' in the TV series *Fiji Survivor*. It's never locked, so look inside.

The northern beach and the western beach (known as Sunset Beach) are quite good for snorkelling, with lots of tiny, colourful fish. Go to the small drop-off and follow it around. Also check out the south-beach pier for a night snorkel; the fish go into a frenzy under the wharf lights. Two dive operations are based at Mana. **Aqua-Trek Mana** (☎ 666 9309; www.aquatrekdiving.com) works exclusively for Mana Island Resort. A two-tank dive here costs $212 and a PADI Open Water Course $700, including equipment. Yoshi, the very capable dive instructor, has produced a great resource of photographs and detailed dive-site descriptions.

Ratu Kini Divers (☎ 942 9318) services Mana's backpacker resorts (and anyone who ducks around the resort fence). It offers two-tank dives for $190 and PADI Open Water Courses for $630 including gear.

Sleeping
BUDGET & MIDRANGE

The backpacker resorts are sewn into a ramshackle Fijian village that grew up after local landowner, Ratu Kini, built a couple of demonstration *bure* to show the Japanese next door how it was done. Most of the resorts sell their accommodation in Nadi, getting clients to commit to long stays before they have had a chance to see the state of the rooms. It is better to arrive and then book a bed after shopping around. Savvy travellers go to Malolo or the Yasawas where standards are far higher for much the same price.

Activities on offer at all the budget resorts include snorkelling trips ($25 per person plus $10 snorkel hire), kayaking ($5 to $10 per hour), hand-line fishing trips ($20) and island hopping ($70 per person). Nightly activities are as much about beer consumption as they are about entertainment. That said, the fire-walkers and knife dancers at Mana Lagoon Backpackers were very good (Monday, Wednesday and Saturday; nonguests $5).

To reach the backpacker resorts, get off at the ferry wharf and when your toes hit sand, turn right. From west to east they are as follows:

Ratu Kini Backpackers (☎ 672 1959; www.ratukini .com; dm incl meals $53-65, d incl meals $153-176; 🖵) No-fuss, no-frills dorms sharing cold-water showers. The doubles are in a long block that's almost indistinguishable from the village. Ask to see the 'deluxe' rooms, which are even further back from the water but considerably smarter. The lively bar here is the centre of backpacker nightlife, since (a) it overlooks the beach and (b) there is a TV.

Mana Lodge (☎ 620 7030, 921 4368; dm incl meals $60, d incl meals $150-180) Without the Nadi marketing arm this place is often quiet, even when the others are full.

Sereana Backpackers (☎ 931 6372; dm incl meals $60) The least professional of the four; the day we called the staff were unsure of the prices and it was completely vacant. They assured us they were open.

Mana Lagoon Backpackers (☎ 929 2337; dm/d/tr/ q incl meals $55/130/155/200) The newest (but not newly built) of the backpacker places, this lodge has some nice touches, like thatched-roof beach shelters and a restaurant-cum-bar with a sand-covered floor. The restaurant-bar doesn't have any dedicated toilets (and none of the rooms have private bathrooms), which results in a constant and annoying stream of partygoers trekking through the dorm at 1am in search of the loo. The buffet-style meals feature lots of rice and pasta and, as they occasionally run short, it pays to get in early.

TOP END
Mana Island Resort (☎ 665 0423, 666 1455; www.man afiji.com; island/ocean-front/beachfront bure incl breakfast $317/587/823, r/ste incl breakfast $470/764; ⊠ 🖭 🖵 🖵) One of the oldest and largest island resorts in Fiji, the 82 hotel rooms and 70 *bure* span the low-lying ground between the north and south beaches. Even though Mana attempts to cater for everyone – couples, honeymooners and families, it is the latter that dominate. It's particularly popular with Australian, New Zealand and Japanese children. Despite its size, it's not as impersonal as you might imagine and the Fijian and Japanese staff (it's Japanese owned) are genuinely friendly. The rooms come in a variety of configurations and are constantly getting refurbished. In 2008, the 'island *bure*' had their turn and are currently good value. Even nicer are the 'ocean-front *bure*', which were designed with couples in mind and have polished floors, cane furniture and baths as well as showers in the en suites. There are also some hotel-like suites in blocks of four, each with a bedroom on the mezzanine floor.

Meal plans are available and there are three mediocre restaurants (buffets cost $34 for adults; children eat free) and three bars (beer $8). Resort facilities include a circular pool, a horizon pool, a new day spa, tennis courts and a great kids club for three- to 12-year-olds (a one-time fee of $20 applies).

Getting There & Away
Mana is one of the few resort islands with a wharf, and one of only two with an airstrip. Flying with Pacific Sun (p143) is the quickest (only 12 minutes) and most scenic way to get to the island. South Sea Cruises' catamarans (p143) cost $83/42 per adult/child one way. Guests of Mana Lagoon and Ratu Kini Backpackers can use the resorts' own *Mana Flyer* transfer boat ($60 one way, 55 minutes), which leaves Nadi's New Town Beach daily at noon.

MATAMANOA
Matamanoa is a small, high island just to the north of Mana.

Matamanoa Island Resort (☎ 672 3620; www .matamanoa.com; d unit/bure incl breakfast $386/622; 🖭 🖵 🖵) has 20 *bure* overlooking a lovely, white-sand beach. All *bure* have a verandah and beach views (half facing sunrise, half sunset). There are also 14 good-value, but not nearly as nice, air-conditioned, hotel-style units with garden views. The resort does not cater for children under 12 and, as there are no day trippers allowed, it is best suited to couples who want a relaxing holiday. Daily meal plans cost $57 for dinner, or $81 with lunch included. There is a three-night minimum stay. As usual, all nonmotorised water sports are free. Other activities include trips to the nearby pottery village on the island of Tavua and diving with Aqua-Trek (see p141).

Most guests arrive via the South Sea Cruises catamarans (p143).

MONURIKI

Tiny, uninhabited Monuriki (and ironically not Castaway Island) featured in the 2001 Tom Hanks movie, *Cast Away*, and every resort worth its cabanas and cocktails sells day trips to what is increasingly referred to as the **Tom Hanks Island**. The trips cost from around $40 to $70 depending on how far the boat has to travel to get there and what kind of lunch, if any, is included. The island is quite beautiful and the wide lagoon is perfect for snorkelling. And who knows? You may even see one of the endangered hawksbill turtles or banded iguanas that live here. Wilson, alas, has moved on.

Seaspray (p142), a two-masted schooner, also sails here as a day trip from Mana.

TOKORIKI

The small, hilly island of Tokoriki has a beautiful, fine-white-sand beach facing west to the sunset and is the northernmost island in the Mamanuca group.

Amunuca Resort (☎ 664 0642; www.amunuca.com; bure rainforest/island/garden/beachfront $252/381/487/605, f/ste $487/663; ✖ ▢ ☎) sports dark timber floors and fashionably worn leather couches, and a series of blindingly white pavilions overlook a cobalt sea. This newbie opened in 2007 and the architects have done a great job splicing white-washed, Greek island–like buildings with traditional thatched Fijian-style roofs. It sounds odd but the resulting blend is a treat for style gurus and it allows all three restaurants to enjoy the views (meal plans are $75/38 per adult/child per day). Rooms range wildly in quality from the adults-only, spilt-level suites dominated by a two-person spa bath to sparsely furnished *bure* with little more than beds and a TV. The beach is very nice, although the coral shelf is very high here and much of the reef is exposed at low tide. There's a kids club, a

40-seat movie theatre and two pools. Diving is provided by Reef Safari (p141).

If you're not married when you arrive at **Tokoriki Island Resort** (☎ 672 5926; www.tokoriki .com; d bure $862, d villas $1150; ✖ ▢ ☎), there is a good chance you will be by the time you leave. This place is the ideal romantic getaway. The whole place drips with orchids, there are queen-sized beds with old-fashioned mosquito-net canopies as well as a gorgeous island-style wedding chapel of stone, wood and stained glass. The 30 beach-front *bure* have indoor and outdoor showers, and it's only a few steps past the hammock to the beach. The five newer villas have private plunge pools, beautiful interiors and large sandstones terraces. Lunch is served in the pleasant terrace-and-pool area while the gourmet, candle-lit dinners (mains $32 to $43) are served in the restaurant. Meal plans cost $137 per person per day. It is so romantic that it is unlikely couples would be allowed to return nine months later – children are not allowed. **Dive Tropex** (☎ 666 6649; www.tokorikidiving.com) has an interesting clam-farming dive site nearby and also runs snorkelling to Paradise Point, an incredible coral garden ($40 per person). A two-tank dive/ PADI Open Water Course costs $235/780.

Most guests take the South Sea Cruises' catamaran (p143) or a flight on a seaplane or helicopter from Nadi (see p143).

CASTAWAY ISLAND

Reef-fringed, 70-hectare Castaway Island, also known as Qalito, is 27km west of Denarau island and just short of paradise. The resort covers about one-eighth of the island – the best bit, on a wide tongue of sand stretching from a bush-clad hill.

ourpick Castaway Island Resort (☎ 666 1233; www.castawayfiji.com; island/oceanview/beach/f bure $625/735/845/1690; ✖ ▢ ☎), the oldest and still one of the best family destinations, is making a splash in the couples market. The 66 spacious *bure* have two rooms to accommodate those with children (kids stay free), small verandahs and intricate *masi* (bark cloth with designs printed in black and rust) ceilings. The rooms were last renovated in 2006, which accounts for their simple but stylish interiors. There's a swimming-pool bar, an open-air pizza shack and a great dining terrace overlooking the ocean (all-day casual meals $11 to $25, dinner $30 to $40). Alternatively, pay $105 per adult and $53 per child, per day, for the unrestricted meal plan once you arrive. The excellent kids club will take three- to 12-year-olds off your hands so you can make use of the well-maintained, and complimentary, nonmotorised water sports. The dive centre here charges $130 for a single-tank dive and $820 for an open water course.

Castaway Island is serviced by South Sea Cruises' catamarans (p143).

WADIGI

Pint-sized (1.2 hectares) and privately owned, Wadigi may beckon but it's off limits to all but a few.

Wadigi Island Lodge (☎ 672 0901; www.wadigi.com; island charter per day incl meals $2500; ❌ ▣ ▣) could be your own private island. Guests (maximum group size of six) are whisked here by helicopter to unwind in sybaritic seclusion. The luxury three-bedroom suite is perched atop the single hill with gorgeous sea views from the living areas and decks. It has its own infinity-edged pool, two small beaches and seven staff including two gourmet chefs and a boat captain.

MALOLO

Malolo is the largest of the Mamanuca islands and has two villages from which the resorts lease their land. The island's highest point is Uluisolo (218m), which was used by locals as a hill fortification and by US forces in 1942 as an observation point and from here there are some great panoramic views.

Diving is offered by Subsurface Fiji (p141), which is based at Malolo Island Resort but will happily take guests from neighbouring hotels as well. Malolo is also within striking distance of the great **surfing** spots mentioned on p141.

Sleeping
BUDGET & MIDRANGE
Funky Fish Beach Resort (☎ 651 3180; www.funky fishresort.com; dm/d $30/80, 1-/2-bedroom bure $120/$240; ▣ ▣) Funky Fish brings some much needed professionalism to the budget/midrange spectrum of the Mamanuca market and is run by former Fiji rugby coach and All Black, affable Brad Johnston. The dorms here are modern, spotlessly clean and partitioned into groups of four. The 'rock lobster' bure are small, bright orange constructions with thatched roofs and outdoor showers, while the larger, beachside 'grand grouper' bure can accommodate four. Tasty meals ($50/60 for two-/three-meal

packages) are served in an impressive hillside bure that enjoys panoramic views over the extremely tidal lagoon in front of the resort. The beach here is only average and many people who stay here come for the surfing or kiteboarding trips ($40 per person; Cloudbreak $70 per person, Saturdays only).

Resort Walu Beach (☎ 665 1777; www.walubeach .com; dm, s & d per person incl meals $95, bure per person incl meals $140; ❌ ▣ ▣) Walu Beach was built for the Australian reality TV show, The Resort, and, now that the show has been cancelled, it's a bit of an orphan. While the owners figure out its future, Walu Beach is offering some fantastic deals. You get all the facilities of a three-star resort for only slightly more than backpacker rates. The bure come in one-, two- and three-bedroom options but were being let out on a per-person basis and the hillside lodges were going for the same price as the dormitory. A short walk past the small beach brings you to 'The Rocks', the resort's second bar, built on a small point. The resort's main restaurant has Sky TV and bar; the included meal package features three-course evening meals.

TOP END
Malolo Island Resort (☎ 672 0978; www.malolois land.com; oceanview/beachfront/f bure $595/695/1120; ❌ ❌ ▣ ▣) Malolo describes itself as having 'plantation-style duplex accommodation reminiscent of the colonial era', which is a fairly accurate description of the 49 bure with their '90s bright-blue detailing. If the rooms

are slightly tired, the families that stay here don't seem to care and there is no faulting the white-sand beach or lush tropical gardens. There are two pools (one for grownups only) and a free kids club. Tariffs include all the usual water activities and are for two adults and up to two children. There are three restaurants (mains $25 to $40), a day spa, an adults-only lounge, walking trails and a Subsurface Fiji (p141) dive shop. Optional meal packages are $85 for adults and $42.50 for children, per day.

Likuliku Lagoon (☎ 672 4275; www.likulikulagoon .com; garden/beachfront/deluxe beachfront/overwater bure $1250/1500/1700/2100; ✗ ✗ ❑ ✦) The first (and so far only) Fijian resort with overwater *bure* opened on this impossibly azure lagoon in 2007. For couples with the cash to splash, the intimacy and privacy to be had here extend almost scurrilously far beyond a do-not-disturb sign on the door. At the risk of sounding like a promotional advert, even Likuliku's second-tier accommodation boasts private plunge pools, thatched lounging pavilions, his and hers closets and inside and outside showers. As you would expect in this five star–plus category, a gourmet chef prepares the food and the canapés are tiny and ambrosial.

Getting There & Away
Pacific Sun (p143) flies to the airstrip on nearby Malololailai where the *Malolo Cat* (p143) also docks. Small resort boats will collect their clients from Malololailai. Alternatively, South Sea Cruises' catamaran (p143) sails directly to Malolo Island Resort and again, other resorts are happy to collect clients from this dock.

Although Likuliku's guests can just as easily arrive by boat, many prefer to charter seaplanes ($235 per person one way) or helicopters ($273 per person one way). For contact details for the companies providing these services see p143.

MALOLOLAILAI
Tranquil Malololailai is approximately 20km west of Denarau island and, at 2.4 sq km, is the second-largest island of the Mamanuca Group. This has long been popular with yachties who anchor in the protected lagoon and make use of the facilities at the marina. All three resorts are built on the shores of a beautiful, but extremely tidal, lagoon. The beach outside Musket Cove Island Resort is the

most affected, and that outside Lomani Island Resort the least affected, by these tides.

Sights & Activities
MUSKET COVE MARINA
Yachties flock (or should that be school) to the excellent **Musket Cove Marina** (☎ 666 2215 ext 1279; VHF Marine channel 68; mcyc@musketcovefiji.com) to avail themselves of the excellent services here. There are 26 moorings ($15 per day), 25 marina berths ($2 per metre, per day), dockside fuel and water (although this can get scarce in the dry season), postal services, a laundry ($6 per load), rubbish disposal, hot showers, book swap, a noticeboard and limited repair services.

In September each year, the Musket Cove Yacht Club hosts **Fiji Regatta Week** and the **Musket Cove to Port Vila yacht race**. Traditional nautical sports such as wet T-shirt, hairy-chest and beer-drinking contests feature in the program.

The **Musket Cove Trader** (General Store; ☎ 666 2215; ☾ 8am-7pm) is probably the best-stocked shop in the Mamanucas – but it doesn't sell alcohol. Yachties can stock up on groceries, meat and vegetables, although not at mainland prices. The Trader also runs a small cafe overlooking the marina, called the **Coffee Cove** (lunch $12.50; ☾ 10am-6.30pm).

SURFING
While there is no official transport to the excellent surf breaks described on p141, the resorts on Malololailai are good bases for surfers because locals **Suju Tukutuku** (☎ 973 5885; sujisurf@yahoo.co.uk; based at Musket Cove), Jacob (also known as Scobie; ask at the marina for him to be contacted) and **Small John** (☎ 930 2262; based at Plantation Island Resort) all make a living transferring thrill-seekers to the breaks for $40 per person (Cloudbreak costs $70 per person, Saturday only; spots are limited – see p141 for more information). They may even do tow-ins. We suggest a 'rashie' of chain-mail might be appropriate if you try this.

FISHING & SAILING
Where there are boats, there are fishing opportunities – and the blackboards outside the activities shed on the marina list all the fishing and yacht charters available. **Take A Break Cruises** (☎ 925 9469; contact@takeabreakcruises.com) offers a variety of outings, including 'dolphin and snorkelling safaris' ($70 per person) on

Mondays and Thursdays; and 'sunset cruises' ($60 per person including drinks and 'nibbles') on Tuesdays and Fridays, on a luxury 14m catamaran. Sport-fishing trips ($125 per person, four hours) or private fishing charters ($250 per hour, maximum of six anglers) are also arranged here.

Sleeping

Musket Cove Island Resort (☎ 666 2215; www.musketcovefiji.com; r $275, d garden/lagoon/beachfront bure $505/505/617, q villas $758; 🖳 🖭) Musket Cove offers several types of accommodation, from hotel rooms to self-catering thatched *bure*. The newer Armstrong Island villas – clustered on an artificial island linked to the mainland by a bridge – have overwater verandahs and a private pool. The lagoon *bure* have a fridge and breakfast bar and are nicely decorated with traditional weavings. The lagoon here is very tidal and, to avoid being disappointed, we recommend asking for the high-tide times before making a reservation. To compensate, there are free snorkelling trips twice daily, along with the usual array of free water sports (but no kids club). Diving is provided by Subsurface Fiji (p141). Named after the owner, Dick's Place (mains $26 to $37), by the pool, often has theme nights including the popular 'pig-on-a-spit' (although not so popular with the pig). The casual Ratu Nemani Island Bar is linked to the resort by a walkway and is the place for do-it-yourself barbecues, cold beers and colourful banter with the yachties.

Plantation Island Resort (☎ 666 9333; www.plantationisland.com; d garden/beachfront $281/413, studio/2-bedroom/beachfront bure $413/522/606; 🕱 🖳 🖭) There are kids spilling out everywhere here; they're in the sea, in the pool, painting T-shirts, climbing plaster cows, egg-and-spoon racing, watching TV and eating chips. Most of them are with the free Club Coconut and look to be having a great time. There are three swimming pools: one for kids (with water slide), one essentially for adults and one for all ages. Like Mana Island Resort, this place is huge (850 people can stay here) and has a slight holiday-camp feel about it. You may have to line up for your buffet or set meal ($68 per adult, and $40 per child, full-meal packages), which is preferable to braving the pretty appalling snack bar (burgers $8) down by the dive shop (a two-tank dive is $164 and a PADI Open Water Course $670). Your best

option is Ananda's Restaurant (mains $22 to $30, dinner only) down by the airstrip. The rooms come in a dizzying array of options. For starters, there are hotel-style rooms that you'll find bright and cheerful, or dated and passé depending on your fashion sense. Or you could try the two-bedroom garden *bure*, which feature twin beds in the front, a big lounge area and a master bedroom out the back. It would be nicer though if the internal walls reached the ceiling.

Lomani Island Resort (☎ 666 8212; www.lomaniisland.com; r/ste incl breakfast $630/690; 🕱 🖭) Lomani is David to the Goliath next door. This small, adult-only resort has a huge pool, a classy colonial-style bar and a decent outdoor restaurant (meal plans $80 per person). The blocks of rooms have a Mediterranean feel to them due to their stucco walls and arched doorways. They're equipped with divan lounges, fridges and DVD players but characterised by the bamboo, four-poster, king-sized bed. Owned by the same family as Plantation Island Resort, the two properties work closely together and guests here piggyback on the other's activities.

Getting There & Away

Pacific Sun (p143) has a shuttle service from Nadi to Malololailai ($142 return). The resorts jointly operate the comfortable *Malolo Cat*, a catamaran that runs three times daily from Port Denarau ($100/50 per adult/child return, 50 minutes), which is why they seldom advise guests of the plane option.

NAMOTU

Namotu, a tiny (1.5 hectares) and pretty island next to Tavarua, is first and foremost a surfing resort.

Namotu Island Resort (☎ 670 6439; www.namotuisland.net; 🕱 🖳 🖭) is a little bit of Bali in Fiji. If you're jetlagged, you might think you're in the wrong country – there are Balinese decorations everywhere. If you don't surf – or at least fish – you might think you're on the wrong planet. Surf breaks include Swimming Pool, one of Fiji's cleanest waves, the consistently surfable Namotu Lefts (these two are exclusive to the resort) and Wilkes Passage (see p141 for more on these breaks). Diving can be arranged with Subsurface Fiji (see p141). Generally, guests are in groups and book package deals in advance through **Waterways Surf Travel** (☎ in US 310-584-9900; waterways@waterways.com), but Namotu does occasionally take 'walk-ins' to fill up a group. No children under 12.

TAVARUA

This small coral island is at the southern edge of the Malolo Barrier Reef, which encloses the southern Mamanucas. It is 12 hectares, rimmed by beautiful white-sand beaches and has great surf nearby at Cloudbreak and Restaurants (p141).

Tavarua Island Resort (☎ 670 6513; www.tavarua .com; ✕ 🔆 🖵 🖭) is American-run and most of the guests are US surfers on week-long package deals. Accommodation is in simple, elevated *bure* along the beach. Rates include all meals, transfers from Nadi and boat trips to great surf breaks. Drinks are extra. Bookings are handled exclusively through **Tavarua Island Tours** (☎ in US 805-686-4551; fax 805-683-6696) in California. Reservations generally need to be made well in advance, although in the low season (December to February) the resort may accept 'walk-ins'. Diving can be arranged with Subsurface Fiji (see p141).

Yasawa Group

The Yasawas pick up where the Mamanucas left off. They're grander in stature, more isolated in location and mellower in temperament. And even though the Yasawas are just as beautiful as the Mamanucas they have, until relatively recently, long been overshadowed by those bolder upstarts nearby.

But times change. In the 1990s the Yasawa chain was considered prohibitively isolated and, apart from a few hardy souls and an occasional cruise ship, these islands saw few travellers. Today a high-speed catamaran threads its way between these rugged volcanic islands, pulling into one blue lagoon after another to offload passengers into a waiting armada of small boats.

The Yasawas have it all – abundant sunshine, exquisite beaches, friendly locals and just enough creature comforts to ward off any hankerings for an early return to 'civilisation'. The quality of resorts here varies dramatically. A *bure* could be anything from a hut that you could blow down with a hair dryer to an upmarket villa with an outdoor shower. A new wave of midrange and top-end accommodation options is now enticing families and well-heeled couples into what has traditionally been the stomping ground of backpackers. Before long, they too are nudged surreptitiously into the true meaning of 'Fijian time', where anything more than two snorkels a day and half an hour on the volleyball court constitutes a busy day at the beach.

The Yasawa chain is composed of 20 or so sparsely populated and surprisingly barren islands. There are no roads, cars, banks or shops and most of the locals live in small, isolated villages, surviving on agriculture and tourism for their livelihoods.

HIGHLIGHTS

- Frolic in the **Blue Lagoon** (p161) waters that helped shoot Brooke Shields to fame and then catch a water taxi to the **Sawa-i-Lau Cave** (p164) where she swam

- Island-hop on a **Bula Pass** (p155) to see if the sand is any whiter at the other end of the island chain

- Dive off a boat and do your best to keep up with the giant **manta rays** (p158)

- Don a snorkel or tank and cavort with turtles, reef sharks and other vivid marine life around **Tavewa** (p160), **Nacula** (p163) or **Nanuya Lailai** (p161)

- Suit up in your Sunday best for a **village church service** (p163) on Nacula, or hang out with the locals during **Friday afternoon rugby** (p156)

- POPULATION: 5000
- AREA: 135 SQ KM

Geography & Geology

The Yasawas stretch for around 90km, beginning about 40km northwest of Viti Levu. The group forms a roughly straight line within the Great Sea Reef. The land is mostly hilly; four of the larger islands have summits close to 600m above sea level. While the relatively dry climate is a plus for visitors, the land is prone to drought. During such times locals and visitors need to conserve water and you may be asked to take fewer and shorter showers.

History

There is archaeological evidence to suggest that some of the Yasawa islands were occupied thousands of years ago, but with a paucity of fresh water and the threat of tribal war, people have come and gone over that time. The present *mataqali* (extended family or land-owning group) of Waya island, for example, are believed to have arrived about five generations, or around 250 to 300 years, ago.

At that time most people lived in the mountains, only occasionally venturing down to the foreshore in search of food and fish. Once Christianity was introduced and the wars subsided, the villagers moved down to the sea and have remained there ever since.

Information

The Yasawas are still remote and there are no shops, banks, postal or medical services, although increased mobile phone ranges mean that if you stand in the right spot, and hold your tongue just so, you might get a signal.

A dozen or so resorts in the Nacula Tikina (ie on Nacula, Tavewa, Nanuya Lailai and Matacawalevu islands) have banded together and, with the help of Turtle Island Resort management, formed the **NTTA** (Nacula Tikina Tourist Association; www.fijibudget.com) to promote their area. The website provides reliable information on accommodation, transport and activities for budget travellers.

For detailed information on diving in the Yasawas, see p68.

Tours

CRUISES

The floating hotel/cruise ships are an excellent midrange to top-end option for visiting the Yasawas. With good food and comfortable accommodation laid on, you can take it easy aboard your luxury vessel, pop overboard for excellent snorkelling and diving, drop in on beautiful white-sand beaches and stop to visit local villagers.

Captain Cook Cruises (☎ 670 1823; www.captain cook.com.au; 15 Narewa Rd, Nadi) offers a three-night Mamanuca and southern Yasawa cruise, a four-night Yasawa cruise, and a seven-night combination cruise onboard the MV *Reef Escape*. The 68m cruise boat has a swimming pool, bars, lounges and air-conditioned accommodation spread over three decks. Accommodation options include cabins with bunk beds, staterooms and deluxe staterooms. Prices per person, twin-share, for cabins/staterooms including all meals and activities (except diving) are $1410/1758 (three nights) or $3125/3896 (seven nights). Children under two years travel free of charge; those up to 15 years pay $480/840 for a three-/seven-day trip, regardless of the type of accommodation. Those who book early qualify for a 20% discount. Cruises depart from Denarau Marina on Denarau island, west of Nadi.

Blue Lagoon Cruises (Map p94; ☎ 666 1662; www .bluelagooncruises.com; 183 Vitogo Pde, Lautoka) offers three-, four- and seven-day Club Cruises to the Yasawas aboard huge motor-yachts. Club Cruises cost from $1364/2810 for two/four nights per twin-share cabin. Seven-day Gold Club Cruises aboard the luxury MV *Mystique Princess* start at $5342 for a twin-share cabin on the saloon deck. Children under 15 pay 11% to 15% of the full fare depending on the cruise, and those aged under two travel for free. Transfers, on-board activities and food are included but drinks, snorkelling and diving are extra. Cruises depart from Lautoka's Queens Wharf on Viti Levu.

Blue Lagoon Cruises also has a seven-day Luxury Dive Cruise aboard the *Fijian Princess*. It includes all the activities (village visits, *kava* ceremonies, shore excursions, walks etc) and comforts of a luxury cruise in addition to 15 dives. The dive sites are scattered from the southernmost to the northernmost tips of the island group and take in some of the most pristine areas. Prices start at $7691 per cabin, if both occupants are diving.

Awesome Adventures Fiji (☎ 675 0499; www.awe somefiji.com) offers three-night cruises on board the 27m *Wanna Taki* for $363/541 per person in a dorm/double room. Rates include all meals, transfers and activities. The boat's bunk-bed dorm accommodates 27 people and the three doubles are areas partitioned off from the main sleeping area by a curtain.

Berths are tight but clean, and fresh seafood is sometimes on the menu. Although the boat looks snug, these trips are fun and relaxed. Travellers rave about the snorkelling and swimming offshore. The boat, however, travels only a short distance between its two moorings. For more information about Awesome Adventures Fiji see the boxed text, opposite.

SAILING

Captain Cook Cruises (☎ 670 1823; www.captaincook.com.au; 15 Narewa Rd, Nadi) has sailing trips to the southern Yasawas aboard the tall ship SV *Spirit of the Pacific*. Swimming, snorkelling, fishing, island treks, village visits, campfire barbecues and *lovo* (feasts cooked in a pit oven) are all part of the deal. Accommodation is in simple *bure*

ashore, or aboard in fold-up canvas beds below the deck cabins. Twin share prices, per person, are $510/680 for a three-/four-day trip.

Robinson Crusoe Island Resort (☎ 628 1999; www.robinsoncrusoeislandfiji.com) offers a four-night sailing cruise from Port Denarau to the southern Yasawa islands on the 15m yacht, *Pelorus Jack*. It costs $500 per person and includes all meals and dormitory-style accommodation on the boat. This is popular with backpackers.

Yachts can also be chartered from Musket Cove Marina (p149), located on Malololailai in the Mamanucas.

KAYAKING

Australian-operated **Southern Sea Ventures** (☎ in Australia 02-8901 3287; www.southernseaventures

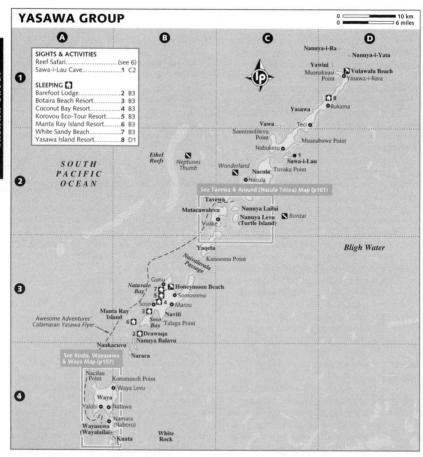

YASAWA GROUP

0 ——————— 10 km
0 ——————— 6 miles

SIGHTS & ACTIVITIES
Reef Safari..............................(see 6)
Sawa-i-Lau Cave.....................1 C2

SLEEPING
Barefoot Lodge.......................2 B3
Botaira Beach Resort...............3 B3
Coconut Bay Resort.................4 B3
Korovou Eco-Tour Resort........5 B3
Manta Ray Island Resort.........6 B3
White Sandy Beach.................7 B3
Yasawa Island Resort..............8 D1

SOUTH PACIFIC OCEAN

Nanuya-i-Ra
Nanuya-i-Yata
Yawini
Muantakuasi Point
Vulawalu Beach
Yasawa-i-Rara
8
Yasawa
Bukama
Vawa
Teci
Saunimofilevu Point
Muanabuwe Point
Nabukeru
1
Sawa-i-Lau
Tuvaka Point
Ethel Reefs
Neptunes Thumb
Wonderland
Nacula
Nacula

See Tavewa & Around (Nacula Tikina) Map (p161)

Tavewa
Matacawalevu
Nanuya Lailai
Nanuya Levu (Turtle Island)
Bonzai
Vuake
Yaqeta
Katasomu Point
Naisalavala Passage
Bligh Water
Gunu
Naturalo Bay
7
Honeymoon Beach
5
Somosomo
Soso
4
Marou
Manta Ray Island
3
Naviti
6
Soso Bay
Talaga Point
2
Drawaqa
Nanuya Balavu
Naukacuvu

Awesome Adventures'
Catamaran Yasawa Flyer

See Kuata, Wayasewa & Waya Map (p157)
Narara
Nacilau Point
Koromasoli Point
Waya Levu
Waya
Yalobi
Natawa
Namara (Naboro)
Wayasewa (Wayalailai)
Kuata
White Rock

THE YASAWA FLYER

Most people travelling to the Yasawas choose to go by the *Yasawa Flyer* (also called the *Yellow Boat*) operated by **Awesome Adventures Fiji** (☎ 675 0499; www.awesomefiji.com; Port Denarau). Half the fun of staying in the Yasawas is getting on and off the *Flyer* as it works its way up the chain towards Nacula. The comfortable high-speed catamaran departs at 9.15am daily from Denarau Marina on Viti Levu, calling in at some of the Mamanuca islands (South Sea Island, Bounty Island, Beachcomber Island and Vomo) before reaching the Yasawa Group. It takes about 1¾ hours to Kuata or Wayalailai ($95 per person, one way), two hours to Waya ($95), three hours to Naviti ($105), and 4½ hours to the lagoon shared by Tavewa, Nanuya Lailai and Nacula ($115). Children aged between six and 15 travel half price. In the afternoon it follows the same route back to the mainland, calling in at all of the resorts once more.

As the boat pulls into each island, it is met by a swarm of dinghies that pull alongside to take turns collecting and depositing guests, bags and mail. It's worth keeping an eye on your luggage as bags are occasionally offloaded onto the wrong boat.

On board the *Flyer* is a tour desk that can call ahead to book island accommodation. The service is excellent and they accept credit cards, which saves on carrying large amounts of cash. Be warned, your choice of accommodation may be limited to the budget end of the quality scale as some of the more desirable options get booked out in advance. So, if you've got a firm idea of what you want, you're better off booking your own accommodation separately.

If you want to linger in the islands without a prebooked itinerary then a **Bula Pass** (seven/14/21 days $279/389/459) can be a good deal. The pass enables unlimited island-hopping within the time period but only one return trip to Denarau. Awesome Adventures Fiji also offers four-/five-/11-night packages. With names such as A Lazy Threesome (six days, five nights, three islands; dm/tw $639/819 per person), A Great Pair (five days, four nights, two islands; dm/tw $500/570 per person) and Tropical Awegasm (12 days, 11 nights, five islands and *Wanna Taki* cruise; dm/tw $1199/1599 per person), the packages include accommodation, meals and transport. But as you don't have the choice of where you stay, it's less flexible than a Bula Pass.

The Accommodation Pass costs $300 and entitles the bearer to stay for five nights at certain resorts, but since these resorts cost $60 a night if you book independently, it doesn't save you any money.

.com) offers eight-day kayaking safaris along the Yasawa chain of islands. The trips (May to October) cost A$2150 per person for a maximum of 10 people per group. The price includes all meals, two-person fibreglass kayaks and safety and camping gear. The pace of the tour is dictated by the weather and the fitness of the group. There are five days of kayaking, during which you'll follow in Bligh's oar strokes, stopping along the way for snorkelling and village visits. Expect to paddle for three to four hours daily.

Another Australian company offering similar tours is **World Expeditions** (☎ in Australia 02-8270 8400; www.worldexpeditions.com). Tours cost around A$2166 and run from May to September.

Getting There & Around

Turtle Airways (☎ 672 1888; www.turtleairways.com) has seaplanes flying daily from Nadi (from Turtle Airways Base in New Town, 20 minutes' drive west from Nadi International

Airport) to Turtle Island Resort (p164). The flight takes about 35 minutes and costs US$888 return per couple. The seaplanes are also available for charter and the islands and reefs look spectacular from above. If you do arrive by seaplane, be sure to inform your resort so they can send their boat to collect you.

For information on getting around the islands by boat, see the boxed text, above.

KUATA

Petite Kuata is the first stop in the Yasawa string. It's quite spectacular, with unusual volcanic rock formations, caves and coral cliffs in the waters off the southern end, which is also where you'll find the best snorkelling. The climb to the summit takes a hot and sticky 20 minutes, and although the resort recommends a guide ($10), you'll be able to manage by yourself as long as you know which way is up. Kuata is separated from Wayasewa by a deep channel and kayaking

---

TIPS FOR BUDGET TRAVELLERS

■ Double rooms are popular; if you want some time to yourself, consider prebooking these to avoid ending up in a dorm.

■ Some of the budget resorts offer their own, cheaper boat transfers to the Yasawas; however, be aware that the trip is quite long, that it's across an exposed stretch of water, and that weather conditions can change quickly. Check for life jackets.

■ Snorkelling equipment costs about $10 per day to hire. Avid snorkellers may want to bring their own.

■ Bring a padlock; security is often relaxed and few resorts have safe-deposit boxes so locking your bags may be your best security option.

■ Mobile (cell) phone coverage is patchy. Ask the locals for the best spots.

■ Meals are included but are fairly basic – bring snacks if you are a big eater.

■ Expect intermittent electricity, and usually only at night; there is often no electricity at all during the day.

■ Don't keep food in your backpack – it attracts rats and ants.

■ Carrying a tent will not significantly save you money.

■ The resorts appreciate it if you make direct bookings, as they then don't have to pay commissions.

■ The quality of accommodation rises and falls like the tide. Work the grapevine on the *Yasawa Flyer* to see which places are currently good value.

■ Be prepared for the accommodation to be no more than simple, thatched *bure* with concrete bathrooms or bunk dorms with shared bathrooms. Mosquito nets are a given, although the cheaper the tariff the larger the holes.

■ Activities such as village visits, snorkelling trips and hiking all cost around $15 per person.

■ Sundays are quiet on the islands but the church services go off.

---

between the two islands is a great way to spend an afternoon.

Kuata Natural Resort (☎ 620 3874; sites per person/dm incl meals $45/60, d incl meals $150-180) is not a collection of condominiums, but that's about as far as the 'natural' tag stretches. Sitting behind a coarse sandy beach with Wayasewa hovering in the near distance, Kuata appeals to that unfussy backpacker with a taste for beer and the simple life. The resort has 20-bed and 10-bed dorms and many traditional-style double *bure* with private bathrooms and fans. The standards are pretty modest and the price range reflects the age and subsequent quality of the *bure*. Water here is potable and all the beds have mosquito nets. The shark snorkelling trip ($25/15 with/without snorkelling-gear hire) described opposite, in the Wayasewa section, is also available here.

WAYASEWA

Wayasewa, also known as Wayalailai (Little Waya), is dominated by a massive volcanic plug (Vatuvula; 349m) that towers dramatically over the beaches below. The sunrise **summit walk** ($10) also takes in a 'wobbling rock' and is highly recommended. The views towards Kuata, Vomo and Viti Levu are phenomenal.

The Fijian Government declared Namara village unsafe and moved it to its present location in 1975 after a rock slide damaged some of the buildings. The new **Namara**, also known as Naboro, has high grassy hills to the south that form a theatrical backdrop for *meke* (dance performances enacting stories and legends) and *kava* ceremonies. **Rugby** kicks off every Friday afternoon at Namara school. The rugby field is in poor condition, the teams unruly and the atmosphere great – we highly recommend attending. Resort staff from neighbouring islands also attend and, if you are willing to cheer for their team, will happily bring guests with them.

Yameto, on the eastern side of the island, also receives tourists on village visits. It is far more low-key and the villagers are unlikely to perform any *kava* ceremonies here. Visitors should expect a stroll through the village, a look at the small church and occasional stalls selling shells and jewellery. All of the activities described here can be organised by the Wayalailai Eco Haven Resort.

A 35-minute boat drive away at a local reef there's a spot renowned for **shark snorkelling**. The sharks, which are mostly white-tip reef sharks, are totally harmless but their sleek looks and stealth-like appearance make for a thrilling outing. The local divers are able to grab hold of their tails by distracting the sharks with food hidden in rock crevices. For more on the issue of shark feeding, see the boxed text, p69. Snorkelling with

the sharks costs $25, including masks and fins, and can be arranged through **Dive Trek Wayasewa**, which is based at the Wayalailai Eco Haven Resort. A two-tank dive/PADI Open Water Course costs $150/550.

Sleeping & Eating

Wayalailai Eco Haven Resort (☎ 628 3292; www.way alailairesort.com; sites per person/dm/f incl meals $45/60/170, d incl meals $150-180) Owned and operated by the Wayasewa villagers, this rustic budget resort was one of the first backpackers to open in the Yasawas. Over the years it has grown, and accommodation now ranges from older singles and doubles in the ageing former schoolhouse to a new 'English dorm' that is light and airy. Some of the lodges here sleep six and are large enough for families. Sitting squarely at the base of Vatuvula's granite facade, the property has a dramatic setting and is tiered over two levels above the beach. Buffet meals are served in a restaurant with a lovely raised deck overlooking the beach and shaded by sails. This place lacks the homely welcome of the smaller establishments but it's an excellent introduction to things to come further up the line.

WAYA

Waya is exquisite on the eyes, with some postcard scenery. It has rugged hills, beautiful beaches and lagoons, and a periphery that alternates between long, sandy beaches and rocky headlands. Waya is also unusually blessed with natural springs that percolate up through the volcanic rock so it is unlikely you will face water restrictions here. There are four villages (Nalauwaki, Natawa, Yalobi, and Waya Levu), a nursing station and a boarding school on the island. Nalauwaki has close ties with Octopus Resort and, thanks to the generosity of the owner, the community has benefited enormously from its donations, including textbooks and school transport.

As tempting as it may be, hiking unguided across the island is no longer recommended. The land is privately owned, the terrain unforgiving and the hiking trails largely overgrown as islanders now rely on motorised boats to get around. The best opportunity to work the pins is the trek (three hours return) to the summit of **Ului Nakauka**. The track from Nalawauki village circles around the back of a huge rock outcrop before ascending to its summit. The views south across Waya and

KUATA, WAYASEWA & WAYA

0 — 5 km
0 — 3 miles

To Tavewa (45km)

Nacilau Point
Koromasoli Point
Nova Bay
Nalauwaki Bay
Vatukavika Point
Bekua Point
Rurugu Bay
Ului Nakakau
Waya Levu
Likuliku Bay
Nalauwaki
Octopus Resort
Varaguru Reef
Naiyala Reef
Waya (429m)
(567m)
Liku Bay
Yalobi Hills
Motukuro Point
Bavu Reef
Adi's Place
Batinareba (510m)
Yalobi
Bayside Budget Resort
Natawa
Bligh Water
Yalobi Bay
Vunadilo Point
Nativaga Point
Sunset Beach Resort
Bonini Point
Loto Point
Namara (Naboro)
Yameto
Tubucikawa Reef
Yegusu Reef
Awesome Adventures Catamaran Yasawa Flyer
Wayasewa (Wayalailai)
Vatuvula (349m)
Naqalia Eco Adventure
Ilo Reef
Old Namara
Wayalailai Eco Haven Resort
Naqalia Point
SOUTH PACIFIC OCEAN
Likunivisawa Point
Kuata Natural Resort
(171m)
Yakawe Reef
Kuata
Nacilau Point
Lotoikuata Point
To Nadi (52km)

YASAWA GROUP

FAST FOOD

On 29 April 1789, mutineers set Captain William Bligh and 18 loyal crew members adrift of the HMS *Bounty* in an open boat just 7m long and 3m wide. The epic journey that followed passed through treacherous waters littered with shallow reefs and islands inhabited by cannibals; two Yasawa war canoes put to sea from Waya in pursuit of them. Fortunately a squall swept in some much-needed wind to raise the mainsail and blow them to the safety of the open sea. This body of water is today referred to as Bligh Water and whilst the Yasawas remain relatively undeveloped, the locals are considerably friendlier.

---

north towards Naviti are spectacular and you may even spot one of the half-wild goats.

A thick rim of coral follows Waya's shoreline and provides great **snorkelling** just off the beaches, particularly near Sunset Beach and Octopus Resorts. Yachties often anchor on one side or the other (depending on the wind) of the **natural sand bridge** that has formed between Waya and Wayasewa.

Sleeping & Eating

our pick Octopus Resort (☎ 666 6337; www.octopus resort.com; dm $42-59, d $169-290; ✗ ⊠) Everyday feels like a lazy Sunday at Octopus. The laid-back vibe, chilled tunes, cold beers, swaying hammocks and a wide sandy beach peppered with thatched sun huts and padded sun loungers make it a small wonder that we ever left. Compared with your average Yasawa backpackers, Octopus is more than a few notches up the coconut tree in terms of quality and yet still retains its unpretentious charms. The compulsory meal package ($45) includes excellent à-la-carte lunches and set dinners in a sand-floored restaurant. A multitude of activities are posted daily on the blackboard, including hand-line fishing (half/full day $30/50), guided walks ($20), quiz nights and movies by the pool. There's a raft of accommodation options: two categories of immaculate dorms, and simple but modern lodges with shared facilities, as well as traditional *bure* with private outdoor showers so you can stargaze as you wash. Diving at Octopus costs $185/595 for a two-tank dive/PADI Open Water Course; they also provide direct transfers from Vuda Point

Marina in a solid, covered boat for $92/45 per adult/child one way. Our only disappointment was that there's an additional charge for snorkel equipment ($5 per day) and kayaks ($10).

YALOBI BAY

It is possible to walk between all the resorts in Yalobi Bay at low tide, but you'll have to scramble over rocks to do so.

Bayside Budget Resort (☎ 666 6644, after the beep dial 6383; dm incl meals $60) Just around the corner from Sunset, and looking two hurricanes shy of being blown away completely, is this tiny backpackers. Apparently it was still open but the mattresses looked mouldy and the place deserted when we called.

Sunset Beach Resort (☎ 666 6644, after the beep dial 6383; dm/d incl meals $60/140) This low-key backpacker camp has one of the most beautiful settings in the Yasawas, overlooking the thin and photogenic sand bridge that connects Waya to Wayasewa. The thatched *bure* doubles and large, 12-bed dorm are fairly rudimentary, but while the standards are basic, the staff here – including the dog – are very hospitable. Moses performs nightly tricks with spoons, the boys do a whip-round for a *kava* kitty, and the dog is impossible to evict from the dormitory. Nightly meals often comprise fish and rice, and if you are lucky you'll get pancakes for breakfast – and spend all day on the volleyball court trying to work them off. Transfers from the *Yasawa Flyer* cost an additional $5.

Adi's Place (☎ 665 0573; dm incl meals $60, d incl meals $130-180) The advantage of staying here is that you are practically in Yalobi, so it affords a great opportunity to experience village life. The word 'rickety' best sums up the accommodation, although the building that houses the doubles is more robust than the rest – it even has some furniture in addition to its beds. The beach itself is tidal and not as nice as Sunset's.

NAVITI & AROUND

One of the largest (33 sq km) and highest (up to 380m high) of the group, Naviti has a rugged volcanic profile.

The island's main attraction is an amazing snorkelling site where you can swim with **manta rays**. The best time to see the giant rays is between June and August, although they may be spotted as early as May and as late as September, cruising the channel near the aptly named Manta Ray Island. All the resorts in the area offer snorkelling trips to the rays for around $25 per person plus snorkel hire; but only Mantaray Island Resort employs spotters, sending the boat out only when they are assured of a successful encounter. Once the rays are spotted, everyone dives overboard and it will be up to you to keep up with the rays. If they are swimming against the current you'll have to kick like an Energizer bunny to stay anywhere near them. It can be a bit of a free-for-all – watch for the flipper in the face. If you are able to free dive the seven-or-so metres down to the rays, don't be tempted to touch them. By touching a manta ray you can damage its mucus membrane, causing it to develop lesions and infections; and although they may be virtually harmless, their powerful wings could cause damage if they were to get a fright. See the boxed text, p160, for more on manta rays.

Diving is courtesy of **Reef Safari** (664 5301; www.reefsafari.com.fj), which is based at Mantaray Island Resort but will pick up from anywhere in the Naviti area as well as from the *Wanna Taki*. A two-tank dive/PADI Open Water Course costs $200/575 including equipment.

Awesome Adventures Fiji offers day trips to Naviti that include return transport, lunch and three hours at Botaira Beach Resort, as well as operating the *Wanna Taki* cruise in this area. See p153 for details.

Sleeping & Eating

Mantaray Island Resort (Map p154; 664 0520; www.mantarayisland.com; sites per person incl meals $85, dm incl meals $90, d incl meals $212-269;) One of the newest of the Yasawa resorts, Mantaray occupies its own wee island, spreading over a small hill between two pretty beaches. The sand here isn't as fine nor as white as that found on other Yasawa beaches, but the excellent snorkelling and its proximity to the manta rays' favoured stomping grounds is a huge plus. The modern dorm is divided into cubicles of four bunk beds and each contains its own fan and light. The cheaper 'treehouse' *bure* share the self-composting toilets and hot showers with the dorm, while the 'jungle' *bure* have private bathrooms. This place is professionally run and deservedly popular so it's worth booking ahead. Mantaray is also a party destination – the music is played loud and late and this noise, along with the background drone of the dive compressors, generators and

desalination plant, can all be heard whilst in the dormitory.

Barefoot Lodge (Map p154; 670 1823; www.captaincook.com.au; bure per person incl meals $99) The *bure* here, made with thatched walls and without lights (so bring a torch), are owned and operated by Captain Cook Cruises (p153). Most who stay here spend their days on prearranged 'sailing safaris', returning only in the afternoon to make use of Drawaqa's three beaches. If you are looking for a quiet, simple alternative, close to the mantas, this is an excellent choice. The *bure* accommodate two and all facilities are shared.

Botaira Beach Resort (Map p154; 603 0200; www.botaira.com; dm/d incl meals $100/418) Botaira targets the more discerning traveller and while it is undoubtedly flashier than your average Yasawa resort, the jump in price is not commensurate with the facilities offered. Apart from a beautiful, open-air restaurant with elevated decks, other amenities – like a pool and the option to deviate from set menus – are conspicuous by their absence. Botaira does, however, have plenty of space and privacy. There are only 11 *bure* here: nine are new and stylish, two more basic and older (ask for a discount). The beach extends over a long cove, thick with palm trees, and the snorkelling along the reef edge is very good, although as it's tidal this can only be accessed via a concrete path at low tide.

NATUVALO BAY

Three backpacker resorts, Korovou Eco-Tour Resort, Coconut Bay Resort and White Sandy Beach, all share a protected, long stretch of white sand about halfway up the west coast of the island. Unfortunately the swimming is only just possible at high tide here – low tide exposes a wide bank of dead, ugly reef and mosslike seaweed. Fortunately a short track (around a 10-minute walk) next to White Sandy Beach crosses over a hill to the pretty and secluded Honeymoon Beach. Visitors need to make a $1 donation to the village to visit this little cove but the pay-off is calm and tranquil waters and great snorkelling. The resorts all have generators, which usually operate between 10am and 1pm and then again from 6pm until bar closing. From north to south they are as follows.

White Sandy Beach (Map p154; 666 4066, 666 6644, after the beep dial 1360; dm incl meals $65, d incl meals $150-200) A slow, mellow budget resort with a

SWIMMING WITH THE DEVIL

It's hard not to feel a little nervous at the sight of a large dark object approaching from the depths towards you, but the graceful flying carpet that emerges is something to admire, not fear. Also known as devil rays (because of their horn-like pectoral fin extensions) manta rays are the largest of the rays and typically measure 4m to 5.5m across at maturity. The largest recorded specimen was a massive 7.6m (2300kg) and due to their size, only four aquariums in the world have ever kept them successfully. Despite their bulk, manta rays are capable of great speed and are known to leap out of the water, landing with a resounding slap – but mostly they glide effortlessly in seemingly synchronised swimming manoeuvres.

clean, 11-bed dorm and several simple *bure*. A small dive centre here offers two-tank dives for $170.

Korovou Eco-Tour Resort (Map p154; ☎ 651 3173, 603 0049; korovoultk@connect.com.fj; dm/d/villas incl meals $70/180/350) In stark contrast to its neighbours, Korovou can accommodate a small army and is frequently packed with young and sociable troops. The 24-bed dorms have wooden bunks and fans. The newly built stone and wooden villas each have a separate lounge, fridge and stone bath. The cheaper wooden lodges have their own verandahs and bathrooms, and are spotlessly clean. Activities here tend to be more reliably organised and the food of a better standard than at the other Natuvalo Bay options.

Coconut Bay Resort (Map p154; ☎ 666 6644, after the beep dial 1300; dm/d incl meals $60/150) You'll spot this place from the *Yasawa Flyer*. It's painted lime green and has a string of beachside, spacious, but very basic, *bure*. The dorm sleeps 14 but is seldom full. The staff are incredibly laid-back.

TAVEWA

Tavewa is a small (3 sq km), low island right in the middle of the Yasawa Group but it houses some of the group's northernmost resorts. A pleasant beach unfurls itself on the southeastern coast of the island but it's often plagued by buffeting trade winds (which are great, however, for kiteboarders). You need to head west to the beach around the bend of Savutu

Point to find relief from the gales and you're best off doing so at low tide. The snorkelling just offshore here is excellent. An ambling ascent of the central crest affords photogenic views of the Yasawa chain, which is particularly spectacular at sunset. The track joins the path connecting Coral View Resort and the southeastern beach.

All the resorts listed here offer boat trips to the Blue Lagoon (opposite; $15 per person) and trips to Sawa-i-Lau caves (p164; $45). Based at Coral View, **Dive Yasawa Lagoon** (☎ 666 2648; VHF Marine channel 72; www.diveyasawalagoon.com) will also pick you up from other resorts (transfer fees apply) on nearby islands. Recommended dive spots include the big wall dives at the Zoo and Bonsai and the swim-throughs and tunnels at the Maze. Every Saturday and Wednesday, Dive Yasawa Lagoon operates a shark dive, where you are likely to see two resident 4m lemon sharks and, occasionally, 2m grey reef sharks. A two-tank dive/PADI Open Water Course costs $175/650 including equipment.

Sleeping & Eating

Coral View Resort (☎ 922 2575; www.coralviewfiji.com; dm/d incl meals $60/210; 🖵) This well-run budget resort is often full to the brim with young Brits returning from their antipodean adventures. Having failed to drink New Zealand and Australia dry, they make a good attempt at polishing off this island and the nightly entertainment often features beach parties and bonfires. The three dormitories range from an older, cramped, 18-bed dorm with a separate cold-water shower block, to a new, clean six-person dorm in a converted *bure*. The small, stone cottages, with their high-pitched roofs, and *masi*-and-bamboo–lined interiors are excellent value; they even have 24-hour electricity. There is interesting snorkelling to be had right offshore but, as the virtually nonexistent beach loses the afternoon sun (thanks to the low hills behind the resort), you'll need to cover the short distance to the southeast beach for serious sunbaking.

Kingfisher Lodge (☎ bookings through Otto & Fanny's 666 6481; d $100) Kingfisher Lodge has just one comfortable, fan-cooled cottage in a junglelike garden. You can order meals in advance or duck down the beach to Otto & Fanny's.

Otto & Fanny's (☎ 666 6481; www.ottoandfanny.com; dm/d incl meals $100/210; 🖵) On a sprawling property, amidst a former copra plantation, this quiet, homely place has a small village of *bure* with private bathrooms and a spacious, 12-bed dorm. The flat, grassy grounds are inundated with coconut trees but offer plenty of wide open spaces. Travellers talk up the meals here and the afternoon tea of banana cake or scones (for only $2) is legendary. This place has a real family feel to it and is one of the best budget resorts in the island chain. Otto and Fanny's is also the closest one to Tavewa's best patch of beach. They charge $20 return for *Yasawa Flyer* transfers.

NANUYA LAILAI

This is it folks – home to that celebrity of all the Yasawas' beaches, the **Blue Lagoon**. Crystalline and glossy, it doesn't disappoint the bevy of swimmers, snorkellers, divers, and people on cruise boats or yachts who dabble in its gorgeous, lucent depths. Actually, it's not dissimilar to many of the lagoons scattered around the Yasawas and the snorkelling here is rich in fish but the coral has taken a hammering over recent years. Travellers are advised by signs enforced at times by security staff to stay clear of Nanuya Levu as well as the section of Blue Lagoon beach used by **Blue Lagoon Cruises** (p153).

The settlement of **Enadala** and several budget resorts reside on the eastern side of Nanuya Lailai, and the beach here is buffeted by strong winds. Connecting the Blue Lagoon and Enadala beaches, and snaking over the mass of gently sloping hills of the island's interior, is a well-trodden **track**. It takes about 30 minutes to walk from one beach to the other by using this track or following the coastline at low tide. But what could possibly draw anyone away from the Blue Lagoon's bright water? Cake could. **Lo's Tea Shop**, next door to Kim's Place, sells banana cake and chocolate cake with sugary sauce for $2.50 a slice. Eat inside astride benches or, better still, outside with your toes in the sand. Both Lo's and **Grandma's Shell Market**, a few doors down, sell seashells by the seashore (along with sarongs and jewellery).

Westside Watersports (☎ 666 1462; www.fiji-dive .com) is located at Nanuya Island Resort and is an experienced dive operation. It caters to guests at resorts on nearby islands including the upmarket Turtle Island Resort, as well

YASAWA GROUP

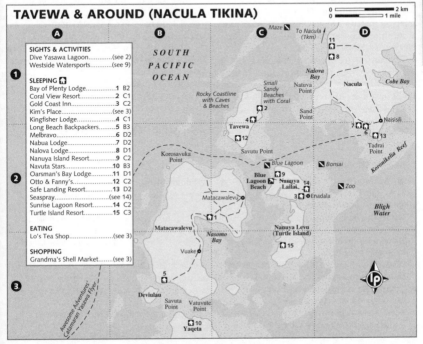

TAVEWA & AROUND (NACULA TIKINA)

0 —————— 2 km
0 —————— 1 mile

SIGHTS & ACTIVITIES
Dive Yasawa Lagoon.............(see 2)
Westside Watersports...........(see 9)

SLEEPING
Bay of Plenty Lodge.................**1** B2
Coral View Resort....................**2** C1
Gold Coast Inn.........................**3** C2
Kim's Place.............................(see 3)
Kingfisher Lodge........................**4** C1
Long Beach Backpackers.........**5** B3
Melbravo...................................**6** D2
Nabua Lodge...............................**7** D2
Nalova Lodge..............................**8** D1
Nanuya Island Resort.................**9** C2
Navuta Stars.............................**10** B3
Oarsman's Bay Lodge................**11** D1
Otto & Fanny's..........................**12** C2
Safe Landing Resort..................**13** D2
Seaspray.................................(see 14)
Sunrise Lagoon Resort..............**14** C2
Turtle Island Resort.................**15** C3

EATING
Lo's Tea Shop.......................(see 3)

SHOPPING
Grandma's Shell Market........(see 3)

SOUTH PACIFIC OCEAN

Maze
To Nacula (1km)

Small Sandy Beaches with Coral
Rocky Coastline with Caves & Beaches

Nalova Bay
Natuva Point
Nacula
Cobe Bay
Sand Point

Tavewa
Korosavuka Point
Savutu Point
Naisisili
Tadrai Point

Koronikelia Reef

Blue Lagoon
Bonsai
Blue Lagoon Beach
Nanuya Lailai
Zoo
Matacawalevu
Enadala

Bligh Water

Matacawalevu
Nasomo Bay
Nanuya Levu (Turtle Island)

Vuake

Awesome Adventures/ Catamaran Yasawa Flyer
Deviulau
Savuta Point
Vatuvute Point
Yaqeta

as Blue Lagoon Cruises passengers. A two-tank dive/PADI Open Water Course costs $165/635. Westside visits the same sites (including the combined, twice weekly shark dive) described in the Dive Yasawa Lagoon listing (p160).

Sleeping & Eating

Gold Coast Inn (☎ 665 1580, 666 6644, after the beep dial 7777; dm/d incl meals $60/150) Offering the highest standard of accommodation in this strip of budget resorts, the private timber *bure* at the Gold Coast Inn have a double and single bed as well as their own bathrooms. This resort is a smallish affair – there are only seven bungalows and a small dormitory – but it's run by a family with a big heart. If you stay over the weekend when Nicky is home from school, it is likely he will sing for your supper and provide the nightly entertainment.

Sunrise Lagoon Resort (☎ 666 6644, after the beep dial 9484; dm/d incl meals $60/150) Camper than a row of pink tents and more fun than a bowl of *kava*, Sunrise is a hit with budget travellers, if for no other reason than that the two men, Queenie and Bridget, who run the place, are so refreshingly unique. The pervading atmosphere is chatty and welcoming, although the accommodation and bathrooms are a little on the rustic side.

Seaspray (☎ 666 8962; dm/d incl meals $70/120) If Seaspray cops much more spray, there may be not much of it left. Very basic and very quiet. Right next door to Sunrise.

Kim's Place (☎ 9361228; dm/d incl meals $70/140) Quiet option with traditional *bure* complete with swinging beds.

ourpick **Nanuya Island Resort** (☎ 666 7633; www.nanuyafiji.com; d incl breakfast $239-401; 💻) A short walk, even in flippers, from the azure waters of the Blue Lagoon, this swish and understated resort is the kind of place you picture when you dream of indulgence, beachside cocktails and exquisite vistas. The *bure* are Fiji-nouveau; the roofs may be thatched but the interiors are chic and elegant. All are fan-cooled and have their own bathroom with solar-heated hot water. Wedding packages are available and, as this place oozes romance, it's a favourite spot for couples (no children under seven) although the *bure* can accommodate families of up to four. It's worth noting that older guests may find the path to the hillside villas too steep and, if you are serious about staying here, you will need to book at least four months in advance. The beachside restaurant is very atmospheric and the à-la-carte fare (mains $24 to $35) deliciously inventive.

MATACAWALEVU & YAQETA

Matacawalevu is a 4km-long hilly volcanic island protected by the large Nasomo Bay on its eastern side. Nanuya Levu (Turtle Island) is to the east, and to the south, across a protected lagoon used for seaweed farming, is Yaqeta. The island has two villages, Matacawalevu on its northeast end and Vuake in Nasomo Bay.

At the time of research, the whole of **Long Beach Backpackers** (☎ 666 6644, after the beep dial 3032; sites/dm incl meals $50/60, d incl meals $150-200) was being upgraded. There were several new *bure* (all with private bathrooms), a new 20-bed dorm and a large beachside restaurant in the pipeline. If they only remember to replace the sheets along with the buildings,

---

BEACH BUSINESS

All the resorts in the Yasawas are on the waterfront but not all can claim idyllic beaches. If white sand, turquoise depths and simmering in a sun-coma are what you came for, the following resorts should be just the ticket.

Oarsman's Bay Lodge (opposite) It's on the best of the Yasawas' resort-based beaches. Protected from the trade winds, the water is still, clear and deep. A large bank of coral provides excellent snorkelling.

Nanuya Island Resort (above) The resort occupies an enviable and isolated position on a quiet beach in front of the renowned Blue Lagoon.

Sunset Beach Resort (p158) At the southern hook of Waya Island, Sunset Beach has a 270-degree bend of beach with plenty of sand. There's great snorkelling in the small passage between Waya and Wayasewa.

Octopus Resort (p158) The beach in this protected cove is beautiful for swimming at high tide and great for sunbaking and wandering at low tide.

Botaira Beach Resort (p159) Botaira's beach is a length of soft white sand with ample room to park a towel. The calm water has a good stretch of shallows before it drops into the deep.

Long Beach has the potential to become one of the best budget resorts in the Yasawas. The big draw here is the long, horseshoe-shaped beach. When the tide is low you can wade to Deviulau island and scramble to the top for great views; although watch for sting rays that sleep in the sandy shallows.

The hillside villas at **Bay of Plenty Lodge** (☎ 995 1341; bayofplentylodge@yahoo.com; dm/d incl meals $60/100) were opened in 2008 and have tiled floors, attached bathrooms, excellent views and are soundly constructed. The mangrove-fringed beach has brownish sand and, being extremely tidal, resembles an estuary for much of the day. Clients are picked up ($10 return transfer) from the *Yasawa Flyer's* Blue Lagoon drop-off point.

Boutique **Navutu Stars** (☎ 664 0553; www.navutustarsfiji.com; d $587-998; ✗ ▣ ▤) specialises in opulent decadence, Pacific-style – with petal-sprinkled baths, intimate sunset dining and complimentary massages on arrival. The whitewashed villas have king-sized beds, exquisitely detailed 7m-high roofs, and fantastic views north from their private decks. Children aged under 14 are not permitted and the food is fabulous (meal packages are available from $100 per person per day). The best beach, however, is a short walk away at a nearby point.

NACULA

Nacula, a hilly volcanic island, is the third-largest in the Yasawas. Blanketed with rugged hills and soft peaks, its interior is laced with well-trodden paths leading to villages and small coves. It is possible to follow a well-defined trail inland through mangroves from the resorts on the southern point to those at Long Beach. Keep an eye out for **mudskippers**, an amphibious fish that has uniquely evolved to be able to breathe out of water. They live in the tidal streams amongst the mangroves.

There are four villages on Nacula island, including Nacula, home of Ratu Epeli Vuetibau, the high chief of Nacula Tikina. The *tikina* (group of villages) includes the islands of Nacula, Tavewa, Nanuya Levu, Nanuya Lailai and Matacawalevu, and is home to about 3500 people. Catching a Sunday **church service** in one of the villages is a real treat; most resorts will arrange free transport for their guests.

Beach devotees will be ecstatic to know that Nacula also has some of the finest swimming in Fiji, particularly at Long Beach.

Sleeping & Eating

The beach around Safe Landing Resort, Nabua Lodge and Melbravo is quite tidal and only a narrow strip of sand between rocky promontories is left exposed at high tide.

Safe Landing Resort (☎ 664 0031; slr@yahoo.com; sites per person incl meals $45, dm/d incl meals $60/185) This place had been closed since 2006 but was only weeks away from reopening when we called. The prices quoted here are indicative only but, from what we saw, Safe Landing promised to have some of the smartest dorms and *bure* in the area. The restaurant has been moved from its former exposed position and now overlooks the resort's trademark sandy cove: a pretty little beach framed between two rocky outcrops.

Melbravo (☎ 924 6610, 978 0407; dm incl meals $60, d with/without bathroom incl meals $150/120) Named after three brothers, Melbravo has seen better days. It has a good reputation for friendly staff but the dining room is dark and dreary and the accommodation more beach shack than beach *bure*.

Nabua Lodge (☎ 666 9173; nabualodgefiji@connect.com.fj; dm incl meals $68, d with/without bathroom incl meals $180/135) Just west of Safe Landing on a nicely landscaped plot of grass with strategically placed hammocks, this lodge may not be the Ritz but it is the place to switch to 'Fiji time' and adopt the local, laid-back attitude. Accommodation is plain and simple – so is the food. You will need to bring your own snorkelling gear, as it is not possible to hire any here.

LONG BEACH

Imagine a long swathe of powdery sand easing into a glassy, cerulean sea and you will have some idea of what to expect at one of the best beaches in the Yasawas. And, unlike other beaches, it's possible to swim here at low tide without trudging over an exposed coral shelf to do so. The snorkelling area, however, which is sectioned off with rope and buoys, is not in the same league and is only average.

Oarsman's Bay Lodge (☎ 672 2921; www.oarsmansbay.com; dm/d incl meals $88/295, f $264; ✗ ▣) Sharing the same prime slice of sandy real estate as Nalova Lodge, Oarsman is one of the Yasawas' most popular resorts (book ahead). The *bure* are clean and crisp, with modern bathrooms and private verandahs, and several have interconnecting rooms ideal for families. The food here is very good, and dinner usually comprises three small courses, but be wary of the Mexican chicken – it has more kick than a Tijuana zebra. The dorm is built directly above the restaurant in the apex of the 2nd storey, and since they both face towards the setting sun, drinks on the deck below are preferable to lingering upstairs in the cramped dorm.

Nalova Lodge (☎ 672 8267; nalova_resort@yahoo .com; d incl meals $180-250) Right next door to Oarsman's Bay Lodge, this teeny resort has been in the making for years. There are six spacious and homey *bure* that are now comparable to those found next door (although don't expect 24-hour electricity) and the price range is governed by their differing sizes. The cheapest do not have private facilities. There's no restaurant or central bar, so meals are served on your own *bure* porch and guests usually join in with the Oarsman's for activities, or ask for a water taxi to be called.

Getting There & Away
The resorts on Nacula charge for their transfers to and from the *Yasawa Flyer*. Nabua Lodge and Melbravo both charge $10 return, whereas Oarsman's Bay Lodge charges $21 and Nalova Lodge $30.

NANUYA LEVU (TURTLE ISLAND)
Nanuya Levu is a privately owned island (2 sq km) with protected, sandy beaches and rugged, volcanic cliffs. The 1980 film *The Blue Lagoon,* starring Brooke Shields, was partly filmed here, as was the original 1949 version starring Jean Simmons. It is off limits to all but resort guests.

One of the world's finest and most famous resorts, **Turtle Island Resort** (☎ 672 2921; www .turtlefiji.com; d from $3135) lures the celebrities, romantics and flush from around the world to its exclusive shores. The resort is owned by American Richard Evanson, who, after making his fortune in cable TV, bought the island in 1972 for his personal hideaway. The 14 two-room *bure* are spaced along the beach. Rates include all food, drinks and most activities including horse riding,

scuba diving and big game fishing. Recent developments here include a hydroponic and organic vegetable garden to supply the kitchen and green initiatives to protect local fauna. Transfers are by Turtle Airways seaplane charter ($1540 return per couple), a 30-minute flight from Nadi.

SAWA-I-LAU
Sawa-i-Lau is the odd limestone island amid a string of high volcanic islands. The underwater limestone is thought to have formed a few hundred metres below the surface and then uplifted over time. Shafts of daylight enter a great dome-shaped **cave** (Map p154) – 15m tall above the water surface – where you can swim in a natural pool. With a guide, a torch and a bit of courage, you can also swim through an underwater passage into an adjoining chamber. The walls have carvings, paintings and inscriptions of unknown meaning. Similar inscriptions also occur on Vanua Levu in the hills near Vuinadi, Natewa Bay and near Dakuniba on the Tunuloa (Cakaudrove) Peninsula.

Most Yasawa budget resorts offer trips to the caves for around $45 per person but you should check if this includes the $10 entrance fee.

YASAWA
Yasawa, the northernmost island in the group, has six small villages and a fabulous, five-star resort.

Remote, five-star **Yasawa Island Resort** (Map p154; ☎ 672 2266; www.yasawa.com; d from $1500; ⊗ ⊗ ⊚) is set on a gorgeous beach. The 18 air-conditioned *bure* are spacious, with separate living and bedroom areas, outdoor showers and their own private beach hut. Rates include lobster omelettes for breakfast and all à-la-carte meals (drinks extra) and activities (except for diving, game fishing and massage). The resort has its own dive shop and day spa. Recommended activities include 4WD safaris and picnics to secluded beaches. Transfers are by charter flight from Nadi ($420 per person one way, 30 minutes).

Lomaiviti Group

The laid-back pace of life in the Lomaiviti (Middle Fiji) Group belies their action-packed history. These islands had a starring role to play in the creation of the Fijian nation. Fiji's legendary last cannibal king, Ratu Seru Cakobau, cemented his power base here and the islands also made headlines as the epicentre of early British colonial action.

Historic Ovalau is the group's administrative centre. There are few good beaches here; the island's beauty lies in its landscape – a mixture of tumbling hills, vibrant forest and wild, craggy coastline. At its heart, the proud village of Lovoni rests in a wide, green valley formed out of an extinct volcanic crater. Spellbinding Levuka, Ovalau's main town, was Fiji's earliest European settlement and the country's first capital. Wandering the historic, timber-fronted main street and imagining the town during its lawless past is a highlight of a visit to Ovalau. When you've had your fill of history, there's plenty of hiking, diving, snorkelling and river swimming to get on with; and from May to September the annual migration of a pod of humpback whales brings these creatures along the east coast of Ovalau.

Basking in the warm waters around Ovalau are several small resort islands. To the north is shark tooth–shaped Koro (with fantastic diving and rainforest hikes), family-oriented Naigani and the luxury resort of Wakaya island. Three tiny coral backpackers islands lie to the south: Leleuvia, Yanuca Lailai and Caqalai. They are each blessed with desert island–fantasy looks, good snorkelling and simple budget resorts.

HIGHLIGHTS

- Enjoy a never-ending stream of breakfast delights at **Levuka Homestay** (p173)
- Hang out with the local expats on Tuesday nights at the **Ovalau Club** (p173) in Levuka
- Delve into Ovalau's interior village, **Lovoni** (p174), situated in a fractured volcanic crater
- Commune with the ghosts of Ovalau's rambunctious past on Levuka's **colonial streets** (p169)
- Don a mask and snorkel and explore the outstanding underwater vistas around **Caqalai** (p175)
- Lounge on the perfect, soft, white beach at the lovely budget resort of **Leleuvia** (p176)
- Dive the **Levuka Passage** (p166), just minutes from the shore, if you're an experienced diver
- Climb up Gun Rock and look for **whales** (p172) in Levuka's harbour, from May to September

- POPULATION: 15,000
- AREA: 409 SQ KM

History

In the 19th century the town of Levuka was a bolt-hole where embittered sailors jumped ship, escaped convicts hid out, polygamous drunks took strings of island brides and disputes were settled with the musket.

As early as 1806, European sandalwood traders stopped at Levuka in search of supplies. However, foreigners did not begin to settle here until the 1830s, when it became a popular whaling centre. The newcomers built schooners and traded for bêche-de-mer (sea cucumber), turtle shells and coconut oil. Some settled down with several Fijian women at a time, explaining to the local people that this was the custom where they came from.

The Lovoni people, warriors of the caldera in the centre of Ovalau, saw the settlers as interlopers and repeatedly burned down their timber town. The Europeans lived under the protection of the chief of Levuka, who was murdered by raiding Lovoni in 1846.

Levuka grew, and by the 1850s it had a reputation for drunkenness, violence and immorality. It attracted beachcombers and freebooters, con men and middlemen, dreamers and crooks. In the 1870s a flood of planters and other settlers came to Fiji, and the booming town reached a population of about 3000 Europeans, with 52 hotels for them to drink in. The cotton boom was brief and its aftermath bitter. A short-lived Ku Klux Klan was formed in Levuka with the (quickly frustrated) aim of installing a white supremacist government.

In 1825 the coastal villagers ended their alliance with the chief of Verata (a village on Viti Levu's Rewa Delta) and gave allegiance to Ratu Seru Cakobau, the powerful chief of Bau (an island off the southeast coast of Viti Levu). Cakobau attempted, unsuccessfully, to form a national government in 1871. In 1874 Great Britain acted on an earlier offer by Cakobau and Fiji was ceded to the Crown (for more information on this period see p34). Fiji thus became a British colony and Levuka was proclaimed its capital. The government was officially moved to Suva in 1882, and by the end of the 19th century trade was also shifting to Suva. With copra markets plummeting in the 1930s, Levuka declined further.

While the northern end of town was swept away in the hurricanes of 1888 and 1905, many of the boom-time buildings remain.

Climate

The climate of these islands is sunnier and drier than the east coast of Viti Levu, although Levukans say that if it doesn't rain for a week it's considered almost a drought.

Activities

For information on cycling see p168.

DIVING & SNORKELLING

The Lomaiviti waters offer some wonderful, little-visited dive sites where you can encounter manta rays, hammerheads, turtles, white-tip reef sharks and lion fish. Blue Ridge, off Wakaya Island, is famous for its bright-blue ribbon eels. There is stunning soft coral at Snake Island, just off Caqalai, in the Moturiki Channel, and excellent hard coral at Waitovu Passage. The Pipeline, two minutes by boat from town at Levuka Passage, is for experienced divers only. Here the fishy waste from the Pafco tuna plant attracts giant groupers, eagle rays and bull sharks. The following dive operators will take you to the aforementioned sites. The famous E6 in the Vatu-i-Ra Channel and Nigali Passage off Gau island can usually only be accessed on a live-aboard (see p72).

Ovalau Watersports (☎ 344 0166; www.owlfiji.com; Beach St, Levuka; ⏱ 8.30am-4pm Mon-Fri, till 1pm Sat) Two-tank dives/PADI Open Water Courses cost $150/650, including gear (minimum of two divers). Instruction is in English or German. Reef-snorkelling trips, accompanying divers, cost $40 per person including equipment. The outfit regularly dives to Wakaya reef including Blue Ridge, Moturiki Channel and Pipeline.

Viti Watersports (Map p167; ☎ 343 0366; www .vitiwatersports.com/caqalai; Caqalai) Another good dive operator; offers two-tank dives/PADI Open Water Courses for $170/575 including gear. It dives around the Moturiki Channel.

YACHTING

Levuka is a port of entry into Fiji for yachties and there are a few good spots to put down anchor in the Lomaiviti Group. You can anchor in Levuka harbour to explore Ovalau, and good desert-island spots to park include Leleuvia island and Dere Bay on Koro island. You will find resort facilities at both of these spots. Try VHF Marine channel 16 to reach the appropriate authorities if entering the country at Levuka, but if no one answers, anchor near Queen's Wharf and make your way ashore. Formalities are usually simpler here than in Suva. There

LOMAIVITI GROUP

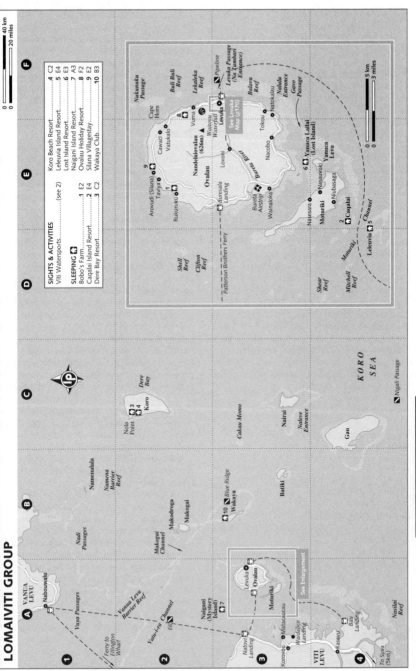

SIGHTS & ACTIVITIES
Viti Watersports.................(see 2)

SLEEPING
Bobo's Farm.........................1 E2
Caqalai Island Resort..........2 E4
Dere Bay Resort..................3 C2

Koro Beach Resort..............4 C2
Leleuvia Island Resort.........5 E4
Lost Island Resort...............6 E3
Naigani Island Resort..........7 A3
Ovalau Holiday Resort.........8 F2
Silana Villagestay...............9 E2
Wakaya Club.....................10 B3

0   40 km
0   20 miles

See Levuka Map (p170)

5 km
3 miles

is a customs house by the main wharf and ship supplies and repairs are available here. Call ahead if arriving outside normal working hours.

Getting There & Around

For flights, head to the office of **Air Fiji** (Map p170; ☎ 344 0139; fax 344 0252; Beach St, Levuka; ☼ 8am-4pm Mon-Fri), next to Levuka Amusement Centre at the Pafco end of town. From Ovalau, Air Fiji flies to Suva (adult/child $65/32 one way, 12 minutes, twice daily Monday to Saturday, once only on Sunday) but will book onward flights throughout Fiji. Credit cards are accepted. The airstrip is about 40 minutes' drive from Levuka. Minibuses to the airstrip ($5 per person) will pick you up from outside the Air Fiji office or from your hotel on request. A taxi costs about $30.

Patterson Brothers Shipping (Map p170; ☎ 344 0125; Beach St, Levuka; ☼ 8.30am-4.30pm Mon-Fri, to noon Sat) has a bus-ferry-bus service from Levuka to Suva via Natovi Landing ($25, four hours, gather at 4.30am for 5am departure daily). You can also opt to stay on the boat from Natovi to Nabouwalu (on Vanua Levu) and then continue by bus to Labasa ($55). **Venu Shipping** (Map p116; ☎ 339 5000; Rona St, Walu Bay, Suva) has direct services from Levuka to Walu Bay in Suva a couple of times a week but the timetable can be erratic.

For information on getting around Levuka, see opposite.

OVALAU

Ovalau is the largest island in the Lomaiviti Group. The island itself is not as pretty as the little brothers and sisters scattered around it, but the capital, Levuka, is captivating and is the only place in the Lomaiviti Group with decent banks, shops and services.

The Bureta Airstrip and Buresala Landing (for ferries) are on the western side of Ovalau, while Levuka is on the eastern coast. A gravel road winds around the perimeter of the island and another follows the Bureta River inland to Lovoni village.

Activities

For information on diving, snorkelling and yachting, see p166.

Levuka and its surrounding area is compact and it is easy to get around by bike – especially if you're heading south, as the road is quite flat. Head north and the road starts to get very hilly around Cawaci. If you're reasonably fit, it will take you about a day to cycle around the island. You can rent mountain bikes from Ovalau Watersports (p166) half-/full day $10/15) in Levuka.

Tours

You can book a number of tours through Ovalau Watersports (p166), including whale watching in season (May to September) and the following options. As a general rule you will be able to arrange pick-up from your hotel when booking.

Epi's Midland Tour (☎ 602 1103, 923 6011; lovoni@owlfiji.com; full day per person $35; ☼ departs 10.30am-11.30am Mon-Sat) takes you to Lovoni village in the crater of an extinct volcano deep in the heart of Ovalau (although it resembles a flat valley floor surrounded by hills rather then anything prehistoric). Epi, who runs the tour, is a Lovoni married to an Englishwoman and will take you through forest and past streams, pointing out all kinds of plants, bush food and local medicine along the way. The scenery is beautiful and Epi will regale you with the history and legends of the island and the Lovoni people. Once you've reached the village and presented your *sevusevu* (gift) to the village chief – assuming the chief is around – you can take a dip in the river. A delicious lunch in one of the village homes is laid on. Price includes transfers and lunch but requires a minimum of four people.

Round Island 4WD Tours (per person $35; ☼ departs 10am) takes you around the island in a 4WD, taking in the major historical sites around Levuka, the village of Lovoni, and the Solomon Islanders' settlement at Wainaloka. You'll call in at Bobo's Farm in Rukuruku for refreshments, hike out to a waterfall and swim in the Bureta River. The tour includes a picnic lunch and requires a minimum of four people.

Silana Village Tour (per person $35) requires a minimum group of six, runs every Wednesday and includes a *meke* (dance performance that enacts stories and legends), a *lovo* (feast cooked in a pit oven) and a chance to make your own handicrafts from coconut and pandanus leaves. The guide, Seru, will also take you around Silana any time for $15 (including lunch).

Day trips to Leleuvia (p176) or Caqalai (p175) cost $70 per person, including lunch.

Ovalau Tourist Information Centre (see right) can book **Tea & Talanoa Tours** (per person $15) with Fijian grandmother Bubu Kara or long-term expat resident Duncan Chrichton (Mr Duncan). *Talanoa* means 'to chat'. Bubu makes delicious scones and Mr Duncan has a fabulous garden and some funky pets. They also offer 90-minute town tours ($8). Book in advance.

A range of **walking tours** (per person from $15) in and around Levuka, including a historical town tour, a walk to the Waitovu Waterfall and the Peak Trail (a hike up a big hill behind town) are also available from Nox, the personable gardener at Levuka Homestay (see p173).

LEVUKA
pop 3750

There's no denying Levuka's visual appeal. It's one of the few places in the South Pacific that has retained its colonial buildings: along the main street, timber shop-fronts straight out of a Hollywood western are sandwiched between blue sea and fertile green mountains. The effect is quite beguiling – you can almost taste the wild, frontier days of this former whaling outpost, in the air.

It is an extremely friendly place and you will be warmly welcomed by the mixture of indigenous Fijians, Indo-Fijians, Chinese Fijians, part-European Fijians and sometimes-eccentric expats who inhabit this sleepy town. Nearly everyone is welcoming to visitors, and if you stay for a week, you'll meet half the town. There are a few good restaurants and cafes here, as well as a good local bar, and the food is surprisingly good.

Levukans have been trying to protect the town's heritage by applying for Unesco World Heritage status, though they have so far been unsuccessful. The government will nominate Levuka again in 2009, and Unesco will make a final decision in 2010.

Orientation

Levuka has one main street, Beach St, which runs parallel to the water (although there's no beach in sight). The north of town is marked by one of two boulders going by the name of Gun Rock. Follow the wafting aroma of fish to the Pafco tuna cannery at the southern end of town.

Being so tiny, Levuka is easy to get around on foot. There is a taxi stand opposite the Westpac bank, from which carriers depart for Lovoni. Carriers to Rukuruku leave from a second taxi stand opposite Emily's Café on Beach St. Mountain bikes can be hired in town (see opposite).

Information

Levuka has the Lomaiviti Group's only tourist facilities. Fast, cheap internet is available at Ovalau Watersports, and the Royal Hotel (p172) also has a computer in its office where you can get online.

Dial ☎ 911 for the ambulance or police.

Colonial National Bank (Beach St, Levuka) Exchanges travellers cheques and currency.

Levuka Hospital (☎ 344 0221; Beach St, Levuka; ⊗ outpatient treatment 8am-1pm & 2-4pm Mon-Fri, to noon Sat, emergencies only after hours) A good, new hospital at the northern end of town. Efficient doctors will treat tourists from around $3.

Ovalau Tourist Information Centre (☎ 330 0356; Levuka Community Centre, Morris Hedstrom Bldg, Levuka; ⊗ 8am-1pm & 2-4.30pm Mon-Fri, to 1pm Sat) Has an information board detailing Ovalau's accommodation and food options and also organises Levuka town tours.

Ovalau Watersports (☎ 344 0166; www.owlfiji.com; Beach St, Levuka; ⊗ 8.30am-4pm Mon-Fri, to 1pm Sat) A dive shop, information centre, internet provider and tour-booking office.

Police station (☎ 344 0222; Totoga Lane, Levuka)

Post office (Beach St, Levuka) Near Queen's Wharf at the southern end of town; there's a cardphone outside.

Westpac Bank (Beach St, Levuka) Has the only ATM in Lomaiviti; also exchanges travellers cheques and foreign currency, and gives cash advances on Visa or MasterCard.

Sights

Levuka is small enough that you can see the sights in a single day of walking. Start your walking tour at Nasova, about 10 minutes' stroll south of the Pafco cannery. The Deed of Cession, handing over Fiji to Britain, was signed here in 1874. **Cession Site**, a memorial commemorating the event, is a pair of anchors and a scattering of plaque-bearing stones.

Across the road are faded **Nasova House**, once the governor's residence, and the thatched **Provincial Bure**. Prince Charles made his headquarters in the Provincial Bure when he represented Her Majesty's government during the transition to independence in 1970. It later served as a venue for Lomaiviti council meetings. A large, new meeting venue has

LOMAIVITI GROUP

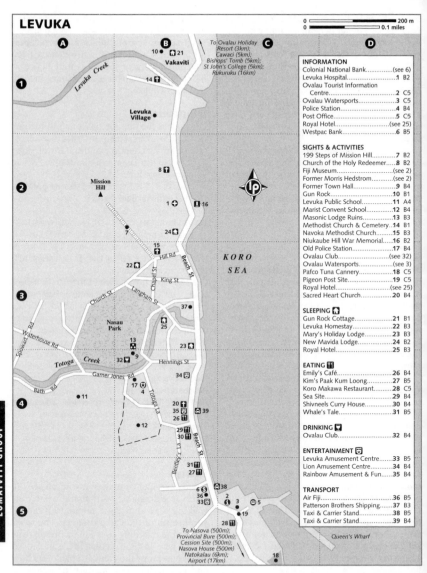

LEVUKA

To Ovalau Holiday Resort (3km); Cawaci (5km); Bishops' Tomb (5km); St John's College (5km); Rukuruku (16km)

0 —————— 200 m
0 —————— 0.1 miles

Levuka Creek

Vakaviti

Levuka Village

Mission Hill

KORO SEA

Hill Rd

Beach St

King St

Langham St

Church St

Chapel St

Waterhouse Rd

Spowart Rd

Totoga Creek

Garner Jones Rd

Bath Rd

Nasau Park

Hennings St

Totoga La

Bentley's La

Beach St

To Nasova (500m); Provincial Bure (500m); Cession Site (500m); Nasova House (500m); Natokalau (6km); Airport (17km)

Queen's Wharf

INFORMATION
Colonial National Bank...............(see 6)
Levuka Hospital..............................1 B2
Ovalau Tourist Information
Centre...2 C5
Ovalau Watersports.....................3 C5
Police Station................................4 B4
Post Office.....................................5 C5
Royal Hotel.............................(see 25)
Westpac Bank...............................6 B5

SIGHTS & ACTIVITIES
199 Steps of Mission Hill..............7 B2
Church of the Holy Redeemer.......8 B2
Fiji Museum..............................(see 2)
Former Morris Hedstrom.........(see 2)
Former Town Hall.........................9 B4
Gun Rock....................................10 B1
Levuka Public School..................11 A4
Marist Convent School................12 B4
Masonic Lodge Ruins..................13 B3
Methodist Church & Cemetery..14 B1
Navoka Methodist Church..........15 B3
Niukaube Hill War Memorial......16 B2
Old Police Station........................17 B4
Ovalau Club.............................(see 32)
Ovalau Watersports..................(see 3)
Pafco Tuna Cannery....................18 C5
Pigeon Post Site..........................19 C5
Royal Hotel............................(see 25)
Sacred Heart Church...................20 B4

SLEEPING
Gun Rock Cottage.......................21 B1
Levuka Homestay........................22 B3
Mary's Holiday Lodge..................23 B3
New Mavida Lodge......................24 B2
Royal Hotel.................................25 B3

EATING
Emily's Café................................26 B4
Kim's Paak Kum Loong................27 B5
Koro Makawa Restaurant............28 C5
Sea Site......................................29 B4
Shivneels Curry House.................30 B4
Whale's Tale...............................31 B5

DRINKING
Ovalau Club................................32 B4

ENTERTAINMENT
Levuka Amusement Centre..........33 B5
Lion Amusement Centre..............34 B4
Rainbow Amusement & Fun.......35 B4

TRANSPORT
Air Fiji...36 B5
Patterson Brothers Shipping........37 B3
Taxi & Carrier Stand....................38 B5
Taxi & Carrier Stand....................39 B4

been built next door, constructed in time for a 2006 Great Council of Chiefs meeting that never got off the ground because of the 2006 coup. According to our guide, it has yet to be used.

The **Pafco tuna cannery** at the southern end of Levuka employs almost 1000 townspeople and gives the whole town its distinctive odour.

It was occupied by Lovoni villagers during the 2000 coup as part of a dispute about unloading cargo.

Head north along **Beach St** where the streetscape dates from the late 19th and early 20th centuries. Just in front of the post office is the site of the original **Pigeon Post**, marked by a nondescript drinking fountain in the centre of the road. From the timber loft that stood here, pigeons provided the first postal link between Levuka and Suva. The birds flew the distance in less than 30 minutes, and were considerably faster and more reliable than Post Fiji.

A few doors away stands the 1868 **former Morris Hedstrom** (MH) trading store, the original MH store in Fiji. Behind its restored facade are the Levuka Community Centre, a library and a branch of the **Fiji Museum** (admission $2; ⏰ 8am-1pm & 2-4.30pm Mon-Fri, 9am-1pm Sat), which holds a small exhibition detailing the history of Levuka, including some wonderful old photos of the town from colonial days.

Sacred Heart Church (Beach St) dates from 1858. The clock strikes twice each hour, with a minute in between. Locals say the first strike is an alarm to warn people who are operating on 'Fiji time'. The light on the spire guides ships through Levuka Passage. From the church, head west along Totoga Lane to explore the backstreets.

The **Marist Convent School** (1882) was a girls school opened by Catholic missionaries and run by Australian and French nuns. It is now a lively coed primary school. It was built largely out of coral stone in an attempt to protect it from the hurricanes that have claimed so many buildings in town, and it remains an impressive monument against the mountain backdrop.

The little weatherboard building on the corner of Garner Jones Rd and Totoga Lane was Levuka's original **police station** (1874), and across Totoga Creek in Nasau Park you'll find Fiji's first private club – the 1904 colonial-style timber Ovalau Club (p173). It's well worth stopping in for a beer, if it's open. Next door to the Ovalau Club is the **former town hall** (1898), built in typical British colonial style in honour of Queen Victoria's silver jubilee.

Alongside the former town hall you'll find the stone shell of the South Pacific's first **Masonic lodge**. Lodge Polynesia (1875) was once Levuka's only Romanesque building, but it was burnt to a husk in the 2000 coup by villagers egged on by their church leaders. Local Methodists had long alleged that Masons were in league with the devil and that tunnels led from beneath the lodge to Nasova House, the Royal Hotel and through the centre of the world to Masonic headquarters in Scotland. Surprisingly, this turned out not to be the case.

Return across the creek and follow Garner Jones Rd west to the **Levuka Public School** (1879). This was Fiji's first formal school and many of Fiji's prominent citizens were educated here, including Percy Morris and Maynard Hedstrom. If you continue up the steps behind the school, you can join some locals for a chat at a popular resting spot. Walk back down to Garner Jones Rd, turn left into Church St and pass Nasau Park. There are many old colonial homes on the hillsides, and the romantically named **199 Steps of Mission Hill** are worth climbing for the fantastic view – although if you count them, you might find there are closer to 185 steps. The very simple, coral-and-stone, Gothic-style **Navoka Methodist Church** (1864), near the foot of the steps, is one of the oldest churches in Fiji.

Head down Chapel St then left along Langham St. The **Royal Hotel** (1860s) is Fiji's oldest hotel, rebuilt in 1903. It is the lone survivor of the once-numerous pubs of that era. Originally it had an open verandah with lace balustrading, but this was built in to increase the size of the rooms. Check out the fantastic old snooker room, and play a game of hunt-the-Royal-Hotel-staff.

Back on Beach St, continue north to **Niukaube Hill**, on a point near the water. This was once the site of Ratu Cakobau's Supreme Court and Parliament House. This is also where the first indentured Indian labourers landed in Fiji, after being forced to anchor offshore for several weeks in an attempt to control an outbreak of cholera. The site now has a memorial to locals who fought and died in WWI and WWII.

North of here is the Anglican **Church of the Holy Redeemer** (1904), with its colourful stained glass and altar of *yaka* and *dakua* wood. Tidy little **Levuka village**, once the home of Tui (Chief) Cakobau, is about 200m further north. In the **cemetery** next to the village's **Methodist Church** is the grave of former American consul John Brown Williams. It was his claim for financial compensation that led Cakobau to hand over Fiji to Britain (see p33 for more on this significant event in Fiji's history).

With the chief's permission you can climb one of two local sites known as **Gun Rock** for a great view over Levuka. In 1849 Commodore Charles Wilkes, of the US exploring expedition, pounded this peak with canon fire from his ship in an attempt to impress the chief of Levuka. Commodore James Graham

---

WARRIORS IN CHAINS: FIJI'S ONLY SLAVES

The saddest exhibit in the Fiji Museum at Levuka is the photograph of a 'dwarf' priest and two Lovoni warriors who were sold by Tui Cakobau to the Barnum & Bailey circus in the USA. In 1870 and 1871 Cakobau fought battle after battle with the ferocious Lovoni highlanders, who regularly sacked the settlement of Levuka and did not accept Cakobau's claim to be king of all Fiji. After repeated failed attempts to penetrate their hill, Cakobau sent a Methodist missionary to subdue the people. The Lovoni put their trust in a 'dwarf' (actually just a short bloke) priest who had the ability to foresee the future. The priest was the first to notice the approaching missionary and, seeing a brightness emanating from him, believed he came in peace. The missionary read from the Bible in Bauan, referring to the Lovoni villagers as the lost sheep of Fiji. He then invited them to a reconciliation feast with Cakobau.

On 29 June 1871, the Lovoni people came down from the safety of their village to Levuka and, in good faith, put aside their weapons. However, as they started their meal, Cakobau's warriors caught them off guard, quickly surrounding and capturing them.

Cakobau humiliated his captives horribly, then sold them as slaves for £3 a head. His takings helped him form his government. Families were separated as the villagers were dispersed as far as Kavala (in the Kadavu Group), Yavusania (near Nadi on Viti Levu), Lovoni-Ono (in the Lau Group) and Wailevu (on Vanua Levu). The Lovoni were the only Fijians ever to suffer this fate. When the British administration took over Fiji it freed the Lovoni slaves, and the blackbirding of other Pacific Islanders (see p33) began instead.

Goodenough repeated the 'entertainment' in 1874. You can still find cannonball scars on the rock. (The other Gun Rock is much smaller, and named for the canon mounted upon it in the 1850s.) Gun Rock is a good place to spot **whales**, which swim past between May and September.

Walk, cycle or take a taxi the 5km north to Cawaci, where you'll find the **Bishops' Tomb** (1922), a beautiful, fading, gothic-style construction on a grassy point overlooking the ocean, where Fiji's first two Roman Catholic bishops are entombed. Our taxi driver told us that ghosts had been 'spotted' up here by locals and it's not hard to see how this place, with its Latin inscriptions, spooky acoustics, and a swaying cross on one of the graves in the foreground, could play upon the imagination. From here you can see the limestone-and-coral **St John's College** (1894), originally where the sons of Fijian chiefs were educated in English. These days girls are educated here too. The boys' and girls' dormitories are separated by a bridge that no student is allowed to cross after 6pm.

Sleeping

Ovalau Holiday Resort (Map p167; ☎ 344 0329; ohrfiji@ connect.com.fj; camping per person $10, dm/s/d $12/15/28, self-contained bungalow s/d $45/77, extra person $25; ⛾) Three kilometres north of town, near Vuma, the Ovalau Holiday Resort consists of a few candy-coloured *bure* on a gentle slope across from the beach. There is a swimming pool here and the larger *bure* have kitchens and would make a good base for a family with a car. A taxi from Levuka will cost $5. A carrier (every half hour from town) costs $1. The resort was up for sale at the time of research.

Mary's Holiday Lodge (☎ 344 0013; Beach St; dm/s/d with shared bathroom incl breakfast $15/20/35) Mary's has the cheapest rooms in town, which are pretty basic and tired, as are the shared, cold-water bathrooms. It's friendly enough though and there's a breezy verandah to relax on.

New Mavida Lodge (☎ 344 0477; Beach St; dm/d inc breakfast $25/80) The New Mavida is an imposing (by Levuka standards) cream building sitting behind a white picket fence. Pass through the gleaming-floored and high-ceilinged lobby to find comfortable rooms with hot-water bathrooms, TV and balconies, and a six-bed dorm. It was reopened in 2006 after a fire in 2003.

our pick **Royal Hotel** (☎ 344 0024; www.royallevuka .com; s/d/tw $29/43/43, cottages from $85; ⛾ ▢ ⛾) The Royal is the oldest hotel in Fiji, dating back to the 1860s (though it was rebuilt in the early 1900s after a fire) and it's got the character to back it up. This proud timber building is thick with colonial atmosphere, from the creaking wooden floorboards to the hallways plastered with black-and-white photographs of Levuka in times past. Upstairs each room is different and full of quirky old furniture, with iron bedsteads and sloping floors. The wonderful, semienclosed private verandahs come complete with old-fashioned white cane chairs and wooden shutters. There are also some modern cottages in the grounds, which are more comfortable but don't quite match the charm of the main building.

Levuka Holiday Cottage (☎ 344 0166; d $80) About a 15-minute walk north of town ($2 by taxi), this is the only self-catering option close to town. There's a well-equipped kitchen with a washing machine and a good supply of hot water, and it's right in the middle of a pretty, tropical garden under Gun Rock cliff. You can swim out from the sea wall in high tide and snorkel around the rock under the beacon. Dolphins occasionally pass this way.

our pick **Levuka Homestay** (☎ 344 0777; www .levukahomestay.com; Church St; s/d incl breakfast $126/148, extra person $42) This is a great choice – a multi-level house with four large, comfortable, light-filled rooms with terraces, each one on its own level. The laid-back owners live on the highest level and regularly invite their guests to share a drink with them on their enormous deck overlooking the harbour (favourite drink-time activity at the time of research: whale spotting). You won't forget the breakfasts here in a hurry. Start with fruit, cereal, toast, cheese and homemade relish, followed by banana pancakes and passionfruit butter, then, if you're not stuffed enough already, bacon and eggs. There is a high chair and a cot here for little ones.

Eating

See the boxed text, below, for the locals' favourite eateries.

Shivneels Curry House (☎ 344 0616; Beach St; mains $4; ☺ breakfast, lunch & dinner before 6pm Mon-Sat) Exhausted Chinese and Indian food lies collapsed all day in the bain-marie, but if you give the owners an hour's notice and $10, they will prepare you a delicious curry plate comprising a fish or chicken curry, dahl, vegetables, pappadums, rice and rotis, served with a cup of masala tea.

Emily's Café (☎ 344 0382; Beach St; lunch/pizzas $4/7; ☺ breakfast, lunch & dinner Mon-Sat, dinner Sun) Serves coffee and a selection of home-baked cakes and fresh bread, as well as fast-food favourites like rotis and pies.

Sea Site (☎ 344 0382; Beach St; meals $4.50; ☺ lunch & dinner) Grab a tasty chicken-curry roti or an ice cream from this otherwise unexciting locals' cafe.

SELF-CATERING

On Thursdays local villagers come to sell fresh fruit and vegetables alongside the waterfront roughly opposite Shivneels on Beach St. You can get almost everything else at the numerous general stores on Beach St.

Drinking & Entertainment

Ovalau Club (Nasau Park; ☺ 4-9.30pm Mon-Thu, 2pm-midnight Fri, 10am-midnight Sat, 10am-9.30pm Sun) Since the Levuka Club closed down, this is the main place in town to go for a drink. Fiji's first gentlemens club, it's extremely atmospheric

---

THE LOCALS' FAVOURITE EATERIES

Kim's Paak Kum Loong (☎ 344 0059; Beach St; mains $8; ☺ lunch & dinner) This is 'hands down the best place to get Chinese food in Levuka'. There are two menus here – one with standard Chinese dishes, another with a mixture of Fijian-style fish and meat dishes and a selection of Thai curries. This place is usually busy and there's a good street-side balcony for voyeurs. Sunday night is buffet night so come prepared to be stuffed.

Koro Makawa Restaurant (☎ 344 0429; Beach St; pizzas from $9; ☺ breakfast, lunch & dinner) You can get curries, fish and chips, and other European meals here, but locals recommend it because of the pizza, which is, apparently, very hit and miss – 'either one of the best pizzas you've ever tasted or a total disaster' was one comment. If you're willing to take the risk, go for one of the many fishy toppings – the tuna is the most fitting since the cannery's right on the doorstep.

Whale's Tale (☎ 344 0235; Beach St; breakfast $6, lunch sandwiches $8, mains $12; ☺ lunch & dinner Mon-Sat) Ask a local to recommend a place to eat and they'll probably send you right here. This is a perennial favourite serving 'the best fish and chips in Fiji' as one local resident told us. There are excellent burgers and sandwiches, an astoundingly good-value set-dinner menu ($17) and pretty good carafes of wine ($14). It's a cute little place with big windows for watching the world go by and a little bamboo thatched kitchen area at the back.

and the white timber colonial-style building is a sight in its own right. It's no longer a colonial club in any respect, but local residents (mostly expats) get together for a drink at 6pm every Tuesday and tourists are always welcome to join them. There's a snooker table, and at the weekend things can get pretty lively and local bands often play. Ask the bar staff to show you a letter written by Count Felix von Luckner during WWI, just before his capture on nearby Wakaya. Von Luckner cruised the South Seas in a German raider disguised as a Norwegian merchant ship, sinking Allied supply boats. When he lost his ship he tried to avoid arrest by disguising himself as an English writer on a sporting cruise. He signed the letter 'Max Pemberton'.

There are a number of pool halls where locals like to pot balls to pop music. Those looking for amusement and fun can try **Rainbow Amusement & Fun** (Beach St; ⊙ 10am-10pm Mon-Sat). Two similar places, the Lion and Levuka Amusement Centres, offer amusement and the same opening hours without the fun.

LOVONI

Lovoni village is surrounded by thick, green rainforest in the centre of a flat-bottomed valley that is actually an extinct volcano crater. It is the island's beating heart and the centre of indigenous culture. There's no accommodation for travellers here but guided tours are available from Levuka (see p168). Wear sturdy shoes and be prepared to face down some serious mud if it rains (which it does often, and suddenly). Your guide should provide a *sevusevu* for the chief (if the chief's around) and point out the **chiefs' burial site** opposite the church and the **Korolevu hill fortification** high on the crater rim, where villagers took refuge in times of war.

The Lovoni villagers are extremely proud of their heritage and our guide described them as the strongest and bravest people in all of Fiji. The fact that Chief Cakobau was only able to defeat them with trickery (see the boxed text, p172) is held up as proof of this. On 7 July each year the enslavement of the Lovoni people is commemorated. People of all religions gather in one church and the history is read out.

There is a Levuka–Lovoni truck, which leaves Levuka at 7am and 11am Monday to Saturday and returns at about 3pm.

RUKURUKU

Rukuruku village is a 17km drive north of Levuka, up a rough road with fantastic ocean vistas along the way. Near the village is a black-sand beach with a view of Naigani island, and there's a small waterfall about 15 minutes' walk up the valley. It's best to arrange a day out there with Bobo (see p168) to avoid trespassing on village property. Schoolchildren might sing you a song and old people will share a bowl of *kava*. Tours are free to house guests at Bobo's Farm. A taxi will cost about $30 each way.

Bobo's Farm (Map p167; ☎ 993 3632, 344 0166; www .owlfiji.com/bobosfarm; Rukuruku; s/d $38/56) is an impossibly tranquil, solar-powered, two-room cottage, 15 minutes away from Rukuruku and surrounded by thick rainforest on a massive farm leading down to the sea. There's a shared living room and tiny kitchen, so you can self-cater if you wish, but the organic, homemade meals here are excellent (breakfast $8, lunch $10, dinner $14). You can also sit on the large main deck of Bobo and Karin's house, which often sets the stage for some *kava* drinking sessions with people from the local village.

You can walk to a nearby black-sand beach or the local waterfall, and there's a freshwater stream for bathing or prawn catching. Bobo will gladly escort you to all of these and the village. He can also arrange island-hopping, snorkelling and fishing trips. Book ahead through Ovalau Watersports (p166) in Levuka. Bobo can pick you up by boat from Bureta Airstrip ($15) or Buresala Landing ($20). You could also get a taxi to the turn-off to the farm ($30) from where it's a five-minute walk down to the cottage.

AROVUDI (SILANA)

About 70 people live in this small village, which has its own little patch of pebbly beach. It's pretty quiet though, as many villagers, including the chief, work away in Suva, leaving several houses empty. The **Methodist village church** (1918) is made of coral cooked in a *lovo*. A *tabua* (whale's tooth) hangs by the side of the altar; it was presented to the village by the first missionaries to come here. A crypt of stones overlooking the beach was the grave site of a chief, but it frightened the children so the villagers moved the body to the hills where their other ancestors are buried. There is one place to stay, run by the enterprising Seru, who also organises regular tours from Levuka (see p168).

Close to the beach the **Silana Villagestay** (Map p167; ☎ 344 0166; silana@owlfiji.com; sites/dm/bure per person $20/25/35) is a basic wooden cabin *bure* (sleeping four) with shared cold-water facilities and space for pitching tents. The owners will cook lunch and dinner ($7), or you can self-cater from the kitchen. During the day you can fish, hike and snorkel. Evenings are for hanging out with the local villagers and drinking *kava*. The carrier from Levuka takes about 40 minutes and costs $3.

OTHER LOMAIVITI ISLANDS

Lomaiviti's smaller islands are beautiful and welcoming, although some are looked after better than others.

YANUCA LAILAI

Yanuca Lailai (Lost Island) is the nearest to Ovalau of the small islands. Much of the shoreline is rocky but there is a patch of golden sand, good snorkelling from the shore, and a small mountain at the island's centre, which you can clamber up for fantastic views out to sea and of Ovalau.

Lost Island Resort (Map p167; www.owlfiji.com/los tisland.htm; sites/dm/bure per person incl meals $30/45/58) is the smallest of the Lomaiviti backpacker resorts, with just three double *bure* and a dorm. The *bure* share a cold-water shower and there is a small shop and bar on the premises. Meals are good here, mostly Fijian fare, and there is plenty of fresh seafood on offer. There are fantastic views of sunrise from the beach and sunset from 'The Rock', which is a five-minute scramble from the resort. Book through either Ovalau Watersports (p166) or the Ovalau Tourist Information Centre (p169) in Levuka. Transfers from the airstrip or Levuka are $25 one way. Transfers from Waidalice on Viti Levu (southeast of Korovou) cost $50.

MOTURIKI

The lush, hilly island of Moturiki is just southwest of Ovalau and home to 10 villages. Although it has no accommodation for travellers, both Leleuvia and Caqalai resorts will take guests to the village of **Niubasaga** for a typical Sunday church service. Be prepared: one of your party will have to get up and introduce the group to the congregation.

WHAT LIES BENEATH

Don't tempt the spirits of Gavo Passage. If you head out to the islands south of Ovalau, your boat will likely travel through a break in the reef. Many indigenous Fijians believe that beneath the waters of Gavo Passage lies a sunken village inhabited by ancestral spirits. Stories of fishermen hooking newly woven mats are whispered around Levuka. When passing over the *tabu* (sacred) site, Fijians remove their hats and sunglasses and talk in hushed tones. They believe the spirits will avenge any act of disrespect. Stay on the safe side, take off your baseball cap and give your sunnies a rest. Even if there are no spirits to annoy, irreverent behaviour might put the wind up your boatman.

CAQALAI

Teeny little Caqalai island lies just south of Moturiki. It only takes 15 minutes to walk around the island perimeter's beautiful **golden-sand beaches**, which are fringed with palms and other large trees.

Run by the Methodist Church, **Caqalai Island Resort** (☎ 343 0366; www.fijianholiday.com; sites/dm/bure per person incl meals $35/45/55) is a great little backpacker haven. Accommodation is in basic thatched *bure*, scattered between the palm trees, some with electricity, some without. There are lovely palm-thatched, cold-water showers that are open to the elements. Food here is good and the vibe is friendly – in the evenings there's usually some singing and dancing followed by the odd *kava* drinking session. There's a small shop here but no alcohol, so you'll need to bring your own. Snorkelling right off the beach is fantastic but for an even more impressive underwater adventure it's possible to walk out to Snake Island (named after the many black-and-white–banded sea snakes here) and drift slowly back to Caqalai. Take some reef shoes though (and something to secure them while you're swimming), as the walkway can be hard on the feet. There's a handy, hand-drawn map in the main *bure* showing the best snorkelling spots. Viti Watersports (p166) runs a dive shop here. Also on offer are village trips to Moturiki ($5), boat trips to tiny Honeymoon Island ($15) and day trips to Leleuvia ($10).

LOMAIVITI GROUP

Getting There & Away

If you're coming from Levuka, you can book transport and accommodation from Ovalau Watersports (p166) or call for a pick-up. One-way transfers cost $30 per person. Transfers from Caqalai to Bureta airstrip on Ovalau cost $50 for one person, or $25 per person for two or more.

From Suva, catch a bus heading down the Kings Road from the main bus terminal and get off at Waidalice Landing, which is next to Waidalice Bridge. You need to call ahead for a boat from Caqalai to pick you up here ($30 per person).

LELEUVIA

Just south of Caqalai sits beautiful Leleuvia, another palm-fringed coral island (slightly larger than Caqalai) wrapped in white, powdery beaches with outstanding views out to sea. At low tide a vast area of sand and rock is exposed – it's a good time to explore the island's tidal pools. It's also possible to swim off the western side or do some good snorkelling and great diving. Watch out for the currents as they can be quite strong.

Leleuvia Island Resort (Map p167; ☎ 336 4008, 359 5150; info@leleuvia.com; dm/bure per person incl all meals $40/50) came under new management in 2007. The place has been slowly renovated and things are looking great. A large, open, sand-floored bar and restaurant area serves cold beer and tasty meals (curry night is a favourite) and at the resort's 'entrance' is a gorgeous wide stretch of beach with strategically placed sun loungers and kayaks for hire. An assortment of pretty, thatched *bure* (with electricity) and rooms are centred around a clearing, and along the beach. There are a couple of good family units and an attractive thatched bathroom area with spotless showers and toilets. It's incredibly relaxing here. The staff are very friendly and put on all kinds of entertainment (such as *kava* drinking and beach bonfires). Whilst the snorkelling is not on a par with Caqalai, it is still good and you can hire equipment. Village trips, diving and fishing excursions are also possible.

Getting There & Away

Boat transfers to/from Waidalice Landing are $30 each way (call in advance for a pick-up. Waidalice is about a 1½-hour bus ride from Suva). Transfers to/from Levuka (one hour) also cost $30 each way. Call in advance

for a pick-up or you can book via Ovalau Watersports (p166).

WAKAYA

About 20km east of Ovalau, Wakaya is a privately owned island visible from Levuka. It has forests, cliffs, beautiful white-sand beaches, and archaeological sites, including a **stone fish trap**. In some areas you'll find feral horses, pigs and deer roaming freely; in others there are millionaires' houses.

Wakaya Club (☎ 344 8128; www.wakaya.com; garden/ocean view d $3300-6000) is one of Fiji's most exclusive resorts. If you've got several thousand dollars to spare, you can live it up here with the likes of Bill Gates, Pierce Brosnan and Crown Prince Felipe of Spain. There is a five-night minimum stay.

Getting There & Away

The island is a 20-minute speedboat ride from Levuka; however, as it's private, you'll need an invite to visit. Call ahead to the Wakaya Club to see if you'll be welcome.

KORO

Many villages are nestled in the lush tropical forests of Koro, northwest of Ovalau. Roads over the mountainous interior provide plenty of thrills and wonderful views. A portion of the island is freehold, so plenty of foreigners have bought up land to build their second homes.

At Dere Bay a wharf allows you to walk out to good swimming and snorkelling; inland is a waterfall and natural pool. The resorts listed here are surrounded by residential developments and have been aimed at people visiting or building real estate on the island, although they are gearing up to be more tourist friendly.

Koro Beach Resort (☎ 331 1075; fijimiller@connect .com.fj; d bure per person incl meals $100; 🔊), next door to Dere Bay, was in the process of reopening at the time of research. There will be space for tents as well as simple thatched *bure*.

Dere Bay Resort (☎ 331 1075; korobeach@connect .com.fj; d bure per person incl meals $200; 🔊) has well-designed *bure* with soaring ceilings, 360-degree outlooks and spacious verandahs. There's also a fantastic deck and pier. There are plans to offer activities and diving.

Getting There & Away

Air Fiji flies Koro–Suva on Thursdays (adult/child $125/62.50 each way), and **Turtle Airways**

(☎ 672 1888; www.turtleairways.com) or **Pacific Island** (☎ 672 5644; www.fijiseaplanes.com) seaplanes will fly you in from Nadi. Ferries run by **Consort Shipping** (Map p118; ☎ 330 2877) leave Suva twice weekly, stopping at Koro on their way to Savusavu. From Savusavu, the Dere Bay boat costs $100 one way. Enquire about transport when you book your accommodation. Pick-up from the ferry/airport is $20/30.

NAIGANI

Naigani (Mystery Island) is a mountainous island about 10km offshore from Ovalau. The island has white-sand beaches, lagoons, a fringing coral reef, the remains of a **precolonial hillside fortification** and 'cannibal caves'.

Naigani Island Resort (☎ 330 0925; www.naiganiisland.com; studios/villas $170/200; ⬛) is a former copra plantation (the main bar and restaurant are the restored homestead of Mr Riley, the Irishman who established the plantation) and a friendly, unpretentious, family resort popular with antipodean time-sharers. The villas have clean, white, airy interiors and are strung out along palm-lined paths in an arrangement that's reminiscent of a retirement village. There's a pretty beach, and good snorkelling about 50m out from the shore.

The best snorkelling, though, is the next bay over at Picnic Beach. You can walk over at low tide (take a sturdy pair of shoes), take a kayak or get the resort boat to drop you off and pick you up a couple of hours later. The more adventurous can follow a path over the mountains from the resort to Picnic Beach. Get detailed directions at the resort beforehand. The path isn't clear and the hills are very steep.

The food here is OK (mostly bland, European-style food) and there's a *lovo* every Saturday night. There's a small pool with a kids' slide, a baby pool and several inflatables. There's also a kids club in the holidays. Babysitting costs $5 an hour.

The generator is turned off from 10am to 4pm every day. One of the empty units serves as an internet cafe with (slow) internet access for $10 an hour. There's a gift shop selling a few T-shirts and souvenirs but it is permanently locked and you'll have to get someone to unlock it if you need anything.

Return boat transfers to/from Suva, via Natovi Landing, or to/from Taviya village, near Rukuruku on Ovalau, are $50/25 per adult/child. Transfer to Ovalau takes around 30 minutes, or more if the weather is poor.

LOMAIVITI GROUP

Vanua Levu

Vanua Levu (Big Island) may be second in size to Viti Levu, but the languid pace of life, dreamy, peaceful landscapes and lack of tourist infrastructure give it a very different feel. The only pocket of tourist activity here is pretty Savusavu – a small town set in a sweeping bay on the island's south coast, and a haven for expats and yachties.

What it lacks in tourist conveniences, Vanua Levu makes up for with seclusion and unspoilt beauty. Here you'll find peaceful countryside, traditional villages and calm, relaxing resorts. A mountainous spine cuts across the island. To the north are sunny hillsides, native forest and sugar-cane and pine plantations. Many Indo-Fijians live here, concentrated around hot, hard-working Labasa. In the mainly indigenous Fijian south are coconut plantations, ocean views and the majority of the island's tourist lodges and facilities. The north and west hardly see any tourists and much of the western coast is accessible only by boat.

The island has a reputation for poor beaches, which is a little unfair. Whilst they may not match up to the glittering stars of the Yasawas, you'll still find kilometre after kilometre of wild, deserted, palm-lined sands. It's under the water, though, that Vanua Levu really shines. Diving is terrific and Jean-Michel Cousteau set up a resort here. Savusavu Bay has great sites for snorkelling and diving, and nearby Rainbow Reef has some of the best dive sites in the South Pacific. Vanua Levu's many deep bays are fantastic for kayaking, and Natewa Bay, the longest in the South Pacific, is frequented by spinner dolphins. Those who aren't water babies can head into the lush, rugged interior for hiking and birdwatching.

HIGHLIGHTS

- Explore the rough roads of the **Tunuloa Peninsula** (p189) by 4WD
- Gaze out at yachts anchored in the bay as you enjoy a sunset drink at the **Savusavu Yacht Club** (p187)
- Look for spinner dolphins in **Natewa Bay** (p186)
- Brave rough roads to visit remote and beautiful **Wainunu Bay** (p195)
- Redefine your image of cruises with a trip on the elegant **Tui Tai** (opposite) departing from Savusavu
- Soak up the colonial atmosphere on the deck of Savusavu's **Planters' Club** (p187)
- Explore Savusavu Bay by **kayak** (p183)
- Snorkel with heaps of colourful fish at **Split Rock** (p183) in Savusavu Bay

- POPULATION: 139,510
- AREA: 5587 SQ KM

Getting There & Around

AIR

Flying is the best way to get to Vanua Levu and both Air Fiji and Pacific Sun have regular flights from Nadi or Suva to either Labasa or Savusavu. You can also fly between Savusavu and Taveuni. See p245 for details.

BOAT

There are several boat services to and from Vanua Levu but unless you've got plenty of time on your hands it's not really worth it – you won't save much money and the trip is significantly longer. Bligh Water Shipping, Consort Shipping and Patterson Brothers Shipping all service Vanua Levu from Viti Levu, Ovalau, Koro and Taveuni. Grace Ferry operates a bus and boat service from Labasa and Savusavu via Buca Bay to Taveuni. See p248 for schedules and ticket prices.

Charters & Cruises

For those looking to charter their own boat, **SeaHawk Yacht Charters** (☎ 885 0787; www.seahawkfiji .com) rents out a beautiful 16m yacht with captain and a cook/crew from $250 to $420 per person per day depending on the season and level of service required. You can go practically anywhere in Fiji and the crew can help you arrange activities such as diving.

A trip with **Tui Tai Adventure Cruises** (Map p182; ☎ 885 3032; www.tuitai.com) combines the comfort, relaxation, fantastic food and luxury of an intimate, upscale resort with an ever-changing South Pacific backdrop. If you're put off the idea of cruising by visions of a cheesy behemoth, never fear: the *Tui Tai,* an elegant, motorised sailboat, is sexy as hell, and the small number of guests keeps the mood friendly and relaxed. You can lounge about in stylish, curved rattan chairs or day beds and spot dolphins from the deck; relax in the onboard spa and eat delicious meals by lantern light or under the stars on a nearby beach. And then there are the activities – including snorkelling, kayaking, biking, diving, fishing and meeting local villagers. Setting off from Savusavu, a typical itinerary includes Taveuni, Kioa and Rabi islands, and provides the only way of reaching the Ringgold Isles (a beautiful, mostly uninhabited group of islands northeast of Vanua Levu), although your itinerary may vary according to the weather. All accommodation is in cabins with private bathroom and air-con. A five-night cruise costs from $5608/3738 per person single/double up to $12,476/8317 for the Oversea Veranda Suite, including all meals and activities except diving. Cheaper rates are available for singles willing to share a cabin. There's also a seven-night option. Tui Tai also funds several community projects, has regular 'humanitarian' tours and uses ecofriendly practices.

ROAD

Vanua Levu's remote, tropical roads are crying out to be explored by 4WD. Hire cars are available in Labasa (see p194) and Savusavu (see p188). Given the bumpy terrain, though, the available vehicles won't always be in top condition. There are unsealed roads around most of the island's perimeter. The road from Labasa to Savusavu is sealed but showing plenty of wear and you'll have to do a fair amount of pothole dodging. The first 20km of the Hibiscus Hwy from Savusavu along the scenic coast is similarly paved. Unfortunately, the rest of the highway is much rougher. Avoid driving at night as there are lots of wandering animals and there is often fog in the mountains. Petrol stations are scarce and usually closed on Sundays, so plan to fill up in Labasa, Savusavu or Seaqaqa. It's also a good idea to take some food with you on the road.

Just remember, you cannot wander on foot through the countryside without permission from the landowners.

It's also possible to navigate the island by bus but timetables can be erratic and it takes far longer.

SAVUSAVU & AROUND

Savusavu (population 4970) is Vanua Levu's liveliest and prettiest settlement, nestled against a sweeping bay, backed by sloping green hills and strung out along a main street dotted with decorative plant pots and flowers. There are several good restaurants, bars, stores and internet cafes catering to a significant expat community. Many foreigners have snapped up land here in recent years in order to build second homes and lodges in the hills and surrounding coast.

Savusavu is also the sole port of entry on Vanua Levu for yachts, and one of the most popular places in Fiji for visiting yachties to put down anchor. There are two excellent marinas here and Savusavu Bay fills up with vessels during the high season. A new marina complex (see www.marinavillagefiji.com) is planned on the waterfront east of town. It will

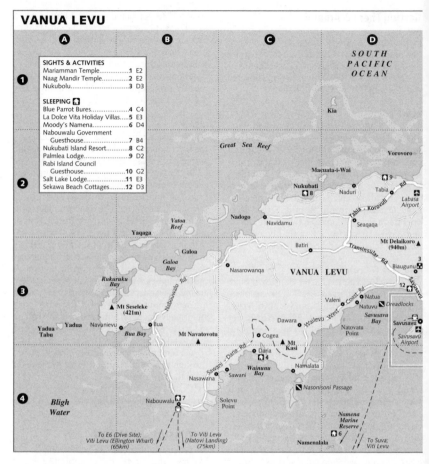

VANUA LEVU

SIGHTS & ACTIVITIES
Mariamman Temple................1 E2
Naag Mandir Temple.............2 E2
Nukubolu..............................3 D3

SLEEPING
Blue Parrot Bures.....................4 C4
La Dolce Vita Holiday Villas.....5 E3
Moody's Namena....................6 D4
Nabouwalu Government
  Guesthouse.........................7 B4
Nukubati Island Resort...........8 C2
Palmlea Lodge........................9 D2
Rabi Island Council
  Guesthouse.........................10 G2
Salt Lake Lodge....................11 E3
Sekawa Beach Cottages........12 D3

SOUTH PACIFIC OCEAN

include an international marina, luxury villas and apartments, bars and cafes.

East of Savusavu the Hibiscus Hwy stretches for 70 miles up the coast. It's a stunning (if bumpy) drive through avenues of palm trees, past spectacular bays and old plantations.

Orientation & Information

All of Savusavu's accommodation and facilities are based along one main road, so you won't get lost, despite the lack of street names. Maps of the area are available from the **Yacht Shop** (Map p182; ☎ 885 0040; Copra Shed Marina; ☺ 8am-1pm & 2-5pm Mon-Fri) and there's an informal little desk in the Bula Re Café (p187) that provides advice on the local area as well as tourist flyers and brochures.

Being an official point of entry for yachts, there are customs, immigration, health and quarantine services available. **Customs** (Map p182; ☎ 885 0727; ☺ 8am-1pm & 2-5pm Mon-Fri) is located west of the marinas on the main street.

ANZ, Colonial National and Westpac banks all have branches in the main street. They all change currency and travellers cheques and give cash advances on major credit cards, as well as having ATMs on site that accept all major debit and credit cards.

Other places of interest:

Curly Cruising & Internet (Map p182; ☎ 885 0122; curly@connect.com.fj; ☺ 8am-5pm Mon-Fri, to noon Sat) A yachting information centre and tour office.

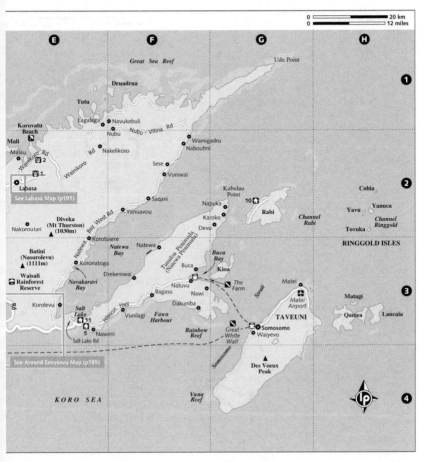

Great Sea Reef

Udu Point

Druadrua

Tutu

Korovatu
Beach

Lagalaga ● Navukebuli

Mali

Malau
Nubu

Nubu - Vitina Rd

Wainigadru
Naboutini

Nakelikoso

Sese ● Vuniwai

Labasa

See Labasa Map (p191)

Kubulau
Point

Saqani

Napuka

Karoko

Rabi

Cobia

Channel
Rabi

Yavu
Yanuca

Channel
Ringgold

Tovuka

RINGGOLD ISLES

Diveka
(Mt Thurston)
(1030m)

Nakoroutari

Yanuavou
Devo

Tunuloa Peninsula
(Natewa Peninsula)

Batini
(Nasorolevu)
(1111m)

Korotasere

*Natewa
Bay*

Natewa

Koronatoga
Drekeniwai

*Buca
Bay*

Kioa

Waisali
Rainforest
Reserve

*Navakaravi
Bay*

Bagasu
Natuvu
Nawi

Matei

Matei
Airport

Matagi

Korolevu

Salt
Lake
11

Vunilagi
Dakuniba

Qamea
Laucala

TAVEUNI

Salt Lake Rd

Naweni

*Fawn
Harbour*

*Rainbow
Reef*

*Great
White
Wall*

Somosomo

Waiyevo

See Around Savusavu Map (p185)

Des Voeux
Peak

KORO SEA

*Vuna
Reef*

Hospital (off Map p185; ☎ 885 0444) The hospital is 1.5km east of town on the road to Labasa. Call the hospital if an ambulance is required.

Laundry Service is available at the Copra Shed and Waitui Marinas (see right).

Pharmacist (Map p182; ☺ 9am-5pm Mon-Fri, to noon Sun) The staff in this pharmacy, next door to the Siloah Clinic, are very helpful.

Police (off Map p182; ☎ 885 0222) The police station is 600m past the Buca Bay Rd turn-off.

Post Office (Map p182) At the eastern end of town near Buca Bay Rd.

Savusavu Computers (Map p182; Waterfront Complex; per hr $4; ☺ 8.30am-5pm Mon-Fri, to 1pm Sat)

Siloah Clinic (Map p182; ☎ 885 0721; ☺ 9am-5pm Mon-Fri) This private health centre is behind Savusavu Wines & Spirits on the main road.

Xenographic Solutions (Map p182; Copra Shed Marina; internet per hr $6; ☺ 8.30am-9pm) There's another branch on the main street next to Savusavu Wines & Spirits.

Sights & Activities
MARINAS

Copra Shed Marina (Map p182; ☎ 885 0457; coprashed@ connect.com.fj) started life as a copra mill back in the late 1800s but now serves as a focal point for Savusavu's tourists and expats. You can arrange all sorts of things here – from car hire to day trips – and when you're done, you can brush up on your Savusavu history at a small display, check your email, munch on a burger or enjoy a beer whilst looking out over the bay. If you've fallen in love with the place, you can even browse for properties at the local

VANUA LEVU

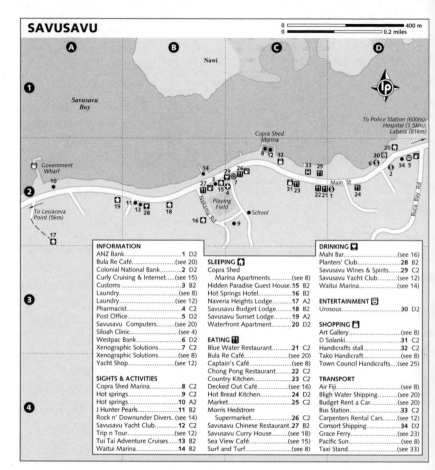

SAVUSAVU

INFORMATION	
ANZ Bank	**1** D2
Bula Re Café	(see 20)
Colonial National Bank	**2** D2
Curly Cruising & Internet	(see 15)
Customs	**3** B2
Laundry	(see 8)
Laundry	(see 12)
Pharmacist	**4** C2
Post Office	**5** D2
Savusavu Computers	(see 20)
Siloah Clinic	(see 4)
Westpac Bank	**6** D2
Xenographic Solutions	**7** C2
Xenographic Solutions	(see 8)
Yacht Shop	(see 12)

SIGHTS & ACTIVITIES	
Copra Shed Marina	**8** C2
Hot springs	**9** C2
Hot springs	**10** A2
J Hunter Pearls	**11** B2
Rock n' Downunder Divers	(see 14)
Savusavu Yacht Club	**12** C2
Trip n Tour	(see 12)
Tui Tai Adventure Cruises	**13** B2
Waitui Marina	**14** B2

SLEEPING	
Copra Shed	
Marina Apartments	(see 8)
Hidden Paradise Guest House	**15** B2
Hot Springs Hotel	**16** B2
Naveria Heights Lodge	**17** A2
Savusavu Budget Lodge	**18** B2
Savusavu Sunset Lodge	**19** A2
Waterfront Apartment	**20** D2

EATING	
Blue Water Restaurant	**21** C2
Bula Re Café	(see 20)
Captain's Café	(see 8)
Chong Pong Restaurant	**22** C2
Country Kitchen	**23** C2
Decked Out Café	(see 16)
Hot Bread Kitchen	**24** D2
Market	**25** C2
Morris Hedstrom	
Supermarket	**26** C2
Savusavu Chinese Restaurant	**27** B2
Savusavu Curry House	(see 18)
Sea View Café	(see 15)
Surf and Turf	(see 8)

DRINKING	
Mahi Bar	(see 16)
Planters' Club	**28** B2
Savusavu Wines & Spirits	**29** C2
Savusavu Yacht Club	(see 12)
Waitui Marina	(see 14)

ENTERTAINMENT	
Urosous	**30** D2

SHOPPING	
Art Gallery	(see 8)
D Solanki	**31** C2
Handicrafts stall	**32** C2
Tako Handicraft	(see 8)
Town Council Handicrafts	(see 25)

TRANSPORT	
Air Fiji	(see 8)
Bligh Water Shipping	(see 20)
Budget Rent a Car	(see 20)
Bus Station	**33** C2
Carpenters Rental Cars	(see 33)
Consort Shipping	**34** D2
Grace Ferry	(see 23)
Pacific Sun	(see 8)
Taxi Stand	(see 33)

estate agent. There are hot showers available for yachties ($4) and there's also a laundry service ($10 a load). Moorings in the pretty harbour between Savusavu and Nawi islet cost $10/260 per day/month in high season, and $8/210 per day/month in low season.

Close by is **Waitui Marina** (Map p182; ☎ 885 0536; waituimarina@connect.com.fj), with showers ($3), laundry ($8 a load) and a private club in a beautiful, restored boat shed. Moorings cost $10/225 per day/month in high season. The marina is closed on Sundays.

Currently in the planning stages, the **Savusavu Marina** (☎ 885 3543; info@marinavillagefiji .com) will have space for 79 yachts, a club-house, laundry facilities, showers and lock-up facilities, just outside town, to the east.

Use VHF Marine channel 16 for assistance in locating moorings on arrival. The marinas can arrange for the relevant officials to visit your boat to process your arrival into Fiji.

HOT SPRINGS

Those vents of steam you see along the water's edge are evidence of Savusavu's geothermal heritage and the volcanic activity that still simmers below the town's surface. There are hot springs (Map p182) behind the playing field and near the wharf. Don't even think about bathing in them as they're literally boiling.

DIVING & SNORKELLING

There are some great, safe diving spots around Savusavu. The best sites include Dreamhouse,

VANUA LEVU

where you'll see schools of barracuda, king-fish, tuna and sometimes hammerheads; Dreadlocks in the centre of Savusavu Bay, a site that's suitable for beginners as well as advanced divers and has a wonderfully photogenic coral garden; and, for experienced divers, Nasonisoni Passage, an incredible drift dive where you'll be sucked along by a strong current. All of the following operators regularly visit these sites.

KoroSun Dive (Map p185; ☎ 885 2452; www.koro sundive.com; Hibiscus Hwy) is on the jetty opposite Koro Sun Resort. Two-tank dives/PADI Open Water Courses, including all gear, cost $190/750. There are special rates for multi-day diving and it also offers day trips to the Somosomo Strait or the Namena Marine Park near Namenalala.

L'Aventure Diving(Map p185; ☎ 885 0188; laventure fiji@connect.com.fj) at the Jean-Michel Cousteau Fiji Islands Resort (p186) has excellent daily dives and top-class equipment. Two-tank dives/PADI Open Water Courses cost $280/860 with gear included.

Dive Namale (Map p185; ☎ 885 0435; www.namalefiji .com; Namale Resort & Spa, Hibiscus Hwy) offers two-tank dives/PADI Open Water Courses, including all gear, for $220/850.

Rock n' Downunder Divers (☎ 885 3447, 932 8363; Waitui Marina) offers two-tank dives/PADI Open Water Courses, including all gear, for $195/600. Favourite spots include Dreadlocks.

J Hunter Pearls (☎ 885 0821; www.pearlsfiji.com) offers snorkelling with a difference – among black pearls on a working pearl farm. Tours depart at 9.30am and 1.30pm weekdays ($25; 1½ hours). Staff members give talks on how pearls are made and afterwards you can head to the shop to buy pearls and shell jewellery. Bring your own snorkel.

Split Rock (Map p185), close to the Jean-Michel Cousteau Fiji Islands Resort (p186), is a deep crevice containing gorgeous soft coral, which attracts hordes of equally colourful fish. You can easily swim out from the beachfront beside the road and snorkel. Ask the locals how to find it.

OTHER ACTIVITIES

Savusavu Bay is a great area for kayaking. Rock n' Downunder Divers (above) offers kayaks for rent for $40 per day. You can also rent mountain bikes ($35 per day) and catamarans, and it can arrange a number of activities including village visits ($60 per person),

beach cruises ($70), sunset cruises ($40) and boat charters ($60 per hour).

SeaHawk Yacht Charters (p179) offers cruises around Savusavu Bay, including full-day picnic cruises ($85), half-day sail-and-snorkel trips ($55), sunset cruises ($50) and overnight cruises ($720 per couple).

Trip n Tour (Map p182; ☎ 885 3154; tripntour@ connect.com.fj; Copra Shed Marina) offers a range of tours around Vanua Levu including one to a copra plantation, full-day Labasa tours and fishing trips.

See p179 for details of the activities offered by Tui Tai Adventure Cruises.

Sleeping

The best sleeping options are out of town, either on Lesiaceva Point to the southwest or along the Hibiscus Hwy to the east. Buses service both these locations (see p188).

BUDGET
In Town

Hidden Paradise Guest House (Map p182; ☎ 885 0106; s/d $25/50, with air-con $30/60; ✸) This has the cheapest rooms in town and is the best place to meet other budget travellers. It's a no-frills deal, with a shared bathroom and cold-water showers, but the rooms are spotless and the owner full of advice about the local area. Breakfast is included in the price and you can watch life pass by from the Sea View Café (p187) at the front of the guesthouse.

Savusavu Sunset Lodge (Map p182; ☎ 885 2171; s/d/f $30/40/60, d with air-con $70, extra person $20; ✸) Set back from the road in grassy gardens this place has simple rooms with hot-water bathrooms and not much else. Plump for a room upstairs if you can – these open up onto a balcony with great sea views. Prices include breakfast.

Savusavu Budget Lodge (Map p182; ☎ 885 3127; fax 885 3157; s/d $30/50, s/d/tr with air-con $55/70/105, extra person $20; ✸) Small, dark and cramped rooms with private bathrooms are the name of the game here, but thankfully there's an upstairs lounge and a balcony overlooking the street, if you need some breathing space. Breakfast is included. The lodge's Indo-Fijian owner also runs a good curry restaurant downstairs at the back (see p187).

Hot Springs Hotel (Map p182; ☎ 885 0195; www .savusavufiji.com; Nakama Rd; dm $36, r with fan/air-con incl breakfast $80/125; ✸ ⚌) The main thing going for this hotel is the view. Every room has a little balcony with fantastic, picture-postcard views over Savusavu Bay – perfect for watching the sunset. The rooms are clean and spacious, but have a whiff of identikit motel about them (it *did* used to be a Travelodge) and several of the bathrooms could do with a refit. Unless you're a stickler for cold air it's not really worth getting an air-con room as they aren't any nicer. The hotel also has a bar, cafe (see Decked Out Café, p187) and pool with a view.

Out of Town

Yau Kolo (Map p185; ☎ 885 3089; yaukolo@yahoo.com; Hibiscus Hwy; sites per person $12, s/d on-site tent $20/30, dm $20) This wonderful camping ground is about 13km from Savusavu and set in a vibrant garden with stunning lagoon views. There are plenty of tent sites here, and a few dorm beds as well as cold showers and compost toilets. There are also a couple of permanent tents complete with mattresses and bedding. You can snorkel in the lagoon and there's also a creek, freshwater swimming hole and small waterfall a short amble away. There's a cafe serving cheap, good meals (there are no self-catering facilities) and a bar in the garden for cold beers. Breakfast is included. It's a $12 taxi ride from town or $1.50 by bus.

Olivia's Homestay (Map p185; ☎ 885 3099; silina@connect.com.fj; Nagigi; cabin per person $18) Guests at Olivia's live the village life at Nagigi. They have to, really, because there's nothing else around. Olivia, who has lived in California, tries to educate her guests in the Fijian way of doing everything from cookery to massage. No activity costs more than a few dollars, and both Olivia and the villagers are extremely welcoming. The no-frills homestay is a single cabin with four simple bedrooms and a cold-water shower. Children are adored. Buses from Savusavu to Nagigi ($1.80, 40 minutes) leave about every two hours, or take a taxi (about $20).

Bayside Backpacker Cottage (Map p185; ☎ 885 3154; tripntour@connect.com.fj; Lesiaceva Rd; s/d $40/50) A good deal for a couple who want their own place for a few days, this sweet little cottage is in the grounds of travel agent Eddie Bower's home and comes equipped with two single beds and a decent kitchen with a gas stove, TV and DVD player. There's a beach across the road but it's not fantastic; bring a snorkel, though, as underwater it's a different story. The cottage is a little way out of town but you can borrow mountain bikes to cycle the 3km.

Otherwise, it's a $3 to $4 taxi ride. There's a minimum two-night stay.

Hans' Place (Map p185; ☎ 885 0621; www.fiji-holiday.com; Lesiaceva Rd; Yasiyasi studio per day/week from $90/630, Yaka cottage per day/week $100/500) Sitting on Lesiaceva Point amongst vibrant green lawns, a skip and a jump away from the ocean, are two cosy, self-contained cottages with comfortable decks. Yasiyasi is a studio built using native hardwoods. Yaka is a one-bedroom cottage, with the bed partitioned off from the living room. Both sleep two people. Each has a kitchenette with a gas stove and fridge, TV and DVD player. They are fan-cooled and have hot showers. Long-term guests are preferred and local meals are available on request. It's a $4 taxi ride from town and bikes are available for hire at $10 a day.

MIDRANGE

In Town

Naveria Heights Lodge (Map p182; ☎ 851 0157; just naveria@connect.com.fj; Naveria Pde; r incl breakfast $130; ⊗) Want to combine breathtaking views with breathless activity? Head straight for Naveria Heights. The owners are exercise junkies and can arrange a whole range of activities to keep their guests on the go, from mountain biking to hiking up in the hills or fitness classes on the deck. They're also happy to prepare low-calorie meals. The two simple rooms here are lovely, with polished wood floors and beautiful vistas. The steep, 15-minute walk up the hill to reach the lodge would get you in the mood, but it's best to call for a pick-up as it is hard to find. There's a crib available for babies.

Copra Shed Marina Apartments (Map p182; ☎ 885 0457; coprashed@connect.com.fj; Copra Shed Marina; r $165; ⊗ ⊗) The marina has two luxury units with good views in the most convenient location in town. They are a bit overpriced, but worth it if you plan to spend a lot of time in the Yacht Club – which you might well end up doing anyway.

Waterfront Apartment (Map p182; ☎ 885 0307; Waterfront Complex; r $165; ⊗ ⊗) This compact studio apartment, with a TV and DVD player, queen-size bed, decent bathrooms and large windows on two sides, is located in the waterfront complex above the Bula Re Café. There's plenty of light and great views over the water.

Out of Town

Daku Resort (Map p185; ☎ 885 0046; www.dakuresort.com; Lesiaceva Rd; budget r $60, oceanview bure s/d $140/150,

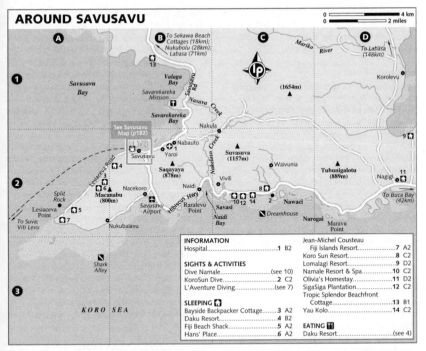

AROUND SAVUSAVU

INFORMATION		Jean-Michel Cousteau	
Hospital	1 B2	Fiji Islands Resort	7 A2
		Koro Sun Resort	8 C2
SIGHTS & ACTIVITIES		Lomalagi Resort	9 D2
Dive Namale	(see 10)	Namale Resort & Spa	10 C2
KoroSun Dive	2 C2	Olivia's Homestay	11 D2
L'Aventure Diving	(see 7)	SigaSiga Plantation	12 C2
		Tropic Splendor Beachfront	
SLEEPING		Cottage	13 B1
Bayside Backpacker Cottage	3 A2	Yau Kolo	14 C2
Daku Resort	4 B2		
Fiji Beach Shack	5 A2	EATING	
Hans' Place	6 A2	Daku Resort	(see 4)

2-bed bure $220, 4-bed pool house $200, 3-bed beach house $230; 🖳 🏊) A resort-cum-self-improvement centre, Daku attracts guests from around the world to participate in a surprisingly diverse array of courses from gospel singing to watercolour painting, meditation and yoga. If you'd rather sit back and relax than expend your creative juices, Daku still has plenty to offer. There's neat accommodation (in *bure* with sea-green-and-white tin roofs), a sweeping sea view, a pleasant pool and a good restaurant and bar (see p187). The beach across the road is pebble rather than sand, but at high tide you can swim out and find top-notch fish viewing. A taxi from town will cost about $3.

SigaSiga Plantation (Map p185; ☎ 885 0413; www .theultimateparadise.com; Hibiscus Hwy; d bure $95, 2-bed-room villa $250) This fine oceanfront villa, 11km from Savusavu and set back from a 1.6km-long, white-sand beach, sleeps up to six guests. In the grounds are two better-than-basic *bure* with excellent bathrooms and spacious, modern kitchens. It's a $10 taxi ride from town and the bus passes by as well.

Sekawa Beach Cottage (Map pp180-1; ☎ 851 0154, 993 2841; nasekawa@hotmail.com; cottages per day/week $140/750, extra person per night $20; 🗙) If you're looking for your own private slice of rainforest, Sekawa Beach Cottages hits the spot rather nicely. Perfect for families with young children, there are 2 hectares of grounds for gallivanting in and it's a five-minute walk to a 2km-long private beach. Accommodation is in a pretty, one-bedroom, plantation-style house with a wraparound deck. There's a microwave, a DVD player, and twin beds in the lounge for the kids. There's a fishing boat for hire and there are free kayaks. A four-night minimum stay applies. It's 18km north of Savusavu town and a $14 taxi ride, or $1.60 by bus.

Fiji Beach Shack (Map p185; ☎ 885 1002; www.fiji beachshacks.com; house per day/week $240/1580; 🏊) This seriously glam, two-level holiday home down by Lesiaceva Point is nicknamed the House of Bamboo. Furnishings are contemporary chic and there are two bedrooms and a fabulous bathroom complete with a sunken bath big enough for two and sea views from two large windows. There's a great DVD library and a good selection of children's board games. Outside there is a plunge pool with a deck, and a day bed. It's not suitable for very young children though, as the pool isn't fenced off. You can snorkel out to Split Rock (p183) from the beachfront across the road. A taxi from town costs $7, or the bus costs $0.75.

TOP END

All of Savusavu's top-end accommodation is a taxi ride from the town centre.

Tropic Splendor Beachfront Cottage (Map p185; ☎ 851 0152; www.tropic-splendor-fiji.com; Savusavu Rd; cottages per day/week $360/2160) This is a good option for a couple seeking something with privacy but still within reach of town. It's a charming, one-bedroom, beachfront cottage with a large deck and small pool overlooking the ocean. There's a full kitchen and lounge with a selection of DVDs and books, and a funky, outdoor, bamboo shower.

Koro Sun Resort (Map p185; ☎ 885 0262; www.korosunresort.com; Hibiscus Hwy; s/d bure from $460/560, 2-bedroom bure from $600; 🞬 🞬 🞬) The Koro Sun has several lavish *bure* overlooking a clear, blue lagoon; some on the beach, others hidden in the hillside undergrowth. A few have outdoor rock showers. Food is included in the price, as are numerous activities – there's a pool, tennis courts, a nine-hole golf course, kayaks, bikes and snorkelling gear, all of which are free to guests. If you fancy being slathered with papaya, there's a 'rainforest spa'. The little ones can amuse themselves with sandcastle building, water-slide competitions and trips to nearby Bat Island (less ominous than it sounds) courtesy of an excellent kids club. Diving is available through KoroSun Dive (p183), which operates from a jetty across the road. The resort is 13km east of Savusavu, and costs about $12 by taxi.

Lomalagi Resort (Map p185; ☎ 851 0585; www.lomalagi.com; Salt Lake Rd; d incl meals from $780; 🞬) This is the only resort at Natewa Bay, and what a spectacular setting it enjoys. Timber promenades wind their way through avenues of impossibly tall palm trees to a collection of *bure* built on a sunny hillside, all with unbeatable views. The beach is grey coral but the snorkelling is great and there's a 1km, white-sand beach about 3km up the coast. A major reason to stay here is the spinner dolphins that frequent the bay, providing one of the best opportunities in Fiji to swim with the creatures. The villas have uninspired decor but are large, with decks, and there's also a swimming pool. The resort was up for sale at the time of writing but it's worth checking to see if it's still

operating because the setting is truly lovely. If you're driving, take the Salt Lake Rd turn-off, about 24km east of Savusavu, not far from where the Hibiscus Hwy turns south.

Jean-Michel Cousteau Fiji Islands Resort (Map p185; ☎ 885 0188; www.fijiresort.com; d bure from $1000; 🞬 🞬) This outstanding, luxury ecoresort is owned by the son of Jacques Cousteau. As you'd expect, it attracts divers from around the world and the dive outfit is superb. The *bure* are deluxe, with handmade furnishings, large decks and private garden areas. Great gourmet meals are included in the price. There's a nice beach and good snorkelling from the shore. If you can afford it, this is a wonderful place to bring the kids. They're lavished with attention with their own Bula Club, which organises fun, educational and cultural activities, and children's meals. There's also their own, private, kids pool and play area and the services of nannies on-hand if need be. All activities, except diving, are included in the rate. The resort is on Lesiaceva Point, where Savusavu Bay meets the Koro Sea. A taxi ride from town will cost $7.

Namale Resort (Map p185; ☎ 885 0435; www.namalefiji.com; Hibiscus Hwy; s/d bure from $1300/1550, grand villa from $2700; 🞬) Namale is a hugely exclusive and pricey resort right by the water, 9km from Savusavu. Accommodation ranges from tropically delicious *bure,* hidden amongst the rainforest and reached by wooden walkways, to a jaw-droppingly luxurious grand villa complete with a mini movie theatre, and private stretch of beach. You won't be able to drop by to sneak a peak though, because they shun the attentions of day trippers or drop-by visitors. The price includes all meals and activities except diving. Dive Namale operates here. Owned by self-help–guru extraordinaire, Anthony Robbins, the resort has several *bure* set aside for workshop attendees to unleash their inner giants.

Eating

Chong Pong Restaurant (Map p182; ☎ 885 0588; mains $5; ⏰ lunch & dinner) Chong Pong serves your standard Chinese food such as chow mein, sweet-and-sour pork and noodle soup. Up a long flight of stairs, it's simple but has nice views across the main road to the market and sea beyond.

Blue Water Restaurant (Map p182; meals $5-6; ⏰ breakfast, lunch & dinner Mon-Sat, dinner only Sun) Provides a comprehensive menu of very tasty curries and Chinese dishes served in a no-frills dining room on the main street of town. Food is good value and plentiful.

Country Kitchen (Map p182; ☎ 927 1372; breakfast $2-3, meals $6; ✆ breakfast, lunch & dinner) One step up from a hole-in-the-wall, this place is popular with local Indo-Fijians for its sweets and also cooks Chinese standards and fresh, tasty, boneless (if you request them) curries, in dilapidated surrounds.

Savusavu Chinese Restaurant (Map p182; mains $6-11; ✆ lunch & dinner) This place serves big portions of all your Chinese favourites in a garishly bright dining room.

Savusavu Curry House (Map p182; ☎ 885 3127; Savusavu Budget Lodge; meals $7; ✆ lunch & dinner) Looking for an authentic curry in Savusavu? This is where you'll find it. Curries are rich and spicy. The only downside is the dark back-room setting.

Bula Re Café (Map p182; ☎ 885 0377; meals from $8; ✆ 10am-10pm; 🖳) Sit inside or on a breezy, plant-filled terrace overlooking the water. Food includes sandwiches, crêpes, pasta, schnitzel and grilled fish. There's live Fijian music every Sunday night, and Wednesday is *lovo* (a feast cooked in a pit oven) night. There's free wi-fi and one internet terminal ($8 per hour).

Sea View Café (Map p182; ☎ 885 0106; Hidden Paradise Guest House; meals $8-10; ✆ breakfast daily, lunch & dinner Mon-Sat) Here you'll get cheap, cheerful, travellers food, served by the endlessly helpful Elenoa.

Daku Resort (Map p185; ☎ 885 0334; lunch/dinner $7/15; ✆ lunch & dinner) It's a short taxi ride out of town but worth it for the lovely poolside setting. At lunchtime you can get fish and particularly good homemade chips, sandwiches and salads. In the evening heavier steaks, curries and fish dishes come into play and there are regular curry and barbecue nights. Call ahead to see what's on offer.

Captain's Café (Map p182; ☎ 885 0511; Copra Shed Marina; pizza from $15, lunch/dinner $8/16; ✆ breakfast, lunch & dinner) A more informal affair than neighbouring Surf and Turf, this joint serves pizzas, pancakes, full-on fry-ups and burgers as well as some seriously tasty milkshakes. It's even attracted the odd celeb (look for the signed note from Brooke Shields on the wall). There's an outside deck for soaking up the rays and you can buy drinks, including cheap draught beer, from the Savusavu Yacht Club (right) next door.

Decked Out Café (Map p182; ☎ 885 0195; Hot Springs Hotel; meals $19; ✆ breakfast & dinner) The restaurant at the Hot Springs Hotel has a menu of homemade pizza, Fijian fish dishes, quesadillas and salads. You can eat out on the deck with a view over town, but the place is usually quiet and lacking in atmosphere, except at weekends and on the occasional pool-barbecue nights.

Surf and Turf (Map p182; ☎ 885 0511; Copra Shed Marina; lunch/dinner from $8/20; ✆ lunch & dinner) This is the poshest restaurant in Savusavu Town, with a lovely outside space overlooking the water. There are great wines available by the bottle or the glass, and tasty pasta, steaks, lobster and crayfish dishes and daily specials. Lunch is a lighter affair with burgers and sandwiches on offer. Surf and turf (lobster tail and fillet mignon) is $40 at dinner.

Savusavu has a few grocery stores, including a well-stocked Morris Hedstrom Supermarket (Map p182). The market (Map p182) has fruit and veggies as well as lots and lots of *kava* root, which is used to make the narcotic drink of the same name. The **Hot Bread Kitchen** (Map p182; ✆ 6am-8pm Mon-Sat, 6am-1pm Sun) has fresh loaves daily.

Drinking

Savusavu Yacht Club (Map p182; ☎ 885 0685; Copra Shed Marina; ✆ 10am-10pm Sun-Thu, to midnight Fri & Sat) Tourists are considered temporary members of this friendly little drinking hole. There are tables out by the waterside, and a TV showing international sporting events inside. There's plenty of cold beer and it's a good place to meet local expats and visiting yachties. You can order meals from the Captain's Café (left).

Waitui Marina (Map p182; ☎ 885 0536; ✆ 10am-10pm Mon-Sat) Sit on the balcony upstairs to enjoy classic South Pacific views of the yacht-speckled, palm-lined bay. The club is friendly and comfortable, the bar is well stocked and all foreigners on holiday are considered temporary members.

Planters' Club (Map p182; ☎ 885 0233; ✆ 10am-10pm Mon-Sat, to 8pm Sun) This was traditionally a place for planters to come and drink when they brought in the copra, and some of their descendants can still be found clustered around the bar today. You can taste the history in the air as you taste the beer in your glass. Happy hour is from 5.30pm to 6.30pm. Once a month, the club holds a Sunday-lunch *lovo*. The bar staff will sign in tourists.

Mahi Bar (Map p182; ⏲ 10am-11pm) Come during the week and you can practically see the tumbleweed rolling around the room. Things get livelier at the weekend though, and there's occasional live music. There is also an outstanding view.

Savusavu Wines & Spirits (Map p182; ☎ 885 3888; ⏲ 8am-6pm Mon-Fri, to 1pm Sat) A popular, well-stocked bottle shop on the main street, this is the place to come for imported wines and beers. There are a couple of tables outside if you wish to sit down and imbibe.

Entertainment

Urosous (Map p182; admission $3-5; ⏲ noon-10pm) The only viable clubbing option in town is above a fast-food chicken restaurant. It's a small-ish room up a dark flight of stairs and plays a mix of local and international music. It's good fun.

Shopping

Art Gallery (Map p182; ☎ 885 3054; Copra Shed Marina) Head here for postcards, paintings and sculptures by local artists, freshwater-pearl jewellery and the odd item of clothing.

Tako Handicraft (Map p182; ☎ 885 3956; Copra Shed Marina) This place also has local handicrafts and postcards.

D Solanki (Map p182; ☎ 885 0025) Head to this draper's for bargain-priced, beautifully tailor-made, double-stitched, lined saris. It also sells traditional Fijian dress and Western clothes.

Next door to the Copra Shed is a handicrafts stall (Map p182) where a local man sells his wooden carvings. At the back of the market is Town Council Handicrafts (Map p182), devoted to local, woven and wooden handicrafts.

Getting There & Around

For flights, head to the office of **Air Fiji** (Map p182; ☎ 885 0538) or **Pacific Sun** (Map p182; ☎ 885 2214) in the Copra Shed. Savusavu airstrip is 3km south of town. Local buses pass the airport every so often; however, a taxi there from Savusavu only costs $2. See p245 for more flight information.

For boat travel, **Bligh Water Shipping** (Map p182; ☎ 885 3192), **Consort Shipping** (Map p182; ☎ 885 0279) and the agent for Grace Ferry (Map p182), the Country Kitchen (p187), are all in the main street. See p248 for more details on boats.

There is an abundance of taxis in Savusavu. There is a taxi stand (Map p182) in the centre

of the town, near the market, but they can also be hailed on the street or booked. You can also hire small carriers from the bus station; they're very reasonable if you're travelling in a group.

Carpenters Rental Cars (Map p182) can be booked through Trip n Tour (p183) and prices start at $110 for a two-door 4WD. A Yamaha scooter costs $45. Bula Re Café is an agent for **Budget Rent a Car** (Map p182; ☎ 881 1999), where prices start at about $100 per day for a sedan and $120 for a 4WD.

BUS

The Savusavu bus station (Map p182) is in the centre of town, near the market. Buses travelling the scenic, sealed (yet bumpy) highway from Savusavu over the mountains to Labasa ($7, three hours, four times daily) depart from 7.30am to 3.30pm. Some buses take the longer route from Savusavu to Labasa along Natewa Bay, and these depart at 9am ($13, six hours).

Buses from Savusavu to Napuca ($7, 4½ hours), at the tip of the Tunuloa Peninsula, depart at 10.30am, 1pm and 2.30pm daily. The afternoon bus stays there overnight and returns at 7am. A 4pm bus only goes as far as Naweni ($3). There is no bus from Savusavu to Nabouwalu; you have to catch a morning bus to Labasa and change buses there.

From Monday to Saturday there are five bus services from Savusavu to Lesiaceva Point ($1, 15 minutes) between 6am and 5pm. For confirmation of bus timetables in the south, ring **Vishnu Holdings** (☎ 885 0276).

NORTH OF SAVUSAVU

The **Waisali Rainforest Reserve** (Map pp180-1; ☎ 828 0267; Savusavu Rd; adult/child $8/2; ⏲ 8am-5pm Mon-Sat) is nestled in the mountains north of Savusavu. It's not particularly exciting but there's a pleasant enough 30-minute walk through dense greenery down to a waterfall (but watch out for its death trap–slippery rocks). You can enter the park 20km north of Savusavu, directly off the road to Labasa. Bus drivers should know where to drop you off (ask before you board), as should most carrier and taxi drivers. If you are driving, it's at km/culvert 14.4, which is also a good viewpoint.

Deep in the mountains north of Savusavu, reachable by 4WD, lies the ruins of **Nukubolu**, an ancient Fijian village, whose old stone foundations, terraces and thermal pools are in surprisingly good condition. The setting is lovely:

a volcanic crater with steaming hot springs in the background. Nukubolu has myriad uses for the local villagers, who dry *kava* roots on corrugated-iron sheets laid over the pools and use the hot springs as a healing aid. The ruins are on the property of the village of Biaugunu, so take a *sevusevu* (gift) for the chief and ask permission before wandering around. The turn-off is about 20km northwest of Savusavu; continue about 8km inland and over a couple of river crossings. You can also rent a carrier from town to take you there; combine it with a trip to Waisali Rainforest Reserve.

TUNULOA PENINSULA

Tunuloa Peninsula, also known as Natewa or Cakaudrove Peninsula, makes up the southeastern section of Vanua Levu. Lush and scenic, it's an excellent area for exploring by 4WD. If you can arrange a guide in Savusavu, or from your resort, the area can also offer some great birdwatching and hiking. The bumpy, mostly dirt, Hibiscus Hwy runs from Savusavu to Napuka, passing copra plantations, old homesteads, waving villagers and thriving forests. The road becomes extremely slippery in the rain; if you've rented a vehicle, check the tyres are good before you set out. There are no restaurants or shops along this route; pack a lunch and bring water.

About 20km east of Savusavu, the Hibiscus Hwy veers right (south). The turn-off to the left (north) follows the western side of Natewa Bay, an alternative 4WD route to Labasa. About 35km further along the highway from this intersection is the turn-off into the village of **Drekeniwai**, where the former prime minister, Sitiveni Rabuka, was born.

Once you hit Buca Bay, the highway turns left (north), becoming more potholed as it heads through the Tunuloa Silktail Reserve, the habitat of the rare **silktail bird**. Found only on this peninsula and on Taveuni, the silktail has sadly made it onto the world's endangered-species list, with logging being its major threat. The average bird is about 8cm high and is black with a white patch on its tail.

If you turn right (south) at Buca Bay, you'll head through Natuvu village and then up over the mountain to the next village, **Dakuniba**. The road is one big pothole and the going is slow, but you'll be rewarded with dazzling views over the forest and out to sea. In a beautiful forest setting, just outside Dakuniba, **petroglyphs** are inscribed on large boulders. They are thought

to be of ceremonial or mystical significance. Be sure to bring a *sevusevu* for the village chief and read up about village etiquette before you arrive (see the boxed text, p42). The people of Dakuniba are very friendly and may offer to take you to a nearby beach to swim, fish or snorkel. The famous Rainbow Reef (p199) is offshore from Dakuniba, but is more easily accessible from the island of Taveuni.

Sleeping

Salt Lake Lodge (Map pp180-1; ☎ 828 3005; www .saltlakelodgefiji.com; Hibiscus Hwy; tw/q bure $70/90) The lake is the centre of everything at this gem of a lodge. There are just two bungalows, Kingfisher and Riversong. Built with local tropical timber, they sit on stilts at the edge of a lake with a beach bar, a lounge and an eating area between them and an outdoor kitchen complete with gas grill. Other than lazing about, there's tubing, snorkelling, biking, kayaking and for fishing enthusiasts, barracuda, trevally and other impressive fish lurk in the waters. There's a strong eco ethos here. All toilets are compost, rainwater is used for bathing and cooking, and there's solar power. The larger bungalow sleeps four and has a private deck up in the treetops; the other sleeps two and has a separate bathroom down a garden path.

La Dolce Vita Holiday Villas (Map pp180-1; ☎ 851 8023; ladolcevitafiji.com; Hibiscus Hwy; d villas $350) La Dolce has gorgeous, round, wooden *bure* with vaulted ceilings, great decking, large, modern bathrooms and fabulous sea views. Rates include all meals. There is a bar and dining room, and even a pizza oven complete with thatched roof. Golfers are kept happy with a six-hole course, and if that doesn't float your boat there's boules, horse riding, jet skiing, bushwalking, snorkelling and trips with a 'dolphin caller' to see (and sometimes swim with) spinner dolphins. A taxi from Savusavu costs about $25.The power is on only from 5.30pm to 11pm.

Dolphin Bay Divers Retreat (p203) and Almost Paradise (p2040) are southeast of Buca Bay. Accessible only by boat, they are most easily reached from Taveuni.

OFFSHORE ISLANDS
Kioa
pop 600

The island of Kioa (25 sq km) is inhabited by Polynesians originally from the tiny, coral-reef island of Vaitupu in Tuvalu. Because of weak soil and overcrowding on their home

BÊCHE-DE-MER

European traders flocked to Fiji in the early 19th century to hunt the lucrative bêche-de-mer (sea cucumber). It fetched huge profits in Asia, where it's still considered a delicacy and aphrodisiac.

You are likely to see some of these ugly, sluglike creatures while snorkelling or diving. They feed on organic matter in the sand and serve an important role as cleaners in the lagoon ecosystem. There are various types: some are smooth and sticky, some prickly, some black and some multi-coloured. After being cut open and cleaned, they are boiled to remove the salt, then sun-dried or smoked. Many find the taste revolting but they are highly nutritious, being 50% to 60% protein.

Bêche-de-mer numbers have been depleted in Asian waters but they are still prevalent in the South Pacific. They make for a lucrative commodity, both for local use and for export, and unscrupulous traders are delivering dive equipment to remote areas and promising high rewards. Villagers of the Bua region are renowned for harvesting the creature. Usually untrained and unaware of the risks, they are encouraged by the traders to dive in deep waters, risking their lives by using dodgy scuba equipment. Many end up with the bends and a stint in the Fiji Recompression Chamber and several have died.

island, they decided that the best idea would be to buy another, more fertile island and start a relocation program. The people of Vaitupu had earned some money during WWII working for American soldiers who had occupied their islands, and in 1947 they purchased Kioa for the grand sum of $15,000. It was with some trepidation, however. Those living on Kioa today speak wryly of their initial fears about how they would deal with the climate and whether they would be eaten by Fijian cannibals.

The residents of Kioa were finally granted Fijian citizenship in 2005. They are very warm and traditional people. Women make woven handicrafts that are sold to tourists on Taveuni and Vanua Levu, and fishing is done from small, traditional *drua* (double-hulled canoes). The people of Kioa have a speciality called *toddy,* which is a tradition that they imported from Tuvalu. It's a sweet syrup taken from coconut sap and can be made into a thick, spreadable syrup or fermented into a pungent alcoholic drink.

There is no accommodation or facilities for tourists; however, Tui Tai Adventure Cruises (p179) and Blue Lagoon Cruises (p153) do make stops here. Alternatively, the Taveuni ferry might be able to drop you off on its way past. For snorkellers and divers, the **Farm**, off the most easterly point of the island, has fantastic corals.

Rabi
pop 4500

Rabi (66 sq km), east of the northern tip of the Tunuloa Peninsula, has four villages popu-

lated by Micronesians originally from Banaba, in Kiribati. At the turn of the 20th century the islanders of Banaba were first tricked and then pressed into selling the phosphate mining rights of Banaba for a small annual payment, and their tiny island was slowly ruined by the subsequent mining and influx of settlers. WWII brought further tragedy when the Japanese invaded Banaba and massacred many villagers. Following the war, Rabi was purchased for the Banabans by the British Government – with money from the islanders' own Provident Fund, set up by the British Government in 1931 for phosphate royalties – and 2000 survivors were resettled here. However, as they were dropped in the middle of the cyclone season with only army tents and two months' rations, and had never been so cold (Banaba is on the equator), many of the original settlers died.

If you're interested in visiting Rabi, you must first ask permission from the **island council** (☎ 881 2913). If you're extended an invitation, catch a bus from Savusavu to Karoko where small boats wait for passengers to Rabi ($70 one way). The **Rabi Island Council Guesthouse** (☎ 881 2913; dm $50; Mon, Wed & Fri) has beds in basic, four-bed rooms. You'll eat with the villagers.

LABASA
pop 24,100

Labasa is sweltering, dusty and almost tourist free. It's a service and administrative centre and an industry town. Sitting about 5km inland on the banks of the winding Labasa River, the fertile river banks and reclaimed mangrove swamps have made this area a centre for the sugar industry since colonial days.

VANUA LEVU

A large sugar mill sits on the outskirts of town, a sugar-transporting railway runs through the centre, and approaching the centre from the airport you'll pass by flat cane fields and smell the scent of molasses in the air, most prevalent during sugar-crushing season (from May to December). Labasa's population is predominantly Indo-Fijian, many of whom are descendants of *girmitiyas* (indentured labourers brought from India to work on the plantations; see p34 for more on *girmitiyas*). The town's main street is bustling. Bollywood music blasts out of stores selling trinkets, bangles and saris, while store owners and shop assistants stand chatting in the doorways.

The town doesn't really have much in the way of tourist attractions but it's a nice enough place to spend a couple of hours and, if you hire a 4WD, the surrounding area is great for exploring.

Information

Nasekula Rd serves as the town's main drag and it is here that you will find the majority of Labasa's shops and services. ANZ, Colonial National and Westpac banks all have branches in the main street. They will change currency and travellers cheques and have 24-hour ATMs that accept all major debit and credit cards on site.

Govinda Internet Café (☎ 881 1364; Nasekula Rd; per min $0.15; ⏲ 8am-7pm Mon-Sat, from 5pm Sun) This air-conditioned cafe has five computers with cheap internet access.

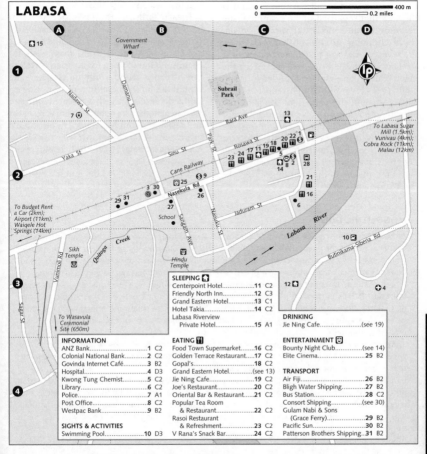

LABASA

SLEEPING	
Centerpoint Hotel	11 C2
Friendly North Inn	12 C3
Grand Eastern Hotel	13 C1
Hotel Takia	14 C2
Labasa Riverview Private Hotel	15 A1

DRINKING	
Jie Ning Cafe	(see 19)

INFORMATION	
ANZ Bank	1 C2
Colonial National Bank	2 C2
Govinda Internet Café	3 B2
Hospital	4 D3
Kwong Tung Chemist	5 C2
Library	6 C2
Police	7 A1
Post Office	8 C2
Westpac Bank	9 B2

SIGHTS & ACTIVITIES	
Swimming Pool	10 D3

EATING	
Food Town Supermarket	16 C2
Golden Terrace Restaurant	17 C2
Gopal's	18 C2
Grand Eastern Hotel	(see 13)
Jie Ning Cafe	19 C2
Joe's Restaurant	20 C2
Oriental Bar & Restaurant	21 C2
Popular Tea Room & Restaurant	22 C2
Rasoi Restaurant & Refreshment	23 C2
V Rana's Snack Bar	24 C2

ENTERTAINMENT	
Bounty Night Club	(see 14)
Elite Cinema	25 B2

TRANSPORT	
Air Fiji	26 B2
Bligh Water Shipping	27 B2
Bus Station	28 C2
Consort Shipping	(see 30)
Gulam Nabi & Sons (Grace Ferry)	29 B2
Pacific Sun	30 B2
Patterson Brothers Shipping	31 B2

VANUA LEVU

Hospital (☎ 881 1444; Butinikama-Siberia Rd) The hospital is southeast of the river.

Kwong Tung Chemist (☎ 881 4611; Nasekula Rd; ◷ 8am-6pm Mon-Thu, to 7pm Fri, to 3pm Sat) Has a decent supply of medicines and vitamins.

Library (Jaduram St; ◷ 9am-1pm & 2-5pm Mon-Fri, to noon Sat) At the Civic Centre, the library has a limited collection of books.

Police (☎ 881 1222; Nadawa St)

Post office (Nasekula Rd; ◷ 7.30am-4pm Mon-Fri, 8am-noon Sat) There are several cardphones outside.

Sights & Activities

The **Wasavula Ceremonial Site** is just south of town, on Vunimoli Rd. At the entrance to the site there is a sacred monolith that villagers believe grew from the ground. Behind the standing stone is the village cemetery, surrounded by a small garden. Beyond is the area that was used during cannibalistic ceremonies, and has a flat *vatu ni bokola* (head-chopping stone), another rock where the severed head was placed and a bowl-like stone in which the brain was placed for the chief. Unless you are given a guided tour you could probably walk right past most of these stones without noticing. The site is on the left, about 800m south off Nasekula Rd. For more on the rituals conducted on this site see the boxed text, below. About 3km past the airport are the **Waiqele hot springs**, which are pretty average but might be worth a visit if you're a big fan of the bubbling stuff. Take the Waiqele bus ($1).

Nonguests can use the pool at the Grand Eastern Hotel (opposite) to escape from the sweltering heat, if they buy lunch or a drink from the hotel bar. There is also a public **swimming pool** (☎ 881 6387; Butinikama-Siberia Rd; admission $1.50; ◷ noon-5pm Mon-Thu, 9am-6pm Fri-Sun) southeast of town.

Sleeping

Labasa Riverview Private Hotel (☎ 881 1367; fax 881 4337; Nadawa St; dm $15, s/d with bathroom $40/55, s/d without bathroom $30/40, s/d with air-con & bathroom $60/80; ⊠) The five-bed dorm here is good value, with a clean, well-equipped kitchen and a balcony overlooking the river. The hotel bar isn't bad either. With nice views, it is a good place to enjoy a sundowner. The double rooms, however, are cramped, dark and basic, and the welcome is far from warm.

Friendly North Inn (☎ 881 1555; fni@connect.com.fj; Butinikama-Siberia Rd; s/d with fan $35/45, s/d with air-con $45/55, apt with air-con $65; ⊠) To escape from the noise and bustle of central Labasa, walk for 20 minutes out of town to the Friendly North Inn, which is wonderfully quiet. There are several duplex villas set in a mellow, flower-studded garden, all with a private bathroom and kitchenette. The hotel has a large, open bar and restaurant, but meals need to be ordered in advance. A taxi into town will cost $3.

Centerpoint Hotel (☎ 881 1057; cenhotel@connect .com.fj; Nasekula Rd; s/d with fan $50/65, s/d with air-con $60/80, extra person $10; ⊠) Bang in the centre of town, this place has large, if gloomy, rooms

---

MONOLITHIC GODS

Although the Wasavula Ceremonial Site (above) is shrouded in mystery, it is thought to be related to similar sites of the *naga* (snake) cult found in Viti Levu's Sigatoka Valley. In the old religion those who betrayed ceremonial secrets would face insanity and death from the ancestral spirits and gods, so what is known about such places is mostly based on hearsay and vague memories.

Before the arrival of Christianity ceremonial sites were venues for communicating with ancestral gods. Rituals performed at the sites provided a spiritual link between the people and the earth, time, crops and fertility. It is believed that this was where chiefs and priests were installed, where male initiation rites took place and where a *bokola* (the dead body of an enemy) was offered to the gods.

Stone monoliths at the sites were seen as actual gods or as the shrines of gods. These stones were often used for refuge; if someone who had committed a crime made it to the monolith before being caught, their life would be spared.

While the rituals of long ago are no longer practised at Wasavula Ceremonial Site, the ancestral gods haven't been evicted so easily. It is still revered as a sacred place by the village people and is now where they bury their dead. Some people continue to see the monolith as supernatural; it is said that in photos of villagers with the monolith, the villagers have often vanished from the developed pictures.

Book your stay at lonelyplanet.com/hotels

with self-contained bathrooms. It's basic but it's the cheapest place in the town centre.

Hotel Takia (☎ 881 1655; hoteltakia@connect.com.fj; Nasekula Rd; s/d with fan $54/64, s/d with air-con $95/105; 🔀) Rooms here are large and clean with a TV, fridge and kettle. There's a restaurant that dishes out hefty servings of Chinese and Indian food for around $15 and a bar that's open from 6pm to 9pm daily, though the drinkers can get rowdy. There's also a nightclub here, and sound carries, so it's not the place to stay if you need your peace and quiet.

Grand Eastern Hotel (☎ 881 1022; grest@connect .com.fj; Rosawa St; standard/deluxe/executive r $77/103/128; 🔀 🛒) This is the plushest hotel in Labasa. There's a pleasant, colonial atmosphere and the hallways are plastered with black-and-white photos of times past. Standard rooms have small porches facing the river, but it's worth paying the extra for the newer, deluxe rooms that have large double beds and sofas, and open out onto the courtyard swimming pool. All rooms are slightly careworn, however. There's also a restaurant (see right).

Palmlea Lodge (Map pp180-1; ☎ 828 2220; www .palmleafarms.com; Tabia-Naduri Rd; s & d from $110; 🔀) This ecoresort is 15km out of town, just off the road that heads down to Savusavu, and overlooks the Great Sea Reef. Spacious *bure* with vaulted ceilings and large verandahs sit on a gentle green slope leading down to the sea. Fruit and veg is grown on an on-site organic farm and every effort is made to manage the resort in an ecofriendly fashion. There are snorkels and kayaks available as well as a number of activities including hiking, fishing and crabbing with a local guide.

Eating

Labasa is full to the brim with basic cafes serving cheap plates of Indian and Chinese food. Note: most restaurants, although open for dinner, close by 7pm.

V Rana's Snack Bar (☎ 881 4351; Nasekula Rd; snacks $0.70; 🕑 7am-6pm Mon-Fri, to 4pm Sat) This place is friendly and has comfortable booths where you can snack on bhajis, samosas and Indian sweets.

Popular Tea Room & Restaurant (Nasekula Rd; snacks $1; 🕑 7am-8pm Mon-Thu & Sun, to 8.30pm Fri & Sat) Has fresh bread, cakes, savoury pastries and a few curries and Chinese dishes. Oh, and tea of course.

Golden Terrace Restaurant (☎ 881 8378; Nasekula Rd; meals $4; 🕑 breakfast, lunch & dinner) Serves dishes

taken from Labasa's three main cuisines: Chinese, Indian and Greasy.

Rasoi Restaurant & Refreshment (Nasekula Rd; curries/mains $4/6; 🕑 breakfast, lunch & dinner) Rasoi has basic plastic chairs and tables and a cafeteria atmosphere, but serves some of the best homemade curries in town. If Indian isn't your bag you can get pretty-good fried rice as well as more substantial European grills such as lamb chops. There's also a small counter selling Indian sweets and pastries.

Joe's Restaurant (☎ 881 1766; Nasekula Rd; meals $6, pizza $10; 🕑 lunch & dinner) It's a Chinese restaurant but you'll find pizza and fish and chips on the menu alongside typical Chinese dishes.

Jie Ning Cafe (Nasekula Rd; dishes $8; 🕑 breakfast, lunch & dinner) Chinese favourites such as chow mein and sweet-and-sour are dished up here in stomach-satisfying portions.

Oriental Bar & Restaurant (☎ 881 7321; Jaduram St; meals $8; 🕑 lunch & dinner Mon-Sat, dinner Sun; 🔀) Look for the bright-orange door and pink balcony overlooking the bus station. Although you wouldn't guess it from the outside, this is one of Labasa's most upmarket and atmospheric restaurants, with a strong Chinese twist to its Fijian decor. The bar is fairly well stocked and the menu has a wide choice of tasty Chinese dishes, including plenty of veggies and a few Fijian options. No caps or vests allowed.

Gopal's (Nasekula Rd; thali $10; 🕑 breakfast, lunch & dinner) Specialises in vegetarian Indian food, and has fantastic thalis. There's also a sweets counter with a nice selection of sinful Indian treats.

Grand Eastern Hotel (☎ 881 1022; Rosawa St; lunch/dinner $15/25; 🕑 breakfast, lunch & dinner) The restaurant at the Grand Eastern serves Western-style food such as steaks and burgers. The interior is decorated with photos of Labasa back in colonial times. You can also eat out on the patio overlooking the swimming pool.

For supplies there are several supermarkets near the bus station, including the **Food Town Supermarket** (Jaduram St; 🕑 8am-6pm Mon-Fri, to 4pm Sat).

Drinking & Entertainment

There's not much going on in town.

Elite Cinema (☎ 881 1260; Nasekula Rd; adult/child $3/1) shows older films, the majority of which are in Hindi.

You might try the bar at the Grand Eastern Hotel for a poolside drink, or brave the caged bar at the **Bounty Night Club** (8pm-1am Wed-Sat). The owners assure us it's safe, but not only is the bar in a cage, the disco mirror ball is in a cage of its own! A night out at the Labasa Club or the Farmers Club is definitely *not* a good idea.

Getting There & Around

For flights, head to the office of **Air Fiji** (881 1188; Nasekula Rd) or **Pacific Sun** (881 1454; Northern Travel Service office, Nasekula Rd). The airport is about 11km southwest of Labasa. The turn-off is 4km west of Labasa, just past the Wailevu River. To reach the airport, catch the Waiqele bus from Labasa bus station; it departs between 6am and 4.15pm ($0.80, four services daily) Monday to Saturday and as per flight schedules on Sundays. A taxi from Labasa costs $12. See p245 for more information.

For boat tickets **Consort Shipping** (881 1454; Northern Travel Service office), **Patterson Brothers Shipping** (881 2444), **Bligh Water Shipping** (881 8471; www.blighwatershipping.com.fj) and the agent for **Grace Ferry** (881 1152), Gulam Nabi & Sons, are all along Nasekula Rd. It is also possible to buy tickets in Labasa for bus-boat combinations to Suva and Lautoka. See p248 for more information on reaching Labasa by boat.

There are regular buses between Labasa and Savusavu ($7, three hours, five times Monday to Saturday, four on Sunday) departing between 7am and 4.15pm. There is also a 9am bus that takes the long route ($13, six hours) to Savusavu around the northeast, following Natewa Bay. Buses to Nabouwalu depart three times per day Monday to Saturday ($9, six hours).

The majority of shops, businesses and hotels in Labasa are within walking distance of the centre. If you are going further afield, there is no shortage of taxis. You'll find the majority of them at the main stand near the bus station. **Budget Rent a Car** (881 1999; Vakamaisuasua) has an office a little way west of town where you can rent sedans/4WD from $100/120 per day.

AROUND LABASA

The area around Labasa is a great place to explore by 4WD. There are a few points of interest; however, it's definitely the adventure of finding them rather than the sights themselves that make it worthwhile. For all of these sights, you'll need to turn left onto Wainikoro Rd, just past the sugar mill and across from a secondary school. This is the main road out of town to the east.

Sights & Activities

Sacred **Cobra Rock** (so called because the 3m-high rock vaguely looks like an oversized cobra about to attack), housed inside the vibrant **Naag Mandir Temple**, is the area's most interesting attraction. The rock is constantly covered with bright, flower-and-tinsel garlands, and offerings of fruit, fire and *lolo* (coconut cream) are placed at its base. This is because, the locals told us, many people believe that the rock can cure the sick and the infertile. We were also told that the rock has magically grown bigger over the years and that the roof has had to be raised four times since the 1950s to accommodate it! Remove your shoes outside the beautifully tiled temple. A few buses pass the temple, including those to Natewa Bay ($1.20). A taxi costs about $10. If you're driving, the temple is 10km from the turning for Wainikoro Rd; you'll pass two smaller temples before you reach Naag Mandir. The temple is heaving on Sunday mornings. If you're going to Cobra Rock, you may wish to take a short detour to the **Mariamman Temple** (Map pp180-1) in Vunivau (just east of Labasa), where the Ram Leela (p235) festival is held around October.

Down through dense coconut trees and past the lounging cows lies **Korovatu Beach** (admission per car $5), which is the closest stretch of beach to Labasa and makes a pleasant side trip if you're in the area for a few days. Bring your own water and snacks.

Just off the northern coast of Vanua Levu, about 40km west of Labasa, you can walk around **Nukubati**, a privately owned island (actually two small islands linked by mangroves), in about 30 minutes at low tide. Once occupied by Fijian villagers, in the 19th century a local chief gave the island to a German gunsmith who settled here with his Fijian wife.

If you're looking for seclusion, **Nukubati Island Resort** (Map pp180-1; 881 3901; www.nukubati .com; d bure beachfront/honeymoon $1240/1500) should do the trick. *Bure* face a white-sand beach but are a little old-fashioned for the price. The prices include gourmet meals, all drinks (including alcohol) and most activities, including tennis, sailing, windsurfing and fishing. Game fishing, diving and massages cost extra. There's also a massive library if you plan to spend your time reading on the beach. A seaplane charter from Nadi costs $3000 or a 4WD-speedboat return transfer from Labasa airport is $370 per couple. There is a maximum of 14 guests and only adults are accepted, unless you book the whole island for $8200 per night, in which case children are accepted. A minimum five-night stay is required. Two-tank dives are $220 plus equipment hire (one-off $60 fee). Guided surf trips to the Great Sea Reef are possible from November to March.

NABOUWALU & AROUND

Nabouwalu is a small settlement on the island's southwestern point. Early in the 19th century, European traders flocked to nearby **Bua Bay** to exploit *yasi dina* (sandalwood), which grew in the hills. Today, the ferry landing is about the only draw for travellers. Nabouwalu has administrative offices, a post office, a small market and a store. Offshore to the northwest, the island of **Yadua Tabu** is home to the last sizeable population of the rare and spectacular crested iguana. It became Fiji's first wildlife reserve in 1980. It might be possible to visit the iguanas with a local guide, weather permitting, but there are no organised tours.

Boats that arrive here are met by buses heading for Labasa but if you want to stay in Nabouwalu, there is a basic, clean **government guesthouse** (☎ 883 6027; r per person $20). It's an old timber cottage on a steep hill and the view is beautiful. It's often booked out with government workers so be sure to call ahead to the district officer. There is a kitchen but no food and it's a good idea to bring along some of your own supplies as there are no eateries nearby.

For ferries to Nabouwalu, see p249. Nabouwalu can only be reached by bus from Labasa, not from Savusavu. The ferry bus is much quicker than the local bus.

The road from Nabouwalu around the southern coast to Savusavu (127km) is barely passable by 4WD or carrier.

NAMENALALA

The volcanic island of Namenalala rests on the Namena Barrier Reef, now a protected marine reserve, 25km off the southeastern coast of Vanua Levu and about 40km from Savusavu. Namenalala has lovely **beaches** and the island is a natural sailors' refuge. There is an old **ring fortification** but the villages disappeared long ago. Today there's just one small, upmarket resort.

Moody's Namena (Map pp180-1; ☎ 881 3764; www .moodysnamenafiji.com; all-inclusive packages for 5 nights incl transfers from Savusavu per person sharing from $2650, s supplement per night $200; 🏵 closed March & April) has six bamboo-and-timber *bure* on a forested ridge. Diving here is excellent and costs $200 per two-tank dive (divers must be certified). Other activities, which include windsurfing, fishing, snorkelling, reef excursions, barbecues, volleyball, and use of canoes and paddle boards, are included in the rate. The island has a nature reserve for birdwatching and trekking and is home to seabirds, red-footed boobies and a giant-clam farm. From November to February hawksbill and green turtles lay their eggs on Namenalala beaches. There is a five-night minimum stay; no children under 16 years old are allowed.

WAINUNU BAY

Hardly any travellers make it over to Wainunu Bay. The road here is poor and the land has escaped commercial logging, so the surrounding landscape – a patchwork of forest and waterfalls – remains untouched, for the most part. Wainunu River, the third-largest river in Fiji, flows into Wainunu Bay. Pioneer David Whippy led the whites of Levuka here when Cakobau briefly expelled

---

VOROVORO – TRIBE WANTED

Tribe Wanted (☎ 992 0428; www.tribewanted.com) is a 'unique community tourism project' founded by two young English entrepreneurs who, in 2006, signed a three-year lease on Vorovoro island, offshore from Vanua Levu. The idea is to create a virtual tribe of up to 5000 members who could then pay to visit the island and, working with the local community, participate in the building of an ecovillage and a real life tribe on Vorovoro. At the time of writing, some 700 members had visited Vorovoro. When the lease is up in September 2009 the Fijian chief and landowner will determine Vorovoro's future. Seven days on Vorovoro (the minimum stay), including meals and pick-up and drop-off at Labasa, costs $600 and includes a one-year membership of the tribe.

them in the mid-19th century. Tea was grown on Wainunu Tea Estate, the longest-surviving tea estate in Fiji, until the 1920s. Subsequent attempts to grow other crops in the area failed and today it is mostly populated with Fijian subsistence farmers who make money selling timber and *kava*.

Tiny **Blue Parrot Bures** (Map pp180-1; blueparrot bures@yahoo.com; dm/d $75/195) is owned and run by Joe Whippy, a third-generation member of the Whippy family. The property is actually an island at the point where two rivers meet to form a creek. Joe and his wife, Robin, have built two traditional thatched *bure* with bamboo walls, bathrooms, cold-water showers and flush toilets. Each *bure* has its own jetty onto the river. There are also four beds in the dorm-style loft in the main building. Rates include all meals and nonmotorised tours. Book via email, but be aware that emails are only answered about every two weeks. The reefs are teeming with fish. Children are accepted only if you book the entire resort.

Wainunu is three hours by very, very bad road from Savusavu, and about an hour from Nabouwalu. (It's actually closer to Viti Levu than Savusavu.) You can hire a carrier for around $150 in Savusavu, and arrange to have them pick you up again at the end of your stay, or arrange to have Joe pick you up. You could also contact Trip n Tour (p183), which can usually help with packages to the lodge.

Taveuni

It's easy to see why Taveuni is called the Garden Island. Hot, steamy and often wet, this luscious strip of land is a carpet of green palms and tropical wildflowers, and its dense, prehistoric rainforest is a magnet for colourful bird life. Taveuni is proud of its natural heritage. A massive swathe of the island's eastern side is a protected national park and here you can get sweaty on hillside hikes, cool off under waterfalls, enjoy a coastal walk along an impossibly beautiful beach trail or glide through clear waters on a traditional *bilibili* (bamboo raft). Dotted around the island's perimeter are black-sand beaches, evidence of the island's volcanic past. If it's sheer indulgence you're after, the nearby islands of Laucala, Matagi and Qamea have stunning white beaches and luxury resorts.

It's not just on dry land that Taveuni makes an impression, though. The island's beauty descends below the water's surface, attracting divers from across the globe – all of them eager to explore the dazzling corals and diverse marine life of the world-famous Somosomo Strait.

Taveuni is also politically important, as it is the chiefly island for the northern part of the country. The Tui Cakau (King of the Reef), the third-highest chiefly title in Fiji, is based in Somosomo.

Taveuni doesn't have any major towns. The island's main income comes from agriculture: mostly copra and to a lesser extent *dalo* (taro plant) and *kava* (Polynesian pepper shrub, the aromatic roots of which are used to make a mildly narcotic, muddy and odd-tasting drink) crops. The land here was once a single copra plantation, since subdivided and sold off.

HIGHLIGHTS

- Experience phenomenal marine life around the world-famous **Rainbow Reef** (p199)
- Snorkel sublime **Vuna Reef** (p199)
- Belt out a song with the locals at Sunday Mass at **Wairiki Catholic Mission** (p201)
- Trek where the forest meets the beach on the **Lavena Coastal Walk** (p209)
- Work up a sweat hiking to the **Tavoro Waterfalls** (p208), then wash it all off under the pounding waters
- Hop on a traditional *bilibili* and snorkel in crystal waters at **Waitabu Marine Park** (p208)
- Experience an adrenalin rush and gain a few bruises at the **Waitavala Water Slide** (p202)
- Soak up the laid-back atmosphere and excellent food of expat-magnet **Matei** (p205)

| ■ POPULATION: 12,000 | ■ AREA: 442 SQ KM |

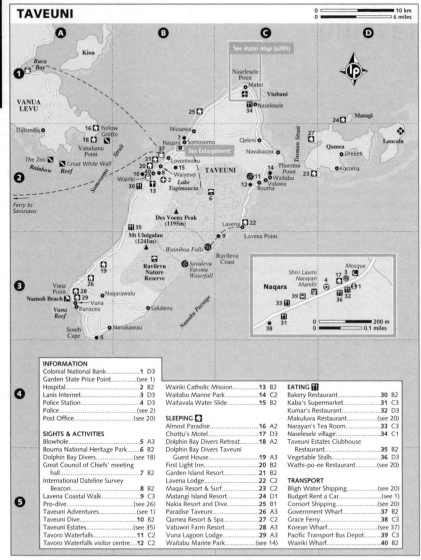

TAVEUNI

INFORMATION
Colonial National Bank..................1 D3
Garden State Price Point.............(see 1)
Hospital...2 B2
Lanis Internet................................3 D3
Police Station.................................4 D3
Police...(see 20)
Post Office..................................(see 20)

SIGHTS & ACTIVITIES
Blowhole...5 A3
Bouma National Heritage Park......6 B2
Dolphin Bay Divers...................(see 18)
Great Council of Chiefs' meeting
    hall...7 B2
International Dateline Survey
    Beacon......................................8 A2
Lavena Coastal Walk.....................9 C3
Pro-dive.....................................(see 20)
Taveuni Adventures..................(see 1)
Taveuni Dive................................10 B2
Taveuni Estates........................(see 35)
Tavoro Waterfalls........................11 C2
Tavoro Waterfalls visitor centre...12 C2

Wairiki Catholic Mission..............13 B2
Waitabu Marine Park....................14 C2
Waitavala Water Slide..................15 B2

SLEEPING
Almost Paradise............................16 A2
Chottu's Motel.............................17 D3
Dolphin Bay Divers Retreat.........18 A2
Dolphin Bay Divers Taveuni
    Guest House.............................19 A3
First Light Inn...............................20 B2
Garden Island Resort...................21 B2
Lavena Lodge...............................22 C2
Maqai Resort & Surf....................23 C2
Matangi Island Resort..................24 D1
Nakia Resort and Dive.................25 B1
Paradise Taveuni..........................26 A3
Qamea Resort & Spa...................27 C2
Vatuwiri Farm Resort...................28 A3
Vuna Lagoon Lodge.....................29 A3
Waitabu Marine Park..............(see 14)

EATING
Bakery Restaurant........................30 B2
Kaba's Supermarket.....................31 C3
Kumar's Restaurant......................32 D3
Makuluva Restaurant...............(see 20)
Narayan's Tea Room.....................33 C3
Naselesele village.........................34 C1
Taveuni Estates Clubhouse
    Restaurant...............................35 B2
Vegetable Stalls............................36 D3
Wathi-po-ee Restaurant...........(see 20)

TRANSPORT
Bligh Water Shipping.................(see 20)
Budget Rent a Car......................(see 1)
Consort Shipping......................(see 20)
Government Wharf.......................37 B2
Grace Ferry...................................38 C3
Korean Wharf...........................(see 37)
Pacific Transport Bus Depot........39 C3
Wairiki Wharf...............................40 B2

Geography & Geology

Much of Taveuni's coastline is rugged, set against some of Fiji's highest peaks. Des Voeux Peak reaches up 1195m and the cloud-shrouded Mt Uluigalau, at 1241m, is the country's second-highest summit. The volcanic soil and abundant rainfall make Taveuni one of Fiji's most fertile areas. While the northeast of Taveuni is fringed by reefs, the southwest has deep water close to shore.

Orientation

The majority of visitors fly into Matei airport at the island's northernmost point, where most of the island's hotels, restaurants and dive shops are based. Head southeast from Matei and you'll eventually hit Bouma National Heritage Park, where the road stops at Lavena. Head southwest from Matei and you reach the towns of Somosomo, Naqara and Waiyevo where there's some budget accommodation, shops and services but not much of interest to tourists. If you arrive by boat it will be at one of the two wharves in the Waiyevo area. Further south there are a few resorts near the village of Vuna. The road then goes only as far as the blowhole on South Cape, making much of the southeast coast almost inaccessible.

Dangers & Annoyances

Theft can be an issue on Taveuni. Always lock your door when sleeping and keep valuables out of sight. Don't wander around alone at night.

All of Taveuni's electricity is supplied by generator. Upmarket resorts have 24-hour power; however, some budget and mid-range places only run their generators in the evening, usually between 6pm and 10pm. Keep a torch handy.

Activities

DIVING & SNORKELLING

Taveuni has achieved mythical status among divers, who come to the Somosomo Strait to see incredible coral, a profusion of fish and the occasional shark, turtle or even pilot whale from September to November. The most famous of the vibrant soft-coral sites is **Rainbow Reef**, which fringes the southwest corner of Vanua Levu but is most easily accessed from Taveuni. Highlights include the luminescent Great White Wall. See p71 for more details. The island is especially hot and humid in January and February and the water clarity is reduced due to plankton blooms and northerly winds from the equator.

There is plenty for snorkellers, too. **Vuna Reef**, off southern Taveuni, boasts dazzling coral and improbable creatures. The three small islands immediately offshore from Naselesele Point in Matei also have good snorkelling (the third is known as the local 'Honeymoon Island'). You can also snorkel happily at Prince Charles or Beverly Beaches.

There are a number of dive operations on Taveuni, and the upmarket resorts on the offshore islands of Matagi and Qamea

have diving for their guests. All of the following companies organise dives in the Somosomo Strait.

Garden Island Dive Centre (☎ 345 0324; www.gardenislandresort.com) was set to open at the Garden Island Resort in early 2009. A two-tank dive/PADI Open Water Course will cost $185/650.

Dolphin Bay Divers (☎ 992 4001, 828 3001; www.dolphinbaydivers.com) operates from Dolphin Bay Divers Retreat (p203), which is located on Vanua Levu but is more easily accessed from Taveuni. It offers two-tank dives/PADI Open Water Courses for $215/620 including equipment. The gear is in excellent condition.

Pro-dive (☎ 888 0125; www.paradiseinfiji.com) is based at Paradise Taveuni (p204). Two-tank dives/PADI Open Water Courses cost $270/630, including gear. There's fantastic snorkelling offshore at the outfit's house reef.

Jewel Bubble Divers (☎ 888 0586; www.jeweldivers.com), near Beverly Beach in Matei, provides high-quality gear and is locally owned and run. Two-tank dives cost $230, and PADI Open Water Courses $680, including equipment.

Taveuni Dive (☎ 828 1063, 888 0063; www.taveunidive.com) is a good, professional set-up located on Taveuni's southwest coast, in Wairiki and Taveuni Estates. A two-tank dive/PADI Open Water Course costs $270/660 including equipment.

Vunibokoi Divers (Dive Taveuni; Map p205; ☎ 888 0560; www.tovutovu.com), Tovu Tovu Resort's dive operation in Matei, is ecstatically recommended by customers. Popular dive master Tyrone Valentine (scion of an old colonial family) has logged an incredible 14,000 dives, mostly around Taveuni. Dives are in the Rainbow Reef area and a two-tank dive/PADI certification costs $215/750 including equipment. The outfit is proud of its 'eco' credentials and does everything possible to avoid damaging local ecosystems.

HIKING

Taveuni's wild interior makes it perfect for exploring on foot. Bouma National Heritage Park (p208) is the place to head for hiking action. Here you can amble beachside on the Lavena Coastal Walk (p209), hike up and down hills to the Tavoro Waterfalls (p208) or take in the guided Vidawa Forest Trail (p208). If that's not hard-core enough you can slog it up to Des Voeux Peak (p202) or around Lake Tagimaucia (p202).

WILDLIFE WATCHING

Taveuni is one of Fiji's best areas for birdwatching. Over 100 species of bird can be found here. Try Des Voeux Peak (p202) at dawn for a chance to see the rare orange dove (the male is bright orange with a green head, while the female is mostly green) and the silktail. Avid birdwatchers also recommend the Vidawa Rainforest Trail (p208). On the Matei side of the village, follow a 4WD track for 3.5km up the mountain. Here you might see parrots and fantails, particularly in August and September when they're nesting. The deep-red feathers of the kula parrot were once an important trade item with the Tongans. The forested Lavena coast is also a good spot to see orange or flame doves, Fiji goshawk, wattled honeyeater, and grey and white heron. Vatuwiri Farm Resort (p204) at Vuna Point in the south is a great place for viewing fruit bats. Down south you can also see and hear magpies, introduced to control insects in the copra plantations.

OTHER ACTIVITIES

Tango Fishing Adventures (Map p205; ☎ 332 4303, 888 0680; makaira@connect.com.fj) can be booked through Makaira by the Sea (p206) and takes you fishing for big game aboard the *Tango* with Captain John Llanes Jr, who has over 30 years' experience. The boat has GPS, VHF and seven rod holders. A half/full day costs $600/1000.

Taveuni Estates (☎ 888 0441) welcomes visitors to its nine-hole golf course ($40 green fee – if there are two of you a free pizza at the local restaurant is included), four tennis courts ($15) and a swimming pool.

Peckham Pearl Farm tours (☎ 888 2789) organises snorkelling tours of the island's only saltwater black-pearl farm, in the Naselesele lagoon. Tours leave at 10am Monday to Friday from Audrey's Beach in Matei (opposite Audrey's Island Coffee & Pastries) and last for 1½ hours ($25/12 per adult/child). You can then browse the wares (pearls $24 and up).

Taveuni Adventures (☎ 888 1700; www.taveuniadventures.com; 1st fl, Garden State Price Point Bldg), based in Naqara, can organise a range of activities including birdwatching excursions, hiking trips to Des Voeux Peak or Lake Tagimaucia, village tours and sunset cruises. It also acts as a booking agent for several accommodation options on the island.

Getting There & Away

AIR

At Matei airport, **Pacific Sun** (☎ 6720 888) has two flights a day to/from Nadi ($168 one way, 1½ hours), as well as flying to Savusavu ($225). **Air Fiji** (☎ 888 0062) has one to two flights daily to/from Nadi ($253 one way, 1½ hours) and Suva ($182 one way, 45 minutes), but be aware that both routes are often heavily booked. See p245 for more details on travelling by air in Fiji.

BOAT

The Wairiki Wharf, for large vessels such as the MV *Suliven*, is about 1km south of Waiyevo. Smaller boats depart from the Korean Wharf, about 2km north. **Consort Shipping** (☎ in Suva 330 2877) and **Bligh Water Shipping** (☎ 888 0261, in Suva 331 8247) have regular Suva–Savusavu–Taveuni ferries with competitive rates – a ticket between Taveuni and Savusavu should cost around $25. Bligh Water is the more comfortable and reliable service. **Grace Ferry** (☎ 888 0320; Naqara) runs a bus-boat trip to Savusavu and Labasa ($20 to $25). The boat departs from the Korean Wharf at 8.45am. The booking office is in Naqara.

For more information about these ferries see p248.

Getting Around

The one main road in Taveuni follows the coast, stretching from Lavena in the east, up north and around to Navakawau in the south. It is sealed from Matei to Wairiki, and there's also a sealed (though slightly potholed) section through Taveuni Estates. There are also a couple of inland 4WD tracks. Getting around Taveuni involves a bit of planning – the main disadvantage being the sporadic bus service. To get around cheaply and quickly you need to combine buses with walking, or take taxis. You can rent 4WDs in Naqara; however, it's better value to hire a taxi for the day and the driver will probably act as a tour guide too!

TO/FROM THE AIRPORT

From Matei airport expect to pay about $20 to Waiyevo, and $60 to Vuna (about one hour) in a taxi. Most upmarket resorts provide transfers for guests.

BUS

Pacific Transport (☎ 888 0278) has a depot in Naqara, opposite the Taveuni Central Indian School. From Monday to Saturday, buses run from Wairiki to Bouma at 8.30am, 11.30am and 4.20pm. The last bus continues to Lavena where the first bus of each morning starts out at 5.45am. On Tuesday and Thursday all buses go as far as Lavena. On Sunday there is one bus at 3.30pm from Wairiki to Lavena, and one from Lavena to Wairiki at 6.45am.

Going south from Naqara, buses run to Navakawau at 9am, 11.30am and 4.45pm Monday to Saturday, returning at 5.30am and 8.15am. On Sunday a bus departs Navakawau at 6.45am and returns from Naqara at 4pm. From Matei, buses run to Wairiki at 11.30am Monday to Saturday and also at 7am and 3pm Monday to Friday during school terms.

The bus schedule is very lax: buses may show up early or an hour late. Be sure to double check the time of the return bus when you board, just to make sure there is one.

CAR

In Naqara, **Budget Rent a Car** (☎ 888 1999; garden state@connect.com.fj; Garden State Price Point Bldg; ⏰ 8am-5pm Mon-Fri, till 1pm Sat & Sun) has 4WDs for between $135 and $185 per day.

TAXI

It's easy to find taxis in the Matei, Waiyevo and Naqara areas, though on Sunday you might have to call one in advance. Hiring a taxi for a negotiated fee and touring most of the island's highlights in a day will work out cheaper than hiring a car. You should be able to get one for around $150 for the day. For destinations such as Lavena you can go one way by bus and have a taxi pick you up at the end at a designated time (but arrange this before you go).

WAIYEVO, SOMOSOMO & AROUND

This isn't the most beautiful part of Taveuni but it is a good place to get things done and holds most of the island's facilities. It's also politically important – Somosomo is the largest village on Taveuni and headquarters for the Tui Cakau (high chief of Taveuni). The **Great Council of Chiefs' meeting hall** (*bure bose*) was built here in 1986 for the gathering of chiefs from all over Fiji. Just south of Somosomo is Naqara, Taveuni's metropolis – if you take metropolis to mean a few supermarkets, a

budget hotel, internet cafe and a bank. Head another 2km down the coast and you'll hit Waiyevo, which is Taveuni's administrative centre and home to the hospital, police station, more ferry links and a resort. About 2km further south of Waiyevo is Wairiki village, which has a general store and a beautiful old hilltop Catholic mission.

Information

Colonial National Bank (☎ 888 0433; Naqara; ⏰ 9.30am-4pm Mon, from 9am Tue-Fri) The only bank on the island will exchange currency and travellers cheques and has an ATM.

Garden State Price Point (☎ 888 0291; Naqara; per min $0.50; ⏰ 8am-5pm Mon-Fri, till 1pm Sat & Sun) One pricey computer for internet access.

Hospital (☎ 888 0444; Waiyevo)

Lanis Internet (Naqara; per min $0.20; ⏰ 8am-8pm Mon-Sat) Next to Chottu's Motel.

Police (☎ 888 0222; Waiyevo) The main police station is at the government compound behind the Garden Island Resort in Waiyevo. There is also a police station in Naqara.

Post office (☎ 888 0027; Waiyevo; ⏰ 8am-1pm & 2pm-4pm Mon-Fri) Among the shops beneath the First Light Inn.

Telephone You'll find a cardphone at the post office as well as outside the supermarkets in Naqara.

Sights

INTERNATIONAL DATELINE

The International Dateline twists its way around Fiji, but the 180-degree meridian actually cuts straight through Taveuni, about a 10-minute walk south of Waiyevo. Along the side of the road to Wairiki, a small, red survey beacon marks the spot. If you take the road uphill from Waiyevo (towards the hospital) and cross the field on the right, you'll find a big, wooden Taveuni map that's split in two to mark the two sides of the dateline. If you're easily amused you'll enjoy jumping from one day to another.

WAIRIKI CATHOLIC MISSION

This faded beauty has bags of colonial charm, and the setting is equally beguiling – standing on a slope peering over the Somosomo Strait. Its interior has an impressive beam ceiling and beautiful stained glass, reputedly from France. In the presbytery there's a painting of a legendary battle in which a Catholic missionary helped Taveuni's warriors defeat their Tongan attackers. It's worth attending Mass at 7am, 9am or 11am on Sunday when the

---

THE LEGEND OF THE TAGIMAUCIA

There once lived a young girl with a wild spirit and a tendency to be disobedient. On one fateful day, her mother lost her patience with the girl and beat her with a bundle of coconut leaves, saying she never wanted to see her face again. The distraught girl ran away until she was deep in the forest. She came upon a large vine-covered *ivi* (Polynesian chestnut) tree and decided to climb it. The higher she climbed, the more entangled she became in the vine and, unable to break free, she began to weep. As giant tears rolled down her face they turned to blood and, where they fell onto the vine, they became beautiful white-and-red *tagimaucia* flowers. Calmed by the sight of the flowers, the girl managed to escape the forest and, upon returning home, was relieved to find an equally calm mother.

---

congregation lets it rip with some impressive vocals. There are no pews here though; the congregation sits on woven mats on the floor. And you'll have to take off your shoes.

The mission is about 20 minutes' walk south along the coast from Waiyevo. You can't miss it on the hill to the left. A dirt track behind leads up to a huge white cross. The views from here are superb.

WAITAVALA WATER SLIDE

If you've always wanted to launch yourself down a series of mini waterfalls, then here's your chance. You can slide down on your bum or attempt to do it standing up, surfer style, like the local kids. Either way, you'll end up (perhaps a little battered) in a small pool at the bottom. It could be a good idea to watch a local go down before you attempt it yourself – there are usually a few kids around to show you how. Be warned though: on our visit the local kids told us never to attempt to begin your slide from the very top of the falls. Even they don't do it, as it can be pretty dangerous.

The slide is a 20-minute walk from Waiyevo. With the Garden Island Resort on your left, head north and take the first right at the bus stop. Take another right at the branch in the road, pass a shed and then go left down a hill. You'll see a 'waterfall' sign. The river is on the Waitavala estate, which is private land, so if you pass anyone on your way there, ask if you can visit.

LAKE TAGIMAUCIA

Lake Tagimaucia is in an old volcanic crater in the mountains above Somosomo. Masses of vegetation float on the lake, which is situated 823m above sea level, and the national flower, the rare *tagimaucia* (an epiphytic plant), grows on the lake's shores. This red-and-white flower blooms only at high altitude from late September to late December.

It is a difficult trek around the lake as it is overgrown and often very muddy; you'll need a stick (to find firm ground) and a guide. Ask around in Naqara or arrange a guide through your accommodation as it's easy to get lost on your way up. Taveuni Adventures (p200) also organises day trips. The track starts from Naqara. Take lunch and allow eight hours for the round trip.

DES VOEUX PEAK

At 1195m, Des Voeux Peak is the island's second-highest mountain. On a clear day, the views from the peak are fantastic: it's possible to see Lake Tagimaucia and perhaps even the Lau island group. Allow three to four hours to walk the 6km up, and at least two to return. It's a steep, arduous climb in the heat, so it's best to start out early. Try to make it up there by dawn if you are a keen birdwatcher. To get here, take the inland track just before you reach Wairiki Catholic Mission (coming from Waiyevo). Alternatively, arrange for a lift up and then walk back at your leisure.

Sleeping

BUDGET

First Light Inn (☎ 888 0339; firstlight@connect.com.fj; Waiyevo; r with fan/air-con $56/66; 🖳) Convenient for the ferries, this is a relaxed and friendly place with a spotless self-catering kitchen for guests and satellite TV. Try to ring before you turn up as it might not always be staffed.

Chottu's Motel (☎ 888 0233; Naqara; budget s/d/tr $40/50/60, deluxe s/d $58.75/70.50) Chottu's has two types of room: budget, which are basic and share cold-water bathrooms; and deluxe, which are still pretty bare bones but have small TVs, private facilities and kitchenettes.

TOP END
Garden Island Resort (☎ 888 0286; www.garden islandresort.com; s/d/tr $240/270/330; 🛏 🖳 🖭) At the time of writing, this resort had come under new ownership and was in for a full revamp of rooms and public areas, and a new dive shop. It's the only resort in the area and has great views over the Somosomo Strait to Vanua Levu and beyond.

Nakia Resort and Dive (☎ 888 1111; www.nakiafiji .com; bure $340-530) Four simple, yet luxurious, *bure* sit on a grassy hillside looking out to sea at this raved-about ecoresort. These guys use alternative energy wherever possible, are into composting and recycling, and have a large organic garden where they get fresh fruit and veg for their restaurant. The owners go out of their way to create a family-friendly environment. They will even make homemade baby food for the little ones and a babysitting service is available. At the time of research a full dive shop was being set up at the resort.

Eating & Drinking
Kumar's Restaurant (☎ 888 1005; Naqara; breakfast/ meals $2/4; 🕑 breakfast, lunch & dinner before 7pm Mon-Sat) Kumar's is a cute, blue, boxlike place serving good curries, and cheap omelettes for breakfast.

Narayan's Tea Room (Naqara; snacks $3-5; 🕑 8am-6pm Mon-Sat) Next to the bus station, this simple but good cafe offers cakes, snacks and the odd curry.

Wathi-po-ee Restaurant (☎ 888 0382; Waiyevo; meals $4-7; 🕑 breakfast, lunch & dinner Mon-Fri, breakfast & lunch Sat & Sun) A basic place that serves big plates of chow mein, curries and Fijian dishes as well as eggs, bacon and toast for breakfast. You can eat your food on tables outside looking over towards the old Cannibal Café with its notorious slogan, 'We'd love to have you for dinner', is still at the back.

Makuluva Restaurant (☎ 994 5394; Waiyevo; lunch/dinner $5/10; 🕑 8am-4pm & 6-8pm Mon-Fri & Sun) There's a small fish market in a shed opposite the Garden Island Resort with a simple cafe at the back. Order dinner in advance, before 4pm (you can either drop off your order at the fish shed or call the owner on her mobile). Makuluva is run by Seventh Day Adventists, and may be one of the few places open on Sunday.

Bakery Restaurant (Wairiki; lunch/dinner $10/15; 🕑 breakfast, lunch & dinner) This new place, next

to Taveuni Dive, serves good breakfasts, burgers and coffee.

For self-caterers, **Kaba's Supermarket** (☎ 888 0088; Naqara; 🕑 8am-5pm Mon-Fri, till 1pm Sat & Sun) is fully stocked. There is also a large MH Supermarket in Somosomo (which sells alcohol, but not on Saturday afternoon or Sunday) or the Wairiki supermarket, which is open on Sundays. For fresh fruit and vegetables try the vegetable stalls along the main street of Naqara, where there are also a couple of bakeries.

SOUTHERN TAVEUNI
The southern part of the island isn't well serviced by public transport but it's a beautiful place to visit. Check out the **blowhole** on the dramatic, windswept South Cape. As the water jumps up through the volcanic rock it creates rainbows in the air. Southern Taveuni is also home to Vuna Reef, which is perfect for snorkellers and novice divers. The main villages on southern Taveuni are Naqarawalu, in the hills, and, on the southern coast near Vuna Reef, Kanacea, Vuna and Navakawau.

Sleeping
BUDGET
Dolphin Bay Divers Retreat (☎ 828 3001, 926 0145; www.dolphinbaydivers.com; Vanaira Bay, Vanua Levu; sites per person/safari tents/bure $15/50/90; 🖳) Just a bay over from Almost Paradise on Vanua Levu, this is a friendly place with simple *bure*, space for camping and some permanent safari tents; some new *bure* were being built at the time of research. It's very popular with divers, who make up most of the guests, but there's also good snorkelling from the beach. The food here is good, plentiful and eaten family style. You can also help yourself to snacks throughout the day. Transfers from Matei cost $60 one way. Meal plans are $60 per day with snacks. Important: Dolphin Bay connects through Vodafone and there is no Vodafone connection and no mobile-phone reception at Buca Bay on Vanua Levu. Do not turn up at Buca Bay and expect to phone Dolphin Bay Divers. You will be stranded, although the locals will put you up for the night.

Dolphin Bay Divers Taveuni Guest House (☎ 888 0531; www.dolphinbaydivers.com; dm/d $15/55) This is a big, spotless house with two double bedrooms with shared bathroom. It is generally used by guests of Dolphin Bay Divers before or after their stay at the resort. You'll share the house

DRUA

For assisting him in a war against the people of Rewa, Ratu Cakobau presented King George of Tonga with a *drua* (traditional catamaran). Named Ra Marama, the *drua* was built in Taveuni in the 1850s. It took seven years to complete, was over 30m long and could carry 150 people. Hewn from giant trees, it could outsail the European ships of the era.

Building *drua* could involve entire communities; some boats could carry up to 300 people. Their construction often involved ceremonial human sacrifices, and the completed vessel was launched over the bodies of slaves, which were used as rollers under the hulls. The last large *drua* was built in 1913 and is on display at the Fiji Museum in Suva. If you visit the island of Kioa, north of Taveuni, you can still see fishermen out in small, one-person *drua*.

with a friendly Indo-Fijian family who cook delicious Indian food and are happy to act as tour guides around the island.

Vuna Lagoon Lodge (☎ /fax 888 0627; dm/s/d $22/48/65) This place is a cross between home-stay and private rental. It's a simple, blue, wooden house a few steps from the beach with a self-catering kitchen and laundry facilities. It's also just a couple of minutes from the Fijian village of Vuna, so it's a great place to hang out and make friends with the locals. Good, home-cooked meals are available for between $7 and $12. To find the lodge, turn down the dirt lane towards the coast at Vuna village; it's the last blue house on the left. It's best to call ahead.

MIDRANGE

Almost Paradise (☎ 828 3000, 992 6782; www.almost paradisefiji.com; Vanua Levu; s/d $155/195; ▢) This place is in a sheltered bay on Vanua Levu, but is accessible only by boat and this is more easily done from Taveuni. There are just a few wooden bungalows here with en suites, rain-water showers, solar power and teeny kitchenettes. There's no beach, but there are some sun loungers on a grassy lawn overlooking the water. There's hiking, good snorkelling at the house reef and you can hire kayaks and paddle in the mangroves up a small river. Diving can be arranged at nearby Dolphin Bay Divers. Transfers from Taveuni cost $45. It was closed for renovation at the time of writing.

TOP END

Paradise Taveuni (☎ 888 0125; www.paradiseinfiji.com; s/d inc all meals from $400/500; ▢) Set on a former plantation on an elevated piece of land, this place has stunning sea and sunset views and plenty of strategically placed hammocks and sun loungers from which to enjoy them. The *bure* are luxury all the way with large decks,

day beds, separate living and sleeping quarters, and huge bathrooms, some with the added bonus of outdoor Jacuzzis and rock showers. The place is run with military precision and any problems are fixed with startling efficiency. There's diving through Pro-dive (p199) and incredible snorkelling right off the shore on the house reef. Activities include fishing, jet skiing, guided walks and wild-boar hunting.

Vatuwiri Farm Resort (☎ 888 0316; vatuwirifiji.com; d cottages incl meals $500) This one is different: a huge estate, one of the last in the South Pacific still in the hands of the founding family, offering the rare opportunity to stay on a working farm in Fiji. The Tartes produce copra, beef, cocoa and vanilla. Accommodation is in two small cottages down by the water's edge and companionable dinners are taken in the main house with the Tarte family, including home-made food with vegetables and meat from their own farm. They are a fascinating family and are happy to talk about their family's and Fijian history. There's plenty to do on the farm such as birdwatching, horse riding, swimming or just enjoying the peace and quiet.

Eating & Drinking

Taveuni Estates Clubhouse Restaurant (☎ 888 0441; breakfast/lunch/dinner $10/15/25; ☺ breakfast & lunch daily, dinner Fri-Sun & only if booked Mon-Thu) Taveuni Estates is a development of private, expat housing about 8km south of Waiyevo, but the restaurant, bar and sporting facilities are open to the public. The restaurant has a wood-fired pizza oven and makes excellent pizza and there's great fresh coffee and fresh croissants at breakfast time. The organic burgers are pretty good too. The bar is a good place for a beer or cocktail if you happen to be in the area.

MATEI

A residential area on Taveuni's northern point, Matei has a string of guesthouses, hotels and rental properties strewn along a long stretch of road crowned by stately palm trees and skirted by beach. The airport is tiny and, if you're travelling light, it's a real thrill to be able to step off the plane and wander down the street five minutes later. Only a couple of beaches are suitable for swimming and sunbathing, but this is a good place to base yourself for diving. This is also the best place on the island to have a meal, with a handful of places to choose from. It's a very warm place and it's easy to fall into conversation with locals and expats in the street.

Information

Matei doesn't have much in the way of services. There are cardphones at the airport and outside the Bhula Bhai & Sons Supermarket and Sonal Shopping Centre. The larger supermarkets and top-end resorts accept credit cards, but you may be charged extra. Some resorts will also change travellers cheques.

Police There is a police post at the airport.

Tovu Tovu (☎ 888 0560; internet per min $0.25) There's one slow computer terminal in the restaurant area of this resort.

Sleeping
BUDGET

Beverly Campground (☎ 888 0381; sites per person/permanent tent/dm $10/15/15) One of those magical spots where everybody makes friends easily and camping isn't a chore, this small site is set on a white-sand beach, beneath fantastic, huge poison-fish trees. The camp has very basic facilities including flush toilets, showers and a sheltered area for cooking and dining. The owner sometimes brings around fresh fruit and vegetables in the morning. He can also provide equipment for snorkelling, fishing and kayaking. Beverly Beach is about 15 minutes' walk west of the airport.

Bibi's Hideaway (☎ 888 0443; sites per person $15, bure s/d/f/honeymoon $70/90/100/110) A rambling five-acre hillside plot hides a selection of *bure* in varying sizes amongst the fruit and palm trees. There are self-catering facilities here and plenty of room for pitching tents. The resort was started by its affable Fijian owners on the suggestion of the author of the first Lonely Planet guide to Fiji. They are extremely friendly and the prices are always up for negotiation.

Tovu Tovu Resort (☎ 888 0560; www.tovutovu.com; bure with/without kitchen $100/85, f bure $130) This is the best budget place in town, with a selection of wooden *bure* with little wooden verandahs, kitchenettes, hot-water bathrooms and fans. It is built on a subdivided copra estate, and owned by the Petersen family, which once ran the plantation. There's even a family chapel – still in use – on a hill overlooking the *bure*. The best thing is the vibe – it's a very welcoming place and they'll go out of their way to make sure you're as comfortable as possible. There's also a family *bure* here and babysitting can be arranged. The excellent Vunibokoi Divers (p199) is based here. The resort is a 20-minute walk

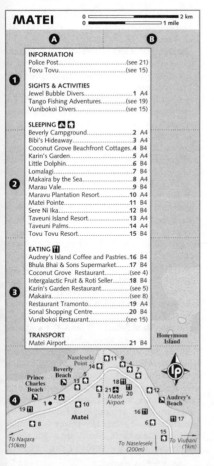

MATEI　0 — 2 km / 0 — 1 mile

INFORMATION	
Police Post	(see 21)
Tovu Tovu	(see 15)
SIGHTS & ACTIVITIES	
Jewel Bubble Divers	1　A4
Tango Fishing Adventures	(see 19)
Vunibokoi Divers	(see 15)
SLEEPING	
Beverly Campground	2　A4
Bibi's Hideaway	3　A4
Coconut Grove Beachfront Cottages	4　B4
Karin's Garden	5　B4
Little Dolphin	6　B4
Lomalagi	7　B4
Makaira by the Sea	8　A4
Marau Vale	9　B4
Maravu Plantation Resort	10　A4
Matei Pointe	11　B4
Sere Ni Ika	12　B4
Taveuni Island Resort	13　A4
Taveuni Palms	14　B4
Tovu Tovu Resort	15　B4
EATING	
Audrey's Island Coffee and Pastries	16　B4
Bhula Bhai & Sons Supermarket	17　B4
Coconut Grove Restaurant	(see 4)
Intergalactic Fruit & Roti Seller	18　B4
Karin's Garden Restaurant	(see 5)
Makaira	(see 8)
Restaurant Tramonto	19　A4
Sonal Shopping Centre	20　B4
Vunibokoi Restaurant	(see 15)
TRANSPORT	
Matei Airport	21　B4

SPENCER TARTE, PLANTATION OWNER

Spencer Tarte's family came to Taveuni in 1871. They came from Birmingham, England, via Australia, to plant cotton, which was at a premium price because of the American Civil War. His family chose Taveuni because of its fertile soil, he says, and bought Vatuwiri Farm – using it first for cotton, then sugar and later, cattle. These days, he says, the farm is still a copra plantation and cattle farm as well as a tourist lodge. Four members of the Tarte family are involved with the running of the farm today. On a typical day, they get up early in the morning to help with activities on the farm, which include looking after the cattle, buildings and grounds maintenance, and copra cutting. They are also working towards improving farming techniques on Taveuni. The best thing about living on Taveuni and Vatuwiri, he says, is that it is unspoilt, with all traditional aspects still in place.

southeast of Matei airport, past the Bhula Bhai & Sons Supermarket.

Little Dolphin (☎ 888 0130; www.littledolphintaveuni .com; d cottage $100) This tiny, two-storey top-heavy cottage has a breezy bedroom and a verandah overlooking the ocean. Downstairs is a kitchen and hot-water bathroom. There are a couple of shelves of books, and snorkels and kayaks can be borrowed for free.

MIDRANGE & TOP END

Makaira by the Sea (☎ 888 0680; fijibeachfrontat makaira.com; bure per day/week from $240/1400) Makaira has two *bure:* one has a living room and panoramic views from both the deck and the bath; the other is smaller, with an outdoor 'jungle shower'. They both come equipped with kitchenettes for self-caterers but there's also a small cafe where breakfast and dinner can be provided, given sufficient notice. On Tuesday nights it's 'fresh fish night' and guests from outside the resort visit for dinner. Makaira is a $3 taxi ride from Matei airport, but only a three-minute walk from Restaurant Tramonto. The generator runs from 7am till 10pm. The family that runs Makaira also owns Tango Fishing Adventures (p200) across the road.

Matei Pointe (☎ 888 0422; www.taveuniresort.com; d bure per day/week from $260/1500, beach house per day/week from $460/2900; ✕ ▣) Walk across the road from the airport and you're at Matei's most conveniently located accommodation. There are three spacious *bure* here with kitchens and fantastic viewing platforms looking out to sea. The main beach house is huge – with 2.5 bedrooms, a kitchen and a sprawling patio with an outdoor dining table and thatched roof for when it rains. There are great walk-in rates to be had.

Coconut Grove Beachfront Cottages (☎ 888 0328; www.coconutgrovefiji.com; bure $300-390) A stone path

studded with fish mosaics leads down to three calm and comfortable cottages and a quiet slice of golden sandy beach. Two of the *bure* have rock showers with sea views and the restaurant here is one of the best on the island. The Californian owner, Ronna, is friendly, knowledgable and efficient.

Maravu Plantation Resort (☎ 332 4303; www .maravu.net; s/d/tr standard bure from $310/450/520, deluxe bure $380/580/700, s/d/tr oceanview villas $590/1000/1180; ⊠ ▣) A former copra plantation across the road from the beach, this isn't as swish as the other luxury resorts, but some of the *bure* do have pretty ocean views and the more expensive have outdoor Jacuzzis and showers. There's a nice, wood, jungle-style bar and restaurant – but it all feels rather soulless. Free activities include horse riding, mountain biking and kayaking. Meal plans offer two/three meals per day for $30/50.

Karin's Garden (☎ 888 0511; www.karinsgardenfiji .com; cottages from $320) A beautiful, wooden, two-bedroom cottage (one double and one twin) in the grounds of the owner's house, with views out towards the reef and beach (which you can access from this property), a kitchen, a sitting room and a verandah. The rooms are big and cosy, the owners affable and relaxed, and there is a two-night minimum stay. There's a small cafe and restaurant here too.

Taveuni Island Resort (☎ 888 0441; www.taveuni islandresort.com; bure per person $680-750, honeymoon villa $2500; ▯ ▣) A luxury jaw dropper, Taveuni Island Resort has 12 *bure* with polished-wood floors, wicker furniture, outdoor rock showers and complete privacy, balanced on a hill. If you've serious cash to splash, there's a private villa complete with plunge pool and your own private team of staff. The resort is popular with honeymooners. Meals are a gourmet's delight, are included in the price and can be taken on the beach, by the pool or in your *bure*. No children under 15 are allowed.

Taveuni Palms (☎ 888 0032; www.taveunipalms fiji.com; d villas $2000, per extra person/child $440/260; 🔀 🖵 🗲) Breathtakingly beautiful, completely tasteful and directly on the beach, Taveuni Palms boasts two villas, each on their own private half-acre with a private beach, a spa, a swimming pool and staff, including a personal chef. The cook will prepare a five-course meal for you every night, but the villas have kitchens anyway. One villa has an attached sleepout for kids, and the resort provides a free nanny (who may even stay over in the sleepout). Both villas are fitted with incredible entertainment centres with big TVs, DVD players and stereos. Activities include kayaking, snorkelling and cooking lessons.

Long-time Taveuni resident **Bob Goddess** (☎ 888 0522; www.fiji-rental-accommodations.com) rents out three family-friendly beachfront holiday homes; all have full kitchen, polished wood floors, great outside deck areas, plenty of lush garden as well as beach access. Rates include a housekeeper:

Lomalagi (d per day/week $310/2000, extra person $25) Lovely Lomalagi has steps that go down to a private cove, and has ocean kayaks available.

Sere Ni Ika (per day/week $430/2800, extra person $25) Has three bedrooms, and the whole front of the house can be opened out to the fresh air. Ocean kayaks are available.

Marau Vale (d per day/week $490/3100, extra person $25) Bob's own house with a fantastically equipped kitchen, and an outdoor rock shower.

Eating & Drinking

There are several good choices in Matei. If you're here on a Wednesday, try the *lovo* (feast cooked in a pit oven) or buffet (complete with entertainment) at Naselesele village (Map p198; your accommodation will be able to arrange this for you). Profits go to the local school.

Coconut Grove Restaurant (☎ 888 0328; lunch $7-22, dinner $14-35; 🕑 breakfast, lunch & dinner) Take off your shoes and enjoy the sea views from the deck of this guesthouse's lovely restaurant. The menu includes wonderfully fresh vegetarian dishes, homemade pasta, soups, salads and fish. You can just turn up for breakfast or lunch but you'll have to let them know you're coming for dinner. They pin up the night's choices on the restaurant door during the day, and you have to write your name down before 4pm. There are usually only three or four choices,

always including one fish and one meat. There is a good-value 'Island Tunes and buffet night' on Saturdays, which is great washed down with a jug of their potent sangria.

our pick Audrey's Island Coffee and Pastries (☎ 888 0039; coffee & cake $10; 🕑 10am-6pm) You can sit on the deck of US-born Audrey's house and enjoy fabulous cakes (moist chocolate cake and white-chocolate coconut slabs are just a couple of the possibilities – it depends on what she's been baking) and coffee whilst looking down the sweeping coast road and out to sea. If you're lucky, she may break out the kahlua and offer you a shot or three. She'll even let you have the recipe.

Vunibokoi Restaurant (☎ 888 0560; dinner mains $18; 🕑 breakfast, lunch & dinner) Tovu Tovu Resort's restaurant has large windows overlooking the island of Viubani. At lunch there are burgers and sandwiches, and there a few choices (usually changing daily) on the dinner board in the evenings, including delights such as crab curry, stir-fried prawns and *rourou* (boiled taro leaves in coconut cream) soup. Food is tasty and very good value and, on Friday, there's a popular 'buffet and music night' ($20).

Karin's Garden Restaurant (☎ 888 0705; mains $30; 🕑 lunch & dinner Mon-Sat) Karin's Garden has opened a tiny cafe and restaurant on the grounds of its guesthouse. Simple snacks are served during the day, but if you want to eat in the evening you'll have to book by lunchtime as everything is made to order. There is one choice per night and the food is mostly European. Possible choices include marinated lamb, goulash and roast pork.

Restaurant Tramonto (☎ 888 2224; pizza from $25, meals $20-25; 🕑 lunch & dinner) If you're in the market for a pizza the size of a small child, then Tramonto won't disappoint – they're huge and mightily topped. You can consume said pizza in a nice raised building overlooking the water. If cheesiness turns you cold then there are a couple of other well-prepared dishes available daily, including fish 'n' chips and lamb shanks. On Sunday there's a buffet dinner ($25) and on Wednesday, a barbecue ($20); reservations are required.

Makaira (☎ 888 0680; dinner $20-30; 🕑 dinner Tue) During high season this tiny resort opens to the public for 'seafood night' on Tuesdays, where you'll be presented with delicious fresh seafood (staff can sometimes prepare nonseafood dishes too, if told in advance) and can bob your head to the groove of a Fijian band. You'll need to book by lunchtime.

Bhula Bhai & Sons Supermarket (☎ 888 0462; ۞ 7.30am-6pm Mon-Sat, 8am-11am & 3-5pm Sun) sells a range of groceries (including disposable nappies, but not beer), phonecards, stationery and film, and accepts Visa and MasterCard (10% commission, $90 limit). It has a public phone and a petrol pump (petrol is not served on Sundays). **Sonal Shopping Centre** (☎ 888 0431; ۞ 7.30am-6pm Mon-Sat, 8-11am Sun), near Matei Point, is another well-stocked supermarket that doesn't sell beer. There are a couple of pool tables outside.

Look out for the man across the road from Coconut Grove who shouts and jumps around to get your attention. He means you no harm. He is the Intergalactic Fruit & Roti Seller and has come from another planet to sell you fresh fruit or fish roti from his small gate-side stall.

Really good rotis ($1.50) can be bought at Matei airport.

EASTERN TAVEUNI

The local landowners of beautiful eastern Taveuni have rejected logging in favour of ecotourism, under the banner of the Bouma Environmental Tourism Project. Scenes for the 1991 movie *Return to the Blue Lagoon* were filmed at Bouma National Heritage Park's Tavoro Waterfalls and at Lavena Beach.

Bouma National Heritage Park

This **national park** (www.bnho.org) protects over 80% of Taveuni's total area, covering about 150 sq km of rainforest and coastal forest.

TAVORO WATERFALLS

There are three waterfalls here, each with natural swimming pools.

The first waterfall is about 24m high and has a change area, picnic tables and barbecue plates and is only 10 minutes' gentle stroll along a flat, cultivated path from the **visitors centre** (☎ 888 0390; falls admission $12; ۞ 9am-4pm). Don't be fooled however, getting to the other falls isn't so easy – it's a good 40-minute, leg-punishing climb up and down hills to the second one. Luckily there are a few lookout points where you can stop and rest along the way. What's more, as you approach the waterfall you'll have to make like a frog and jump from boulder to boulder to cross a river; there's a rope you can use to balance but be

careful as the rocks are very slippery. It's not quite as big as the first but is more secluded and beautiful. Getting to the third fall involves a hike along a less-maintained, often muddy, path through the forest for another 40 minutes, and if it's been raining it can be difficult to access. Smaller than the other two (about 10m high), it has a great swimming pool and rocks for jumping off (check for obstructions first!). If you bring your snorkelling gear, you'll be able to see the hundreds of prawns in the water.

VIDAWA RAINFOREST TRAIL

If you are a keen walker, try this full-day, guided trek led by shamans. Beginning at Vidawa village, it passes through the historic fortified village sites of Navuga and follows trails into the rainforest where you'll see lots of bird life. The trek then takes you to the Tavoro Waterfalls. You can only do this walk with a guide and need to book in advance. The trip runs Monday to Saturday and can take a maximum of eight people ($40). It includes guides, lunch, afternoon tea and park admission fee. Book through the Tavoro Waterfalls visitor centre.

If you are in the mood for a marathon, it is possible to catch the early morning bus to Bouma (45 minutes from Matei, 1½ hours from Naqara), make a flying visit to all three waterfalls and catch the early afternoon bus at about 1.40pm on to Lavena. In a rush, you can also do the coastal walk before dark and either stay overnight at Lavena or be picked up by a prearranged taxi. But this is Fiji – you'll be the only one rushing. For transport information see p201.

WAITABU MARINE PARK

This area has decent snorkelling and a gorgeous white-sand beach. It is only possible to visit the park with a guide. The village of Waitabu has set up a half-day tour that includes a local guide, guided snorkelling, a *bilibili* ride, and afternoon tea and singing in the village ($40 per person, or $35 each for a group of four or more). There's also a Backpackers' Tour with guided snorkelling ($20 per person). You can't just turn up though and will have to book in advance, as trips will depend on the tides that day. Bookings are taken on ☎ 888 0451 or 820 1999. You can also arrange to stay the night at the new **campground** (per person with own tent $10, incl hire tent $15). There are toilets and showers and you can order a meal for $10. A return trip in a taxi should cost about $50.

LAVENA COASTAL WALK

The 5km Lavena Coastal Walk follows the forest edge along stunning white-sand Lavena beach (known as Blue Lagoon Beach to the locals ever since the movie was filmed here, our guide told us), then a volcanic-black beach, past peaceful villages, before climbing up through a landscape straight out of Jurassic Park to a gushing waterfall. There's some good snorkelling and kayaking here and Lavena Point is fine for swimming.

The path is well maintained and clearly marked. About halfway along the trek, watch for the *vatuni'epa,* bizarre rock pedestals formed by the erosion of the coral base along the coast, which, according to our guide, the locals refer to as mushrooms because of their shape. Past these, the path seems to disappear at Naba settlement: follow the path onto the beach, then follow the shore past the *bure* and cross the stream to where the path reappears. Further ahead is a suspension bridge and eventually the trail takes you up the ancient valley of Wainibau Creek.

To reach the falls at the end of the trail, you have to clamber over rocks and swim a short distance through two deep pools. Two cascades fall at different angles into a deep pool with sheer walls. The hardy can climb up the rocks to the left-hand side and jump into the deep pool. If you're visiting in the rainy season, the rocks near the falls can be slippery, if not flooded; it can be difficult and dangerous to reach the falls at this time. Ask at Lavena Lodge for current conditions. At any time of year (even if it hasn't been raining), violent flash floods can occur and readers are advised staying to the left of the pool, where you can make an easier getaway.

The walk is managed through Lavena Lodge. Entrance is $12, or $15 including a guide. You can also take a guided sea-kayak journey and coastal walk for $40 (including lunch). You can also arrange to take a boat one way and walk back ($120). Usually you can order a meal for when you return to the lodge ($10) but it's a good idea to bring along some food and definitely bring water.

Lavena village is about 15 minutes' drive past Bouma, 35 minutes from Matei.

However, by local bus it takes about one hour from Matei or just under two from Waiyevo. Expect to pay about $60 for a taxi to/from Matei. See p200 for more information on transport services.

Sleeping & Eating

Lavena Lodge (☎ 888 0116; tw per person incl Lavena Coastal Walk $30) Run by friendly, informative staff, the lodge has basic, clean rooms and a shared kitchen and bathroom. Electricity is supplied in the evening. There's a bench and table underneath a tree on the gorgeous beach from which to watch the sun go down, and when everything is quiet in the late afternoon it seems like a perfect slice of paradise. Meals are available ($7 breakfast, $10 lunch or dinner). There's a tiny shop in the village, but if you're planning to cook, bring your own supplies.

OFFSHORE ISLANDS

Qamea, Laucala and Matagi are a group of islands just east of Thurston Point, across the Tasman Strait from northeastern Taveuni. All three of the islands have lovely, white-sand beaches.

MATAGI

Tiny, horseshoe-shaped Matagi (1 sq km), formed by a submerged volcanic crater, is 10km off Taveuni's coast and just north of Qamea. Its steep rainforest sides rise to 130m. The bay faces north to open sea and there is a fringing reef on the southwest side of the island.

The *bure* at **Matangi Island Resort** (☎ 888 0260; www.matangiisland.com; d standard island bure US$525, d beachfront bure US$690, d treehouses US$900, 2-bed villas US$1050; 💻 🍽) are huge, vaulted-ceilinged affairs with massive beds, tons of windows to let in the light and separate seating areas. Each *bure* is surrounded by a neat tropical garden. It's romance run amok in the 'treehouses', perched 5m up in the tree canopy with wraparound decks, views to the beach, outdoor Jacuzzis, lanterns aplenty and daybeds. The pretty restaurant, where all meals are taken, looks over Qamea and out to the ocean. Rates include all meals, most activities and transfers to and from Taveuni. Matangi boasts 30 dive spots within 10 to 30 minutes of the island; a two-tank dive is $225 (including gear) at the

TAVEUNI

resort's dive shop. The resort is not suitable for children under the age of 12.

QAMEA

The closest of the three islands to Taveuni is Qamea (34 sq km), only 2.5km east of Thurston Point. Its coastline is riddled with deep bays and lined with white-sand beaches; the interior is fertile, green and rich in bird life. The island is also notable for the *lairo* (annual migration of land crabs). For a few days from late November to early December, at the start of their breeding season, masses of crabs move from the mudflats towards the sea.

The magnificently thatched *bure* at **Qamea Resort & Spa** (☎ 888 0220; www.qamea.com; d/tr bure $1250/1540, d premium villas $1910; ✶ ✿) lie on a long stretch of beautiful, white-sand beach. Refurbished in 2007, the huge, air-conditioned *bure* are decorated with Fijian art, and some have plunge pools, spa baths or rock showers. Rates include meals and transfers to and from Taveuni; children under 16 are not accepted

unless you book the entire resort! There is excellent snorkelling just offshore as well as windsurfing, sailing, outrigger canoeing, nature walks, village visits and fishing trips. There's a dive shop where two-tank dives/PADI Open Water Courses cost $260/950, including gear.

Maqai Resort & Surf (☎ 990 7900; www.maqai.com; sites per person $20, dm $30, s/d/tr bure $60/80/100) is a new surf resort on a beautiful stretch of beach overlooking three surf breaks. Accommodation is basic – in safari tents and a dorm. There's a boat to take you out to the breaks, beach volleyball, *lovo* and beach barbecues.

LAUCALA

Just 500m east across the strait from Qamea, 30-sq-km Laucala was once owned by the estate of the late US millionaire Malcolm Forbes. The resort was purchased by Red Bull billionaire Dietrich Mateschitz in 2003. At the time of writing the finishing touches were being put on a seven-star luxury resort, although details were being kept under wraps.

Kadavu Group

Sitting sleepily 100km south of Viti Levu, the ruggedly beautiful Kadavu Group offers a slice of wild and untamed Fiji, with few visitors and even fewer amenities. There is one small town here and next-to-no roads. As your plane from the main island touches down on a tiny airstrip surrounded by luminescent sea, volcanic peaks and intense forest, you'll feel as if you're embarking upon something special. Your flight will likely be followed by a long, and sometimes bumpy, boat ride to your resort of choice, but the feeling of seclusion and the stunning, almost-prehistoric landscape make it more than worthwhile.

Snaking its way around the islands, the Great Astrolabe Reef is justifiably renowned in diving circles. People come from all over the world to sample its underwater delights. Handsome stretches of long, sandy beach and sheltered coves ring the islands' perimeters. In the interior you'll find all manner of bird life, including the colourful Kadavu musk parrot, thriving in an impossibly green rainforest that's ripe for scrambling up hillsides, splashing about under waterfalls and kayaking through mangroves.

The group is made up of several islands including Kadavu (the country's fourth-largest island), Ono, Galoa and Yaukuve Levu. Kadavu is irregular in shape and is almost split into three by deep bays along its length. At its southern tip sits its highest peak, the impressive, 838m-high Nabukelevu (Mt Washington).

There are some 70 villages in the Kadavu Group, all relying largely on subsistence agriculture and the export, to the main island, of local produce. Each village has its own fishing grounds, which resorts negotiate use of for diving, surfing or fishing.

HIGHLIGHTS

- Experience underwater nirvana at the **Great Astrolabe Reef** (p213)
- Grab a guide and head into the interior to look for Kadavu's indigenous **bird life** (p214)
- **Hike** (p213) into the rainforest for a swim in one of the Kadavu Group's many waterfalls or spend an afternoon with the locals in one of Kadavu's many villages, such as **Tiliva** (p213)
- Soak up island paradise at a **top-end lodge** (p215) on Kadavu
- Unleash your inner surfer dude and sample the breaks at **Cape Washington** (p213)
- Dive with the manta rays at **Buliya** (p213)
- **Kayak** (p213) around beautiful Ono island's secluded bays

- POPULATION: 12,000
- AREA: 411 SQ KM

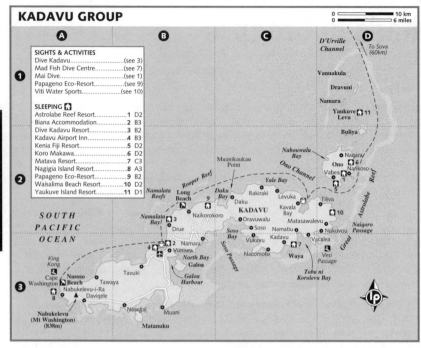

KADAVU GROUP

SIGHTS & ACTIVITIES
Dive Kadavu...................(see 3)
Mad Fish Dive Centre..............(see 7)
Mai Dive.....................(see 1)
Papageno Eco-Resort...............(see 9)
Viti Water Sports..................(see 10)

SLEEPING
Astrolabe Reef Resort............1 D2
Biana Accommodation............2 B3
Dive Kadavu Resort.............3 B2
Kadavu Airport Inn.............4 B3
Kenia Fiji Resort............5 D2
Koro Makawa...............6 D2
Matava Resort............7 C3
Nagigia Island Resort.........8 A3
Papageno Eco-Resort..........9 B2
Waisalima Beach Resort......10 D2
Yaukuve Island Resort.......11 D1

ORIENTATION

Most visitors will stay on Kadavu, where you'll find the bulk of the accommodation and the group's only town, petite Vunisea. There's not much to interest tourists here but it's the Group's administrative centre, and is where you'll find the police station, post office and hospital (all on the top of the hill), and airstrip. It is on an isthmus with Namalata Bay to the west and North Bay to the east.

Other islands in the Kadavu Group are Ono, Buliya, Yaukuve Levu, Namara, Dravuni and Vanuakula. Of these, Ono and Yaukuve Levu are the only islands set up to receive tourists.

INFORMATION
Emergency & Medical Services

Hospital (☎ 333 6008) Opened in 1996 with the help of Australian aid, Vunisea's hospital only has limited services. For more serious ailments, you're better off heading back to Viti Levu. Divers suffering from the bends can be transferred to the Fiji Recompression Chamber Facility (see p117) in Suva by Medivac helicopter service.
Police (☎ 333 6007)

Money

Some resorts, especially the more upmarket ones, accept credit cards but check before you fly out. You'll more than likely need cash for the budget resorts. You can't change foreign currency in Vunisea and there's no ATM so bring however much money you'll need.

Post & Telephone

The **Vunisea post and telephone office** (◷ 8am-3pm Mon-Fri) is on top of the hill, a short walk from the airstrip. It also sells some groceries, clothes and stationery. Kavala Bay, at the northeastern end of the island, also has a post office.

DANGERS & ANNOYANCES

The ferry trip to Kadavu from Suva can be rough and the timetable is erratic. It's better to fly instead. The small boats used by budget resorts for transfers to/from the airstrip sometimes don't have covers, life jackets or radios. The Group often falls prey to rough weather and the southeast coast in particular is often assaulted by wind and rain. The weather can be especially rough from April to August.

ACTIVITIES

The Kadavu Group's rich landscape and underwater seascapes make it a perfect destination for nature lovers, divers, hikers and birdwatchers.

Hiking

Kadavu's hilly rainforest interior is sprinkled with waterfalls and hiking trails. There are good treks into the interior from several of the resorts. Resort staff will act as guides for the tougher treks. For shorter journeys you can set off on your own, but be sure to ask locals beforehand if a track is safe. The strip of coast between Waisalima Beach Resort (p214) and Tiliva village makes for a scenic walk at low tide. The isolated villagers are very traditional, so when visiting a village ask to speak to the *turaga-ni-koro* (hereditary chief) first, remove your hat and don't carry things on your shoulders. See the boxed text, p42, for more information on village etiquette.

Diving & Snorkelling

The famous **Great Astrolabe Reef**, which is a major pull for most visitors to Kadavu, hugs the eastern side of the Group, and is bisected by the Naiqoro Passage. It's home to brilliantly coloured soft and hard corals, a fantastic assortment of tunnels, caverns and canyons, and a variety of marine life, including plenty of reef sharks and graceful manta rays. Particularly recommended are Broken Stone, Split Rock and, for novice divers, Yellow Wall. The weather often dictates which sites are suitable to dive, and visibility can range from 15m to 70m. Most of the resorts will also take snorkellers out to the reef.

Buliya island, just north of Ono, is a great manta dive site, where you're pretty much guaranteed an amazing encounter with the rays. Many of the resorts in the area also arrange trips to Buliya to snorkel with the manta rays.

For more information on Kadavu's diving sites, see p72. The following operators have excellent equipment and instructors.

Mad Fish Dive Centre (☎ 333 6222) at the Matava Resort (p214) offers dives all over the reef system, including fantastic manta ray, cave and shark dives. Two-tank dives/PADI Open Water Courses cost $200/610 including equipment. It strongly supports reef conservation and environmentally friendly diving practices.

Papageno Eco-Resort (☎ 603 0466) has knowledgable instructors who will take you to the best sites, taking into account weather conditions and what you want to see. It's also within easy reach of the tanker wreck *Pacific Voyager*. A two-tank dive/PADI Open Water Course costs $160/620 including equipment. It uses fixed moorings for its dives and encourages tourists to help protect the reefs.

Dive Kadavu (☎ 368 3502; www.divekadavu.com) has fast boats with up to four dives per day. A favourite haunt is Namalata Reefs, which is about 5km off the west coast of the island and more sheltered from the prevailing winds than the Great Astrolabe Reef. Expect to pay $150/650 for a two-tank dive/PADI Open Water Course including equipment. This operation, which is based at the Dive Kadavu Resort (p215), was the first dive resort on the island to use fixed moorings.

Mai Dive (☎ 603 0842) is a new operation serving the Astrolabe Reef Resort (p215) and other resorts on Ono island. A two-tank dive/PADI Open Water Course including equipment costs $180/580.

Viti Water Sports (☎ 331 7281), based at Waisalima Beach Resort (p214), is a well-equipped operation with excellent instructors. It charges $185/650 for a two-tank dive/PADI Open Water Course, with equipment.

Fishing

Many of Kadavu's resorts offer game and sport fishing and will take you out beyond the reef to look for yellow fin tuna, *mahi-mahi* and *walu* (butter fish). You may be able to take some of your catch home for dinner.

Surfing

The best surfing in Kadavu is found around **Cape Washington**, at the southernmost end of Kadavu. It gets plenty of swell activity year-round, including the excellent King Kong Lefts, off Nagigia island. **Vesi Passage**, near Matava Resort, also has powerful surf, but the waves often get blown out.

Keen surfers should head for Nagigia Island Resort at Cape Washington, which has daily boats heading out to the surf as well as several private breaks suitable for beginners.

Sea Kayaking

Organised kayaking trips take place from May to September. **Tamarillo Sea Kayaking** (☎ in New Zealand 04-239 9885; www.tamarillo.co.nz/fiji) offers

KADAVU GROUP

kayak tours, which are interesting and well-organised, around Kadavu. The seven-day tours cost about $2400 per person. All tours include meals and accommodation in budget resorts as well as a villagestay. It also offers a nine-day Kadavu extreme expedition that aims to completely circumnavigate Kadavu island, and a seven-day family-friendly expedition.

All of the resorts have two-person ocean kayaks for hire.

Birdwatching
The lush rainforests, especially on Kadavu's eastern side, are home to a wide variety of bird life, including the indigenous Kadavu honeyeater, Kadavu fantail, velvet fruit dove and the colourful Kadavu musk parrot. Most of the resorts will be able to arrange a guide.

Yachting
Whilst there are no facilities aimed directly at yachties, Kadavu has several sheltered bays that are suitable for putting down anchor, including Daku Bay near Papageno Eco-Resort, Toba ni Korolevu Bay near Kadavu village, and Nabouwalu Bay on Ono island. Yachties are usually welcome to have a meal or a drink, get laundry done or arrange a dive course at a nearby resort. **Fiji Safari** (☎ 921 1403; www.fijisafari.net) offers yacht charters around Kadavu on a 36ft Jeaneau. Yacht charters can also be arranged through Matava Resort (right).

SLEEPING
Take into account the time and cost of transfers when choosing your accommodation. In Kadavu most of the places to stay are a fair way from the airport, and the only way to get there is by boat.

Kadavu
BUDGET & MIDRANGE
Waisalima Beach Resort (☎ 331 7281; www.waisalimafiji.com; sites/dm per person $10/25, s/d with bathroom per person $100/150, s & d without bathroom per person $75) A quintessential laid-back backpacker's beach fantasy, Waisalima is all about simple pleasures. The thatched *bure* are far from glamorous but have solar-powered lighting, comfy beds and hot showers. Hammocks are strewn along a long stretch of beach and there's a shady, well-stocked beach bar and great views over to Ono island. The food (meal plan per adult/child is an additional $50/25 per day) is

good and includes plenty of fresh fruit, home-baked pastries, fresh fish, and vegetables and herbs from the garden. When relaxing on the beach gets old you can visit a waterfall ($40 per person), use kayaks, visit the local village or try a barbecue booze cruise ($60). Return boat transfers from Vunisea airstrip cost $100 per adult, $50 per child. There's also a dive shop, Viti Water Sports (p213), here.

Matava Resort (☎ 333 6222; www.matava.com; d with/without bathroom per person $220/120; ✗) Matava wins glowing reviews from travellers for its well-considered mix of budget and midrange accommodation, friendly vibe and enthusiastic hosts who know all the best diving spots. Rustic, airy, thatched-and-timber *bure,* framed by wide decks looking out to sea, clamber up the neat hillside grounds. The furnishings are simple but comfortable. For that extra bit of luxury you could opt for a honeymoon *bure,* which has bigger beds, better furnishings and even-more-impressive views. The resort runs on solar power, has a large organic garden and employs strict recycling policies. Meals, using vegetables and herbs from the organic garden, are eaten communally in the big restaurant-bar *bure,* which is beautifully lit by lanterns in the evening.

The resort doesn't have a sunbather-friendly strip of beach, but there are suitable spots a short kayak away and there is plenty of space to lounge in the grassy grounds. A reef links Matava to Waya, a picturesque offshore island, which makes for a great snorkelling or kayaking trip. Aside from diving (see p213), you can arrange hiking trips, village and waterfall visits, game fishing or a meeting with the local medicine man. Boat transfers from Vunisea airstrip cost $50 per person one way and take around an hour. Budget travellers can opt to share a *bure* with other single travellers for $30 a night and buy their meals separately. There's no formal babysitting service but a local sitter can easily be arranged.

Staying in Vunisea really defeats the purpose of coming to Kadavu but if you get stuck here, **Biana Accommodation** (☎ 333 6010; s/d $45/65), about 2km north of the airport, near the wharf, has basic rooms with mosquito nets. Rates include breakfast; lunch or dinner is $5. There's a budget lodge called the **Kadavu Airport Inn** (dm $25) right outside the airport gates, with a couple of dorms and *bure.* It was deserted at the time of writing but its operators hoped to reopen it in the future.

TOP END

Nagigia Island Resort (☎ 603 0454; www.fijisurf.com; dm/s/d/tr per person from $115/263/206/160; ✗) This place had lost its way for a while, with guests complaining of poor upkeep and service, but under new management things are looking up. The outstanding setting is a good start. Nagigia's home is a remote and staggeringly photogenic island on the far western side of the island group, near Cape Washington (see p213). *Bure* and dorms have dramatic reef, surf and mountain views, and hang so close to the water they're practically dipping their toes into the sea. There's no beach to speak off but there are sufficient spots for sunbathing and lots of little wooden platforms with steps leading into the water. Nagigia is known as a surfers' resort and has a choice of five breaks that produce ridable waves year-round, with bigger swells during midyear. For those who are not surfboard savvy there's fabulous snorkelling in the lagoon, village visits, windsurfing, kite surfing and plenty of great walks, including one to Cape Washington lighthouse for a swim in the Nasoso Beach caves. The resort can also arrange trips with Dive Kadavu (p213).

Papageno Eco-Resort (☎ 603 0466; www.papagenoecoresort.com; s/d from $300/420; ✗) Low-key Papageno is the stuff of island fantasies. Large, dark-wood *bure,* with decks looking out to sea, are spread sparingly (to ensure plenty of privacy) around manicured tropical gardens. Towards the back of the resort are four connected 'garden rooms', which share a single verandah, are surrounded by greenery and overlook a small stream. All rooms are decked out with local artwork and have bigger-than-average bathrooms. The welcoming central lodge has a small bar, some comfy chairs and an excellent selection of books. The resort prides itself on its ecocredentials, using solar and microhydro energy to complement its generator, composting organic waste on site, and investing heavily in environmental-development and local community projects. The food is excellent and plentiful, and breakfasts alone – gargantuan feasts including eggs from the resort's own hens, homemade pastries, pancakes, sausage, fresh fruit, juices, porridge and an array of cereals – could set you up for the day. *Kava* (a mildly narcotic, muddy and oddtasting drink made from the aromatic roots of the Polynesian pepper shrub) ceremonies, sea kayaking and hiking are all free. Snorkelling, fishing and surfing are extra. There are family rooms here and a babysitting service is available ($25 daily, $3 an hour).

Dive Kadavu Resort (☎ 368 3502; www.divekadavu.com; s/d/tr/f $320/560/780/980; ✗) This appealing resort has unfussy *bure* with comfortable beds, verandahs, hot water and tidy bathrooms. Most of the visitors are here on dive packages (mostly from the US), but it's a nice place to relax for a few days even if you don't dive. Sheltered from the prevailing southeasterly winds, it boasts an excellent beach where the snorkelling and swimming is wonderful, regardless of the tide. There's also a social, oceanfront bar that hosts regular *lovo* (feast cooked in a pit oven), barbecue and curry nights. The staff is friendly and efficient, and rates include meals and airport transfers. You can also arrange birdwatching tours and village visits.

Meal plans are an additional $60 per person. Return boat transfers from Vunisea airstrip are $70 per person.

Ono

Kenia Fiji Resort (☎ 360 7951; www.keniafijiresort.com; sites per person $10, dm/d from per person $25/60) The only budget resort on Ono island is run by a very friendly Senegalese-Fijian couple and their family. It features basic thatched *bure* with shared facilities and a basic dining *bure* and bar with views out over the water. A meal package (three meals) is $45. The attraction here is the spectacular beachfront – one of the best in the Kadavu Group. The sea is incredibly vibrant and the beach is wide and curved, with views over to the breaks of the Great Astrolabe Reef. You can take hikes into the interior and clamber over rocks to jump into a deep, bright-blue pool. There's no dive outfit here but dives can be arranged through Mai Dive at neighbouring Astrolabe Reef Resort. There are plans to upgrade the *bure* and the facilities.

Astrolabe Reef Resort (☎ 603 0842; www.maidive.com; sites per person incl meals $75, s/d incl meals $180/270) Pretty, pale-green, wooden bungalows line the beach at this new resort run by a young Australian family. All have wooden verandahs and are right by the water so you can gaze out at the view whilst lying in bed. Showers at the back of each *bure* are open to the elements so you can wash under the stars. Even the loos have ocean vistas. Return airport transfers are

THE BATTLE OF THE SHARK & OCTOPUS GODS

Dakuwaqa, the Shark God, once cruised the Fiji islands challenging other reef guardians. On hearing rumours of a rival monster in Kadavu waters, he sped down to the island to prove his superior strength. Adopting his usual battle strategy he charged at the giant octopus with his mouth wide open and sharp teeth prepared. The octopus, however, anchored itself to the coral reef and swiftly clasped the shark in a death lock. In return for mercy the octopus demanded that the people of Kadavu be forever protected from shark attack. In Kadavu the people now fish without fear and regard the shark as their protector. Most won't eat shark or octopus out of respect for their gods.

$140 per adult. Children under 16 stay free if with two or more adults, otherwise they pay $60. Accommodation is cheaper if you stay more than three nights.

Koro Makawa (☎ 603 0782; www.koromakawa.com .fj; per person per night $450) A drop-dead luxurious family pad with two bedrooms, a wraparound deck, a plunge pool and private sea views. If you're not content with enjoying the good life on your private beach, your private staff can arrange diving, snorkelling, secluded beach picnics and nature walks, and they can provide a nanny service, amongst other things. You can snorkel with manta rays five minutes away. All activities except game fishing are included.

Yaukuve Levu

This beautiful, reef-fringed volcanic island was set to see its first luxury resort in mid-2009. **Yaukuve Island Resort** (☎ 327 0011; www.yaukuve .com) looks very promising. Swish *bure* have living rooms, plasma TVs, sunken baths and rain showers, and there's a gym, spa, screening room, and a couple of good restaurants on the island.

EATING

The airport has a kiosk selling snacks, drinks and rotis. There are small grocery stores in Vunisea and Kavala Bay, and a regular weekday market in Vunisea. Most of the resorts are very remote, so even if all your meals are provided it may be an idea to take along snacks, especially to the budget resorts.

GETTING THERE & AWAY
Air

Air Fiji (☎ 331 3666; suvasales@airfiji.com.fj) has daily return flights from Suva to Kadavu ($220, 30 minutes). **Pacific Sun** (☎ 672 0888; www.pacificsun .com.fj) has daily flights to Kadavu from Nadi ($220 return, 45 minutes). It is advisable to check timetables and confirm flights the day before departure.

Transfers to Yaukuve Levu take 45 minutes from Nadi by private seaplane or helicopter, which can be organised through your resort.

Ideally, have your accommodation and transfers booked in advance, otherwise you could be stranded in Vunisea.

Boat

Venu Shipping (Map p116; ☎ in Suva 339 5000, 330 7349; Rona St, Walu Bay, Suva) operates a Suva–Kadavu ferry, MV *Sinu-i-Wasa*, from $55 per person one way. This service is mostly for cargo and local use, and it is irregular and unreliable. It visits Kavala Bay (handy for the resorts on northern Kadavu and Ono island), Vunisea and Nabukelevu-i-Ra. The trip can be bearable or terrible, depending on the weather you strike. The ferry sails on Tuesday nights.

GETTING AROUND

Kadavu's few roads are restricted to the Vunisea area, except for one rough, unsealed road to Nabukelevu-i-Ra around the southern end of Kadavu. It's easy to walk around Vunisea or hitch a ride. Small boats are the island group's principal mode of transport. Each resort has its own boat and will pick up guests from Vunisea airstrip. Make sure you make arrangements in advance. Boat trips are expensive due to fuel costs and mark-ups. In rough weather it can be a wet and bone-crunching trip to the more remote resorts.

To get to Ono island you'll have to fly to Vunisea on Kadavu, where you'll be picked up by your resort. Transfers take anything from one to two hours.

Lau & Moala Groups

Fiji's final frontier, the Lau islands are strewn across the southwest corner of Fiji's vast archipelago like a rash of green spots on the skin of the Pacific. Few visit here, but those who do report countless bays; deserted, reef-rimmed atolls; and sparsely populated islands with hilly interiors. For the hardened and patiently adventurous, Lau and Moala offer the opportunity to create your own trail and go where few outsiders have been.

The 57 isles of Lau are subdivided into northern and southern Lau and it is said that on the southern-most island of Ono-i-Lau you can see Tonga on a clear day. This proximity to its Pacific neighbour has had a profound influence on the group's cultural development. The southeast trade winds made it easy for Tongan warlords to reach Fiji and with them came Tongan language, food, decoration and architecture. The winds that blew them so favourably over were less inclined to blow them back and Lau islanders still bear the names and physical traits of their Tongan ancestors.

Vanua Balavu and Lakeba are the only two of the 30 or so inhabited islands that see a slow dribble of visitors. Both have basic amenities, weekly flights and a simple guesthouse.

Although much closer to the mainland, the Moala Group is even further removed from the reaches of tourists and has no facilities whatsoever. To visit islands as remote as these requires a lot of luck and an invitation.

There is little opportunity to get ahead on these islands (beyond copra farming) and urban drift has resulted in the greater part of the population now living on Fiji's mainland.

LAU & MOALA GROUPS

HIGHLIGHTS

- Weigh anchor in a kayak, dinghy or yacht in the spectacular **Bay of Islands** (p219)
- Rub shoulders with the locals on **Vanua Balavu** (p219), home to a unique fusion of Tongan and Fijian cultures
- Charter a local's boat, grab some **snorkelling** (p218) gear and head to the nearest reef that takes your fancy
- Sidestep the 'roaches and battle the bats to marvel at the limestone walls of **Oso Nabukete** (p221) and **Vale Ni Bose** (p219)

Bay of Islands ★
★ Vale Ni Bose
★ Vanua Balavu

Oso
Nabukete
★

- POPULATION: 11,500
- AREA: 114,000 SQ KM

History

Lau first came into contact with Europeans in 1800 when the American schooner *Argo* was wrecked on Bukatatanoa Reef east of Lakeba. Fijians from Oneata island looted the wreck for muskets and gunpowder, and the sailors lived with the islanders until they were killed in disputes.

The greatest influence, though, came from Lau's eastern Pacific neighbour, and by the mid-19th century the whole region was dominated by Tonga. In 1847, Tongan nobleman Enele Ma'afu, cousin of King Taufa'ahau of Tonga, led an armada of war canoes to Vanua Balavu to investigate the killing of a preacher. Six years later the king appointed Ma'afu governor of the Tongans in Fiji. After the later murder of 17 Wesleyans, Ma'afu took Vanua Balavu by force and subjugated its inhabitants. He then established Sawana village near Lomaloma as his base. The Tongans assisted in local Fijian wars in return for protection by Chief Cakobau of Bau. By 1855 Ma'afu had become a powerful force in the region and influential throughout much of Fiji. He was one of the signatories to the Deed of Cession to Britain and became officially recognised as Roko Tui Lau (Protector of the Tongans of Vanua Balavu). After his death in 1881, Tongan power weakened, the title passed to the Tui Nayau (Traditional Fijian Chief of Lau) and many Tongans returned to their home country.

The chiefs of the Lau Group have always been surprisingly influential; those with the title Tui Nayau have included the late Ratu Sukuna and Ratu Mara.

Information

There is little infrastructure for locals, let alone for travellers, but you will find a couple of general stores and schools in Lomaloma and on Lakeba. Currently there is only spotty Vodafone mobile coverage on Vanua Balavu. There is the **Lomaloma post office** (☎ 889 5000) on Vanua Balavu, and the **Tubou post office** (☎ 882 3001) on Lakeba. Tubou also has a **police station** (☎ 882 3043), telephone exchange and **hospital** (☎ 882 3153).

Activities & Tours

The biggest draw is the isolation of the islands; a chance to interact with local communities and experience firsthand a way of life seldom seen by outsiders. **Hiking** is the most accessible

activity and easily arranged, and as long as you follow polite etiquette (see the boxed text, p42) you will be well received.

Lau Group is still relatively unexplored in terms of **diving**. The Fijian Government protects the waters, and commercial fishing is prohibited in the area. Most serious divers arrive on independent yachts or live-aboard charters.

In the absence of diving companies, **snorkelling** is the next best way to experience the sizeable reefs and their marine life. Guesthouses should be able to arrange for local boats to run you out to the reefs and they may even have snorkelling gear, but it's a long way to come if they haven't.

Sailing around the Lau Group requires a special permit, issued in Suva by the **Lau Provincial Council** (Map p118; ☎ 330 5368, 331 0230; Yatu Lau Arcade), opposite Suva's main bus station. Boats arriving from Tonga must proceed directly to Suva to get this rather elusive permit (see p239) and clear customs and immigration. You can read an account of how one captain got his on his website http://starsonthesea.com/laugp.htm.

Earth River (☎ in the USA 1800-643-2784, 845-626-2665; www.earthriver.com) is an adventure company offering 10-day kayaking expeditions that encompass Pacific Harbour, Beqa and four days of kayaking around Vanua Balavu. There are only about one or two trips a year, but they are a fantastic opportunity to snorkel and swim in areas that would be difficult for independent travellers to get to. Accommodation on Viti Levu is in hotels, but around Vanua Balavu it's village stays and beach camping. Rates (US$2900 per person) include all meals and accommodation.

Getting There & Away

Air Fiji (☎ 347 8077; www.airfiji.com.fj) flies between Suva and Vanua Balavu on Fridays ($170 one way, 1½ hours), Lakeba on Mondays ($171, 1½ hours) and Moala on Tuesdays ($159, 45 minutes).

If you have plenty of time and a masochistic streak, you can also reach the Lau and Moala Groups by cargo/passenger boats

Saliabasaga Shipping (Map p116; ☎ 331 7484), which operates from the dark-green shipping container on Muaiwalu Wharf, Suva, has slow monthly trips from Suva to the Lau and Moala Groups, including Vanua Balavu, Lakeba, Moala, Matuke and Totoya. Expect

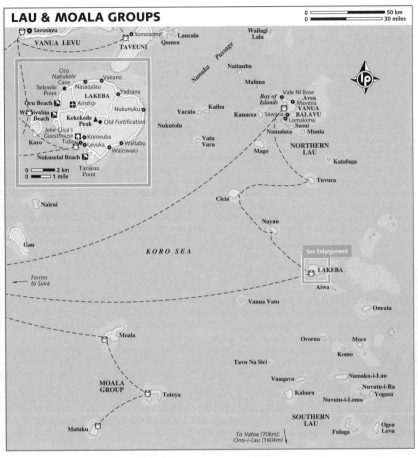

LAU & MOALA GROUPS

LAU & MOALA GROUPS

to spend about a week on board to travel to the far reaches of the southern Lau Group. One-way fares, including meals, start at $100. For more detail on Lau see p248, and on Moala, p248.

LAU GROUP

VANUA BALAVU

Vanua Balavu, 355km east of Nadi, about halfway to Tonga, is Northern Lau's largest island, and has a grass airstrip.

Arguably also the most scenic of Lau's islands, it is enigmatic in shape and substance. Averaging about 2km wide, it resides with eight other smaller islands inside a barrier reef. The islands curl their way around the surrounding water like an inverted 'S', creating sheltered bays and corridors of calm sea. The interior of Vanua Balavu is scattered with rugged hills and pristine, sandy beaches ring the group's perimeter. The celebrated **Bay of Islands**, also known as Qilaqila, sits in the northwest pocket and is a spectacular site for diving, kayaking and swimming. It's also a lovely place for yachties to draw anchor and a known hurricane shelter. Within the rugged limestone hills is **Vale Ni Bose** (literally the Meeting House of the Gods), a gaping cave with limestone walls and a pool of crystalline water. On clear days the hazy green shape of Taveuni is visible across a 115km stretch of open sea.

KNOW BEFORE YOU GO

■ The Lau and Moala islands are Fiji's wild frontier. There are no hotels, bars, restaurants, dive shops, banks or tourist shops. Only two islands, Vanua Balavu and Lakeba, have guesthouses. Neither accepts credit cards.

■ Meals will be mostly whatever the locals can catch or grow. Expect fresh seafood of various kinds and local fruits and (often starchy) vegetables.

■ Book flights well in advance and confirm your reservation. Flights are infrequent, sometimes rescheduled and generally full. If it rains and the grass on the landing strip is dangerously slippery, the plane will return to Suva.

■ Boats can run weeks behind their published timetables and if they do, the local shops will run out of goods. BYO snacks.

Vanua Balavu's largest village is **Lomaloma** on the southeast coast. In the mid-19th century Tonga conquered the island, and the village of Sawana was built next to Lomaloma. Fifth-generation Tongan descendants still live in **Sawana**, and the houses with rounded ends show the influence of Tongan architecture.

At one time ships trading in the Pacific regularly visited Lomaloma and it had the first port in Fiji. In its heyday, Lomaloma had many hotels and shops, as well as Fiji's first botanical gardens, though little remains of its past grandeur. The Fijian inhabitants of Vanua Balavu trace their ancestry to Tailevu (southeastern Viti Levu) and Cakaudrove (eastern Vanua Levu and Taveuni).

One week after the full moon in November, the people of Vanua Balavu witness the **annual rising of the balolo** (tiny green and brown sea worms). At sunrise the Susui villagers collect worms by the thousands. The catch is first soaked in fresh water, then packed into baskets and cooked overnight in a *lovo* (pit oven). The fishy-tasting baked worms are considered a delicacy.

Sleeping

Now that Nawanawa Estate has closed, there is only one place to stay on Vanua Balavu.

Moana's Guesthouse (☎ 822 1148, 820 1357; www .moanasguesthouses.com; r per person incl meals $75, children

under 12yr $50; ✕ 💻) covers all the basics with beach *bure* and guesthouse options. The three simple *bure* are a 1km walk from Sawana village and mere metres from a tidal beach. The *bure* are simple, thatched affairs with mosquito nets, solar power, private bathrooms and mats laid over concrete floors. Back in Sawana, Tevita and Carolyn Fotofili also offer homestay-style accommodation in a Tongan-style cottage that can accommodate two couples or a family, in two bedrooms sharing a communal lounge. Moana's can arrange boat, snorkelling and fishing trips and collects travellers from the airstrip for $40 return. There is internet but it's slow and not always working.

OTHER NORTHERN LAU ISLANDS

Mago island made headlines in 2005 when Hollywood actor Mel Gibson bought the former copra estate for nearly US$15 million from a Japanese hotel chain, making it one of the largest privately owned islands in the world. The Yavusa Vuaniivi clan, who claimed their ancestors were cheated by 19th-century British settlers who allegedly gave the islanders 2000 coconut plants in return for Mago, challenged the sale's validity.

Meanwhile, over on **Naitauba** island, controversial cult leader and self-declared divine avatar, Adi Da Samraj, holds spiritual retreats for members of the cult group, The Fellowship of Adidam.

Kaibu is another privately owned island in the northern Lau Group, 55km west of Vanua

FATAL ATTRACTION

There is a freshwater lake near the village of Mavana, on the northeast corner of Vanua Balavu, which is considered sacred. The people of Mavana gather here annually for a fun ceremony authorised by their traditional priest. Naked except for a leaf skirt, they jump around in the lake to stir up the muddy waters. This provokes the large fish known as *yawa* (a type of mullet usually only found in the sea) to spring into the air. It is believed that the male fish are attracted to the female villagers and thus easily trapped in the nets. Legend has it that the fish were dropped into the lake by a Tongan princess while flying over the island on her way to visit her lover on Taveuni.

Balavu. It has a grass airstrip, shares a fringing reef with the larger island of Yacata and is home to the now defunct, but previously exclusive, Kaimbu Island Resort. It has been in a state of renovation and sale for several years and conflicting rumours of its imminent operation or demise abound.

Air Fiji also flies to **Cicia**, a 34-sq-km dot in the Pacific southwest of Vanua Balavu, every Thursday ($162 one way) to service the five small villages that are evenly spaced around its perimeter. There is no place to stay on the coconut-covered Cicia.

LAKEBA

Lakeba, being the hereditary seat of the Tui Nayau (Chief of Lau), is the most important island in southern Lau. It is a roughly circular volcanic island, approximately 9km in diameter, with a small peninsula at its southern end. Its 54-sq-km area is home to about 2000 people. In days of yore the islanders lived in an interior hilltop fort, far from marauding neighbours. Today they live in the eight coastal villages that are connected by a road that circles the island. To the east is a wide **lagoon** enclosed by a barrier reef.

Yams, coconuts and *kumala* (sweet potatoes) grow well along the fertile coast and the interior is covered with grasslands, pandanus and pine plantations.

Lakeba was historically a meeting place for Fijians and Tongans; it was also the place where Christian missionaries first entered Fiji via Tonga and Tahiti. Two missionaries, Cross and Cargill, developed a system for written Fijian here and produced the first book in that language. Lakeba was frequently visited by Europeans before the trading settlement was established at Levuka in the Lomaivitis.

The **provincial office** (☎ 882 3164) for the Lau Group is in **Tubou** at the southern end

of Lakeba. There is also a guesthouse, post office, police station and hospital here, and some of the nearby **beaches** are good for snorkelling and swimming. For transport you can utilise the carriers and buses that circle the island. Enele Ma'afu, the once-powerful Tongan chief, is buried here, as is Ratu Sir Lala Sukuna, formerly an influential Tui Lau who established the Native Lands Trust Board in 1940.

The island has caves worth visiting, especially **Oso Nabukete**, which translates as 'too narrow for pregnant women'. Adorned with huge pillars of limestone stalactites and inhabited by bats, it's an awesome example of nature's might. Take some *kava* (mildly narcotic, muddy and odd-tasting drink made from the aromatic roots of the Polynesian pepper shrub) as a *sevusevu* (gift) to Nasaqalau village, where you can arrange a guide (bring your own torch). There is also an **old fortification** in the middle of the island at Kekekede Peak where the people retreated to during times of war.

Small **Jeke Qica's Guesthouse** (☎ 820 3177; r per person incl meals $65) in Tubou offers two rooms with private bathrooms inside 'Jack's house'. Meals are simple but filling and Jack can provide interesting commentary on the area's culture and history.

OTHER SOUTHERN LAU ISLANDS

There are 16 other southern Lau islands, mostly within a radius of 100km southeast of Lakeba. Vatoa and Ono-i-Lau are more isolated and much further south.

The islanders of southern Lau are well known for their crafts: Moce, Vatoa, Ono-i-Lau and Namuka-i-Lau produce *masi* (bark cloth) and the artisans of Fulaga are excellent woodcarvers. You may be able to purchase crafts from villages on the islands or from handicrafts shops in Suva.

SHARK CALLING

Traditionally, the villagers of Nasaqalau performed a shark-calling ritual in October or November each year. About a month prior to the ceremony, the spot was marked by a post and a flag of *masi* (bark cloth) and a traditional priest ensured no one went near the post or fished in the nearby area. On the designated day the caller, standing neck-high in the water, would chant for up to an hour. A school of sharks, led by a white shark, would be drawn to the place. All of the sharks except the white shark would be killed and eaten by the villagers.

Reports on whether shark calling is still performed here vary from village to village, like a wild rural myth. However, the general consensus seems to be that the ritual has not been enacted in earnest for some 100 years.

MOALA GROUP

The three islands of this Group – Moala, Totoya and Matuku – are geographically removed from Lau, but administered as part of the Eastern Division. They are about halfway between Kadavu and the southern Lau Group. The islands are the eroded tops of previously submerged volcanic cones that have lifted more than 3km to the sea surface. Totoya's horseshoe shape is the result of a sunken volcano crater forming a land-locked lagoon. The volcano was active 4.9 million years ago. Matuku has rich volcanic soil, steep wooded peaks and a submerged crater on its western side. However, this beautiful island is generally inaccessible to visitors. Each of the islands has villages.

MOALA

Moala (65 sq km) is the largest and most northerly of the group. It is about 160km from Suva. The island is roughly triangular in shape, with a deeply indented coast. The highest peak reaches 460m and has two small **crater lakes**. It has extremely fertile soil and supports nine villages. The villagers produce copra and bananas, which they send to Suva, a night's sail away. The ancestors of Moala's inhabitants came from Viti Levu.

Moala has no tourist infrastructure and although you don't need to be formally invited as such, your only option for accommodation is with a local family. You will need to organise this with a friend or member of the family before you arrive. You should also ask beforehand what kind of *sevusevu* to take with you.

Rotuma

Far flung and isolated, the tiny volcanic island of Rotuma drifts in the Pacific 460km north-west of Viti Levu. The vast distance between its tiny frame and the mainland is an accident of geography, but the divide that separates is also the schism that nurtures, and it is this isolation that has allowed the Rotumans to develop such an inimitable culture.

Ethnically and linguistically distinct from Fiji, the Rotuman culture more closely resembles that of the Polynesian islands to the east than the Melanesians on the mainland. Strong emphasis on communal sharing and *kainaga* (kinship), combined with a slow pace of life, mean that visitors encounter a close-knit people with an elastic sense of time. And that is how the Rotumans prefer it to remain.

In 1985, wary of Western influence, 85% of Rotumans voted against opening the island up to tourism and while it's perfectly feasible to visit, genuine travellers here are few. Most who do so have been invited or are returning residents visiting 'home' to renew ties with families and friends.

There are more than twice as many Rotumans living abroad than there are left on Rotuma. Most have left to find work and opportunities in Fiji, New Zealand and Australia, and this mass exodus means that young people can seem relatively scarce on this beautiful island outpost.

Physically, Rotuma resembles a whale, with the larger body of land linked to the small tail end to the west by the Motusa isthmus. Like bubbles in a fish's trail the seabird island rookeries of Uea, Hatana and Hofliua follow in Rotuma's wake. Uea is a high, rocky island and the spectacular Hofliua is also known as 'Split Island' because of its unusual rock formation.

ROTUMA

HIGHLIGHTS

- Share a bowl of *kava* and a slice of **Polynesian culture** and **hospitality** (p224)
- Join the dancers traversing from house to house 'asking' those inside to join them on the street and celebrate the summertime festival of **Fara** (p224)
- Stare out at an endless ocean from **Mt Suelhof** (p224), Rotuma's highest peak
- Explore the ancient graves of kings at **Sisilo Hill** (p224)

Mt Suelhof ★

★ Sisilo

- POPULATION: 3000
- AREA: 43 SQ KM

HISTORY

Tongans invaded Rotuma during the 17th century and the Tongan influence is evident to this day in its language and dance. In 1791 Europeans on the HMS *Pandora* stopped here to search for mutineers from the *Bounty* and by the mid-19th century Rotuma had become home to traders, runaway sailors and escaped convicts. Following closely behind came the clergy, in the form of Tongan Wesleyan (in 1842) and Marist Roman Catholic (in 1847) missionaries, although their good intentions did not last – 30 years later the various Christian factions were warring. In response to the unrest, the Rotuman chiefs decided to cede their home to Britain, and Rotuma became joined politically to the Fijian colony in 1881. Today Rotuma relies on subsidies and copra, which is processed at the mill near Savusavu on Vanua Levu.

INFORMATION

The driest and most comfortable months to visit are between July and September, although the best time to visit is during the Fara festival (December to mid-January). There are no banks on Rotuma, but in Ahau there are shops and a **post office** (☎ 889 1003), which also acts as a Western Union agent.

The island's first **internet cafe** (✆ 8am-1pm Mon-Fri) opened in May 2008 in the Post Fiji building in Ahau and an insightful and informative website designed for Rotumans can be found at www.rotuma.net.

SIGHTS & ACTIVITIES

Rotuma's volcanic curves offer excellent hiking and there are spectacular views from **Solroroa Bluff** and **Mt Suelhof** (256m), Rotuma's highest peak. Between Losa and Solroroa Bluff is **Mamfiri**, a volcanic vent that drops around 25m.

Twenty stone tombs were recorded at **Sisilo Hill** in 1824 and this archaeological site is also known as The Graveyard of Kings. The area is largely overgrown but the huge Ki ne he'e ceremonial platform and Tafea Point stone walls remain. With the help of a guide (recommended), you should be able to find the cannon that was used as a headstone for the last man to be interred here. Before visiting Sisilo Hill seek permission from the town elders and during your visit remember that it's a cemetery, not a playground. If you're lucky, you may spot some endemic wildlife including the Rotuman gecko and the red-and-black Rotuman honeyeater.

Rotuma also has some of the loveliest **beaches** in Fiji. The best are at Oinafa, Losa and Vai'oa, west of Solroroa Bluff. There are also some fine surfing areas around the island; locals will be able to point you in the right direction to best exploit the conditions. Between Else'e and Oinafa are two *fuliu* (freshwater springs), which are popular swimming holes.

This beautiful remote island is not just for outdoors addicts though, and one of the most rewarding experiences is simply staying with villagers. An annual festival known as **Fara** begins on 1 December, during which the strong work ethic adopted throughout the year is replaced with six weeks of dancing, parties and general revelry. The festival coincides with Christmas and the emphasis is on hospitality and celebrating friends, family, visitors, life and love. At this time the population increases by around one-third; it's undoubtedly the best time to be on the island.

SLEEPING & EATING

The easiest way for you to stay on Rotuma is to organise a homestay through a Rotuman contact. If you're lucky enough to be invited to the island, discuss with your contact how best to compensate the family during your stay. Failing that, contact the Fiji Visitor Bureau in either Nadi or Suva (see p239) for updated information and their advice. Staff

ROTUMA

0 — 4 km
0 — 2 miles

Uea

Hatana

Solroroa Bluff

Freshwater Springs

Rotuma Air Strip

Else'e

Oinafa

Vai'oa Beach

Maftoa

Ahau (Government Station)

Mt Suelhof (256m) ▲

Sisilo Hill

Maka Bay

Mamfiri

Jasmine's Accommodation

Hofliua

Mojito's

Barfly

Motusa

ROTUMA

Losa

Kalvaka

Anmosega Point

To Suva (450km)

will be able to provide you with the appropriate contact details for the Rotuman Island Council – the body you should approach if you want to visit.

Another option would be to post a message on www.rotuma.net. This online forum is used by Rotumans to keep in contact across the globe and somebody there may be willing to offer a homestay.

Mojito's Barfly (☎ 889 1144; Motusa) has simple rooms with shared facilities but they are generally reserved for government workers. Mojito's will provide meals on request, but you need to give them plenty of notice.

Travellers stay at **Jasmine's Accommodation** (Motusa) from time to time in simple rooms. Phone the **District Office** (☎ 889 1011) to arrange in advance.

GETTING THERE & AWAY
Air
Air Fiji (☎ 331 5055; www.airfiji.com.fj) flies from Suva to Rotuma on Wednesdays for $375 one way and the trip takes two hours. As this is a turnaround flight you have to stay for at least a week and from time to time scheduled departures have been cancelled. Adopt a Rotuman attitude and be flexible.

Boat
Western Shipping (Map p116; ☎ 331 7484; Yellow Shipping Container on Muaiwalu Wharf, Suva) operates

---

THE ORIGIN OF ROTUMA

Rotumans believe their ancestors came from Samoa. The spot where the island presently lies was nothing but open sea until the arrival of Samoan chief, Raho, and his favourite grandchild. The little girl was unhappy in her homeland as her cousin was always annoying her. To escape his torment, she convinced her grandfather to take her away to live on another island. For days and nights their entourage sailed westward in an outrigger canoe, but failed to find land. Eventually the chief threw some Samoan soil overboard. The soil grew to form a beautiful, fertile island, which he named Rotuma. Some of the soil scattered, forming the other small islands. Rotumans commemorate this legend in their dance and song.

---

the *Cagi Mai Ba* to Rotuma (deck/seat/cabin $125/155/190) once a month. The journey takes 36 hours and the conditions on board are very basic.

Yachts occasionally visit the island and to anchor they must obtain permission from the Ahau government station in Maka Bay, on the northern side of the island. Note that yachties can't make Rotuma their first port of call; see p239 for details.

Directory

CONTENTS

Accommodation	226
Activities	228
Business Hours	232
Children	232
Climate Charts	233
Customs Regulations	233
Dangers & Annoyances	233
Discount Cards	234
Embassies & Consulates	234
Festivals & Events	234
Food	235
Gay & Lesbian Travellers	235
Holidays	236
Insurance	236
Internet Access	236
Legal Matters	236
Maps	237
Money	237
Post	237
Shopping	238
Telephone & Fax	238
Time	239
Tourist Information	239
Travellers with Disabilities	239
Visas	239
Volunteering	240
Women Travellers	240
Work	240

ACCOMMODATION

Five-star hotels, B&Bs, hostels, motels, resorts, treehouses, bungalows on the beach, campgrounds and village homestays – there's no shortage of accommodation options in Fiji.

Rates quoted in this book include Fiji's 12.5% value-added tax (VAT) and the 5% hotel turnover tax. Also, they are peak season rates, which tend to be 10% to 20% higher than those for the low season.

Useful accommodation websites:
- www.fiji-backpacking.com
- www.fijibudget.com
- www.4hotels.co.uk/fiji
- www.fiji4less.com
- www.fiji.pacific-resorts.com
- www.travelmaxia.com
- www.wotif.com.au
- www.fijibeaches.com

Budget

Budget travellers in Fiji can expect to pay $25 to $35 for a dorm bed and between $70 and $135 for a double. Dedicated single rooms are few and far between and solo travellers wanting privacy usually end up forking out for a double. Campsites are provided at some budget resorts, but as they are only a few dollars cheaper than dormitories the hassle of carrying a tent seems hardly worth it (see p228 for more information).

Facilities at budget places are usually shared. Many backpacker resorts in places such as Nadi and the Coral Coast on Viti Levu have their own restaurants, bars, laundries, internet access and tour desks. Some midrange resorts have converted a room or two into dorms – often a great bargain as you'll have access to all of the resort's facilities. On the outer islands amenities become simpler, and sometimes hot water and electricity is a luxury.

Budget resorts in the Yasawa and Mamanuca islands often include three meals in their tariffs, as generally they do not provide self-catering facilities and there is nowhere else to eat. An accommodation-and-meal package costs between $60 and $95.

Budget accommodation standards vacillate wildly during the lifetime of each edition of this guide. What can be a particularly nice *bure* (traditional thatched dwelling) one day, can be tattered and torn within hours by hurricanes and tropical storms. See the boxed text, p156, for what to expect on the outer islands. If possible, quiz other travellers, check Lonely Planet's **Thorn Tree** (www.lonelyplanet.com/thorntree) or browse through the comments book in the office of the Fiji Visitors Bureau (FVB; p239) to get the latest low-down on a particular place.

BOOK YOUR STAY ONLINE

For more accommodation reviews and recommendations by Lonely Planet authors, check out the online booking service at www.lonelyplanet.com/hotels. You'll find the true, insider low-down on the best places to stay. Reviews are thorough and independent. Best of all, you can book online.

PRACTICALITIES

- The **Fiji Times** (☎ 330 4111; www.fijitimes.com), the **Daily Post** (☎ 327 5176; www.fijidailypost.com) and the **Fiji Sun** (☎ 330 7555; www.sun.com.fj) are the country's principal newspapers; all are based in Suva.

- **Fiji Magic** (☎ 330 0591; www.fijilive.com/fijimagic) is a free, monthly publication with details and prices of accommodation, restaurants, activities and tours.

- The government-sponsored **Fiji Broadcasting Commission** (www.radiofiji.com.fj) has stations in English (2Day FM – Suva 100.4 FM and Nadi 107.4 FM), Fijian (Radio Fiji 1 – 558AM) and Fiji-Hindi (Radio Fiji 2 – 620AM and 98 FM).

- Bula FM (Suva 100.2 FM and Nadi 102.4 FM) plays an eclectic mix of pop, rock, reggae, dance, folk, country and local music. Radio Fiji Gold (Suva 100.4 FM and Nadi 94.6 FM) appeals to an older generation.

- The video and DVD system used in Fiji is PAL, which is the same as in Australia, New Zealand, Europe, the UK and most of Asia and the Pacific. The US video and DVD system is NTSC, which is incompatible.

- Electricity is supplied at 240V, 50Hz AC. Many resorts have universal outlets for 240V or 110V shavers and hairdryers. Outlets use flat two- or three-pin plugs as in Australia or New Zealand.

- Fiji follows the metric system: kilometres, kilograms, litres and degrees in Celsius.

If you're making reservations at budget places while you're on the road, don't be surprised if you show up and nobody's heard of you. Administration can sometimes be a little less-than-organised and reservations don't always make it into the book. However, Fijians do take such disorganisation in their stride, and a bed will invariably be found for you, but it might be in the dormitory.

Midrange

The bulk of accommodation in Fiji falls under the midrange banner. Options include hotels, motels and resorts ranging from $135 to $250 for a room, regardless of whether occupied by one or two adults. Guests can expect bathrooms, TVs, bar fridges and tea and coffee facilities in hotels, while many lodges and resorts offer self-contained units with kitchens. These rooms are often more tired than one might expect from the price. A midrange hotel in Fiji is likely to be below the standard found in the developed world (although entirely comfortable), but significantly more expensive. If you're looking to stay a bit longer and want to move around, avoid paying too much in advance and keep your options open.

However, on remote islands such as Kadavu, where there are few places to stay and the main form of transportation is by small boat, it is better to book ahead. This will avoid you being left stranded without a vacancy in your price range, and ensure you'll be met at the airport or ferry.

Top End

Fiji's top-end options do not suffer the same comparatively low-standard/high-price issues as its midrange hotels. The resorts are generally five-star chains or upmarket island resorts with rooms that equal anything else in the world. Expect day spas, landscaped pools, stylish restaurants and complimentary nonmotorised water sports. Prices range from $250 for a double to sky's-the-limit tariffs. Children aged under 12 generally stay free (and sometimes even eat free) at the family-oriented resorts while others are strictly adult-only affairs. The prices quoted in this book are 'rack rates' and you will almost certainly be able to make a booking for less by exploring a few options, such as the following:

- Consider prebooking your accommodation as a package deal with a travel agent. Because of their buying power, they are sometimes given rates not available to the general public.
- Some hotels discount heavily on websites like those mentioned at the start of this section, or on their own web page.
- Other places offer cheap rates to those who phone, on the assumption that they are speaking to someone within Fiji. Ask for the 'local rate'.

DIRECTORY

■ In the quieter months of February and March some resorts offer cheap walk-in rates to fill vacant rooms.

Types of Accommodation
CAMPING

You should never just set up camp without permission. Most of Fiji's land, even in seemingly remote areas, is owned by the indigenous population, *mataqali* (extended families) or villages. If you are invited to camp in a village, avoid setting up your tent next to someone's *bure*. Doing so can be misinterpreted as implying that you feel the house is not good enough for you to stay in. Ask where the best place to pitch your tent is, and provide a *sevusevu* (gift).

Elsewhere, you can pitch your tent at some of the budget lodges on the Yasawa and Kadavu islands, Vanua Levu, Taveuni and Viti Levu's Coral Coast. In the Yasawas expect to pay around $55 per person per night, which will include three meals.

HOSTELS

The Cathay chain has budget accommodation at Lautoka, Saweni Beach, the Coral Coast and Suva. It gives discounts for HI (Hostelling International) and Nomad cardholders.

RENTAL ACCOMMODATION

Most of the long-term rental accommodation is on Viti Levu – in Suva and Pacific Harbour, and to a lesser extent in Nadi. There are also a number of houses for rent on Taveuni. Renting apartments or rooms with weekly rates may be a cheap option if you are looking for a fixed base from which to take day trips.

RESORTS

The term 'resort' is used loosely in Fiji and refers to accommodation ranging from backpacker-style to exclusive luxury. If you are prepared to put up with rudimentary facilities and services, you can find yourself an inexpensive (by Fijian standards) piece of paradise.

Most resorts offer meal plans, which are fixed-price packages that generally include breakfast, lunch and dinner, and these can be good value if you are a large eater. The downside is that if the food isn't up to par, there is little that you can do about it. It's worth asking when booking if you can 'upgrade' to a meal plan once you have arrived (and tested it first).

Whether catering to the high or low end of the 'resort' spectrum, most resorts feature *bure*-style accommodation. The word *bure* (when used in this context) refers to a stand-alone room with a thatched roof and other traditional architecture. This could mean anything from a luxury, air-conditioned unit to a beach shack that a hungry goat could eat in an afternoon.

In the midrange and top-end price brackets, nonmotorised activities tend to be included in resort rates; but diving, parasailing, water-skiing, jet-skiing, fishing and island-hopping excursions generally cost extra.

There are many backpacker resorts on the offshore islands, including the Yasawas, Mana in the Mamanucas, Kadavu, Nananu-i-Ra, and Leleuvia and Caqalai near Ovalau. For those who are happy to spend up to a few hundred dollars per day for extra comfort, services and activities, there are many popular resorts in the Mamanucas, on Viti Levu's Coral Coast, on Taveuni, and some exclusive movie-star hang-outs on remote islands.

ACTIVITIES

Fiji has plenty to offer the adventurous and active. The archipelago's warm, clear waters and abundance of reef life make it a magnet for divers and snorkellers. Underwater visibility regularly exceeds 30m, though this is reduced on stormy days or when there is a heavy plankton bloom.

Birdwatching

Fiji features some brilliant members of the feathered family. Taveuni is home to more than 100 species, including the rare orange dove. See p200 for information regarding the best birdwatching sites. Kadavu (p214) is also home to a diversity of bird life, including the Kadavu musk parrot.

On Vanua Levu, the Tunuloa Peninsula is home to the rare silktail (p189), while the rainforests around Savusavu are popular bird hang-outs. On Viti Levu, Colo-i-Suva Forest Park (p121) near Suva is very accessible and Kula Eco Park (p104) on the Coral Coast offers birders a chance to get nose-to-beak with the rare, native, Pacific black duck. For more about Fiji's birds, see p62 and consider picking up a copy of *Birds of the Fiji Bush,* by Fergus Clunie and Pauline Morse of the Fiji Museum (available in the gift shop of the Fiji Museum, see p117).

FIJIAN HITCH

Fiancées and honeymooners flock to Fiji like bees to a honey convention. The tropical beaches, amber sunsets, secluded resorts, island singing – this archipelago smacks of romantic paradise, and 'don't it know it'. Many resorts cater to the almost- and newly-I-dos with irresistible honeymoon and wedding packages and can provide you with much of the information and planning you need. Regardless of how you go about it there are some fundamentals you'll need in order to tie the knot.

Essentials for a marriage licence to be issued in Fiji include: someone of the opposite sex (same-sex marriage is not legal in Fiji), birth certificates, passports (although it would be tricky getting into the country without one anyway) and, if you're under 21, a document of consent signed by your folks. If (and this is a little prickly) this is your second (or more) time round, you'll also need to produce a copy of divorce papers, a decree nisi or a death certificate.

You'll need to present all of the above documentation to a Registry Office prior to your actual marriage in order to obtain a marriage licence. This process only takes around 20 minutes, but it's a good idea to make an appointment if you're not getting a resort or travel agent to organise the whole shebang for you. The **Registrar General's office** (Map p116; ☎ 331 5280; Ground fl, Suvavou House, Victoria Pde; 🕑 8.30am-3.30pm Mon-Fri) is in Suva, but there are also **Divisional Registrars** (Lautoka ☎ 666 5132; 1st fl, Rogorogoivuda House, Tavewa Ave; 🕑 9am-3pm Mon-Fri; Nadi ☎ 670 0101; Korivolu Ave; 🕑 8am-1pm & 2-4pm Mon-Fri). There's a $22 fee and you have 21 days to then get hitched.

A less official, but equally important, consideration is the weather. Regardless of the wording, your vows will lose some of their romantic impact if you end up reciting them beneath a golf umbrella in gale-force winds (see p21 for more climate information). And if you have dreams of you, your betrothed and a priest alone on a secluded beach, you may want to check your resort's occupancy before you book.

Lastly, it's a good idea to get some perspective, advice and tips from the romance experts. The following websites can help you plan the perfect Fijian wedding or honeymoon, if not organise it outright:

- http://destination-weddings-abroad.com/fiji/
- www.fijihoneymoon.com
- www.holidaysforcouples.com.au/pacificocean-fiji.html
- www.weddings-in-fiji.com

Cycling

Cycling is a good way to explore Viti Levu, Vanua Levu (the Hibiscus Hwy) and parts of Ovalau and Taveuni. With the exception of the Kings and Queens Roads, most roads, especially inland, are rough, hilly and unsealed, so mountain bikes are the best option. Serious cyclists would be well advised to bring their own bike as there is only one company (Stoney Creek Resort near Nadi, see p90) that rents bikes of a standard suitable for a multi-day ride. The circular route around Viti Levu would be a great trip and there are plenty of accommodation options to boot. You could also cycle along Vanua Levu's unsealed roads from Savusavu along Natewa Bay (no accommodation around here) and along the Hibiscus Hwy from Buca Bay, where you can take the ferry over to Taveuni. Ovalau also has a scenic, unsealed (mainly flat) coastal road.

Diving & Snorkelling

The dive industry in Fiji is well established and covered in depth on p67. For information on diving insurance, see p256.

However, some of Fiji's most spectacular scenery is just below the surface, where the water is warm, making snorkelling also an activity not to be missed. Although the coral took a hammering in 2000 during a bout of severe coral bleaching, the reefs have recovered extremely quickly.

Often some of the best underwater gardens are very close to the coast, making snorkelling a relatively inexpensive and easy pastime compared with diving. Just remember to wear a T-shirt and waterproof sunscreen, as it is easy to become absorbed by the spectacle, lose sense of time and scorch your back and legs.

The following tips are also useful to remember:

- If you have not snorkelled before or are not a confident swimmer, familiarise yourself with the equipment first in a pool or shallow water.
- Learn how to clear your snorkel, so that you don't panic and tread on the fragile coral.
- It is common to see reef sharks but don't be alarmed, they're probably more scared of you than you are of them.
- The most beautiful creatures can be poisonous, so avoid touching anything.
- Avoid being washed against the reef as coral cuts can turn into nasty infections.
- Night snorkelling with a light is a fantastic experience if you can overcome your fear of the unknown!

Most resorts offer snorkelling equipment, although budget places will often charge for it (between $5 and $20). It may be worthwhile buying your own gear as it can be frustrating if you are in a gorgeous location without any (or poor) equipment.

In many places there is fine snorkelling directly off the shore, but these reefs can become exposed at low tide and it can become a belly-scraping ordeal to return to land. Resorts (and dive operators) often run snorkelling trips to the outer reefs ($25 to $40 per person) where the coral is intact and more spectacular. Do your bit to keep it that way and wear a life jacket to avoid standing up.

The best sites on Viti Levu are at Natadola Beach, Nananu-i-Ra and Beqa Lagoon. Viti Levu's Coral Coast – despite the name – is not that great for snorkelling as it is usually a fair way to the drop, much of the reef is dead and swimming is mostly tidal.

The best snorkelling sites are on the outer islands. Notable sites include the Mamanucas and Yasawas (particularly the manta-ray trip, see p158); Vanua Levu's rocky coastline, especially near Maravu Point, southeast of Savusavu; Taveuni's Vuna Reef (p199); offshore from Matava Resort in Kadavu (p214); and the Lomaiviti Group's Caqalai and Leleuvia.

Fishing

Villages have rights over the reefs and fishing in Fiji, so you cannot just drop a line anywhere: seek permission first. Many of the more expensive resorts offer game-fishing tours and boat chartering. On Viti Levu, resorts at Nadi

(p82), Pacific Harbour (p110) and Nananu-i-Ra (p136) all offer fishing trips. From the far end of the Yasawas to the other end of the Mamanucas, resorts (large and small) can organise boats and tackle, although this could be anything from a simple hand line in the Yasawas to a big game charter at Musket Cove (p149). There is also a reputable fishing-tour company based at Taveuni – see p200 for details.

Hiking

It is culturally offensive to simply hike anywhere in Fiji – you need to ask permission, be invited or take a tour. To ensure that you are not being culturally insensitive, see the boxed text, p42, and ask local villagers or hotel staff to organise permission and a guide. Good boots are essential for hiking year-round. Carry plenty of water, good maps, a compass, a warm jumper and a waterproof coat; and be sure to tell others where you are heading in case you get lost or have an accident.

Koroyanitu National Heritage Park (p96) and Colo-i-Suva Forest Park (p121) on Viti Levu offer the best trekking opportunities on the mainland. The tour companies in Navua (p112) can offer more challenging multiday tracks to those who are that way inclined. If you plan to be in Fiji for a while, consider contacting the Rucksack Club in Suva – contact details are available from the FVB (p239) – which organises regular walks and excursions.

On Taveuni, the Lavena Coastal Walk (p209) is an excellent marked trail.

Horse Riding

The locals around Natadola Beach (p98) make a living out of saddling-up day trippers, while horse riding is also a common resort activity along the Coral Coast. Other opportunities crop up at Vatuwiri Farm in Taveuni (p204) and at Bulou's Eco Lodge (p138) in the Nausori Highlands.

Kayaking

Top-end resorts have kayaks for guest use free of charge; others hire them at about $20 and $30 for a half- and full day respectively. The islands of the Mamanucas, Vanua Levu, the Yasawas, Nananu-i-Ra and Kadavu are all great for kayaking. Some keen kayakers paddle Taveuni's rugged Ravilevu Coast, but generally the western sides of the islands are preferred as they're sheltered from the southeast trade winds.

There are also special sea-kayaking tours available during the drier months, between May and November. Some combine paddling with hiking into rainforests, snorkelling, fishing and village visits. For more information on Yasawa kayaking tours see p154, on remote Lau tours see p218 and for Kadavu tours see p213.

River Trips

Spectacular *bilibili* (bamboo rafting) trips can be made on the Navua River in the Namosi Highlands of Viti Levu; see p112 for details. Adrenalin Jet (p88) at Denarau has speedboat tours through the island's mangroves.

Sailing

Yachties are often looking for extra crew and people to share costs. Approach the marinas, ask around and look on the noticeboards. See the boxed text, p245 for more information.

Fiji's marinas include the Royal Suva Yacht Club (p122); Vuda Point Marina (p91); Port Denarau (p88); Musket Cove Marina (p149), on Malololailai in the Mamanucas; and the Copra Shed Marina and Waitui Marina (p181), both at Savusavu on Vanua Levu.

The designated ports of entry for Fiji are Suva, Levuka, Lautoka and Savusavu. Yachties intending to sail to the outer islands, such as the Lau Group, will require a customs permit and a permit to cruise the islands. This is obtained from the Ministry of Fijian Affairs, or from the commissioner's office in Lautoka, Savusavu or Levuka. Seek advice from a yachting agent or yacht club in Fiji before applying for the permit. See p239 for more details.

The main yachting season is June to August, but there are races and regattas throughout the year. Obviously the Fijian reefs necessitate good charts and crews with sailing experience.

For organised cruises and charters, refer to the individual island chapters. Musket Cove Marina (p149) hires out a range of vessels for sailing around the Mamanucas and Yasawas, including some that are fully crewed with skipper and cook. There are also private boats for sail and adventure cruises from Savusavu's marinas. By Fijian law you must have a local guide on all chartered boats.

Contact individual yacht clubs for further information, and pick up a copy of the *Yacht Help Booklet, Fiji*, available from the FVB. *Landfalls of Paradise – The Guide to Pacific Islands*, by Earl R Hinz, and Michael Calder's *Yachtsman's Fiji* are also popular references.

Surfing

Most surf pitches over outer reefs and in passages, and is for intermediate to advanced surfers only. For these reefs you need boats and guides. Marine safety can be lax so ask for oars, life jackets and drinking water as well as a mobile (cell) phone on board. Southerly swells are consistent from May to October, but there is surf year-round. The trade winds are southeast and offshore at the famous breaks. Northerlies, from November to April, are offshore on the Coral Coast.

The best surf spots are along Viti Levu's south coast (particularly the Sigatoka River mouth, see p101), the Mamanuca Group (see p141) and Frigates (p113) near Yanuca island. There are some remote breaks at Kadavu (see p213). The dry season (May to October) is the best time to go, due to low pressures bringing in big surf. Keen surfers should bring their own board, although these can be rented at Fiji Surf Company (p82) in Nadi.

You should be aware that Fijian villages usually have fishing rights to, and basically own, adjacent reefs. Some resorts pay the villages for exclusive surfing rights, which has led to disputes between competing surfing and diving operations. If you would like to explore lesser-known areas, you will need to respect local traditions and seek permission from the local villagers.

Some lesser-known spots include Suva, which has a reef-break at the lighthouse (you need a boat to get there) and Lavena Point on Taveuni (although the waves here are less consistent).

Click onto www.globalsurfers.com/fiji.cfm for more useful information, and http://mag icseaweed.com/Tavarua-Surf-Report/669/ for swell conditions.

Visiting Villages

Many tours include a village visit in their activities. Some villages have become affected by bus loads of tourists parading through their backyards every other day and the *sevusevu* ceremony and *meke* (a dance performance that enacts stories and legends) can seem somewhat put on. Other village tours, especially those run by the villagers, are smaller

DIRECTORY

in scale with perhaps not so much going on; however, the whole experience can feel much more genuine.

The village tours to Lovoni (p168) on Ovalau are fantastic and Navala (p137), in Viti Levu's highlands, is one of Fiji's most picturesque villages.

Windsurfing

Nananu-i-Ra (p136) is a wind machine between May and July when the trade winds are consistently strong. Care is needed here (and elsewhere) to avoid shredding your sail and yourself on sharp coral.

BUSINESS HOURS

Fijians are not known for their punctuality, often observing 'Fiji time'. Post offices and most shops and cafes open between 8am and 9am and close at around 5pm weekdays, or 1pm on Saturday. Banks are open 9am to 4pm on weekdays, though some close at 3pm on Friday. A few internet cafes and shops are open for limited hours on Sunday, but the general rule is to assume everything will be closed. For indigenous Fijians it is a day for church, rest and spending time with family.

Restaurants generally open for lunch (11am to 2pm) and dinner (6pm to 9pm or 10pm) from Monday to Saturday, as well as dinner on Sunday. Many remain open from 11am to 10pm. Bars in Suva and Nadi are open from late afternoon to around midnight on weeknights but extend their hours into early morning from Thursday to Saturday. Resort bars have more flexible schedules and cater to guests' drinking preferences (eg daiquiris at 10am).

Government offices are open from 8am to 4.30pm Monday to Thursday, and 8am to 4pm Friday.

Many places in Fiji close for lunch from 1pm to 2pm.

CHILDREN

Fiji is a major family destination and is very child-friendly; Fijians love children and children love Fijians. Children are valued in Fiji and child care is seen as the responsibility of the extended family and the community. Everyone will want to talk with your kids and invite them to join activities or visit homes. Babies and toddlers are especially popular – they may tire of having their cheeks pinched! Fijian men

play a large role in caring for children and babies, so don't be surprised if they pay a lot of attention to your kids. Fijian children are expected to be obedient and spend lots of time playing outdoors. Backchat and showing off is seen as disruptive to the fabric of the community, so when visiting a village, try to curb any crying, tantrums and noisy behaviour.

Lonely Planet's *Travel with Children* has useful advice on family travel, and has a section on Fiji.

Practicalities

Travelling around with kids in Fiji is fairly easy. The large chain car-rental companies can provide baby seats, but local companies and taxis don't. If you intend to take public transport, a backpack for transporting infants is a good idea. Also bear in mind that local buses have bench seating, no seat belts and can be fairly cramped, so may not be particularly conducive to travelling with small children or babies.

Many resorts cater well for children, with free kids club for four to 12 year olds and child-friendly pools. Babysitting for toddlers and infants is easily arranged for between $5 and $15 per hour. Smaller exclusive resorts on the other hand tend not to accept children, or at least relegate them to a specific period during the year. Some resorts are on multiple levels with sand paths, which can make using prams and strollers difficult.

Many restaurants in cities and tourist areas, such as the Coral Coast on Viti Levu and well-equipped resorts in the Yasawas and Mamanucas, have cots and high chairs.

Long-life milk is readily available, as is bottled spring water and fruit juice. Fiji is a fairly conservative and demure society and while breast feeding is common among the local population, you'll seldom see it, so follow their example and find a private place to do so. Nappies, formula and sterilising solution are available in pharmacies and supermarkets in the main cities and towns, but if you are travelling to remote areas or islands, take your own supplies. Consider using cloth nappies wherever you can.

Many small boats don't carry enough life jackets and never have child-sized ones; if you're planning to island hop in small boats, you might want to consider bringing your own.

For ideas on keeping the kids content, see the boxed text, p80.

CLIMATE CHARTS

Fiji's wet season is from November to April, with the heaviest rains falling between December and mid-April. Fiji has a mild average temperature of 25°C, but it can climb to above 30°C in summer (December and January) and sink to 18°C in winter (July and August). See p21 for information about the best time to visit Fiji.

CUSTOMS REGULATIONS

If you are travelling with an expensive camera or computer equipment, carry a receipt to avoid possible hassles with customs when arriving home.

Visitors can leave Fiji without paying VAT on the following: up to $400 per person of duty-assessed goods; 2L of liqueur or spirits; or 4L of wine or beer; 500 cigarettes or 500g of cigars or tobacco, or all three under a total of 500g; and personal effects.

Pottery shards, turtle shells, coral, trochus shells and giant clamshells cannot be taken out of the country without a permit. You can bring as much currency as you like into the country, but you need to declare any amount over $10,000 and you can't take out more than you brought in.

Importation of vegetable matter, seeds, animals, meat or dairy produce is prohibited without a licence from the Ministry of Agriculture & Fisheries. If you're taking a domestic pet into Fiji you need to write to the **Director of Animal Health and Production** (☎ 331 5322; fax 330 5043; GPO Box 15829, Suva) and send them your animal's details including an up-to-date vet report. The department will send you a licence or approval to take your pet into Fiji. Otherwise staff will quarantine your pet for a few weeks on arrival.

DANGERS & ANNOYANCES

Fiji is still a pretty safe place for travellers. When you're in Nadi or Suva, though, do not walk around at night, even in a group, as muggings are common. Locals catch cabs after dark in these cities and you should do the same. Don't hitchhike; while it's commonly done by locals, as a foreigner you're a sitting duck for muggers. As a precaution, use a money belt and keep your valuables in a safe place.

While it's unlikely that you'll be robbed, it does happen, so try to keep all valuables out of sight and lock your door while you're out

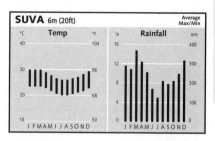

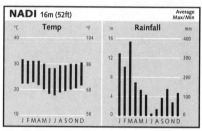

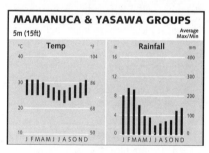

or sleeping. Most resorts have a safe where you can store your money belt. You can also avoid becoming utterly destitute by stashing a small amount of cash or a couple of travellers cheques in a separate place to where the bulk is stored.

As you exit customs at Nadi airport, you'll likely be swarmed by touts who will do their best to get you into their shuttle van and on the road to their employer's resort. It's advisable to have at least your first night of accommodation booked, but if you're unsure of where you want to stay and want to avoid these mobs while you consider your options, head to the FVB desk.

Sword sellers are not as common as they used to be, but if anyone becomes overly friendly, wants to know your life story and begins carving your name on a long piece of wood, just walk away, even if they pursue you claiming that you have to pay for the rubbishy item. Male travellers in particular are likely to be approached and asked if they want marijuana (see p236) and/or prostitutes.

If you are unlucky enough to be caught in a natural disaster such as a cyclone or flood, ask locals for advice on where to seek protection from the elements.

If driving, there are some road hazards you should be aware of; see p250 for more information.

Contrary to Fiji's image promoted overseas, many beaches, especially on the large islands, aren't great for swimming. The fringing coral reefs often become too shallow at low tide. Avoid swimming or snorkelling alone and be very careful of currents and tidal changes. Always seek local advice on conditions. For safety precautions regarding marine life see p256.

DISCOUNT CARDS

STA Travel and other student-travel agencies give discounts on international airfares to full-time students who have an International Student Identity Card (ISIC). Application forms are available at these travel agencies. Student discounts are occasionally given for entry fees, restaurants and accommodation in Fiji. You can also use the student health service at the University of the South Pacific (USP) in Suva.

Several backpacker resorts also accept VIP cards. Click onto www.vipbackpackers.com to purchase a card and find out about discounts.

We didn't come across any instances where people with seniors cards received any discounts.

EMBASSIES & CONSULATES

It's important to understand what your own embassy – the embassy of the country of which you are a citizen – can and can't do to help you if you get into trouble. Generally speaking, it won't be much help in emergencies if the trouble you're in is remotely your own fault. Remember that the laws of the country you are in bind you. Your embassy will not be sympathetic if you end up in jail after committing a crime locally, even if such actions are legal in your own country.

In genuine emergencies you might get some assistance, but only if other channels have been exhausted. For example, if you need to get home urgently, a free ticket home is exceedingly unlikely – the embassy would expect you to have insurance. If all your money and documents are stolen, the embassy might assist with getting a new passport, but a loan for onward travel is out of the question.

The following countries have diplomatic representation in Fiji. All embassies are in Suva, although the Americans are on the move – due to the congestion caused by heightened security they may move to a bombproof bunker at Tamavua Heights.

Although most consulates and embassies open from 9am to 4pm, Monday to Friday, many only take visa applications during designated sessions (usually in the morning) and are closed for their own state holidays. It is worth phoning ahead before fronting up.

Australia (Map p116; ☎ 338 2211; 37 Princes Rd, Tamavua)

China (Map p116; ☎ 330 0251; 147 Queen Elizabeth Dr)

European Union (Map p118; ☎ 331 3633; 4th fl, Fiji Development Bank Centre, Victoria Pde)

Federated States of Micronesia (Map p118; ☎ 330 4566; 37 Loftus St)

France (Map p118; ☎ 331 2233; 7th fl, Dominion House, Thomson St)

Germany (Map p118; ☎ 331 2927; 82 Harris Rd)

Japan (Map p118; ☎ 330 4633; 2nd fl, Dominion House, Thomson St)

Korea (Map p118; ☎ 330 0977; 8th fl, Vanua House, Victoria Pde)

Malaysia (Map p118; ☎ 331 2166; 5th fl, Air Pacific House, Butt St)

Nauru (Map p118; ☎ 331 3566; 7th fl, Ratu Sukuna House, Macarthur St)

Netherlands (Map p118; ☎ 330 1499; 1st fl, Crompton Solicitors Suite, 10 Victoria Arcade)

New Zealand (Map p118; ☎ 331 1422; 10th fl, Reserve Bank Bldg, Pratt St)

Tuvalu (Map p118; ☎ 330 1355; 16 Gorrie St)

UK (Map p118; ☎ 322 9100; Victoria House, 47 Gladstone Rd)

US (Map p118; ☎ 331 4466; 31 Loftus St)

Canadians have access to an **Honorary Consul** (Map p81; ☎ 972 2400; Nadi airport, Nadi) in Nadi, Mr Janna Bai Vyas .

FESTIVALS & EVENTS
February–March
Hindu Holi (Festival of Colours) People squirt coloured water at each other either in late February or early March; mostly in Lautoka.

March–April

Ram Naumi (Birth of Lord Rama) A Hindu religious festival and party on the shores of Suva Bay during late March or early April. Worshippers wade into the water and throw flowers.

Fiji International Jazz Festival Three-day jazz festival showcasing musicians from around the world. Held early to mid-April along the Coral Coast.

July

Bula Festival One of Fiji's biggest festivals – held in Nadi with rides, music, shows and the crowning of 'Miss Bula'.

Fiji Ocean Swim (www.fijiswim.com) International swim event attracting athletes from around the world who compete in teams or individually in 1km, 2.3km or 18km races.

August

Hibiscus Festival Held in Suva, with floats, food stalls, fair rides and the crowning of 'Miss Hibiscus' (p124).

Hindu Ritual Fire Walking Performed by southern Indians in many temples, including Suva's Mariamma Temple (p124; also see p44 for a participant's insight).

September

Fiji Regatta Week (www.musketcovefiji.com) Annual regatta luring avid yachties from around the world. Held at Musket Cove.

Lautoka's Sugar Festival Lautoka comes alive with fun fairs, parades and the crowning of the Sugar Queen.

October–November

Diwali (Festival of Lights) Hindus worship Lakshmi (the goddess of wealth and prosperity); houses are decorated and business is settled. Candles and lanterns are set on doorsteps to light the way for the god. Held in late October or early to mid-November.

Ram Leela (Play of Rama) Primarily a Hindu festival; theatrical performances celebrate the life of the god-king Rama and his return from exile. It's held at the Mariamman Temple (in Vunivau, near Labasa) around the first week of October, and has been celebrated here for more than 100 years.

South Pacific World Music Festival Acclaimed Fijian and international musicians treat Savusavu to five days of global harmony. Held in late November.

Armistice Day Also known as Remembrance Day, Suva observes a minute's silence at 11am on 11 November, although sometimes it might actually be something like 10.50am, depending on the accuracy of the clocks.

FOOD

Dining options for the larger centres are divided into restaurants, cafes and quick eats and self-catering categories in their respective destination chapters. The listings under each category are in order of budget based on the average price of a main course.

Budget travellers can pay around $15 for a meal, although quick-eat options such as bakeries and cheap curry joints are considerably cheaper. To really save money, visit the local markets and eat locally grown vegetables. Self-caterers could expect to get by on about $15 a day. Midrange travellers can expect to pay $10 to $25 for lunch or dinner at a good cafe or restaurant. In the cities and upmarket resorts meals tend to cost anything from $25 to $50.

See p56 for more information about food and drink in Fiji.

GAY & LESBIAN TRAVELLERS

In 1997, Fiji became the second country in the world to protect against discrimination based on sexual orientation in its constitution and, precoup, Chaudhry's government was all for legalising homosexual activity. However, this sentiment evoked a heated reaction from the present conservative and very Christian government. In 2002, the debate about legalising homosexuality was once again sparked when a new Family Law bill was put forward. Sadly, this stirred greater hostility and two prominent gay men (the Red Cross leader John Scott and his partner) were murdered in July 2002.

There is some indication of changing attitudes in the community. A large number of openly gay men work in the hospitality industry, and some nightclubs in Lautoka, Nadi and Suva are gay-tolerant. Occasionally you'll come across a Fijian so obviously gay that he'll make Boy George seem like the Marlboro Man. Furthermore, in 2005 the Fijian High Court acquitted two gay men who had been previously convicted and sentenced for having a sexual relationship. The judge who gave the ruling also urged the Fijian Law Commission to address reform in legislation regarding homosexuality in Fiji.

It's important to remember, however, that sodomy and other homosexual acts remain illegal in Fiji and as such, the police have the right to arrest and prosecute on these grounds. Public displays of affection in general are considered offensive in Fiji; as a gay or lesbian couple, the risks of receiving unwanted attention for outwardly homosexual behaviour are high. But gay couples who are relatively private are extremely unlikely to have any trouble in Fiji. Gay singles should exercise some caution; don't give anyone an excuse to even think you are paying for sex, and be very careful not to give the impression you are after young Fijian men.

The website www.globalgayz.com/g-fiji .html tracks gay developments in Fiji.

HOLIDAYS

Fijians celebrate a variety of holidays and festivals; for details of the latter, see p234. New Year's Day is celebrated all over Fiji: in villages, festivities can last a week or even the whole month of January. There is also a day commemorating Ratu Sir Lala Sukuna, considered Fiji's greatest statesman.

Public Holidays

Annual public holidays include the following:
New Year's Day 1 January
Easter (Good Friday & Easter Monday) March/April
Prophet Mohammed's Birthday March
National Youth Day March
Ratu Sir Lala Sukuna Day Late May or early June
Queen's Birthday Mid-June
Fiji Day (Independence Day) Early October
Diwali Festival October/November
Christmas Day 25 December
Boxing Day 26 December

School Holidays

School holidays in Fiji, Australia and New Zealand can have an impact on the availability of accommodation in Fiji. In Fiji school holidays generally last for two weeks, from late April to early to mid-May and mid-August to early September. Summer holidays run from early December to late January.

For details on school holidays in Australia and New Zealand, click onto www.school -holidays.com.au and www.minedu.govt.nz.

INSURANCE

Having a travel-insurance policy to cover theft, loss and medical problems is a very good idea. There are many policies available and your travel agent will be able to recommend one, but always check the small print. You may prefer a policy that pays doctors or hospitals direct, rather than you having to pay on the spot and claim later. If you have to claim later, make sure you keep all the documentation. See p252 for more information. It's a smart idea to email a copy of your insurance

to yourself. That way, should everything be lost, you can access the information online (ditto for passports).

Some policies specifically exclude so-called 'dangerous activities', which can include diving, motorcycling and even hiking. If you're planning to dive, it's best to purchase either comprehensive cover or pay extra for this activity; see p256. A motorcycle licence acquired in Fiji may not be valid under some policies.

Check that the policy covers ambulances and an emergency flight home. The Australian Department of Foreign Affairs and Trade warns travellers that some insurance companies will not pay claims that arise when travellers have disregarded the government's travel advice.

Worldwide travel insurance is available at www.lonelyplanet.com/travel_services. You can buy, extend and claim online anytime – even if you're already on the road.

INTERNET ACCESS

Internet cafes are fairly prolific in Suva, Lautoka and Nadi and competition means that you can jump online with broadband access for as little as $3 per hour. Budget resorts in Nadi also have internet access; some using prepay cards that deduct credits in 15-minute allotments. This works out at around $10 an hour. Outside of the urban centres access is more limited, slower and pricier (up to $8 an hour in internet cafes), but thanks to the new VTSat, a satellite-based telecommunication network, even the remote islands like Rotuma now have internet access.

If you're carrying your own laptop you can sign up to a dial-up account with a service provider such as **Connect** (www.con nect.com.fj) or with a wireless (wi-fi) provider like **Unwired Fiji** (☎ 327 5040; www.unwired.com.fj), which enables users to connect to the internet without the use of a phone line (but you'll need to purchase a special modem from them).

Many midrange and top-end resorts have internet connections, so you simply need to plug your computer in.

LEGAL MATTERS

The only drug you are likely to come across when travelling in Fiji is marijuana – which is illegal. Don't seek it out or buy it, as the consequences if you are caught can be serious – it is not uncommon for drug users in Fiji to be imprisoned in the psychiatric hospital.

It's also illegal to drink and drive. See p235 for information on gay and lesbian legal restrictions.

Most travellers manage to avoid any run-ins with the local authorities. If you are arrested, though, you have the right to contact your embassy or consulate, which will be allowed to provide you with legal representation but can do little else.

MAPS

The best place to buy maps of the Fiji islands is the **Map Shop** (Map p118; ☎ 321 1395; Room 10, Department of Lands & Surveys, Government Bldgs, Southern Cross Rd) in Suva. It sells big (1:50,000) and detailed topographic maps of each island or island group, as well as maps of Suva.

The front of the telephone book has a series of excellent city and town maps. At the FVB, or specialist book and map shops overseas, you can usually purchase the latest Hema map of Fiji. Specialist marine charts are usually available at Fijian ports but are expensive; try to buy them overseas.

MONEY

The local currency is the Fiji dollar ($); it's fairly stable relative to Australian and New Zealand dollars. See the inside front cover for exchange rates. All prices quoted in this book are in Fiji dollars unless otherwise specified.

The dollar is broken down into 100 cents. Bank notes come in denominations of $50, $20, $10, $5 and $2. There are coins to the value of $1, $0.50, $0.20, $0.10, $0.05, $0.02 and $0.01 although the latter two are seldom used.

It's good to have a few options for accessing money – take a credit card, a debit card, some travellers cheques and a small amount of foreign currency. The best currencies to carry are Australian, New Zealand or US dollars, which can be exchanged at all banks.

Before you head out to remote parts of Fiji, check in the appropriate destination chapter to make sure you can access money, exchange currency or cash travellers cheques.

ATMs

ATMs are common in major urban areas and most accept the main international debit cards including Cirrus and Plus. The ANZ bank has an ATM at Nadi International Airport. Although they are increasingly commonplace, you won't find ATMs in remote areas, including the Yasawas, so plan ahead.

Credit Cards

Restaurants, shops, midrange to top-end hotels, car-rental agencies and tour and travel agents will usually accept all major credit cards. Visa, Amex and MasterCard are widely used. Some resorts charge an additional 5% for payment by credit card. Cash advances are available through credit cards at most banks in larger towns.

Tipping

Tipping is not expected or overtly encouraged in Fiji; however, if you feel that the service is worth it, tips are always appreciated. At many resorts you can drop a tip in the 'Staff Christmas Fund' jar.

Travellers Cheques

You can cash travellers cheques in most banks and exchange bureaus, and at larger hotels and duty-free shops. It's a good idea to take travellers cheques in both small and large denominations to avoid being stuck with lots of cash when leaving.

The 24-hour ANZ bank at Nadi International Airport charges $2 on each transaction. Other banks and exchange bureaus don't normally charge a fee.

POST

Post Fiji (www.postfiji.com.fj) is generally quick with its actual delivery, if a little slow at the counter, and has offices throughout the country.

To mail a letter within Fiji costs $0.20 and double that if you want it sent Fast Post. Postcards sent internationally cost $0.40, while letters (up to 15g) cost $0.65.

Sending mail is straightforward; by the time you've reached the front of the queue, you'll know the process by heart. Airmail can usually make it to Australia or New Zealand within three days and Europe or North America within a week. If you're really in a hurry, there's an international express-mail service available through the main post offices.

It's possible to receive mail at poste restante counters in all major post offices. Mail is held for up to two months without a charge. It's also possible to receive faxes at **Fintel** (Fiji International

INTERNATIONAL PHONE CODES	
Country	**Code**
Australia	☎ 61
Canada	☎ 1
France	☎ 33
French Polynesia	☎ 689
Germany	☎ 49
Japan	☎ 81
New Zealand	☎ 64
Tonga	☎ 676
UK	☎ 44
USA	☎ 1
Vanuatu	☎ 678

Telecommunications; Map p118; ☎ 331 2933; 158 Victoria Pde) in Suva and major post offices (see right).

DHL (Map p116; ☎ 337 2766; dhlinfo@fj.dhl.com; Grantham Rd, Suva) has representatives throughout the country, as well as its main office in Suva. A 5kg package to New Zealand, Australia, US or UK costs $187, $218, $256 or $234 respectively, not including insurance.

SHOPPING
The main tourist centres of Nadi, the Coral Coast and Suva have lots of handicraft shops. Savusavu (on Vanua Levu) and Lautoka also have lots of handicraft shops, which are quieter and where the salespeople are less pushy. You can also buy interesting handicrafts direct at villages, particularly woven goods and carvings.

Traditional artefacts, such as war clubs, spears and chiefly cannibal forks, are popular souvenirs. So too are *kava* (*yaqona*; a Fijian narcotic drink) bowls of various sizes (with miniature ones for salt and pepper), woven pandanus mats, baskets from Kioa, sandalwood or coconut soap, and *masi* (bark cloth) in the form of wall hangings, covered books and postcards. Stuffed, *masi*-patterned teddies called Bula Bears are Taveuni and Ovalau specialities and are quite cute. Pottery can be a good buy – if you can get it home in one piece. Don't buy any products derived from endangered species such as turtle, and avoid the temptation to buy seashells. Also be cautious about buying wooden artefacts. A label reading 'Treated Wood' doesn't guarantee an absence of borers. Inspect items closely for holes or other marks, or you may end up paying more for quarantine in your own country than you did for the actual piece.

Clothing shops in Suva and Nadi have *bula* shirts (a *masi*- or floral-design shirt) and fashion items by local designers. There are also vibrant saris and Indian jewellery on sale. Fijian ceramic jewellery is sold in the Government Crafts Centre (p129) in Suva.

Bargaining
Indigenous Fijians generally do not like to bargain, however, it's customary in Indo-Fijian stores, especially in Nadi and Suva. Indo-Fijian shop owners and taxi drivers consider it bad luck to lose their first customer of the day, so you can expect an especially hard sales pitch in the morning.

TELEPHONE & FAX
There are no area codes within Fiji. To dial a Fijian number from outside of Fiji, dial the country code (☎ 679) followed by the local number. To use International Direct Dial (IDD), dial ☎ 00 plus the country code.

You'll find a phone in most midrange and top-end hotel rooms. While local calls are often free, hefty surcharges are added onto long-distance calls. **Fintel** (Map p118; ☎ 331 2933; 158 Victoria Pde) in downtown Suva is the only provider of international VOIP (voice over internet protocol) calls and these are a fraction of the cost ($0.20 per minute) of using traditional lines.

The easiest way to make local calls within Fiji is to buy a Transtel Tele Card, available in denominations from $3 to $50. Dial ☎ 101 and enter the code on the card by following the automated instructions (in English). Local calls cost $0.36 for the first 20 minutes (and then $0.18 per minute thereafter), national calls cost $0.34 per minute and mobile calls cost $0.63 per minute.

Collect calls are more expensive and a surcharge applies when using operator assistance (☎ 010) or international operator assistance (☎ 022). Outer islands are linked by cable and satellite to worldwide networks.

You can send and receive faxes from major post offices. If you're faxing internationally, try Fintel in Suva. At post offices, incoming faxes cost $1.50 per page and sending a local, regional or international fax costs $1.65, $9.65 or $12.15 respectively, per page. Additional pages are usually a little cheaper. Check out the website of **Post Fiji** (www.postfiji .com.fj) for further information and locations offering fax services.

Mobile Phones

Vodafone (www.vodafone.com.fj) is the only mobile-phone company in Fiji. It operates a GSM digital service and has roaming agreements with Vodafone in Australia, New Zealand and the UK, as well as Optus in Australia. Ask for rates charged in Fiji for your mobile-phone calls before you leave home – you may end up paying international rates for local calls.

Mobile phones can be rented from **Vodafone Rentals** (Map p81; ☎ 672 6226; Nadi airport concourse) for $6 per day, but as you can buy a cheap phone in town for $20 including $40 free talk-time, there is little sense in renting one. SIM cards can be purchased for $9.95, including $10 free talk-time.

Mobile phone numbers in Fiji generally start with ☎ 9.

TIME

Fiji is 12 hours ahead of GMT/UTC. When it's noon in Suva, corresponding times elsewhere are as follows:

Add one hour to these times if the other country has daylight saving in place.

City	Time
Same Day	
Sydney	10am
Auckland	noon
Honolulu	2pm
Previous Day	
London	midnight
Los Angeles	4pm
New York	7pm

TOURIST INFORMATION

The **Fiji Visitors Bureau** (FVB; www.fijime.com; Nadi Map p81; ☎ 672 2433; Suite 107, Colonial Plaza; Suva Map p118; ☎ 330 2433; cnr Thomson & Scott Sts) is the primary tourist information body in Fiji. The Nadi office is the head office. At the time of research there was talk of rebranding this organisation as Tourism Fiji.

The **South Pacific Tourism Organisation** (Map p118; ☎ 330 4177; www.spto.org; 3rd fl, Dolphin Plaza, cnr Loftus St & Victoria Pde, Suva) promotes cooperation between the South Pacific island nations for the development of tourism in the region including Fiji.

TRAVELLERS WITH DISABILITIES

In Pacific countries disabled people are simply part of the community, looked after by family where necessary. In some cities there are schools for disabled children but access facilities, such as ramps, lifts and Braille, are rare. Many resorts are designed with multiple levels, lots of stairs and sandy paths, making them difficult for some people to use. Buses do not have wheelchair access and pavements have high kerbs.

Nevertheless, people will go out of their way to give you assistance when you need it. Airports and some hotels and resorts have reasonable access; before booking a particular resort, check if it suits your needs. Access-friendly resorts include Tokatoka Resort Hotel (p85) and the Beachside Resort (p85) in Nadi, and Treasure Island Resort (p144) in the Mamanucas. On the Coral Coast, Hideaway Resort (p108) will also cater to special needs.

Organisations

For pretrip planning advice try the internet and disabled people's associations in your home country. The **Fiji Disabled People's Association** (Map p118; ☎ 331 1203; 3 Brown St, Toorak, Suva) may also be able to provide advice.

Australian-based **Travelaffare Hove** (☎ in Australia 08-8278 7470; www.e-bility.com/travelaffare) can assist disabled people with information on international holidays, including to Fiji.

VISAS

You'll need to have an onward ticket and a passport valid for at least three months longer than your intended stay to get a visa. A free tourist visa for four months is granted on arrival to citizens of more than 100 countries, including most countries belonging to the British Commonwealth, North America, much of South America and Western Europe, India, Indonesia, Israel, Japan, Mexico, Philippines, Russia, Samoa, Solomon Islands, South Korea, Tonga, Tuvalu, Vanuatu and many others. Check www.fiji.gov.fj/publish/fiji_faqs.shtml for a full list.

Nationals from countries excluded from the list will have to apply for visas through a Fijian embassy prior to arrival.

Those entering Fiji by boat are subject to the same visa requirements as those arriving by plane. Yachts can only enter through the designated ports of Suva, Lautoka, Savusavu and Levuka. Yachts have to be cleared by immigration and customs, and are prohibited from visiting any outer islands before doing so. Yachties need to apply to the **Ministry for**

Fijian Affairs (www.fiji.gov.fj/publish/m_fijian_affairs
.shtml) for special written authorisation to visit
the Lau Group.

Visitors cannot partake in political activity
or study, and work permits are needed if you
intend to live and work in Fiji for more than
six months. Foreign journalists will require a
work visa if they spend more than 14 days in
Fiji (see right for more details).

Visa Extensions

Tourist visas can be extended for up to six
months by applying through the **Immigration
Department** (☎ 331 2672; Government Bldgs, Suva).
You'll need to show an onward ticket and
proof of sufficient funds, and your passport
must be valid for three months after your
proposed departure.

VOLUNTEERING

Cocooning yourself in five-star resorts, dining
at exclusive restaurants and sipping on poolside cocktails all help pump much-needed dollars into the cash-strapped economy, but these
experiences bear little resemblance to the day-
to-day life of most Fijians. If you are eager to
spend your time as well as your money helping
the locals, a vacation incorporating some vol-
unteer work might be the way to go. Different
organisations are on the lookout for different
skill sets, so do your research well. If at all possible, make contact with the volunteers who
went before you to see if they felt the work
they participated in was rewarding. It is safe to
assume that volunteering often takes place in
fairly remote locations under fairly primitive
conditions. If you are liable to faint at the sight
of a gecko clinging to the roof of your thatched
hut, it may not be for you.

Lonely Planet's **volunteering website** (www
.lonelyplanet.com/volunteer) has excellent resources
and advice for helping you to get started.
Tribe Wanted (see the boxed text, p195) is a
community-based eco-project near Labasa
that may appeal to some. The following organisations all have volunteering opportunities within Fiji.

Fiji Aid International (www.fijiaidinternational.com)
Greenforce Fiji (www.volunteerabroad.com/listingsp3
.cfm/listing/30444)

Mad Venturer (www.madventurer.com)
Peace Corps (www.peacecorps.gov)

WOMEN TRAVELLERS

Fiji is a fairly male-dominated society, but it
is unlikely that solo women travellers will experience any difficulties as a result. Be aware,
however, that men in this environment may
view the influence of Western women as a
threat to their own position, and therefore
might discourage their wives from talking
with you.

If you're travelling alone, you may experience whistles and stares but you're unlikely
to feel threatened. Nevertheless, some men
will assume lone females are fair game and
several female readers have complained of
being harassed or ripped off, particularly in
touristy areas.

Generally speaking though, female travellers will find Fijian men friendly and helpful,
especially if you are travelling with a male
partner. Both men and women'll treat you
with more respect if you follow the local dress
codes (see p42).

For information on health matters, see
p254.

WORK

Those travelling to Fiji for reasons other than
a holiday must declare this on their arrival
card. They will be given a visa for 14 days
and will have to apply for subsequent extensions. Those wishing to live or work in Fiji for
more than six months will require a working
visa. These can be difficult to get and need
to be organised at least two months prior to
travelling to Fiji. Application forms can be
obtained from any Fijian embassy and must
be completed and sent by the applicant to
the immigration authorities in Fiji. Your application will normally only be approved if
supported by a prospective employer and if
a person with your skills cannot be found
locally. Unemployment is a problem in Fiji
and consequently finding work once you're
in the country is difficult. If you want to conduct business in Fiji, contact the **Fiji Trade &
Investment Board** (☎ 331 5988; www.ftib.org.fj; 6th fl,
Civic Tower, Government Bldgs, Victoria Pde, Suva).

Transport

CONTENTS

Getting There & Away	**241**
Entering the Country	241
Air	241
Sea	244
Getting Around	**245**
Air	245
Bicycle	247
Boat	247
Bus	249
Car & Motorcycle	249
Hitching	251
Local Transport	251
Taxi	251
Tours	251

GETTING THERE & AWAY

Centrally situated in the South Pacific, Fiji is one of the main airline hubs of the Pacific region (Hawaii is the other). Many travellers visit on round-the-world (RTW) tickets or stopovers between North America and Australia or New Zealand. Most agents will allow those on package deals to extend their stay on either side of the accommodation package.

Flights and tours can be booked online at www.lonelyplanet.c om/travel_services.

ENTERING THE COUNTRY

Make sure you have a valid passport and, if necessary, an appropriate visa before arriving in Fiji. See p239 for more details. Immigration procedures are straightforward and it's highly unlikely that travellers will experience difficulty.

In general, visitors do not need to show immunisation cards on entry, although it's always wise to check with your local authorities before leaving in case this changes.

AIR
Airports & Airlines

Most visitors to Fiji arrive at Nadi International Airport (NAN), situated 9km north of central Nadi. Nausori Airport (SUV) near Suva is used mainly for domestic

> ### THINGS CHANGE...
> The information in this chapter is particularly vulnerable to change. Check directly with the airline or a travel agent to make sure you understand how a fare (and ticket you may buy) works and be aware of the security requirements for international travel. Shop carefully. The details given in this chapter should be regarded as pointers and are not a substitute for your own careful, up-to-date research.

flights; however, some flights to neighbouring South Pacific countries fly from here.

On arrival at Nadi International Airport a sea of smiling faces and guitar serenading will greet you. Most of these people will be representing local accommodation or the many travel agencies in the airport.

Nadi International Airport has a 24-hour ANZ bank with currency exchange. There are many travel agencies, airline offices and car-rental offices in the arrivals area, as well as a post office, cafeteria, restaurant, duty-free shop, newsagency and luggage storage area. Luggage storage costs $3 to $6 per day.

Nausori Airport, about 23km northeast of downtown Suva is used for domestic flights by Pacific Sun and Air Fiji.

Code-sharing arrangements mean that Qantas ticket holders are carried on Air Pacific planes and United Airlines passengers are carried by Air New Zealand. The following international airlines fly to and from Fiji. Phone numbers are those in Fiji unless otherwise stated.

Air New Zealand (airline code NZ; ☎ 331 3100; www .airnewzealand.co.nz; hub Auckland, New Zealand)

Air Pacific (airline code FJ; ☎ 672 0888, 330 4388; www.airpacific.com; hub Nadi, Fiji)

Air Vanuatu (airline code NF; ☎ 672 2521, 331 5055; www.airvanuatu.com; hub Port Vila, Vanuatu) Local sales agent is Air Fiji.

Aircalin (airline code SB; ☎ 672 2145; www.aircalin .nc; hub Noumea, New Caledonia) Local agent is Aviation Travel International.

Korean Air (airline code KE; ☎ 672 1043; www.korean air.com.au; hub Seoul, Korea)

CLIMATE CHANGE & TRAVEL

Climate change is a serious threat to the ecosystems that humans rely upon, and air travel is the fastest-growing contributor to the problem. Lonely Planet regards travel, overall, as a global benefit, but believes we all have a responsibility to limit our personal impact on global warming.

Flying & Climate Change

Pretty much every form of motor travel generates CO_2 (the main cause of human-induced climate change) but planes are far and away the worst offenders, not just because of the sheer distances they allow us to travel, but because they release greenhouse gases high into the atmosphere. The statistics are frightening: two people taking a return flight between Europe and the US will contribute as much to climate change as an average household's gas and electricity consumption over a whole year.

Carbon Offset Schemes

Climatecare.org and other websites use 'carbon calculators' that allow jetsetters to offset the greenhouse gases they are responsible for with contributions to energy-saving projects and other climate-friendly initiatives in the developing world – including projects in India, Honduras, Kazakhstan and Uganda.

Lonely Planet, together with Rough Guides and other concerned partners in the travel industry, supports the carbon offset scheme run by climatecare.org. Lonely Planet offsets all of its staff and author travel.

For more information check out our website: lonelyplanet.com.

Pacific Blue (airline code DJ; ☎ 672 0777; www.flypacificblue.com; hub Brisbane, Australia)

Qantas Airways (airline code QF; ☎ 672 2880, 331 3888/1833; www.qantas.com.au; hub Sydney, Australia) Code shares with Air Pacific.

Solomon Airlines (airline code IE; ☎ 672 2831; www.flysolomons.com; hub Honiara, Solomon Islands)

United Airlines (airline code UA; ☎ in Australia 131 777; www.united.com; hub Chicago, USA) Code shares with Air New Zealand.

Tickets

High-season travel to Fiji is between April and October as well as the peak Christmas and New Year period. Airfares peak between April and June, and in December and January. If you book well enough in advance, however, it's possible to escape the seasonal price variations. As Fiji is a popular destination for Australian and New Zealand families, school holidays in these countries are considered high periods in Fiji. See p236 for further information about antipodean holiday periods.

A $30 departure tax will be incorporated into your ticket.

Recommended websites for bookings:

Cheap Flights (www.cheapflights.com) Informative site with specials, airline information and flight searches from the US and other regions.

Cheapest Flights (www.cheapestflights.co.uk) Cheap worldwide flights from the UK.

Expedia (www.expedia.msn.com) Mainly US-related travel site.

Flight Centre International (www.flightcentre.com) Respected operator with sites for Australia, New Zealand, the UK, the US and Canada.

Jet Abroad (www.jetabroad.co.nz) The New Zealand site for this travel service.

Opodo (www.opodo.com) Reliable company specialising in fares from Europe.

Orbitz (www.orbitz.com) Excellent site for web-only fares.

STA (www.statravel.com) Prominent in international student travel, but you don't have to be a student; site linked to STA sites worldwide.

Travel.com (www.travel.com.au) Good site for Australian travellers.

Travelocity (www.travelocity.com) A US site that allows you to search fares (in US dollars) to/from practically anywhere.

Trip Advisor (www.tripadvisor.com) Good site for flights from the US.

INTERCONTINENTAL (RTW) TICKETS

RTW tickets are often real bargains. They are usually put together by two or more airlines permitting you to fly anywhere on their routes as long as you don't backtrack. Most tickets are valid for up to one year. A common route from London to Australia and New Zealand via Asia and the US costs around £700/1600 (plus taxes) low/high season, although many factors (not least fuel prices) influence this.

The cheaper RTW tickets usually have more restrictions such as fewer choices of where you can stop, large fees to change flight dates and mileage caps. It's also worth checking the minimum and maximum number of stops you can make and how many different airlines you can use. An alternative type of RTW ticket is one put together by a travel agent using a combination of discounted tickets.

Circle Pacific tickets use a combination of airlines to…circle the Pacific – they generally include stops in the US, South Pacific, Southeast Asia, New Zealand and Australia. As with RTW tickets, there are advance-purchase restrictions and limits as to how many stopovers you can make. These fares are likely to be about 15% cheaper than RTW tickets.

Online ticket sales for RTW and Circle Pacific fares:

Airbrokers (www.airbrokers.com) A US company.

Just Fares.com (www.justfares.com) A US company.

Roundtheworld.com (www.roundtheworldflights.com) This excellent site allows you to build your own trips from the UK with up to six stops.

Usit (www.usit.ie) An Irish company.

Western Air (www.westernair.co.uk) A UK company.

World Travellers' Club (www.around-the-world.com) A US company.

Asia

There are direct flights to Nadi from Japan with Air Pacific and from South Korea with Korean Air. Low-/high-season return airfares from Tokyo to Nadi are around US$1500/2600; from Seoul to Nadi they are about US$1549/1653. Fares are typically more expensive in December/January, and July/August.

Most flights to/from Southeast Asia go via Australia or New Zealand. Return airfares from Hong Kong to Nadi are around US$1600/2200 for low/high season. Most countries offer fairly competitive deals – Bangkok, Singapore and Hong Kong are good places to shop around for discount tickets.

Recommended agencies in Japan:

No 1 Travel (☎ 03-3205 6073; www.no1-travel.com)

STA Travel (☎ 03-5391 2922; www.statravel.co.jp)

Australia

Qantas, Air Pacific and Pacific Blue operate between Australia and Fiji. Qantas planes don't actually fly to Fiji but the airline sells tickets and code shares seats on Air Pacific

flights. The flight time is about four hours from Sydney and 4½ hours from Melbourne.

Fares from Sydney or Brisbane are typically A$700/1350 return for low/high season. Flights from Melbourne cost from A$100 to A$200 more. The further in advance you book, the cheaper your ticket is likely to be.

Agencies in Australia with specialist Fiji knowledge:

Fiji & Pacific Specialist Holidays (☎ 02-9080 1600; www.pacificholidays.com.au)

Hideaway Holidays (☎ 02-8799 2500; www.hideawayholidays.com.au)

South Pacific Holidays (☎ 1300 997 287; www.tropicalfiji.com)

Talpacific Holidays (☎ 1300 137 727; www.talpacific.com)

Continental Europe

Generally there is not much variation in airfares for departures from the main European cities, but deals can be had, so shop around. Expect to pay around €1100/2000 for low-/high-season travel.

Useful agencies:

Adventure Travel (www.adventure-holidays.com) German agency specialising in South Pacific travel.

Anyway (☎ 0892 893 892; www.anyway.fr) French site.

BarronTravel (☎ 020-625 8600; www.barron.nl) Dutch agency operating 3 Oceans Travel, which specialises in the South Pacific.

OTU Voyages (☎ 08 2081 7817, 01 4441 3850; www.otu.fr) French network of student-travel agencies; supplies discount tickets to travellers of all ages.

Voyageurs du Monde (www.vdm.com)

Wereldcontact (☎ 0343-530 530; www.wereldcontact.nl) Dutch agency.

New Zealand

Air Pacific flies from Auckland, Wellington and Christchurch to Nadi. Air New Zealand also flies between Nadi and Auckland and has shared services on the other routes. From Auckland to Fiji (three hours) costs about NZ$600/1200 (including taxes) for low/high season. Flights from Wellington and Christchurch tend to cost around NZ$200 extra.

Good booking agencies:

Air New Zealand (☎ 0800 737 000; www.airnewzealand.co.nz)

Flight Centre (www.flightcentre.co.nz)

Go Holidays (☎ 0800 464 646; www.goholidays.co.nz) South Pacific specialists for accommodation and packages.

TRANSPORT

House of Travel (www.houseoftravel.co.nz) Nation-wide travel agency.

STA (www.statravel.co.nz)

Talpacific Holidays (☎ 09-914 8728; www.travel arrange.co.nz) South Pacific specialists.

Travel Online (☎ 0800 000 747, 09-920 6000; www .travelonline.co.nz)

Zuji (www.zuji.co.nz) Online booking service.

Pacific Countries

In the not-so-distant past it was possible to buy air passes that allowed travel within the South Pacific. The different terms and conditions varied from pass to pass but the general idea was that you could work your way around several island nations provided that you met certain mileage requirements. The three most popular passes – Air Pacific's Triangle Fare and Visit South Pacific pass and the Qantas Boomerang Pass have all been cancelled. It is, however, worth keeping an eye out for such passes as they can offer good value to those who plan to explore the Pacific.

Currently the only flights between Fiji and its Pacific neighbours are the Air Pacific flights to Samoa ($430 one way), Tuvalu ($477 one way), Solomon ($548 one way), Hawaii ($894 one way), Tonga ($355 one way), Vanuatu ($416 one way) and Kiribati ($656 one way). These prices include taxes.

Pacific island nations' airlines that fly directly to Fiji are Air Vanuatu (from Port Vila, Vanuatu), Aircalin (from Noumea, New Caledonia) and Solomon Airlines (from Honiara, Solomon islands). All of these airline websites are listed on p241.

UK & Ireland

London is the travel-discount capital of Europe. Airline-ticket discounters are known as bucket shops in the UK and many advertise in the travel pages of weekend newspapers, such as the *Independent* on Saturday and the *Sunday Times*. Also check the travel section of the free magazine, *TNT*. A return ticket from London to Nadi costs about £600/1600 (plus taxes) in low/high season. Some agencies to check out:

Ebookers (☎ 0871 223 5000; www.ebookers.com)

Trailfinders (☎ 0845 058 5858; www.trailfinders.co.uk)

Travel Bag (☎ 0800 804 8911; www.travelbag.co.uk)

US

Fiji is a major stopover between the west coast of the US and Australia or New Zealand. Fiji is about six/12 hours from Hawaii/West Coast US. Fares from the US vary greatly depending on the season and ticket restrictions. Los Angeles to Nadi with Air New Zealand is about US$1200/1800 for low/high season.

The following agents specialise in travel to Fiji and the South Pacific:

All Travel (☎ 800 300-4567, 310-312-3368; www .all-travel.com)

Fiji Travels (www.fijitravels.com)

South Pacific Direct (www.southpacificdirect.com)

Sunspots International (☎ 800-334-5623, 503-666 -3893; www.sunspotsintl.com)

SEA

Travelling to Fiji by sea is difficult unless you're on a cruise ship or a yacht.

Cargo Ship

Few of the shipping companies will take passengers on cargo ships and those that do will usually charge hefty rates. It is virtually impossible to leave Fiji by cargo ship unless passage has been prearranged. A useful American company is **Freighter World Cruises** (☎ 800-531-7774; www.freighterworld.com), which can organise travel on a freighter ship around the South Pacific. You could also try asking your local shipping agents, or go to the docks and personally approach the captains.

Yacht

Fiji's islands are a popular destination and stopover for yachts cruising the Pacific. The best time to sail is in the 'winter' from early November to late April when the southeasterly trade winds are blowing. During the 'summer' months (May to October), winds change direction more often and the chance of finding yourself in a storm or cyclone is greater.

Strict laws govern the entry of yachts into Fiji and yachties should immediately make for a designated port of entry (Suva, Lautoka, Levuka or Savusavu) to clear customs, immigration and quarantine. Be sure to have a certificate of clearance from the previous port of call, a crew list and passports. Before departing, you'll again need to complete clearance formalities (within 24 hours), providing inbound clearance papers, your vessel's details and your next port of call. Customs must be cleared before immigration, and you must have paid all port dues and health fees. For more information see p239.

Other marinas in Fiji include Vuda Point Marina (between Nadi and Lautoka)

IT'S A SAILOR'S LIFE FOR ME

Crewing on a yacht across the blue of the Pacific can sound romantic, and often it is – remote beaches, pristine reefs and the soft slap of the ocean against the hull. It all sounds fab but before you grab that bottle of rum and train a parrot to whistle sea shanties have a scan through these tips.

- Long passages between landfalls, cooped up with strangers, can get mighty boring on a 15m-long piece of fiberglass. Spend as much time with the captain as possible before committing. This way you can both see how compatible you are likely to be with the rest of the crew.

- Expect to share a room. Yachts are semiprivate at best.

- Fresh water on a boat is a premium. It is unlikely that you will use it to wash with.

- Your attitude is supremely important. Once at sea you can't get off. Be willing to do all kinds of jobs and know that a yacht is no place for lofty creature comforts.

- Discuss in detail the skipper's expectations of you and if you are expected to contribute to the kitty before you leave.

- Expect to take your turn at night watches.

- To find a crewing position be proactive, use the noticeboards at marinas, knock on doors and learn where the boats will be at different times of the year. It is no use looking in Fiji if all the boats are still in Tonga.

- To enter the Pacific islands you need to prove onward transportation, which means the skipper must vouch for you. They are well within their rights to hold your passport or deny you shore leave.

- Try to gauge the experience of the skipper and the condition of the boat. Your life depends on it.

and Port Denarau (Denarau Marina) on Viti Levu, and Musket Cove Marina on Malololailai (Plantation Island) in the Mamanucas. Yachties are often looking for extra crew and people to share day-to-day costs. If you are interested, ask around the marinas and look on the noticeboards. For more details on travelling by yacht see p231 and visit www.noonsite.com/Countries/Fiji, which details port facilities and has a library of online trip accounts.

Yatch Help (Map p88; ☎ 675 0911; VHF Marine channel 16; www.yachthelp.com; Shop 5, Port Denarau) is an extremely efficient aid to skippers. It can arrange Lau cruising permits, assemble provision orders and contact tradesmen, and it publishes the *Fiji Marine Guide*.

The Coconut Milk Run is a popular route cruising from California to New Zealand via Hawaii, Tahiti, Rarotonga, Vava'u and Fiji. To make the most of the weather most yachts depart California in February and reach Fiji in July or August.

Boats from New Zealand often time their departure to coincide with the Auckland-to-Fiji yacht race in June. By the end of October most yachts head south to Australia and New Zealand via New Caledonia to spend the summer there.

GETTING AROUND

By using local buses, carriers (small trucks) and ferries you can get around Fiji's main islands relatively cheaply and easily. If you'd like more comfort or are short on time you can utilise air-conditioned express buses, rental vehicles, charter boats and small planes.

AIR

Viti Levu's airports at Nadi and Nausori (near Suva), are the main domestic hubs. Other domestic airports include Savusavu and Labasa on Vanua Levu, Matei on Taveuni, Vunisea on Kadavu, Bureta on Ovalau in the Lomaiviti Group, and Malololailai and Mana in the Mamanucas. Many other small islands also have airstrips. There are flights to some outer islands where there is no accommodation for tourists and an invitation is needed to visit – in some cases it is illegal to turn up uninvited. Rotuma, Gau and Koro in the Lomaiviti

TRANSPORT

FIJI AIR FARES

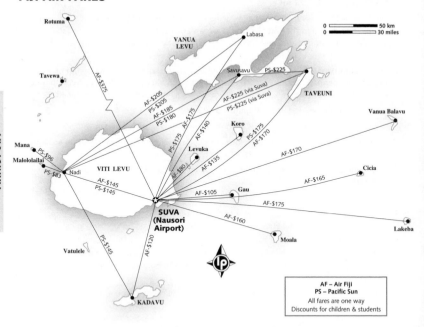

AF – Air Fiji
PS – Pacific Sun
All fares are one way
Discounts for children & students

Group, Moala and Vanua Balavu (in the Moala Group), and Lakeba in Lau have airstrips but receive few visitors, while other islands such as Vatulele (off Viti Levu), Yasawa and Wakaya (in the Lomaiviti Group) have their own airstrips that serve the upmarket resorts.

Airlines in Fiji
Fiji is well serviced by frequent Air Fiji and Pacific Sun internal flights. Some may find the light planes scary, especially if it's windy or turbulent, but the views of the islands, coral reefs and lagoons are fantastic. Most flights are turnaround flights that return to Suva after unloading and reloading passengers. As some flights only go once a week it is advisable to book well in advance to secure a seat.

Air Fiji's services operate out of Nausori Airport near Suva and have a less-than-stellar record when it comes to customer satisfaction. In 2008 the planes were grounded for two weeks leaving countless people stranded on remote islands.

Pacific Sun was formed when Fiji's international carrier, Air Pacific, bought Sun Air in 2006. Pacific Sun often transports passengers' luggage in a separate plane, and arriving before or after your possessions is a common occurrence. It is a smart policy to take a change of clothes and all your valuables in your carry-on luggage. Prices on routes shared by the airlines are almost identical.

Air Fiji (☎ 331 5055; www.airfiji.com.fj) operates flights from Suva to Nadi, Kadavu, Koro, Labasa, Lakeba, Levuka, Moala, Rotuma, Savusavu, Taveuni, Vanua Balavu, Cicia and Gau. From Nadi, there are flights to Suva, Labasa, Savusavu and Taveuni. There is also a flight between Savusavu and Taveuni.

Pacific Sun (☎ 330 4388; www.pacificsun.com.fj) domestic routes are from Suva to Nadi, Labasa and Taveuni, and from Nadi to Suva, Kadavu, Labasa, Malololailai, Mana, Savusavu and Taveuni.

Air Passes
Air Fiji has a 30-day air pass that is sold only outside Fiji. It costs US$270 for those living in the USA and $517 for everyone else. The pass includes four flights but you can buy additional legs for $100 per sector. It's best to book your seats because the small planes

often fill up quickly. Children under 12 get a 25% discount, while infants are charged 10% of the full fare. There is a $100 predeparture-cancellation fee, and reimbursement is minimal once in Fiji. If you change your mind it will cost $100 to reissue your ticket.

Charter Services

Charter services are most commonly used by those wishing to maximise their time at island resorts.

Island Hoppers (☎ 675 0670; www.helicopters.com.fj) offers transfers to most of the Mamanuca islands' resorts, as well as helicopter flights departing from Denarau island and Nadi airport. A flight to Vomo, Castaway Island, Waidigi or Tokoriki Resorts by helicopter costs $294 one way per person.

Turtle Airways (☎ 672 1888; www.turtleairways.com) has a fleet of seaplanes departing from New Town Beach or Denarau, near Nadi. As well as joy flights, it provides transfer services to the Mamanucas, Yasawas, the Fijian Resort (on the Queens Road), Pacific Harbour, Suva, Toberua Island Resort and other islands as required. Turtle Airways also charters a five-seater Cessna and a seven-seater de Havilland Canadian Beaver. Contact the airline for rates.

Pacific Island Seaplanes (☎ 672 5644; www.fijiseaplanes.com) also offers transfers to islands in the Mamanuca, Yasawa and Lau Groups.

BICYCLE

Cycling not only allows you to see the countryside at your own pace but you'll reduce your carbon footprint at the same time. While not popular, cycling is certainly feasible. See p229 for information on suggested routes.

The best time to go is the drier season (May to October), and note that the eastern sides of the larger islands receive higher rainfall. Mountain bikes are best for exploring the interior. If you intend to cycle around Fiji as a main form of transport, bring your own bike, helmet, waterproof gear, repair kit and all other equipment. It is difficult to get bike parts in Fiji. If you wish to take a bike on a domestic flight, make sure it is demountable.

The biggest hazard for cyclists is the unpredictable traffic – drivers can be pretty manic and are not used to cyclists. Avoid riding in the evening when visibility is low. Travel light but carry plenty of water – it can be hot and dusty or humid. You can usually buy

coconuts and bananas from villages along the way. The cheapest place to store bikes is at backpacker hostels.

BOAT

With the exception of the Mamanuca and Yasawa Groups, and upmarket resort islands, often the only means of transport to and between the islands is by small local boats, especially for the backpacker resorts. Life jackets are rarely provided on the small boats and usually they have no radio-phones. If the weather looks ominous or the boat is overcrowded, consider postponing the trip or opting for a flight.

In other areas, it is difficult to explore and hop from island to island unless you have a charter boat or yacht. On Kadavu, for example, transport is mostly by small village- or resort-owned boats. Apart from the Suva to Kadavu ferry, there is no organised transport.

Ferry

Regular ferry services link Viti Levu to Vanua Levu and Taveuni, and also Viti Levu to Ovalau. The Patterson Brothers, Beachcomber Cruises and Consort Shipping boats are large roll-on, roll-off ferries carrying passengers, vehicles and cargo. They have canteens where you can buy drinks, snacks and light meals. Ferry timetables are notorious for changing frequently, plus boats sometimes leave at odd hours and there is often a long waiting period at stopovers. The worst thing about the long trips is that the toilets can become disgusting (take your own toilet paper). There are irregular boats that take passengers from Suva to Lau, Rotuma and Kadavu.

NADI–MAMANUCAS

South Sea Cruises (☎ 675 0500; www.ssc.com.fj) operates two fast catamarans from Denarau Marina to most of the Mamanuca islands, including Malolo, Walu Beach, Castaway Island, Mana, Treasure Island, Beachcomber Island, Bounty Island, South Sea Island, Matamanoa and Tokoriki. See p143 for information on these services.

NADI–YASAWAS

Awesome Adventures Fiji (☎ 675 0499; www.awesomefiji.com), which is the same company as South Sea Cruises, operates the lurid yellow *Yasawa Flyer,* a large catamaran that services all of the resorts on the Yasawa islands plus some of the Mamanuca resorts, daily. It's a large boat with a comfortable interior including a snack shop and toilets, but you'll still feel the swell on choppy days. See the boxed text, p155 for more details.

SUVA–KORO–SAVUSAVU–(LABASA)–TAVEUNI

Consort Shipping (Map p118; ☎ 330 2877; fax 330 3389; consortship@connect.com.fj; Ground fl, Dominion House Arcade, Thomson St, Suva) runs twice a week from Suva to Savusavu ($90/60 for cabin/seat) via Koro ($85/55 for cabin/seat), departing Suva at 5pm on Tuesdays and 6pm on Fridays. It takes 12 hours to reach Savusavu, and then continues for another four hours on to Taveuni ($110/70 from Suva for cabin/seat). On the way back it departs Taveuni around 4pm on Wednesdays and 9am on Sundays, arriving in Suva at around 11am on Thursdays and 6am on Mondays. This boat often runs late. For those bound for Labasa, a bus meets the boat at Savusavu. A Suva to Labasa fare including the bus costs $110/70 for a cabin/seat.

SUVA–SAVUSAVU–(LABASA)–TAVEUNI

Bligh Water Shipping (Labasa Map p191; ☎ 881 8471; Shop 4, Sangam Complex; Lautoka Map p94; ☎ 666 8229; Shop 3, Nede St; Savusavu Map p182; ☎ 885 3192; 1st fl, Water Front Bld; Suva Map p116; ☎ 331 8247; www .blighwatershipping.com.fj; 1-2 Matua St, Walu Bay; Taveuni Agents – Tima Ltd Map p198; ☎ 888 0261) departs Suva at 6pm on Mondays, Wednesdays and Fridays to Savusavu. For those bound for Labasa a bus meets the boat at the wharf. The MV *Suilven* then departs Savusavu at 6am on Tuesdays, Thursdays and Saturdays arriving at Taveuni at 10.30am. The boat returns to Savusavu on the same day, leaving at 2.30pm and arriving in Savusavu at 7pm before returning to Suva at 8pm. Adult fares from Suva to Savusavu/ Taveuni/Labasa are $67/78/73. A fare for the Savusavu-to-Taveuni leg costs $45.

Grace Ferry (Labasa Map p191; Gulam Nabi & Sons; ☎ 881 1152; Nasekula Rd; Savusavu Map p182; Country Kitchen; ☎ 927 1372) operates a bus/boat trip from Taveuni to Savusavu and Labasa ($20 to $25). See p200 for more information.

(SUVA)–NATOVI–LEVUKA–NABOUWALU (VANUA LEVU)

Patterson Brothers Shipping (Labasa ☎ 881 2444; Nasekula Rd; Lautoka ☎ 666 1173; 15 Tukani St; Levuka ☎ 344 0125; Beach St; Nabouwalu ☎ 883 6002; Nausori ☎ 347 8335; Suva Map p118; ☎ 331 5644; fax 330 1652; Suites 1 & 2, Epworth Arcade, Nina St) operates a daily service ($25 one way), which involves a 1½-hour bus ride from Suva (Western Bus Terminal, Rodwell Rd) to Natovi Landing, followed by a ferry to Buresala Landing (one hour) and another bus to Levuka (one hour). Buses depart Suva at 2pm and Labasa at 5am. It is possible to travel on to Nabouwalu on Vanua Levu, where you can continue by bus to Labasa ($55).

(SUVA)–BAU LANDING–LELEUVIA–LEVUKA

There are services from Suva to Leleuvia via Bau Landing ($30 one way) and from Leleuvia to Levuka ($20 one way). See p176 for more information.

SUVA–KADAVU

Venu Shipping (Map p116; ☎ 339 5000; Rona St, Walu Bay, Suva) runs once-weekly passenger services on the MV *Sinu-i-wasa* (deck/cabin $55/75 one way). See p216 for more information.

SUVA–LAU GROUP

Saliabasaga Shipping (Map p116; ☎ 331 7484; Dark green shipping container on Muaiwalu Wharf, Suva) has monthly trips aboard the MV *Tunatuki* to Lakeba, Nayau, Cicia, Tuvuca, Vanua Balavu and occasionally Komo, Namaku-i-Lau, Moce and Oneata. The one-way fare to Vanua Balavu is $120/160 for deck/cabin including meals.

Western Shipping (Map p116; ☎ 331 7484; Yellow Shipping Container on Naryan Jetty, Suva) operates the *Cagi Mai Ba* to the islands in the Lau Group (deck/seat/cabin $104/115/130) once a month. Phone for departure times and dates.

SUVA–MOALA GROUP

There is no accommodation for visitors on the Moala islands – you need to be invited by a local to stay.

Saliabasaga Shipping (see above) runs monthly trips on the MV *Tunatuki* to Moala, Matuke and Totoya in the Moala Group. The journey takes about eight hours and a one-way fare is $100/130 for deck/cabin.

SUVA–ROTUMA

Western Shipping (see above) operates the *Cagi Mai Ba* to Rotuma (deck/seat/cabin $125/155/190) once a month. The journey takes 36 hours; phone for departure times and dates.

(LAUTOKA)–ELLINGTON WHARF–NABOUWALU (VANUA LEVU)–(LABASA)

This Patterson Brothers Shipping (opposite) service was suspended in 2008 but it is likely that it will restart. It involved a bus ride from Lautoka (3½ hours), a trip on the *Ashika* ferry (3¾ hours) and another bus to Labasa (four hours). Buses departed from outside the Lautoka office at 4am on Fridays and Mondays, and from Labasa at 6am on Sundays and Wednesdays. The fare was $60.

LAUTOKA–SAVUSAVU

Bligh Water Shipping (opposite) boats depart Lautoka every Monday, Wednesday and Friday at 4pm although you should report at 2pm. The boat, MV *Westerland,* arrives in Savusavu between 3am and 4am but passengers can stay aboard until it gets light. The boat then departs Savusavu for Lautoka on Tuesdays, Thursdays and Sundays at 9pm, arriving around 9am. Fares cost $64 one way. This service connects with the MV *Suliven* service to Taveuni.

Yacht

Yachting is a great way to explore the Fiji archipelago. It is possible to charter boats or hitch a ride at a marina. See p244 and the boxed text, p245, for more information.

BUS

Fiji's larger islands have extensive and inexpensive bus networks. Local buses are cheap and regular and a great way to mix with the locals. While they can be fairly noisy and smoky they are perfect for the tropics, with unglazed windows and pull-down tarpaulins for when it rains. There are bus stops but you can often also just hail buses along the road, especially in rural areas. Most drivers prefer to go downhill at the maximum speed that their vehicle allows to make up for the excruciatingly slow speed that they travel at uphill. It's a lot like being on a roller coaster, only cheaper.

Air-conditioned express buses run on some major routes such as Nadi to Suva.

Sunbeam Transport and Pacific Transport are the main carriers on Viti Levu; see p78 for more information. Pacific Transport also operates services on Taveuni (see p201). Coral Sun's Scania coaches only stop at the major resorts between Nadi airport and Suva. The buses are more comfortable than those of the other operators, are only a few dollars more expensive and are predominantly used by tourists (see p78 for more information). Local companies operate buses on Vanua Levu but they can be slow and their timetables can be erratic.

Reservations are not necessary for local buses. If you are on a tight schedule or have an appointment, though, it's a good idea to buy your ticket in advance, especially for bus trips and tours over longer distances (eg Suva to Nadi). Pacific Transport and Sunbeam issue timetables (available from the Fiji Visitors Bureau; FVB) but for most of the local buses you should just ask around at the bus stations.

CAR & MOTORCYCLE

About 90% of Fiji's 5100km of roads are on Viti Levu and Vanua Levu, of which about one-fifth are sealed. Both of these islands are fun to explore by car, 4WD or motorcycle.

Driving Licence

If you hold a current driving licence from an English-speaking country you are entitled to drive in Fiji. Otherwise you will need an international driving permit, which should be obtained in your home country before travelling.

Fuel

Petrol stations are common and easy to find on Viti Levu and Vanua Levu. They are most prolific and competitive in the cities. Once you get off the beaten track, however, they become fewer and further between. If you plan to do some driving by 4WD into Viti Levu's interior you should take a full tank with you. If you do run out of fuel it might be available in village shops (but don't assume so).

Hire

Rental cars are relatively expensive in Fiji. Despite this, it is a good way to explore the larger islands, especially if you can split the cost with others.

Some rental agencies will not allow their cars to be driven on unpaved roads, which greatly limits your ability to explore the highlands. It is possible to take vehicles on roll-on, roll-off ferries to Vanua Levu or Taveuni but again, some companies do not allow this. The ferry costs are pretty expensive and vehicles are available to rent on both of these islands anyway. If you do take a car on a ferry to Vanua Levu it's best if the car's a 4WD.

The shorter the hire period, the higher the rate. Delivery and collection are often included in the price. Rates for a week or more with an international company start at around $85 per day, excluding tax, but the same car can cost twice as much per day for just one or two days' hire. Some companies will hire at an hourly rate or per half day, while some have a minimum hire of three days. It's usual to pay a deposit by credit card. If you don't have a credit card you'll need to leave a hefty cash bond.

A valid overseas or international driving licence is required. The minimum-age requirement is 21, or in some cases 25.

Ask the FVB about the various companies. Generally, the larger, well-known companies have better cars and support but are more expensive. Consider what's appropriate for you, including how inconvenienced you might be if the car breaks down, what support services are provided, the likely distance to services, cost of insurance, if value-added tax (VAT) is included and the excess or excess-waiver amount. Regardless of where you rent from, check brakes, water and tyre pressure and condition before heading off.

The easiest place to rent vehicles is on Viti Levu. Most rental agencies have offices at Nadi International Airport; the established companies also have offices in other towns and rental desks at larger hotels. Car-rental agencies on Vanua Levu and Taveuni have mostly 4WDs due to the islands' rough roads.

Some of the more reputable car-rental agencies on Viti Levu:

Avis Rent a Car (www.avis.com.fj) Korolevu (☎ 653 0833); Korotogo (Map p102; ☎ 652 0144); Nadi airport (☎ 672 2233); Nausori airport (☎ 337 8361); Suva (Map p116; ☎ 337 8361)

Budget Rent a Car (www.budget.com.fj) Labasa (☎ 881 1999); Nadi airport (☎ 672 2636); Nausori airport (☎ 347 9299); Savusavu (☎ 881 1999); Sigatoka (Map p100; ☎ 650 0986); Suva (Map p116; ☎ 331 5899); Taveuni (☎ 888 0291)

Hertz (www.hertzfiji.net) Nadi airport (☎ 672 3466); Suva (Map p116; ☎ 338 0981)

Thrifty Car Rental (www.thrifty.com) Nadi airport (☎ 672 2935); Suva (Map p118; ☎ 331 4436)

Although not widely available, motorcycles and scooters are not a bad way to travel in Fiji. Similar traffic rules and rental conditions as mentioned previously for car rental apply to motorcycles and scooters. Rental per day starts at around $55/65 for scooters/125cc motorcycles.

INSURANCE
Third-party insurance is compulsory. Some car-rental companies include it in their daily rates while others add it at the end (count on $22 to $30 at least). Personal accident insurance is highly recommended if you are not already covered by travel insurance. Renters are liable for the first $500 damage. Common exclusions, or problems that won't be paid for by the insurance company, include tyre damage, underbody and overhead damage, windscreen damage and theft of the vehicle.

Road Conditions
The perimeter of Viti Levu is easy to get to know by car. The Queens Road and most of the Kings Road are sealed, although the section between Korovou and Dama is still unsealed. It takes about 3½ hours to drive the 200km from Nadi International Airport to Suva (via the Queens Road) but this depends on how many lorries you get caught behind on the hills. Roads into Viti Levu's interior are unsealed and a 4WD is generally necessary.

There are unsealed roads around most of Vanua Levu's perimeter, but there's a sealed road from Labasa to Savusavu and the first 20km of the Hibiscus Hwy from Savusavu along the scenic coast is also paved. The remainder of the Hibiscus Hwy is quite rough.

Road Hazards
Some locals drive with a fairly heavy foot on the accelerator pedal and many ignore the whole idea of sticking to the left-hand side when navigating bends (particularly along the Coral Coast). Local drivers also tend to stop suddenly and overtake on blind corners, so take care, especially on gravel roads. Buses also stop where and when they please. There are lots of potholes and sometimes the roads are too narrow for two vehicles to pass, so be aware of oncoming traffic.

Watch for sugar trains in the cane-cutting season because they have right of way. Dogs wandering onto the road can be a major hazard so observe the speed hump–enforced 20km/h rule when driving through villages. Avoid driving at night as there are many pedestrians and wandering animals – especially along the southeast coast of Viti Levu, on Vanua Levu and on Taveuni.

Road Rules

Drive on the left-hand side of the road. The speed limit is 80km/h, which drops to 50km/h in villages. Many villages have speed humps to force drivers to slow down. Seatbelts are compulsory for front-seat passengers. Parking fines in Suva are generally around $2.

HITCHING

Hitching is never entirely safe in any country and we don't recommend it. Travellers who decide to hitch should understand that they are taking a small but potentially serious risk.

Hitching in Fiji, however, is common. Locals do it all the time, especially with carriers. It is customary to pay the equivalent of the relevant bus fare to the driver. Hitchhikers will be safer if they travel in pairs and let someone know where they are planning to go. Crime is more prevalent around Suva, although there have been cases of hitchhikers being mugged around Nadi.

LOCAL TRANSPORT

Many locals drive small trucks (known as carriers) with a tarpaulin-covered frame on the back. These often have passenger seating and some run trips between Nadi and Suva. You can pick one up in Nadi's main street; they leave when they are full and are quicker and only slightly more expensive than taking the bus.

Minivans are also an increasingly common sight on the road. Popular with locals, they're also quicker and more expensive than a bus but much cheaper than a taxi. Your ride won't necessarily be more comfortable, though – it's generally a sardine-type affair. Minivans plough up and down the Queens Road around Nadi.

TAXI

You will find taxis on Viti Levu, Vanua Levu, Taveuni and Ovalau. The bus stations in the main towns usually have taxi depots and there is often an oversupply of taxis, with drivers competing for business. There are some good cabs, but most are rickety old dinosaurs bound for or retrieved from the wrecker. Most taxi drivers are Indo-Fijians keen to discuss life and local issues. They invariably have relatives in Australia, New Zealand or Canada.

Unlike in Suva, the taxi drivers in Nadi, Lautoka and most rural areas don't use their meters. First ask locals what an acceptable rate for a particular trip is. Then, if there is no meter, confirm an approximate price with the driver before you agree to travel. Cabs can be shared for long trips. For touring around areas with limited public transport such as Taveuni, forming a group and negotiating a taxi fee for a half or full day may be an option.

Always ask if the cab is a return taxi (returning to its base). If so, you can expect to pay $1 per person or less, as long as the taxi doesn't have to go out of its way. To make up for the low fare the driver will usually pick up extra passengers from bus stops. You can usually recognise a return taxi because most have the name of their home depot on the bumper bar.

TOURS

Fiji has many companies providing tours within the country, including trekking, cycling, kayaking, diving, bus and 4WD tours. Cruises to the outer islands such as the Mamanucas (p141) and Yasawas (p153) are popular. There is also a sailing safari on the *Tui Tai* from Savusavu to Taveuni, Kioa and Rabi (p179).

Activity-based tours, such as hiking and kayaking are discussed more fully on p228.

Feejee Experience (☎ 672 3311; www.feejeeexperience.com) offers coach transfers for budget travellers that allow you to hop on and off the route as you like within six months. The six-day Lei Low ($558) includes Natadola Beach, sandboarding down the Sigatoka Dunes, the Coral Coast, highland trekking, tubing on the Navua River, Suva nightclubs, *bilibili* (bamboo raft) trips, the mud pools at Sabeto, kayaking, snorkelling at Volivoli (Rakiraki) and Beachcomber Island. The four-day Hula Loop ($396) includes slightly less, and a third option, Tribal Loop ($1399), includes seven nights with the Tribe Wanted sustainability project in Vanua Levu (see the boxed text, p195). These tours are popular with the 20-something crowd who do not want to use the public buses. Nightly activities are catered to this age group and are very social, fortified with alcohol and are lots of fun. Feejee Experience has a stellar reputation and those who sign up for a tour rave about their experiences. The tours include the cost of all of the activities mentioned here but do not include any accommodation or food. Before you book, however, it is worth keeping in mind that a perfectly comfortable Sunbeam Bus will also take you around the island for $31.50.

TRANSPORT

Health Dr Michael Sorokin

CONTENTS

Before You Go	**252**
Insurance	252
Recommended Vaccinations	252
Medical Checklist	252
Internet Resources	253
Further Reading	253
In Transit	**253**
Deep Vein Thrombosis (DVT)	253
Jet Lag & Motion Sickness	253
In Fiji	**254**
Availability & Cost of Health Care	254
Infectious Diseases	254
Traveller's Diarrhoea	255
Environmental Hazards	256

Rabies is no danger in any of the Fijian islands. And there are no crocodiles. There is also no malaria in Fiji, a huge health plus. Mosquitoes do exist, though, and the main danger from them is dengue fever. Health facilities are good in Fiji; however, this is a small country with a limited budget so 'good' does not necessarily equate with the facilities in a well-developed country.

BEFORE YOU GO

Prevention is the key to staying healthy while abroad. A little planning before departure, particularly for pre-existing illnesses, will save trouble later. See your dentist before a long trip, carry a spare pair of contact lenses and glasses, and take your optical prescription with you. Bring medications in their original, clearly labelled, containers. A signed and dated letter from your physician describing your medical conditions and medications, including generic names, is also a good idea. If carrying syringes or needles, be sure to have a physician's letter documenting their medical necessity.

INSURANCE

If your health insurance policy does not cover you for medical expenses abroad, consider taking supplemental insurance. (Check www.lonelyplanet.com/bookings/insurance.do for more details.) Find out in advance if your insurance plan will make payments directly to providers or reimburse you later for overseas health expenditures. (In Fiji most treatment requires payment in cash, though.)

Really serious illness or injury may require evacuation, eg to Auckland or Sydney; make sure that your health insurance has provision for evacuation. Under these circumstances hospitals will accept direct payment from major international insurers.

RECOMMENDED VACCINATIONS

The World Health Organization (WHO) recommends that all travellers be covered for diphtheria, tetanus, measles, mumps, rubella and polio, regardless of their destination. Since most vaccines don't produce immunity until at least two weeks after they're given, visit a physician at least six weeks before departure. A recent influenza vaccination is always a good idea when travelling. If you have not had chicken pox (varicella) consider being vaccinated.

MEDICAL CHECKLIST

It is a very good idea to carry a medical and first-aid kit with you, in case of minor illness or injury. The following is a list of items you should consider packing.

- acetaminophen (paracetamol) or aspirin*
- adhesive or paper tape
- antibacterial ointment, eg Bactroban, for cuts and abrasions (prescription only)
- antibiotic plus steroid eardrops (prescription only), eg Sofradex, Kenacort Otic
- antibiotics (prescription only), eg ciprofloxacin (Ciproxin) or norfloxacin (Utinor; Noroxin)
- antidiarrhoeal drugs, eg loperamide
- antigiardia tablets – tinidazole (prescription only)
- antihistamines (for hay fever and allergic reactions)
- anti-inflammatory drugs, eg ibuprofen
- bandages, gauze, gauze rolls, waterproof dressings
- DEET-containing insect repellent for the skin

REQUIRED & RECOMMENDED VACCINATIONS

If you have been in a country affected by yellow fever within six days of arriving in Fiji, you will need an International Certificate of Vaccination for yellow fever to be allowed entry into the country. Vaccinations are recommended for hepatitis A, hepatitis B and typhoid fever.

All injected vaccinations can produce slight soreness and redness at the inoculation site, and a mild fever with muscle aches over the first 24 hours. These are least likely with hepatitis A and a little more common with hepatitis B and typhoid inoculations. Typhoid inoculation can cause a sensation of nausea within 24 hours and the hepatitis B vaccine can produce temporary joint pains.

An allergy to eggs or poultry is a condition that makes the yellow-fever vaccination inadvisable; an exemption certificate can be issued. Very rarely, an acute allergic (anaphylactic shock) reaction can occur within minutes of any vaccination. More commonly a flulike illness of varying severity may occur at any time up to 10 days after vaccination. In the elderly, encephalitis has been recorded.

- iodine tablets (for water purification)
- oral rehydration salts, eg Gastrolyte, Diarolyte, Replyte
- Permethrin-containing insect spray for clothing, tents and bed nets
- pocket knife+
- scissors, safety pins, tweezers+
- steroid cream or hydrocortisone cream (for allergic rashes)
- sun block
- syringes and sterile needles (prescription only), and intravenous fluids if travelling in very remote areas
- thermometer

*Aspirin should not be used for fever – it can cause bleeding in sufferers of dengue fever
+ Do not take on planes in carry-on luggage

INTERNET RESOURCES

There is a wealth of travel health advice on the internet. For further information, www.lonelyplanet.com is a good place to start. WHO produces a superb free, online text, *International Travel and Health,* which is available at www.who.int/ith/. Other websites of general interest are MD Travel Health at www.mdtravelhealth.com, which provides complete travel health recommendations for every country (updated daily), also at no cost; the Centers for Disease Control and Prevention at www.cdc.gov; and Fit for Travel at www.fitfortravel.scot.nhs.uk, which has up-to-date information about outbreaks and is very user-friendly, and www.traveldoctor.com.au, a similar Australasian site.

It's also a good idea to consult your government's travel-health website:

Australia (www.dfat.gov.au/travel/)
Canada (www.hc-sc.gc.ca/)
New Zealand (www.mfat.govt.nz/travel)
UK (www.doh.gov.uk) Click on Policy and Guidance, then on Health Advice for Travellers.
USA (www.cdc.gov/travel/)

FURTHER READING

Good options for further reading include *Travel with Children* by Cathy Lanigan; *Healthy Travel Australia, New Zealand and the Pacific* by Dr Isabelle Young; and *Your Child's Health Abroad: A Manual for Travelling Parents* by Dr Jane Wilson-Howarth and Matthew Ellis.

IN TRANSIT

DEEP VEIN THROMBOSIS (DVT)

Blood clots may form in the legs during plane flights, chiefly because of prolonged immobility. The longer the flight, the greater the risk. The chief symptom of DVT is swelling or pain of the foot, ankle or calf, usually but not always on just one side. When a blood clot travels to the lungs, it may cause chest pain and breathing difficulties. Travellers with any of these symptoms should immediately seek medical attention.

To prevent the development of DVT on long flights you should walk about the cabin, contract the leg muscles while sitting and drink plenty of nonalcoholic fluids.

JET LAG & MOTION SICKNESS

To avoid jet lag (common when crossing more than five time zones) try drinking plenty of nonalcoholic fluids and eating light meals. Upon arrival, get exposure to natural sunlight and readjust your schedule (for meals, sleep and so on) as soon as possible.

Antihistamines such as dimenhydrinate (Dramamine) and meclizine (Antivert, Bonine) are usually the first choice for treating motion sickness. Ginger is a herbal alternative.

IN FIJI

AVAILABILITY & COST OF HEALTH CARE

Fiji has readily available doctors in private practice and standard hospital and laboratory facilities with consultants in internal medicine, obstetrics/gynaecology, orthopaedics, ophthalmology, paediatrics, pathology, psychiatry and general surgery. Private dentists, opticians and pharmacists are also available. The further you get from main cities the more basic the services.

Private consultation and private hospital fees are approximately equivalent to Australian costs. Fees for government-provided services vary from modest to negligible but waiting times can be very long. Direct payment is required everywhere except where a specific arrangement is made, eg in the case of evacuation or where a prolonged hospital stay is necessary; you will need to contact your insurer. Although hospitals will accept credit cards, there might be difficulty with the more-remote small hospitals. If a credit card is not accepted you should be able to arrange cash on credit through local banks.

Except in the remote, poorly staffed clinics, the standard of medical and dental care is generally quite good even if facilities are not sophisticated. The overall risk of illness for a normally healthy person is low; the most common problems being diarrhoeal upsets, viral sore throats, and ear and skin infections – all of which can mostly be treated with self-medication. For serious symptoms, eg sustained fever, chest or abdominal pains, it is best to go to the nearest clinic or doctor straight away.

Family Health

Tampons and pads are readily available in main centres but do not rely on getting them if you travel to one of the outer islands. Dengue fever, especially in the first three months of pregnancy, poses a hazard because of fever but otherwise there is no reason why a normal pregnancy should prevent travel to the region. However, unless necessary, immunisation in the first three months of pregnancy is not recommended.

For young children, it is again dengue fever that could be a problem. The disease tends to come in epidemics mainly in the hotter, wetter months so it should be possible to plan holidays accordingly.

Medications & Contraception

Most commonly used medications are available. Private pharmacies are not allowed by law to dispense listed drugs without prescription from a locally registered practitioner, but many will do so for travellers if shown the container or a prescription from home. Oral contraceptives are obtainable without prescription in Fiji, as is the 'morning after' pill. Most anti-inflammatories, as well as asthma inhalers, are also available over the counter. However, it is best to have a sufficient supply of a regularly taken drug as a particular brand may not be available and sometimes quantities can be limited. This applies particularly to psychotropic drugs such as antidepressants, antipsychotics, anti-epileptics or mood elevators. Insulin is available even in smaller centres, but you cannot guarantee getting a particular brand, combination or preferred administration method. If you have been prescribed 'the very latest' oral antidiabetic or antihypertensive make sure you have enough for the duration of your travel.

INFECTIOUS DISEASES

Despite the long list following, the realistic risks to visitors from infectious diseases are very low with the exception of dengue fever.

Dengue Fever

Dengue fever is a virus spread by the bite of a day-biting mosquito. It causes a feverish illness with headache and severe muscle pains similar to those experienced with a bad, prolonged attack of influenza. Another name for the disease is 'break bone fever' and that's what it feels like. Danger signs include prolonged vomiting, blood in the vomit and a blotchy rash. There is no preventive vaccine and mosquito bites should be avoided whenever possible. Self-treatment involves paracetamol, fluids and rest. Do not use aspirin. Haemorrhagic dengue fever has been reported only occasionally, manifested by signs of bleeding and shock, and requires medical care.

Eosinophilic Meningitis

Eosinophilic meningitis is caused by a microscopic parasite – the rat lungworm – which contaminates raw food. It's a strange illness manifested by scattered abnormal skin sensations, fever and sometimes by the meningitis (headache, vomiting, confusion, neck and spine stiffness), which gives it its name. There is no proven specific treatment, but symptoms may require hospitalisation. For prevention pay strict attention to advice on food and drink.

Hepatitis A

This is a virus disease causing liver inflammation spread by contaminated food or water. Fever, nausea, debility and jaundice (yellow coloration of the skin, eyes and urine) occur and recovery is slow. Most people recover completely but it can be dangerous to people with other forms of liver disease, the elderly and sometimes to pregnant women towards the end of pregnancy. Food is easily contaminated by food preparers, handlers or servers, and by flies. There is no specific treatment. The vaccine is close to 100% protective.

Hepatitis B

Hepatitis B is a virus disease causing liver inflammation but the problem is much more serious than hepatitis A and frequently goes on to cause chronic liver disease and even cancer. It is spread, like HIV, by mixing body fluids, ie sexual intercourse, contaminated needles and accidental blood contamination. Treatment is complex and specialised but preventive vaccination is highly effective.

Hepatitis C

This is a virus similar to hepatitis B that causes liver inflammation, which can progress to chronic liver disease or result in a symptomless carrier state. It is spread almost entirely by blood contamination from shared needles or contaminated needles used for tattooing or body piercing. Treatment is complex and specialised. There is no vaccine available.

HIV/AIDS

The incidence of HIV infection is on the rise in the South Pacific and is fast becoming a major problem in Fiji. Safe-sex practice is essential at all times. If an injection is needed in a smaller clinic it is best to provide your own needles. Blood transfusion laboratories do tests for HIV.

Leptospirosis

Also known as Weil's disease, leptospirosis produces fever, headache, jaundice and, later, kidney failure. It is caused by a spirochaete organism found in water contaminated by rat urine. The organism penetrates skin, so swimming in flooded areas is a risky practice. If diagnosed early it is cured with penicillin.

Typhoid Fever

Typhoid is a bacterial infection, which can be acquired from contaminated food or water. The germ can be transmitted by food handlers or flies, and can be present in inadequately cooked shellfish. Typhoid causes fever, debility and late-onset diarrhoea. Untreated it can produce delirium and is occasionally fatal, but the infection is curable with antibiotics. Vaccination is moderately effective, but care with eating and drinking throughout your time in Fiji is equally important.

TRAVELLER'S DIARRHOEA

Diarrhoea (frequent, loose bowel movements) is caused by viruses, bacteria or parasites present in contaminated food or water. In temperate climates the cause is usually viral, but in the tropics bacteria or parasites are more usual. If you develop diarrhoea, be sure to drink plenty of fluids, preferably an oral rehydration solution (eg Diarolyte, Gastrolyte, Replyte). A few loose stools don't require treatment, but if you start having more than four or five stools a day, you should start taking an antibiotic (usually a quinolone drug) and an antidiarrhoeal agent (such as Loperamide). If diarrhoea is bloody, persists for more than 72 hours or is accompanied by fever, shaking, chills or severe abdominal pain you should seek medical attention. Giardiasis is a particular form of persistent, although not 'explosive', diarrhoea caused by a parasite present in contaminated water. One dose (four tablets) of tinidazole usually cures the infection.

To prevent diarrhoea pay strict attention to the precautions regarding food and water; see p257 for details.

HEALTH

ENVIRONMENTAL HAZARDS

Threats to health from animals and insects are rare indeed but you need to be aware of them.

Bites & Stings

Fiji is blessedly free of dangerous land creatures. There are some land snakes but these are very rarely seen.

JELLYFISH

The notorious box jellyfish (seawasp) has not been recorded, but the blue-coloured Indo-Pacific 'Man o' War' is found in Fijian waters. If you see these floating in the water or stranded on the beach it is wise not to go in. The sting is very painful. Treatment involves ice packs and vinegar; do not use alcohol. Smaller cubo-medusae are abundant and are found particularly on still, overcast days. They usually produce only uncomfortably irritating stings but can cause generalised symptoms, especially in someone with poorly controlled heart disease, although this is rare.

POISONOUS CONE SHELLS

Poisonous cone shells abound along shallow coral reefs. Stings can be avoided by handling the shell at its blunt end only and, preferably, using gloves. Stings mainly cause local reactions but nausea, faintness, palpitations or difficulty breathing are signs flagging the need for medical attention.

OTHER MARINE LIFE

As in all tropical waters, sea snakes may be seen around coral reefs. Unprovoked, sea snakes are extremely unlikely to attack and their fangs will not penetrate a wetsuit. First-aid treatment consists of compression bandaging and splinting of the affected limb. Antivenom is effective, but may have to be flown in. Only about 10% of sea-snake bites cause serious poisoning.

Some of the most beautiful sea creatures, such as the scorpion fish and lionfish, are also highly venomous. Avoid the temptation and keep your hands to yourself! Sea urchins, crown-of-thorns starfish and stonefish can be poisonous or cause infections. Barracuda eels, which hide in coral crevices, may bite. Sea lice or stingers can also be a nuisance.

Shark attacks on divers and snorkellers are rare in Fiji. Reef sharks don't normally attack humans for food, but they can be territorial. Avoid swimming near waste-water outlets, areas where fish are being cleaned and the mouths of rivers or murky waters. If you are lucky enough to see a shark, just move away calmly.

Coral Cuts

Cuts and abrasions from dead coral cause no more trouble than similar injuries from any other sort of rock, but live coral can cause prolonged infection. If you injure yourself on live coral don't wait until later to treat it. Get out of the water as soon as possible, cleanse the wound thoroughly (getting out all the little bits of coral), apply an antiseptic and cover with a waterproof dressing. Then get back in the water if you wish.

Coral Ear

This is a commonly used name for inflammation of the ear canal. It has nothing to do with coral but is caused by water entering the canal, activating fungal spores resulting in secondary bacterial infection and inflammation. It usually starts after swimming, but can be reactivated by water dripping into the ear canal after a shower, especially if long, wet hair lies over the ear opening. Apparently trivial, it can be very, very painful and can spoil a holiday. Apart from diarrhoea it is the most common reason for tourists to consult a doctor in Fiji. Self-treatment with an antibiotic-plus-steroid eardrop preparation (eg Sofradex, Kenacort Otic) is very effective. Stay out of the water until the pain and itch have gone.

Diving Decompression

Because Fiji has wonderful opportunities for scuba diving, it is easy to get overexcited and neglect strict depth and time precautions. The temptation to spend longer-than-safe times at relatively shallow depths is great and a major cause of decompression illness (the 'bends'). Early pains may not be severe and may be attributed to other causes but any muscle or joint pain after scuba diving must be suspect. A privately run compression chamber is available in Suva but transport to it can be difficult. Even experienced divers should check with organisations such as **Divers' Alert Network** (DAN; www.diversalertnetwork.org) about the current site and status of compression chambers, and insurance to cover costs both for local treatment and evacuation. Novice divers must be especially careful. If you have not taken out

HEALTH

FISH POISONING

Ciguatera is a form of poisoning that affects otherwise safe and edible fish unpredictably. Poisoning is characterised by stomach upsets, itching, faintness, slow pulse and bizarre inverted sensations, eg cold feeling hot and vice versa. Ciguatera has been reported in many carnivorous reef fish, especially barracuda but also red snapper, Spanish mackerel and moray eels. There is no safe test to determine whether a fish is poisonous or not. Although local knowledge is not entirely reliable, it is reasonable to eat what the locals are eating. However, fish caught after times of reef destruction, eg after a major hurricane, are more likely to be poisonous. Treatment consists of rehydration, and if the pulse is very slow medication may be needed. Healthy adults will make a complete recovery, although disturbed sensation may persist for some weeks.

insurance before leaving home you may be able to do so online with DAN.

Food & Water

The municipal water supply in Suva, Nadi and other large towns can usually be trusted, but elsewhere avoid untreated tap water, and after heavy rain it's worth boiling the water before you drink. In some areas the only fresh water available may be rainwater collected in tanks and this should certainly be boiled. Food in restaurants, particularly resort restaurants, is safe. Be adventurous by all means but expect to suffer the consequences if you succumb to adventurous temptation by trying raw fish or crustaceans as eaten by some locals.

Heat Exhaustion

Fiji lies within the tropics so it is hot and often humid. Heat exhaustion is actually a state of dehydration associated to a greater or lesser extent with salt loss. Natural heat loss is through sweating, making it easy to become dehydrated without realising it. Thirst is a late sign. Small children and old people are especially vulnerable. For adults, heat exhaustion is prevented by drinking at least 3L of water per day and more if actively exercising. Children need about 1.5L to 2.5L per day. Salt-replacement solutions are useful as muscle weakness and cramps are due to salt as well as water loss and can be made worse by drinking water alone. The powders used for treating dehydration due to diarrhoea are just as ef-

fective for heat exhaustion. Apart from these, a reasonable drink consists of a good pinch of salt to a pint (0.5L) of water. Salt tablets can result in too much salt being taken, causing headaches and confusion.

Heat Stroke

When the cooling effect of sweating fails, heat stroke ensues. This is a dangerous and emergency condition characterised not only by muscle weakness and exhaustion, but by mental confusion. Skin will be hot and dry. If this occurs 'put the fire out' by cooling the body with water on the outside and, if possible, with cold drinks for the inside. Seek medical help as a follow-up, or urgently if the person can't drink.

Sunburn

It should go without saying that exposure to the ultraviolet (UV) rays of the sun causes burning of the skin with accompanying pain, dehydration and misery (with the long-term danger of skin cancer) but experience shows that reminders are necessary. The time of highest risk is between 11am and 3pm and remember that cloud cover does not block out UV rays. Neither does a pleasant breeze. The Australian *Slip, slop, slap* slogan is a useful 'mantra' – slip on a T-shirt or blouse, slop on a sunscreen lotion (of at least 15-plus rating) and slap on a hat. Treat sunburn like any other burn – cool, wet dressings are best. Severe swelling may respond to a cortisone cream.

HEALTH

Language

CONTENTS

Fijian	**258**
Pronunciation	258
Further Reading	259
Accommodation	259
Conversation & Essentials	260
Directions	260
Health & Emergencies	260
Numbers	260
Shopping & Services	261
Time & Dates	261
Transport	261
Fiji-Hindi	**261**
Pronunciation	261
Conversation & Essentials	262
Directions	263
Health & Emergencies	263
Numbers	263
Time & Dates	263
Transport	263

One of the reasons many visitors from the English-speaking world find Fiji such a congenial place to visit is that they don't have to learn another language – the majority of the local people they come in contact with can speak English, and all signs and official forms are also in English. At the same time, for almost all local people, English is not their mother tongue – at home, indigenous Fijians speak Fijian and Indo-Fijians speak Fiji-Hindi (also known as Fijian Hindi and Fiji Hindustani). If you really wish to develop a better understanding of the Fijian people and their culture, it's important that you know something of the Fijian languages; no matter how poor your first attempts at communicating, you're sure to receive plenty of encouragement from Fijians.

FIJIAN

The many regional dialects found in Fiji today all descend, at least partly, from the language spoken by the original inhabitants. They would have come from one of the island groups to the west, either the Solomons or Vanuatu, having left their Southeast Asian homeland at least 1000 years previously and spread eastwards by way of Indonesia, the Philippines and Papua New Guinea. From Fiji, groups left to settle the nearby islands of Rotuma, Tonga and Samoa, and from there they spread out to inhabit the rest of Polynesia, including Hawaii in the north, Rapa Nui (Easter Island) in the east, and Aotearoa (New Zealand) in the south. All the people in this vast area speak related languages belonging to the Austronesian family.

There are some 300 regional varieties (dialects) of Fijian, all belonging to one of two major groupings. All varieties spoken to the west of a line extending north–south, with a couple of kinks, across the centre of Viti Levu belong to the Western Fijian group, while all others are Eastern Fijian.

Fortunately for the language learner there is one variety, based on the eastern varieties of the Bau–Rewa area, which is understood by Fijians throughout the islands. This standard form of Fijian is popularly known as *vosa vakabau* (Bauan), though linguists prefer to call it standard Fijian. It's used in conversation among Fijians from different areas, on the radio and in schools, and is the variety used in this chapter.

In Fijian, there are two ways of saying 'you', 'your' and 'yours'. When speaking to someone who is your superior, or an adult stranger, you should use a longer 'polite' form. This form is easy to remember because it always ends in *-ni*. In all other situations, a shorter 'informal' address is used.

PRONUNCIATION

Fijian pronunciation isn't especially difficult for the English speaker, since most of the sounds found in Fijian have similar counterparts in English. The standard Fijian alphabet uses all the English letters, except 'x'. The letters 'h' and 'z' are used for borrowed words only and occur rarely.

The Fijian alphabet was devised relatively recently (in the 1830s) by missionaries who were also competent linguists. As a result it

---

'FIJINGLISH'

Here are a few English words and phrases used in Fijian but with slightly different meanings:

Fijian English	English
grog	*kava*
bluff	*lie, deceive*
chow	*food, eat*
set	*OK, ready*
step	*cut school, wag*
Good luck to ...!	*It serves ... right!*
Not even!	*No way!*

---

is economical and phonetically consistent – each letter represents only one sound, and each sound is represented by only one letter.

In common with all Pacific languages, Fijian's five vowels are pronounced much as they are in languages such as Spanish, German and Italian:

a	as in 'father'
e	as in 'bet'
i	as in 'machine'
o	as in 'more'
u	as in 'flute'

Vowels have both short or long variants, with the long vowel having a significantly longer sound. In this guide a long sound is written as a double vowel, eg **aa**. An approximate English equivalent is the difference between the final vowel sound in 'icy' and 'I see'. To convey the correct meaning of a word it's important that vowel length is taken into account in your pronunciation. For example, *mama* means 'a ring', *mamaa* means 'chew it', and *maamaa* means 'light' (in weight). Note that *maamaa* takes about twice as long to pronounce as *mama*.

Most consonants are pronounced as they are in English, but there are a few differences you need to be aware of:

b	pronounced with a preceding nasal consonant as 'mb'
c	as the 'th' in 'this' (not as in 'thick')
d	pronounced with a preceding nasal consonant as 'nd'
g	as the 'ng' in 'sing' (not as in 'angry')
j	as the 'ch' in 'charm' but without a following puff of breath
k	as in 'kick' but without a following puff of breath
p	as in 'pip' but without a following puff of breath
q	as the 'ng' in 'angry' (not as in 'sing')
r	trilled as in Scottish English
t	as in 'tap' but without a following puff of breath, often pronounced 'ch' before 'i'
v	pronounced with the lower lip against the upper lip (not against the upper teeth as in English) – it's somewhere between a 'v' and a 'b'

Occasionally on maps and in tourist publications you'll find a variation on the spelling system used in this guide – it's intended to be easier for English speakers to negotiate. In this alternative system, Yanuca is spelt 'Yanutha', Beqa 'Mbengga', and so on.

FURTHER READING

A good introduction to the language is Lonely Planet's *Fijian Phrasebook*, which provides all the essential words and phrases travellers need, along with grammar and cultural points. Lonely Planet's *South Pacific Phrasebook* covers the languages of many South Pacific islands – ideal if you intend visiting a few countries in one trip. Those interested in further studies of Fijian will find George Milner's *Fijian Grammar* (Government Press, Suva, 1956) an excellent introduction to the language. Likewise, Albert Schutz's *Spoken Fijian* (University Press of Hawaii, Honolulu, 1979) is a good primer for more advanced studies.

ACCOMMODATION

Where is a ...?	*I vei ...?*
hotel	*dua na otela*
cheap hotel	*otela saurawarawa*

A note of caution. The term 'guesthouse' and its Fijian equivalent, *dua na bure ni vulagi*, often refer to establishments offering rooms for hire by the hour.

I'm going to stay for...	*Au na ...*
one day	*siga dua*
one week	*maacawa dua*

LANGUAGE

I'm not sure how long I'm staying.
Sega ni macala na dede ni noqu tiko.
Where is the bathroom?
I vei na valenisili?
Where is the toilet?
I vei na valelailai?

CONVERSATION & ESSENTIALS

Hello.	*Bula!*
Hello. (reply)	*Io, bula/Ia, bula.* (more respectful)
Good morning.	*Yadra.*
Goodbye.	*Moce.* (if you don't expect to see them again)
See you later.	*Au saa liu mada.*

You may also hear the following:

Where are you going?
O(ni) lai vei? (used as we ask 'How are you?')
Nowhere special, just wandering around.
Sega, gaade gaa. (as with the response to 'How are you', there's no need to be specific)
Let's shake hands.
Daru lululu mada.

Yes.	*Io.*
No.	*Sega.*
Thank you (very much).	*Vinaka (vakalevu).*
Sorry.	*(Ni) Vosota sara.*
What's your name?	*O cei na yacamu(ni)?*
My name is ...	*O yau o ...*
Pleased to meet you.	*Ia, (ni) bula.*
Where are you from?	*O iko/kemuni mai vei?*
I'm from ...	*O yau mai ...*
How old are you?	*O yabaki vica?*
I'm ... years old.	*Au yabaki ...*
Are you married?	*O(ni) vakawati?*
How many children do you have?	*Le vica na luvemu(ni)?*
I don't have any children.	*E sega na luvequ.*
I have a daughter/ a son.	*E dua na luvequ yalewa/tagane.*
I don't speak Fijian/English.	*Au sega ni kilaa na vosa vakaviti/vakavaalagi.*
Do you speak English?	*O(ni) kilaa na vosa vakavaalagi?*
I understand.	*Saa macala.*
I don't understand.	*E sega ni macala.*
May I take your photo?	*Au tabaki iko mada?*
I'll send you the photo.	*Au na vaakauta yani na itaba.*

DIRECTIONS

I want to go to ...	*Au via lako i ...*
How do I get to ...?	*I vei na sala i ...?*
Is it far?	*E yawa?*
Can I walk there?	*E rawa niu taubale kina?*
Can you show me (on the map)?	*Vakaraitaka mada (ena mape)?*
Go straight ahead.	*Vakadodonu.*
Turn left.	*Gole i na imawi.*
Turn right.	*Gole i na imatau.*

Compass bearings (north, south etc) are never used. Instead you'll hear:

on the sea side of ...	*mai ... i wai*
on the land side of ...	*mai ... i vanua*
the far side of ...	*mai ... i liu*
this side of ...	*mai ... i muri*

HEALTH & EMERGENCIES

Help!	*Oilei!*
Go away!	*Lako tani!*
Call a doctor!	*Qiria na vuniwai!*
Call an ambulance!	*Qiria na lori ni valenibula!*
Call the police!	*Qiria na ovisa!*
I'm lost.	*Au saa sese.*
I need a doctor.	*Au via raici vuniwai.*
Where is the hospital?	*I vei na valenibula?*
I have a stomach-ache.	*E mosi na ketequ.*
I'm diabetic.	*Au tauvi matenisuka.*
I'm allergic to penicillin.	*E dau lako vakacaa vei au na penisilini.*
condoms	*rapa, kodom*
contraceptive	*wai ni yalani*
diarrhoea	*coka*
medicine	*wainimate*
nausea	*lomalomacaa*
sanitary napkin	*qamuqamu*

NUMBERS

0	*saiva*
1	*dua*
2	*rua*
3	*tolu*
4	*vaa*
5	*lima*
6	*ono*
7	*vitu*
8	*walu*
9	*ciwa*
10	*tini*
11	*tinikadua*
12	*tinikarua*

20	ruasagavulu
21	ruasagavulukadua
30	tolusagavulu
100	dua na drau
1000	dua na udolu

SHOPPING & SERVICES

I'm looking for ...	Au vaqaraa ...
a church	na valenilotu
the market	na maakete
the museum	na vale ni yau maaroroi
the police	na ovisa
the post office	na posi(tovesi)
a public toilet	na valelailai
the tourist office	na valenivolavola ni saravanua

What time does it open/close?	E dola/sogo ina vica?
Where are the toilets?	I vei na valelailai?
How much is it?	E vica?
That's too expensive.	Au sega ni rawata.
I'm just looking.	Sarasara gaa.
bookshop	sitoa ni vola
clothing shop	sitoa ni sulu
laundry	valenisavasava
pharmacy	kemesi

TIME & DATES

What time is it?	Saa vica na kaloko?
today	nikua
tonight	na bogi nikua
tomorrow	nimataka
yesterday	nanoa

Monday	Moniti
Tuesday	Tusiti
Wednesday	Vukelulu
Thursday	Lotulevu
Friday	Vakaraubuka
Saturday	Vakarauwai
Sunday	Sigatabu

TRANSPORT

Where is the ...?	I vei na ...?
airport	raaraa ni waqavuka
(main) bus station	basten
bus stop	ikelekele ni basi

When does the ... leave/arrive?	Vica na kaloko e lako/ kele kina na ...?
bus	basi
plane	waqavuka
boat	waqa

FIJI-HINDI

Fiji-Hindi (also known as Fijian Hindi and Fiji Hindustani) is the language of all Indo-Fijians. It has features of the many regional dialects of Hindi spoken by the Indian indentured labourers who were brought to Fiji from 1879 to 1916. (Some people call Fiji-Hindi 'Bhojpuri', but this is the name of just one of the many dialects that contributed to the language.)

Many words from English are found in Fiji-Hindi (such as room, towel, book and reef), but some of these have slightly different meanings. For example, the word 'book' in Fiji-Hindi includes magazines and pamphlets, and if you refer to a person of the opposite sex as a 'friend', it implies that he/she is your sexual partner.

Fiji-Hindi is used in all informal settings, such as in the family and among friends, but the 'Standard Hindi' of India is considered appropriate for formal contexts, such as in public speaking, radio broadcasting and writing. The Hindu majority write in Standard Hindi using the Devanagari script with a large number of words taken from the ancient Sanskrit language. The Muslims use the Perso-Arabic script and incorporate words from Persian and Arabic. When written this way, it is considered a separate language, Urdu, which is the principal language of Pakistan. Indo-Fijians have to learn Standard Hindi or Urdu in school along with English, however they all speak Fiji-Hindi informally.

Some people say that Fiji-Hindi is just a 'broken' or 'corrupted' version of Standard Hindi. In fact, it is a legitimate dialect with its own grammatical rules and vocabulary unique to Fiji.

PRONUNCIATION

Fiji-Hindi is normally written only in guides for foreigners, such as this, and transcribed using the English alphabet. Since there are at least 42 different sounds in Fiji-Hindi and only 26 letters in the English alphabet, some adjustments have to be made. The vowels are as follows:

| a | as in 'about' or 'sofa' |
| aa | as in 'father' |

LANGUAGE

e	as in 'bet'
i	as in 'police'
o	as in 'obey'
u	as in 'rule'
ai	as in 'hail'
aai	as in 'aisle'
au	as the 'o' in 'own'
oi	as in 'boil'

The consonants **b**, **f**, **g** (as in 'go'), **h**, **j**, **k**, **l**, **m**, **n**, **p**, **s**, **v**, **y**, **w** and **z** are similar to those of English. The symbol **ch** is pronounced as in 'chip' and **sh** is pronounced as in 'ship'.

The pronunciation of the consonants 't' and 'd' in Fiji-Hindi is a bit tricky. In 't' and 'd' in English, the tip of the tongue touches the ridge behind the upper teeth, but in Fiji-Hindi it either touches the back of the front teeth (dental) or is curled back to touch the roof of the mouth (retroflex). There are also two 'r' sounds, both of which differ from English. In the first, the tongue touches the ridge behind the upper teeth and is flapped quickly forward, similar to the way we say the 't' sound in 'butter' when speaking quickly. In the second, the tongue is curled back, touching the roof of the mouth (as in the retroflex sounds) and then flapped forward. In this chapter we've used a simplified pronunciation guide and haven't made these distinctions. You can substitute the English 't', 'd' and 'r' for these sounds and still be understood.

Finally, there are 'aspirated' consonants. If you hold your hand in front of your mouth and say 'Peter Piper picked a peck of pickled peppers', you'll feel a puff of air each time you say the 'p' sound – this is called aspiration. When you say 'spade, spill, spit, speak', you don't feel the puff of air, because in these words the 'p' sound is not aspirated. In Fiji-Hindi, aspiration is important in distinguishing meaning. Aspiration is indicated by the use of an 'h' after the consonants – for example:

pul/phul	bridge/flower
kaalaa/khaalaa	black/valley
taali/thaali	clapping/brass plate

Other aspirated consonants:

bh	as in 'grab him' said quickly
chh	as in 'church hat' said quickly
dh	as in 'mad house'

gh	as in 'slug him'
jh	as in 'bridge house'
th	as in 'out house'

CONVERSATION & ESSENTIALS

There are no exact equivalents for 'hello' and 'goodbye' in Fiji-Hindi. The most common greeting is *kaise* (How are you?). The usual reply is *tik* (fine). In parting, it's common to say *fir milegaa* (We'll meet again).

More formal greetings are: *namaste* (Hindus) or *salaam alaykum* (Muslims) – the reply to the latter is *alaykum as-salaam*.

There are no equivalents for 'please' and 'thank you'. To be polite in making requests, people use the word *thoraa* (a little) and a special form of the verb ending in *naa*, eg *thoraa nimak denaa* (Please pass the salt). For 'thanks', people often just say *achhaa* (good). English 'please' and 'thank you' are also commonly used. The word *dhanyavaad* is used to thank someone who has done something special for you. It means something like 'blessings be bestowed upon you'.

The polite form of the word 'you', *ap*, should also be used with people you don't know well. The informal mode uses the word *tum*. Polite and informal modes of address are indicated in this guide by the abbreviations 'pol' and 'inf', respectively.

Yes.	ha
No.	nahi
Maybe.	saayit
I'm sorry. (for something serious)	maaf karnaa
What's your name?	aapke naam kaa hai? (pol)
	tumaar naam kaa hai? (inf)
My name is ...	hamaar naam ...
Where are you from?	aap/tum kaha ke hai? (pol/inf)
I'm from ...	ham ... ke hai
Are you married?	shaadi ho gayaa?
How many children do you have?	kitnaa larkaa hai?
I don't have any children.	larkaa nahi hai
Two boys and three girls.	dui larkaa aur tin larki
Do you speak English?	aap/tum English boltaa? (pol/inf)
Does anyone here speak English?	koi English bole?
I don't understand.	ham nahi samajhtaa

DIRECTIONS

Where is the ...?	*... kaha hai?*
shop	*dukaan*
airport	*eyapot*
(main) bus station	*basten*
market	*maaket*
temple	*mandir*
mosque	*masjid*
church	*chech*

You can also use the English words hotel, guesthouse, camping ground, toilet, post office, embassy, tourist information office, museum, cafe, restaurant and telephone.

I want to go to ...	*ham ... jaae mangtaa*
Is it near/far?	*nagich/dur hai?*
Can I go by foot?	*paidar jaae saktaa?*
Go straight ahead.	*sidhaa jaao*
Please write down the address.	*thoraa edres likh denaa*

By the ...	*... ke paas*
coconut tree	*nariyal ke per*
mango tree	*aam ke per*
breadfruit tree	*belfut ke per*
sugar-cane field	*gannaa khet*

HEALTH & EMERGENCIES

Help me!	*hame madad karo!*
Call the doctor/police.	*doktaa ke/pulis ke bulaao*
Go away!	*jaao!*
Where is the hospital?	*aaspataal kaha hai?*
I'm diabetic.	*hame chini ke bimaari hai*
I'm allergic to penicillin.	*penesilin se ham bimaar ho jaai*
I have a stomach-ache.	*hamaar pet piraawe*
I feel nauseous.	*hame chhaant lage*
condom	*kondom/raba*
contraceptive	*pariwaar niyojan ke dawaai*

medicine	*dawaai*
sanitary napkin	*ped, nepkin*
tampon	*tampon*

NUMBERS

1	*ek*
2	*dui*
3	*tin*
4	*chaar*
5	*paanch*
6	*chhe*
7	*saat*
8	*aath*
9	*nau*
10	*das*
100	*sau*
1000	*hazaar*

English is normally used for numbers from 20 to 99.

TIME & DATES

What time is it?	*kitnaa baje?*
It's ... o'clock.	*... baje*
When?	*kab?*
today	*aaj*
tonight	*aaj raatke*
tomorrow	*bihaan*
yesterday	*kal*

English days of the week are generally used.

TRANSPORT

When does the ... leave/arrive?	*kitnaa baje ... chale/pahunche?*
ship	*jahaaj*
car	*mottar*

You can also use the English words bus, plane and boat.

Glossary

This glossary is a list of Fijian (F), Fijian-Hindi/Hindi (FH) and other (O) terms you may come across in Fiji.

See p60 for some useful words and phrases dealing with food, and the Language chapter, p258, for some other useful words and phrases.

balabala (F) – tree fern with the unique property of not igniting over hot stones (good for fire-walking rituals)
bêche-de-mer (O) – elongated, leathery sea cucumber, with a cluster of tentacles at the mouth – sound appetising? Considered a delicacy in Asia; you may find it on your menu
beka (F) – flying fox or fruit bat
bete (F) – priests of the old Fijian religion
bhajan (FH) – a style of Hindu devotional music
Bharat Natyam (FH) – Indian classical dance
bilibili (F) – bamboo raft
bilo (F) – drinking vessel made from half a coconut shell
bokola (F) – the dead body of an enemy
bua (F) – frangipani
bula (F) – cheers! hello! welcome! (literally, 'life')
bula shirt (F) – *masi-* or floral-design shirt
bure (F) – traditional thatched dwelling or whatever your resort decides it to be
bure bose (F) – meeting house
bure kalou (F) – ancient temple
bure lailai (F) – 'little house'; toilet

cibi (F) – death dance
copra (O) – dried coconut kernel, used for making coconut oil

dadakulaci (F) – banded sea krait, Fiji's most common snake
dakua (F) – a tree of the kauri family
dele (F) – a dance where women sexually humiliate enemy corpses and captives; also called *wate*
drua (F) – double-hulled canoe; traditional catamaran

fuliu (F) – freshwater springs
FVB – Fiji Visitors Bureau

girmitiya (FH) – indentured labourer; the word comes from *girmit,* the Indian labourers' pronunciation of agreement

ibe (F) – a mat
ibuburau (F) – drinking vessels used in *kava* rites

io (F) – yes
ivi (F) – Polynesian chestnut tree

kacua (F) – petrel
kainaga (F) – kinship
kaivalagi (F) – 'people from far away'; Europeans
kaiviti (F) – indigenous Fijian
kanikani (F) – scaly skin from excessive *kava* use, often accompanied by a tranquil grin
kathak (FH) – Indian classical dance
kava (F) – *Piper methysticum* (Polynesian pepper shrub); more importantly the mildly narcotic, muddy, odd-tasting drink made from its aromatic roots; also called *yaqona*
kerekere (F) – custom of unconditional giving based on the concept that time and property is communal; also means 'please'
koro (F) – village headed by a hereditary chief
kula – a type of parrot; Fiji's national bird
kumala (F) – sweet potato

lairo (F) – annual migration of land crabs
lali (F) – a large slit drum made of resonant timbers
lau toka (F) – spear hit
lehenga choli (FH) – skirt, blouse and veil, Bollywood style
lovo (F) – Fijian feast cooked in a pit oven

malo (F) – see *masi*
mana (F) – spiritual power
masi (F) – bark cloth with designs printed in black and rust; also known as *malo* or *tapa*
mataqali (F) – extended family or landowning group
meke (F) – dance performance enacting stories and legends
mithai la gaadi (FH) – Indian sweet stall

naga (F) – snake
NAUI (O) – National Association of Underwater Instructors
nokonoko (F) – casuarina tree; also known as ironwood
noni (F) – an evergreen tree that produces a warty, foul-smelling, bitter-tasting fruit gaining credibility worldwide for its ability to help relieve complaints including arthritis, chronic fatigue, high blood pressure, rheumatism, and digestive disorders

ota (F) – edible fern

PADI (O) – Professional Association of Diving Instructors
pandanus (O) – a plant common to the tropics whose sword-shaped leaves are used to make mats and baskets

pelagic (O) – large predatory fish, or whale
Puja (O) – Hare Krishna prayer

qawali (FH) – a style of Muslim devotional music

rara (F) – ceremonial ground
ratu (F) – male chief

salwaar kameez (FH) – pants and dress, Bollywood style
sega (F) – no
sevusevu (F) – presentation of a gift to a village chief and, consequently, the ancestral gods and spirits; the gift is often *kava (yaqona);* however *tabua* is the most powerful *sevusevu;* acceptance of the gift means the giver will be granted certain privileges or favours
sulu (F) – skirt or wrapped cloth worn to below the knees

tabla (F) – percussion
tabu (F) – forbidden or sacred, implying a religious sanction
tabua (F) – the teeth of sperm whales, which carry a special ceremonial value for Fijians; they are still used as negotiating tokens to symbolise esteem or atonement
tagimaucia (F) – a flower with white petals and bright red branches; Fiji's national flower
talanoa (F) – to chat, to tell stories, to have a yarn
tanoa (F) – *kava* drinking bowl
tapa (F) – see *masi*
tikina (F) – a group of Fijian villages linked together
toddy (O) – a sweet syrup from coconut sap, which can be made into a thick, spreadable syrup or fermented into a pungent alcoholic drink (a tradition imported from Tuvalu)
trade winds (O) – the near-constant (and annoying) winds that buffer most of the tropics

tui (F) – king or chief
tui qalita (F) – direct descendants of a chief
turaga (F) – chief
turaga-ni-koro (F) – hereditary chief

vale (F) – a family house
vale ne bose lawa (F) – parliament house
vanua (F) – land, region, place
vatu ni bokola (F) – head-chopping stone used during cannibalistic rituals
vatuni'epa (F) – rock pedestals formed by the erosion of the coral base along the coast
veli (F) – a group of little gods
vilavilairevo (F) – fire-walking (literally, 'jumping into the oven')
vinaka (F) – thank you
Viti (F) – the name indigenous Fijians used for Fiji before the arrival of Europeans (whose mispronunciation gave Fiji its current name)
voivoi (F) – pandanus leaf
vulagi (F) – visitors; also *kaivalagi*
vutu (F) – a tree flowering only at night with highly scented, white and pink blooms with a distinctive fringe; flowers traditionally used as fish poison

waka (F) – bunch of *kava* roots
waqa tabus (F) – double-hulled canoe
wate (F) – see *dele*

yaka (F) - breadfruit tree
yaqona (F) – see *kava*
yasi dina (F) – sandalwood
yavu (F) – base for housing
yawa (F) – a type of mullet usually only found in the sea

The Authors

DEAN STARNES
Coordinating Author, Viti Levu, Mamanuca Group, Yasawa Group, Lau & Moala Groups, Rotuma

Dean was an impressionable six when he first travelled to Fiji. The week he spent bobbing above the Mamanuca reefs in a leaky mask and a pair of floaties ignited a passion for travel that has since taken him to over 85 countries. With several visits to Fiji now under his weight belt, Dean knew it was time to come home when he started preferring *kava* to beer. He now lives in Auckland where he alternates between writing for Lonely Planet, freelancing as a graphic designer and shirking responsibilities. His book, *Roam; the Art of Travel,* and his website, www.deanstarnes.com, feature photography and stories about his wayfaring ways.

GEORGE DUNFORD
History, The Culture

A Melbourne-based writer, George Dunford has worked on travel guidebooks for Lonely Planet as well as *Micronations* and *The Big Trip*. He's also contributed to several publications including *Meanjin, Wanderlust,* the *Big Issue* and others. He wrote the first blog for Lonely Planet's website, produced podcasts (www.lonelyplanet.com/podcasts), acted as a commissioning editor for Northeast Asia and continues to blog about travel, tech and writing at hackpacker.blogspot.com.

NANA LUCKHAM
Lomaiviti Group, Vanua Levu, Taveuni, Kadavu Group

Nana's first visit to Fiji was a two-week stopover on the way to New Zealand, when she lived it up in the Yasawa islands and won a 'bula bula' dance competition. This time around she was happy to see the quieter side of life in some of the country's less-visited regions. Nana has worked full-time as a travel writer for the past few years, after time spent as a UN Press Officer in New York and Geneva and an editor in London. She has contributed to several other guidebooks. When not on the road she lives in the exotic wilds of southwest London.

LONELY PLANET AUTHORS

Why is our travel information the best in the world? It's simple: our authors are passionate, dedicated travellers. They don't take freebies in exchange for positive coverage so you can be sure the advice you're given is impartial. They travel widely to all the popular spots, and off the beaten track. They don't research using just the internet or phone. They discover new places not included in any other guidebook. They personally visit thousands of hotels, restaurants, palaces, trails, galleries, temples and more. They speak with dozens of locals every day to make sure you get the kind of insider knowledge only a local could tell you. They take pride in getting all the details right, and in telling it how it is. Think you can do it? Find out how at **lonelyplanet.com**.

CONTRIBUTING AUTHORS

Clement Paligaru wrote the Indo-Fijian History & Culture chapter. An Indo-Fijian journalist, he has reported on Asia Pacific affairs for the Australian Broadcasting Corporation for over 15 years. Clement is a presenter on ABC Radio Australia's *In the Loop* program and the Australia Network's program *Pacific Pulse,* which profile the peoples and cultures of Oceania.

Jean-Bernard Carillet wrote the Diving chapter. Born with restless feet and fins, his journeys have led him to the best dive destinations in the world, including French Polynesia, New Caledonia, the Red Sea, the Caribbean and, lately, Fiji and Vanuatu. As a dive instructor and incorrigible traveller, Jean-Bernard has written widely for various French publications, including *Plongeurs International* magazine. He has also coordinated and coauthored two Lonely Planet diving guides: *Tahiti & French Polynesia* and the *Red Sea.*

Michael Sorokin wrote the Health chapter. Dr Sorokin has extensive experience as a physician and GP in South Africa, the UK, the Pacific Islands and rural South Australia. He has special interests in rheumatology, infectious diseases and preventative medicine. Dr Sorokin was awarded the Order of Fiji in recognition of his services to health care in Fiji. He is partly responsible for the maintenance of the Traveller's Medical & Vaccination Centre (TMVC) database and helps with reference material for the continuing education of TMVC medical staff.

Behind the Scenes

THIS BOOK

Lonely Planet's guide to Fiji was first published in 1986. We've had a small army of authors work on this book since then, with the last edition written by Justine Vaisutis (coordinating author) plus the Fiji-ophile team of Mark Dapin, Claire Waddell and Virginia Jealous (Suva-based provider of wine, pasta and inside information to authors and commissioning editors alike). This 8th edition was written by Dean Starnes, Nana Luckham and George Dunford, and Clement Paligaru called on his family and friends in Fiji once more to update the special chapter on Indo-Fijian History & Culture. This guidebook was commissioned in Lonely Planet's Melbourne office, and produced by the following:

Commissioning Editors Suzannah Shwer, Judith Bamber, Tashi Wheeler
Coordinating Editor Angela Tinson
Coordinating Cartographer Simon Goslin
Coordinating Layout Designer Wibowo Rusli
Managing Editor Sasha Baskett
Managing Cartographers David Connolly, Shahara Ahmed
Managing Layout Designer Laura Jane
Assisting Editor Victoria Harrison
Assisting Cartographers Alissa Baker, Peter Shields, Jacqueline Nguyen, Andy Rojas

Cover Designer Marika Mercer
Project Managers Fabrice Rocher, Craig Kilburn
Language Content Coordinators Quentin Frayne, Branislava Vladisavljevic

Thanks to Glenn Beanland, Sally Darmody, Nicole Hansen, Geoff Howard, Corey Hutchison, Rachel Imeson, Geoff Stringer, Andrew Smith, Marg Toohey

THANKS
DEAN STARNES

Fiji is a friendly place, and I owe a large *vinaka vakalevu* (and probably a few Fiji Bitters) to all the people who helped me out while I was on the road. I'm particularly grateful to Chris Keehn, Peter Kohler and Martin Garea-Balado for their invaluable advice on yacht crewing and to Fabia Lonnquist, Janelle Morey and Anna Scanlan for their insights into Suva. This book is far richer for the expertise lent by Céline Cottille, Iliana Lagi Naigulevu, Laurent Bloc'h, Julika Bourget, Jonathan Prasad, Helen Sykes and Vasemaca Rakabu Driso.

It wouldn't be right not to acknowledge the legacy of work from previous editions and the help and assistance from fellow author Nana Luckham, commissioning editor Judith Bamber and managing cartographer David Connolly.

THE LONELY PLANET STORY

Fresh from an epic journey across Europe, Asia and Australia in 1972, Tony and Maureen Wheeler sat at their kitchen table stapling together notes. The first Lonely Planet guidebook, *Across Asia on the Cheap,* was born.

Travellers snapped up the guides. Inspired by their success, the Wheelers began publishing books to Southeast Asia, India and beyond. Demand was prodigious, and the Wheelers expanded the business rapidly to keep up. Over the years, Lonely Planet extended its coverage to every country and into the virtual world via lonelyplanet.com and the Thorn Tree message board.

As Lonely Planet became a globally loved brand, Tony and Maureen received several offers for the company. But it wasn't until 2007 that they found a partner whom they trusted to remain true to the company's principles of travelling widely, treading lightly and giving sustainably. In October of that year, BBC Worldwide acquired a 75% share in the company, pledging to uphold Lonely Planet's commitment to independent travel, trustworthy advice and editorial independence.

Today, Lonely Planet has offices in Melbourne, London and Oakland, with over 500 staff members and 300 authors. Tony and Maureen are still actively involved with Lonely Planet. They're travelling more often than ever, and they're devoting their spare time to charitable projects. And the company is still driven by the philosophy of *Across Asia on the Cheap*: 'All you've got to do is decide to go and the hardest part is over. So go!'

My warmest thanks, however, is reserved for my wife, Debbie, who not only had to spend a wet New Zealand winter alone, but supported me tirelessly through the write-up period and without whom I wouldn't have met a single deadline.

NANA LUCKHAM

Thanks so much to Suzannah Shwer for giving me a dream commission and to Judith Bamber and Angela Tinson for editing. Thanks also to my excellent coordinating author Dean Starnes. In Fiji, thank you to Terri at Paradise Taveuni, to Spencer Tarte for his local voices interview, to Ali on Ono Island for taking us on a jaunt in his boat, to John and Marilyn at Levuka Homestay and to Nox for his excellent tour of Levuka. More thanks go to everyone at Papageno Resort for helping me get around Kadavu, the guys at Tovu Tovu Resort on Taveuni for their incredible hospitality and to Ben Swift for spending yet another holiday on Lonely Planet assignment. My biggest thanks go to Kobin Luckham for making the long trip over from London to keep his little sister company on the road.

OUR READERS

Many thanks to the travellers who used the last edition and wrote to us with helpful hints, useful advice and interesting anecdotes:

Jared Alston, Sophie Bannister Martin, Chris Barnes, Sally Baughn, Daniel Blackburn-Huettner, Andrew Boyle, Judith Buchser, Gerry Buitendag, Quill Cheyne, Janis Couvreux, Cecily Daroux, John Davies, Cathy Degaytan, Mark Degaytan, Robert Drake, Sandrine Fauconnet, Lin Fong, Kuan Foo, Terri Gortan, Pierre Guibor, Md, Henry Hatherly, Caroline Helbig, Mark Hillhouse, Juan Hoffmaister, Lisa Ichiyama, Rebecca Johinke, Linda Jones, Anne Juhl, Rachel Jung, Sharon Kelly, Adrian Kelly, Bruce Kennedy, Jack Korporaal, Linda Koss, Jenny Laahs, Paul Laviers, Matthieu Louvrier, Hilda Mcleod, Deb & Graham Merrett, Veronica Nakyanzi, Margery Nash, Rusi Naulivou, Kelly Navitio, Henriette Nielsen, Andre Nies, Sue Oakley, Danielle Ohlson, Stephanie Parsons, Palvi Patel, Daniel Paull, Dina Priess Dos Santos, Daniel Schmitt, Jonathan Schultz, Carolyn Smith, Gary Spies, Toby Sprunk, Rogowski Stephen, Christine Tawake, Ian Thomson, Maggie Thorssell, Tom Tindal, Nic Turrentine, Chris Van Wyk, Julia Von Meiss, Maria Walker, Judith Walker, Tony Wheeler, Neil Wing, Kimm Woodward

SEND US YOUR FEEDBACK

We love to hear from travellers – your comments keep us on our toes and help make our books better. Our well-travelled team reads every word on what you loved or loathed about this book. Although we cannot reply individually to postal submissions, we always guarantee that your feedback goes straight to the appropriate authors, in time for the next edition. Each person who sends us information is thanked in the next edition – and the most useful submissions are rewarded with a free book.

To send us your updates – and find out about Lonely Planet events, newsletters and travel news – visit our award-winning website: **lonelyplanet.com/contact**.

Note: we may edit, reproduce and incorporate your comments in Lonely Planet products such as guidebooks, websites and digital products, so let us know if you don't want your comments reproduced or your name acknowledged. For a copy of our privacy policy visit lonelyplanet.com/privacy.

ACKNOWLEDGMENTS
Many thanks to the following for the use of their content:

Globe on title page ©Mountain High Maps 1993 Digital Wisdom, Inc.

Internal photographs; p4 (top), p12 (top), p14 (top), p15, p16 Dean Starnes; p4 (bottom) Nana Luckham; p8 De Agostini/Getty Images; p12 (bottom) Photodisc/Alamy; p13 LOOK Die Bildagentur der Fotografen GmbH/Alamy. All other photographs by Lonely Planet Images, and by Casey Mahaney p5, p10 (bottom), p11; Holger Leue p6 (top); Mark Daffey p6 (bottom); Manfred Gottschalk p9; Liz Thompson p10 (top); Robyn Jones p14 (bottom).

Index

A

accommodation 22, 226-8, *see also* adults-only resorts, child-friendly resorts, private resorts, *individual locations*

activities 228-32, *see also individual activities*

adults-only resorts
Mamanuca Group 146, 147, 150
Taveuni 206, 209, 210
Vanua Levu 194, 195, 196
Viti Levu 98
Yasawa Group 163

Air Fiji 246

air travel 241-4, 245-7
airlines 241-2, 246
charter services 247
to/from Fiji 241-4
within Fiji 245-7, **246**

Alliance Party 50

animals 61-3, 104, *see also individual animals*

annual rising of the *balolo* 220

architecture 46-7
colonial 15, 46-7, 169, 14
Dravidian 15, 80, 14
modern 47
traditional 15, 46, 48, 137-9, 15

area codes 238

Armistice Day 235

Arovudi (Silana) 174-5

arts 44-6, *see also* dance, film, literature, music

ATMs 237

Auckland to Fiji yacht race 245

Australian Polynesia Company 32, 34, 115

B

Ba 137

Bainimarama, Commodore Frank (Josaia Voreqe) 19, 37, 38-9, 50

Baker, Reverend Thomas 33, 138

bargaining 238

bark cloth, *see masi*

Bau 131-2

000 Map pages
000 Photograph pages

Bavadra, Dr Timoci 50

Bay of Islands 219

Beachcomber Island 7, 144, 6-7

beaches 7, 6-7
Beachcomber Island 7, 144, 6-7
Blue Lagoon 13, 161, 13
Botaira Beach Resort 159
Caqalai 7, 175
Deuba Beach 109
itineraries 30, **30**
Korovatu Beach 194
Laucala 210
Lavena Beach 209
Leleuvia 176
Likuliku Lagoon 7, 149
Long Beach 7, 163
Matagi 209-10
Monuriki 7, 147
Natadola Beach 13, 98, 12
Navini 7, 145
Ono Island 7, 215-16
Qamea 210
Robinson Crusoe Island 97-8
Rotuma 224
Tokoriki 7, 147
Vomo 7, 144-5
Waitabu Marine Park 208
Wakaya 176
Waya 7, 157-8

bêche-de-mer 32, 190

Beqa 113

Beqa Lagoon 68, 109, 113-14

Biausevu 106

bicycle travel, *see* cycling

birds 62
kacau 62
kula parrot 200
orange dove 200
silktail 189

birdwatching 62, 228
Colo-i-Suva Forest Park 121
Kadavu Group 214
Taveuni 200
Vanua Levu 189, 195
Viti Levu 104

bites 256

black Christ mural 133

blackbirding 33-4

Bligh, Captain William 31, 158

Bligh Water 69-71

blowholes 203

Blue Lagoon 13, 161, 13

Blue Lagoon, The 164

boat travel, *see also* cruises, ferry services, river trips
children, travel with 232
travel to/from Fiji 244-5
travel within Fiji 247-9
Yasawa Flyer 155

Bollywood 55, 191

books, *see* literature

bookshops 23, 117

botanical gardens 121

bougainvillea festival 137

Bouma National Heritage Park 208-9

Bounty 31

Bounty Island 143-4

Bua Bay 195

Bukuya 139

Bula Festival 24, 235

Buliya 213

bus travel 200-1, 249

business hours 232, *see also inside front cover*

C

Cakaudrove Peninsula 189

Cakobau, Ratu Seru 32, 33, 34, 115, 131-2

camping 228

cannibalism 31, 103, 133, 134, 192

Cape Washington 213

Caqalai 7, 175-6

car travel 249-51
insurance 250
internet resources 250
carriers 251

Cast Away 7, 147

Castaway Island 147-8

Castle Rock 96

casuarina 64

caves
Meeting House of the Gods 219
Naihehe 103
Oso Nabukete 221
Sawa-i-Lau 13, 164
Vale Ni Bose 219
Wailotua Snake God Cave 132

Celebrity Love Island 144

Charlot, Jean 133

charter flights 247
Chaudhry, Mahendra 38, 50
child-friendly resorts
  Amunuca Resort 147
  Castaway Island Resort 147
  Fiji Beach Resort & Spa Managed
    by the Hilton 89
  Hideaway Resort 108
  Jean-Michel Cousteau Fiji Islands
    Resort 186
  Koro Sun Resort 186
  Malolo Island Resort 148
  Mana Island Resort 146
  Naigani Island Resort 177
  Nakia Resort & Dive 203
  Naviti Resort 107
  Outrigger on the Lagoon 105
  Plantation Island Resort 150
  Radisson Resort Fiji 89
  Shangri-La's Fijian Resort 99
  Sonaisali Island Resort 92
  Tovu Tovu Resort 205
  Treasure Island Resort 144
  Warwick Fiji Resort & Spa 108
children, travel with 232, see also
  child-friendly resorts
  boat travel 232
  food 59, 232
  health 254
  Viti Levu 80
churches
  Arovudi (Silana) 174
  Bau 131
  Levuka 171
  Lovoni 9, 174, 9
  Suva 122, 124
  Tavua 136
Cicia 221
cinemas 95, 129, 193
climate 21-2, 61, 233
Cobra Rock 194
Coconut Milk Run 245
Colo-i-Suva Forest Park 9, 121, **121**, 8
colonial period 34-5
cone shells 256
consulates 234
Cook, Captain James 31
coral 62, 63, 70
Coral Coast 99-114
Coral Coast Scenic Railway 98
coral cuts 256
coral ear 256
costs 22, see also inside front cover
coups 36-9
Cousteau, Jean-Michel 186

crafts
  masi 47-8
  Oceania Centre for Arts & Culture
    44
  pottery 47, 102, 131
  weaving 44, 48
  woodcarving 44, 47
credit cards 237
crested iguanas 62, 65, 104, 195
cruises, see also boat travel
  Mamanuca Group 141-3, 149
  Vanua Levu 179, 183
  Viti Levu 93
  Yasawa Group 153-4
culture 40-8, see also Fijian culture,
  Indo-Fijian culture
customs regulations 233
cycling 90, 168, 189, 229, 247

D
Dakuniba 189
Dakuwaqa 216
dance 46
dangers 233
decompression 256
Deed of Cession 169
Denarau 88-90, **88**
dengue fever 254
Dere Bay 176
Des Voeux Peak 202
Deuba Beach 109
diarrhoea 255
disabilities, travellers with 239
discount cards 234
dive sites 67-73
  Beqa Lagoon 68, 109, 113-14
  Bligh Water 69-71
  E6 70
  Great Astrolabe Reef 72-3,
    213
  Kadavu Group 72-3, 213
  Lau & Moala Groups 218, 219
  Lomaiviti Group 69-71, 166
  Malolo Barrier Reef 68
  Mamanuca Group 68, 141
  Nananu-i-Ra 135
  Rainbow Reef 72, 199
  Rakiraki 134
  Shark Reef 68, 69
  Somosomo Strait 71-2, 199
  Taveuni 71-2, 199
  Vanua Levu 71, 182-3, 195
  Viti Levu 68, 97, 106, 109, 113-14,
    134-5
  Yasawa Group 68

diving 11, 67-74, 229-30, 10
  beginners 67, 74
  decompression 256
  dive centres 73
  drift diving 73
  Fiji Recompression Chamber
    Facility 117
  health 256
  manta rays 69, 213
  responsible diving 71
  with sharks 69, 70, 72, 109,
    166, 213
Diwali (Festival of Lights) 24, 54, 235
dolphins 61, 186, 189
Drekeniwai 189
drinks 56
  kava 57
  toddy 190
  water 56, 257
driving, see car travel
drua 204

E
E6 70
economy 33-4, 35, 36, 37, 40-1, 115
education 41
electricity 199, 227
embassies 234
Emperor Gold Mining Company 137
environmental issues 23, 65-6, see
  also GreenDex
  transport 242
  Tribe Wanted 195
eosinophilic meningitis 255
European traders 31-2
events, see festivals & events
exchange rates, see inside front cover

F
Fara 15, 224
fax services 238
Feejee Experience 251
Femlinkpacific 54
ferry services 247-9
Festival of Lights (Diwali) 24, 54, 235
festivals & events 16, 24, 234-5
  annual rising of the *balolo* 220
  Auckland to Fiji yacht race 245
  bougainvillea festival 137
  Bula Festival 24, 235
  Diwali (Festival of Lights) 24,
    54, 235
  Fara 15, 224
  Fiji International Jazz Festival 235
  Fiji Ocean Swim 235

INDEX

festivals & events *continued*
Fiji Regatta Week 24, 149, 235
food 57
Hibiscus Festival 15, 24, 124, 235
Hindu Holi (Festival of Colours)
24, 234
Karthingai Puja 81
lairo 210
Lautoka's Sugar Festival 24, 235
Musket Cove to Port Vila yacht
race 149
Panguni Uthiram Thiru-naal 81
Ram Leela festival (Play of Rama)
24, 54, 235
Ram Naumi (Birth of Lord Rama)
24, 235
shark-calling ritual 221
South Indian fire-walking festival
16, 54, 124, **16**
South Indian Sangam convention
55
South Pacific World Music Festival
24, 235
Thai Pusam 81
Fiji International Jazz Festival 235
Fiji Labour Party 36
Fiji Military Force 35
Fiji Museum 15, 119-20, 171, 172
Fiji Ocean Swim 235
Fiji Recompression Chamber Facility
117
Fiji Regatta Week 24, 149, 235
Fiji Survivor 145
Fiji time 20
Fiji Women's Crisis Centre 44
Fiji Women's Rights Movement 44
Fijian Alliance Party 35, 37
Fijian Association 36
Fijian culture 24, 40-8
Fijian language 258-61
Fiji-Hindi language 261-3
film 24, 45
Blue Lagoon, The 164
Bollywood 55, 191
Cast Away 147
cinemas 95, 129, 193
*Journey to the Dawning of the
Day* 122
Return to the Blue Lagoon 208
fire-walking 16, 44, 54, 109, 124, **16**
fish 63

fish poisoning 257
fishing 230
Kadavu Group 213
Mamanuca Group 149
Taveuni 200
Vanua Levu 189, 194, 195
Viti Levu 82, 106, 110
food 56-60, 235
Frigate Passage 113

G
Garden of the Sleeping Giant 13, 90, **12**
Gavo Passage 175
gay travellers 235-6
geography 61
geology 61, 64-5
girmitiyas 34-5, 49, 171
golf 42
golf courses
Taveuni 200
Vanua Levu 186, 189
Viti Levu 85, 98, 108, 110, 123
Grand Pacific Hotel 122
Graveyard of Kings 224
Great Astrolabe Reef 72-3, 213
Great Council of Chiefs 19, 37-9
Great Council of Chiefs' meeting
hall 201

H
Hanks, Tom 7, 147
Hare Krishna 93
health 252-7
books 253
children, travel with 254
internet resources 252, 253
heat exhaustion 257
heat stroke 257
Hedstrom, Maynard 171
hepatitis 255
Hibiscus Festival 15, 24, 124, 235
Hibiscus Hwy 180
hiking, *see* walking
Hindu Holi (Festival of Colours) 24,
234
Hinduism 35, 49, 80-1, 82
history 31-9
Australian Polynesia Company 32,
34, 115
blackbirding 33-4
Cakobau, Ratu Seru 32, 33, 34,
115, 131-2
colonial period 34-5
coups 36-9
Deed of Cession 169

European traders 31-2
girmitiyas 34-5, 49, 171
independence 36
Indo-Fijians 34-5, 49-55
missionaries 32-3, 131, 138,
218, 221
Viti 31
voting 36
whaling 33
WWI 35, 36, 174
WWII 35, 36
hitching 251
HIV/AIDS 255
HMS Bounty 158
holidays 22, 236
horse riding 13, 98, 204, 206, 230, **12**
hot springs 90, 182, 189, 192

I
Iloilo, President Ratu Josefa 39
Indo-Fijian culture 34-5, 36, 49-55
insurance
car 250
health 252
travel 236
International Brotherhood of
Magicians 135
International Date Line 61, 201
internet access 236
internet resources 23, 25, 226
car rental 250
health 252, 253
travel insurance 236
ironwood 64
itineraries
beaches 30, **30**
Lomaiviti Group 29, **29**
Mamanucas & Yasawas 26, **26**
natural attractions 30, **30**
Vanua Levu 28, **28**
Viti Levu 27, **27**

J
jellyfish 256
Joske's Thumb 122
Journey to the Dawning of the Day 122

K
kacau 62
Kadavu Group 211-16, 248, **212**
Kaibu 220
Kalevu Cultural Centre 99
Karthingai Puja 81
kava 57
Kavu Kavu Reef 113

INDEX

kayaking 11, 230-1, **10**
  Kadavu Group 213-14
  Lau & Moala Groups 218, 219
  Vanua Levu 183
  Viti Levu 95, 110
  Yasawa Group 154
Keiyasi 103
kerekere 42
kids clubs, *see* child-friendly resorts
Kings Road 130-9
Kingsford Smith, Charles 120
Kioa 189-90
kiteboarding 136, 160
Koro 176-7
Korolevu 105-8, **106**
Korotogo 104-5, **102**
Korovatu Beach 194
Korovou 132
Koroyanitu National Heritage Park
  9, 96
Ku Klux Klan 166
Kuata 155-6, **157**
Kula Eco Park 104
kula parrot 200
Kulukulu 101

L
Labasa 190-4, **191**
lairo 210
Lake Tagimaucia 202
Lakeba 221
land ownership 23, 34, 35, 36, 38,
  49-50
languages 258-63
  Fijian 258-61
  Fiji-Hindi 261-3
  food vocabulary 59
Lau & Moala Groups 217-22, 248, **219**
Laucala 210
Lautoka 92-6, **94**
Lautoka Sugar Mill 93
Lautoka's Sugar Festival 24, 235
Lavena Coastal Walk 9, 209
Lawai 102
legal matters 236-7
Leleuvia 176
leptospirosis 255
lesbian travellers 235-6
Levuka 15, 166, 169-74, **170**, **14**
Likuliku Lagoon 7, 149
literature 23, 45, 54
  bookshops 23, 117
  health 253
  Indo-Fijian 45, 54
  sailing 231

Lomaiviti Group 165-77, **167**
  beaches 175, 176
  cycling 168
  diving 69-71, 166
  ferry services 248
  itineraries 29, **29**
  sailing 166
  snorkelling 166, 175, 176
  tours 168-9
  travel to/from 168
  travel within 168
  village visits 168
  walking 169
Lomaloma 220
Lomolomo Guns 90
London Missionary Society 32
Long Beach 7, 163
lovo 57
Lovoni 9, 174, **9**
Lovoni people 166, 172

M
magazines 227
Mago 220
Malolo 148
Malolo Barrier Reef 68
Malololailai 149-50
Mamanuca Group 7, 140-51, **142**
  cruises 141-3, 149
  diving 68, 141
  ferry services 247
  fishing 149
  itineraries 26, **26**
  surfing 141, 149, 150, 151
  tours 141-3
  travel to/from 143
  travel within 143
Mana 145-6
mangroves 64
Manta Ray Island 159
manta rays 69, 158, 160, 166, 213
maps 237
Mara, Ratu Sir Kamisese 38, 50
Mariamma Temple 124
Mariamman Temple 194
marijuana 236
masi 47-8
Masons 171
Matacawalevu 162-3
Matagi 209-10
Matamanoa 146-7
Matei 205-7, **205**
Mateschitz, Dietrich 210
Matuku 222
Maunivanua Point 101

Mavana 220
measures 227
Meeting House of the Gods 219
meke 46
Methodist Church 39, 171, 175
metric conversions, *see inside front
  cover*
missionaries 32-3, 131, 138, 218, 221
missions
  Naililili Catholic Mission 131
  Naiserelagi Catholic Mission 133
  Wairiki Catholic Mission 15,
    201-2
Moala Group, *see* Lau & Moala
  Groups
mobile phones 239
Momi Bay 96-7
Momi Guns 97
Monasavu Dam 137
money 237, *see also inside front cover*
Monuriki 7, 147
Morris, Percy 171
Moturiki 175
Mt Batilamu 96
Mt Koroyanitu 96
Mt Lomalagi 137
Mt Uluigalau 198
music 45-6
  Fiji International Jazz Festival 235
  South Pacific World Music Festival
    24, 235
Musket Cove Marina 149
Musket Cove to Port Vila yacht race
  149
myths & legends
  Dakuwaqa 216
  Gavo Passage 175
  Mavana 220
  Navatu Rock 133
  Rotuma 225
  tagimaucia 202

N
Naag Mandir Temple 194
Nabouwalu 195
Nacula 163-4
Nadarivatu 137
Nadi 78-88, **81**, **83**
  accommodation 82-6
  activities 80-2
  drinks 87
  food 86-7
  internet access 79
  medical services 79
  shopping 87

Nadi *continued*
  sights 80-2
  tourist offices 79-80
  tours 82
  travel to/from 87-8
  travel within 87-8
naga (snake) cult 192
Naigani (Mystery Island) 177
Naihehe cave 103
Naililili Catholic Mission 131
Naisali 92
Naiserelagi Catholic Mission 133
Naitauba 220
Nakabuta 102
Nakauvadra Range 133
Namena Barrier Reef 195
Namenalala 195
Namosi Highlands 113
Namotu 150
Nananu-i-Ra 134-6, **135**
Nanuya Lailai 161-2
Nanuya Levu (Turtle Island) 164
Naqara 201
Nasaqalau 221
Nasilai village 131
Natadola Beach 13, 98, 12
Natewa Peninsula 189
National Federation Party 36, 51
national parks & reserves 65
  Bouma National Heritage Park
    208-9
  Colo-i-Suva Forest Park 9, 121,
    121, 8
  Koroyanitu National Heritage
    Park 9, 96
  Kula Eco Park 104
  Sigatoka Sand Dunes 9, 101
  Tunuloa Silktail Reserve 189
  Yadua Tabu 195
Native Land Trust Board 36
Natovi Landing 132
Nausori 131-2
Nausori Highlands 137-9
Navai 137
Navala 15, 137-9, 15
Navatu Rock 133
Navini 7, 145
Navua 112
newspapers 43, 227
Nukubati 194
Nukubolu 188

O
Oceania Centre for Arts & Culture 44,
  54, 121
Ono 7, 215-16
orange dove 200
orchids 90, 12
Oso Nabukete 221
Ovalau 168-75

P
Pacific Harbour 108-12, **110**
Pacific Sun 246
pandanus 48, 64
Panguni Uthiram Thiru-naal 81
parliament complex 120
Party of Policy Makers for Indigenous
  Fijians 37
passports 241, *see also* visas
People's Charter 39, 51
petroglyphs 189
phonecards 238
planning 21-5, 236
  health 252-3
plants 63-4
politics 19, 35-9
  Alliance Party 50
  coups 36-9, 50, 115
  female representation 43-4
  Fiji Labour Party 36
  Fijian Alliance Party 35, 37
  Fijian Association 36
  Great Council of Chiefs 19, 37-9
  independence 36
  Indo-Fijian 49-51
  land ownership 23, 34, 35, 36,
    38, 49-50
  National Federation Party 36,
    51
  parliament complex 120
  Party of Policy Makers for
    Indigenous Fijians 37
  People's Charter 39, 51
  Soqosoqo-ni-Vakavulewa-ni
    Taukei 37
  voting 36
population 41
postal services 237-8
pottery 47, 102, 131
private resorts 148, 194, 196, 210

Q
Qalito 147-8
Qamea 210
Qarase, Lasenia 37, 38-9, 50
Qilaqila 219

R
Rabi 190
Rabuka, Lieutenant Colonel Sitiveni
  37-9, 50, 189
radio 43, 227
rafting 231
Rainbow Reef 72, 199
Rakiraki 133-4, **133**
Ram Leela festival (Play of Rama) 24,
  54, 235
Ram Naumi (Birth of Lord Rama)
  24, 235
religion 35, 43
  Hare Krishna 93
  Hinduism 35, 49, 80-1, 82
  Methodist Church 39, 171, 175
  naga (snake) cult 192
reserves, *see* national parks & reserves
Resort, The 148
resorts 22, 227, 228, *see also* adults-
  only resorts, child-friendly resorts,
  private resorts
Return to the Blue Lagoon 208
Rewa River 131
river trips 11, 231
Robbins, Anthony 186
Robinson Crusoe Island 97-8
rock climbing 122
Rotuma 223-5, 248, **224**
Royal Suva Yacht Club 122
rugby union 41, 129
Rukuruku 174

S
Sabeto Mountains 13, 90, 12
sailing 11, 231, 244-5, 11
  Fiji Regatta Week 24, 149, 235
  Kadavu Group 214
  Lau & Moala Groups 218
  Levuka 166
  Musket Cove Marina 149
  Musket Cove to Port Vila yacht
    race 149
  Royal Suva Yacht Club 122
  Vanua Levu 179, 181
  Viti Levu 91
Samraj, Adi Da 220
sandalwood 32, 195
Savusavu 179-88, **182**
Savusavu Bay 179
Sawa-i-Lau 13, 164
Sawana 220
Sayed-Khaium, Attorney General
  Aiyaz 51
scenic flights 89

sea cucumbers 32, 190
self-catering 58
sevusevu 42, 57
Shark Reef 68, 69
shark-calling ritual 221
sharks 63
    diving 69, 70, 72, 109, 166, 213
    feeding 69, 109
    shark-calling ritual 221
    snorkelling 157, 213
Shobna Chanel Dance Group 54
shopping 238
Shree Laxmi Narayan Temple 122
Sigatoka 99-101, **100**
Sigatoka Sand Dunes 9, 101
Sigatoka Valley 102-3
Silana, *see* Arovudi (Silana)
silktail 189
Snake Island 175
snorkelling 11, 229-30, 11
    Kadavu Group 213
    Lau & Moala Groups 218
    Lomaiviti Group 166, 175, 176
    manta rays 69, 213
    sharks 157, 213
    Taveuni 199
    Vanua Levu 182-3, 195
    Viti Levu 95, 106, 135
    Vuna Reef 199
    Yasawa Group 69, 157, 160
Somosomo 201-2
Somosomo Strait 71-2, 199
Soqosoqo-ni-Vakavulewa-ni Taukei 37
South Cape 203
South Indian fire-walking festival 16, 54, 124, 16
South Indian Sangam convention 55
South Pacific World Music Festival 24, 235
South Sea Island 143
Speight, George 38, 115
sports 41-2
Sri Krishna Kaliya Temple 93
Sri Siva Subramaniya Swami Temple 15, 80-1, 14
stings 256
student discounts 234
sugar industry 93, 190
Sukuna, Ratu Sir Lala 36
sunburn 257
surfing 11, 231
    Beqa Barrier Reef 113
    Cape Washington 213
    Cloudbreak 141, 149, 151
    Desperations 141, 149

Frigate Passage 113
    internet resources 231
    Kavu Kavu Reef 113
    Kulukulu 101
    Mini Clouds 141, 149
    Momi Bay 97
    Namotu Left 141, 149, 150
    Natadola Beach 82
    Restaurants 141, 149, 151
    Sigatoka beach 82
    Swimming Pools 141, 149, 150
    Uciwai Landing 92
    Vesi Passage 213
    Waidroka Surf & Dive Resort 107
    Wilkes Passage 141, 149, 150
    Yanuca 114
sustainable travel, *see* GreenDex
Suva 15, 114-30, **116**, **118**
    accommodation 125-6
    activities 122-4
    cinema 129
    drinking 128-9
    festivals & events 124
    food 126-8
    history 115
    internet access 117
    medical services 117
    orientation 116
    shopping 129
    travel to/from 130
    travel within 130
    walking tour 123-4, **123**
Suva Municipal Market 120

T
tabu 33
tabua 33
tagimaucia 63, 202
Tarte, Spencer 206
Tasman, Abel 31
Tavarua 151
Taveuni 9, 197-210, **198**
    birdwatching 200
    cruises 200
    dangers 199
    diving 71-2, 199
    electricity 199
    ferry services 248
    fishing 200
    snorkelling 199
    tours 200
    travel to/from 200
    travel within 200-1
    walking 9, 199, 208, 209

Tavewa 160
Tavoro Waterfalls 208
Tavua 136-7
Tavuni Hill Fort 103-4
taxes 22, 233
taxis 251
telephone services 238, *see also inside front cover*
temples 82
    Mariamma Temple 124
    Mariamman Temple 194
    Naag Mandir Temple 194
    Shree Laxmi Narayan Temple 122
    Sri Krishna Kaliya Temple 93
    Sri Siva Subramaniya Swami Temple 15, 80-1, 14
    Tavua 136
Thai Pusam 81
Thurston, John Bates 64
Thurston Gardens 120
Tiliva 213
time 239
tipping 59, 237
Toberua 132
toddy 190
Tokoriki 7, 147
Tomanivi 137
Totoya 222
tourist information 239
tours 251
    Coral Coast 100, 106, 109, 110-11
    Denarau 89
    Kadavu Group 214
    Koroyanitu National Heritage Park 96
    Lomaiviti Group 168-9
    Mamanuca Group 141-3
    Nadi 82
    Nausori Highlands 137
    Navua River 112
    Taveuni 200
    Vanua Levu 183
travel insurance 236
travel to/from Fiji 241-5
travel within Fiji 245-51, **246**
travellers cheques 237
Treasure Island 144
Tribe Wanted 195
Tui Cakau 201
Tui Viti, *see* Cakobau, Ratu Seru
Tunuloa Peninsula 189
Tunuloa Silktail Reserve 189
TV 43

INDEX

TV show locations
    Celebrity Love Island 144
    Fiji Survivor 145
    Resort, The 148
typhoid fever 255

U
Uciwai Landing 92
Udreudre, Ratu 133, 134
Udreudre's Tomb 133
University of the South Pacific 120-1
    Oceania Centre for Arts & Culture
        44, 54, 121
Uru's Waterfall 132

V
vaccinations 252, 253
Vaileka 133
Vale Ni Bose 219
Vanua Balavu 219-20
Vanua Levu 178-96, **180-1**
    birdwatching 189, 195
    cruises 179, 183
    diving 71, 182-3, 195
    ferry services 248, 249
    fishing 189, 194, 195
    itineraries 28, **28**
    kayaking 183
    sailing 179, 181
    snorkelling 182-3, 195
    tours 183
    travel to/from 179
    travel within 179
    village visits 189
    walking 189
    windsurfing 194, 195
Vatukoula 137
Vatulele 114
vatuni'epa 209
vegetarian travellers 58-9
Vidawa Rainforest Trail 208
video systems 227
village etiquette 42
village visits 15, 231-2
    Coral Coast 102, 107, 110
    Kadavu Group 213
    Koroyanitu National Heritage
        Park 96
    Lomaiviti Group 168
    Navala 137-9

Ovalau 174
Rotuma 224
Vanua Levu 183, 189
Viseisei 90-1
Waitabu 208
Yasawa Group 156
visas 239-40, *see also* passports
Viseisei 90
Viti 31
Viti Levu 75-139, **76-7**, *see also* Nadi
    & Suva
    birdwatching 104
    children, travel with 80
    diving 68, 97, 106, 109, 113-14,
        134, 135
    fishing 106, 110
    itineraries 27, **27**
    kayaking 95, 110
    snorkelling 95, 106, 135
    surfing 92, 97, 101, 107, 109,
        113-14
    tours 82, 89, 96, 100, 106, 109,
        110-11
    travel to/from 78
    travel within 78
    village visits 90, 96, 102, 107,
        110, 137-9
    walking 90, 96, 112, 135
    windsurfing 95, 136
volunteering 240
Vomo 7, 144-5
von Luckner, Count Felix 174
Vorovoro 195
voting 36
Vuda Point 91-2
Vuda Point Marina 91-2
Vuna Reef 199
Vunisea 212

W
Wadigi 148
Wailotua Snake God Cave 132
Wainunu Bay 195-6
Wainunu Tea Estate 196
Wairiki Catholic Mission 15, 201-2
Waisali Rainforest Reserve 188
Waitabu 208
Waitabu Marine Park 208
Waitavala Water Slide 13, 202
Waiyevo 201-2

Wakaya 176
walking 230
    Kadavu Group 213
    Lau & Moala Groups 218
    Lomaiviti Group 169
    Rotuma 224
    Taveuni 9, 199, 208, 209
    Vanua Levu 189
    Viti Levu 90, 96, 112, 135
Wasavula Ceremonial Site 192
water 56, 257
Waya 7, 157-8, **157**
Wayalailai 156-7
Wayasewa 156-7, **157**
weather, *see* climate
weaving 44, 48
websites, *see* internet resources
weddings 229
weights 227
whales 61, 172
whaling 33
Wilkes, Charles 33, 148
Williams, John Brown 33, 171
windsurfing 11, 232
    Vanua Levu 194, 195
    Viti Levu 95, 136
women in Fiji 43-4, 45
women travellers 240
    health 254
woodcarving 44, 47
work 240
WWI 35, 36, 174
WWII 35, 36

Y
yacht permits 244-5
yachts, *see* sailing
Yadua Tabu 195
Yanuca 98-9, 113-14
Yanuca Lailai (Lost Island) 175
Yaqeta 162-3
yaqona, see kava
Yasawa Flyer 155
Yasawa Group 7, 152-64, **154**, 6
    costs 156
    itineraries 26, **26**
Yaukuve Levu 216

Z
ziplines 110

INDEX

GreenDex

The following Fijian attractions, tours and accommodation options have been identified by the authors as demonstrating an active sustainable-tourism policy. Some are involved in environmental and wildlife protection; many have taken steps to protect the fragile coral ecosystems that so many travellers visit Fiji to enjoy. Others are particularly economical with resources and have implemented ecofriendly initiatives such as using solar energy, the environmentally sound management of wastes, and low-impact, sustainable eco-tours.

We've also included community-owned initiatives that make a point of employing local people, maintaining and preserving local identity and culture and ensuring that locals enjoy at least some of the economic benefits of tourism.

We want to keep developing our sustainable-tourism content. If you think we've omitted someone who should be listed here, or if you disagree with our choices, email us at talk2us@lonelyplanet .com.au and set us straight for next time. For more information about sustainable tourism and Lonely Planet, see www.lonelyplanet.com/about/responsible-travel.

KADAVU
accommodation
  Matava Resort p214
  Papageno Eco-Resort p215
activities
  Dive Kadavu p213
  Mad Fish Dive Centre p213
  Papageno Eco-Resort p213

LOMAIVITI GROUP
accommodation
  Bobo's Farm p174

MAMANUCA GROUP
accommodation
  Navini Island Resort p145

TAVEUNI
accommodation
  Almost Paradise p204
  Nakia Resort & Dive p203
activities
  Vunibokoi Divers p199

VANUA LEVU
accommodation
  Jean-Michel Cousteau Fiji Islands
    Resort p186

Palmlea Lodge p193
Salt Lake Lodge p189
activities
  L'Aventure Diving p183
  Tribe Wanted p195
tours
  Tui Tai Adventure Cruises p179

VITI LEVU
accommodation
  Bulou's Eco Lodge p138
  Namatakula Village Homestay
    p107
  Natalei Eco-Lodge p132
  Navua Upriver Lodge p112
  Raintree Lodge p125
  Stoney Creek Resort p90
  Tiri Villas p111
  Viseisei Village Homestays p91
  Waidroka Surf & Dive Resort p107
  Yanuca Island Resort p114
activities
  Aboard-A-Dream Nautilus Dive p98
  Beqa Adventure Divers p109
  Fiji Surf Company p82
  Kaiviti Divers p134
  Ra Divers p134
  Scuba Bula p97

sights
  Kula Eco Park p104
tours
  Adventures in Paradise p100
  Discover Fiji Tours p112
  Sigatoka River Safari p100
  Wilderness Ethnic Adventure Fiji
    p124

YASAWA GROUP
accommodation
  Korovou Eco-Tour Resort p160
  Mantaray Island Resort p159
  Nanuya Island Resort p162
  Navutu Stars p163
  Octopus Resort p158
  Sunset Beach Resort p158
  Turtle Island Resort p164
  Wayalailai Eco Haven Resort p157
tours
  Southern Sea Ventures p154
  World Expeditions p155

MAP LEGEND

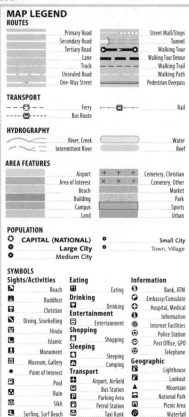

ROUTES

Primary Road	Street Mall/Steps
Secondary Road	Tunnel
Tertiary Road	Walking Tour
Lane	Walking Tour Detour
Track	Walking Trail
Unsealed Road	Walking Path
One-Way Street	Pedestrian Overpass

TRANSPORT

Ferry	Rail
Bus Route	

HYDROGRAPHY

River, Creek	Water
Intermittent River	Reef

AREA FEATURES

Airport	Cemetery, Christian
Area of Interest	Cemetery, Other
Beach	Market
Building	Park
Campus	Sports
Land	Urban

POPULATION

CAPITAL (NATIONAL)	Small City
Large City	Town, Village
Medium City	

SYMBOLS

Sights/Activities
- Beach
- Buddhist
- Christian
- Diving, Snorkelling
- Hindu
- Islamic
- Monument
- Museum, Gallery
- Point of Interest
- Pool
- Ruin
- Sikh
- Surfing, Surf Beach

Eating
- Eating

Drinking
- Drinking

Entertainment
- Entertainment

Shopping
- Shopping

Sleeping
- Sleeping
- Camping

Transport
- Airport, Airfield
- Bus Station
- Parking Area
- Petrol Station
- Taxi Rank

Information
- Bank, ATM
- Embassy/Consulate
- Hospital, Medical
- Information
- Internet Facilities
- Police Station
- Post Office, GPO
- Telephone

Geographic
- Lighthouse
- Lookout
- Mountain
- National Park
- Picnic Area
- Waterfall

LONELY PLANET OFFICES

Australia
Head Office
Locked Bag 1, Footscray, Victoria 3011
☎ 03 8379 8000, fax 03 8379 8111
talk2us@lonelyplanet.com.au

USA
150 Linden St, Oakland, CA 94607
☎ 510 250 6400, toll free 800 275 8555
fax 510 893 8572
info@lonelyplanet.com

UK
2nd fl, 186 City Rd,
London EC1V 2NT
☎ 020 7106 2100, fax 020 7106 2101
go@lonelyplanet.co.uk

Published by Lonely Planet Publications Pty Ltd
ABN 36 005 607 983

Mixed Sources
Product group from well-managed forests and other controlled sources
www.fsc.org Cert no. SGS-COC-005002
© 1996 Forest Stewardship Council
FSC

Although the authors and Lonely Planet have taken all reasonable care in preparing this book, we make no warranty about the accuracy or completeness of its content and, to the maximum extent permitted, disclaim all liability arising from its use.